People and Politics:

An Introduction to American Government

Twelfth Edition

People and Politics:

An Introduction to American Government

Twelfth Edition

Mary Kate Hiatt
Delta College
University Center, Michigan

Gregory Publishing Company   Wheaton, IL 60187

Design and Production: Gregory Publishing Company
Typeface: AGaramond
Typesetting: Gregory Publishing Company
Cover Art: Sam Tolia

People and Politics:
An Introduction to American Government

Twelfth Edition, 2005
Printed in the United States of America
Translation rights reserved by the authors
ISBN 0-911541-76-4

Revision Authors

Special thanks and recognition go to the following professionals who serve as revision authors for *People and Politics*.

Thomas Boudrot
Delta College, University Center, Michigan

Steve Candee
Lane Community College, Eugene, Oregon

Charles P. Hiatt
Central Florida Community College, Ocala, Florida

Dina Krois
Lansing Community College, Lansing, Michigan

Ron Lane
University of Texas, Brownsville, Texas

Carl Luna
San Diego Mesa College, San Diego, California

Dick Mahood
University of Memphis, Memphis, Tennessee

Joe Mac McKenzie
San Diego Mesa College, San Diego, California

Ed Millican
San Bernardino Valley College, San Bernardino, California

Dorothy Stanton Pelton
Henry Ford Community College, Dearborn, Michigan

Santiago Peregrino
Delta College, University Center, Michigan

Greg Rabb
Jamestown Community College, Jamestown, New York

Jack Waskey
Dalton State College, Dalton, Georgia

Tony Wege
Coastal Georgia Community College, Brunswick, Georgia

Contents in Brief

Table of Contents

PART TWO: THE POLITICS OF PARTICIPATION

CHAPTER 5—Political Parties: Donkeys, Elephants and "Long Shots"   85

CHAPTER 6—Interest Groups: The Politics of Numbers   107

Preface

I have often wondered if anyone actually reads the preface to a book. I must admit that I do not always, because some of them seem too long and too filled with details for me to take the time. Therefore, it is with a bit of anxiety that I write this preface to the twelfth edition of *People and Politics*. If you are still reading, I can promise you that I will be brief and that I will put as much of my personality into this writing as I can so you can get the *feel* for who I am and why this book came about.

Educators like to attend conferences with other educators. It is not that we enjoy one another's company that much. Rather, we like to attend because we get to tax deduct our expenses to that conference, which just happened to be in a city we'd like to visit, such as San Francisco or Chicago or Miami. I attended one of these *delightful* events more than twelve years ago where a discussion took place concerning introductory American government textbooks. No, the discussion was not part of the conference. As usual, the most meaningful things at these conferences occur in the lobby of the hotel or in the bar. The conclusion that this particular group of educators came to that October day in Chicago was that students were not reading most of these textbooks because they were not written for students. On the contrary, most were written by professors for *other* professors. We "profs" wanted our peers to "Oh" and "Ah" and go on about how wonderful our book was. How comprehensive! How definitive! We lost sight of our real audience—students. How good is a book if students do not read it? How good is it if students do not understand it even if they do read it? I had just enough ego to think I could probably write a textbook that students could really understand. Thus, the concept *of People and Politics* was born.

With this twelfth edition, I and a group of very talented and dedicated community college teachers of American government have continued that tradition of trying to make this book as readable as we can for our students. We know that other professors already understand what is contained in these pages. We want *you* to understand it. We want *you* to "catch the fire," so to speak, and to become the educated, attentive citizen that you can be. After all, it is to the benefit of us all for you to do so. We are not naïve enough to think that this one book will transform you from a vegetative state when it comes to politics to one where "the news" becomes your primary focus on TV, radio, or the Internet. However, we do hope that, if you understand what you read here in these pages, you will be intrigued enough to continue to pay attention to what's going on around you in the political arena, to make informed decisions, and to act responsibly.

Mary Kate Hiatt, Ph.D.
May 1, 2005
Saginaw, Michigan USA

Chapter One

Challenges to America:
Thinking About What
Lies Ahead

The year 2005 marked the 218th anniversary of the writing of the Constitution of the United States. Although this constitution was not the first one used in this country, it is the oldest written constitution still in force in the world today. We can rightly wonder how much Americans really know about the Constitution, the foundation upon which our system of government rests, or about the government that this document created so long ago.

If a poll conducted on the 200th anniversary of the writing of the Constitution of over a thousand Americans is accurate, the Constitution is indeed a mystery to many of us.[1] The survey found that only a small majority knew that the Constitution created the government and defined its powers; a similarly small majority did not know that the Bill of Rights is the first ten amendments to the Constitution. Moreover, more than half of the people questioned believed that the statement, "From each according to his ability, to each according to his need," was contained in the document when in reality it is found in Karl Marx's *Communist Manifesto.*

Not only did the survey discover that Americans are woefully ignorant about the general ideas in the Constitution, but it also illustrated that many do not know a great deal about the powers the document grants to various branches or officials of the government. Almost half of the respondents stated (incorrectly) that the president possesses "emergency powers," which allow him or her to suspend constitutional rights during war or other national emergencies. Furthermore, about 60 percent believed (also incorrectly) that the president can appoint justices to the Supreme Court without anyone else's consent; and by a

64-percent margin these Americans believed (incorrectly once again) that the Constitution made English the official language of the United States.

While those responding to the poll were in error about most things relating to the government and the Constitution, they did manage to redeem themselves in some areas, particularly criminal justice issues. However, when we examine why they seemed to know so much about this aspect of the government, we conclude that television has had an impact. Ninety-two percent knew that all persons accused of a crime had to be provided with an attorney free of charge if they could not afford one, and 83 percent knew that everyone had the right to a trial by jury.

Yet despite these "right" answers, there were a number of aspects of constitutional rights that were a bit more muddied. Seventy-five percent asserted that everyone is guaranteed a free, public education through high school; about half stated that the Constitution gives citizens the right to own a handgun, while only 44 percent knew that the Constitution's free speech guarantees include freedom to preach violent revolution. However, 60 percent did know that the Supreme Court is the part of the government that interprets what the Constitution means, but fewer than half correctly identified who the current Chief Justice of the Supreme Court is or what the famous Supreme Court cases *Brown* v. *Board of Education*, *Miranda* v. *Arizona*, or *Roe v. Wade* were all about.[2]

THE GREAT EXPERIMENT

To fill in some of the gaps in our knowledge about the American government and to correct some of the inaccuracies, we should begin with the basic idea that the United States government, created by the Constitution when it went into effect in 1789, was an experiment in many ways. After all, we must remember that the idea of democracy—people governing themselves—was relatively new, and certainly a federation-type government such as the Constitution prescribes was unique in the world at the time. In addition, no other country had a head of state like the president, and no others had a high court that could determine the constitutionality of governmental actions. In other words, governmentally speaking, the United States was unique for its time, and, in many respects, it still is.

This country is unique in other ways. **First**, unlike the European countries of the day, the United States was, and still is, a multinational state. Whereas in Spain, for example, one found primarily Spaniards, in the United States there were many different nationalities and races represented. This situation makes the country a bit more difficult to govern at times perhaps, but many people feel it is also one of America's greatest strengths.

Second, the original settlers of this country were quite different from those who set off for the Spanish, French, or Portuguese colonies. The men and women who came to the English colonies along the coast of North America fell pre-

Dressed in the garb of early patriots, these marchers remind their fellow citizens of our nation's struggle for freedom and liberty.

dominantly into three categories: (1) those seeking to make their fortunes— adventurers, (2) political and religious dissenters, and (3) poor people who left their native lands to seek a better life in the colonies. The British, unlike the Spanish and the French, looked upon the "New World" as a place to send their excess population, as a source of raw materials for their growing industries, and as a market for their manufactured goods. The Spanish, the French, and the Portuguese saw the Americas primarily as places to exploit for the benefit of the mother country and severely restricted who could settle there. To the colonists who settled in what later became the United States, the New World was indeed a promised land—a land alive with hope and opportunity for them. Leaving the "old world" behind, the Americans, according to the viewpoint of the French in that time, were trying to build a new land. Although they were not driven westward across the Appalachian Mountains by economic ambition, the trail blazers who marched toward the mighty Mississippi took democratic ideals along and recreated that which they had east of the mountains. America was, indeed, a dynamic place, no less so in the wilderness than in the cities.

In the years since the present Constitution was put in place, the United States has enjoyed an enviable reputation of stability. Unlike many other countries in the Western Hemisphere (North and South America), this country has had but one violent, political upheaval (War Between the States, 1861-1865). Despite national traumas such as the Great Depression of the 1930s and the assassinations of four presidents (Lincoln, Garfield, McKinley, and Kennedy), the United States government has remained on a stable course without disruption of the governmental processes. In fact, even when confronted with massive political and economic woes after the Revolution, the Americans still leisurely took two years to find a solution in a new constitution and as De Tocqueville recounts, ". . . without its costing humanity a single tear or drop of blood." Although we do not have the highest standard of living in the world today, Americans still enjoy more economic advantages than most of the people of the world. This economic and political stability may, in part, explain why the United States has escaped some of the radical, sociopolitical movements such as Marxism or anarchism, which seem to plague many countries around the world.

Challenges to American Democracy

If, indeed, we assert that the United States is a democratic country—one that allows the overwhelming majority of its citizens to participate in the governing process—then we certainly must also recognize that it is relatively easy to govern ourselves when things are going well. It is quite another matter when serious problems arise for which there are probably no quick or simple solutions. A number of such serious challenges confronts the American government in the first decade of the twenty-first century.

Military Challenges. The United States began the twentieth century as an emerging great power. Combining its military might with that of other countries, the United States fought two world wars in the first half of the twentieth century. The Allied victory in World War II in 1945 did not mean an end to the need for a strong military. On the contrary, the threat to world peace was thought by some to be even greater since the United States, soon followed by the Soviet Union (U.S.S.R.), had nuclear capabilities. For approximately forty-five years after the end of that great war, the U.S. and the U.S.S.R. fought what was described as a "cold war." While neither country usually confronted the other's armies directly, both countries and their allies built up massive military capabilities and expended vast amounts of national wealth to maintain the so-called arms race.

With the collapse of the Soviet Union in 1991 and the end of the cold war, it appeared, for a short time, that military threats to American interests were in retreat. As both the 1991 Gulf War and the tragic events of September 11, 2001, demonstrated, the end of the cold war has not eliminated external threats to the United States. **Terrorism** has emerged as the major threat to American security. Moreover, as one noted scholar points out, America's position as the sole remaining great superpower may invite a backlash from many peoples around the world, and terrorism provides a mechanism for that backlash.[3]

Terrorism has no nationality. Unlike dealing with an action undertaken by a particular country's military, dealing with a terrorist incident can be a particularly frustrating endeavor since often it is not known who did the deed or where the terrorist can be found. Even if the governments of certain countries such as Afghanistan, Iran, Syria, or North Korea can be identified as supporters of and havens for terrorists, it is quite difficult to tie these countries directly to a terrorist incident; therefore, retaliation becomes a moot point. The destruction of the World Trade Center in New York in 2001 by Al Qaeda terrorists was quickly tied to the Taliban regime in Afghanistan, but this case was unusual. Many times identifying and then finding the culprits never happens.

World opinion is more often than not against such retaliation for a number of reasons. **First**, some of these countries supply our allies with substantial amounts of necessary items such as oil. **Second**, these countries purchase numerous products, not the least of which is military hardware, from these allies. **Third**, retaliation against a country as Iran, frequently identified as a supporter of terrorism, could have serious consequences for the United States since the Iranians have some sophisticated weaponry of their own and share a border with Russia. If military action occurred in Iran, Russia or other parties might be drawn into the conflict.

The Department of State defines terrorism as ". . . premeditated, politically motivated violence perpetrated against noncombatant targets by subnational groups or clandestine state agents. International terrorism is terrorism involving citizens or territory of more than one country." Put another way, terrorism is the ability of a person or a group of people to extract compliance from another person or group through the use of force or the threat of it illegally[4] or without regard for human rights; i.e., terrorism aims to extract this compliance through massive intimidation to bring about specific changes in the behavior, thought processes, and emotions of the masses. These desired changes include pity, sympathy, indignation, and hatred, depending upon who the terrorist targets are. Such a definition is much more neutral in that it can be applied to any form of terrorism, whether from a relatively small, unorganized group, an individual, or from the power of the state itself. As defined, terrorism challenges the ability of the United States to protect its citizens at home and abroad. The use of civilian airliners to destroy the World Trade Center and damage the Pentagon in 2001, as well as earlier attacks on American targets in Sudan, Yemen and Kenya, fully underscore the nature of this threat.

While it appears that very few people have claimed to have the answer to what causes terrorism, everyone seems to agree that at least one contributing factor is unequal distribution of the world's resources. In plain language, the highly industrialized countries such as the United States and most Western European countries have accumulated most of the world's wealth. Poorer countries perceive this situation as unfair, and that perception provides a fertile breeding ground for terrorism. Other major contributing factors to terrorism are ideological, religious, and cultural differences. As the influences of democratic capitalism, with its emphasis on individual rights and ambitions, spread around the world, they pose uncomfortable challenges to established cultures and political regimes. In so far as one becomes "modern," one may lose one's traditional ideological or religious identity. Asian societies, such as Japan and Singapore, seem to have made this transition more successfully than more traditional societies in Africa and the Middle East. In these societies, people who find it most difficult to cope with modern changes may strike out, hence, the rise in political terrorism by religious fundamentalists around the world, such as with the Taliban in Afghanistan and the Al Qaeda terrorist network of Osama bin Laden. As global capitalism continues to develop, this conflict between "new" and "old" ways of organizing societies will continue to grow. Much the same thing occurred in Western Europe when the medieval period gave way to the Renaissance and the beginnings of modern capitalism.

In contrast to the focus by the Clinton administration during the 1990s on global economic issues, the Bush administration has been compelled to switch the focus of American foreign policy to military and terrorist threats. This shift has caused a reevaluation of the United States' relationships with other countries, such as the states of the former Soviet Union. The disintegration of the Soviet Union into its component parts—Russia being the most significant—as well as the emergence of Boris Yeltsin as the first democratically elected president of Russia seemed at the time a "good" thing from an American perspective since the United States would no longer have to contend with a united, powerful, and hostile Soviet Union. The Yeltsin administration, while marked by a closer personal relationship with U.S. President Bill Clinton, was marred by

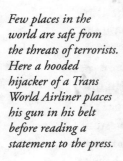

Few places in the world are safe from the threats of terrorists. Here a hooded hijacker of a Trans World Airliner places his gun in his belt before reading a statement to the press.

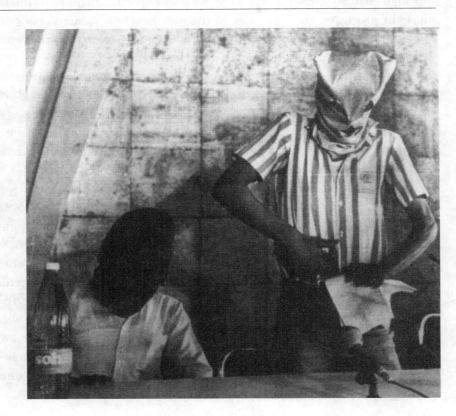

corruption, a major economic downturn in 1998, and a bloody, ethnic war in the break away Muslim republic of Chechnya.

One of the consequences of the September 11 terrorist attacks has been a strengthening of ties between the U.S. and states of the former Soviet Union, particularly Russia. These countries and the United States have found common cause in allying with the "war" on terrorism proclaimed President Bush after these attacks. Russian voters elected Vladimir Putin, a former KGB (secret police) officer, as president in 2000. Communists continue to hold high positions in a number of other, former members of the old Soviet bloc such as in Byelorussia and Muslim central Asian republics such as Uzbekistan and Tahkistan. Yet despite these lingering ties to the past, the U.S. has cultivated the support of these governments in the war on terrorism. How long this "togetherness" will last is uncertain since there are still major differences among these countries in terms of their interests and ideologies.

Moreover, with the collapse of communism in Eastern Europe, long-standing, ethnic rivalries resurfaced that had been squelched for the past half century by the strong police states that existed in that part of the world. In 1999, the U.S and its NATO allies fought a brief war with Serbia over the treatment of Muslims in Kosovo. When President Clinton committed troops to the area in his second term as president, he assured the American public that the soldiers "would be home by Christmas." They are still there, and the hostilities are still evident. This area, known collectively as the Balkans, continues to be a significant challenge to European stability. Ethnic conflicts such as these have taken on a new significance as they provide a potential breeding ground for terrorist organizations.

The War on Terrorism has become either the motivation for or the justification for the increased use of American power around the world. In the spring of 2002, President Bush announced a shift in American national security policy. The "**Bush Doctrine**" announced to the world that the United States has the option of preemptive (first) strikes against any threat to American security interests. This new approach is different from previous American policy never to strike first. (See Chapter Fourteen.) The first test of this doctrine was the invasion in 2001 of Afghanistan and the overthrow of the Taliban fundamentalist government, from which Al Qaeda terrorists arose under the leadership of Osama bin Laden. The second example of the United States' new policy came in March 2003. The U.S. and its coalition allies invaded Iraq and removed the government of dictator Saddam Hussein, who, according to the Americans, the British, and others, threatened the use of chemical and biological weapons.

In addition to terrorism and ethnic tensions, more traditional conflicts continue to threaten global stability. Problems continue in the Middle East, such as the issue of Iran, an Islamic fundamentalist republic historically at odds with the U.S., pursuing nuclear weapons, and rising pro-democracy movements in

Arab states such as Egypt, Lebanon, and Syria since the U.S. invasion of Iraq and the holding of democratic elections. Since the Middle East is a major supplier of the world's oil, this continuing instability in the region is a potent threat, not only to United States' national interests but also to those of most of the rest of the world.

Economic Challenges. Economic issues have always underscored the American domestic, political debate and have made or broken political careers. While there have been periods of economic recession during this time, for the most part the country has experienced prosperity and economic growth. Presidents and members of Congress delight in taking credit for the good times and point the finger elsewhere during the bad.

The rising global economy has had a profound and expanding influence on America's economy. From the infamous triangle trade of the eighteenth century, to the clipper ships of the nineteenth, to its role as the world's industrial and technological giant in the twentieth, the United States has always been a country built on trade. Over the past generation, globalization and its impact on domestic economic performance has only intensified. In the 1970s, the U.S. suffered from "**stagflation**," an economic condition characterized by high unemployment and high inflation. This stagflation, although mild compared to that experienced by many other countries, was still very upsetting to the public at large. One of the major causes of that economic disaster of the '70s was the oil embargoes by the Oil Producing and Exporting Countries (OPEC) and the resulting massive increase in energy costs. The price of oil and natural gas once again plague everyone's budget in the new millennium.

America's economic problems in the 1970s were further compounded by **increasing global competition**. The European and Japanese economies, now fully recovered from the damage of WW II, joined by the developing industrial economics in East Asia, began to put more pressure on American manufacturers, who had been somewhat insulated from such competition in the decades after World War II. During this period increased foreign competition, especially from lower-paid wages abroad, caused a significant loss of good paying factory jobs in the United States. In the 1980s this job loss particularly hit blue collar workers in the manufacturing sector. The American manufacturing sector lost about 1 million jobs between 1981 and 1986. By the 1990s the erosion of good-paying jobs seeped into the high tech, middle management and services sector, the "holy grail" of middle-class job security. To try and become more competitive in the emerging global economy, major corporations began "downsizing" (a euphemism for "laying-off," which is the practical equivalent of "firing") large numbers of relatively well-paid, middle-class workers.

In 1960, President John F. Kennedy proclaimed "a rising tide lifts all boats," meaning that traditionally in America, when the economy is doing well, everyone prospers. This has been part of the social glue that has held this country together for over two hundred years. For a number of reasons, not the least of which is the changing of the economy from an industrial one to an informational one, the lowest economic class lost ground in the competition for accumulation of wealth. The unprecedented economic boom of the 1990s with the resulting build up of large fortunes by some corporate elites, the collapse of the dot.com stock bubble in the spring of 2000, and the Enron corporate scandal produced a relatively negative image of capitalism. The result was that average Americans do not trust a good portion of the corporate world.

From the 1970s through the 1990s, Asian industrial states—first led by Japan and later China—began to emerge. Using an export-led strategy of development, these economic "tigers," as they were called in the press, increasingly target the U.S. market for their goods. In addition, the United States faces serious competition for the **European Union (EU)**, which in 1992 formed an even stronger trade confederation than already existed. Some analysts see this move as a much greater challenge to American economic dominance than anything the Japanese could do. In response to this challenge, the United States joined with Canada and Mexico in the **North American Free Trade Agreement (NAFTA)**, which is an economic confederation similar to the EU.

But, if other countries' economic success may come at American expense, their economic failures can cause even more problems for the U.S. After rapid expansion in the 1980s, the Asian "tigers," beginning with powerhouse Japan, slipped into an increasingly deep recession. The near-collapse of formerly prospering economies in Malaysia, Indonesia, and other Asian countries and their weak economic recovery are a major concern for U.S. economic policy makers. They fear that future economic downturns like the 1997 "Asian flu" could spread like a contagion across the world, potentially triggering a global depression. No less a figure than, international financier George Soros has argued that the world faces a potentially disastrous economic downturn due to the increasing volatility of global trade and finance.[5] Weak economies in Asia, Latin America and Eastern Europe all are looking to the United States, as both a source of aid, as well as an export destination, to help their flagging economies.

The American economy, however, showed signs of weakness by the spring of 2000 when it slipped into a mild recession. Productivity of nonfarm and non-supervisory workers has been increasing at the rate of about 3 percent per year. Economists say that much of this increase in productivity reflects the billions of dollars spent on computers and high tech equipment over the last decade. The problem now is that companies continue to face global competition. One bright spot stands out. The productivity of the American worker (nonfarm) rose in the fourth quarter of 2000 at an annual rate of 3.5 percent, and stands at 2.3 percent annual rate since the official beginning of the recession in March 2000.[6] Continued productivity increases are dependent on the workers' environment, in which training and equipment play significant roles.

A sign of the global economy. A manufacturing plant once associated with the production of American goods now bears the sign of foreign ownership— "Mataushita Electric Corporation of America." The "buying of America, as it is termed by those concerned with foreign investments in the United States, is a major economic problem facing this country in the coming years.

The American economy, moreover, is fueled by consumer spending. To maintain this spending rate, the average American has been increasingly dipping into savings. In September 1998, for the first time since statistics on savings began to be gathered 40 years ago, the savings rate dipped into negative numbers and has continued at that level. The economic slowdown in Asia has had a domino affect on numerous American exporters to the region, especially in the western United States. Global financial insecurities, uncertainty over the Japanese economy and the new European currency (the **EURO**), as well as extreme fluctuations in the energy markets, such as in California, have also made the U.S. stock market volatile. It is the technology sector that drove the huge market gains of the last decade. Continued weakness in this sector drags down the entire economy, as does lingering fears over the war on terror.

The future economy of the United States seems a mixed bag. The major trends are number one, the growth of the size of the American economy. If you drew a map of the world in economic terms, practically the only thing on it would be the United States. As of 2005, the United States had a 11.3 trillion dollar economy, twice the size of Japan at 4.3 trillion and 9 times the size of China.

The second major trend is the creation of a permanent two tier or two class economy, the very aristocracy that Americans prohibited in their federal Constitution. On the one hand, there is a massive excess of global workers, which keeps wages down.[7] On the other hand, there has been a systematic cutting of the tax rates of the wealthiest Americans. From John Fitzgerald Kennedy through Ronald Reagan, income tax rates were cut from 90 to 28 percent and George W. Bush has persuaded the Republican Congress to reduce them even further. Governor Schwarzenegger in California has even proposed no sales tax on yachts. Today a rising economic tide lifts only the yachts.

The third major trend is the explosion of the M3 money supply by Alan Greenspan, Chairman of the Federal Reserve. M3 is the sum of the U.S. monetary base and the non-gold international reserves held by central banks. M3 is being created by Chairman Greenspan at a rate of 17 billion dollars a week or almost a trillion dollars a year. This explosion in M3 contributes to the decline in the value of the dollar in 4 years from 1 Euro being equal to 85 cents to 1 Euro equaling $1.35. This inflation is causing central banks to switch from the dollar to the Euro as the basis of stored value.[8]

The fourth major trend is the decline of the technological advantage held by the United States in various non-military areas. For example, by the end of 2005, Toyota's entire line of cars, trucks and SUV's is supposed to be hybrids attaining 38-55 miles per gallon. Obviously, a number of American auto workers will lose their jobs, which will have an adverse economic effect.

A fifth major trend is the rising U.S. trade and budget deficit and the falling value of the American dollar over the past several years. When George W. Bush assumed the presidency in 2001, the American government was projected to run a budget surplus (where revenues exceed expenditures) of more than three trillion dollars by the end of the decade. A combination of declining government revenues due to the recession that followed the collapse of the Dot.Com bubble, tax cuts initiated by the president, and increased government spending on social programs and the war on terrorism resulted, by 2005, of the government running deficits in excess of $300 billion dollars a year and projected accumulated deficit of three to four trillion dollars over the next deficit. Economists worry that excessive government deficits have two adverse effects on the American government. First, deficits increase domestic spending, which can drive up inflation. Second, excessive government borrowing leaves less money for the private sector to borrow, driving up interest rates, which can slow down both consumption and investment, slowing the American economy. Domestic interest rates, however, remained historically low through the 2004 election year, in large part because foreign countries—especially Asian countries that sell massive quantities of products to the United States—have loaned hundreds of billions of dollars to the U.S. to offset its deficits. These countries fear a decline in the U.S. economy can adversely affect their exports to America. But, when you add the amount of money foreign countries have been loaning the U.S. to the U.S. trade deficit—the amount the U.S. buys from the world subtracted from the amount it sells to the world—the U.S. has been running over $600 billion dollars per year in the red. Foreign investors around the world increasingly feel the U.S. economic position is unsustainable. This has been manifested by a major drop in the value of the dollar against other currencies, especially the Euro. The dollar (and the U.S. economy) might well drop precipitously should Asian countries decide the U.S. is no longer a good investment bet over the next several years.

Equality. Not only is the United States challenged to maintain its economic prowess, but it is also challenged to create a society where all people are treated equally regardless of their race, ethnic background, religion, sex, or political views. One difficulty seems to be that many Americans do not see the connection between the concept of equality and its application in real life. Whether referring to equality for women or minority groups such as blacks, Hispanics, or native Americans, the problem remains the same: How do we ensure that everyone is treated fairly? The question sounds almost simplistic. However, if we look at the history of this or any other country in trying to provide equal treatment for all its people, we observe that the road to equality is long and difficult.

The grand American experiment to which we referred earlier occurred not only in the area of governmental structure but also in the realm of ideals. The United States was the first country to unite two ideals that, until that day, were thought to be incompatible—equality and liberty. In the mind of a European, equality meant an equal sharing of money and property. On the other hand, liberty meant the right of individuals to pursue their own ambitions without governmental interference—thus, creating a situation whereby some acquired more wealth than others. Accordingly, the two concepts clashed. How then was it possible to believe in equality and liberty at the same time?

For the most part, the American thinkers resolved the dilemma by accepting the traditional view of liberty while rejecting that of equality. Instead, equality was assigned a new meaning—one relying upon morality and politics rather than the traditional economic one. From the American perspective, true also to its strict, Protestant views, human beings stood as equals before the eyes of their Creator. Consequently, no person had the right to hold himself or herself above another in terms of human worth. Likewise, since people were moral equals, it then followed that no person had the right to enslave another or, for that matter, deny to another political and civil rights. Regarding material rewards, American thinkers rejected the strict view of equal wealth and instead focused on equal opportunity. Here each member of the society would be free to compete openly and fairly for the riches of society. Although it would be true that some would inevitably obtain more than others, such inequities would be deemed just and tolerable so long as everyone was afforded the opportunity to compete fairly. In summary then, equality in the American definition implied the following: (1) **political equality**, (2) **social equality**, and (3) **equality of opportunity**. Viewed in this context, liberty and equality were not only compatible but indispensable to each other. If liberty implied the right of individuals to pursue their own ambitions, then they must be afforded the opportunity to exercise their talents free from governmental interference. If not, then liberty would be meaningless.

Political thinkers have long recognized the importance of ideals to the survival of nations. In essence, ideals are the glue that binds a society together. A nation lacking either an agreement upon its ideals or a belief that these ideals are fairly applied is destined for continual upheaval. A reading of any daily paper with its account of civil war throughout the world bears witness to this assertion. What then does the future hold for America? Will women and racial and ethnic minorities become increasingly more discontented with their lot? The United States is presumably committed to a course of equality for all. To avoid future problems, then, we must reaffirm our belief in our ideals by expanding opportunities so that all of our citizens may share equitably in the riches of our society. On this point agreement is fairly common. On how it is to be accomplished, consensus breaks down. Nevertheless, the challenge remains before us.

Confidence in Government. While economic and social problems present significant challenges to democracy in the United States, a series of events over the last four decades has produced perhaps a more serious threat. Americans in the past usually had great confidence in the government's integrity, honesty, and fairness. Now, however, there is apparently a rather pervasive attitude that all politicians are "crooks"; the people who serve in the government are either dishonest or incompetent. This attitude was not produced overnight but has been fueled by a number of significant political events over the last several decades.

First, for most of the post-World War II period, political parties have declined in influence. As we shall see in later chapters, where parties once served to organize opinion and action in the citizenry, as well as in the government, political parties had lost much of their ability to "capture" a voter for more than one election. In other words, the public seemed to have become independent of party loyalties. Many people apparently were inclined to align themselves from election to election with candidates who appealed to them at the moment, rather than to stick with a particular political party. This trend was somewhat reversed during the 1990s by the increasing polarization of the American "right" and "left," but large numbers of Americans continue to see themselves as political "independents." If the results of the elections of 1994, 1996, 1998, 2000 and 2004 are indicative, it would appear that, at least at some levels, a significant social divide has emerged in American politics, increasingly polarizing the major parties. The inability of voters to clearly indicate a preference between the two major parties in the 2000 and 2004 elections, the former one of the closest in history and the latest the narrowest reelection margin for an incumbent since Woodrow Wilson, is seen by some commentators as evidence of an electorate split down the middle but closely tied to the moderate middle. Demographic analysis of the election, however, can be interpreted differently.

George W. Bush, the Republican candidate for president in 2004, overwhelmingly won in predominantly white, agrarian, church-going rural counties. Al Gore, the Democratic candidate, won heavily in the more multicultural, industrial and post-industrial secular urban counties. In the states in which Mr. Gore won the electoral vote, such as California, Illinois and New Mexico, Mr. Bush still won most of the rural counties. Similarly, Mr. Gore won most of the urban areas in states that went for Mr. Bush. Such a result may indicate the emergence of a much greater cultural and political division within American society that has not been seen before for the past century. In this polarized environment partisan politics has intensified. (Witness the Clinton impeachment process.) Yet, as the political environment becomes increasingly partisan, true moderates may well find themselves increasingly marginalized by both parties. The 2004 election repeated this "Red State" (Republican) "Blue State" (Democrat) divide, with George W. Bush winning 93 percent of votes of Republican voters and Democrat John F. Kerry, senator from Massachusetts, winning 90 percent of his party's vote. Moderate voters who might vote for either party seem an increasingly endangered species in America.

Second, the decline of party loyalty and the rise of partisanship have produced a change in the expectations of the American electorate toward people's attention. The president has now assumed that predominant spot. He or she will be expected to be all things to all people—to be the leader, economically, politically, and morally, not only within the United States but also in the world. He or she must be "squeaky clean." When failure or human weakness appears on the scene, the public becomes disillusioned and apathetic.

To lay the blame totally on the shoulders of the masses would not really tell the whole story about this crisis in confidence toward the government. It is undeniably true that the public's attitude has been fostered by a number of events. For example, the Vietnam War succeeded in driving a deep wedge between the government and the people, as well as between segments of the population who supported the war and those who did not. Revelations about misleading or inaccurate reporting of North Vietnamese troop strength and the commitment of the South Vietnamese to keeping the communists out caused much confusion, dismay, and disillusionment among the masses on both sides of the question. That this country "lost" that war in a most ignominious fashion did not help matters either. Americans believed they were invincible. After all, hadn't "we" defeated the Nazis and the Japanese? How could we then turn around and be driven out of South Vietnam by a "pip-squeak" country like North Vietnam?

Still reeling from the Vietnam fiasco, Americans were treated to "Watergate," in which the President of the United States, Richard Milhouse Nixon, lied to hide his and others' involvement in illegal campaign activities and the attempted cover-up of those activities. On the verge of impeachment and removal from office, he became the first American president to resign his office. Melodramatic as this may sound, discovering that the president had probably committed a criminal act produced some of the same feelings in the public at large that might be experienced by children who discovered their father was "cheating" on their mother: shock, anger, disillusionment.

Similarly, "Irangate" during the last two years of the Reagan administration did not increase public confidence in the government. While former President Reagan was not implicated in any criminal activity, others in his administration were. According to testimony given at Senate hearings on the matter, the United States directly and indirectly sold arms to Iran (a country that the United States has long maintained supports worldwide terrorism) in exchange for American hostages held in Lebanon and subsequently used the profits from these sales to supply Nicaraguan rebels. If nothing else came out of the Iran/Contra scandal, the American public seemed to conclude that the president certainly was not very diligent about finding out who was doing what, when, and how in his government and showed poor judgment concerning the sale of weapons to Iran.

Public questioning of presidential competence has not been limited to Republican presidents. Prior to Reagan's election in 1980, the United States was treated to 444 days of the Iran Hostage Crisis during the one-term administration of President Jimmy Carter. Not only was the public frustrated with Carter's inability to secure freedom for the hostages, they were not at all certain that he was doing anything other than sitting in the White House waiting for Iran to do something. In retrospect, such a stance on the part of the president was probably the best one to take if he hoped eventually to see those hostages released alive. However, the American electorate is not known for its inordinate patience nor its ability to withstand humiliation at the hands of yet another (in their opinion) "pip-squeak" country. President Carter was viewed as highly incompetent as a result of the hostage crisis, which probably was a major contributor to his resounding defeat in 1980.

The Clinton presidency was marked by a never-ending train of allegations and investigations of the president, the First Lady Hilary Clinton, and various members of the administration. These allegations ended in articles of impeachment being brought against the president; however, the senate failed to convict Mr. Clinton; therefore, he continued on as president. Later, the former president's licence to practice law was taken away after Mr. Clinton was convicted of lying to a grand jury during the investigation of one of his "sexcapades."

The administration of George W. Bush itself began in the controversy surrounding the 2000 election problems. The collapse of Enron, the seventh largest corporation in the United States, amid charges of accounting fraud and the loss of billions of dollars in stockholder value and employee pensions further dogged the new administration. Revelations that Enron executives had contributed heavily to both political parties, but especially to the Bush campaign, and the seemingly close relationship between Enron executives and members of the administration created a negative public impression.

There is also a general feeling among the people that the government no longer does anything really well. The Veterans Administration is viewed as highly inefficient in dealing with the problems of those who served in the armed forces. The Congress is looked upon by many as being composed of self-serving individuals who can only agree on salary increases for themselves and when to adjourn for vacation. The Courts are seen as agents of injustice where criminals are set free to continue preying on society. Police, particularly in big cities, are viewed as corrupt, willing to look the other way on dope or prostitution as long as they are paid off by the criminal element. Without doubt, these attitudes and economic, social, and political problems that beset the United States put severe strains on this system of government we call democracy.

President Bush's remarkably high public support following September 11 helped to restore some degree of public confidence in the American government. But President Bush's approval ratings dropped dramatically over the next several years. The Bush administration used claims that Saddam Hussein, dictator of Iraq, was developing weapons of mass destruction and actively supported terrorists like Al Qaeda as justification for its 2003 invasion of that country. Subsequent to the invasion, it became apparent to the American public that neither of these allegations were true. Allegations of American abuse of Iraqi prisoners and continued violence in Iraq necessitating an apparently open ended American military occupation further undermined public support for both the war and the president. By the 2004 election year, Bush's approval rating had fallen to barely 50 percent. In general, the increase of the American public's confidence in its government has been declining over the last three years back to pre-9/11 levels. Whether this trend will continue remains to be seen.

Illegal Drugs. Unless the United States government and, more importantly, the American people themselves find a way of dealing successfully with the "drug problem," none of us will have to worry about war, poverty, equality, or whether we have confidence in the government. In the past it could be said that illegal distribution and use of drugs were found only in the "bad" neighborhoods or the "bad" schools. Now one can find "horse," "nose candy," "crack," or "ice" almost anywhere including places operated by the government such as prisons. The stuff is sold in school yards to kids in the third grade by kids who are in the fourth grade! Drug addiction is an "equal opportunity employer" in that it does not discriminate on the basis of race, creed, color, sex, national origin, place of residence, or occupation. The amount of money lost by American business because of drug-abusing employees, the amount of money spent by police agencies and prisons on drug-related crimes, the amount of money spent on trying to rehabilitate users, and the amount of money spent in trying

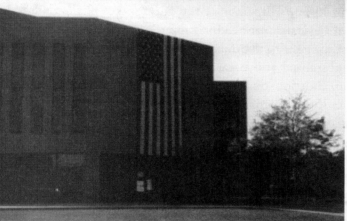

After the September 11 attacks on the World Trade Center and the Pentagon, the public displayed American flags in a show of patriotism and support for the "war on terrorism."

to educate people about the dangers of drugs are almost incalculable. However, the real tragedy lies in the number of wasted lives because of drug abuse. Some of these countless dead are innocent of any wrongdoing—the person who just happened to be in the wrong place at the right time when drug dealers decided to shoot at each other, or the baby who was born addicted to "crack" because the mother was a user.

Some argue that the drug problem is caused by foreigners who grow the crops from which the drugs are made. Colombia, Cuba, Panama, Mexico, and Nicaragua are frequently denounced as "drug-trafficking" countries. It is true that these and other countries supply many of the drugs that reach the American market. Let's not forget who the buyers are. If Americans didn't buy illegal drugs, there would be no market here and, hence, no drug problem for us domestically. It should also be remembered that marijuana, although illegal, is a huge, domestic cash crop in the United States. A number of people make their living growing "pot" as other people grow wheat. It seems then that perhaps our task should be to stop trying to lay the blame for our drug habits on the Colombian drug lords or others and seek the solutions in our own back yard.

The Abortion Question. No issue since the slavery issue of the nineteenth century has divided Americans into such extreme positions as has abortion. While polls show that a majority of Americans support freedom of choice on abortion, there is a substantial and vocal segment of the population who are vehemently opposed to abortion. Some oppose abortion even in cases of danger of death to the mother if the pregnancy continues. Both the "pro-choice" and "anti-choice" sides accuse the other of wrongdoings. Anti-choice groups often refer to pro-choice groups as murderers. In 1993, 1994, and again in 1998 physicians who performed abortions were murdered by members of anti-abortion groups. In 1995, two workers in clinics providing abortion services were shot to death by an anti-abortion extremist. Numerous abortion clinics have been bombed or have received bomb threats. On any given day throughout the country anti-choice groups picket clinics where abortions are performed, and pro-choice groups picket the picketers! The question seems to be irreconcilable since neither side seems willing to compromise. Regardless of the outcome of the abortion question—and there will be many political clashes among various branches of the federal government on this issue—it has raised the specter of extremism in the United States to a level that has not been seen since just prior to the civil war. Scientific inquiries into such areas as human cloning and stem cell research only serve to further cloud and inflame the issue.

UNDERSTANDING GOVERNMENT

It is obvious from the previous discussion of some of the challenges the United States government and its people face that these kinds of problems just don't go away over the course of time. On the contrary, they usually get worse. The easiest thing to do, of course, would be to continue going along the path we have been, saying: "*They* ought to do something." However, if we are to continue under the relatively democratic system that we now have, these challenges must be faced, not by *them* but by *us* since the word democracy comes from the Greek words *demos*, meaning people, and *cratein*, meaning rule. How are we to do this? The first step is in understanding government, in general, and the United States government, in particular: its origins, purposes, and functions.

The Nature of Government

Definition. To begin with, government can be defined in many different words. The words used here are not necessarily the ones you might choose to use, so feel free to phrase your own definition, just so long as you understand what the words mean and can express that meaning to yourself and others. Government is the legal structure that contains the formal "rulers," who initiate and pass laws (rules), execute and administer laws, and interpret the laws and resolve disputes. In other words, governments, regardless of what kind they are (democratic or nondemocratic), have three functions: a legislative function, an executive function, and a judicial function. Not all governments perform these functions in the same way, but they all do perform the same functions.

Origin of the State and Government. Human beings, being the rather curious animals that they are, have wondered, often in lengthy written works, where government originated. It is apparently disquieting to many people not to know exactly the origins of everything that exists or ever existed. With this mind set, political theorists have created many possible scenarios as to the origin of government.

Depending on how loosely the term government is defined, some people contend that governments have existed since the time that at least two people existed: one was the leader and the other the follower. Since the "leader" made and enforced the rules, and resolved any disputes that arose, he or she was the government. As people became more numerous, families organized into clans (related families), clans organized into tribes (related clans), tribes into nations (related tribes), and nations ultimately into states, such as the United States, Mexico, Kenya, or Kuwait. Along the way as the societal organizations became more complex, so did the governments that ruled these societies. This kind of theory of the origin of states and governments is often referred to as the **evolutionary theory**.

Other people, not being satisfied with the evolutionary theory, decided that governments and states originated by force: hence, the **force theory**. These people contend that at some point in the early history of human beings, one man was so much stronger and probably more psychologically intimidating than the others in the group that he forcibly imposed his will on them. "You do what I say or I'll beat you with my big club and then stab you with my Saber-Toothed

Tiger bone!" (You got the picture?) This "tough guy," in turn, then recruited other, lesser "tough guys" as his enforcers. In return for their services, they would receive property, which was probably taken from those they governed. (Does this scenario sound like some of the things that go on today?)

Then there are those good-natured souls who just cannot buy that the origin of the state and the government could have come about in either of these haphazard or crude ways. These folks are called social contract theorists. They say that the evolutionists and the force people are all wrong. What really happened is this. Way back in the dark days of history, human beings existed in a state of nature—no government, free to do as they pleased, except as limited by the laws of nature. However, when things started getting a little crowded, human beings, being rational (thinking) animals, realized that forming an organized society and having someone to govern it was necessary. Therefore, these people sat down and drew up a contract, an agreement, among themselves to form this organized society that today we call the **state**. Then they made a contract with one of their members to be the ruler. This person (Let's call him George) could be the ruler as long as he governed fairly. If George began to do things that were not fair to the people of the state, then those people could revolt, kick old George out, and get a new ruler. In other words, governments were created with the consent of the people to be governed, and the people could withdraw their consent if the government became arbitrary (not governing according to the agreed-upon rules).

This theory of the origin of the state and the government, the **social contract theory**, was first asserted in 1689 by John Locke, an Englishman, who was trying to justify two revolutions that had occurred in England in the previous forty years. It was also used to justify the American Revolution in 1776. Let's take a look at the social contract theory in use in the Declaration of Independence.

> *We hold these truths to be self-evident; . . . that they [people] are endowed by their Creator with certain unalienable rights . . . .*
>
> *That to secure these rights, governments are instituted among men, deriving their just powers from the consent of the governed;*
>
> *That whenever any form of government becomes destructive of these ends, it is the right of the people to alter or to abolish it, and to institute new government. . . .*

You can see that the author of the Declaration, Thomas Jefferson, was quite familiar with the social contract theory. Jefferson knew that the political leaders of England would also understand what the Americans were saying because politicians in England had used these arguments less than one hundred years before to justify their own revolutions against tyrannical kings! Jefferson, to say the least, was a pretty smart cookie to use their own arguments against them.

John Locke, an English philosopher, greatly influenced the thinking of our Founders and provided the rationale for our break with England.

Purposes of Government. If we accept that the social contract theory is the foundation of the American government, then the purpose of government must be to protect our inherent, "unalienable" natural rights. We can also look to the Constitution of the United States itself to see other purposes that the Founding Fathers believed to be important in 1787.

The Preamble to the Constitution states the purposes of government, besides those mentioned above, to be: **(1)** "to establish Justice," **(2)** "to promote the general Welfare," and **(3)** "to secure the Blessings of Liberty to ourselves and our Posterity." If we read the entirety of the Constitution, we find that the terms "justice," "the general welfare," and "liberty" are not clearly defined anywhere in the document. Over the years the meanings have been clarified by laws and court decisions. We must keep in mind that the meanings and, therefore, the purposes of government change over the years. For example, it is doubtful that the people of Washington's day interpreted the meaning of "promote the general Welfare" to mean that the government would provide Medicare, Medicaid, unemployment compensation, aid to dependent children, public education, guaranteed student loans, and the like. Today many take these things for granted as legitimate functions of government in providing for the "general Welfare."

However, we must bear in mind that not everyone in the world sees things the same way. Some view the purposes of government to be much more invasive of citizens' personal lives than we do. For example, workers in Singapore routinely submit to weekly drug tests without batting an eyelash. (Singapore, it might be noted, has very little problem with drug abuse, but it is also illegal to chew gum in Singapore!) Nevertheless, in the minds of most Americans today the United States government exists to do those things that we cannot do very readily for ourselves (e.g., defend against foreign enemies) and increasingly many things that we habitually did for ourselves or formerly were not done at all.

THE AMERICAN GOVERNMENT

Representative Democracy. Throughout the world, both the purposes of governments and their structures may differ. The United States government is, at least ostensibly, a **representative democracy**. Instead of individuals deciding for themselves what the government should do (**direct democracy**), we elect or appoint others to make these decisions, i.e., to represent us in making these decisions. Not only are these "representatives" located in the legislative branch of government (Congress), but they are also found in the executive branch in the person of the president, vice president, and cabinet members, as well as in the judicial branch in the person of judges. By living in this society, we have given up our right to do whatever we want, whenever we want. We have given the government the authority to make, enforce, and interpret the "rules of the game," so to speak. Our particular government does these things, as we noted, in a democratic manner through representatives.

Constitutionalism. However, the representatives are not free to make, enforce, or interpret rules as they see fit. Rather, we have constitutions, national and state, which set limits on the ruling authority of our representatives, as well as limits on individual behavior to some extent. Governments that are limited in this manner are said to be constitutional governments, meaning they are limited by constitutions. Whether democratic or nondemocratic, almost all governments today have some form of written constitution. Yet, we can readily

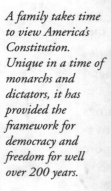

A family takes time to view America's Constitution. Unique in a time of monarchs and dictators, it has provided the framework for democracy and freedom for well over 200 years.

A prerequisite for democratic government is an informed, knowledgeable citizenry and participation. Here, Senator Dick Durbin (D-IL) is talking to a group of students visiting the capital.

see that a constitution is not worth more than a piece of used gum unless people are willing to abide by its provisions. Unfortunately throughout the world there are people who will disregard constitutions or any other form of laws and run the country for their own purposes. The Philippine Islands under former "President" Ferdinand Marcos is an example of a government disregarding the laws to suit the dictator's own purposes. The goal of President Marcos in governing the Philippines was to ensure his political power and family wealth. Political scientists refer to this form of government as a "kleptocracy": the rule of thieves.

Separation of Powers, Federalism, Check and Balance System. To try to prevent similar occurrences in the United States, the government is constructed in such a way that governmental power is highly decentralized. Here we mean that not only is the national government divided into parts (legislative, executive, and judicial branches—**separation of powers**), but the government is also divided on a geographic basis: one central government and currently fifty state governments (**federalism**). In addition, at the national level, as well as at the state level, each branch of government is given approximately equal amounts of authority, as well as some power to control or, at least, prevent the action of the others (**check and balance system**). As we shall see in later chapters, this system of checks, while apparently warding off some abuses of governmental authority, tends also to slow the governing process down, often to a crawl. Despite this drawback, however, many people believe that without these constitutional checks and limitations of power, the United States would not be considered the leader of the "free world" today.

AMERICA'S FUTURE

There are always people running around who are willing to prophesy gloom and doom. In fact, it is often easier to be pessimistic than optimistic about the future since pessimism does not require us to do anything but to sit around moaning and groaning. On the other hand, optimism demands action, demands that we get off our duff and *do* something. We cannot expect someone else to do things for us; we must be responsible for our own future. We Americans have chosen and now have a long tradition of democratic government. You will recall the origin of the word democracy: *demos*, meaning people, and *cratein*, meaning rule. Democracy is not the easiest form of government to have; in practice it may be the most difficult since it requires us, the people, to *do* something. What does democracy and, indeed, our future and the future of the country we live in require us to do? It requires that we do three things, none of which are necessarily easy. **First**, democracy requires that we educate ourselves so that we will have the tools with which to gather information to apply and interpret it. **Second**, democracy requires that we inform ourselves about what is going on so that our decisions are not based on incorrect or inadequate data. **Third**, democracy requires that we become involved. We can be quite educated and informed and still do nothing.

If all of us or even just a majority of us in the United States were to become educated, informed, and involved, the problems we face would not seem so insurmountable. We may, indeed, never eliminate poverty or war, for example, which would be sad, but never to have tried would be tragic. If we Americans truly wish to do something about these challenges, rather than just sit around and complain about how "they" are not doing anything, then the first step is to become educated about how the government works. That, my friends, is the point of this book.

Chapter One Notes

[1]Survey conducted by the Hearst Corp. and reported by the *Washington Post*, March 1987.

[2]School desegregation, the rights of criminal suspects, and abortion, respectively.

[3]Chalmers Johnson, *Blowback: The Costs and Consequences of American Empire.* (New York: Henry Holt & Company, 2000).

[4]This definition suits terrorism although it was used to define the term *power* in Harold Lasswell's political analysis. See, Harold Lasswell, *Politics: Who Gets What, When and How.* New York: McGraw-Hill, 1936.

[5]George Soros. *The Crisis of Global Capitalism: Open Society Endangered* (New York: Public Affairs, 1998).

[6]"Industrial Production Slips 0.1%, Strongest Showing in Six Months," *The Wall Street Journal Online*, 19 February 2002. http://online.wsj.com/article print/0,4287,SB1013779489963701840,00.html.

[7]*Wall Street Digest*, June 2004 p.4.

[8]*Wall Street Digest*, May 2004 p.1.

Suggested Readings

Bachrach, Peter. *Theory of Democratic Elitism: A Critique*. Boston: Little, Brown & Co., 1967.

Corbett, Michael. *Political Tolerance in America: Freedom and Equality in Public Attitudes*. New York: Longman, 1982.

Dahl, Robert A. *Modern Political Analysis*. 4th ed. Englewood Cliffs, N.J.: Prentice Hall, 1984.

Easton, David. *The Political System: An Inquiry into the State of Political Science*. New York: Alfred A. Knopf, 1953.

Huntington, Samuel. *American Politics: The Promise of Disharmony*. Cambridge, Mass.: The Belknap Press, 1981.

Lasswell, Harold. *Politics: Who Gets What, When and How*. New York: McGraw-Hill, 1936.

McClosky, Herbert, and John Zaller. *The American Ethos: Public Attitudes Toward Capitalism and Democracy*. Cambridge: Harvard University Press, 1985.

Medcalf, Linda, and Kenneth Dolbeare. *Neopolitics: American Political Ideas in the 1980s*. Philadelphia: Temple University Press, 1985.

Mills, C. W. *The Power-Elite*. New York: Oxford University Press, 1956

Ohmae, Kenichi. *The Borderless World: Power and Strategy in the Interlinked Economy*. New York: HarperCollins, 1990.

Part One
Building a Nation

Original blueprint for the Statue of Liberty

In our first major section, we pause for a brief look at our country's history. Are you wondering "Why study history?" Generations of government students have entertained precisely the same question. Why then spend the time?—for a number of reasons. First, we study history because it's fun. Yes, that's right—fun! It is a rare student, indeed, who has not sat around a kitchen table listening to accounts of his/her family history. We hang on every word, devour every detail, and then carry the stories with us for a lifetime, eventually passing them on to our own children. The same is true of the history of this country. As Americans, we share a common heritage that is exceedingly rich and colorful, and its study can be just as entertaining as our family heritage. In addition, we study history so as not to repeat the mistakes of the past. America's record is good but not perfect. Policy makers and citizens must be aware of past errors if we are to improve the future. Finally, we study history to reaffirm our beliefs in the ideals upon which the United States was founded. A country without ideals is endlessly doomed to internal strife and civil war. History allows us to reacquaint ourselves with these ideals and, thus, maintain the commonalty that makes us distinctively American.

Our venture into the past is divided into three separate chapters. In chapter two, we explore the development of our country and the factions that influenced its structure. In chapters three and four, we explore how this structure has evolved and changed over time. Each in its own special way shows us where we are today and points new directions for the future.

Chapter Two

The American Experience
New Ideas for a New Nation

> Men and nations behave wisely once they
> have exhausted all the other alternatives.
> —Abba Eban

It was a Sunday late in January 1776. The Reverend Peter Muhlenberg stood before his Lutheran congregation at Woodstock, a community in the Great Valley of Virginia. For his sermon he had chosen a passage from Ecclesiastes 3: 1-8: "To every thing there is a season, and a time . . . a time of war, and a time of peace." The young minister who was also a community leader and, likewise, served in the House of Burgesses proceeded to explain to his German flock exactly what was at stake in the Revolutionary War. Closing the service, he dramatically shed his clerical gown and stood before them dressed in the uniform of a colonel of the Virginia militia. For the remainder of the war, Reverend Peter Muhlenberg served as commander of the 8th Virginia Regiment, a fighting unit composed mostly of Germans from the settlements along the Shenandoah.[1] The Revolution had begun. All across the country, men and women, like the Reverend Muhlenberg, were committing themselves to the dream of independence. Seven years later, after seven thousand Americans had sacrificed their lives, the dream of independence became reality when the British signed the Articles of Peace and sailed home from the shores of a land they had held for nearly two hundred years.

THE AMERICAN REVOLUTION ════════════════════

Our study of the historical background of our government picks up with the Revolution. This is not meant to imply that the colonial experience is not worth examination. It is an exceedingly rich and colorful period. Only time and space limitations prevent a discussion of it here. So, on with the Revolution!

Why Revolution?

Exactly why did the colonies find it necessary to break with their mother country of Great Britain? Surprisingly enough, considerable disagreement can be found among historians regarding this point. In general three major themes are accepted, though the degree of emphasis for each varies with the scholar. One of the most frequently mentioned factors is a sense of political discontent among the colonists. Whether true or not, they perceived that they were being treated unfairly by the British Crown. The representative governments that they had established faced constant interference from England; they were subjected to laws and taxes from a distant government in which they had little or no voice, and seemingly on every front, their financial well-being was pushed aside in favor of the economic interest of the mother country.

It is also fair to assume that not everyone who immigrated to the "New Land" was a loyal subject. Many had come to escape religious persecution. Others came in search of a new and better life away from the rigid and confining aristocratic structure of English society. And still others came because they were "kicked out" of the old country and forcibly exiled to the new land (slaves, criminals, indentured servants, debtors). It is estimated that nearly half of all immigrants to America moved against their will.[2] Few of these had an overwhelming love for their motherland.

Finally, some experts insist the Revolution would have occurred even if the British had eased-up on the colonists and had given in to many of their demands. A sense of provincial pride was developing in the colonies. Whether it was "Americanism" or a loyalty attached more to their colony, the colonists no longer felt British. Three thousand miles of treacherous ocean separated them from their mother country, and they had, in spirit and in fact, become distinctively different. As this nationalistic fever began to take hold and spread throughout the colonies, revolution was probably inevitable.

The Justification

Once fighting broke out, the leaders of the Revolution felt compelled to justify their actions—to the British, to the world, and, most importantly, to themselves. The justification would be found in the writings and theory of an English philosopher named John Locke. Locke maintained that initially individu-

"The Struggle of Concord Bridge." A portrait illustrating what many believe to be the opening shots of the Revolutionary War with England.

als lived in a "state of nature." In this state the individual existed in perfect freedom, governed only by "natural law." This law, insisted Locke, was universal and the product of unchanging reason. The single most important principle of natural law was that humans were born free and possessed, by right of birth, certain "natural rights"—life, liberty, and property. To insure that these rights were safeguarded, a "social compact" was enacted among individuals that led to the creation of government. Once created, governments had the responsibility of preserving natural rights while individuals had the responsibility of obeying the government. In other words, each had rights and each had responsibilities. The most radical conception of this mutual relationship was Locke's notion that individuals had the right to break the compact if the government failed to live up to its obligation of protecting natural rights. This might not sound too revolutionary to us today, but remember this was the age of kings, queens and "divine right." It was this theory, with few alterations, that Thomas Jefferson offered to the world in the Declaration of Independence as the justification for the American Revolution.

WE WON. WHAT NOW?

Few Americans are aware that our present form of government is our second attempt at governing ourselves. Our first attempt was the Articles of Confederation, a government similar to our present one in some ways but radically different in others. Obviously, it was the radically different ones that caused the problems.

The Articles of Confederation

In June of 1776, Richard Henry Lee introduced two key proposals to the Continental Congress. The first called for a declaration of independence; the second proposed the creation of a confederated system of government that would bind the states together in a permanent "league of friendship." Lee's first proposal was accepted immediately and resulted in Thomas Jefferson's writing of the Declaration of Independence. His second proposal, however, was assigned to committee for further study. In the meantime, the states continued to govern themselves as they had always done, and the Continental Congress carried on with its main duty of directing the war effort. However, during the war, it became apparent to everyone that a more lasting, formal governmental arrangement that would more closely bind the states together was necessary. In 1777, the Articles of Confederation were submitted to the states for ratification, and in 1781, just two years before the conclusion of the war, they became our first constitutional government.

Structure of the Articles

Under the Articles of Confederation, the states retained all powers that they had previously enjoyed. To coordinate the states in matters of mutual concern, a single-house legislative body was created and constituted the only agency of the national government; there were no executive or judicial branches of government. Each state received one vote in Congress. The states would remain sovereign (independent) in all matters except in those areas specifically explained in the Articles. In brief, they included the following:

Matters of foreign policy. The national government was to be the sole decision-maker in those areas concerning foreign governments. It alone could declare war, negotiate treaties, and regulate international trade. Likewise, it alone was empowered to handle Indian affairs.

Responsibility for matters necessary for the common good of all states. The national congress was permitted to engage in certain activities that needed national coordination. These included: establishing a postal system, fixing weights and measurements, regulating the value of coinage, borrowing money and issuing bills of credit, and settling disputes between states over land and boundaries.

Providing for national security. All governments must be able to protect themselves from external threat. (This was certainly true during a period where nations were attempting to establish colonial empires.) Consequently, the national government was permitted the power necessary to raise and equip an army and navy.

Not a bad list of powers, right?—wrong! Although it may appear that the national government possessed sweeping powers, it didn't. No sooner had the Framers of this government finished slapping one another on the back for a job well done, than did the problems begin.

Problems with the Articles of Confederation

One of the first major problems with the Articles was that the national government was not given the power to tax the people directly. To raise money to carry forth with its responsibilities, the national congress had to rely upon voluntary contributions from the states. As any church minister could well explain, such is not the most stable source of income. In many cases states were faced with their own fiscal problems and had little left over to contribute to national debts. In other cases, disputes developed between the national government and the states and, to gain leverage, the state would refuse to release funds in an attempt to force the national government into a compromising position.

Regarding its power to raise an army, the national government was again in the position of relying upon voluntary state participation. Each state was assigned a troop quota, but, as in the case of taxation, it was up to the state legislature to meet their quota or not.

The national government was denied the power to regulate commerce among the states. The period immediately following the end of the Revolution saw a tremendous growth in economic activity as trade sanctions imposed on the colonists by Britain disappeared. Some states, eager to gain an advantage for their newly created businesses or to protect those enterprises that were not faring well against outside competitors, imposed discriminatory regulations, taxes, or both on goods from other states. Naturally, the state on the blunt end of these practices retaliated with similar measures. Before long, it was economically impossible to move goods from one end of the country to the other. Free trade was dead, and the national government was powerless to correct the problem.

The national government lacked executive leadership. The only constitutional agency of the national government was a one-house congress. Without an executive branch the national government was unable to carry out its directives (the primary function of an executive branch). As such, the national congress could legislate all it wanted, but policies, once agreed upon, proved ineffective because there was no one there to insure that they would be carried out.

A CALL FOR CHANGE

After struggling with the Articles of Confederation for nine years, it was apparent to many that America was on the brink of losing its freedom because of the internal chaos generated by the Articles. At nearly every turn, the country courted disaster. Economic depression resulted in hungry and disgruntled farmers angry with governmental foreclosure on their property. States were pressed to issue more paper money that, in turn, only deepened the severity of prevailing economic depression. Consequently, many feared a new revolution pitting those at the bottom of society against those at the top.

States, on their own initiative, opened negotiations with foreign powers on trade and policy matters. Likewise, George Washington feared that efforts were underway to persuade Kentucky to secede and join Spain.[3] Also, due to the sad state of America's military forces and economic conditions, there was fear that Great Britain might reopen the war to regain its lost colonies. (Actually such fears were not unfounded as the suggestion had been advanced in the British Parliament.)

With all this in mind James Madison was successful in convincing his fellow state legislators of the necessity of national action. Thus, in September of 1786, Virginia called for a national meeting of all states to be held at Annapolis, Maryland, for the sole purpose of reviewing economic conditions and proposing changes. Unfortunately, only five states showed up; consequently, little action could be taken. However, one delegate from New York, Alexander Hamilton, used the meeting to argue forcefully for a convention in which a stronger national government could be created. Brilliant, articulate, and committed to more centralized government, Hamilton, together with Madison, persuaded the members of the meeting to urge the states to call for a constitutional convention to take place in Philadelphia in May 1787.

The Philadelphia Convention

Initially many of the states had second thoughts about the wisdom of a national convention. Many believed the problems of the country were merely a result of worldwide economic conditions and would soon pass. Others felt that those speaking out angrily were small in number and constituted little more than "rabble-rousers" discontent with their poor luck in life. However, all disagreements on the severity of the problem were laid to rest with **Shays' Rebellion** of 1786-87. Angered over land foreclosures, Massachusetts farmers rallied around Daniel Shays, a former captain in the American Revolution, to prevent their land from being seized by the courts. At first, Shays' efforts were confined to disrupting court proceedings—judges were forced from their courtrooms, and jails were stormed to free debtors. However, later, when Shays determined that such efforts were futile in the long run, he committed himself and his followers to open rebellion. On January 25, 1787, Shays, along with eight hundred of his rebels, marched into Springfield, Massachusetts, with intentions of seizing the federal arsenal to obtain weapons in support of his cause. Unfortunately for the rebels, the army was waiting with cannons, and many were killed in the initial assault. The rebels retreated to Petersham, where they finally were defeated with little difficulty. Most of the rebels were pardoned by the government before the end of the year. Shays, for his part in the uprising, was condemned to death but escaped to Vermont. A year later he too was pardoned. Although the revolt failed, its intensity was enough to convince many state leaders that the time for action was now.

Setting

The convention was officially opened May 14, 1787. However, since many of the delegates arrived late (same old story, huh?), a quorum was not achieved until May 25, and it is this date that is taken as the actual start of the convention's work. The East Room of the State House was used as a meeting hall, the same chamber in which the Declaration of Independence was signed eleven years previously. By all historical accounts the summer of '87 was an intolerably hot one. We can appreciate the suffering endured by those within, sitting around small tables, windows closed tightly, and little or no ventilation. It was under such conditions that the shape of America's new government began to take form.

Preconvention Issues

From the outset, three issues were critical to the success of the convention. The **first** was the need to establish an air of legitimacy. This was accomplished simply by inviting George Washington and electing him presiding officer. In fact, the notice of the convention received little attention until it was learned that

Shays' Rebellion provided the Federalists with the issue they needed to call for the Philadelphia Convention.

Washington would attend. Seven other states immediately agreed to send delegates and Congress, which had been indecisive on the matter, agreed to pass along its blessings to the proceedings. Likewise, so well revered and trusted was Washington by the common man that his presence at the convention dispelled suspicious notions of foul play. In addition, Washington's attendance guaranteed that any final document produced in his presence would stand a good chance of ratification. Certainly the members of the convention were aware of Washington's enormous popularity, and, according to the records of the proceedings, it was generally recognized that Washington would be the country's first president. Even the discussion of presidential powers was done within the context of the Washington personality.

Interestingly, the **second** major issue was one contemporary politicians fight over—the need for secrecy. (However, since secrecy carries a negative connotation, we now refer to it as "closed debate.") Those in attendance were very much aware of political realities. It was agreed that, unless they were free to speak their minds openly without fear of reprisals, the inevitable course of the convention would be political grandstanding, self-serving speeches, and voting alignments based more upon constituents' demands rather than reason and foresight. To avoid this dilemma, the convention imposed a rule of secrecy that would last more than fifty years after the convention had finished its work. Only convention delegates could enter the building, windows were closed tightly (an insufferable condition for summer), and only delegates were permitted to examine the convention records kept tirelessly by James Madison. Did the delegates speak their minds? Most certainly! Consider Charles Pinckney's statement: "No one should be president who is not worth one hundred thousand dollars." Or the statement of the aristocratic Gouverneur Morris who spoke of the common man with contempt: "The mob begins to think and reason. Poor reptiles! They bask in the sun, and ere noon they will bite, depend on it." Or Roger Sherman whose advice to the convention was "It is advisable that the people have as little to do as may be about government." Or Alexander Hamilton, in reference to the ability of the common man to rule, stated: "The turbulent and changing masses seldom judge or determine right." And finally, even George Washington's advice to convention delegates: "Do not produce a document of which you yourself cannot approve just to please the people." Certainly, plucked out of context and lacking appropriate background, such comments, if printed and circulated by the press, would have destroyed the convention. Not only did secrecy allow convention delegates to speak freely, it also promoted a give-and-take atmosphere in which members were able to compromise on the more troublesome issues of the times.

The **third** major issue concerned the purpose of the convention. Originally the convention had been called to revise the Articles of Confederation. This could be accomplished by strengthening the national government while still retaining state sovereignty, which was so important to a confederated arrangement. However, from the very start of the convention it was apparent a hidden agenda existed. Many of the convention's delegates, later to be termed **Federalists** (Actually the term "nationalists" would have been more appropriate.), arrived with the intention of dumping the confederated system in favor of a stronger national government that we today refer to as federalism. In essence a flip-flop would occur in the power relationship between the states and the national government. Under the Articles of Confederation the states were supreme; under federalism the national government would become dominant in many areas. The Federalists generally included larger business interests, financiers, and merchants, those who had suffered the most under the Articles of Confederation. On the opposite side were the **Anti-Federalists**, consisting primarily of successful farmers, independent businesses, debtors, and laborers. Obviously, the latter group had done very well under the existing government and, likewise, mistrusted a more centralized and powerful government. They were more inclined to favor sticking to the original mandate of the convention—namely, a revision of the Articles. The dispute was settled more by default than anything else. Because the Anti-Federalists were satisfied with the way things were progressing, they felt no sense of urgency to change. Hence, they were poorly represented at the convention. Similarly, many influential members of this group, like Patrick Henry, refused to participate, claiming that he "smelt a rat." Rhode Island, perhaps the most strongly opposed to change, boycotted the proceedings altogether. Consequently, in terms of numbers the Federalists dominated the convention.

The Convention at Work

Surprisingly, a considerable amount of agreement existed among convention delegates. For example, from the outset a majority of delegates agreed that conditions had so deteriorated under the Articles nothing less than a complete change of government would improve matters. Thus, with the convention less than one week old, the delegates voted overwhelmingly in favor of a resolution that proclaimed that "a national government ought to be established consisting of a supreme legislative, executive, and judiciary." The importance of this resolution is twofold. **First**, it formed the basis for switching to a federal government, and **second**, it established the concept of "separation of powers" as the means of controlling power within government. Additionally, the delegates were of one mind on the need to protect property (not surprising, since most of the delegates were men of wealth and property). And **third**, on the issue of how much power to give the common man, the delegates overwhelmingly favored a republican government in which the people would rule through elected representatives. This concept was essentially a check on the "evils" of direct democracy.

Things seemed to be humming along nicely, but then, as life would have it, problems developed. Three major conflicts surfaced as the delegates got down to the "nuts and bolts" of the government they were about to create. **First**, on the issue of representation in the national legislature, the large states and the small states found themselves pitted against each other. **Second**, the structure and the power of the executive divided the delegates into two camps—one side favoring a strong executive, the other fearful of the potential for abuse. And **third**, as always, slave and nonslave states fought bitterly over the institution of slavery.

The **Virginia Plan** was first to address the above conflicts. Arriving first, and with the conference delayed, the Virginia delegation used the time to organize. On May 29, the 33-year-old governor of Virginia, Edmund Randolph, seized the initiative and offered a stunned convention a series of fifteen resolutions drawn primarily from the thinking of James Madison. The move was a stroke of political genius. By being first, the Virginia Plan became the working model for the convention. Basically it proposed:

1. a bicameral (two-house) legislative body in which the people would elect members to the lower house. In turn, this elected body would select members to an "upper house" from nominees from the states. Representation to these legislative bodies would be based on population, and its laws would be supreme over any conflicting state law;

2. a national executive to carry out the laws of Congress. The legislature would select the executive, but, once selected, the executive would function independently;

3. a national judicial system would be established—also selected by the legislature.

During the next two weeks the Virginia Plan was vigorously debated with the smaller states becoming increasingly alarmed. From their point of view, the plan exceeded the boundaries within which the convention was to function, namely, a revision of the Articles. Too, the distribution of seats in the national legislature on the basis of population meant the smaller states would be at the mercy of the larger states on virtually every policy issue. Furthermore, the proposal for a strong executive, the exact make-up of which was not specified, aroused fears of monarchy. To counter these fears, William Paterson of New Jersey set before the convention an alternative proposal. Termed the **New Jersey Plan**, it proposed the following outline for government:

1. a unicameral Congress (one house) would be created with each state receiving one vote;

2. the national government would be strengthened, but the Articles of Confederation would be continued. Congress would have the power to

regulate trade, impose taxes, and establish national laws that the states would be forced to obey;

3. an executive branch would be created, but the powers of the office would be shared by more than one person. Congress would be given the responsibility of electing the executives;

4. a supreme court would be established, and its members would be appointed by the executive branch.

Although the New Jersey Plan addressed all the fears associated with strong central government, the main concern was the issue of small states versus large states. Unorganized and fewer in number, the supporters of the New Jersey Plan were defeated when the Virginia Plan passed 7 votes to 3. New York, New Jersey, and Delaware (the three states that had cast their votes against the Virginia Plan) refused to accept defeat. Since they were centrally located in the country, any attempt to continue without their support meant that the nation would be divided into two separate parts. Debate continued, accusations were exchanged, and tempers flared in the sweltering heat, but neither side would budge. The convention had reached a critical stage. A near fatal collapse of the convention was avoided when a Connecticut delegate, Roger Sherman, offered what is now referred to as the **Great Compromise** (sometimes referred to as the **Connecticut Compromise**). It resolved the deadlock by proposing the establishment of a bicameral legislative body. The first house would be based upon population, thus, giving the large states a greater percentage of delegates. To protect the interests of the small states, a senate was to be created with each state receiving two members regardless of size. The measure passed, and the work of the convention moved forward.

Other Compromises

In debate over the Great Compromise, the thorny issue of slavery surfaced. Naturally, finding it to their advantage, the slave states wished to count the slaves as people. However, for purposes of taxation, they wished to exclude slaves, considering them property rather than "human." Nonslave states insisted that this proposal was unfair. In the end, both for purposes of representation and taxation, slaves were counted as "three-fifths" of a person.

Slavery as an institution required compromise. A number of delegates were firmly opposed to its continuation. Terming it "infernal traffic," George Mason argued passionately against slavery, stating that it "...will bring the judgment of heaven on a country. As nations cannot be rewarded or punished in the next world they must in this. By an inevitable chain of cause and effects Providence punishes national sins, by national calamities."[4] It is interesting, however, that Mason just happened to be one of the largest slave owners at the convention. Perhaps this is one reason the slave states were unmoved by his eloquence. More importantly though, the slave states saw the abolition of slavery as a threat to their economic livelihood and, thus, would have nothing to do with ending it. Again, compromise was in order. Congress was forbidden to end the importation of slaves (not slavery itself) until 1808.

Another source of conflict that had to be ironed out centered on a difference of economic interest between the North and the South. The economy of the southern states was heavily dependent upon agriculture. Consequently, they feared that the more industrial North would attempt to impose export taxes on the crops they shipped abroad. To alleviate this fear, the South demanded that the national government be legally restricted from levying export taxes. The North agreed, but, in return, the South was forced to surrender to the national government the right to regulate commerce both among states and with other nations.

With the tough issues resolved, the delegates assigned the task of hammering out the exact language of the Constitution to a committee and recessed. George Washington took the opportunity to head for his favorite fishing hole with pole in hand. Seeing the inevitable course of events to follow, some delegates returned home; others simply rested and waited in anticipation of the final document. In a matter of weeks the document was ready for inspection. Debate followed; minor changes were made, and on September 17, 1787, thirty-nine of the fifty-five delegates signed it. It is fair to say that as a group most of those signing were not altogether pleased. Compromise had diluted almost everyone's expectations—except perhaps for Benjamin Franklin's. For, having confessed that he had wondered throughout the convention whether the sun that was painted on the back of Washington's chair in the convention hall was rising or setting, he finally concluded: "I have the happiness to know that it is a rising and not a setting sun."

Ratification

The work of the convention was far from over. Ahead lay the difficult task of selling the new Constitution to the rest of the country. The battle for ratification proved to be one of the most interesting chapters in our nation's history.

Before departing Convention Hall, two critical decisions were made by those who had written and supported the new government. **First**, the decision was made that a unanimous vote would not be required to ratify the new Constitution—nine votes would be sufficient. **Second**, it was decided to bypass the state legislatures in the ratification process in favor of state conventions. Politically, this decision was strikingly brilliant because the state legislatures were packed solidly with Anti-Federalists. Bear in mind these two decisions were not difficult to enact since most of those offended by the thought of a strong national government had either not attended the convention or had left early in disgust. (There is a lesson to be learned here.) Also, the Anti-Federalists were disadvan-

taged because they had little information about the new government. Remember that the proceedings of the convention were confidential. Only those present could review the records. This automatically cast the Anti-Federalists in a defensive position in all ratification debates.

The strategy of the Federalists was to move quickly. Realizing their opponents were grossly unorganized and politically fragmented, they sought to ratify the new Constitution in as many states as possible before their opposition had a chance to react. If successful, they reasoned, the sheer weight of their momentum might carry the day in those states most opposed to the new government. This strategy proved effective. Ratifying conventions were hurriedly organized in Delaware, Pennsylvania, and New Jersey; and, before the year was up (less than four months), ratification was achieved in these states. Stunned, the Anti-Federalists frantically attempted to organize their forces. One month later in January, two more states ratified: Georgia and Connecticut. Massachusetts fell the following month. By now six states had ratified the Constitution, and momentum was on the side of the Federalists. In April and May, Maryland and South Carolina, respectively, voted to join the new government, and now only one additional state was needed. On June 21, 1788, New Hampshire cast its historic vote for approval and, thus, the Constitution was ratified. But the government itself was not put in place at this time because two key states had not yet voted to ratify: Virginia and New York. Without their support the new government could not survive. Over the summer both states voted to ratify by narrow margins, and the new government was officially born on March 4, 1789.

By this time North Carolina and Rhode Island remained the only holdouts. North Carolina first voted overwhelmingly against the new Constitution (2 to

1 margin) but reconsidered later and ratified it November of 1789. For its part, Rhode Island, after considering what life would be like as an independent country or the possibility of being forcibly dragged into the union by the other twelve states, reluctantly ratified by a vote of 34 to 32 on May 29, 1790.

The fight for ratification pitted two groups against each other. Those favoring the new government tended to be from various moneyed groups—bankers, exporters, and large agricultural interests. Too, in terms of geography, support for the Constitution was strongest in smaller states. Opposition was primarily in the larger states and from small farmers. Although the arguments were bitter and the rivalry between the two factions hostile, two significant contributions emerged in their struggles. The first was *The Federalist*,[5] a series of articles written by Alexander Hamilton, James Madison, and John Jay to convince the voters in New York to support the ratification of the new Constitution. Not only is this collection of writings regarded as one of the most profound political works produced in all the centuries of history, it is, in essence, the single most important guide we have to the thinking of those who created our government. The second contribution was that in the debates over ratification, the Anti-Federalists objected that nowhere in the Constitution was there a bill of rights protecting the people against the abusive power inherent in the tendency of centralized government. The Federalists disagreed. They pointed to parts in the documents that prohibited the national government from passing **ex post facto** laws and **bills of attainder** or from suspending the **writ of habeas corpus**. Likewise, trial by jury in criminal cases was preserved as well as a narrow definition of treason. These were sufficient they insisted. Still, the Anti-Federalists refused to budge. When it became apparent that their support was critical in Virginia and New York, the Federalists agreed to incorporate a bill of rights once ratification was achieved.

A Different Interpretation

Despite the bitterness generated over ratification of the Constitution after passage, the country settled into it with relative ease. In fact, within a decade of institution, both in terms of practice and stature, the Constitution had been elevated to the position of a "secular religion." Thus, it was a surprise when, over a hundred years later in 1913, a historian named Charles Beard published a blistering attack on the document. In his work, *An Economic Interpretation of the Constitution*,[6] Beard attempted to paint the delegates of the Philadelphia Convention as a group of petty, self-interested individuals bent on creating a government that would serve their narrowly defined economic interests. To support his contention, Beard documents that the delegates were, as a whole, members of the propertied class whose financial interest had suffered under the Articles of Confederation. Those with the most to lose by abandoning the Articles were the small and large farmers and the common nonpropertied person whose presence at the convention was notably absent—a condition that has its roots more in design rather than coincidence.

Although Beard's work has been heavily criticized, perhaps the most cited is the book, *We the People*,[7] by Forrest McDonald, first published in 1958. McDonald points out that a strict economic view of the Constitution is much too simplified. An examination of the ratification battle demonstrates that many wealthy individuals ended up in the opposition's camp because of the commitment to individual rights. For example, Elbridge Gerry of Massachusetts, one of the nation's richest men and signer of the Declaration of Independence, refused to sign the document at the Philadelphia Convention and worked hard against its ratification in his own state. In sharp contrast, Madison and Hamilton, men of modest means and heavily in debt, were instrumental in its passage.

Which view is right?—probably neither one, at least totally. As with most arguments, the right answer lies somewhere in the middle. The human being is an enormously complex creature. Rarely are actions based upon a single emotion or need. The men in attendance at the Philadelphia Convention were human and undoubtedly concerned with their own future. But it must also be remembered that these men, for the most part, were the same men who slightly more than ten years earlier had put their lives on the line for a new nation. It is unlikely that they were devoid of passion for their country. Too, they were intelligent and had the foresight to understand that wrecking the nation for their own materialistic desires would, in the long run, destroy their own financial well-being. However, it is easy to understand how they, being human, might have been inclined to look for solutions that solved both their own needs for security as well as the nation's problems. What is important, though, is that, for whatever reasons, they chose a path that ultimately has led us to our present government—very democratic, very stable, and one that proudly boasts the oldest working constitution in the world today.

AND NOW LET THE MUSIC PLAY

Almost universally, the Constitution written in Philadelphia was and still is regarded as a truly unique document. Structurally, its uniqueness revolves around four concepts built into the United States government.

Constitutionalism

The American government was the first to use the concept of a written constitution. Certainly, other countries had employed constitutions, but in an "unwritten" format. An unwritten constitution is not a single document but, rather, one made up from a series of laws, declarations, legislative acts, and commonly accepted customs. Similarly, an unwritten constitution is open ended, meaning that each new act of legislature or parliament is automatically incorporated into the constitution. If conflicts exist, the newer act is taken as the current law. The Americans were much more precise. To them the Constitution was the supreme law of the land incorporated into a single document. In very specific language it set the limits in which government could exercise power, and all legislative acts and judicial decisions had to conform to these predetermined constitutional limits.

Separation of Powers

Besides dividing the power of government horizontally into two parts (federalism), the Framers decided to hedge their odds against abusive government with vertical cuts. At the national level, the operations of government were divided into three distinct branches: legislative, executive, and judicial. Article I of the Constitution states, "all legislative Powers herein granted shall be vested in a Congress of the United States." Article II, directs that "the executive Power shall be vested in a President of the United States." And Article III, mandates that "the judicial Power of the United States, shall be vested in one supreme Court, and in such inferior Courts as the Congress may from time to time ordain and establish." The above arrangement is referred to as **separation of powers**. In essence, it is additional insurance against one individual or group gaining too much power.

It should be mentioned that, constitutionally speaking, the states are not required to follow a similar arrangement in separating their power. However, all states have voluntarily chosen to follow the national model.

Checks and Balance System

The Constitution also limits the power of government by means of **checks and balance system**. The mechanics of this device are that it makes all three branches dependent upon one another to carry out their own responsibilities. For example, Congress is assigned the responsibility to enact laws, but the president has the right to veto them. However, the power of the veto is not absolute. If Congress so chooses, it can override the president's veto by a two-thirds vote in both houses. The Supreme Court can check the power of Congress by declaring that a law is unconstitutional. To curb this power, the Constitution provides for presidential appointment of federal court members. Thus, presidents exercise some influence on the court by appointing judges that agree with their political philosophy. But this power is restrained by the fact that the Senate must confirm all such appointments to the federal bench. Likewise, Congress controls the size and funds of the courts—a further check on the power of the judicial branch. The executive branch has the power to negotiate treaties, but final approval must be given by the Senate for them to be binding.

The electoral system itself is an example of checks and balances. The Constitution specifies that different constituencies select different elected officials in our government. Members of the House of Representatives are elected by small districts within the states, whereas senators are chosen by the entire state. On the other hand, the entire nation is the constituency of the president. Moreover, the Constitution also set different terms for each—two years for a representative, six years for a senator, four years for the president, and life tenure for federal judges. The thinking of the writers of the Constitution was that, in staggering the terms of office, it would be difficult for any one group who might enjoy a brief period of popularity to capture the national government and dominate completely at the expense of others. Likewise, since they were elected at different periods, it would be natural to assume that each group would represent a different set of issues. The life tenure of judges was to insulate them from political pressure (discussed further in chapter 11) and provide some continuity in the government.

Although numerous other examples could be offered, the point should be clear—under a system of checks and balances no one branch of the government is capable of carrying out its function without the support and cooperation of the others. Nor does any branch exercise its responsibility exclusively. This may well contradict the conception of many students that the powers of each branch are rigidly and precisely defined. For example, although the responsibility of lawmaking is primarily assigned to Congress, it is also shared with the executive and judicial branches. The same holds true for each of the other two branches in terms of their prime responsibilities.

Judicial Review

The last major concept employed by the writers of the Constitution was that of **judicial review.** Simply stated, this allows the judicial branch to strike down an act of Congress if it, in the opinion of the court, conflicts with the Constitution. Although judicial review was not specifically written into the Constitution, there is good reason to believe that the Framers believed that such a right did exist. Otherwise, why institute constitutionalism as a major aspect of our government? If the Constitution was to be the supreme law of the land, then some agency within the government would have to assume the responsibility of upholding it. And since the court had already, under the Articles of Confederation, been utilized in this manner, it is only natural to believe that the Framers of our government felt they should continue the practice. In 1803, under Chief Justice John Marshall, the Court reaffirmed its ability to strike down acts of Congress as unconstitutional in the precedent setting case of *Marbury v. Madison*.[8] Seven years later, the Court again acted, only this time at issue was a state law that conflicted with our national Constitution. As was true in the first case, judicial review was used to justify the action of the Court.

SURVIVING THE TEST OF TIME

While the Framers of our government might have been long on debate, they were remarkably short on ink when penning the final document. Written in approximately 1800 words, the Constitution of the United States is the "hands down" winner for brevity of any other similar document in the modern world. Yet, despite its shortness, our Constitution is the oldest working constitution in the world today. How is it possible that a document so short has endured for so long? Basically three factors have contributed to its long life.

Interpretation

Perhaps the single most important reason that the American Constitution has withstood the test of time lies in the fact that it is so brief. Had they instead written at length and in very specific language, there is little doubt that it would have outlived its usefulness in a short period of time, and a new constitution would have been required. However, in choosing to be brief, the Framers outlined the basic structure of our government and left the job of interpreting it to future generations. Consequently, as times change, the Constitution can be reinterpreted to fit the conditions and problems of that particular generation of Americans.

Custom and Usage

In some instances more than interpretation was required. For example, at the beginning of our nation's history, there were no political parties. Indeed, many of our country's early leaders, like George Washington, believed political parties were unnecessary evils, promoting division and hatred. As such, they were excluded from the Constitution. If an individual wanted to run for office, he would simply announce his candidacy and begin "politicking." This might have been feasible when the country was small, but in a nation of 260 million people it would be sheer chaos. The problem was resolved as the nucleus for political parties began to form around the battle between the Federalists and Anti-Federalists over ratification. As we shall see later (Chapter 5), our basic two-party system emerged naturally, without amendments or interpretation. Another example of change through practice can be seen in the electoral college. Although in the Constitution, the electoral college was originally viewed as a check on the power of the common man. The Framers believed that those chosen by the people as electors would exercise an independent role in the selection of the president and would vote, not necessarily for the person the people wanted but, rather, for the best and most qualified individual. However, this was not the way it worked in practice. The people voted for individuals loyal to the candidate associated with their political party and, hence, the job of elector ended up being largely ceremonial. Again, the point is that in practice the system often

How The Constitution May Be Amended

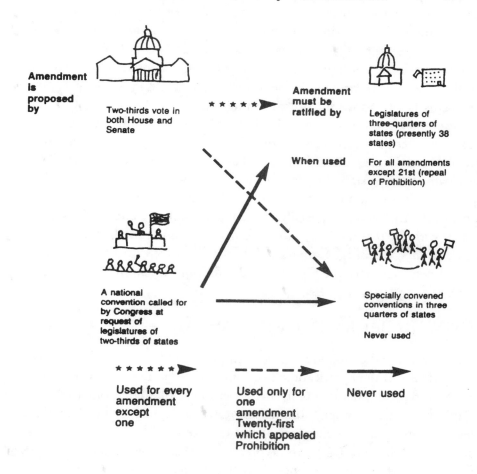

Amendment is proposed by

Two-thirds vote in both House and Senate

★ ★ ★ ★ ★ ▶

Amendment must be ratified by

Legislatures of three-quarters of states (presently 38 states)

When used

For all amendments except 21st (repeal of Prohibition)

A national convention called for by Congress at request of legislatures of two-thirds of states

Specially convened conventions in three quarters of states

Never used

★ ★ ★ ★ ★ ★ ▶   - - - - ▶   ───▶

Used for every amendment except one   **Used only for one amendment Twenty-first which appealed Prohibition**   **Never used**

changes to meet the demands and customs of those practicing it. In essence the system adapts gradually to the demands of the times and eliminates the need for constant revision.

Amendments

The last means used to keep the Constitution alive and workable is the amendment process. It is last on our list because it is the least used process. In over two hundred years, only twenty-seven amendments have been added. And when considering that the first ten were adopted immediately after ratification (the Bill of Rights) and two others essentially cancel each other out (the Eighteenth prohibiting the sale and distribution of alcohol and its repeal by the Twenty-first), one must be impressed that in only a few instances have we had to "surgically fix" the Constitution by opening it up and inserting new language. This is not to imply that numerous attempts have not been made to amend the Constitution. In fact, several thousand amendments have been suggested during our history, but only a relatively few have even remotely had a chance of passing. One of the main reasons is that the amendment process is not easily executed.

Amending the Constitution involves a two-step procedure. First, an amendment must be proposed. This may be handled in two different ways. In the first, the national legislature by a two-thirds vote of both houses calls for the consideration of the proposed amendment. Should either house fail to obtain the necessary two-thirds majority, the amendment automatically dies. The second method entails having two-thirds of the state legislatures call upon Congress to convene a national convention for the express purpose of proposing the amendment. To date, all amendments have been proposed by Congress. Having cleared the first step, the proposed amendment must be ratified. Again, two options exist. In the first, three-fourths of the state legislatures must vote to approve. In the second, specially elected state ratifying conventions are used and, as with the first method, a three-fourths vote is required. Who determines which method is used?—Congress. With the lone exception of the Twenty-first Amendment (repeal of the Eighteenth Prohibition Amendment), all have been ratified through state legislatures.

LOOKING BACK—LOOKING AHEAD

If the Framers of the United States government could be transported in time to see the results of their work some two hundred years later, they would be both amazed and proud. Undoubtedly, the government they envisioned and created during that hot and muggy summer of 1787 functions much differently than they had intended. Some aspects of this change would probably alarm them. For ex   the emergence of the presidency over Congress as the dominant branch in government would not sit well with many of them. Nor would the rise of political parties and their strangle hold on the electoral process have them clapping uncontrollably. However, other aspects would most certainly please them. The importance of the Bill of Rights in our lives, for instance, would have the Anti-Federalists elbowing the Federalists with a "See! I told you so" expression. The Federalists, for their part, would be smiling and reminding their worthy counterparts of their doomsday predictions for the country under federalism. But above all else, the Framers would have to be enormously pleased that the government they created has stood the test of time so well. In part, this is due to the brilliant construction of the Constitution as an instrument of government. But also, it is due to the attitude and values of Americans both now and then. Historical records show that no one at the Philadelphia Convention was totally satisfied with the Constitution in its final draft. What is important, though, is that each understood the need to compromise for a greater goal—a workable, republican government.

Certainly, the Constitution is no less controversial today than it was in 1787. However, like our founding ancestors, most of us understand no one individual can have it all his/her own way. Compromise is important. When we Americans, individually or collectively, lose an election or court battle, we do not run home and drag our shotguns out of the closet. We win some and we lose some, but, above all else, Americans recognize the importance of constitutional government.

Will the Constitution continue to serve future generations of Americans as well as it has done in the past? Although it is impossible to foretell the future, history presents a powerful argument that the answer is yes. Over two hundred years have elapsed since our forefathers pinned their hopes for a brighter future on the Constitution. During this time, it has survived wars, economic depressions, technological advances that would boggle the mind of its writers, political scandals, and a host of other changes too numerous to mention here. Yet, despite all of these events, the Constitution still functions today because of its unique flexibility, coupled with the American people whose political character demands orderly democratic government, provides a winning combination that almost certainly guarantees a bright future—both for the Constitution and the country.

Chapter Two Notes

[1] Carl Bridenbaugh, *The Spirit of '76: The Growth of American Patriotism Before Independence 1607-1776* (New York: Oxford University Press, 1975), 148.

[2] M.B. Norton, and others, *A People and a Nation: A History of the United States,* 2d ed. (New York: Houghton Mifflin Co., 1986), 72.

[3] William H. Riker, *Federalism: Origin, Operation, Significance* (Boston: Little Brown & Co., 1964), 18-20.

[4] Carl Van Doren, *The Great Rehearsal* (New York: Viking Press, 1948), 153.

[5] Alexander Hamilton, James Madison, and John Jay, *The Federalist Papers,* ed. Clinton Rossiter (New York: Penguin, 1961).

[6] Charles A. Beard, *An Economic Interpretation of the Constitution* (New York: Macmillan Co., 1941).

[7] Forrest McDonald, *We the People* (Chicago: University of Chicago Press, 1958), Ch. 8.

[8] *Marbury v. Madison*, 1 Cranch 137 (1803).

Suggested Readings

Bailyn, Bernard. *The Ideological Origins of the American Revolution*. Cambridge: Harvard University Press, 1967.

Becker, Carl. *The Declaration of Independence: A Study in the History of Political Ideas*. New York: Alfred A. Knopf, 1942.

Eidelberg, Paul. *The Philosophy of the Constitution*. New York: Free Press. 1968.

Lipset, Seymour. *The First New Nation*. New York: Basic Books, 1963.

Rossiter, Clinton. *1787: The Grand Convention*. New York: Macmillan Co., 1966.

Storing, Herbert. *What the Anti-Federalists Were For*. Chicago: University of Chicago Press, 1981.

Schumpeter, J.A., ed. *Capitalism, Socialism, and Democracy*. 3d ed. New York: Harper, 1950.

Vaughan, A.T., ed. *Chronicles of the American Revolution*. New York: Grosset & Dunlap, 1965.

Chapter Three

The Federal System:
The Theory of Shared Governance

Perhaps no concept of American government is more misunderstood than that of federalism. Certainly, most Americans know that we have a federal government, but how many could explain what that means? As an academic exercise, we surveyed a number of our own students to see if they could accurately define what this concept of federalism is all about. After all, if anyone should know, American college students should, right? Here is a representative sample of their answers

-a government that controls the state governments

-the government that handles the financial situations

-a system of government that is based on the Constitution—separation of state and local governments

-the branch of government which passes all laws and enforces state laws

-government at the national level that oversees the majority of laws of the nation and its people

-federal government is the term we use to say when we, as citizens, elect representatives to vote for us on major issues

-the government that controls spending and makes capitalistic decisions

-a system of government based on the Constitution

-a government that is higher than the state and rules over the whole country

-a system of government in which the people support the government and, in turn, the government helps the people.

Are any of the above answers right?—obviously not. Imagine that you had been asked. What would have been your definition? Take a minute and write it down on a piece of scratch paper. When you have completed this chapter, look back on your definition, and see how close you came to the correct answer.

One final comment needs mentioning before we begin this chapter. It would be an understatement to say that few students approach the study of federalism with great zeal. There isn't much a writer can do to make the subject thrilling. Nevertheless, try to keep an open mind. The study of federalism is crucial to your understanding of American government. Few problems in America are without federal implications. Consequently, if you are to understand this government and the problems of contemporary American society, it is imperative that you have a basic understanding of this chapter. So, with that in mind, let's begin.

DEFINING FEDERALISM

As we saw in the last chapter, after the colonists formally severed their ties with the English, they were left with the formidable task of replacing governments. Facing them were two distinct choices, each possessing a unique set of consequences. On the one hand, they could have opted for a **unitary** structure of government. Traditionally, this system of government is defined as one in which the central government is the only constitutionally empowered government of the land. Although the national government may elect to create regional governments, such as our states, all policy making powers are determined and assigned by the central government. Likewise, once created, regional governments have no inherent right to exist. They serve at the pleasure of the central government and may be abolished by the mere stroke of the pen. Most true democracies in the world today function under a unitary governmental structure. Great Britain, France, Israel, Sweden, and Norway are only a few examples.

As indicated earlier, the delegates' fear of strong central government, coupled with an intense loyalty to statehood, prevented even the slightest consideration of unitary government at the Philadelphia Convention. Instead, a **federal** system was adopted. A federal system of government differs from a unitary system in that two governments are created within the same society, rather than one: a

Confederation

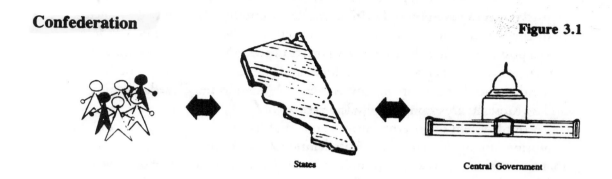

Figure 3.1

States   Central Government

The power of the state is supreme (state supremacy). The national government exercises power over the people indirectly through the states.

Federalism

U.S.A.

State Government   Central Government

The power of the national government is supreme (national supremacy). Both the national government and states receive and exercise power directly in relationship to the people.

Unitary Government

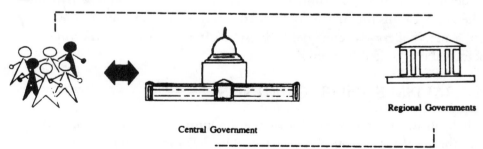

Central Government   Regional Governments

The national government is the only constitutionally empowered government of the society. All regional governments are created by and exist at the discretion of the national government.

central government and regional units, or states. Each government is autonomous in its own sphere of authority and, constitutionally, each is assigned substantial powers and responsibilities independent from the other. Moreover, since both governments derive their source of power from the Constitution, neither is in a position to alter the rights and powers of the other through the normal legislative process (such as a bill introduced and passed in the legislative body of either the central or constituent governments). United States, Canada, Mexico, and Switzerland are examples of federated systems.

A third system of government, and one that has long caused considerable confusion among students, is a **confederation**. The confusion lies in the fact that the architects of the Constitution used the term federation to refer to what political scientists now term confederation. In part the confusion is understandable because the two systems are identical in their overall intent, namely, to limit the power of government by creating two governments within the same society and constitutionally dividing the power between them. The critical difference between the two systems teeters on the issue of supremacy, or, put differently, who has the most power. In a confederation, the regional governments, or states, reign as supreme since they, by constitutional compact, create the national government and set parameters in which the latter may institute policy. One other important difference between the two systems lies in the relationship of the people to the government. As illustrated in Figure 3.1, in a confederation the relationship between the people and the state is direct, whereas the national government's influence is felt only indirectly as it filters through the states. In a federal system, both the state and the national government maintain a direct relationship with the people, gaining power and exercising authority.

As seen in the previous chapter, our first government was a confederation. Although this may seem somewhat alien to twentieth-century Americans, to our Founding Fathers it made perfect sense. After all, the states, as colonies, existed long before the national government was ever conceived. Unfortunately, confederated systems of government have not stood the test of time well, mainly for the same reasons the Articles of Confederation failed the Founders. A good example of a modern-day confederated system can be seen in the governmental structure of the United Nations.

FEDERALISM'S SHORTCOMINGS

Was federalism the best choice for our new country? For many critics of the system the answer is a resounding no. Listed below are a few of the many problems associated with this unique political structure.

Federalism is extremely complicated. As we mentioned in chapter one, democracy is one of the most difficult forms of government to operate. A prerequisite for democratic government is an informed, knowledgeable citizenry and participation. The more difficult the system is to grasp, the more likely that a breakdown in the democratic process will occur. Unfortunately, argue critics, the sheer immensity of the federal system promotes confusion. Few Americans, as indicated by surveys, know the names of their state leaders, city council members, county officials or state judges. In truth, it is difficult for even professional politicians to keep track of all the various offices and elected officials. Too often such confusion leads to apathy that, in turn, becomes the springboard for corruption and mismanagement at the state and local governmental levels.

Federalism can block attempts to solve national problems. Our national legislature is composed of officials selected by state and local constituencies. As such, if they wish to be re-elected, they must please their voters. Often, what this means is voting against needed legislation simply because it conflicts with the more narrowly defined interest of their constituency. The importance of this point is driven home in the annual battle between senators and representatives of farm and urban states. Generally, with rare exception, when farm bills appear on the floor of Congress, the vast majority of those members from highly urbanized areas will vote thumbs down on the bill, not because of anything inherently wrong with the legislation, but rather because the passage of the measure would mean a redistribution of money from urban to rural residents. In terms of re-election this is bad politics, hence, a no vote. A similar fate befalls urban legislation. Thus, in the long run the needs of the nation are unattended. Critics of the system argue that this will always be the case until our leaders and representatives are elected at the national level. This can only be accomplished with the elimination of federalism.

Federalism is the source of disparity in the treatment of citizens of different states. Capital punishment is one such example. In some states it is permitted; in others it is not. Similarly in some states the maximum penalty for the possession of an ounce of marijuana is a $25 fine; in other states the penalty is a year in prison. Is it fair that two citizens who have committed the same crime be treated so differently?—hardly. But it is legal under federalism. Likewise, since it is the state that is responsible for the distribution of societal benefits—education, unemployment, welfare, health benefits—a similar disparity exists. Why does this condition exist? Mainly because states differ in their ability to raise taxes to pay for such services. Consequently, the mere place of birth or residency can determine not only the quality of life but, indeed, life expectancy itself.

Federalism presents problems in taxation. Currently, citizens are taxed at multiple levels by different governmental agencies often for the same purpose as seen in the case of education that is supported by property taxes, sales tax, and a federal income tax. Why are so many taxes needed for one purpose? Because in a federal system the responsibility for education is divided among local school

Not all citizens are treated fairly in a federated system. The distribution of goods and services required by families for a healthy and meaningful existence usually comes from the state. But what happens if the state either refuses to provide such services or, worse yet, decides to distribute them unequally? Does this occur in America? Can you cite some examples?

districts, a state education agency, and a national Department of Education. All, of course, need tax dollars to support their bureaucratic staff. Consequently, millions of dollars are siphoned out of the system that otherwise could be used to improve the quality of education for our children. Similarly, it is important to note that each level of government utilizes different taxes to collect its needed dollars. The national government relies principally upon the federal income tax, which is adjusted according to income levels. Thus, it is a **progressive tax**—one fitting the amount of tax to the ability to pay. Sales tax, the principle instrument of the state, and real estate tax, the primary tax of local governments, have proven to be an extremely **regressive tax**—one in which the burden falls heaviest on the poor. Such a system, argue critics, is unfair and inefficient. In a unitary government, one tax would be levied. Not only would such a tax be more efficient but much fairer.

Federalism promotes unhealthy competition among states. Few state officials would debate the importance of industry in terms of employment opportunities and overall state wealth. Therefore, states are engaged in an ongoing battle to hold on to their existing industry and attract new industries. How is this done?—for the most part through taxation. Businesses eager to maximize profits look favorably upon states with low corporate tax rates. For their part, politicians, eager to grab the credit for fiscal growth, are more than willing to make the needed tax concessions. Thus, a nationwide trend has developed in which industry's share of the tax burden has declined over the last three decades while that of the individual has increased dramatically. It is important to note that interstate competition for industry is not confined to taxation alone. Other concessions include antilabor laws, subsidized buildings, restraints on public spending to hold the tax line, and, even more important, promises to limit regulatory activities. All of these, maintain critics of federalism, serve the interest of industry while jeopardizing the health and welfare of individuals.

Federalism, both from a historical perspective and a contemporary viewpoint, has been the eternal wellspring of racial discrimination. It was the fear of strong central government that motivated the Framers of our government to create a federal system. The state was to be the vanguard protecting individual freedom and civil liberties against the more powerful, intrusive nature of the national government. Ironically, as critics of federalism quickly point out, it has been the state that has been the grand discriminator within the system. On the other hand, the national government has assumed the role of individual protector. Take the right to vote, for example. It was not the national government that prevented blacks or women access to the ballot box; it was the state. Only through federal intervention did the right to vote for these two groups become a reality. Moreover, it was not the national government that segregated our schools, our neighborhoods, indeed, our people; it was the state. Again, only through strong federal intervention have many of these inequalities disappeared. And despite laws to the contrary, much discrimination persists under our federal system.

Federalism renders some states too small and others too large for administrative efficiency. It is true that most unitary systems create smaller units of government to handle the enormous task of government more efficiently. In federalism such divisions are already present. Although this might seem to be an advantage, in practice, just the opposite proves true. In unitary systems, the central government is free to adjust boundary lines when economic and demographic conditions warrant. In a federated system once boundary lines are fixed, they are insoluble. What this means is that despite all the changes that have occurred (technology, communication, transportation, population shifts, etc.) or will occur in the future, America is essentially saddled with the same 50 states with the same fixed boundaries forever. The costs of this inefficiency are incalculable, insist critics.

WHY FEDERALISM?

Fear and loyalty were the dominate themes surrounding the creation of American federalism. On the one hand, as seen in the previous chapter, the fears of the Framers regarding strong central government bordered on paranoia. This led to the creation of a confederacy and, when it failed, it was only natural that the delegates in Philadelphia would embrace federalism rather than unitary government. Working in concert with this fear was an intense loyalty to statehood. In actuality, those attending the convention felt more pride in being a

Most governmental services that we now regard as necessities are delivered by local governments. Here a fire truck arrives at the scene of a disaster. How many other governmental services can you think of offhand?

citizen of their respective state than their country. By today's standards this might seem strange, but one must remember that prior to independence relationships between the colonists were fraught with petty jealousies and divisions. Neither revolution nor eight years of confederate government were enough to mend fences. So, even though some members of the convention might secretly have harbored ideas of creating a unitary state, in the final analysis they also would have had to realize that such a government was beyond political reality for the times. Had it not guaranteed the right of the state to exist as a sovereign partner in the country's government, the newly conceived Constitution would never have been ratified by the state legislatures.

So it was inevitable that America's government would be federal. Let us now turn our attention to an explanation of the federal structure.

AMERICAN FEDERALISM: THE NUTS & BOLTS

The Constitution of the United States attempts to accomplish two broad overriding goals. **First**, it sets the parameters in which government is to exercise power. This is what is referred to as **constitutional government** (limited government). **Second**, it defines the relationship between the national and state governments. Basically this is achieved through grants of powers.

Powers of the National Government

In distributing powers the Framers of the Constitution decided to delegate the powers of the national government and reserve those of the state. (We'll talk about reserved powers later.) Hence, in the first three Articles of our Constitution, the powers of the national government are distributed among the three branches—legislative, executive, and judicial. Three basic grants of power are distinguishable. First, and most obvious, are what we term **enumerated powers**, those powers that are specifically listed in the Constitution as belonging to the national government. In addition, as we shall see later in this chapter, the Court has ruled that the national government also possesses what has come to be called **implied powers**. Such powers are inferred from the "elastic clause" of the Constitution and are, as so ruled by the Court, "necessary and proper" in carrying forth the enumerated powers. More will be said about this later, too.

The Court, in the case *United States v. Curtiss-Wright Export Corporation* (1936),[1] granted the national government a third type of power termed **inherent powers**. As defined by the Court, this power flows not from the Constitution but, rather, from the right of the government to exercise power in certain domains simply because it is a government. All governments regardless of size or power need to interact with other governments in the world. A government lacking these powers would not be able to guarantee its survival in the world community very long. Consequently, the right to wage war, negotiate treaties, regulate foreign commerce, occupy territory, explore space, and others are what the Court has defined "as necessary concomitants of nationality."[2]

Powers of State Government

It would have been an impossible task to set down in writing all powers that government (national and state) was to exercise. Indeed, the list would have been endless. To solve this dilemma, it was decided to list the powers of the national government and reserve those of the state. Where in the Constitution are the powers of the states reserved?—the Tenth Amendment that states:

> *powers not delegated to the United States by the Constitution, nor prohibited by it to the States, are reserved to the States respectively, or to the people.*

What does this mean? Simply, that most of the functions of government we encounter on a day-to-day basis are delivered by the state or an agency acting on behalf of the state (counties, townships, school districts, cities, etc.). The range of these activities includes education, traffic regulation, police and fire protection, aid to the homeless, unemployment compensation, and a host of others too numerous to list. At first glance it might seem as if the state ended up with the lion's share of power, and, indeed, there is good reason to believe that such was the intention of the writers of the Constitution. However, the concept of implied powers, along with additional court rulings, has augmented the power of the national government while restricting the ability of the state to be the sole decision maker in many of the above areas. More about this later.

Another avenue of power available to the states is that which it shares with the national government. Examples include the power to tax and spend, borrow money, appropriate property for public purposes, and establish courts of law. Termed **concurrent powers**, these allow the states to carry forth their obligations as autonomous entities separate from the national government.

Limitations and Obligations of the National Government

In granting power to the national government, the Constitution also establishes barriers to the exercise of power. Article I, Section 9, prohibits the national government from passing **bills of attainder** (acts which single out certain individuals for punishment without trials) and **ex post facto** laws (increasing the penalty of a crime after it has been committed or making the act illegal after it was performed). Likewise, the Constitution limits the government's right to suspend the **writ of habeas corpus**. Thus, individuals being held for an offense must be brought to court and informed of the charges against them. And too, the Constitution specifically states that the government must not infringe upon the civil rights and liberties of citizens.

As to obligation, the Constitution in Article IV imposes three basic guarantees to the state from the national government. They are as follows:

1. guarantee to every state in the union a republican form of government;

2. protect each state against invasion and domestic violence;

3. insure and preserve the territory of each state.

Although seemingly straightforward, the guarantee of a republican form of government has resulted in some confusion among experts. First, nowhere in the Constitution is the term *republican* clearly defined. In addition, the Constitution is silent on the issue of which branch of the national government is to oversee this provision. Historically the courts have been reluctant to enter into this area, claiming that it was a "political" rather than a "judicial" matter better resolved by Congress or the president.

Article IV, Section 4 of the Constitution demands that the national government protect the state against invasion and domestic violence. Invasion is relatively straightforward and agreed upon. Only once in the history of the country (War of 1812 with the British) was the national government obliged to perform this function. In matters of domestic violence, the story is different. On sixteen different occasions, presidents have had to dispatch federal troops to quell domestic riots. Although the Constitution mentions the role of the states in requesting help, presidents have sent troops over strong protest of the governor and state legislature. Examples are seen with President Eisenhower's intervention to quell domestic violence by angry whites over court-ordered integration of a public high school in Little Rock, Arkansas. Similarly after the murder of two civil rights advocates in 1962, President Kennedy was forced to send sixteen thousand federal troops to assist with the enrollment of James H. Meredith,

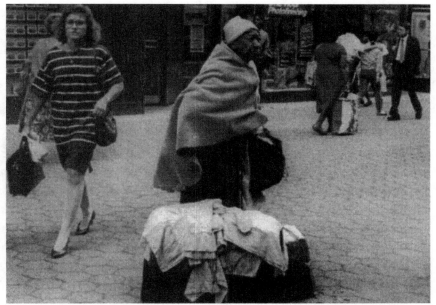

Who has the responsibility for the homeless? Currently, it is the state. However, the growing number of homeless, coupled with the rigid laws of some states, encourage the homeless to move to neighboring states with more generous benefits. These states in turn have lobbied the national government for economic assistance. Do you believe they should receive it?

a black student, into the University of Mississippi at Oxford. One year later, Kennedy was again forced to take action when Governor Wallace followed through with a campaign pledge to stand "in the schoolhouse door" in an attempt to prevent black students from entering the all-white University of Alabama. In all the above cases, intervention was taken over the objections of the governor and state legislature and involved issues with strong racial overtones.

The Constitution also mandates no territory of a state will be taken without its permission to form a new state, nor will two states be combined to form one. Also, Article V guarantees that no state "shall be deprived of its equal Suffrage in the Senate." Thus, six states (Alaska, Delaware, North Dakota, South Dakota, Vermont, and Wyoming) are represented by two senators and only one representative.

Limitations and Obligations of the States to the Union

The principle limitation placed upon the states is that prohibiting succession from the Union—an issue that was tested and settled by the Civil War. Other restrictions, outlined in Article I, Section 10 of the Constitution, limit the states in a wide variety of activities ranging from coining money to engaging in agreements with foreign governments without the consent of Congress. And finally, the inclusions of the Thirteenth, Fourteenth, Fifteenth, Nineteenth, Twenty-fourth, and Twenty-sixth Amendments have served to further restrict the right of states to interfere in the civil rights of certain groups of American citizens.

In the way of obligations, the Constitution requires states to hold elections for Congress, fill congressional vacancies when the need arises, select presiden-

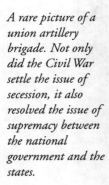

A rare picture of a union artillery brigade. Not only did the Civil War settle the issue of secession, it also resolved the issue of supremacy between the national government and the states.

tial electors, and consider proposed amendments to the Constitution. Perhaps the greatest obligation imposed by the Constitution upon the states is that contained in Article V. Here the states are directed to recognize the supremacy of the Constitution and laws of the national government. Thus, when national and state law conflict, and the law of the national government is deemed constitutional, the state law must give way.

One final note on restrictions. In the eyes of the Constitution, only two governments exist: national and state. Local governments are the stepchildren of the states, adopted for effective and efficient administration of state policy. In a strict theoretical sense the states have formed a unitary relationship with their local governments. Any policy making authority they possess is derived solely from the power of the state. Consequently, all constitutional restrictions that bind states, also bind local governments.

Horizontal Federalism: State to State Obligations

Besides their obligations to the national government, the Constitution also instructs the states regarding their responsibilities toward each other. Undoubtedly, this was an outgrowth of the difficulties experienced under the Articles of Confederation. Article IV of the Constitution outlines three major areas of responsibilities. First, each state must give **full faith and credit** to the civil decisions, official records, and judicial judgments of other states. For example, a group of consumers in Iowa who have successfully brought suit against an unscrupulous business should not be compelled to take their case to court again just because the business moved to Texas to avoid settlement. The Texas court should automatically accept the decision rendered in the Iowa court without subjecting the plaintiffs to a new trial. The same should be true of all cases, including custody decisions resulting from divorce actions. However, in some cases complications develop and the decisions of one state court are not always honored by another state.

States are also required to grant citizens of other states the same **privileges and immunities** accorded to their own citizens. A state may not deny to a citizen of another state full protection of law enforcement, use of the courts, or the right to engage in legitimate business practices so long as it is a right possessed by its own citizens. Nor can a state levy heavier taxes on citizens of different states or place restrictions on them that are not common to its own residents. Although the Constitution seems clear enough on this point, exceptions have occurred and have been, in many cases, accepted by the courts as valid. Nonresident students do not have the same rights to attend a public university in another state as a resident; they must pay higher tuition. Many states also charge a higher fee for hunting and fishing licenses. In addition, states are not required to extend to nonresidents the same political rights afforded their own citizens, such as voting and jury duty. It is noteworthy to mention before leaving this topic that the Supreme Court has recently taken an interest in **durational residency**, requirements imposed by states on individuals to obtain full benefits. Here the Court has tried to determine what residency requirements are justifiable. One year has been viewed as acceptable for university attendance, six months for political privileges, and one day for emergency welfare payment.

The third requirement of states concerns **extradition.** Simply stated, this means that a state, upon request, is obliged to return a fugitive of justice to the state in which the crime has been committed. Although the Constitution appears very specific when it uses the word *shall* in reference to the state's obligation to extradite, they have not always complied. In the celebrated case of Dennis Banks, a native American activist, the state of California refused to extradite him to South Dakota for fear his life was in jeopardy. However, in spite of this case and other examples like it, extradition is usually a routine matter between states. Nevertheless, in 1987, the Supreme Court ruled that states could use the power of the federal courts to force another state to fulfill an extradition request.[2] Likewise, Congress has clarified the process with two acts of its own. **First,** since the Constitution does not specify who in the state shall be responsible for extradition, Congress has designated the governor. And **second**, it has made fleeing across state lines to avoid prosecution a federal offense.

Lastly, the Constitution has allowed states the right to enter into certain types of agreements with other states. They may do so as long as the agreements do not collectively increase the powers of the states over the national government (viewed as contradictory to the concept of national supremacy) or interfere with the right of the national government to carry out its responsibilities. Such agreements, called **interstate compacts,** allow states to solve problems among themselves or to cooperate in some joint venture. For example, the states that border the Colorado River have entered into a successful interstate compact to share the water in that river. Once agreed upon, interstate compacts usually require the approval of Congress and, once given, are deemed legally enforceable contracts by the courts. This is not to imply that once formed all is well. Sometimes the compacts turn out for the worse, and the respective states end up in court anyway.

CONCLUSION

In this chapter we discussed the theoretical aspects of American federalism and why our Founders chose this form of government as opposed to a unitary system. Likewise we pointed out some of the disadvantages of this form of government. In the following chapter we discuss how this system of government evolved when set into practice as well as some of its advantages. Finally, we conclude with some thoughts on the future of American Federalism.

Chapter Three Notes

[1]299 U.S. 304 (1936).

[2]*Puerto Rico v. Branstad*, 483 U.S. 219 (1987).

Suggested Readings

Anton, Thomas. *American Federalism and Public Policy*. Philadelphia: Temple University Press, 1989.

Beer, Samuel H. *To Make A Nation: The Rediscovery of American Federalism*. Cambridge: Harvard University Press, 1993.

Elazar, Daniel J. *American Federalism: A View from the States*, 3d. ed. New York: Harper & Row, 1984.

Henig, Jeffrey. *Public Policy and Federalism*. New York: St. Martin's Press, 1985.

Peterson, Paul E. *The Price of Federalism*. Washington, D.C.: Brookings Institution, 1995.

Riker, W.H. *Federalism: Origin, Operation, Significance*. Boston: Little Brown & Co., 1964.

Walker, David B. *The Rebirth of Federalism: Slouching Toward Washington*. Chatham, N.J.: Chatham House, 1995.

Wills, Gary. *Explaining America*. Garden City, N.Y.: Doubleday & Co., 1981.

Chapter Four

American Federalism:
Putting the Ideas into Practice

It is often stated that the American Constitution is a living document, continually evolving in response to an ever changing world. To a large extent this effect was deliberate. The Framers of the Constitution established the principles upon which the government would operate and outlined the parameters in which power could be exercised. Much of the rest, stated one, would be filled in by history. Nowhere could these words have been more prophetic than in the evolution of American federalism. Generally speaking, two broad classifications can be used to define the relationship between the two governments: competitive and cooperative federalism.

COMPETITIVE FEDERALISM

Undoubtedly for most of our history, the relationship between the national government and the states was characterized by intense conflict and division of responsibilities. The national government and the states were viewed as adversaries, competing for power and responsibility. Overall, three general periods can be distinguished under competitive federalism.

The Rise of the Nationalist: *McCulloch v. Maryland*

As we saw in the last chapter, not everyone was elated over the adoption of a government that emphasized stronger central powers. In fact, the roots of the American political party system can be traced to the fight between the Federalists and the Anti-Federalists over ratification of the Constitution. After ratification the battle continued. The Federalists, led by Alexander Hamilton, urged the national government to exert its powers to resolve some of the difficulties created by the Articles of Confederation.

One such measure, aimed at providing fiscal continuity to the economic chaos left in the wake of the Articles of Confederation, was the creation of a national bank. The thought of a national bank alarmed members of the newly created anti-centralist Democratic-Republican Party of Thomas Jefferson for two reasons. **First**, they believed that the national government was far exceeding its authority. Certainly, within the Constitution, no such power was delegated to the national government and, consequently, if not delegated, the power should belong to the states as directed by the Tenth Amendment. **Second**, they believed the creation of a national bank would provide the Federalists with new economic power that could be used as leverage for a further usurping of states' rights. In spite of these objections the Federalists were successful in their efforts, and in 1809 the first national bank was created. However, the bank became such a source of conflict between the two groups that Congress failed to renew its charter after expiration. Although this was perceived as a major victory for states' rights, it was short-lived. In 1816 the bank was resurrected to cope with new economic problems left by the War of 1812. The reappearance of the bank angered the Anti-Federalists, and new efforts were launched to destroy it. One such effort, initiated by the state of Maryland, was to tax the bank so heavily that it would collapse. James McCulloch, a cashier of the Baltimore branch, refused to pay the tax that amounted to $15,000. The refusal precipitated a constitutional crisis that eventually ended up in the Court of Chief Justice John Marshall. In deciding the case, Marshall outlined two basic questions needing resolution. **First**, did the national government have the right to establish a bank, and, **second**, did the state have a right to tax an agency of the national government? In answer to the first, Marshall ruled that indeed the government possessed the right to establish a bank. Speaking for a unanimous court, Marshall first reviewed the "great" powers provided to the national government by the Constitution, then ruled:

> *...it may with great reason be contended, that a government, entrusted with such ample powers, on the due execution of which the happiness and prosperity of the nation so vitally depends, must also be entrusted with ample means for their execution.*[1]

Where did Marshall find such means? He finds it in the "necessary and proper" clause of Article I, Section 8 ("elastic" clause). In doing so, Marshal advanced the principle of **implied powers** and provided the national government with the means to act beyond the literal language of the Constitution. Regarding the second question, Marshall, again speaking for a unanimous court, ruled:

> *The Court has bestowed on this subject its most deliberate consideration. The result is a conviction that the States have no power, by taxation or otherwise, to retard, impede, burden, or in any manner control, the operations of the constitutional laws enacted by Congress to carry into execution the powers vested in the general government. This is, we think, the unavoidable consequence of that supremacy that the constitution has declared.*[2]

Marshall emphasized that Maryland, in using its taxing power, was really attempting to destroy the United States Bank and that "the power to tax is the power to destroy." Destruction of an agency of the United States government in this fashion was not the intention of the authors of the Constitution. Thus, the law establishing the tax was declared null and void, and the nationalist position prevailed. The total impact of Marshall's decision in *McCulloch v. Maryland*[3] would come to light in two later decisions involving commerce. Here Marshall would broadly interpret the word commerce to include not only those things affecting the movement of goods between states but also any economic action that affected the economy of more than one state. Coupled together, the decisions of the Court concerning implied powers and commerce clearly gave the nationalists the opening rounds in the struggle for dominance. However, the battle was far from over. In the years to come supporters of the states' rights position would continue their fight, both in the courts and on the battlefields of the Civil War.

State-Dominated Federalism

Although the national government had gained substantial powers over the states during Marshall's tenure and, overall, the relationship was characterized by conflict, it would be misleading to imply that no cooperation existed between the national government and the states. After ratification both the national and the state governments worked together to get the new government off to a sound start. National and state laws were brought into alignment, financial relief was given to the states through assumption of their debts, the first grants were offered in the form of land, and each developed compatible revenue sources. However, after the Civil War the atmosphere changed dramatically, and all cooperation seem to halt. At almost every turn the national government and the states found themselves in conflict. Initially the national government maintained its advantage, but the tide was soon to change. Rejecting the Marshallian-Hamiltonian view, the Court unexpect-

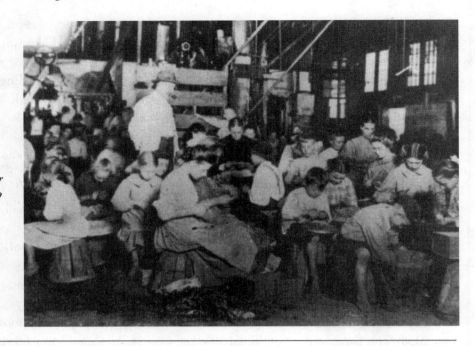

A foreman checks on "backsliders" in a Delaware food processing plant at the turn of the century. Although states had the power to end child labor on their own, few did so because of political pressure from business and industry leaders seeking cheap labor.

edly veered to the right. Turning to the Tenth Amendment, it carved out a broad and exclusive list of state powers untouchable by the doctrine of national supremacy. Suddenly the states found themselves in a commanding position. Ironically the cases that eventually turned back the Federalist interpretation concerned commerce, the same issue used by the Marshall Court to buttress the doctrine of implied powers. In characterizing this period, Edward S. Corwin coined the term **dual federalism**.[4] Under this view, the Court held that the powers of the two governments (national and state) were rigidly defined and fixed by the Constitution, the national government and the states were on equal footing, and the powers of the national government were limited strictly to those expressly delegated within the Constitution. Some political scientists have likened the arrangement to that of a three-layer cake of government, the institutions and functions of each layer being considered separately. To worsen matters for the national government, the Court ruled that corporations enjoyed the same Fourteenth Amendment *due process* protection as did individuals, thus, further limiting the power of the national government to govern interstate commerce. *Hammer v. Dagenhart*[5] epitomizes the posture of the Court during dual federalism. At issue was the validity of the Child Labor Act of 1916, which prohibited the shipment of goods manufactured by children who worked more than eight hours a day. The Court, consistent with its previous decisions, ruled that the national government possessed no such right and, consequently, had intruded upon an area reserved to the states. Unfortunately state legislatures were paralyzed to act, because they were either captives of their own industries or leery of losing a competitive advantage in the marketplace.

Re-emergence of the Nationalists

With the collapse of the stock market in 1929, the economy plunged into one of the worst depressions of our history. Before it would end, 1 out of 4 Americans would be unemployed and homeless, thousands of banks would fail, businesses would be lost, and more than one-third of the farmers would lose their land. In the midst of the chaos, Franklin Delano Roosevelt and the New Deal Democrats would respond with bold, new governmental programs in banking, industry, and social welfare. Initially all would be struck down as the Court held fast to its strict constructionist interpretation. In desperation Roosevelt would mastermind his now famous co*urt-packing* scheme. It too would fail, but shortly thereafter the Court would reverse its position and again return to the Marshallian-Hamiltonian view. Subsequent rulings regarding the national government's rights in interstate commerce and promoting the general welfare of the country would further increase the power of the national government. Advocates of states' rights would launch numerous attempts to curtail the growing influence of the national government in seemingly every aspect of American life. As always, their claim would be rooted in a strict-constructionist interpretation of the Tenth Amendment. But in 1941 with the case of *United States v. Darby*,[6] the Court all but ended any hope states' rights advocates might have harbored when it ruled "all is retained which has not yet been surrendered." Thus, not only did the Court minimize the importance of the Tenth Amendment, it also sounded the death bell for dual federalism.

COOPERATIVE FEDERALISM

Few battles are waged today between the states and the national government over constitutional boundary lines. For the most part the states have accepted a larger federal role in their affairs. Indeed, recent attempts by the national government to retreat from the seemingly dominant role it developed over the last five decades has met almost unanimous resistance by state governors and legislatures. Why the sudden shift in attitude? In general it can be said that both the states and the national government have come to recognize that the world we live in today is far more complex and challenging than could be handled by fifty state governments acting separately. Likewise, the increasing fiscal demands of twentieth century America far outstripped the fiscal capabilities of state governments.

Twenty-First Century Problems

Complexity of interlocking global community. Two world wars, the advent of communism, threats of nuclear holocaust, the international scramble for scarce resources, and the rise of international terrorism have altered the world in rather

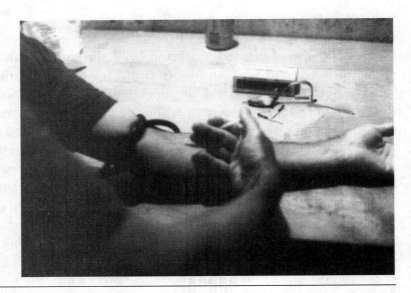

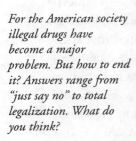

For the American society illegal drugs have become a major problem. But how to end it? Answers range from "just say no" to total legalization. What do you think?

dreadful ways. No longer is it possible for a country to isolate itself from the world community. What happens in one part of the world has dramatic consequences for the rest. In the midst of the global struggles and tension, the United States has risen to the pinnacle of world leadership. Not only are we responsible for our own security but for much of that of the free world. To meet our obligations, the national government has had to assume far greater powers than ever envisioned by the Framers. Many times these powers are only incidentally related to its constitutional power. For example, in 1957, the Russians launched Sputnik I, the first unmanned satellite. Alarmed by the Soviets' spectacular success, America responded with an unprecedented array of programs to ensure its own future in space exploration and technology. In many cases, such programs like those generating special funding for math and science courses, cut across lines traditionally reserved for state control.

Existence of problems that overlapped state boundaries. The industrial society brought with it many problems incapable of being resolved on a state by state basis. Pollution is a good example. It does little good for one state to enact strict environmental controls if neighboring states permit their industries to pollute. Eventually the pollutants will blow their way. Drug enforcement, crime control and prevention, construction of vast transportation and communication networks, energy conservation, inflation, resource management, consumer protection, all represent areas where it's impossible for states, each acting as separate entities, to manage. Only a national plan cutting across state boundaries is capable of resolving the problems.

Inability of states to meet the needs of its citizens. States vary in their access to resources and, hence, in their ability to provide vital services to their citizens. For instance, Mississippi ranks last among all states in per capita income. Likewise, property values and access to tax revenue generated from industry is far below the national norm. Still, Mississippi is expected to provide the same services in education, police and fire protection, workman's compensation, welfare, medical assistance to the elderly and needy, and a host of other costly programs afforded to citizens of wealthier states such as New York and California. Although these services had traditionally been viewed as matters for states, many began questioning the fairness of the inequalities. For example, is it fair that one child's social and economic opportunities be limited because he/she happens to be born in a state incapable of providing the same educational benefits as one living in a wealthier state? Such inequalities eventually necessitated federal action to reduce the discrepancies between the opportunity structures of states. With it came increased federal powers.

Refusal of states to meet the needs of the disenfranchised. In many cases the financial limitations of the states have prevented them from acting. In other cases, it has been an unwillingness, for a variety of reasons, to live up to their responsibility. Race relations in this country are a case in point. In still others, it is more of a matter that certain groups such as the physically handicapped, the mentally retarded, the elderly, etc., lack the necessary political clout to compete successfully for state revenue dollars. Unable to find success at the state level, these groups found their way to Washington, D.C.

Centralization of economic and political power by big business and labor unions has made state governance more difficult. As corporations' and unions' growth accelerated rapidly, so did their capacity to mobilize economic and political power to force upon the states their demands. An example of this can be demonstrated by the fact the UAW (United Auto Workers) has a membership of about 1 million and an annual budget of $217 million. As one can easily imagine, a lone state would be easy prey for a disgruntled corporation or union. Increasingly, states have had to run to big brother (national government) to fight many of the battles they could not possibly win themselves.

Highly mobilized interest group pressure on national government for favorable national legislation. As the national economy became more complex and international in scope, so did the problems faced by industries. No longer could they look to states for solutions. Instead they focused their attention toward Washington, D.C., lobbying for favorable tax legislation, tariffs, subsidies, and other legislative actions that would ensure a stable and healthy business climate. The success of business at the national level stimulated action by competing interests, such as labor, farmers, and environmentalists, who found it impossible to win support for their goals without similar federal backing. Once the national government created legislation to regulate these matters, it was then forced to create a huge bureaucratic organization to enforce compliance. In time the bureaucratic structure itself became a force to further federal expansion as it sought out and established friendly ties with powerful political groups to guarantee its own growth and survival.

National Fiscal Advantage

Concerning the federal fiscal relationship in America, Walter W. Heller has stated, "prosperity gives the national government the affluence and the local governments the effluents." What this implies is, while state and local governments are responsible for many of the services provided to citizens, especially the more costly ones such as health, education, housing, fire and police protection, it is the national government that commands the lion's share of tax revenues. As demonstrated by Figure 4.1, the national government collected 63 percent of tax revenues in 1992, compared to 22 percent for the state and 15 percent for local governments. On the spending side, however, if one excludes military expenditures (which account for approximately 30 percent of total federal spending) and concentrates on direct domestic expenditures, local governments spent 44 percent of governmental moneys compared to the state's 23 percent and 33 percent for the national government.[7] Clearly, local governments could not survive without federal handouts.

This fiscal relationship is principally accounted for by the clear superiority of the federal government in the American tax structure. The major revenue source for the national government is the federal income tax. States rely heaviest upon sales (consumption) tax, while local governments depend upon property taxes. Studies demonstrate that in comparison to sales and property taxes, income taxes are exceedingly more elastic and progressive. **Tax elasticity** is the ability of a tax to grow with the economy without the need for legislative tax increases. **Progressiveness** refers to the capacity of a tax to shift the burden to those most capable of paying. Consequently, as personal earnings have increased over the years, more and more of the population have steadily crept upward into new and higher tax brackets and, hence, have contributed an ever increasing share of their income to the national government. State and local governments have not fared as well. In fact, state and local officials often find themselves in the proverbial "double bind" when faced with citizen demands for increases in government services, on the one hand, and tax revolts on the other. The sensitivity of such officials to the political reality of tax increases, coupled with their concern of the ability of their state to maintain a competitive economic environment with other states, has sent most scurrying off to Washington, D.C., in search of relief.

Marble-Cake Federalism

In the years to come the national government would respond to the ever increasing problems of federalism and the pleas of local and state governments for financial assistance. With each response the national government would gain in both power and influence, and there would come greater cooperation among all three levels of governments. Morton Grodzins, reacting to the layer-cake analogy of American federalism, stated:

> *The American form of government is often, but erroneously, symbolized by a three-layer cake. A far more accurate image is the rainbow or marble cake, characterized by an inseparable mingling of differently colored ingredients, the colors appearing in vertical and diagonal strands and unexpected whirls. As colors are mixed into the marble cake, so functions are mixed in the American federal system.*[8]

Whether the layer-cake analogy was ever appropriate for any time during our federal relationship is questionable. What is important is that as the United States moved deeper and deeper into the twentieth century, the marble-cake analogy became more pronounced. By the 1980s, the "colors," "vertical and diagonal strands," and "unexpected whirls" described so eloquently by Grodzins in 1960 surpassed even his own expectations.

FISCAL FEDERALISM

All of this does not mean, as implied by some writers, that federalism is dead in America. What has occurred is that the relationship between the national government and the states has changed. If anything, it has evolved into a fiscal relationship with the states delivering services and the national government picking up the bill. In fact, many political scientists actually refer to this new relationship as **fiscal federalism**. To understand fiscal federalism, it is important to be aware of how funds are shifted between the various levels of government. Three basic means, each having a different set of consequences, have been used to redistribute money from the national government to state and local governments: categorical grants, block grants, and revenue sharing.

Categorical Grants

Typically **categorical grants** have dominated the grants-in-aid program, accounting for approximately 75 percent to 80 percent of all money distributed to state and local governments in recent years. Simply defined, categorical grants are those in which the federal government specifically earmarks money for designated purposes. In other words, strings are attached, and once state and local governments accept the money, they are legally bound to use it for that particular purpose and in a manner prescribed by federal administrative guidelines. Medicaid and the Food Stamp program are two of the best-known programs funded by categorical grants. Others include education, environment control, highway construction, recreation development, and conservation. An idea of the immense categorical aid structure can be seen in the fact that at last count state and local officials were overwhelmed by 259 separate programs administered by federal agencies. Needless to say, simply keeping current on all the various programs is a Herculean feat.

Two distinct types of categorical grants exist. The most common is the **formula grant**. Here money is available to all eligible governmental units as a matter of right based upon a predetermined formula set by Congress. Hence, it is Congress and not a federal agency that determines guidelines. The formulas set by Congress usually involve population and financial need. Approximately two-thirds of all categorical grants are of the formula type.

Project grants constitute the second category. Project grants differ from formula grants in that only a specified number of dollars are available, and state and local governments must compete with each other for the funds. Hence, a considerable amount of grantsmanship is interjected into application.

Block Grants

Continual complaints over the rigidity of categorical grants led to the emergence of the **block grants** in the mid-1960s. Money distributed under these grants was for use within a broad functional area largely at the recipient's discretion. For example, the national government might grant a state $10 million for crime control. The state would then be in the position of determining exactly how the money might be spent. As expected, state governments tend to favor block grants. Local governments, on the other hand, favor categorical grants since block grants are awarded only to states. In general Democrats have been

Although nearly everyone has a story of someone buying prime beef at the grocery store with federal food stamps, the program is hailed by experts as one of the truly successful federal subsidy programs. Without it, tens of thousands of children and poor would go hungry.

less supportive than Republicans of block grants charging that too much of the money is siphoned away from needy urban areas. In addition, critics also argue that bypassing cities increases the likelihood that the needs of minorities and the poor will be overlooked. Currently, block grants account for about 15 percent of all federal money returned to the states.

Revenue Sharing

On October 20, 1972, President Nixon signed *The State and Local Fiscal Assistance Act*, which became commonly known as **revenue sharing**. In introducing revenue sharing to the nation, Nixon labeled it "new federalism" and forecast that it would launch a "new American Revolution" in which power and authority would be returned to the people. Supported by liberals and conservatives, Democrats and Republicans, revenue sharing was hailed by all as the panacea through which all federal-state fiscal problems would be alleviated.

Put simply, revenue sharing was the return of federal tax dollars to state and local municipalities with almost no strings attached.

Despite all the grandiose promises, revenue sharing failed to be the stimulus for innovative and creative programs. Research by the Office of Revenue Sharing demonstrated that local governments used 80 percent of their money to maintain existing programs. The placement of these funds in operational budgets often allowed local politicians to delay raising local taxes. In 1985, Ronald Reagan acted to end the program, and one year later it was officially eliminated. Reagan also cited the federal deficit as a reason for ending revenue sharing.

Pros and Cons of Fiscal Federalism

The advantages and disadvantages of the grants-in-aid program have been and continue to be hotly debated. Briefly listed below are some of the more salient ones.

The critics of the present grants-in-aid programs argue that:

1. The rules and regulations that come attached to federal money are far too complicated. Often times federal money arrives with code books running into the hundreds of pages. Simply to read and administer federal regulations become a nightmarish task for local officials.

2. Restrictions attached to federal funds make it impossible to implement many programs effectively. Civil rights compliance regulations have dramatically increased the liability problems for businesses participating in programs like the Comprehensive Employment and Training Act

(CETA). Faced with potential and costly law suits from minorities, women, and the handicapped, many businesses simply refuse to join in local efforts to bring federal dollars into the community.

3. Not enough discretionary power is given to local and state officials in the use of federal dollars. The problems of states and local communities vary greatly. Critics maintain that it is impossible for Washington, D.C., bureaucrats to understand local needs. More money, they insist, should come without strings, as is the case with revenue-sharing funds.

4. The grants-in-aid program has been used by the national government to threaten state and local communities with crossover **sanctions**. In other words, the national government will tell a state that unless it institutes policy in one area, it will lose funds in another. Both the 55 mph speed limit and 21-year-old drinking law were instituted by the national government in this manner. The states were informed that unless they complied, no federal highway funds would be forthcoming. Faced with the loss of these vital funds, the states capitulated. The Supreme Court made the legality of this tactic clear in *South Dakota v. Dole*.[9] In the decision the Court argued that Congress can place restrictions on grants-in-aid, under its spending power, without infringing on the reserved powers of the states.

On the other hand, the advantages of the present grants-in-aid system can be summarized in the following arguments:

1. Grants-in-aid help to equalize the difference of wealth between states. As mentioned previously, states vary greatly in their access to resources— some states are very rich, others very poor. The national government through its grants-in-aid program can help alleviate these differences through a process known as **equalization**. Most grants require that states provide matching funds. Richer states are required to put up substantially more money than poorer states. Thus, some measure of parity in needed services (education, health care, unemployment compensation, recreational facilities, etc.) is achieved. The downside to equalization is that it, in a sense, punishes those states that choose to pay for better services. A state that refuses to tax itself can benefit by receiving higher grant amounts.

2. Under the present system of grants the national government is able to target certain national problems for resolution. Generally speaking, state and local officials are more parochial in orientation and less concerned with national problems. Problems nationwide in scope are the concern of the federal government, but to resolve these problems, once targeted, it needs the cooperation of state and local officials since they are the

Due to "crossover sanctions" we now have a national minimum drinking age of twenty-one. Although many states were unhappy about it, they were forced to comply under the threat of loss of federal highway funds. The same tactic was used by the national government to coerce states to comply with a 55 mph speed limit. Many feel that such tactics are abusive and undermine the power of the states. Do you agree?

ones in the position of delivering services. The grants-in-aid system provides the opportunity to entice state and local officials into voluntary cooperation.

3. Grants-in-aid provide for more decentralization. The grants-in-aid system is not a one-way street. State and local officials exert pressure on the national government to adopt items from their own agendas. Thus, as state and local priority items are transformed into national priorities and vice versa, federalism truly becomes a dynamic, reciprocal relationship that invigorates and revitalizes all levels of government. The grants-in-aid system is the medium through which this transfer occurs. For example, there has been some loosening of welfare regulations in recent years. The Clinton administration has granted waivers allowing states to strengthen work requirements in 43 states. This has allowed these states to introduce restrictions on welfare recipients that are enforced at the state level. In other words, it has freed these states to experiment with different ways of removing people from the welfare rolls. This initiative was further strengthened by the Personal Responsibility and Work Opportunity Reconciliation Act of 1996. Without these waivers a state that tried to require welfare recipients to work would have been punished under federal guidelines.

4. Grants broaden the use of the federal income tax. Both sales and property taxes (used principally by state and local governments) are severely restricted in their ability to raise funds and are also extremely regressive. As we have already seen, the federal income tax is much more elastic

(expanding with the economy) and progressive. The grants-in-aid system guarantees that a larger share of the funds used to provide services in needed areas will be generated through the federal income tax that, compared to the alternative of turning over responsibility of these programs to the state, is much fairer to all people in the nation.

5. The grants-in-aid system insures that all citizens have access to tax dollars. Groups lacking political clout often fail to receive their fair share of tax dollars at the state level. Blacks, women, the elderly, homosexuals, and the handicapped are examples of groups who have a difficult time getting state and local governments to spend much tax money on their problems. The national government has proven more responsive and through the grants-in-aid system can pinpoint certain overlooked groups for financial assistance. In many cases the national government has bypassed state and local governments altogether to assist these groups.

Undoubtedly the debate will continue as to the merit of the grants-in-aid system. However, as noted by Reagan and Sazone:

> *What matters for the present purposes is that both constitutionally and politically, we have as a nation accepted the notion that it is appropriate for the national community to embed its scale of values (i.e., those values that a majority of national legislators can agree upon) in programs that offer state and local governments financial inducements to be persuaded that the national scale of values should also be the local priorities.*[10]

One activity by the national government that has been viewed negatively by the states on a number of occasions is the use of **mandates**. When the national government issues a requirement (mandate) for states to do things they don't want to do, the states have raised objections. In recent years, mandates have included handicap access in public accommodation, setting national speed limits, or a national drinking age. States were compelled to obey under threat of civil, criminal or financial penalties, Often the objection is to the cost of performing the mandate. On other occasions the objection has been to the national government's intrusion into the states' rights. On occasion, the Supreme Court has agreed that Congress and its bureaucratic agents have invaded the reserved powers of the states.

The attempt of Republican administrations since the 1980s to transfer power from the national government to the states has met with some success. However, to the surprise of liberals, there has been a trend for many states to set standards for environmental or human rights and consumer and family protections that are higher than those of the national government. Concern with these issues has been a result of the growth of the states themselves.

Cooperative federalism and its financial support through fiscal federalism is getting a new push from the War on Terrorism. The Federal Bureau of Investigation (FBI) was focused upon domestic crime until the terrorist attacks of September 11, 2001. Since then, it has been reoriented to anti-terrorism as its primary task. Criminal prosecution has been shifted more than ever to the states. In addition, the FBI is now engaged in training state and local police forces, as well as other first responders, about the nature of terrorists who might strike inside the United States. The reason is that the law enforcement official who knows the locality the best is the local police officer or deputy. Training in the new environment is being done with the recognition that defense of liberty is the task of all parts of the federal system—local, state, and national.

ASSESSING FEDERALISM

Is Federalism Worth the Effort?

In opening this chapter we pointed to federalism's shortcomings. Throughout the chapter, we have attempted to come to an understanding of how America has attempted to resolve, alleviate, or circumvent all the problems inherent in this form of government. At this point one must wonder—is all the struggle worth the effort? Perhaps, as some critics maintain, the same forces that have driven us toward increasing centralization (stronger national government) will inevitably lead us away from federalism altogether and into a unitary system. Why wait? Perhaps the time has come for another Philadelphia Convention. Do you agree?

Not all problems are easily solved. Here a "street person" picks through the garbage. How do we turn seemingly able-bodied people into productive citizens? An advantage of federalism is that although no one has an absolute answer, states are free to experiment in an attempt to find solutions to this problem, as well as others. If successful, the method can be shared with other states. Thus, an advantage of federalism is its flexibility.

Assessing Federalism's Advantages

Federalism does have problems; no one, not even its advocates, would insist otherwise. However, all governments have problems—no political system is perfect. To assess federalism as a system of government, one must also have an understanding of its advantages.

Federalism is well-suited to large countries. Although we are coming closer to a national culture, major differences still exist among us as a people. This is typical of large countries. Federalism allows for flexibility, permitting people of differing beliefs, attitudes, and values to design public policies more suitable to their convictions while still protecting the rights of minorities at the national level.

Federalism provides a social laboratory for new policies. Unfortunately, we do not have all the answers to life's problems. The hard-core unemployed serve as a good example. Try as we have, nobody yet has arrived at a "sure-fire" way to take such individuals and turn them into productive wage-earning citizens. The advantage of federalism is that it allows for experimentation, and, if successful, the program can be adopted by other states under similar circumstances. Innovation and creativity are not high priority items in unitary governments since programs are normally instituted on a national scale; consequently, failures are more devastating.

Federalism provides a safeguard to freedom. As an instrument of governmental control, federalism has a different connotation to us today than it did to the Framers. To them, the states would provide a military as well as an institutional barrier to the "power-grabbing" tendencies they believed inherent within highly centralized governments. Of course, today with the growth of the national government and military technology, such thoughts would be ludicrous. Does this mean that federalism has lost its utility as a protector of freedom? Not really. In noting that "federalism is, perhaps, as much a state of mind as anything else,"[11] M.J.C. Vile defined it as an attitudinal safeguard. Like separation of powers and judicial review, it is part of our political heritage—a heritage that expects and demands freedom, and its continual presence in our government, though constantly evolving, reinforces our beliefs and commitment in our ideals that, in turn, serves to perpetuate freedom.

Federalism encourages citizen participation. As noted previously, democracy is one of the most difficult forms of government to maintain. Not only does it demand an informed electorate, it also requires participation. Federalism fosters participation by providing more access to government than would a unitary structure. In a unitary system the only critical electoral positions would be those of the national government. This is not true of federalism. Because we have fifty states, we greatly expand the opportunities for citizens to become directly involved in the decision-making process of government. It is also note-worthy to mention that besides government, federalism produces a similar decentralization in the political party system in the United States. Not only does this encourage additional participation, it also helps ensure that a wide range of interest and concern of citizens are represented.

Recent Developments

Recent developments in federalism have included a number of decisions by the U. S. Supreme Court that have restrained the federal government and supported state's rights. These cases have arisen in interpretation of several portions of the Constitution. The Commerce Clause, especially since the Franklin Roosevelt administration, has been used to create regulatory federalism. In recent cases, however, the Supreme Court has restrained the use of the Commerce Clause. For example in *U. S. v. Lopez* (1995) the Court decided that Congress does not have the authority under the Commerce Clause to regulate the possession of a gun within 1000 feet of a school building; this is a state matter. In *United States v. Morrison* (2000), the Supreme Court again limited the ways Congress and the president can use the commerce clause. In *Morrison*, the Court declared the 1994 Violence Against Women Act unconstitutional because its linkage to commerce was too remote.

Other important cases have arisen over the **sovereign immunity** doctrine, which prohibits suits by private persons in state court without the state's permission (cf. the Eleventh Amendment and *Chisholm v. Georgia*). In *Seminole Tribe v. Florida* (1996) the Court held that the federal courts did not have the authority to force a state to comply with the Indian Gaming Regulations Act. In this decision it upheld the right of the state to not be sued over such matters as a violation of the sovereign immunity doctrine. Furthermore, in *Florida Prepaid v. College Saving Bank* (1999) the Court again upheld the sovereign immunity of the states to be protected from suits grounded in the theory that the interstate commerce clause gives Congress the right to override the Eleventh Amendment. Most recently in a decision that curtails the regulatory power of federal independent agencies, the Court decided in *Federal Maritime Commission v. South Carolina Ports Authority* (2002) that private parties cannot sue a state before an administrative law judge in the Federal Maritime Commission because it violates the sovereign immunity of the state. This last decision effectively allowed South Carolina the freedom to decide whether to license or not to license gambling cruise ships operating from South Carolina ports. How it will affect other issues is part of the ongoing struggle for power between the states and the federal government.

Federalism is an ongoing relationship between the federal and state governments. Tensions will always exist because there are always going to be struggles

Table 4.2

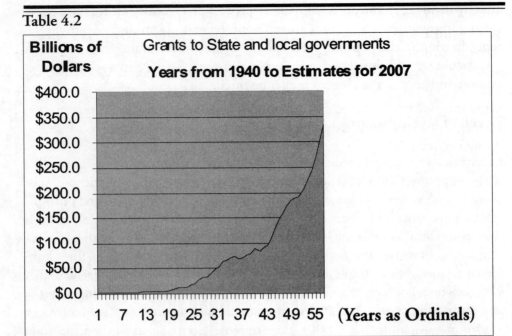

Graph derived from U. S. Budget FY-2003 Table 12.1—SUMMARY COMPARISON OF TOTAL OUTLAYS FOR GRANTS TO STATE AND LOCAL GOVERNMENTS: 1940–2007

for power over a steady stream of issues. Two new issues are: money and education.

The money issue arises because the states tend to be less ready to spend on many projects than the federal government is. Better put, the capacity of interest groups to get the federal government to spend money on projects or issues is more successful with one federal government than fifty state governments. The current money issue is partly about federal mandates and programs that exceed state capacity or interest in funding. Some of these are absolutely necessary despite the indifference of local citizens or local elites. Pollution control, for example, would very likely not occur if the cities and states were not forced to clean up their acts. Atlanta's pollution of the Chattahoochee River with its sewer runoff has resulted in heavy EPA fines. Without that incentive it is unlikely that the downstream towns and cities would ever see clean water. This kind of federal pressure is a plus to many people.

However, the No Child Left Behind Act has left many people very frustrated. The attempt of the federal government to set educational standards is sparking a revolt among the states. The idea of standards and quality education for children is very meritorious. It would be rare to find someone witless enough to argue against the idea of quality education for all children. However, ideals are not political practice. To implement programs that achieve the goal of all children excelling is rhetorically idealistic and financially expensive. When the federal government wants to enter into an area without a doubt reserved to the states with mandates that supply only a tiny proportion of the total money spent to educate a child, it is asking for a revolt. In many localities the average cost may be eight or even ten thousand dollars per year to educate each school child. When the states and localities contribute thousands and the federal government gives two or three hundred and then wants to command the process of education and testing there is a serious mismatch. This is only one issue among many between the federal government and the states.

THE FUTURE OF FEDERALISM

There are about two hundred sovereign states in the world today. Most of these have a unitary form of government. Only about a dozen are federal systems. These federal systems, however, govern about two-thirds of the land area of the world. Many of the world's federal systems, for instance, those in Canada, Mexico, Argentina, Germany, Australia, and elsewhere, have been deeply influenced by the American federal system. In addition, there is currently a debate in Europe over the future of the European Union and whether it should become a federal system rather than a confederal system.

Federalism around the world, like that in the United States, is a product of historical needs, historical challenges, and competing views over the role of government at the local, regional, and national level. These competing views on the proper role of government in meeting historical events will shape the federalism of tomorrow. What are these views?

One view could be called the **unitarist** view. The concerns of the Founding Fathers were to create "a more perfect union," without creating a tyranny. Many Americans today do not share these original concerns. There are those who believe that federalism is merely a phase in the eventual development of an America of the future that will be a unitary state with the states abolished or merged into more efficient administrative units. Those who want this vision of the end of federalism and the coming of a more efficient (and coercive) elitist form of government may get their wish. This model, however, is opposed to the vision of the Founding Fathers because it seeks a sort of "more perfect union" but has no concern about the possibility of tyranny. It was the abuse of power by an English government pretending to absolutism in an Absolutist Age that provoked the American Revolution. That was to be avoided when the federal Constitution was written.

Second is the **pragmatist** view. There are those in American politics who pride themselves on practical issues. Generally these people focus on money that flows from government treasuries. These politicos have sometimes been characterized as "the tax and spend crowd." Their concern is not with federalism as a form of decentralized government that will promote liberty and restrict opportunities for tyranny, but rather with what they can get now. For these actors the system is a cash cow, and the federal cash cow gives the most. For those who hold this view the jobs and monies that the federal treasury can dole out is all that matters, and their support is to the arrangement that will profit them the most.

The third view, **civil libertarian**, focuses on civil rights and civil liberties. Political actors in this category may be liberal, or conservative, or even hold other positions. Quite often they have looked to the federal government to control the states over issues of civil rights and liberties. With a new War Against Terrorism now in progress, there are those who will be supporters of more power to be given to all levels of government to protect against terrorism. Others will be promoters of restraints on governments, especially on the federal government's need to restrict the Bill of Rights to promote national security.

Last the view, **globalists**, share economic, social, and environmental concerns. In this category are promoters of the North American Free Trade Agreement (NAFTA). This agreement strives toward a unified North American economy. It also means, however, a voluntary restricting of the sovereignty of the signers—Mexico, Canada, and the United States. Other agreements such as environmental treaties or global trade agreements restrict the sovereignty of the federal government and the states as well. Political activists in this category are also seeking to limit governmental action and, more often, global corporate action. The outcome of actions in this area is likely to be a diminishing of the traditional dual federalism model.

There are those at all levels of the government that can be seen seeking to keep the balance of dual federalism in some manner. Some of the actors in this category will be local and state officials opposed to unfunded federal mandates. Others will be those opposed to increasing federal regulations (which create regulatory crimes) to govern the lives of people at the local level through the administrative state that arose in the last half of the twentieth century.

The future of federalism in the United States is a future that promises new struggles for defining the ongoing relationships between the federal, state, and local governments with the people. The same struggle is ongoing in other federal systems and in the development of the European Union.

Chapter Four Notes

[1] *McCulloch* v. *Maryland*, 4 Wheaton 316 (1819).

[2] 4 Wheaton 316.

[3] 4 Wheaton 316.

[4] Michael D. Reagan and Johan G. Sanzone, *The New Federalism* (New York: Oxford University Press, 1981).

[5] *Hammer v. Dagenhart*, 247 U.S. 251 (1918).

[6] *United States v. Darby*, 312 U.S. 100 (1941).

[7] Advisory Commission on Intergovernmental Relations, *Significant Features of Fiscal Federalism* (Washington, D.C.: Government Printing Office, 1992.)

[8] Morton Grodzins, "The Federal System," *Goals for Americans* (Englewood Cliffs, N.J.: Prentice Hall, 1960). Grodzins collected a large number of analogies that have been used to describe the federal state relation.

[9] *South Dakota v Dole*, 97 L. Ed. 2nd 171 (1987).

[10] Reagan and Sanzone, 74.

[11] M.J.C. Vile, *The Structure of Federalism* (New York: Oxford University Press, 1961).

Suggested Readings

Bowman, A.M. and Kearney, R.C. *State and Local Government* 2d ed. Boston: Houghton Mifflin Company, 1993.

Derthick, Martha. *The Influence of Federal Grants.* Cambridge: Harvard University Press, 1970.

Elazar, Daniel .J. *American Federalism: A View from the States* 3d ed. Harper & Row, 1984

Engdahl, David E. *Constitutional Federalism in a Nutshell.* 2nd ed. St. Paul Minnesota: The West Publishing Group, 1987.

Henig, Jeffrey. *Public Policy and Federalism.* New York: St. Martin's Press, 1985.

Kettl, Donald F. *The Regulation of American Federalism.* Baltimore: Johns Hopkins University Press, 1987.

Riker, W.H. *Federalism: Origin, Operation, Significance.* Boston: Little, Brown, and Co., 1964.

Wills, Gary. *Explaining America.* Garden City, N.Y.: Doubleday & Co., 1981.

Part Two
The Politics of Participation

The Art of Campaigning

Democracy is one of the most difficult forms of government to institute and manage. The horizon of history is sewed with literally hundreds of countries who have attempted and failed to establish democratic governments. Sporting one of the oldest constitutions in the world, the United States stands out as a beacon of human potential for self-government. Why America? To a large extent, this country has been blessed with a very stable society. Unlike many other countries that are torn by conflicting political philosophies, the United States seems to have settled into a pattern of acceptance. In other words, we tend to agree on the "important things." But, this is not the whole story. Agreement is not enough. To maintain democracy, two key factors must be present constantly. First, the citizenry of a democratic government need to be well educated. If not, then it will be only a matter of time before some political scoundrel with visions of grandeur steals the government from the people. Second, a democratic government demands participation. Democracy is not a passive government; it is active. Citizens need to put their knowledge to work at a variety of levels to ensure that our elected officials run the government correctly and in accordance with the needs and wishes of the public.

In this section we examine how citizens educate themselves and participate in government. The following five chapters explain how Americans keep the gears of government well greased and running smoothly.

Chapter Five

Political Parties
Donkeys, Elephants and Long Shots

James Madison, a major contributor to the Constitution of 1787, warned in *Federalist Number 10* against the dangers of what he called "factions" since they produced "instability, injustice, and confusion." However, it was almost immediate that two such factions, or groups, developed around the issue of ratification of the Constitution. These two groups, the Federalists, who supported approval of the new Constitution, and the Anti-Federalists, who opposed it, eventually developed into this country's first two political parties: the Federalists and the Democratic-Republicans. Despite the fears of James Madison and others, political parties today are a necessary part of the governmental process as we know it in the United States.

DEFINITION

Caution must be used in defining political parties because they are not all the same. However, the following definition is general enough to cover all political parties. A **political party** is any organized group of people who seek to control governmental policy by occupying the positions of authority in the government, either by force or through legitimate elections. In democratic countries, it includes voters who support the party on election day with their votes or with financing and work on behalf of the party's candidates; any government officials who were elected or appointed under the party name (label); and officials of the party organization itself. Sometimes these groups of people overlap. For example, a party leader may also be a government official. Nevertheless, the distinction among party members is useful: voters and workers, government officials, and party officials. In nondemocratic countries, parties include rank-and-file members who support the party, sometimes with violence; government officials and party officials, who are often the same people.

Differences Between Parties and Interest Groups

Many times it becomes confusing to discuss political parties in democratic countries without first making a clear distinction between parties and interest groups. Although interest groups often give major support to political parties through fund raising, attempts to influence public opinion, and votes, there are definite differences between political parties and interest groups.

First, political parties are usually much larger, although not always, than interest groups. For example, the largest interest group is the American Association of Retired Persons (AARP), with about 35 million members; however, people who consider themselves Democrats in the United States might number as many as fifty to sixty million or more at any given time. With these larger numbers, of course, usually comes more money than any single interest group might be able to raise at a particular time.

Second, the main function of a political party is to win elections, thereby, controlling the government. On the other hand, interest groups do not offer candidates themselves. Rather, interest groups seek to influence the officials who are elected or appointed under the party label. Again we need to take note that interest groups do support party candidates with their money, by influencing public opinion, or actual work for the candidates. But they do not offer candidates under their own interest group labels. If they did, then these interest groups would become political parties, according to our definition.

Third, interest groups are usually narrower in their focus than are political parties. The Humane Society of the United States, for example, focuses its efforts on animal welfare and governmental policies to promote animal welfare. It does not deal with such issues as nuclear war, the economy, gay rights, welfare, income taxes, or any of the other innumerable issues that political parties deal with.

Finally, as compared to the two major political parties in the United States, Democrat and Republican, many interest groups are extremely ideological, whereas the two major parties are not.

Before we go on, let's get a clear picture of what the word ideology means. An **ideology** is a way of looking at the world around us. We might say it is like

Images of the world are shaped by ideologies. What do you see here? What does your response say about your ideological beliefs?

a "dye" that colors what we see. For example, if a person wearing green-tinted glasses (Let's call her Tallulah.) were to walk into a room full of people, she would look out at the people and say: "This is a room full of green people." Entering right after Tallulah is Pythias, wearing purple-tinted glasses, who observes the room and says: "This is a room full of purple people." Now they are both looking at the same group of people, but because of the differences in the tint of their glasses, Tallulah and Pythias are seeing the people quite differently. Ideology works the same way. If a person whose ideology is liberalism (a liberal) looks at a group of people who have all been convicted of armed robbery, the liberal might say: "These poor people are all victims of society. If they had had proper upbringing and advantages that others in the society had, then they wouldn't have committed these crimes. They need understanding and help, not punishment." On the other hand, if a person whose ideology is conservative (a conservative) observes the same group of people, the conservative might say: "All people have a free choice either to obey the law or not. These people chose not to obey the law. They are vicious and need to be punished severely so that they don't commit these crimes again." These ways of looking at the world, the dye, so to speak, are what we call ideologies: conservatism, liberalism, communism, pacifism, militarism, authoritarianism—all the different "isms" we can think of. Interest groups are much more likely to have some consistent ideology, or "ism," coloring what they think or do than are the major political parties in the United States, although most people consider Democrats to be generally more liberal than Republicans.

TYPES OF POLITICAL PARTIES ════════════════════════

Political parties can be grouped, or categorized, in several ways. For our purposes, we shall put parties into two categories: democratic parties and nondemocratic parties. (Here the word democratic is used in the generic sense—the common usage of the word.) **Democratic parties** are those that are open to anyone, not just a privileged few, and allow debate on policies the party wishes to pursue at all levels of party activity. On the other hand, **nondemocratic parties** are those that usually are not open to just anyone who wishes to participate; rather, just a select few are allowed to join. Decisions on party policy matters are normally made by the leaders of the party, not the rank-and-file party members.

Democratic parties themselves fall into two different categories: ideological, democratic parties and nonideological, democratic parties. **Ideological parties**, as the name suggests, are those that adhere to a particular ideology, or view of things—the "dye" we spoke of earlier. Some are extremely conservative; some are extremely liberal; while others fall anywhere in between. Regardless of the particular ideology the party follows, however, all ideological, democratic parties are made up of a single group of people (meaning they all have basically the same ideology). They are highly structured and organized, unified, and disciplined. The British political parties in the House of Commons (a legislative body similar to the United States House of Representatives) are good examples of ideological, democratic parties.

When a political party is characterized as highly structured and organized, it means that the party has a definite organization and structure. The party could be diagrammed on a chart in a similar manner to organizational charts used to describe businesses such as General Motors Corporation or IBM. If a party is considered unified and disciplined, it means that the members usually abide by the decisions that the party as a whole has made, even if it means the party member gives up his/her own opinion. To enforce this unity in these kinds of parties, persons can be removed as members of the party if they act too independently. In highly disciplined parties, members who are elected officials of the law-making branch of government, for example, usually vote the way the party wants them to vote in the overwhelming majority of cases. By contrast, in the United States, where the two major parties are not highly disciplined, it is not uncommon to find a Democrat who will vote with Republicans on some issues or a Republican who will vote with Democrats on some issues. After the vote these people are still members of their respective parties. Freedom to make up one's own mind seems to be a "given" in nonideological, democratic parties whereas it is not in ideological, democratic parties; there, party unity must prevail.

Nonideological, democratic parties are characterized as alliances of many different groups, often with different ideologies but with some common interests. Therefore, the party is, more or less, forced not to have a definite ideology to survive. In fact, it is usually the case that these parties try to pursue a middle-of-the-road course so as not to drive away potential supporters. Nonideological, democratic parties, unlike their ideological counterparts, are not structured, not unified, and not disciplined, as a rule. Furthermore, they do not have nearly as much organization, nor as active and as powerful internal structures as ideological parties. In this regard, ideological parties are like canals dug by machines and lined with concrete. The water flows in them very straight and narrow. On the other hand, nonideological parties are like meandering streams we might find in nature. The water flows very much where it wants to—here, there, and everywhere.

Unlike democratic parties, nondemocratic parties are always ideological, highly unified, organized, and disciplined. Prominent examples of this type of party are the Ba'ath Party in Iraq before the fall of Hussein, the Rastakhiz Party during the final years of the Pahlavi monarchy in Iran, the Communist Party in Cuba, and the Nazi Party in Germany prior to and during World War II. These parties usually have youth organizations, women's branches, and other party structures to appeal to various elements of the society in a similar fashion that churches in the United States do. Unlike democratic parties, where debate over the issues can take place at all levels of the party, nondemocratic parties usually do the arguing over what to do at the very top of the party structure. Then the leaders just tell the rest of the party what everyone is going to do. It should be obvious now that these nondemocratic parties are found in countries that are thought of as dictatorships.

FUNCTIONS OF DEMOCRATIC PARTIES

Since the main focus of this text is government, American style, we shall deal with the functions of democratic parties—the kind found in the United States. There are actually ten functions performed by democratic parties.[1]

First, political parties serve as agencies of action, whether for people who share a common ideology or for groups of people who have differing ideologies. In other words, the parties, whether ideological or nonideological, are the doers, the performers of actions of the government.

Second, parties serve as vehicles to bring together the various demands for governmental action made by individual citizens, as well as interest groups. In this capacity, political parties are like huge funnels that catch all these demands and pour them into the government. That way the demands are made much more effectively than if individuals or even groups tried to channel them to the government themselves.

Third, political parties help to formulate, or shape, public opinion. In other words, the parties try to tell the public what the issues are and attempt to tell them how to think regarding these issues. For example, suppose one of the issues brought up by the Democrats in the next election was unemployment. Democratic politicians would be making speeches all over the country pounding away at the unemployment issue. In their speeches they might say that unemployment in the United States was too high and that the government should spend tax money to retrain displaced workers or give the states more money to provide better educational opportunities for the people or create government jobs for those who are out of work or perhaps all four. Republicans might counter by saying that unemployment was at an acceptable level and that jobs must come from the private sector of the economy, not the government. These are the kinds of things parties do when they are trying to formulate public opinion.

Fourth, political parties offer the people political alternatives, or policy choices. As the last paragraph indicates, each party offered a different solution to the problem of unemployment. The same thing is likely to occur on most issues whether the issue is foreign aid, terrorism, social programs, military spending, or whatever. Political parties will usually offer a somewhat, or (rarely) drastically, different solution to the various problems facing the country.

Fifth, political parties bring together in the organization different kinds of people and groups. For example, in both the Democrat and Republican parties one will find different racial, ethnic, and religious groups; different age groups; groups from different regions of the country; groups with differing ideologies. In this regard, parties are like the cage that holds the numbers in a bingo game. The person calling out the numbers turns the cage over several times to mix up the numbers. Then the individual calls them out one at a time. Each number is different, but they are all in the same cage; just as the people and groups who make up political parties are different, but they are all in the same party.

Sixth, political parties run the government, or at least parts of it. They perform this function, for the most part, as professional politicians— professional government runners, so to speak. The members of the parties, who are either elected or appointed to office, usually have chosen politics as their career, not just a one-time thing, not as people might do if they were working their way through school as a dishwasher. (Washing dishes is not something most people would plan to do for the rest of their working lives!) Because political parties run the government, they are also responsible for what the government does. The public can point a finger at the parties, and it is their fault if things don't go well. However, in the United States, because parties are not particularly disciplined or unified, making parties truly responsible for their behavior is sometimes difficult. In other words, politicians frequently depart from the party "line" and support what their constituents want, or they might even support or oppose something just because they themselves want to.

Seventh, political parties act as employment agencies, seeking out people to fill government offices, as well as party offices. However, unlike employment agencies, political parties give their recruits on-the-job training frequently by having a person start out in a very low-level position and letting that person work his or her way up the ladder to a position of real authority. Rarely (except perhaps for diplomatic posts) does one see a political party recruit someone for high government office without that person's having quite a bit of experience in lesser offices.

Eighth, political parties serve as critics of and checks on other political parties, particularly on the party that elected the president. What we're talking about here are the "ins" and the "outs." Usually in the United States the "in" party is the one that holds the presidency, while the "out" party is the one that did not win the presidency. Since the president is very powerful in setting policy for the United States, the opposing party often acts as a stumbling block in the president's way in implementing the program. This party function works like a basketball game. The team that has possession of the ball has the intention of driving down the court and making a basket. If there were no opposing team on the court, then there would be nothing, short of poor shooters, to prevent the team from scoring. Political parties function like the two teams on the basketball court. The "in" party has the ball and wants to make a basket, but the "out" party wants the ball itself so it can score the points. Politics in many respects is like basketball games; you win some and you lose some.

Ninth, parties serve as instruments of peaceful change. By allowing individuals and groups to channel demands to the government through the parties, by helping to formulate public opinion, and by running the government or parts of it, parties create a climate for change in which political violence is kept at a minimum. The contests can be fought at the ballot box and not in the streets.

Finally, political parties act as links between individuals or groups and the government by allowing these people to be party members who help to formulate party policies and by offering their candidates to the voters on election day. In this regard, parties are like the electric cord and plug that connect an appliance to the source of energy. When the cord is plugged in, the electricity flows to the machine. When political parties are "plugged in," then the government flows to the people and vice versa. (Fortunately, unlike this example, electricity usually does not flow back to the outlet!)

POLITICAL PARTY SYSTEMS

Not only can political parties be classified according to whether they are democratic or nondemocratic, but they can also be grouped according to the number of parties competing in the political arena. This classification has three categories: multi-party systems, two-party systems, and one-party systems.

Most democratic countries have what are called **multi-party systems**, in which there are three or more major political parties competing for control of the government and, therefore, control of its policies. The multi-party system is found in countries such as France and Italy. In a multi-party system the political parties are usually ideological and well organized. These parties are frequently leader oriented, meaning that the leader of the particular party exerts very strong influence over the party followers, sometimes more than the party organization itself. As a result, many parties in a multi-party system do not last very long. When the leader dies or retires, for example, the party just folds up its tents, so to speak, and fades away. As a result of having more than two political parties to choose from, sometimes no single party wins a majority of the seats in the legislative branch. Consequently, no single party actually can control the policies of the government. What happens in most instances is that two or more parties will form a **coalition**, or alliance, with one another, so that voting together, they can control, whereas none of them could do so if voting alone. The problem is that, if one of the parties in the coalition decides it does not want to play the game anymore, then the coalition collapses and new elections are held. This kind of activity causes multi-party systems to be less stable than two-party systems or one-party systems.   For the government to function, compromises among the parties must occur after the election if no single party receives a majority of the popular vote.

A **two-party system**, as its name implies, has no more than two major political parties. A two-party system does not mean that there are just two political parties but rather that no more than two political parties have a realistic chance of winning a majority in the legislative branch of the government. This type of party system is found in democratic societies also but less frequently than multi-party systems are. Although somewhat functionally different, the United States, Canada, and Great Britain are examples of countries with two-party systems. In Great Britain and Canada, parties other than the major parties make a greater contribution to the political process than they do in the United States. Nevertheless, both Canada and Great Britain have two dominant parties. Unlike parties in a multi-party system, political parties in a two-party system are either nonideological or much less ideological. Since they are nonideological or less ideological, parties in two-party systems are not made up of single groups. Rather, they are usually alliances of many different groups with differing shades of ideology. These parties are usually more loosely organized than their multi-party-system counterparts. The parties in the two-party system are not leader centered; on the contrary, leaders change rather frequently. If a party leader dies or retires, the party usually continues with a new leader. In other words, parties in the two-party system tend to have longer lives than do parties in a multi-party system. Furthermore, since there are only two parties with a realistic chance of winning a majority in the legislative branch, two-party systems tend to be more stable than multi-party systems. One or the other political party should win a majority; therefore, there should be no coalition

Table 5.1: Comparison of Party Systems

SMD

MULTI-PARTY SYSTEM	TWO-PARTY SYSTEM	ONE-PARTY SYSTEM
More than one major political party	Two major political parties	One major political party
Parties usually ideological	Parties either ideological or non-ideological	Party ideological
Parties usually disciplined, structured	Parties disciplined, organized, structured when ideological; not disciplined, nor highly organized when nonideological	Party highly organized, disciplined, structured
Compromises frequently take place between parties after an election; frequent coalition governments	Compromises occur within the parties before an election; coalitions within the party	Any differences of opinion are ironed out in the top levels of the party and are not publicized
Parties are frequently leader centered	Parties usually not leader centered	Party leader centered
Parties are frequently short lived	Parties exist indefinitely	Party exists indefinitely
Party organization and government organization easily distinguishable	Party organization and government organization easily distinguishable	Difficult to distinguish between party organization and government organization
Found in democratic countries	Found in democratic countries	Frequently found in nondemocratic countries - dictatorships
Governments frequently unstable	Governments stable	Governments stable unless overthrown

governments.[2] Elections are held at regular intervals rather than having elections occur as a result of a failed coalition. Finally, unlike parties in a multi-party system, where compromises frequently occur *after* an election has taken place so that the government can function, parties in a two-party system make their compromises *before* the election to get as many votes as possible to win a majority. These compromises are a result of the generally nonideological nature of these parties. Whenever these parties have developed strong ideological positions that tend to exclude the views of other people with different ways of looking at things, the parties' chances of winning an election are significantly weakened. This kind of thing has happened several times in United States elections, notably in the 1964 Republican Party and the 1968 and 1972 Democratic Party.

One-party systems, or single party systems, obviously contain one major political party. If there is opposition, it is usually minimal. Typically, one-party systems are found in dictatorships but not exclusively so. Communist dictatorships such as Cuba and The People's Republic of China serve as examples of countries with one-party systems. In these countries it is very difficult to determine where the party organization begins and the government organization ends. In other words, the party and the government are frequently one and the same. The leaders of the one political party will also be the leaders of the government. The single party found in one-party dictatorships is ideological, organized, highly structured, and disciplined; that is, it is also a nondemocratic party.

Democratic countries may also adopt one-party systems. Even the United States has operated for short periods of time with a one-party system, not because other parties were not allowed to function but just because they were not there. Mexico, also a democracy, had been considered a one-party system for nearly seven decades. However significant changes have developed over the last few years. In 1999, in largely fair elections, Mexico's voters overthrew 68 years of history. Defecting both to the political right and left, they ended the overall majority of the Institutional Revolutionary Party (PRI) in the lower house of their Congress. Similarly, by a huge majority of voters in the capital, they elected Cuauhtemoc Cardenas, the left-wing candidate, mayor of Mexico City. However, turning to the right, Mexican voters chose Vincente Fox of the center-right National Action Party (PAN) as the President of Mexico, breaking an historic 71-year control of the PRI on the Mexican president's office. If all goes well for Fox and the PAN, the next decade will probably put Mexico securely into the multi-party category.

Table 5.1 compares multi-party systems, two-party systems, and one-party systems in a convenient format.

WHY A TWO-PARTY SYSTEM IN THE UNITED STATES?

There are probably three major reasons why the United States in particular has a two-party system rather than a multi-party system or a one-party system. **First,** the two-party system is traditional. Two political parties actually developed early in the history of this country, having sprung from a group that supported ratification of the Constitution and one that did not support ratification. Besides, the British had a two-party system that served as an example. Once a tradition gets started, it is difficult to change it.

Second, since the United States is considered a democratic country, it would seem inconceivable that a one-party system would be allowed to survive for very long. It would be "un-American," so to speak, to have no real choices on election day.

Third, the United States has an election system that is different from those found in most countries with multi-party systems: the single member district. To understand this concept, we also have to understand its counterpart in multi-party systems: the **multi-member district—proportional representation.** In countries such as Italy, where multiple parties exist, it is relatively easy for small parties to elect candidates to the legislative branch of government because seats in the parliament (legislative branch) are awarded roughly in proportion to the number of votes that each political party received. For example, if Party X received 25 percent of the popular vote, then Party X would be allotted 25 percent of the seats in the parliament. If Party Y received 30 percent of the vote, then it would be awarded 30 percent of the seats. If Party Z received 20 percent of the vote, then that party would have 20 percent of the seats in the parliament. In the United States, with its single-member districts, however, whichever candidate receives the most votes, then that candidate gets elected and the other candidates are just losers. In other words, seats in the Congress (legislative branch) are not awarded in proportion to the number of votes a party received. Rather, seats are awarded to the party's candidates who got the most votes whether those votes were a majority or not (usually). On the other hand, some states require a run-off election if none of the candidates receives a majority of the vote. Since there are traditionally already two major parties, it is very difficult for new, smaller parties to challenge candidates of the major parties because the smaller parties cannot normally pull enough votes to get their nominees in office. Additionally, for a political party candidate for president of the United States to win, he or she must have a majority of the electoral vote. It would be quite an uphill battle (although not impossible) for a third party to win such a majority in the electoral college. There have been no third-party electors selected in any state since the 1968 election. Consequently, unless the electoral system changes in the United States, it is highly unlikely that a multi-party system will develop. The more likely scenario would be that, if a third party actually won the presidency, for example, one of the other two parties would soon cease to exist, and the United States would again have a two-party system.

IMPACT OF THE TWO-PARTY SYSTEM

The two-party system in the United States has had several significant effects. **First**, majority government is assured at all levels of government. Unlike the situation that occurs sometimes in multi-party systems, there are no coalition governments where parties have to join together to achieve a voting majority in the legislative branch. Even in the executive branch, the president must be elected by a majority of the electoral college, whereas the chief executive in countries with multi-party systems can be the result of a compromise among a number of political parties.

Second, the two-party system has produced political parties that are alliances of many different groups, as stated previously. Therefore, the parties are nonideological so as not to lose any potential voters in the next election.

Third, the groups and individuals that make up each of the two political parties are generally similar. Both parties will have conservatives and liberals; Catholics, Protestants, and Jews; blacks, whites, Orientals, and Hispanics, etc. However, it is true at the present time that some groups tend to consider themselves members of one of the parties more so than the other. For example, currently more conservatives are found in the Republican Party than in the Democratic Party. Because the parties are made up of similar types of people, party leaders must compete for support from among the same groups. To highlight the similarity of the two major parties in the United States, George Wallace, former governor of Alabama and former presidential candidate, once stated: "There's not a dime's worth of difference between the two."

Fourth, the two-party system has produced two very similar parties that agree on general goals for the society but may differ merely on the methods that should be used to achieve these goals. For example, both political parties agree that the United States should defend itself against foreign aggressors. But they may disagree about how to do so. Should the United States have a strong nuclear arsenal? Should it involve itself in the affairs of other countries to protect itself? Should it hold talks with such countries as Cuba or North Korea? Should it trade with those countries that are unfriendly to the United States? In other words, the parties tend to agree on the "what" but often disagree on the "how."

Fifth, the two-party system effectively prevents third parties from becoming successful. Third parties, or minor parties, come and go, although some have been in existence for a long time and are usually centered on a single issue or ideology. If the ideas the third party puts forth seem to be catching on with the people, one or both of the major parties will just adopt the minor party's program or parts of it. Therefore, these parties never really have a chance to capture the minds and hearts of the voters.

Sixth, in the two-party system of the United States, the party that loses the presidential election or fails to win a majority of the seats in Congress does not feel worthless or rejected. In fact, the losing party (i.e., minority party) plays the role of watchdog on the activities of the ruling party and, of course, always expects to win on the next go round.

MINOR PARTIES

Although the United States has a two-party system, this arrangement does not preclude the formation of third parties, or minor parties. In fact, these minor parties play a significant role in politics in the United States although they rarely manage to have their candidates elected to office, particularly at the national level.

Functions of Minor Parties

Minor parties essentially do three things in the political arena in the United States. First, and probably most importantly, they bring new ideas to the attention of the public. Since our major parties, Democrats and Republicans, are middle-of-the-road parties, trying to appeal to the largest possible number of voters while alienating as few as possible, minor parties have been in the forefront in the area of new solutions to old problems in society as well as within political parties themselves. Once these ideas "catch on," and become popularized, the major parties usually adopt the ideas themselves. For example, the Anti-Mason Party of the 1830s was the first political party to use a national convention to select the presidential and vice-presidential nominees. In no time at all, this procedure was adopted by the major parties. The Populist Party, formed in 1892, was the first party to advocate direct election of Senators and the right of women to vote—a radical idea for its time! Likewise the Socialist Party, organized in 1901, championed the cause of unemployment compensation, old-age pensions, workman's compensation, and a graduated income tax. When these ideas became popular, they were adopted by the major parties and were later enacted into law. It would not be accurate, however, to assume that everything minor parties advocate eventually comes to pass. The Socialist Party, which championed the cause of unemployment compensation, old-age pensions, workman's compensation, and a graduated income tax, also supported government ownership of the mining, oil, communications, liquor, and transportation industries, as well as government ownership of banks and utilities. The Socialists even wanted to do away with the Supreme Court's power of judicial review—declaring laws unconstitutional. None of these ideas were ever adopted.

Contemporary minor parties advocate positions that are likely to receive the same kind of reaction as did the Socialist Party's failures previously men-

Although America is basically a two-party system, other political parties do exist. Here a member of the "Marxist-Leninist Party" distributes literature on apartheid (segregation in South Africa). This party has few followers and has never been listed on a national ballot.

tioned. Some of the more bizarre ideas are guaranteeing everyone a job at a living wage, a 32-hour/4-day work week, one-year paid leave for every seven years of work (your author's personal favorite), and a guaranteed adequate income for everyone. Those proposals seem mild compared to others advocated by some minor parties such as eliminating the IRS, CIA, FBI, income taxes, and the civil service. So if the American voters get angry enough at the two major parties, they can always vote for the Natural Law Party, which advocates transcendental meditation and Yoga for everyone.

Second, minor parties can hold the balance of power in a close election. When votes are cast for a minor-party candidate or candidates, those votes must come from somewhere—the other two parties usually. If enough of those votes come from one of the two major parties, then chances are the other major party will win. This phenomenon may have occurred in the election of 1912 when third-party candidate Theodore Roosevelt presumably pulled votes from the Republican Taft, thereby enabling the Democrats to win with Woodrow Wilson. It may also have contributed to the victory of Richard Nixon over Hubert Humphrey in 1968 when George Wallace ran as a candidate of the American Independent Party, which had split off from the Democratic Party. It is also possible that, if the popular vote is divided sufficiently among the two major-party candidates and minor party candidates, no one person will get a majority of the electoral vote in a presidential election. If this event comes to pass, then the House of Representatives will choose the president and the Senate will choose the vice president, according to the rules set out in the Constitution. In that event, the "politicking" would be "hot and heavy," to say the least.

The election of 1824 serves as an illustration of this phenomenon when the one and only political party split into four factions!

Third, minor parties allow people who hold a minority opinion to express that opinion through the third party where their voices would be more likely to be heard. Again in their efforts to stick to the middle ground, major parties are not as likely to champion causes with which large numbers of voters are likely to disagree.

After all the "amens" have been said, political scientists have probably paid more attention to minor parties than the electorate has. Only one minor party (the Republican Party) has succeeded in supplanting one of the major parties. Moreover, not counting the Republicans, only five minor parties have managed to win even 10 percent of the popular vote in a presidential election, and only seven have been able to win a single state in a presidential election. Most recently in 1992 and 1996, Ross Perot captured 19 and 8 percent of the popular vote, respectively, but not one electoral vote.

STATE PARTIES

Although state parties often take a back seat to the national parties in the United States in media attention, it is worth noting that many of the American states are larger than a number of countries and even more complicated in some respects. Therefore, it is pertinent to address the characteristics of political parties in the states, as well as those of national parties.

To begin with, political parties at the state level perform the same functions as national parties, but state parties are not duplicates of the national parties although sometimes they are similar. State parties are actually affiliates (associates) of the national parties, but state parties are not dependent on national parties for their existence. State parties possess a high degree of independence and receive no instruction from the national parties concerning candidates or policy positions. Therefore, it is no surprise that, for instance, while the Democratic Party at the national level was pursuing policies of racial integration, state Democratic Parties in the South were struggling to do just the opposite.

State parties can also get away with being more ideological than their national counterparts. In some states, the vast majority of the population is relatively conservative (e.g., Mississippi) or it may be that the people of a state are pretty liberal (e.g., Massachusetts). In that event, the state party would be more likely to align itself where the majority of the voters are on the ideological scale rather than stay strictly in the middle.

Furthermore, unlike the national party level where competition is usually keen between Republicans and Democrats, many states are actually dominated by one or the other party. Some of these states could be said to have a one-party system instead of a two-party system.

As a result of the separation of state parties from national parties, citizens often tend to vote for one party's candidates at the national level, while casting their ballots for the candidates of the other party at the state level. If we do not understand that these state parties are merely affiliates of the national parties and not sub-units of the national parties, then this tendency may seem incomprehensible.

NATIONAL PARTY ORGANIZATION

The organization of political parties at the national level or state/local level is generally characterized as loose. However, since the 1960s a trend toward stronger party organization at all levels and stronger connections among all levels is evident. Still, Republican national, state, and local organization is usually more structured and disciplined than is its counterpart in the Democratic Party.[3] Furthermore, it should be emphasized again that state parties are not mere branches of the national parties; the state parties are affiliates of the national parties. And national parties really only exist every four years to elect a president and a vice president, since these are the only two offices elected by the entire country. Every other office is elected from a state or a part of a state. With these qualifications in mind, let's proceed to the two most important structures of American national parties.

The National Convention

Functions. The national convention, meeting only for about four or five days every four years, is theoretically the supreme legislative organ of the national party, and also theoretically it nominates the presidential candidates and drafts a **platform**—a statement of the party's program and ideals. In reality the national conventions perform a number of functions besides these two. **First,** usually national conventions merely "rubber stamp" the presidential nominee's choice for the vice-presidential nominee rather than actually selecting that person itself. The presidential nominee just makes it known whom he/she wants, and the convention accepts that vice-presidential nominee, often by **acclamation**—a voice vote. **Second,** national conventions serve as agencies to bring about compromise among politicians representing different interest groups and ideologies. These interest groups and ideological interests do manage to soften or strengthen some of the positions taken by the party in its platform. **Third,** the national conventions help to raise money for the parties' candidates by lining up group support, for example, from labor unions or big business corporations. **Fourth,** since national conventions present us with a spectacular event, complete with television coverage, they try to create or solidify strong loyalty to the party among the voters and try to impress the new voter and the independent voter. In other words, they try to convince these voters to join the "bandwagon" or "follow the leader."

Although delegates to these national nominating conventions appear to be free to choose whomever they please as a presidential nominee, in reality most delegates are pledged to vote for a particular candidate on the first ballot at least.

Selection of Delegates. The manner of selection and the number of delegates to each party's convention varies from party to party and from state to state. The Democratic National Convention has about twice as many delegates as the Republican convention. Again, depending on the state and the party involved, delegates are selected by means of **presidential primaries,** wherein the party's voters get to choose the delegates themselves or, at least, express a preference for the party's presidential nominee. Although most states today use primaries to select delegates, some states use **party caucuses** (party meetings held at the local level) or **conventions** within the state.

Those who support the use of primaries for delegate selection assert that primaries are more democratic than caucuses and are more representative of the wishes of the party's voters. Besides, supporters claim that primaries create a solid test of the very skills necessary to be a successful president.

Opponents of primaries argue that, while primaries draw more participants than do caucuses, the quality of the caucus far outweighs that of the primary. While voters may spend a few minutes voting in the primary, people who attend caucuses spend several hours, at least, learning about party politics, listening to the actual candidates or their representatives, and hearing the advice of party leaders and elected officials who have practical, governmental experience. Finally, critics contend, voters may have only superficial knowledge of the candidates in a primary, most of which was gained through reading or hearing about popularity polls and watching television ads.

The validity, or lack of it, of the criticism of primaries as a method of selecting delegates to the parties' national conventions seems largely irrelevant. The trend today is toward the primaries, with some supporters even suggesting regional primaries instead of state-by-state primaries. Ultimately, if all states and the District of Columbia use primaries, the national nominating conventions may become unnecessary.

The National Committee

Although it appears on paper to be a powerful unit of party governance, the national committee is a paper tiger. It does conduct party business when the national convention is not in session and assists during the presidential campaign. Besides, it selects the location and dates of the next convention, helps to raise funds for the party's candidates, and fills vacancies on the party's ticket if they occur after the convention has adjourned. However, the reality of the matter is that power in American political parties resides more at the state-party level than at the national-party level.

The national committee of each party varies slightly in its membership, but both are composed of at least one man and one woman from each state, the District of Columbia, and several territories. Generally speaking, all the members are prominent men and women. In other words, not just any "Joe Blow" off the street gets to be a member of the national committee. In recent years the national committee has increased its influence on state parties somewhat, particularly by means of providing services such as staff, polls and research, voter identification, campaign seminars, rule enforcement, technical assistance, and cash transfers.[4]

The most powerful person on the national committee is the **national chairperson**, who organizes and conducts the presidential campaign for the party, keeps in touch with state and local party leaders, helps raise money for the campaign, tries to keep the party unified behind the candidates, and prepares for the next election. He or she is also active in the years when there are no presidential elections by acting as spokesperson for the party if its candidate did not win the presidency and by assisting the president in "controlling" the party if its candidate did win. In the latter event, he or she plays a prominent role in helping the president reward faithful party members by appointing them to various positions in the government—a practice that is called **patronage**. Many times the chairperson of the national committee from the winning party receives a patronage position in the new presidential administration. Ron Brown, Democratic National Committee Chairman, was appointed Secretary of Commerce by the 1992 presidential election winner, Democrat Bill Clinton. Similarly, Jim Nicholson, Chairperson the Republican National Committee when George W. Bush was elected in 2000, became an ambassador.

STATE PARTY ORGANIZATION

While it may seem odd that national party organization should be separated from state party organization, the fact remains that the national parties and their respective state party counterparts merely create an alliance to form two major political parties every four years to elect a president and vice president. In other words, the national party and the state party are really two different institutions; the state party is not subordinate to—does not take orders from—the national party. Within the state Democratic or Republican parties there are **state committees** with varying degrees of authority over the actions of the party and its members. There are also **county committees**, which usually play a very significant role in local matters, and precinct organizations headed by a **precinct captain**. (A **precinct** is a local voting district, normally consisting of one thousand voters or less.) Where a well-organized political party exists locally,

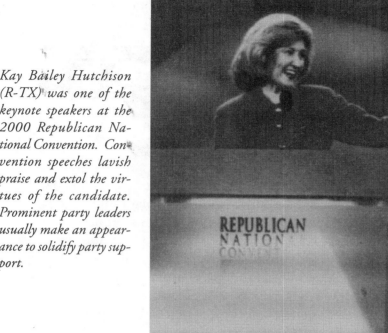

Kay Bailey Hutchison (R-TX) was one of the keynote speakers at the 2000 Republican National Convention. Convention speeches lavish praise and extol the virtues of the candidate. Prominent party leaders usually make an appearance to solidify party support.

the precinct captains are responsible for getting the party's supporters to vote, distributing campaign materials, and generally keeping informed about what is going on politically in the precinct. However, today, because political party organization is still relatively weak, most precincts do not have active captains. Republican Party organization is considered strong in only eight states, while Democratic Party organization is considered strong in only two.[5] The introduction of the mass media as the main vehicle of campaigning today has lessened the need for strong party organization to ensure a candidate's victory at the polls.

POLITICAL PARTY TACTICS

If the goal of a political party is to elect its candidates to public office to make governmental policies, then it follows that the party must have certain ways or methods of accomplishing this objective. These methods or tactics are intended to create a favorable response from the voters, as well as from the party workers themselves. There are many ways of describing party tactics. For our purposes, let's just discuss the major tactic: electioneering.

Electioneering

As the term implies, electioneering from the standpoint of a political party, means all the things political parties could conceivably do in attempting to win an election. First, political parties engage in massive amounts of propaganda, which is defined as the use of words or images (symbols) to communicate ideas to the voters who the party hopes will vote for its candidates. Television, of course, has been a real advantage to political parties in their efforts to propagandize (Parties like to use the term "educate.") the public. Second, electioneering can involve the party organization itself. Usually, the more unified behind its candidates a party is, the better its chances of being successful on election day. Third, patronage—the promise of government jobs—also plays a role in electioneering, although not as strongly as it used to since many government positions are now covered under the Civil Service Merit System. Under this system a person applying for a position with the government must be among the most qualified candidates, which is determined by means of testing and/or education and experience. Fourth, although buying votes is not legal, political parties have been known to resort to this tactic on occasion, purchasing votes for such nominal sums as $0.25 sometimes. According to one source, President Lyndon Johnson would never have been elected senator from Texas if he and his supporters had not "bought" massive numbers of votes, especially from the southern counties in Texas.[6]

EVALUATION OF UNITED STATES PARTIES AND PARTY SYSTEM

As we have seen in the discussion of American political parties at the national level thus far, they are highly decentralized, loose alliances of state parties. As such they must cater to many conflicting ideologies and interests. Also, in the presidential race they must satisfy the frequently opposing interests of the rural parts of the country and the urban centers, as well as all geographic sections of the country, many of which have conflicting concerns. American political parties find themselves having to deal with all races and ethnic groups, whose interests may also collide. As a result, there is frequently no ideological consistency in either domestic policy or foreign policy. For example, the Democrats and Republicans both at various times have adopted a pro-Israeli policy, as well as a pro-oil policy (Arab), a policy of no racial discrimination, as well as a policy of affirmative action, a policy of containment of communism, as well as a policy of "peaceful" coexistence.

The two major parties in the United States also have been relatively ineffective in steering the course of national policy. Unlike their European counterparts, which are highly organized, unified, and disciplined, American parties are unable even to control the nominations of candidates under their own party label and unable to force party members in elected, policy-making positions to follow the party line. Hence, what the parties say they will do when elected and what they actually do are often as far apart as Los Angeles is from Kyoto, Japan. To make matters worse for American parties, the American electoral system focuses more on the candidate than on the political party, especially since the introduction of radio and television. Candidates are nominated and voted upon by the electorate primarily on the candidates' own characteristics and not on party loyalty. The result is that party leaders cannot assure passage of their political agenda even if their party is in the majority. It is indeed true that the American voter clamors for more party responsibility, i.e., having the campaign promises match the policies enacted when the party is elected. However, those voters do not seem to recognize that the entire electoral/political system is geared to giving them exactly what they are getting—relatively little party responsibility. Therefore, if responsible party government is what the voters truly want, then the voters may have to change the system.

Chapter Five Notes

[1] See David Truman, *The Governmental Process: Political Interest and Public Opinion,* 2d ed. (New York: Alfred A. Knopf, 1971); Earl Latham, "The Group Basis of Politics: Notes for a Theory," *American Political Science Review* 46, no. 2 (June 1952): 376-397.

[2] It is possible that a coalition government could occur in a two-party, parliamentary system if a minor party split the votes enough. However, this situation is infrequent.

[3] Cornelius P. Cotter, and others, *Party Organizations in American Politics: American Political Parties and Elections* (New York: Praeger, 1984), 28.

[4] Cotter, 63.

[5] Cotter, 28.

[6] Robert A. Caro, *The Years of Lyndon Johnson: The Path to Power* (New York: Alfred A. Knopf, 1982).

Suggested Readings

Aldrich, John. *Why Parties?* Chicago: University of Chicago Press, 1995.

Beck, Paul Allen, and Frank J. Sorauf. *Party Politics in America*. 8th ed. New York: HarperCollins, 1996.

Burham, Walter Dean. *Politics and Elections in America*. 4th ed. New York: Norton, 1970.

Charles, Joseph. *The Origins of the American Party System*. New York: Harper, 1956.

Cotter, Cornelius P., and others. *Party Organizations in America Politics*. Pittsburgh: University of Pittsburgh Press, 1989.

Epstein, Leon. *Political Parties in the American Mold*. Madison, Wis.: University of Wisconsin Press, 1986.

Key, V.O.,Jr. *Political Parties and Pressure Groups*. 5th ed. New York: Crowell, 1964.

Maisel, L. Sandy. *Parties and Elections in America: The Electoral Process*. Landham, Md.: Rowman & Littlefield, 1999.

Key, V.O., Jr. *Southern Politics*. Knoxville: University of Tennessee Press, 1984.

Reichley, A. James. *The Life of the Parties: A History of American Political Parties*. New York: Macmillan Co., 1992.

Royko, Mike. *Boss: Richard J. Daley of Chicago*. New York: W.W. Norton and Company, 1969.

Sorauf, Frank L. and Paul Allen Beck. *Party Politics in America*. New York: HarperCollins, 1992.

Chapter Six

Interest Groups:
The Politics of Numbers

The United States is a nation of joiners. From the very beginning, Americans have felt that joining together with others in a group was probably the best way to achieve some particular goal, whether that goal was personal, such as building a house in a new settlement, or political, such as securing a new constitution for the United States. In the early 1800s, one foreign observer wrote: "The Americans make associations to give entertainments, to found seminaries, to build inns, to construct churches, to diffuse books, to send missionaries . . . Wherever at the head of some new undertaking you see the government in France, or a man of rank in England, in the United States you will be sure to find an association."[1] As a result of this tendency of Americans to join groups for all kinds of purposes, even political purposes, some people believe we have a system of democracy based on groups rather than individual members of the society. Such a system is often referred to as **pluralist democracy** or **polyarchical democracy**, but for our purposes here, let's just call this type of democracy **group democracy**.[2]

Why Join? Since we do have group democracy, it might be useful for us to understand why people join groups. Although most Americans join groups because they want to, there are some instances when people were more or less forced to join a group in order to pursue some particular line of work. For example, at one time in our history physicians were required to join the American Medical Association in order to work in hospitals. In some states today, lawyers must join the state bar association (lawyers' group) to practice law. Some states also require that people join a labor union at the place where they wish to work in order to be employed there or to maintain their employment there.

Despite those few examples of required joining of groups, most people enter into a group because they want to.[3] Typically groups provide a way of making the individual's voice heard on particular issues and also provide monetary benefits such as group life, health, or auto insurance or discounts on travel expenditures or appliances or clothing. Some groups even publish a magazine or newsletter of special interest to the members of the particular group.

People also join groups for social reasons. At group meetings people can meet and socialize with others who have similar interests. In addition, the groups often provide social events such as dances, banquets, or trips for the members. In today's society, where most of us live in urban areas and move quite frequently, groups can provide a means of meeting and interacting with other people—activities that might be difficult if these groups did not exist.

DEFINITION OF INTEREST GROUPS

So far we have referred to these organizations as just "groups." Let's now call them what they are—interest groups. An interest group, or pressure group as it is sometimes called, is an organization of people who share common goals and concerns and seek, directly or indirectly, to influence public policy on these matters. If there were no interest groups through which people could express their concerns to the public in general and to the government in particular, then an individual's voice might not be heard in the crowd, so to speak. There are just too many people and too many concerns for one individual to accomplish very much on his or her own. So we have groups—strength in numbers.

THE FORMATION OF INTEREST GROUPS

Actually we can easily see how these groups get organized. Any group of people who possess some commonalty is actually a potential interest group. We all know that most people in the United States have brown eyes. Some, however, have blue eyes. Now that fact in itself isn't terribly earthshaking news and doesn't cause the formation of a real interest group. But, if the majority, the brown-eyed people, believed that blue-eyed people were inferior in mental and physical abilities and persuaded the government to pass laws requiring separate schools for the two groups, then we can see how the common interest of blue-eyed people would develop immediately and an interest group would be organized for blue-eyed people. Or we might suppose that our town has a beautiful park where people could go sit under a tree and read, watch birds, or just sit there and do nothing. Our park has swings for children, picnic tables, benches, and a pond with ducks in it. However, one day the city government decides to sell the park land to a man who wants to build a factory on it. All of a sudden

Unfortunately, some issues are not easily resolved. To dramatize their cause against "acid rain," members of Green Peace, an environmental group, hung banners from smokestacks in four different European countries to protest factory emissions.

the people who enjoyed the park have a common concern—saving the park—and an interest group would probably be formed for that purpose. What we are seeing here is that there are uncountable numbers of potential interest groups: blue-eyed people, green-eyed people, short people, tall people, save-the-park people, save-the-old-oak-tree-on-Main-Street people, save-the-snails people, prohibit-gum-chewing-in-public people, etc. And there are literally thousands of real interest groups—those that have actually formed around a particular common interest: save the whales; save the snail darter; prohibit nuclear weapons; help the poor, the alcoholics, other drug abusers, the handicapped, and so forth. Some of these real interest groups remain for a long time, but others fade away when the interest around which they were formed has been resolved one way or the other. Although most interest groups have a basis in fact, some do not. For example, there is an interest group called The Flat Earth Society, which espouses that the planet is really flat, and The God Saves the Earth Flying Saucer Foundation, whose purpose is probably known only to deities or aliens from another galaxy.

CATEGORIES OF INTEREST GROUPS

Interest groups can be categorized (grouped) according to the type of common interest the group has. We shall use a time-honored principal here called the KISS principal, which stands for KEEP IT SIMPLE STUPID. Is the group based mainly on the way the members earn a living or is it not? (It couldn't get much simpler than that!)

Economic Interest Groups

Economic interest groups are those whose common interests revolve around the type of work a person does in order to earn a living. These interest groups can themselves be divided into four categories: business groups, labor groups, agricultural groups, and professional groups. Let's take a look at each one separately.

Business Groups

Business interest groups are the largest (in number) and probably the most powerful of all categories of interest groups. Among the largest and most powerful of such organizations is the United States Chamber of Commerce. Founded in 1912, the Chamber of Commerce represents over 200,000 individual businesses and has about 4000 local, state, and regional chapters and trade associations.

Another of the major business interest groups is the National Association of Manufacturers (NAM), which was organized before the turn of the century around 1896. NAM's membership is mainly composed of big business such as manufacturers of automobiles and steel. Although a bit more conservative than the Chamber of Commerce, the National Association of Manufacturers is usually in agreement with the Chamber of Commerce on major issues of concern to business.

The National Federation of Independent Business (NFIB) represents a relatively more militant voice in behalf of small business. Established in 1943, members are typically small enterprises with six or seven employees—drug stores, convenience stores, and gas station operators. Representing approximately 600,000 members, it is staunchly pro-Republican and anti-big government. It maintains close alliance with congressional Republicans. It was the most tenacious and effective lobby in opposition to President Clinton's health care program in 1993.

Although these three interest groups represent business in general, there are a considerable number of associations that speak for specific business interests: for example, the American Petroleum Institute, the American Bankers Association, the National Restaurant Association, the National Automobile Dealers Association, the National Home Builders Association.

On the surface it may appear that business interest groups present a united front—that they have no conflicts with one another. This proposition is not true in many cases. For example, the producers of electricity may be supportive of government regulation of the gas industry because such regulation may mean the electricity producers could get a larger share of consumers to use electricity instead of gas. Likewise, the automobile producers may well be interested in seeing import taxes lowered or removed from such items as imported steel so that their production costs would be less, while the domestic steel producers would perhaps like to see those import taxes raised so that they could sell more steel at a higher price. Despite these conflicts business interest groups do have substantial influence on the thinking of the American public and on government officials, because governments at all levels affect both the climate in which businesses operate and their profits. In virtually every area of industrial and commercial activity—oil and gas production, import/export activities, new and used car sales, and money and banking—some kind of association exists to provide services to their members and also to lobby in support of regulations favorable to their interests and against those that are not.

Labor Groups

The first successful, national labor union in the United States was the Knights of Labor, which at its height claimed a membership of about 700,000. From the point of view of the workers, they needed representation with management to deal with the immediate issues of wages, hours, conditions of work, and organizing rights. The early years of this century witnessed battles between labor and management over these very issues.

Today, unions are an accepted part of the American economic system. Although union membership has declined from its high in the 1950s, there are still over 16 million union members in the work force. The AFL-CIO, with approximately two-thirds of total membership, is the largest and most authoritative voice for organized labor. Corresponding to some large business lobbies, the federation (AFL-CIO) includes 83 affiliated unions representing a cross section of the traditional work force—electricians, plumbers, chemical workers, teachers, brick layers, farm workers, government workers, and so on. However, there are other unions that do not come under the umbrella of the AFL-CIO with memberships of about another 4 million. The AFL-CIO, as well as these other unions, is primarily interested in economic benefits for labor such as wages, retirement benefits, health care, and working conditions.

In the last two decades, the influence of labor unions has declined for a number of reasons. First, labor's public image has been tarnished in recent years because of its undemocratic system of governance contaminated by corruption and racketeering. Not all union leaders are crooks, but the attitude of some segments of the public has been generalized across the board to cover all unions, not just the guilty ones.

Second, like the interests of business, there are occasions when the interests of various labor groups are not the same. They do not always speak with one voice and will sometimes support different candidates for political office, a circumstance that lessens their ability to influence the government. Similarly, the leadership of the unions will frequently support one group of candidates for political office, while a substantial number of union members vote for another.

Third, membership in labor unions was largely found in the industrial Northeast and Midwest, which have been losing population in recent decades to nonunion areas such as the South and Southwest. Since representation in the House of Representatives is based on a state's population, the voice of unions is much quieter than it used to be.

Unionism in America grew out of the strife between low-paid workers and the greed of capitalism. The struggle for unionization was long and bitter but was eventually won when the government recognized the right of workers to organize. Eugene Debs is shown here addressing railroad workers. He and other union officials were jailed for disobeying a court injunction against the Pullman Strike of 1894.

Finally, some workers feel that labor unions have become too interested in maintaining higher wages for the bulk of union members at the expense of recruiting younger workers and minority workers. This feeling was intensified when, in the 1980s, the United Auto Workers negotiated a two-tier wage scale with auto manufacturers, which meant that newly hired persons would make less for doing the same job as the person with experience. This was not the norm in the auto industry, and the practice was dropped a few years after it began because it was such a divisive issue. In addition, there is a 36 percent gap between the wage received by a full-time employee and the wage received by a part-time employee. Therefore, some potential members see no benefit to themselves in joining a union. It was widely reported during a recent UPS strike, purportedly over the hiring of part-time workers rather than full-time, that it was indeed the Teamsters Union that had negotiated the higher pay for full-timers at UPS years ago at the expense of part-timers. Nor has labor's image been enhanced by its relatively late push for minority rights and its half-hearted recruitment of minority workers into its ranks. Some labor unions have also lost membership because of downsizing within most American companies. The United Auto Workers is a prime example. Unions in general may have to shift their emphasis away from their traditional "backyard," the manufacturing sector of the economy, to a new frontier, namely the service sector.

Today's workers are well aware of the challenges facing them. John J. Sweeny, an insurgent candidate, was swept into office in the fall of 1995, as president of the AFL-CIO. In a sharp break with its past complacency, the AFL-CIO under Sweeny has embarked on an ambitious plan to reverse labor's political fortunes. Under Sweeny's leadership, union members contributed heavily to and worked extensively on behalf of Clinton's re-election in 1996 and in support of Al Gore in 2000. Democratic congressional candidates were also recipients of union support in these two elections. Its representatives maintain a highly visible and active presence on Capitol Hill.

Agricultural Groups

The transformation of the United States from a principally agricultural work force to one heavily dependent on the latest technology has radically altered political organizations representing farmers. Unlike in the past, no single farm organization dominates today. Rather, there are a number of specialized groups that are best classified as protest organizations, multipurpose organizations, or single-issue organizations, examples of which are noted in Table 6.1.

Protest organizations, as their classification implies, want basic changes in agricultural policies that will improve their members' status, such as easier farm loans, maintenance of the traditional farm family, and the phasing out of heavy chemical usage as far as crop production is concerned. The American Agriculture Movement (AAM), for example, wants continued governmental price supports primarily for grain products—corn, barley, oats, etc. In the late 1970s, AAM members drew a good deal of media and public attention to their economic problems when they drove tractors to Washington and set a number of farm animals loose at the capitol. The membership of protest organizations is characteristically small and idealistic; therefore, their activities are limited to little more than protest. Greater opportunities for influence lie in these groups joining forces with other groups with relatively broader economic concerns and more political clout.

Multipurpose organizations, as their title suggests, have a wide range of concerns, as well as a more diverse membership. These organizations maintain permanent staffs who are expert in both policy formation and lobbying. Over a calendar year, it is not unusual for them to address a number of farm issues like price supports, international trade, or government regulations on the use of fertilizers and pesticides. Representatives of the American Farm Bureau Federation or of the Farmers' Union maintain close and continuing contacts with the people who make farm policy, as well as those who enforce it. Due to the relatively broad concerns of these groups, multipurpose organizations range across the political spectrum from liberal to conservative. However, the underlying ideology of these organizations seems to be pragmatic (practical) on most issues. As a result, these groups have gained a stable and consistent image that coincides with the organizations' political purposes and strategies.

Single-issue organizations are relatively more specialized—dairy farmers, fruit farmers, or soybean producers, for example. These interest groups prefer being independent; therefore, they avoid joining forces with other groups. This strategy allows them to maximize their relatively modest funding and to maintain their unique image. However, this same strategy often means that getting what they want takes longer than it might if the organizations were larger.

This brief classification of farm organizations clearly demonstrates how diverse they are—differing in size, specific interest, and political strategies. Like other organized interests, farm-oriented groups have increased in number since

Table 6.1: Categories of Farm Pressure Groups

Protest Organizations

American Agriculture Movement
Family Farm Movement
North American Farmers' Alliance

Multipurpose Organizations

American Farm Bureau Federation
American Farmers' Union
National Cotton Council Processors

Single-Issue Organizations

American Farmland Trust
National Soybean Association
National Peanut Growers Group

the 1960s. They now include an assortment of associated interests like food processors, farm implement dealers, agricultural research foundations, and colleges. This growth has produced a farm lobby that brings a variety of viewpoints—sometimes conflicting—before both legislative and administrative policy makers.

Professional Groups

The last category of economic interest groups, the professional, is, for the most part, specialized according to the particular profession represented. Professions are those occupations that require specialized training usually of a longer duration than other lines of work—medicine, law, teaching, or engineering. All of the professions have their own interest groups, and some of these professions subdivide into smaller categories within their own groups. For example, there are many different kinds of engineers, physicians, or teachers. Each category usually has its own interest group such as the American Society of Chemical Engineers, the Association of Trial Lawyers of America, or the Modern Language Association. However, there are large organizations that embrace the particular profession as a whole. The American Medical Association (AMA), representing the interests of physicians in general, for a long time was the unchallenged authority on matters concerning medicine. Now, however, other medical-related groups, as well as consumer groups, have recently become heavily involved in health-care issues. Still the American Medical Association has played a major role in blocking such legislation as a national health-care program and in shaping such programs as Medicare and Medicaid—government-sponsored programs for the elderly and the poor.

While the AMA represents the interests of physicians, the American Bar Association (ABA) speaks for the lawyers. It is interesting to note that the interests of these two groups have collided recently over the issue of medical malpractice. Many physicians, along with the AMA, are claiming that the cost of medical malpractice insurance is so high as to make it impractical for physicians to have it. (Medical malpractice insurance is a type of insurance that will pay monetary damages awarded by a court if a physician is found to have performed in a negligent manner in treating one of his or her patients.) The physicians say that the insurance rates are so high because juries are awarding huge sums of money to people in malpractice suits. Therefore, the medical profession generally would like to see malpractice awards limited to a maximum amount, for example, $250,000. Attorneys and their interest groups have been successful so far in keeping any such maximum amount from being made into law. They claim that it is unfair to the victim of malpractice or his/her family to place a limit on the amount awarded. However, some maintain that the legal profession may not be as interested in the "poor victim" as it is in enriching his or her lawyer, since most lawyers' fees in these kinds of cases are based on how much the client is awarded! Whether this belief is true or not, the ABA does represent the interests of lawyers. In addition, it advises the president and the Senate on the relative merits of individuals being considered for appointment to federal judgeships and has recommended certain reforms in the court system.

Non-Economic Groups

In addition to groups that are primarily economic, there are those organized around race, religion, sex, national origin, age, ideology, or some single issue or category of issues. Among these would be found the John Birch Society and Americans for Democratic Action, which are both based on conflicting views of how things are and how they ought to be—ideology. The John Birch Society is considered a very conservative group while the Americans for Democratic Action are deemed to be very liberal. In addition, there are the National Association for the Advancement of Colored People, the American Association of Retired People, the Italian Anti-Defamation League, the National Organization for Women, Mothers Against Drunk Drivers, Common Cause, the Congress of American Indians, Veterans of Foreign Wars, and even groups such as the Ku Klux Klan and the American Nazi Party. There are also groups that seek to influence governmental policy toward particular countries. (Pro-Israeli interest groups are notably successful in this regard.) The list is almost endless. If there is an issue or a group of people who in some way is different from other groups of people, there is usually an interest group that will form to address those issues or common concerns. Let's just look at a couple of these noneconomic interest groups.

The National Organization for Women (NOW), established in 1966, offered an emotional refuge for thousands of women who perceived themselves as second-class citizens because of limited job opportunities, low pay, and low esteem. Although a prime purpose of its founders was to create an organization that would develop political strategies for ending sex discrimination, membership offers opportunities for social interaction and discussion of issues of common concern. Currently NOW and other women's rights organizations such as the National Abortion Rights League are pushing for the continuance of abortion rights, affirmative action programs, and maternity leave programs. NOW lost some its support in the recent White House sex scandals when the organization did not support the claims of women who said Mr. Clinton had sexually harassed them.

There are large numbers of non-economic interest groups that are frequently referred to as "public interest" pressure groups. Group members get satisfaction from having contributed to some worthy cause—cleaning up water and air pollution, eliminating government waste, or requiring more citizen participation at all levels of public decision making. These organizations consist of a wide range of groupings including research centers, citizens' lobbies, public interest law firms, and numerous state and local community action groups. They are pursuing public reforms (or supporting some "cause"). In their view, only through greater public participation can the prevailing imbalances favoring private interests be corrected, and government agencies must be sensitized to the welfare of all not just to the powerful few.

One of the most well-known public interest groups is Common Cause, established in 1970 to provide a channel for citizen opposition to the Vietnam War.[4] Initially the organization was mainly anti-war; however, the Watergate scandals of the early 1970s led to public demands for reform. As a result, governmental accountability became the centerpiece of the organization's political objectives. Currently the group supports public funding of congressional campaigns, limiting the amount of political action committee (PAC) money in elections, and tougher controls on lobbying activities.

Although strongly "cause" oriented, Common Cause frequently participates in lobbying coalitions. When environmental legislation is before Congress, it will follow the lead of the Wilderness Society, Friends of the Earth, or the Sierra Club. Consumer legislation will find it allied with the Consumer Federation of America, Public Citizen, or the Consumers' Union. One of the most successful public interest groups on the national scene today, it has activated thousands of middle-class liberals and professionals interested in governmental reform. It, along with similar public interest groups like Physicians for Social Responsibility and the Environmental Defense Fund, have played a major role in securing enactment of consumer, environmental, and occupational health and safety legislation over the past decades.

Recently, gay and lesbian rights activists have appeared on the scene and have established their own organizations. In fact, they are some of the fastest growing interests on the national level at the present time. Although still fledgling organizations, comparatively speaking, nonetheless both their numbers and fundraising abilities are quite noteworthy. Today, more than two dozen organizations exist representing both gays and lesbians including such organizations as the Lambda Defense Fund, Human Rights Campaign, and the Gay and Lesbian Task Force. They are increasingly well-funded and were actively involved in supporting Democratic candidates in both the 2000 and 2004 elections.

As noted in other areas of this text, the attack on and destruction of the New York World Trade Center, along with the severe damage to the Pentagon, have brought about substantive changes in United States politics. With evidence pointing to the involvement of Middle Eastern Muslim extremists in these attacks, there is greater interest in and scrutiny of the U.S. Muslim community with between 5 and 7 million members. Table 6.2 provides a breakdown of the existing domestic Muslim community.

The main politically active groups include the Council on American-Islamic Relations (CAIR), the Muslim Public Affairs Council (MPAC), and the American Muslim Council (AMC). Each of these groups has a distinct agenda: CAIR primarily pursues legal challenges to discrimination against Muslims; MPAC works closely with the Democratic Party on economic and social issues, and AMC focuses on raising Arab political consciousness. All three of these organizations maintain an active Washington presence, and all three endorse George W. Bush. This blanket endorsement comes as a result of his criticism of government attempts to deport immigrants **suspected** of terrorist activity. These organizations also strongly support Bush because of his more conservative politics with emphasis on the family and religious beliefs.

INTEREST GROUP TACTICS

The name of the game for political interest groups is influence. Influence, in the context of group politics, can be defined as the ability of a group (or a coalition of groups) to get others (especially public officials) to do what the group wants. Some groups may resort to violence to gain their ends, but most prefer the traditional methods that have proven successful for others. In this setting, four key political strategies of influence will be discussed: propaganda, lobbying, litigation, and electioneering, as well as violence although it is neither a legal nor a characteristic tactic of interest groups in the United States.

Propaganda

Just about all interest groups engage in **propaganda**; that is, almost all of them present their case with words and pictures in such a way as to create a favorable public image. In this context, modern technology is a key ingredient in the continuing struggle to be influential.

Table 6.2 — GROUP PORTRAIT

Group	HQ/Income	Leader	Base	Priorities
Religious Groups				
Islamic Society of North America	Plainfield, Ind., with many affiliated organizations	Sayyid M. Syeed	Largest immigrant group; includes many ethnic groups, mostly from Asia	Islamic observance, conversion, community-building, political recognition. Leans GOP on social, religious issues.
Muslim American Society	Calumet City, IL	Imam W. Deen Mohammed	African-American Muslims	Religious; also has a public-policy arm, with tie to Democrats
Islamic Circle of North America	Jamaica, N. Y.	President: Zulfiqar Shah	Large, including many from Southeast Asia	Focuses on preaching, to Muslim & others Works with AMA, AMC, and CAIR.
Islamic Supreme Council of America	Washington; claims 23 centers in U.S. & more overseas	Sheik Muhammad Hisham Kabbani	Loose community of Sufi Muslims, including Muslim scholars.	Promotes the Sufi form of Islam; criticizes Islamic radicals in the United States.
Political Groups				
American Muslim Council	Washington;8-person staff; $657,000 in 1998	President: Yahya Basha. Director; AlyAbuzaakouk	Broad membership	Political participation. Opposes sanctions on Iraq, secret evidence, and gay marriages.
Council on American-Islamic Relations	Washington, 40-person staff; $1.2 million in 1998	Director: Nihad Awad. Spokesman: Ibrahim Hooper	Donors and members who support its civil litigation.	Litigation; foreign-policy issues; may create a lobbying arm; opposes secret evidence, anti-terror law.
Muslim Public Affairs Council	Los Angeles; 5-person staff in Washington; $185,000 in 1999	Director: Salam Al Marayati. Political adviser: Mahdi Bray	Strongest in California and among second-generation Muslims.	Building activism on domestic and foreign-policy issues; opposes secret evidence and anti-terror law. Ties to Democratic Party.
Islamic Institute	Washington, 4-person staff; $190,000 in 2000	President: Khaled Saffuri	Largely secular; center-right, Repubican ties	Supports tax cuts, school vouchers; opposes secret evidence, anti-terror law.
Arab Groups and Coalitions				
Arab American Institute	Washington, 18-person staff; $1.1 million 2000	Director: James Zogby	Bipartisan secular Arab-Americans.	Bipartisan political participation; opposes anti-terror law.
American-Arab Anti-Discrimination Committee	Washington, 18-person staff; $1.1 million 2000	President: Ziad Asali	Secular and Christian Arabs.	Some foreign-policy work. Focuses on anti-Arab discrimination, opposes anti-terror law.
National Coalition to Protect Political Freedom	Washington, one part-time staffer. Under $10,000.	President: Sami Al Arian. Coordinator: Kit Gage	Coalition, including MPAC, AMA, CAIR, AMC, Irish Northern Aid (Noraid).	Opposes use of secret evidence in deportation and anti-terror law.

Source: *National Journal*, October 27, 2001, Vol. 33, No. 43, pp. 3301-3388.

The U. S. Muslim community is highly diverse. Up to 40 percent are African Americans and are members of the Muslim American Society. Roughly another 30 percent of Muslims are from Pakistan, India, and Southeast Asia. Only one-quarter of U. S Muslims are Arab; most Arab-Americans are Christian. This chart shows the most prominent religious and political Muslim groups, as well as the largest Arab groups.

One of the most successful and most utilized forms of propaganda is institutionalized advertising. Today just a casual scanning of newspapers, magazines, trade journals, and other mass circulation media reveals numerous expensive, well-designed ads by business associations, manufacturers, environmental organizations, trade unions, and so on. These ads may picture the important role oil companies and their products play in our daily lives, or the ads may emphasize the growing concern of automobile manufacturers for cleaner air. Similarly, an ad placed by business might stress the important contributions its members make to a strong and vibrant economy. The purpose of all these ads is to create and maintain a strong, positive relationship between the organization and the public at large. It is hoped that, when the need arises, this favorable relationship will translate into public support for concerns of these and other comparable organizations. Pages 120 and 121 demonstrate the use of visual propaganda by various organizations.

Lobbying

The First Amendment to the Constitution provides for the right to "petition the Government for the redress of grievances." Current law (the Federal Regulation of Lobbying Act) describes a "lobbyist" as "any person who shall engage himself for pay or any consideration for the purpose of attempting to influence the passage or defeat of any legislation." Since the end of WWII, lobbying has been a growth industry with thousands of lobbyists petitioning the national, state, and local policymakers daily.

In its simplest form, **lobbying** is communication between some interest group spokesperson and a public official. But as a day-to-day activity, lobbying is a highly complex and continuous process involving a range of activities as noted in Figure 6.1 (page 122).

Just about all interest groups lobby but in their own unique ways. Moreover, not all pressure groups have the same level of concern with law or policy making that takes place in Washington or in various state capitals. Today, though, because of the national government's increasingly broad agenda—civil rights, environmentalism, racial discrimination, defense, space exploration, foreign policy—many more groups seek access to Washington. Much of this contact falls into the category of **direct lobbying**. Direct lobbying includes such activities as one-on-one meetings between lobbyists and members of the government or their staffs or testifying at legislative or administrative hearings. Direct lobbying might also involve delegations of farmers, union members, or veterans meeting informally with Washington officials.

Increasingly, though, Washington is the object of **indirect**, or **grassroots**, **lobbying**. Actually grassroots lobbying is nothing new; it was commonplace in various efforts to pass legislation by civil rights groups, environmental organizations, and labor unions. What is new are the various methods used in con-

In some public schools, it's a science textbook. What's taught in Sunday school shouldn't be taught in Monday through Friday school. But that's exactly what's happening. School officials that impose their religious beliefs on your children are in direct violation of the First Amendment. Help us defend your rights. Support the ACLU.   www.aclu.org american civil liberties union

PUBLIC INTEREST LAW

What does the term convey to you? For many it conjures up some "public interest" groups who have used this vehicle for change and social justice to reshape America in their own image. But their image of America is often frightening.

★ In the name of "civil liberties" they seek to censor out of the public square any positions or values informed by faith or which they perceive as "religious."

★ In the name of "free speech" they all too often enforce only the ideology of the new statists and the politically correct police and seek to prevent all other points of view from having access to the marketplace.

★ In the name of "family" they seek to dismantle the family and substitute in its place same sex unions and relationships of convenience.

★ In the name of new found "rights," they endorse, promote and seek to enforce, with our tax dollars, the legalized killing of the unborn up to the day of birth; and the medical extermination of the elderly, the disabled, and the seriously ill. Rather than encourage those who have lost the desire to live to choose life, they encourage them in suicide.

IS THIS ALL REALLY IN THE "PUBLIC INTEREST"?
We don't believe it is and we're convinced you don't either.

We're the AMERICAN CENTER FOR LAW AND JUSTICE, a national public interest law firm and educational organization dedicated to pro-liberty, pro-life and pro-family causes.

★ We believe that the First Amendment protects free speech. That includes religious speech in the public arena and "politically incorrect" speech.

★ We believe that there is an inherent and pre-eminent right to life and that one of the genuine roles of government is to protect, preserve and defend life, not legalize its destruction in the name of new found "rights."

★ We believe that the family is the basic cell of civilization and must be protected and supported if the social order is to remain intact.

★ We practice true public interest law and we're in the battle of our lives.

This message is presented by
THE AMERICAN CENTER FOR LAW AND JUSTICE–NEW HOPE

The American Center for Law and Justice–New Hope is the pro-life project of the American Center for Law and Justice and Catholics United for Life. Write to us at New Hope, Kentucky 40052 or call (502) 549-7020.

Figure 6.1: Direct and Indirect Techniques of Lobbying Congress

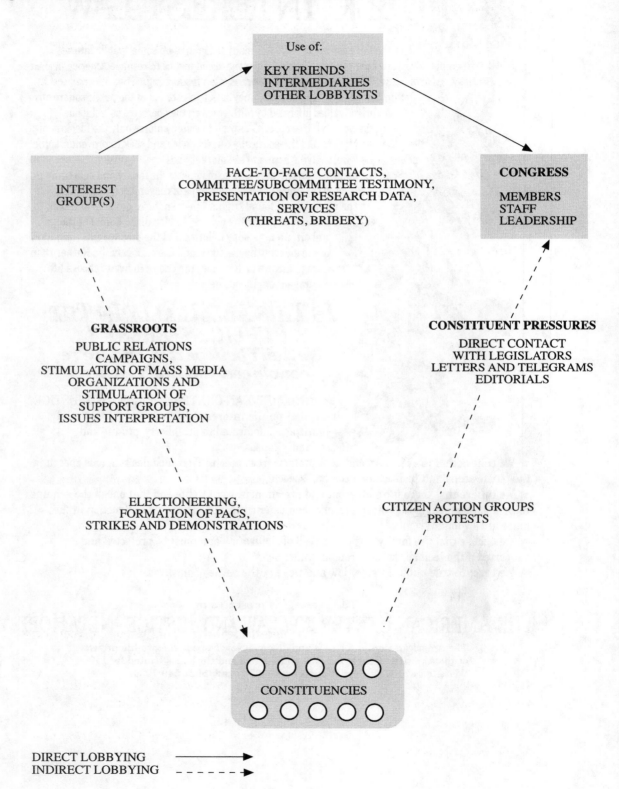

ducting indirect lobbying and the number of pressure groups making use of the indirect approach. Most surprising is the increasing number of highly specialized companies that represent clients before various public officials and forums. These firms provide a wide range of services including consulting, strategic planning, gathering signatures on petitions, telephone and direct mail contacts, and many others. Table 6.3 provides a few of the many possible examples of companies that do this kind of work and some of their client groups.

Grassroots lobbying does not come "cheap." Large sums of money, totaling about $1 billion, are used for expenses within the various interest groups for salaries of employees and similar items, as well as expenses for outside consultants and firms like those in Table 6.3.

Table 6.3: Grassroots Lobbying Firms

Firm Name & Location	Major Clients
APCO Associates Washington, D.C.	American Nurses Association American Tort Reform Association Recording Industry Association of America
Beckel Cowan Washington, D.C.	Federal Express Walt Disney Co. AT & T
Bottenberg & Associates Topeka, Kansas	Phillip Morris Tenneco Glaxo
Bonner & Associates Washington, D.C.	American Bankers Association, Pharmaceutical Research & Manufacturers of America, Pacific Telesis
Business Mail Express, Inc. Reston, Virginia	National Rifle Association Signet Bank Fingerhut Corporation U.S. English
The Carlyle Gregory Company Falls Church, Virginia	American Airlines California Association of Insurance Executives American Broadcasting Association
Chapman Communications Arlington, Virginia	RV Dealers Association of North America Consumers United for Rail Equity

Source: Ron Facheaux, "The Grass Roots Explosion," *Campaigns and Elections* (December/ January, 1995), p. 26.

The recent grassroots lobbying effort of the pressure group Health Insurance Industry of America (HIAA) serves to illustrate exactly how these campaigns work.[5]   The HIAA was a highly visible player in the recent legislative battle over proposed changes to the U.S. health care system. During congressional consideration of various health care bills, HIAA hired field directors in six states—Texas, Louisiana, New York, North Dakota, and Oklahoma—and sponsored a grassroots coalition in all 50 states. In addition to their extensive in-house apparatus, the HIAA hired several consulting firms: The Clinton Group for telephone contact, the RTC Group for direct mail, and Direct Impact enlisted the aid of a small number of people with political influence ("grasstop" efforts), plus two polling firms to measure the influence of their contacts on Capitol Hill.

Another pressure group that has used grassroots lobbying successfully is the National Association of Life Underwriters (NALU), which represents a segment of the life insurance industry. The NALU originally began its lobbying efforts with a core of six hundred activist members that has increased to about three times that many today. The organization currently maintains a network of ten thousand members who serve as contacts to all congressional districts. Local coordinators routinely meet with each member of Congress three or four times a year. Even though the NALU has an extensive in-house lobbying arm, it still employs outside consultants for specialized projects and for help in updating its mailing lists. They also systematically have members contact legislators by phone and fax.

The National Restaurant Association, representing over 100,000 business units, runs an aggressive grassroots campaign. Although the organization directly represents only 12.5 percent of the country's restaurants, its grassroots

A PAC for the NRA sends letters to its constituents to update them on the voting behavior of their legislators. Notice the letter identifying which legislators supported NRA's position on a critical piece of legislation. Members are urged to write to their House and Senate legislators.

efforts speak for the entire industry. In addition to its mail and phone contact programs, the association also employs satellite technology to transmit live contacts throughout the United States. Its BITE-BACK program uses an inbound 800 number capable of informing members of upcoming issues. Recently the organization has set up interactive booths at conventions where members can send messages to public officials by means of a touch-tone phone or computer.

With grassroots lobbying benefiting from new technologies, its use will inevitably increase. On the horizon are technologies such as e-mail, the Internet, and taped video messages. These are deliverable now almost instantaneously and can be integrated with more traditional approaches. Lobbying, like so many other activities, has definitely embraced the most up-to-date technology.

Electioneering

Interest groups have always been interested in who is elected to office and have always been active in political campaigns. Before the 1970s, they channeled most of their activities either through the Democratic or Republican Parties, i.e., labor unions usually worked on behalf of Democrats and business associations usually supported Republicans. They did so with the intent of having some voice in the various policies the newly elected candidates would make. Today the electoral process is less subject to the direction of party leaders and more a product of the candidates' own campaign activities, as well as government regulations.

The processes for influencing voters have changed as well. Radio and television are the principal media through which elections are observed, candidates are judged, and voting decisions are made. Computers, mass mailings, polling, and television ads have revolutionized elections and generated much activity outside the control of political parties. Indeed, there are "messages" from political candidates via e-mail and web sites! All of these activities create opportunities for pressure groups to have a greater say in candidate nominations, to influence party policies, and to affect election results.

The campaign reform laws of the 1970s resulting from the Watergate scandal created further opportunities for interest groups to influence elections and government policy. These laws led to the establishment of political action committees (PACs). PACs raise money and donate that money to various candidates, as well as to grassroots lobbying campaigns "for" and "against" legislative or executive proposals.

PACs are categorized as either **connected** PACs or **non-connected** PACs. Connected PACs are those that have a sponsoring organization that may pay operating and fund-raising expenses. The usual sponsoring organizations are pressure groups, for example, the United Auto Workers, and corporations like Coca-Cola. Reflecting the importance of high technology in today's economy, leaders of the most powerful high-tech companies have formed their own PAC.

Table 6.4: Examples of Large Washington-Based PACs

Connected	Nonconnected
AFL-CIO Committee on Political Education	American Sugarbeet Growers' Assoc. PAC
American Bankers Association PAC	Emily's List
American Dental Political Action Committee	English Language PAC
Carpenters Legislative Improvement Committee	National Abortion Rights League PAC
Committee on Letter Carriers Political Education	National Security PAC
Machinists Non-Partisan Political League	Ruff PAC

Led by a well-known technology venture capitalist and the CEO of Netscape Communications, Technology Network (usually just called TechNet) intends to focus on ensuring that the technology industry has continuing input at state and national levels of government. Formed in 1997, it was only a year later that TechNet was credited with persuading Congress to reduce restrictions on hiring computer-savvy foreigners, securing a temporary ban on Internet taxes, new copyright protections, and even $100 million for the next generation of the Internet.

Non-connected PACs—those that do not have a sponsoring organization—frequently have an ideological agenda, such as the Fund for a Conservative Majority, which supports conservatives and conservative causes in general. Non-connected PACs also include issue-oriented PACs like Americans for Free International Trade or the National Rifle Association. Table 6.4 lists some of the largest Washington-based PACs, both connected and non-connected.

In the two decades that PACs have been around, their number has increased dramatically. Among the connected PACs, those sponsored by corporations now total approximately 1800; union-sponsored PACs about 350; and those sponsored by other groups about 1000. Non-connected PACs have also soared to around 1100, with the total number of PACs now exceeding 40,006.[5] To put it mildly, PACs are part of a "growth industry" in the United States, and the money they raise and contribute to political candidates and causes is substantial as Table 6.6 demonstrates.

By and large, PACs contribute most of their money to congressional candidates, with the larger share going to the House as opposed to the Senate. Because House members must run every two years, their need is more frequent than Senators who serve six-year terms. Over the years, Democrats have been the principal beneficiaries primarily because they have usually held a majority in both Houses. However, in the 1996 election cycle, Republican and Democratic candidates received almost equal contributions from PACs.[6]

At the presidential level, PAC contributions are not as critical. They amount to only about 5 percent of the contributions received by presidential hopefuls.

Table 6.5			TOP 25 LOBBYING FIRMS		

#	Lobbying Firm	Lobbyists	1st Half '04 Revenues	2nd Half '04 Revenues	% Changes 2003-2004
1	Patton Boggs	63	$15,210,000	$14,330,000	+6
2	Akin, Gump, Strauss, Hauer & Feld	50	13,780,000	13,140,000	+5
3	Cassidy & Asso	43	13,280,000	14,320,000	-7
4	Van Scoyoc Asso	46	11,560,000	9,980,000	+16
5	Piper Rudnick	47	8,760,000	9,200,000	-5
6	Dutko Group	36	8,590,000	5,140,000	+67
7	Williams & Jensen	21	8,560,000	8,880,000	-4
8	Greenberg Traurig	22	7,040,000	13,600,000	-48
9	Barbour, Griffith & Rogers	11	6,780,000	5,690,000	+19
10	Clark Consulting	8	6,720,000	4,490,000	+50
11	Hogan & Hartson	NA	6,680,000	6,990,000	-4
12	Swidler, Berlin, Shereff & Friedman	NA	6,660,000	6,160,000	+8
13	Quinn Gillespie	NA	6,410,000	6,320,000	+1
14	PMA Group	NA	6,360,000	4,600,000	+38
15	Washington Council Ernest & Young	NA	6,120,000	6,660,000	-8
16	PodestaMattoon	NA	5,920,000	3,910,000	+51
17	Washington Group	NA	5,430,000	4,640,000	+17
18	Federalist Group	NA	5,300,000	2,240,000	+139
19	Mayer, Brown, Rowe & Maw	NA	5,230,000	3,330,000	+57
20	Alcalde & Fay	NA	4,860,000	3,790,000	+28
21	Carmen Group	NA	4,780,000	4,140,000	+16
22	Clark& Weinstock	NA	4,760,000	3,960,000	+20
23	Livingston Group	NA	4,500,000	2,280,000	+97
24	Holland & Knight	NA	4,310,000	4,570,000	-6
25	Timmons & Co.	NA	3,900,000	3,920,000	-1
25	Wexler Walker Public PolicyAssociation	NA	3,900,000	2,500,000	+56

National Journal December 18, 2004, 3744

Table 6.6 — PAC CONTRIBUTIONS: 1999-2000

	Number of Candidates	All PACs	Corporate PACs	Trade PACS	Labor PACs	Non-connected PACS
ALL CANDIDATES	2416	245,555,860	84,238,115	68,284,501	50,163,846	35,608,832
HOUSE	2083	193,392,428	62,163,202	55,026,570	43,545,309	27,018,226
SENATE	333	51,963,432	22,074,913	13,257,931	6,618,537	8,590,606
Democrats	777	116,798,155	27,116,549	26,123,931	46,022,865	14,471,240
Republicans	812	127,926,750	56,969,816	42,014,028	3,901,331	21,056,556
Others	827	630,955	151,750	146,542	239,650	81,036
Incumbents	*437*	*184,034,484*	*70,546,905*	*55,100,583*	*32,596,929*	*20,047,149*
Challengers	*1,555*	*26,987,927*	*3,829,207*	*4,640,470*	*10,801,393*	*7,175,740*
Open Seats	*424*	*34,333,449*	*9,862,003*	*8,543,448*	*6,765,524*	*8,385,943*
HOUSE						
Democrats	671	98,091,880	22,006,852	22,294,664	39,817,016	11,425,594
Republicans	720	94,690,471	40,016,100	32,585,914	3,489,243	15,518,847
Others	692	610,077	140,250	145,992	239,050	73,758
Incumbents	*408*	*150,518,975*	*33,727,602*	*45,826,979*	*30,256,074*	*15,076,368*
Challengers	*1,337*	*19,895,941*	*2,292,141*	*3,458,421*	*8,036,180*	*5,722,233*
Open Seats	*338*	*22,977,512*	*5,284,638*	*5,741,170*	*5,253,055*	*6,219,625*
Democrat Incumbents	207	76,007,187	20,879,700	19,399,958	26,885,656	6,572,352
Democrat Challengers	357	12,871,427	545,093	1,491,222	7,960,130	2,695.915
Democrat Open Seats	107	9,213,266	582,059	1,403,484	4,971,230	2,157,327
Republican Incumbents	198	74,081,008	33,586,923	26,293,426	3,244,368	8,463,181
Republican Challengers	357	6,963,914	1,736,998	1,957,449	49,050	3,012,518
Republican Open Seats	165	13,645,549	4,692,179	4,335,039	195,825	4,043,148
SENATE						
Democrats	106	18,706,275	5,109,697	3,829,267	6,205,849	3,045,646
Republicans	92	33,236,279	16,953,716	9,428,114	412,088	5,537,709
Others	135	20,878	11,500	550	600	7,251
Incumbents	*29*	*33,515,509*	*15,960,482*	*9,273,604*	*2,340,855*	*4,970,781*
Challengers	*218*	*7,091,986*	*1,537,066*	*1,182,049*	*2,765,213*	*1,453,507*
Open Seats	*86*	*11,355,937*	*4,577,365*	*2,802,278*	*1,512,469*	*2,166,318*
Democrat Incumbents	11	9,469,055	3,424,312	2,311,844	2,058,387	1,360,477
Democrat Challengers	74	5,221,397	646,118	725,844	2,764,213	967,698
Democrat Open Seats	21	4,015,823	3,526,598	2,010,399	128,620	1,456,797
Republican Incumbents	18	24,046,454	12,536,170	6,961,760	282,468	3,610,304
Republican Challengers	48	1,863,261	890,948	455,955	1,000	470,608
Republican Open Seats	26	7,326,564	3,526,598	2,010,399	128,620	1,456,797

Source: Federal Election Commission

Current law does not allow PACs to contribute directly to presidential campaigns, but PACs can play an important role in grassroots activities and voluntary efforts.

What is the impact of all this money? Evidence is quite mixed. Most members of Congress publicly state they are not "for sale." But, at times, there does appear to be some link between campaign contributions and congressional voting on certain pieces of legislation. One study found that committee members devoted more time and effort to issues affecting organized interests in their districts as opposed to issues that did not.[7] Similarly, a relationship was found between the level of PAC contributions and voting: the greater the contribution, the greater the activity. Just how these contributions play out with respect to other members of Congress will, of course, vary.

PACs have both their supporters and their critics. The critics charge that some PACs are stronger than others and, therefore, exercise undue influence on elected officials. They also claim that party leaders and chairs of congressional committees and subcommittees receive disproportionately greater amounts of PAC money because of their status. Finally, the charge is also made that corporations are more numerous and wealthy and can outspend their main adversary, trade unions. This last charge is true as far as it goes, but corporate PACs only outspent labor PACs on average about $30 million in the 1996 presidential election-year cycle.[8] In the overall scheme of things, $30 million is not a significant difference.

Supporters, by contrast, note that PAC money helps finance the costs of elections, thereby reducing the financial burden on taxpayers and the general public. Additionally, PAC money allows more persons to run for office and reach more voters than was possible under the old system of a generation ago. Finally, PACs link voters with their representatives—an important function in a democratic election.

Despite these pros and cons, Congress has considered legislation that would place more limits on PACs. Recent proposals included imposing limits on spending by congressional candidates, lowering or eliminating the amount of money PACs may contribute, and providing public funding for future congressional races. (See Chapter Nine) Thus far, the Supreme Court has allowed limitations on campaign contributions but not on campaign spending, ruling that the latter constitutes a violation of free speech.

527's

A relatively new force in American politics is a non-profit organization established under Section 527 of the Internal Revenue Code, which grants tax-exempt status to political committees at the national, state, and local level. Over recent years, the term has come to refer to a new form of political organization operating in a gray area of the law. These groups actively influence elections and policy debates at all levels of government but cannot coordinate with or contribute to a federal candidate in any way. They also may not expressly advocate for the election or defeat of a specific federal candidate, although 527s are quite free to portray federal candidates in such a way that there is little doubt as to the message. With respect to state candidates, the rules are different. 527 organizations can, and frequently do, give money directly to state and local candidates. In most cases, however, these organizations must abide by state laws including registering with state election authorities and filing financial reports disclosing both the sources and contributions to various candidates. It must be kept in mind, however, that each state has different rules governing 527s. Finally, 527s can buy political ads, depending upon their content, for course. Also they may have to file additional disclosure information with the FEC. Advertising involving federal candidates falls under federal campaign laws. State laws may also apply in some cases. These committees file their financial reports with the Internal Revenue Service (IRS), not with the Federal Election Commission (FEC), as do PACs, for example.

The 527 organizations are the "bastard children" of a loophole opened more than 25 years ago when the IRS broadened its definition of the types of organizations eligible for tax-exemption, as non-profit groups. This expansive classification is larger than that granted to organizations subject to FEC regulations. It thus allows 527 organizations to gain political committee status under tax law, while avoiding regulation under federal election laws.

The most common kinds of 527s are those affiliated with interest groups, unions, or associations of elected officials. Some examples of the following would be:

> AFL-CIO
> Democratic Governors Association
> Republican Governors Association
> Pro-Choice Vote
> EMILY's List
> New Democratic Network
> Citizens for Better Medicare
> National Federation of Republican Women
> Campaign for a Progressive Future
> College Republican National Committee

Additionally, individuals can establish a 527 organization, such as:

George and Susan Soros. International financier and philanthropist. Involved in philanthropic activities in over 50 countries dealing with a range of programs focusing on civil society, education, public health, and human rights. Founded Central European University located in Budapest, Hungary. A heavy contributor to the Democrats in the 2004 election to the tune of over $24 million.

Jane Fonda. Actress and political activist. Visited Hanoi during the Vietnam War to protest American bombing and participation. Generally supportive of the Democrats and contributed over $13 million in the 2004 election.

T. Boone Pickens. Founder and CEO of Mesa Petroleum Company. Mesa is one of the leading oil and gas exploration and production firms in the nation. Has been a strong voice in opposing governmental regulation of the petroleum industry. Contributed over $6 million to Republicans in 2004.

Alice Walton. A multibillionaire as the daughter of the late Sam Walton, founder of Walmart. Not actively involved in the day-to-day operation of the Walmart empire but does indulge in philanthropic activities, such as donating $300 million to the University of Arkansas for graduate education at the school. Contributed over $2 millions to the Republicans in 2004.

John R. Hunting. Outdoorsman and hunter in Wyoming. Activist with regard to preserving the natural environment of the Western state. A frequent guide for groups involving hunting and fishing in the Rocky Mountain states. Contributed approximately $3 million in the 2004 election to the Democrats.

Nothing prevents these and other individuals from raising money without filing as a 527, but 527 status means not having to pay tax on individual donations. The bottom line with respect to either organizational or individual 527s is that it provides a good deal of flexibility.

Are there any financial restrictions on 527s? Yes, but they are very few. There are no upper limits on contributions nor are there spending limits. Any donor may contribute from individuals to union to corporations, even other non-profits. Also, there are no specific prohibitions on foreign contributions. 527s can utilize political ads in support of chosen candidates, but they must file with the FEC. Finally, does McCain-Feingold apply to 527s? Not specifically; but this law's restrictions on advertising close to an election applies to all political organizations.

Litigation

Today's interest groups frequently turn to litigation (lawsuits) when other channels of access are blocked or unprofitable. Both federal and state courts can affect existing policy as the other two branches of government do. However, courts are more passive than the legislative or executive branches for three reasons. First, they must have disputes or questions brought to them before they can act. Second, courts must accept jurisdiction regarding to the question involved (i.e., decide to hear the case). Third, courts follow more prescribed rules and procedures in their decision making than do the other two branches of government.

Generally interest groups litigate in three ways: by bringing suits on behalf of their members, by joining in a suit with others i.e., (**class action law suit**), and by filing an *amicus curiae* brief (friend of the court brief). An *amicus curiae* brief is a written argument, filed with the permission of a court, which provides additional arguments to those presented by the parties involved in the case. They are filed by persons or groups who are not parties to the case but who have an interest in how the case is decided.

An excellent illustration of interest group litigation is the current controversy over abortion. In 1973, the U.S. Supreme Court ruled in *Roe v Wade*[9] that women have the right to abortion on demand up to the third month of pregnancy. Between the third and sixth months of pregnancy, a state could set standards for abortion procedures to protect the health of women but could not prohibit abortions. Only in the final three months could a state limit or prohibit abortions. Predictably this decision produced a strong negative reaction among conservatives. In 1989, in *Webster v Reproductive Health Services*[10] anti-choice (i.e., right-to-life) groups won a partial victory when the Supreme Court allowed states indirectly to place a limited number of restrictions on abortion.

Violence

Although the use of force (violence) is not a legal method of obtaining political goals, it has been used by individuals, as well as groups, for thousands of years. While it is not in widespread use in the United States by interest groups, it has been employed. Most of the interest groups that have utilized violence as a tactic to achieve their aims have been on the fringes of the law throughout most of their existence. The Ku Klux Klan, a group that advocates and believes in the superiority of white people, is one such group.

The Ku Klux Klan had its beginnings immediately after the War Between the States, often referred to as the American Civil War. Organized to frighten black people away from voting, the Klan often used threats, beatings, or even murder to achieve its aim of white control of the political, economic, and social system. Klan activity was not limited only to the South but could also be found in many other states. In fact, in 1989, a former Louisiana Klan leader (David Duke) was elected to Congress as a Republican. However, with the changes brought about in the 1960s and 1970s regarding the civil rights of black people, most, if not all, of the violent activity of the Klan has stopped although the organization does hold rallies, protest marches, and print publications. This and other groups are free to do these things as long as they remain peaceful.

Although its title is the American Nazi Party, this organization is not a political party but an interest group. Having its origins in the 1930s just before American entrance into World War II, the American Nazi Party is interested in seeing that the "white" race, particularly people of Germanic descent, maintains control over the political, economic, and social system in this country. Like the Ku Klux Klan, the Nazis do not like blacks, Jews, Catholics, immigrants, or anyone else who is not of Germanic descent. They usually dress in uniforms similar to those worn by the Nazis in Germany during World War II and have been known to advocate and engage in violent confrontations with any number of people, including the police.

Elements of both these groups have recently joined together in several "hate" groups, as they are sometimes known. The most well known is probably the Aryan Nation, a group that trains its members as a paramilitary force. Others, not quite as organized as the Aryan Nation, have been implicated in the deaths of a number of minorities and immigrants, merely because the victims were minorities or immigrants.

Although most of the violent activity has been confined to groups that might also be called domestic terrorists, sometimes labor unrest has prompted some union members to behave exactly as their more notorious counterparts in the

Klan, the Nazis, or the Aryan Nation. It must also be noted that, although an interest group might officially proclaim a nonviolent agenda, members of some groups have been connected to violent activities. For example, animal rights' activists have illegally entered research laboratories, destroyed files, and released laboratory animals. Likewise, abortion foes have been implicated in the bombings of numerous clinics where abortions are performed, as well as the murder of physicians and others connected with women's clinics where abortions may be performed.

These violent groups and the behavior of some group members are not typical of interest groups in the United States for two fundamental reasons: (1) most Americans do not believe that violence is an acceptable method of bringing about political change in this country; (2) interest groups in the United States, unlike those in some other countries, have access to governmental structures through which they can work to achieve their goals peacefully.

THE FUTURE OF INTEREST GROUPS

Interest groups are now an integral part of our political system. They are not only a means by which citizens can participate in politics, but they also inform public officials about a wide range of issues. In this context, interest groups are contributing to the democratic way of life.

Over the past quarter century, there has been a virtual explosion in both the number and the variety of interest groups. Almost every segment of American society features some associational existence and activity. Liberals in American society assert that business and professional groups have greater influence because they have more money to spend. Conservatives argue that these groups may have more money to spend than public interest groups or farm groups, for example, but the former have certainly not won all or even most of the political battles. The ideological interpretation is evident when both liberals and conservatives point to some of the same legislation as evidence for their accusations. Whether one perceives particular interest groups as having undue influence often depends upon whether the individual speaking is in favor of or against the issue in question.

Regardless of how the relative strength of various groups is perceived, one can hardly maintain that farm lobbies, for example, are not extremely powerful when the issue of commodity price supports are at hand or that such groups as the American Association of Retired Persons (AARP) don't carry the day practically every time the issues of social security and Medicare are brought up. The years immediately ahead will probably not witness a significant reduction in the activities of interest groups. Controversy, however, does exist with respect to PAC formation and their campaign contributions. Despite these and other issues surrounding interest groups, they will continue to play a major role in the politics of the United States in the foreseeable future.

Chapter Six Notes

[1]Alexis de Tocqueville, *Democracy in America* (Garden City, N.Y.: Doubleday, 1969), p. 485.

[2]See, David Truman, *The Governmental Process: Political Interests and Public Opinion* (2d ed.; New York: Knopf, 1971), and Robert A. Dahl, *Who Governs? Democracy and Power in an American City* (New Haven: Yale University Press, 1961); Earl Latham, *APSR*, "The Group Basis of Politics," (June, 1952).

[3]J.Q. Wilson, *Political Organizations* (New York: Basic Books, 1973), chap. 3.

[4]A best source on Common Cause is Andrew S. McFarland, *Common Cause: Lobbying in the Public Interest* (Chatham, N.J.: Chatham House, 1984).

[5]Harold W. Stanley and Richard G. Niemi, Vital Statistics on American Politics, 1997-1998, ed (Washington, D.C.: Congressional Quarterly, Inc., 1998), p. 94

[6]Stanley and Niemi, p. 103.

[7]Richard L. Hall and Frank W. Wayman, "Buying Time: Moneyed Interests and the Mobilization of Bias in congressional Committees," *APSR* 84 (1990).

[8]Stanley and Niemi, p. 96.

[9]410 U.S. 113.

[10]109 S. Ct. 3040.

Suggested Readings

Berry, J.M. *The New Liberalism: The Power of Citizen Groups,* Washington D. C.: Brookings Institution, 1999.

Birnbaum, Jeffrey H. *The Lobbyist.* New York: Random House, 1993.

Cigler, A. J., and B. A. Loomis, eds. *Interest Group Politics.* 6th ed. Washington, D.C.: CQ Press, 2002.

Herrnson, Pauls S., Ronald G. Shaiko, and Clyde Wilcox, (eds.). *The Interest Group Connection: Electioneering, Lobbying, and Policymaking in Washington,* 2nd ed. Washington, D.C.: *Congressional Quarterly Press,* 2005.

Mahood, H. R. *Interest Groups in American National Politics: An Overview.* Upper Saddle River, N.J.: Prentice Hall, 2000.

Walker, Jack, *Mobilizing Interest Groups in America.* Ann Arbor: University of Michigan Press, 1991.

West, Darrell M. *Checkbook Democracy: How Money Corrupts Political Campaigns.* Boston: Northeastern University Press, 2000.

Wolpe, Bruce C., and Bertram J. Levine. *Lobbying Congress: How the System Works.* 2d. Washington, D.C.: CQ Press, 1996.

Chapter Seven

Public Opinion:
Americans Speak

In the year 1798 in Aveyron, a province in France, hunters captured a naked boy in the woods. He was four and a half feet tall and appeared to be about 12 years old. Although he was obviously a human male, he behaved like a wild animal in that he walked on all fours and did not speak. He ate only potatoes, acorns, and chestnuts. Victor, as he was later named, was eventually put into the care of Dr. Jean-Marc Itard, who tried unsuccessfully to teach him to behave like a human being. Victor did learn to walk upright and to speak a few one-syllable words; however, by the time he died in 1826, he was not much different from what he was when he was discovered by the hunters in the woods of Aveyron.[1]

POLITICAL SOCIALIZATION

The point of the story about Victor is that human beings learn to be human beings and that they learn this behavior at a very early age. We call this learning process socialization. When this learning process involves politics, it is called political socialization—the process by which we acquire our attitudes toward political things such as elections, the flag, the army, the police, voting, politicians, etc. While socialization, in general, makes a human being a human being, political socialization makes an American an American, a Russian a Russian, a Nigerian a Nigerian, or a Mexican a Mexican. In other words, these people have probably developed a different set of attitudes about political things because of the environment in which they have grown up. Nigerians would probably have no particular feeling one way or the other about the Mexican flag. In fact, they may not even know what the Mexican flag looks like. On the other hand, Mexican citizens would probably display intense feelings of pride and loyalty when they saw it.

Let's illustrate political socialization in another way. Have you ever noticed that one of the favorite subjects of conversation for Americans is "criticizing the government"? We seem to like to do it just for the fun of it and look upon the activity as our "patriotic" duty. It would be almost un-American to say something nice about the government. On the other hand, if we could transport ourselves to another country such as China, we would observe that Chinese citizens do not spend their time criticizing the government to one another as we do. Criticism of the government is rarely expressed in public—especially after government troops killed protesters in Beijing in 1989—and may not be done much in private either.

This difference in behavior is the result of the difference in political socialization. Americans are taught at an early age, particularly by the example of other Americans, that it is perfectly acceptable to criticize the government in private or in public. The Chinese, by contrast, are taught in the same manner that this behavior is not acceptable and that people who act this way may be either criminals or insane.

Parents march with their children to demonstrate against war. Such early experiences shape the future political attitudes of children.

Types of Political Socialization

Psychologists and sociologists report that most socialization occurs at a very early age. Yet, socialization, in general, and political socialization, in particular, are actually processes that continue throughout a person's lifetime. However, it would be inaccurate to leave the impression that people change political attitudes very swiftly or very radically during their lives. When they do, it is usually as a result of some traumatic political event that affects them personally, such as a war or an economic depression. Even then, most people maintain the same political posture they had for years.

Socialization can be either direct or indirect. Direct socialization is the process by which attitudes and ideas are deliberately taught, perhaps by parents. For instance, parents might tell their children to respect other people as individuals. That kind of lesson would be called direct socialization. Indirect socialization occurs when a person is not taught something intentionally but, rather, when he/she learns it by observing others. Using our earlier illustration, even though the parents might have told the child that he/she should respect other people, the child may observe that the parents always refer to minorities by slang names that indicate a lack of respect. If the child begins to emulate (copy) this behavior, then indirect socialization has occurred. As you can see from the preceding example, sometimes the message conveyed through direct socialization may conflict with one conveyed through indirect socialization. The result of this "mixed message" may create in individuals what psychologists refer to as *cognitive dissonance*.[2]

Sources (Agents) of Political Socialization

The Family. It has long been held that the most important source of political socialization is the family. Most children spend a large part of their early years—their most impressionable years—with family members. Therefore, it should be no surprise that the political attitudes of family members are frequently very similar. Children are great imitators. If they hear parents express political opinions or indicate a preference for a particular political party, it is not unusual for the children to mimic the parents by expressing the same opinion or by declaring that they are members of that political party.[3] It is also true that children who view their parents in a negative way tend to view other authority figures in the same negative light.[4] Until children reach about age ten, they tend to follow the lead of their parents on political matters, whether they understand these issues or not. However, at about ten, the influence of peers and the media become more evident, and children begin to show some divergence from their parents' views, although not completely.

While the family is still probably the major source of political socialization, it may not remain in that position in the future. With more and more parents

The pledge of allegiance. A typical scene in most schools across the nation. In this way children learn the political values of the country and develop pride in their heritage. Such values and commitment are a necessary ingredient to an orderly and just society.

working rather than remaining at home during a child's early years, other institutions, individuals, or groups may take the family's place as the main socializing agent in the United States. We can easily see how a day-care center might take over the family's role. If a very young child is brought to the center about 7:00 a.m. and is picked up by the parents at 5:00 or 6:00 p.m., then chances are the child is exposed to more socialization at the day-care center than he/she is at home.

The School. It is sometimes easy to forget that children spend perhaps as many as 7 or 8 hours a day at school or school-related day-care centers. Educational institutions, usually along with the parents, teach children the fundamentals of politics—American style—although it may not be called politics. Let's look at a few examples.

To begin with, schools teach young children about the flag; they teach the pledge of allegiance and patriotic songs, such as the national anthem. All of these lessons are designed to produce loyalty to the country—the first lesson in politics. Additionally, schools teach orderliness and the rules of fair play and democracy as they are understood in this country. Children often elect class monitors or other assistants very early in their school careers. In higher grades they elect class officers, a student government, and frequently participate in events such as mock nominating conventions or congresses. The lessons learned here are that the democratic way of life—the American way of life—is desirable. Undoubtedly the list of things that are associated with political socialization that educational institutions teach could become quite lengthy. The important concept here is that schools have traditionally been considered the second major source of political socialization and may become even more important depending upon the lifestyle choices of families. It is also important to understand that schools are usually very supportive of the system of government in the United States and attempt to transmit that supportive attitude to the children.

Peers. As far as peers (your friends and associates) are concerned, they can play a significant role in political socialization. Like the family, peer groups can "reward" members with acceptance for "right" thinking and behavior and "punish" them with rejection for "wrong" thinking and behavior. However, in most instances the peer group does not override the political socialization of the family except in areas of particular relevance to the group. For example, many 18-year-olds did not wish to see the legal drinking age raised to 21, while their parents probably supported such a move. Although peers usually do not overcome family socialization, the peer group can actually substitute as the main socializing agent when the family structure is weak. Children who grow up in families where parents are often not present when the children are home will frequently join some group from which they can receive emotional support and guidance. Unfortunately, sometimes the groups may be more accurately described as "gangs." Still, there are other peer groups where young people learn American political values or have those values reinforced. Such groups as the Boy Scouts, Girl Scouts, or Campfire Girls teach many of the same values as do families and schools—such as pride in the country, reverence for the flag, a sense of group cooperation, and fairness.

Of course, as students move up into the higher grades, and especially into college, they become subject to the expression of attitudes, by both peers and teachers, that may challenge the traditional political values promoted in the early grades. This became much more evident in the social and political protests on college campuses in the 1960s and 1970s and has seen a recent resur-

Besides the fun of outdoor life, girl scouts and campfire girls instill many desirable political values of the country. Here a group of girls march in a Fourth of July celebration.

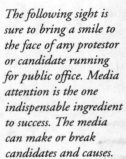

The following sight is sure to bring a smile to the face of any protestor or candidate running for public office. Media attention is the one indispensable ingredient to success. The media can make or break candidates and causes.

gence over issues like "globalization," the environment, and the World Trade Organization. Such protests seem to be a group mindset particularly among college students, who tend to become more "traditional" as they get older. Keep in mind that college professors tend to be much more liberal than the average citizen and will often teach their students to question, if not challenge, existing authority.

The Clergy. If children in the family regularly receive religious instruction, then the clergy, like teachers, can also be agents of political socialization. The ideas of fairness, honesty, hard work, and loyalty can now be connected with the idea that God wants people to possess these qualities. If, as an adult, the person attends a place of worship regularly or even listens to or watches religious programming on radio or television, then they may continue to reinforce the individual's attitudes and behaviors learned as a child. A current illustration of this phenomenon can be seen with the issue of abortion. Many conservative religions have taken a very strong "pro-life" view; consequently, it is not surprising that the majority of their members oppose the Court's position on the right of a woman to terminate her pregnancy. The key here seems to be how involved the individual is with religious activities and how these issues spill over into the political arena.

The Mass Media. In recent years much attention has been given to the role of the mass media, particularly television, in shaping the attitudes and behavior of children. Studies indicate that children and adolescents spend more time watching television than they do in school, frequently much of it alone.[5] Additionally, about two-thirds of the adult population get most of their political information from television.[6] While children and adolescents do not usually pay as close attention to news programs as adults might, the young do get politically socialized by indirect political messages. Positive attitudes toward the space program can be developed by watching reruns of *Star Trek* or the president's announced desire to have manned flights to the moon and Mars. Television, movies, and video games with big name stars (or *virtual* ones) portraying American soldiers actually engaged in military actions via live video streaming on TV or through a computer can do much to generate support for military initiatives and even be an effective recruitment tool. Favorable attitudes about the effectiveness of the police may also be developed by watching police shows like *Law and Order* or *CSI*, since the culprits are usually caught—unlike real life![7] Conversely, distrust of government can certainly be fostered in the young through the influence of certain themes in programs or movies like *Fahrenheit 9/11*, where presidential motives and policies are depicted as less than above board.

While researchers continue to study the role the mass media, particularly television, play in political socialization, it is increasingly apparent that the influence is both direct (on the individual) and indirect (on other agents of political socialization). In other words, if seeing negative political advertising on television has caused you to dislike political campaigns in general, seeing these ads is likely to have had a similar effect on your parents, peers, teachers, etc., (i.e., other socialization agents). These people, in turn, will merely reinforce your negative feelings. According to some researchers, this "double whammy" effect may indeed be responsible for making television *the* most important influence in developing our political attitudes. However, keep in mind that not all researchers agree.

PUBLIC OPINION

Definition

By now you may legitimately be wondering why the phrase public opinion has not been mentioned. It does seem a bit odd since the title of this chapter is "public opinion." Well, here it is—**public opinion consists of beliefs, or opinions, shared by a relatively large number of people on matters of public concern or interest**. Now before we take that definition apart, let's answer two other questions that may have crossed your mind at this point. First, what is the difference between political socialization and public opinion? Second, where does the notion of *ideology* fit into all of this? Although they are definitely related concepts, they actually are two different things. Political socialization, as indicated earlier, is the *process* by which people acquire political attitudes. In other words, political socialization is *how* people learn to think the things they think, based upon the influences in their lives. Ideology (as discussed in chapter five) is their world view, political orientation or lens through which they view the political world based upon how they've been socialized (liberal, conservative, etc.). Public opinion is *what* they actually think, usually about *specific issues*.

To illustrate this difference, let's take children who grow up in a family of working-class people who belong to a labor union. The adults view labor unions quite favorably and always express this idea in the family. These children are being politically socialized by their family—the "how." As a result, their ideology would include a "pro-labor" orientation. Contrast these children with some who grow up in a business-oriented or entrepreneurial family who express rather negative attitudes about unions. These children are also being politically socialized by the family—the "how." But *what* they think about labor unions—public opinion—is quite different. In other words, mainly everyone gets politically socialized in the same ways (or, at least, by the same sources) but the public opinions they may hold as a result of their political socialization may be vastly different.

Now let's go back to the definition of public opinion and look at it more closely. As indicated, public opinion is the beliefs and attitudes about political things shared by a significant number of people. The people whose opinions are part of "public opinion" are not necessarily a majority. In fact, there may be many public opinions on the same issue. Additionally, the people whose opinions are part of public opinion must have expressed their opinions in some way: either verbally to someone—perhaps to family members, friends, or someone taking a poll; or in writing—for example, in a letter to the editor of a newspaper; or by some action—such as joining in a demonstration against nuclear weapons. One way or the other, a person's opinion must be expressed for it to count in what we call public opinion. (Simply because an opinion is not expressed at a particular time does not mean that it will not be voiced at a future date when the issue becomes more important to the individual. These unexpressed "opinions" are referred to as **latent opinions.**) Moreover, the opinion must be on a matter of public concern. If someone were to ask five thousand Americans if they liked the color purple, the answers would indeed be opinions but not public opinions because the color purple has no political significance at the moment. If it ever becomes associated with something political, then perhaps the question might be relevant.

Factors Influencing Public Opinion

Much as most people would like to believe that they form their opinions based on the facts presented, this really isn't the case. The same agents that perform the political socialization function also continue to influence our opinions to a greater or lesser extent throughout our lives. In other words, our opinions are influenced by the family, peers, teachers, clergy, the mass media, or some variation or combination of these factors. Two variations of these factors are opinion leaders and *socioeconomic background.*

Opinion Leaders. Opinion leaders are those people who have a more than usual influence on the opinions of others. They can be people with whom we have face-to-face contact or people we see on television or people we read about. They are people we like and trust: a particular family member, a member of the clergy, a teacher, a movie star, a rock singer, a newscaster, a politician, etc. These people often play the role of interpreter—explaining what we see or experience. The opinion leaders whom we see face-to-face usually have more of an impact on what we think than those we experience indirectly through television or the print media. Advertising agencies have known about opinion leaders for a long time. You may have noticed that famous movie or television stars are often used to sell products on television. George Foreman, who sells the lean, mean fat reducing grilling machine, has a great influence on the buying public. Likewise, Regis Philbin and Ed McMahon have sold life and health insurance to the elderly. These commercials by these opinion leaders are identical to the "commercials" for matters of public concern except for the content. In the 2004 presidential election, Democratic candidate John Kerry's Catholic faith became a controversial issue when it was suggested by Archbishops in both Massachusetts and Colorado that Catholic politicians who support abortion rights (Kerry does) should not be able to take communion.[8] Some Catholic bishops even suggested that parishioners who *voted* for such candidates should also be denied this sacrament. These religious opinion leaders were trying to influence the public's thinking in much the same way that spokespeople for commercial products do. The only difference was the content of the message.

Socioeconomic Backgrounds. As we have already seen, some of these influencing factors affect some groups of people more than others on certain issues. If a survey were conducted to find out what public opinion was among working-class people and among professional people on various aspects of foreign trade, for example, there would probably be a substantial difference of opinion between the two groups as a whole. The most likely influencing factor here would be the socioeconomic backgrounds of the two groups—a combination of family background, education, and income. Within this category, one could also certainly include such factors as a person's race, sex, and region of the country where he or she grew up. Although Americans do not tend to be rigidly class conscious, whether a person comes from the lower, middle, or upper class does tend to "color" their political opinions.

Let's not forget that some of the influences or agents of political socialization influence public opinion as well.

Peers. Friends and associates—peers—also may exert some influence on opinions. We all know how difficult it is to be the "odd man out" in the group—to be the only person who disagrees about something. Since we all tend to seek approval and acceptance from groups that are important to us, it isn't surprising that the opinions of group members are often the same on most political issues. However, we cannot say that groups definitely influence the opinions of the individuals in the group. It could be that people just tend to associate with other people who think as they do. Perhaps the only way we could be certain that people's friends and associates influenced their opinions is if we knew that they believed one thing when they came into the group but later changed their minds as a result of peer pressure.

The Clergy. As indicated previously, churches are agents of political socialization and can be a continuing influence on public opinion. People who attend a church regularly, particularly those churches where obviously political subjects are discussed from the pulpit, may be influenced by what they believe to be the morally "correct" way to think or the way that "God" wants them to think. When religious leaders make statements from their pulpits about the candidate the congregation should vote for, as illustrated in the previous example, they are influencing public opinion. Even if people do not accept the opinion put forth by the particular religious group, they may have been at least influenced to think about the subject and to form some sort of opinion. This concept can be illustrated by the issues of abortion, pornography, or gay marriage that have been kept alive in the minds of the public by various religious organizations. As one pastor of a Washington state church recently remarked, "God wants us to be involved in government . . . . It's not like we're trying to impose our values on the country. We're trying to prevent other people from imposing their values on us."[9]

The Mass Media. Finally the mass media, especially television, play a significant role in the formation of public opinion. While there is still a persistent belief that the media have the ability to make the American public believe anything the media want them to believe, various studies over the years have found that the media primarily functions to *reinforce* already-existing beliefs and do not usually cause a change in beliefs even if these beliefs are challenged by television, newspapers, or magazines.[10] It seems that our previous political socialization is normally strong enough to "filter" what we see and hear and to make it fit what we believe regardless of the real content of the mass communication. This is not to say the media can have no effect in shaping public opinion. In fact, evidence suggests that, *given certain conditions*, the media can produce a particular attitude, belief, or opinion in some segments of the population.[11] One researcher suggests that, if a particular issue is believed to be really important and if the media's "slant" on that issue is presented repeatedly, a person may change even deeply-held, political opinions.[12] The bottom line seems to be that the audience being persuaded at least has to be rather open-minded on the subject being discussed. Media persuasion is also more effective if repeated and if people watching the broadcast or reading the newspaper or magazine have a chance to discuss the issue among themselves or with an opinion leader. Finally,

Trying to influence public opinion, this follower of Louis Farrakhan distributes copies of his organization's newspaper in hopes of attracting new members.

it doesn't hurt the media campaign if the spokesperson is someone the audience trusts and likes (an opinion leader).

Significance of Public Opinion

Thus far, we have discussed how people acquire political opinions through the process of political socialization. Additionally, we have seen what public opinion is and the factors that shape or influence it. But our discussion has failed to bring up why public opinion is important. Why bother having a chapter of this book on public opinion? What difference does it make?

The Traditional View. There are many schools of thought regarding the significance of public opinion. Let's examine two of them. The first is the traditional view, which claims that public opinion plays an important role in shaping public policy. This traditional line of thought further asserts that the role of public opinion is, of course, more pronounced in democratic countries than in nondemocratic ones. Nevertheless, according to this theory, public opinion does influence public policy regardless of the country's form of government. Many supporters of the traditionalist perspective point to the late 1960s and early 1970s to provide examples of how an informed and engaged citizenry were able, through expressions of public opinion and other means, to significantly affect the way that public policies were created and enacted.

In the 1970s there was a big push in this country to build nuclear power plants. Driven by the oil embargo of the early 1970s and the subsequent calls for greater "energy independence," these plants were supposedly a safe and in-

expensive source of present and future needs for electrical energy. In the beginning, few people questioned the need for these power plants or their real safety.
One such facility was begun in a small town in central Michigan. While the
plant was still under construction, a woman wrote a letter to the editor of the
local newspaper in which she questioned the need for, the cost of, and the safety
of the plant. That one letter began a chain of events that ended in the power
company's stopping construction and closing the facility.[13] Why was this one
letter so important? That letter seemingly stirred the residents of the community and the surrounding area to ask the same questions. When the answers
were not satisfactory to the citizenry, public opinion against continuation of
the plant began to be mobilized. Eventually that public opinion was translated
into a governmental order to the powerful electric company to cease construction. After the subsequent "meltdown" of a nuclear reactor in 1979 at Three
Mile Island, Pennsylvania, and the disastrous accident at Chernobyl in the
Ukraine in 1986, nuclear power no longer appeared to be such a good idea to
the public. Today, the debate regarding nuclear power has largely shifted away
from whether or not nuclear power is a good alternative (although we still hear
proposals for it in the U. S. and China) and turned toward the question of what
to do with decommissioned nuclear plants, missiles, and the transporting and
disposal of nuclear (radioactive) waste.

During that same period, public opinion shifted (or became energized)
around other domestic policy issues related to health and safety in the workplace, the value and safety of consumer products and services, and the state of
our natural environment. From 1969 to 1972 grassroots citizens were able to
convince a Democratic Congress and a Republican administration to enact numerous pieces of legislation to protect the safety of the workplace (Occupational Safety and Health Act), consumer products (Consumer Products Safety
Act), the air we breathe (the Clean Air Act), and the water we drink (the Clean
Water Act). Nor was the impact of public opinion limited to only *domestic*
policy issues during this period.

When the United States officially began its involvement in the Vietnam
conflict in 1964, public opinion was generally favorable or at least neutral.
However, as the war dragged on, the mood of Americans shifted. It has been
suggested that part of the shift in public opinion was brought about by the
commentary of Walter Cronkite, an opinion leader of television news and regarded by many as the "most trusted man in America" at one time. Massive
demonstrations occurred in many parts of the country against our continued
involvement in that war. Some of these demonstrations included violent clashes
with the police and the national guard. The 1968 and 1972 presidential elections saw the war in Vietnam as a major political issue, particularly after the
release of a document that became known as the *Pentagon Papers*, in 1970.[14]
The United States ended its involvement in the war in 1974. Even today, what
has become known as the "Vietnam syndrome" (fear of getting involved in

another Vietnam-like situation) still influences public opinion. Perhaps reflecting that fear, in a recent ABC News/ *Washington Post* poll, when asked if "All in all, considering the costs to the U.S. versus the benefits to the U.S., do you think the war with Iraq was worth fighting or not?" more than half the respondents answered in the negative.[15]

According to the traditionalists, public opinion even in nondemocratic countries can have significant impact. From 1976 to 1982, the government of Chile was controlled by the military. Anyone who even remotely seemed to be a threat to the government could be taken away by troops or secret police, never to be seen again. During that period thousands of people just disappeared. Despite the obvious fear that the same thing could happen to them, a few of the mothers of "the disappeared" (*desaparecidos*), as they were called, began to assemble daily in the square in front of one of the government buildings. They all wore white scarves to identify themselves and demanded to know what happened to their children. More and more people began to appear in the square. Others began to take notice and demand that the practice of government kidnapping cease and that those responsible be brought to justice. In 1982 the military rulers were forced out of power, and since then a number of persons were convicted in Chilean courts of involvement in the kidnapping and murder of many of the "disappeared."

And with the world continuing to get "smaller and smaller," with the advent of television and the Internet, it has become more and more difficult for leaders of autocratic nations to keep the images and messages from democratic nations from penetrating the consciousness of their own citizens. The events of the last two decades in Eastern Europe also serve notice that public opinion is potent even in dictatorships. The forced resignation of long-time East German leader Erich Honiker, the destruction of the Berlin Wall, and the establishment of a multi-party system in Poland all illustrate the power of public opinion even in highly undemocratic societies. However, it must also be noted that some governments, from China to the Middle East, still ignore public opinion and continue in their repressive ways. Despite the demonstration of public opinion in favor of more freedom in China, the Chinese government persists in maintaining its dictatorship by extreme force when necessary. For example, Chinese army troops crushed protests in Tiananmen Square, June 3 and 4, 1989, with death-toll estimates of between 500 and 7,000, up to 10,000 injured, up to 10,000 dissidents arrested, and 31 tried and executed.[16]

Those who believe in the traditional theory of how public opinion works could cite those success stories to support their claim that, when people express a political opinion with intensity, it is extremely difficult to ignore it. Government policy makers who ignore public opinion may find themselves merely defeated in the next election, or they may face the same fate as Marie Antoinette, Queen of France, in 1789. When she was told that the French people had no bread (food), she replied: "So let them eat cake." Her head was cut off shortly after she made that famous response to "public opinion."

Elitist View. A second school of thought in regard to the significance of public opinion—we'll call it the elitist view—claims that public opinion is actually not generated by the masses at all. Rather, government policy makers (**formal elites**) and those who influence them (**informal elites**) decide what they want to do and then mold public opinion to suit their policies. In order to understand what is meant here, we must examine the role of mass media once more.

The elitists argue that mass media (newspapers, magazines, radio, television, and most recently the Internet) exercise political power beyond what most people realize in both subtle and obvious ways. To begin with, owners of corporate media decide what the public shall see and hear and, more significantly, what the public shall *not* see and hear both in news and in entertainment. In other words, media "sets the agenda" as to what is important for us to know about and what isn't. For example, in the first month after the scandal broke regarding former President Clinton's "affair" with White House intern Monica Lewinsky, the news media devoted more time to that story (about one-third of all network news time) than to the winter Olympics, a papal visit to Cuba, and growing tensions with Iraq combined![17] Of course, what *should* have been one of the biggest news stories of the 90's went virtually unreported and therefore unnoticed. This was the story of how lobbyists for media conglomerates were able to convince the Congress to literally "give away" to them the *digital spectrum,* a public resource estimated to be valued at over $70 billion, in the **Telecommunications Act of 1996**. In the roughly thirteen months from the time the bill was first introduced in Congress until its final passage, a total of nineteen minutes was estimated to have been devoted to that story.[18]

While the media in its agenda setting function may be the *driver* of public policy in situations like the ones just illustrated, it is also often used as the *vehicle* by policy makers to promote desired outcomes in other situations, whether it be welfare reform, a new prescription drug bill, or engendering support for a new foreign policy initiative. Yet those who hold the elitist view would also point out that, despite the best efforts of both the formal and the informal elites to sway public opinion their way, the public may not always adopt the desired attitudes. One of the critical points of the elite theorists, however, is that even when this opposition appears, the government policy makers may do what they want anyway despite negative public opinion. The elitists point to 1954, when the justices of the U.S. Supreme Court (formal elites) decided that public schools must be integrated and that bussing should be used to achieve it. Despite the fact that a majority of the American public opposed the decision, the policy went into affect anyway. Additional historical examples can easily be found. While facing majority public opposition, the Court declared prayer in the pub-

Jimmy Carter and Omar Torrijos signing the Panama Canal Treaty.
June 16, 1978
Photo credit: Jimmy Carter Library

lic schools unconstitutional in 1963. When President Jimmy Carter signed the treaty giving up the Panama Canal to Panama, public opinion favored keeping the canal. And, while a majority of Americans favored tighter gun control laws, Congress relaxed the laws in 1986 but a few years later reversed itself and tightened them.

Of course, in evaluating how well or how poorly government responds to public opinion (even if it reflects the will of the majority,) it should be remembered that even the founders of this country expressed significant reservations about the notion of a direct democracy that would allow a "tyranny of the majority" to trample the rights of those in the minority. Yet regardless of which view about the significance of public opinion is correct, the traditional or the elitist (perhaps neither or perhaps both, depending on the issue), if we wanted to know what the content of public opinion was on a particular issue, how could we find out?

Measuring Public Opinion

From the very beginnings of societal organizations, the rulers have had ways of finding out what the people think. When governmental organizations were rather small, such as those found in American Indian tribes, there were tribal councils that met with the chiefs. In these meetings the issues at hand were discussed. It was fairly easy for a chief to discover "public opinion" since most of the "public" was at the meeting. But in modern times with millions of people constituting the "public," finding out what public opinion is becomes a bit more of a problem. The "chief" just can't ask 100 million people what they think!

Public Opinion Polls. It was a long time coming, but in the 1930s Elmo Roper and George Gallup developed the first scientific public opinion poll.[19] Gallup predicted that Franklin Roosevelt would be re-elected as president in 1936 when other respected organizations were saying Roosevelt would be defeated.

Scientific public opinion polling today is done by hundreds of organizations using the mathematics of probability connected with random sampling. Let's illustrate random sampling in a simplified manner. Suppose we wanted to know the opinion of 100 students on raising the legal age for drinking alcoholic beverages. If we put all the students' names into a computer program and told the computer to select every third name, it would print out a list of 33 students' names. Now if the laws of probability are at work here (and they usually are), the characteristics of the students selected by the computer should be very close to the characteristics of all 100 students. For example, if 51 percent of the 100 students are females, then about 51 percent of the sample (51 percent of the 33 students selected at random by the computer) should also be female. If 25 percent of the 100 students are Hispanic, then about 25 percent of the sample should be Hispanic and so on. Then we would ask those 33 randomly selected students what their opinion was about raising the legal drinking age. Let's assume that 75 percent believed it should not be raised; 20 percent thought it should; and 5 percent stated that they had no opinion about the matter. Mathematically then, if we were to ask the same question of all 100 students, the percentages should remain approximately the same.

Looking at public opinion polls on a larger scale, we can readily see that public opinion pollsters do not ask the over 270 million people in the United States what they think on any given issue. To do so would be too costly and too time-consuming. However, as we have just seen, they don't have to ask all of the people to determine what the opinion is. Rather, the reputable national polling organizations—the ones that have proved to be quite accurate—merely ask a random sample—usually about 1000 to 2000 people. The answers obtained from this sample of the population will usually be accurate, with a **margin of error** (the difference between the results of our sample and that of the total population) of between + or - 2 percent to 3 percent. This margin of error means that, if 62 percent of those questioned said they believed that current gun control laws were effective in reducing crime, then anywhere from 59 percent to 65 percent (+ or - 3 percent) of the total population should respond the same way if they were asked the same question.

The Problems with Polling

While scientific public opinion polling is a vast improvement over simply "guessing," there are still numerous problems associated with it.

Margin of Error. There will inevitably be some questions that are too close to call. If the question concerned who would win a very close election, it would be difficult for a pollster to predict a winner if the poll revealed a 51 percent to 49 percent split in the vote. The 2000 presidential election was one such race. Combining the closeness of the race and the high percentage of "undecided" voters produced some very volatile polling results. For example, the CNN/ USA Today/Gallup tracking poll showed former Vice President Gore ahead by 11 percent on October 4 and then Governor Bush ahead by 8 percent just three days later on October 7.[20]

Wording of Questions. How the questions are asked can influence the answers or even make the results of the poll subject to differing interpretations. Suppose the pollster asked this question: "Do you think the United States should invade Cuba to restore democracy and remove the godless communists?" The answers obtained might be inaccurate because of the use of the terms "restore democracy" and "communists." There would be a tendency for Americans to want to say "Yes" to that question because to say "No" would be indicating that they wanted communists to remain in Cuba. In other words, the question is biased (or, at least, *ambiguous*); it is designed to get people to say "Yes" and is an example of what is referred to as a "double-barreled" question.

Lack of Knowledge. People have a tendency to sometimes express an opinion even when they know nothing about the subject. Very few people like to appear ignorant about anything; therefore, they will give an opinion on subjects ranging from oil depletion allowances to the International Monetary Fund when they have absolutely no idea what these terms mean.

Every major newspaper in the country devotes space in its editorial section for citizens to voice their views. These editorials are usually lively, informative and entertaining. In addition, they serve as an important means of communication among citizens. Such communication is a vital ingredient to an open and democratic society.

Forced Opinion. Related to the previous problem, people may likewise formulate an opinion when asked, even if they hadn't really thought about the issue previously. In other words, the poll may "create" a public opinion about an issue where there was none previously. This may be particularly evident when a new issue or new information is revealed and people are asked to respond to an "instant poll" before all of the facts are in or a context has been provided.

Contradictory Opinions. People may state contradictory positions in the same poll. For example, in one poll 75 percent of the persons questioned agreed with the following statement: "Professors in state-supported institutions should have freedom to speak and teach the truth as they see it." Yet 75 percent of the same group agreed with this statement also: "Professors who advocate controversial ideas or speak out against official policy have no place in a state-supported college or university."[21]

Lying. Though the practice doesn't appear to be widespread, some people do lie. Three areas where lying might produce inaccuracies are polls conducted about people's prejudices or their illegal activities and those conducted after an election. People do not usually like to admit to something that is socially unacceptable or illegal. For instance, if the poll concerned attitudes about race, some people would lie rather than admit that they are racially prejudiced. Likewise, after an election most people want to appear to have voted for the winner. Therefore, whether these people voted for the winner or not, they may tell the pollster that they did. On the flip side of the coin, however, if the candidate they voted for does not perform well, these same people will deny having voted for him or her. Sometimes we have to wonder how some people ever got elected since no one voted for them! Despite its problems, however, scientific public opinion polling today has significant value in determining what the public thinks about political matters.

Polling and Elections

Although some information about the public mood may be obtained by looking at election results, measuring public opinion by this means is rather difficult for a number of reasons.

First, in most elections issues are not clearly defined by the candidates. Candidates may not take clear-cut stands, particularly on controversial subjects, because they do not wish to lose any potential votes. Therefore, it is difficult for the voter to vote for or against candidates based on their stands on any specific issue that might be important to that voter.

Second, even if the candidates stated their positions on various issues, voters are still faced with making a choice about (or *prioritizing*) which issue is most important to them. In the 1968 presidential election one of the important issues was the war in Vietnam. One presidential candidate, George

McGovern, stated that, if elected, he would remove all United States forces from that country—in other words, end the war. The winning candidate, Richard Nixon, stated that he would remove American troops only if he could achieve "peace with honor." If we were to gauge public opinion on the issue of the Vietnam War based on the 1968 election results, it would appear that the American public was massively supportive of the war in Vietnam because Nixon won by a landslide. However, this conclusion would not be borne out, in fact, since the country was badly divided on that subject. People obviously voted for Nixon for reasons other than his Vietnam War stance. The same might also be said about public opinion regarding the war on terrorism and the Iraq War relative to the presidential candidates in the 2004 election.

Third, a significant number of people do not vote for a number of reasons such as a feeling that their votes do not really matter or because they have not registered. These and other aspects of voter behavior will be discussed in the next chapter.

Fourth, a significant number of people vote for one candidate over another for reasons that appear to be unrelated to political issues: the candidate's appearance or the location of his/her name on the ballot. With these factors in mind, we can see that election results may tell us the general mood of the public—liberal, conservative, etc.—but certainly judging the content of public opinion could prove to be hazardous.

In addition to the more generalized challenges associated with measuring public opinion based upon election results, we have also witnessed some other specific polling problems in the last few presidential elections that are worthy of mention.

Projection Polls in the 1996 Presidential Election

Immediately following the presidential election of 1996, a very well-respected pollster, Everett Carl Ladd, a political scientist and director of the Roper Center for Public Opinion Research at the University of Connecticut, wrote a scathing article in the *Wall Street Journal* saying that polling in that election was worse than in 1948. While he primarily focused on the questionable "methodology" (techniques used to gather and interpret the survey data) used by his colleagues in the polling industry, he also touched on the misinterpretation of the public mood, the overly pessimistic assessment of the GOP candidate, low voter turnout and the sheer volume of national polls as contributing to why so many final projection polls (just prior to the election) were so different from the actual vote. He called for a blue-ribbon panel of experts to review and make recommendations about how polling could be improved.[22]

Not surprisingly, Ladd himself became the focus of much criticism by his colleagues in the polling industry. Yet, he was able to bring about what he wanted: a thorough and rigorous review of the methods and analysis used in the election. Unfortunately, both old and new problems arose in the public opinion polling of the 2000 presidential election.

The "Debacle" of the 2000 Election

Obviously, there will be much to remember (and much that many people would like to forget) about the 2000 presidential election. One thing that will likely stand out is the frustration people felt in watching the networks' election coverage as the networks kept changing their minds over who had actually won the election. Tom Brokaw, anchor for NBC news, in apologizing for switching back and forth over declaring a winner, finally quipped, "We don't simply have egg on our face, we have omelets on our suits." With the election of 2000 turning out to be one of the closest in U.S. history, the electoral outcome hung on just one state, Florida. The frustration and anger, reflected in public opinion polls over the next few weeks, reflected a growing partisan divide over charges of voter fraud, faulty ballot design, political manipulation, and worse. Ultimately, the Supreme Court's 5-4 ruling to stop the recounting of the Florida votes (effectively awarding the election to Mr. Bush) did little to assuage the resentment engendered during the lengthy legal and political process.

In January 2001, CNN (Cable Network News) released an independent report accusing the networks of an "abuse of power," driven by "an overconfidence in experts and polls."[23] A large part of the problem was attributed to exit polls, conducted by Voter News Service and used by all the major networks and the Associated Press, which the report claimed used outmoded technology. One recommendation was that networks stop using exit polls to project winners too early in close races. Despite the recommendation, however, exit polls continued to be used to predict the outcome of every major election in the United States after the 2000 election, and it was exit polls that became the major contentious issue in the 2004 election as well.

Exit Polls, "Moral Values" and the 2004 Presidential Election

By the 2004 presidential election, the Voters News Service had been replaced by Edison Media Research and Mitofsky International as the key pollsters for the National Election Pool, a consortium of news organizations that included FOX news, ABC, NBC, CBS, CNN, and the Associated Press. Throughout the campaign of 2004 these and other organizations reflected a back and forth shift in public support for both the incumbent, George W. Bush, and his Democratic rival, Massachusetts Senator John Kerry, almost up until election day (although the president appeared to enjoy a slight lead throughout).

On election day, early exit polls demonstrated a significant shift in support to Kerry, particularly in "swing states" like Ohio that had been considered too close to call. By the end of the day, however, when the *actual* votes had been counted, President Bush had captured 3 million more popular votes than Kerry, the necessary electoral votes (including Ohio) and another four years in the White House. The early jubilation of the Kerry campaign had turned to despair, and questions of voter fraud, intimidation, and disenfranchisement began to arise, much as they had in 2000.

While we may never completely know all of the reasons for the turn of events that ensued, a couple of explanations may provide some insight as to why the exit polls were so far off:

First, exit poll numbers are *always* off, particularly early ones that have not been weighted to account for sampling bias or reflective of new turnout patterns.[24]

Second, Republican voters tend to be more wary of talking to pollsters (or anyone associated with the perceived "liberal media") and, therefore, may have been significantly underrepresented in the exit polling data.

Third, while much of the media and the "blogosphere" touted the impact of "moral values" in deciding the election, little objective analysis supports this contention. The moral values question appeared in only *one* survey, with no definition of what it was, and alongside other much more discrete variables (terrorism, health care, etc.). It was sort of like throwing in one apple in a bunch of oranges. One columnist concluded that "this hot-button catch phrase had no place alongside defined political issues (and thus) created a deep distortion."[25]

Finally, as Richard Morin of the *Washington Post* suggests, "A few more presidential elections like this one and the public will learn to do the right thing and simply ignore news of early exit poll data.[26]

Focus Group Research

While nearly all of the polls taken, election or otherwise, seek to provide information on *what* people think or *how* they are going to vote, it is also important for us to understand *why* people vote the way they do. In order to address this a more *qualitative* method of research has emerged in the form of *focus groups.* This type of survey research has been proven to be extremely valuable in the fifty years it has been in use. From the testing of people's reaction to political propaganda during World War II to the marketing of consumer products, focus group research has been able to tap into people's *feelings* about a variety of things. More recently it has been used to test campaign messages on homogeneous groups to see which ones get the best response. As Frank Luntz, one of the principle author's of the Republican Party's successful "Contract with America," in 1994 said, "Focus groups are centrally concerned with understanding attitudes rather than measuring them."[27]

Initiatives and Referenda. Initiatives and referenda are types of elections where the voters are asked their opinions on specific issues. It is easier to interpret public opinion in these elections because they are generally limited to a specific question. For example, the voters may be asked to decide whether they want 10-cent deposits on bottled or canned soft drinks sold in their state. Obviously public opinion on that issue would be clear based on the results of that referendum. However, even with these types of elections public opinion may still be a bit clouded. Let's suppose that the voters were asked to approve a small tax increase to support public schools, but the voters rejected the proposal. On the basis of these results, could we say that public opinion on tax increases was negative? No, we couldn't because it may well be that the voters did not see the need for the tax increase or that they were displeased with the public school system. As with other types of elections, great care must be taken when the results of referenda or initiatives are used to interpret public opinion.

Interest Groups and "Grassroots" Contact. Like the use of elections, other methods to ascertain public opinion are also relatively unscientific. Policy makers, such as members of the House of Representatives or the Senate, frequently come in contact with lobbyists for various interest groups. These interest groups obviously have members, and we assume, sometimes incorrectly, that the interest group leaders and their lobbyists speak the opinions of the members. This assumption, as indicated, is not always accurate. For instance, labor leaders normally give the unions' support to Democratic candidates for president. If this statement of support by the president of the union were used to determine how the members of the union would vote, we would undoubtedly conclude that most would vote for the Democratic candidates. However, in presidential elections in the last twenty years or so, many have voted for Republicans or have been widely split between the two candidates despite the unions' support for the Democrats.

Besides contact with lobbyists, members of the Congress have contact with their constituents back home either face-to-face or through letters, faxes, e-mail, or phone calls. Again if 80 percent of the contacts they receive were against raising corporate taxes, for example, could we conclude that about 80 percent of all their constituents back home felt the same way? The answer is "no" because most people do not contact lawmakers unless they are really heavily involved in an issue. Chances are that most of the people who contacted the lawmakers in our example were corporation stockholders who would stand to lose a significant amount of money if taxes were raised.

Mass Media. Sometimes public opinion is measured by taking a look at the content of the mass media such as television, newspapers, and magazines. If we wanted to know how people felt about revising the tax laws in the United

States, we could look at the amount of time spent by television news programs in reporting the issue and how they reported it—whether in a positive light or in a negative one. Furthermore, we could look at the number of favorable and unfavorable letters to editors of newspapers to try to get some kind of handle on the public's feelings on the matter. However, like interest-group and grassroots contact, using this method to measure public opinion is also like playing with loaded dice. People who write letters to newspapers tend to be those who hold extreme opinions[21] (usually negative) and are frequently the more highly educated in our society or those with good writing skills. Most people do not write letters to newspapers or magazines. Likewise, as we have already seen, regardless of the reporting of an issue by the media, the public does not always adopt the desired opinion. To make matters worse, there has been a recent upsurge in mistrust of the news media since the prestigious *New York Times* newspaper had a reporter *making up* the news as he paraded through Iraq and elsewhere.

Intensity and Stability of Public Opinion

When policy makers or students of public opinion look at its content, they will also find it useful to measure the intensity and stability of a particular opinion. Not all public opinions are the same on particular issues year after year or even week after week. In other words, public opinion may be **unstable.** The Vietnam War, as well as other issues, provides a good illustration of public opinion that was supportive of American involvement in the beginning and then shifted to a more negative stance. These shifts in public opinion may occur rather rapidly or they may take a number of years to develop. The public perception of administration policies in Iraq, Afghanistan, and the war on terror also serve as more recent examples of the volatility of public opinion.

For example, do you think that Americans are more religious or less religious today than they were ten years ago? The Graduate Center of the City University of New York recently released a study indicating that the number of adults saying that they subscribed to or identified with no religion (often referred to as secularists) has more than doubled since 1990. Table 7.1 highlights some of the findings in that study.

Table 7.1: American Religious Identification

Religion	Catholic	Protestant	Jewish	Muslim	No Religion
1990	26.5%	60%	2%	.3%	8%
2001	24.5%	52%	1.7%	.6%	14%

Source: Graduate Center of the City University of New York (October 2001).

In the wake of September 11, 2001, there appeared to be a rekindling of religious faith with many people attending houses of worship who had not been there in many years. Yet as reported in another recent survey it appears that almost the same number of people who thought that religion's effect was "in decline" (52 percent) prior to September 11 believed it still to be so three months after the events.[28]

Don't confuse *public opinion* with *popular opinion*. Public opinion is usually well thought out, but **popular opinion** is what we usually get in "instant polls" conducted by television and radio stations or on the Internet in response to a significant story of the day (often before all the facts are in or before people have had a chance to really think about the event).[29] With the rash of shootings by students in a number of schools in the United States in recent years, one might expect a spike in opinion in favor of gun control. In other words, those events would be expected to produce extremely negative *popular* opinion. But in looking at public opinion data, one can readily see that the public has been overwhelmingly supportive of strong gun control measures for many years. Table 7.2 illustrates this point.

Table 7.2: Public Opinion Supporting Gun Control, 1959-1996 (percent)

Year	1959	1967	1975	1985	1990	1996
Percent	75	73	74	72	79	80

Note: Question: "Would you favor or oppose a law that would require a person to obtain a police permit before he or she could buy a gun?"

Adapted from: Harold W. Stanley and Richard G Niemi, *Vital Statistics on American Politics: 1997-1998* (Washington, D.C.: Congressional Quarterly, Inc. 1998), 154

You might legitimately ask: if public opinion does indeed drive government policy, why has it been so difficult to get strong gun control measures passed in the United States. At least part of the answer to that question harkens back to interest groups. You will remember that people in the United States (as well as many other countries) pursue political goals by forming interest groups. One of those groups, the National Rifle Association, has been more effective until recently in blocking many tough gun control laws than their opposition has been in getting these laws passed. Regardless of your own view of this issue, the point is interest groups are powerful political entities.

Public opinion on the Vietnam War also illustrates the concept of intensity (i.e., strength). We all know that not every issue is of equal importance. The more important an issue is to people, the more intense will be their opinion about it and the more likely they are to take action. Those who were around during the 1960s and early 1970s remember massive demonstrations, sometimes quite violent, against the war. We would have to conclude that the people who were willing to get out in the street and perhaps to get themselves injured or killed to demonstrate against the war held that opinion very strongly. At best these "intense" people numbered only about 250,000 or so during the height of the conflict. There were undoubtedly others in the country who opposed the Vietnam War but did not feel that opposition as strongly as the demonstrators; i.e., their opinions were not as intense. Policy makers who merely looked at a public opinion poll from that period of time concerning support for or opposition to the war might be seriously misled if they did not take a look at the intensity of the support or opposition. People who feel very strongly about an issue are quite inclined to vote for or against candidates based on that issue alone and to get actively involved in the campaign.

Studies have shown that the same factors that influence the content of public opinion also influence its intensity. However, there is at least one additional factor involved here: political efficacy. Political efficacy refers to a feeling of political power—a feeling that "What I think and what I do really does make a difference in the behavior of the government." People who feel this way are usually the ones who hold very intense political opinions. Therefore, they are the ones who are likely to vote or demonstrate or perhaps commit illegal acts to get their point across. We can imagine that a "bag lady" on the streets of Chicago and a Wall Street banker may hold negative opinions on the issue of abortion, but of the two the banker is more likely to try to do something to change the laws than the "bag lady" is. She may believe that, because of who *she* is, nothing she thinks will make a difference. On the other hand, the banker may assume that, because of who *he/she* is, what he/she thinks *will* make a difference. Political efficacy is also an important determinant in voter behavior.

"When is a poll *not* a poll?"

Before we leave the topic of measuring public opinion entirely, you should be warned that there are some rather unscrupulous people out there (if you haven't figured this out by now!) who engage in negative campaigning while disguising themselves as researchers or pollsters. A **push poll** is a very devious form of political manipulation that is meant to *change* opinions, not measure them. Typically, a "pollster" will call potential voters and ask which candidate they are supporting. If the respondents say that they are voting for the "other" candidate (not the one supported by the caller) they will be asked a series of questions designed to produce doubt about their preferred candidate in the respondent's mind, such as, "If you knew that your candidate abused their children or liked to kill puppies for sport, would you still support them?" They don't have to actually accuse the candidate of anything, just simply put doubt in your mind as to whether you should continue to support the candidate given that they might abuse children or animals. It is guilt by insinuation—a pretty nasty trick! Unfortunately, these kinds of tactics are frequently used late in a campaign when there is little time to respond to the attack.[30]

THE FUTURE

Although there is some correspondence between public opinion and the policies of the government in the United States, clearly this correspondence is not particularly great. Even when public opinion does match up with certain government policies, it is still possible that some group of elites "created" the public opinion. Conversely, when the public opinion does not coincide with government policy, it is possible that some other group of elites "created" that opinion also.

If the low level of correspondence between public opinion and public policy continues for a relatively long period of time, we might expect that perhaps the citizens of the United States would demand changes resulting in the creation of a government more responsive to public opinion. On the other hand, we might also see an increasing number of people adopting the apathetic attitude that "It doesn't matter what I think" and leaving the discussion of and the decisions about public policy to the "experts." At that point we would have to find some term to describe the United States other than a democracy. Government by "experts" is not democratic. In the next chapter we note that, if voter turnout for elections is any gauge of public apathy, then this country is well on its way to becoming nondemocratic merely because we did nothing.

Chapter Seven Notes

[1]Jean-Marc Itard, *The Wild Boy of Aveyron* (New York: Appleton-Century-Crofts, 1962).

[2]The term "cognitive dissonance" describes a psychological conflict that occurs when a deeply held belief is challenged by new information that significantly contradicts it.

[3]Dawson, R., Prewitt, K., Dawson, K., *Political Socialization.*(Boston: Little, 1977)

[4]Dean Jaros and others, "The Malevolent Leader: Political Socialization in an American Subculture," *American Political Science Review* 62 (1968): 564-575.

[5] Donald F. Roberts et. al. *Kids & Media @ the New Millennium* (Menlo Park: The Henry J. Kaiser Family Foundation, 1999)

[6]*Public Opinion* (August/September, 1979).

[7]Charles K. Atkins, "Communication and Political Socialization," *Handbook of Political Communication*, ed. Dan D. Nimmo and Keith R. Sanders (Beverly Hills, Calif.: Sage, 1981), 317-320.

[8]"Bishop issues Communion warning," *Los Angeles Times,* (May 15, 2004), A4.

[9]"Pastor signing up Christian voters," *Eugene Register-Guard,* (July 19, 2004), C3

[10]Joseph T. Klapper, "The Effectiveness of Mass Communication," in Graber, 27-28.

[11]Denis McQuail, "The Influence and Effects of Mass Media," in Graber, 40-42.

[12]Robert M. Entman, "How the Media Affect What People Think: An Informational Processing Approach." *Journal of Politics.* 51 (May 1989): 361-363.

[13]The plant, located in Midland, Michigan, was ultimately converted to a different fuel.

[14]This was a secret document release by a disillusioned former Department of Defense official, Daniel Ellsberg, which revealed a history of military blunders and misinformation regarding how the war was being conducted.

[15]ABC News/ *Washington Post* poll of December 16-19, 2004, as reported in The Polling Report <www.pollingreport.com> December 23, 2004.

[16]*The World Almanac and Book of Facts,* 1993 ed., s.v. "World History: Revitalization of Capitalism, Demand for Democracy: 1980-89."

[17]James Q. Wilson, *American Government* (Boston: Houghton Mifflin Company, 2000), 78.

[18]*Free Speech for Sale: A Bill Moyer's Special* [videorecording] (Princeton: Films for the Humanities, 1999).

[19]The term "scientific" is applied to these polls and not to the ones that preceded them because Roper and Gallup and others were the first to use the mathematical principles of probability in their sampling techniques. This methodology will be explained later.

[20]"Misty Science," *The Economist* (Oct. 21, 2000), 38-39.

[21]Robert S. Erikson and Norman R. Luttberg, *American Public Opinion: Its Origins, Content and Import* (New York: John Wiley and Sons, 1973), 38.

[22]Everett Carl Ladd, "Pollsters Waterloo," *Wall Street Journal* (November 19, 1996)

[23]"Report Calls Networks' Election-Night Work an 'Abuse of Power,'" *Eugene Register-Guard,* (February 3, 2001), 3A.

[24]Ruy Teixeira, "With Exit Polls: President Dukakis," *The Center for American Progress and the Century Foundation,* (November 17, 2004.)

[25]Dick Meyer, "The Myth Behind the Moral Values Vote," *The Washington Post,* (December 12, 2004.)

[26]Richard Morin, "Surveying the Damage," *The Washington Post,* (November 21, 2004)

[27]Frank L. Luntz, "Focus Group Research in American Politics," *The Polling Report,* (May 16 and May 30, 1994.)

[28]Will Lester, "Poll Shows 9/11 Effect Has Faded," *Eugene Register-Guard* (March 23, 2002), 7A.

[29]Robert Nisbet, "Popular Opinion versus Public Opinion," *Public Interest* (1975), 167.

[30]Glen Bolger and Bill McInturff, "Push Polling Stinks," *Campaigns & Elections* (August 1996) , p70

Suggested Readings

Asher, Herbert. *Polling and the Public*. Washington, D.C.: Congressional Quarterly Press, 1988.

Cantril, Albert H. and Susan Davis Cantril. *Ambivalence in American Public Opinion About Government*. Woodrow Wilson Center Press, 1999.

Dawson, Kenneth Prewitt and Karen Dawson. *Political Socialization*. 2d ed. Boston: Little Brown & Co., 1977.

Elder, Charles D. and Roger W. Cobb. *The Political Uses of Symbols*. New York: St. Martin's Press, 1983.

Frank, Thomas, *What's the Matter with Kansas: How Conservatives Won the Heart of America,* New York.: Henry Holt & Co., 2004

Jennings Kent M. and Richard G. Niemi. *The Political Character of Adolescence: The Influences of Families and Schools*. Princeton: Princeton University Press, 1974.

_____. *Generations and Politics: A Panel Study of Young Adults and Their Parents*. Princeton: Princeton University Press, 1981.

Lakoff, George. *Moral Politics: How Liberals and Conservatives Think*. Chicago: University of Chicago Press, 2002.

Lipset, Seymour and William Schneider, *The Confidence Gap: Business, Labor, and Government in the Public Mind*. New York: The Free Press, 1983.

MacManus, Susan A. *Young v. Old: Generational Combat in the 21st Century*. Boulder, Colo: Westview Press, 1996.

Page, Benjamin I and Robert Shapiro. *The Rational Public: Fifty Years of Trends in America's Policy Preferences*. Chicago: University of Chicago Press, 1992.

Schafer, Bryon E. and William J. M. Claggett. *The Two Majorities: The Issue Context of Modern American Politics*. Baltimore: Johns Hopkins University Press, 1995.

Stimson, James A. *Public Opinion in America*. Boulder, Co.: Westview Press, 1991.

Zaller, John. *The Nature and Origins of Mass Opinions*. New York: The University Press, 1993.

Chapter Eight

VOTER BEHAVIOR:
The Politics of Choice

As we have seen in the chapter on public opinion, there is cause for concern that public policy and public opinion do not often match. According to the traditional view of the significance of public opinion, people are supposed to elect officials who will be responsive to their desires—their public opinions. The problem then becomes how to get people to go to the polls and vote on election day. This chapter will deal with the qualifications for voting, who cannot vote and why, and the reasons people don't vote, as well as the reasons they do vote.

QUALIFICATIONS FOR VOTING

Citizenship

To be eligible to vote in the United States, a person must be a citizen. It does not matter whether the person was born in this country or became a citizen later in life. But he/she must be a citizen. Strange as it may seem, not all countries require that voters be citizens, and at one time in this country non-citizens (aliens) were allowed to vote in some states. Some countries still do allow persons who merely live in the country to vote. However, in all states in the United States citizenship is now a "must."

Registration

Until the late nineteenth century, citizens who wanted to vote and who met other voting requirements just showed up at the polls on election day and voted. However, many people, especially in large urban areas, were paid to vote at a number of polling places or were paid to vote using a dead person's name; then they would vote under their own names later in the day. Most states responded to this voter fraud by passing laws in the late 1800s that required potential voters to register before they voted. This registration presumably helped to eliminate the kinds of cheating just described.

Every state except North Dakota requires that individuals register before voting. Most states also use **permanent registration**, which means that, once people are registered, they remain on the list of eligible voters until they move or die. Some states, however, require **periodic registration** whereby everyone must register every ten years. To register everyone again—**purging**—is an expensive and time-consuming process. Recently one county in Texas was ordered to purge its voter registration list because there were over 6000 dead people still registered to vote in that county! With that many deceased people still on the books, "**voting the graveyard**" could take on a whole new meaning.

Residency

The residency requirement for voting means that the voters actually have to live in the state and locality in which they wish to vote. Such a requirement was also a result of fraud, at least in part. Crooked political bosses would get people to come from outside the voting district on election day to vote for a particular candidate. Residency requirements are also intended to insure that people who vote in local elections are familiar with the issues in that area before they vote.

In the recent past, state residency requirements varied greatly in length from two years in Mississippi to two months in West Virginia. However, the Civil Rights Act of 1970 requires a residency period of no more than 30 days for presidential elections. In 1972, the Supreme Court also declared lengthy residency requirements for state and local elections to be unconstitutional and seemed to suggest 30 days as a maximum.[1] Of those states that do require voter registration, slightly more than half do not demand any residency except that individuals be a resident on the day they register to vote. The remaining states require a residency before registration. This residency obligation varies from state to state, the least being 20 days and the most 30.

Age

Besides citizenship, registration, and residency requirements, a person must be at least 18 years of age to vote in the United States. Until the passage of the

Twenty-sixth Amendment to the Constitution in 1971, age requirements varied from 18 to 21, with most states at 21. However, probably as a result of the Vietnam War, the Twenty-sixth Amendment lowered the voting age in all elections to 18. The reasoning was that, if a person was old enough to be drafted and possibly fight in a war at 18, then he should be old enough to vote. That rationale might be used for males, but females were never drafted; therefore, one must conclude that the age of 18 was still an arbitrary one. Strangely enough, many 18-year-olds do not vote.

WHO CANNOT VOTE

It is obvious from our discussion of the qualifications for voting that those people who are not registered to vote cannot vote; those who have not met the residency requirements, who are not citizens, and who are not at least 18 years of age are not eligible. Most states also exclude persons who have been declared mentally incompetent, prison inmates, convicted felons, and those convicted of election-law violations such as voter fraud. Furthermore, United States citizens who are living outside this country (except military personnel) are excluded unless they go through the sometimes cumbersome process of obtaining an absentee ballot that some states don't even have. There are an estimated 4 to 5 million United States citizens living in foreign countries.[2] The votes of absentee ballots have been known to change the outcome of elections, sometimes illegally, as has been noted in a number of elections over the years in the United States. In other words, absentee ballots have the potential for good or evil.

NONVOTING

On the basis of the qualifications for voting in the United States, the vast majority of Americans aged 18 or over should vote. However, even in presidential elections where the most people vote in this country, only a little more than half of those who were qualified by age actually voted between 1924 and 2004. Voter turnout is highest in the United States during a presidential election. However, since 1912, voter turnout in presidential election years has ranged between 49 percent and 63 percent. It has been much lower in "off-year" (nonpresidential-election year) congressional elections: between 30 percent and 50 percent, and in strictly local elections the turnout has been as low as between 10 percent and 20 percent. Table 8.1 shows where the United States ranks in terms of voter turnout as compared to some other industrialized countries. Not only is present-day turnout in the United States lower than that of most other democracies, it is also much lower than it was in nineteenth-century America. If so many people have died in wars over the last two hundred years to establish or maintain democracies such as the United States, why don't most Americans over the age of 18 vote? The reasons are quite numerous, but basically they fall into two categories: (1) legal reasons and (2) lack of party competition and organization that lead to voter apathy.

Legal Reasons

Noncompulsory Voting Laws. In the first place, in the United States people are not required to vote. Countries such as Costa Rica, Australia, Belgium, Chile, Greece, Italy, and Venezuela impose penalties on citizens who fail to vote. Consequently, voter turnout there is much higher than in the United States where there is no legal penalty for not voting. Costa Rica, for example, increased its voter turnout by about 15 percent when compulsory voting laws were enacted, and voter turnout in the Netherlands decreased about 10 percent when compulsory voting laws were removed.[3]

Registration. As we have seen, in most states people who wish to vote must register in the state and in the locality in which they live. On the surface this requirement may seem quite simple. However, consistently in the United States eligible citizens have failed to register to vote in part because registration involved enough "hassle" in some states that a number of potential voters did not think it was worth the trouble. Voter registration difficulties are exclusive to the United States since many countries automatically register all of their citizens to vote. With the intention of increasing voter registration Congress passed the National Voter Registration Act. This law requires that states allow persons

Table 8.1 Comparison of Voter Turnout in Selected Democracies

Country	Year of Last Election	Voter Turnout
Australia	2001	95%
Belgium	2003	92%
Denmark	2001	89%
Chile	2001	86%
Austria	2002	84%
Italy	2001	81%
France	2002	80%
Germany	2002	79%
Russia	2004	64%
Mexico	2000	64%
Canada	2000	63%
Israel	2001	62%
Japan	2000	62%
Great Britain	2001	59%
United States	2004	55%
Switzerland	1999	43%

Source: Recent issues of *Electoral Studies* contain various election reports in which data such as these can be found. On-line election data can be found at the web site *Elections Around the World* (www.electionworld.org).

to register to vote in a number of locations including, but not limited to, driver licensing bureaus and offices that provide welfare assistance and aid to the disabled. But probably the biggest benefit to voter registration is that the law requires states also to register people by mail when they renew their driving license. In addition, no one can be removed from voter registration lists for not voting, as had been the case in many states previously.

Number of Elections. Another factor that affects voter turnout is the number of elections in one year. Unlike European countries where at most there is usually one election per year, in the United States there may be any number of elections per year. Depending on the state, there may be elections for national offices, those for state offices, presidential primary elections, state primary elections, state runoff elections, municipal elections, school board elections, and possibly separate elections for tax matters or recalls of state officials. It has been consistently true that, when state elections for governor and similar offices are not held at the same time as the presidential elections, turnout for those state elections is always lower—usually below the 50-percent mark. Similarly, since elections for the House of Representatives are held every two years, when they fall in an "off-year," voter turnout is also low.

Absentee Ballots. Some states do not provide for casting an absentee ballot if a potential voter will be out of his/her voting district at the time of the election. Many of the states that do have absentee ballots create a difficult process for obtaining such a ballot. Therefore, in either case, the lack of provision for absentee balloting or the difficulty in obtaining one will affect voter turnout.

Nevertheless, the trend here is also for easing the process for obtaining the use of an absentee ballot. Oklahoma and Iowa recently joined Texas and California allowing anyone, otherwise eligible to vote, to vote by absentee ballot simply by requesting one. Furthermore, very few states still require that absentee ballot signatures be notarized.

Meanwhile, as those voting by absentee ballots increased, so did prosecutions for voter fraud involving such ballots. Federal authorities warned states to be alert to unusual patterns of absentee ballot requests, many absentee ballots sent to single addresses, and high percentages of absentee ballots coming from small areas.[4]

Reasons Based on Party Organization and Competition

As we have seen in the chapter on political parties, American parties are generally not very well organized, and what little organization there is, is quite loosely connected from the local on up to the national level. The nature of our two major political parties results from many factors, some of which are legal factors, as we have seen. The parties must appeal to the largest number of voters as possible while alienating ("turning off") as few as possible. Consequently, the two major parties in the United States tend to appeal to the middle class and to middle-class ways of thinking. Such a situation makes it difficult for the parties to get the lower classes interested in voting because there is no incentive nor is there much organization with which to do it. And it is among the lower classes that a large percentage of nonvoting takes place. Income and educational level are the two most important factors affecting voter turnout. In recent elections, voter turnout among people with college degrees was over 80 percent while turnout among those with less than a high school education was about 35 percent.[5] The less money and education a person has, the less likely he/she is to vote.

You may remember the quote in the chapter on political parties from former Alabama Governor George Wallace in referring to the two major parties in the United States: "There's not a dime's worth of difference between the two of them." This statement accurately reflects an attitude shared by a significant number of Americans who do not vote for that reason. Rightly or wrongly, they think that it does not really matter who wins an election. Things will remain pretty much the same. So they don't make the effort to vote. We call this condition **voter apathy**, and it is a major contributor to the phenomenon of nonvoting. Whatever else can be said about why people do *not* vote, there is one factor political scientists are very certain of: the more education a person has, the more likely he/she is to vote. Formal education is the most powerful predictor of voter turnout.[6]

DETERMINANTS OF VOTER CHOICE

It would seem that every candidate for political office would like to know why voters vote the way they do—what causes a voter to choose one candidate over another. Rationally speaking, it would also seem that the voters look at the issues in the election, decide what they think about them, then choose candidates who think as they do. But this does not appear to be entirely the case. Rather, the candidates' party affiliation, his/her particular characteristics (voter appeal), evaluations of the candidates' ability to handle the "job," and ideology (perhaps) apparently play a larger role than do issues in most cases.

It is interesting that people are likely to think that the candidates they intend to vote for think as they do on the issues that are important to them. To illustrate the point, let's look at the case of Joe Blow. Joe works in the auto industry where competition from foreign imports is threatening his job. He would like to see import quotas and import taxes on all foreign cars so that they would be more costly and, thus, make the American car more appealing to the buyers. Joe likes Esmerelda Tweedy, who is running for President of the United States, and he intends to vote for her. He is quite likely to think that Tweedy agrees with him although she may never have voiced an opinion on the matter or may even have stated something to the contrary. Or she may have said, as many politicians do, "We have to do something to protect the American worker."

Not everyone favored a national amendment allowing women to vote. Here "woman suffrage" is opposed by an organization claiming that giving the women the right to vote will undermine man's natural authority and destroy traditional home values.

Joe then just assumes that Tweedy would do what he wants done. It's the old saying that we believe what we want to believe, not necessarily what is true.

Candidates

The candidates themselves may be a factor in why people vote the way they do. Research indicates that a candidate's *image* with the voters plays a major role in voters' decisions to vote for the candidate.[7] The three most important features of candidate image are integrity, reliability, and competence.[8]

As stated earlier, voters may also evaluate a candidate and decide whom they like based on their idea of the candidate's past or future (projected) performance. Let's look at the 1980 presidential election to see how this works. The two candidates were Democrat Jimmy Carter, seeking re-election for a second term, and Republican Ronald Reagan, who at that time was a former governor of California. According to a 1981 study, Reagan's win was based more on the voters' negative evaluation of Carter's past performance as president rather than on the promises Reagan made about what he would do if he were elected.[9] In other words, Reagan won in part because voters were dissatisfied with what Carter had *already* done rather than because they liked or necessarily believed what Reagan said he *would* do.

Similarly, former President H. W. Bush's image of reliability was seemingly more damaged with the voters when he broke his pledge of "no new taxes" than President Clinton's image of integrity was concerning all the scandals surrounding him, his spouse, and members of his administration. Keep in mind that it is often a combination of image factors (reliability, integrity, and competence) that produces a vote for a candidate. For example, President Carter was apparently always viewed by the voters as honest, but the voters were just as adamant in their characterization of him as incompetent. Competence is the most significant of the three characteristics in determining voter choice based on personal characteristics.

Party Affiliation

Voters may decide how to vote based on the party affiliation of the particular candidate. In the past this was more important than it seems to be today. The day when a voter was a "Democrat" or a "Republican" and would vote accordingly, regardless of whether the party candidate were Porky Pig or the devil himself, is gone. As we have seen in a previous chapter, the fastest growing block of voters is the independent voter. Still, people may consider party when voting because they believe one of the political parties to be better equipped to handle governing than any other party at that particular time. At another point in time, they may choose to vote for another party's candidate. Yet, there are people who vote for a particular political party's candidates because they have a deep attachment to that party. This attachment, although openly denied, can still be seen in the data that show "independents" consistently vote for one party or the other. In other words, they really aren't independent at all.

Ideology

Closely related to party affiliation as a factor in voter behavior is ideology. You will perhaps remember (If you don't, here it is again!) that ideology is the view of how things really are and how a person would like things to be. (Whether he/she is right or wrong is unimportant.) Previously we used the example of a person wearing rose-colored glasses looking at a room full of people. He says, "Ah! These are rose-colored people." Another person comes into the same room wearing green-colored glasses, looks at the same people and says, "Ah! These are green-colored people." They are both looking at the same people, but they are seeing different colors because of the glasses they are wearing. Ideology merely "colors" what we see and hear regardless of what the situation really is. Ideology then can "color" voter behavior. If a voter has a conservative ideology, and if he/she thinks that Republican candidates are more conservative than Democratic candidates, then that voter is more likely to vote for Republicans.

Issues

In the 1940s and '50s, studies that dealt with whether voters considered the issues tended to show that they really didn't. These studies concluded that voters voted the way they did because of party identification and the candidates' perceived appeal and competency more than they did because of the issues. However, later studies, using more complicated mathematics, discovered that it was very difficult to separate issue voting from candidate voting from party voting, etc. It seems that they are all tied up together and affecting one another. However, most studies do agree that the candidates' voter appeal, how competent they seem to be, and what party they belong to tend to have more of an effect on voting than do the issues and the candidates' stands on them—if they have any. That last item—if they have any stands—may be the key to why issues do not affect voting behavior as much as they would seem to. Again we must remember that candidates for office are trying to appeal to as many voters as possible while alienating as few as possible to win the election. So it would be foolish for a candidate to take a clear-cut stand on a controversial issue if he/she could avoid it. The result of this situation is the well-known "political double talk." When asked a direct question on a controversial issue, the candidate is likely to give a five-minute answer. When he/she finally comes to a period, so to speak, we are not at all certain which position the candidate has taken, but it all sounded so good. In recent years, it has become increasingly difficult for candidates for major offices to avoid taking stands on highly volatile issues such as abortion. However, in the early stages of the 2000 presidential election year, Republican presidential hopefuls George Bush, Jr., and Elizabeth Dole both managed a masterful stroke by stating they were against most abortions but felt that the American public was not yet ready to ban them. This position is about as middle of the road as a candidate can get!

Issues cannot play any role at all if the parties or candidates do not differ on the issues. If candidates take the same position (or no position), then we have the "echo chamber effect"—each saying or not saying the same thing.[10] When candidates or parties do not differ on the issues, then issues are unimportant as a factor in voter behavior.

However, one issue in particular seems to have more clout than others perhaps—namely economics. A study of the effect of economic conditions on voter behavior states that ". . . evidence . . . indicates rather convincingly that public support for political authorities . . . responds quite systematically to macroeconomic conditions."[11] In plain English that means people *do* vote their pocketbooks. If the economy stinks, they will usually vote out the people in office at election time and vote in another bunch. (It should be noted that the new bunch may produce an equally stinky economy.) The perception of the American public that the economy was in trouble seemed to be a decisive factor in the election of Bill Clinton, despite George H.W. Bush's strong popularity during the Gulf War in 1991. Economics is often a false issue because in many respects the economy under any given president is more a result of actions by previous administrations and the Federal Reserve Board than it is the actions of the current administration. In other words, the economy does not "go South" overnight, nor does it improve in a flash either.

One final comment about issues as a factor in voter behavior. Not all issues have the same importance to all the voters. Some issues are easier to understand than others are. Consequently, the "hard" issues will only be important perhaps to voters with a great deal of political information. Usually those voters are the ones with higher educational levels. The monetary policy of the Federal Reserve Board would be a "hard" issue.[12] Only people who kept up with what that government agency was doing and what monetary policy means to the economy would consider it in voting. (Even then they might not consider it if they knew that the Federal Reserve Board is not directly controlled by any elected official.) On the other hand, abortion might be considered an "easy" issue,[13] meaning that most anyone whom we might think of as just a "warm body" probably understands what the term means and has formulated some opinion on the matter. According to at least one study, issue voting is more likely to occur in elections where there are many "easy" issues.[14]

Although we have isolated these factors that presumably "cause" people to vote the way they do, we must emphasize that these "causes" cannot be separated as neatly as we have done here. They interact with each other, rather than operating independently of each other. In other words, any given voter may vote in a particular way because of a number of these factors. They are highly intertwined. We cannot say which one was the causal factor any more than we could determine which snowflake of the thousands that fell on someone's roof caused the roof to cave in.

VOTING PATTERNS

When political scientists began to look at voting data, they discovered that there were a number of distinct patterns. Demographic factors (population characteristics) such as religion, social class, race, nationality, sex, age, and place of residence were relatively consistent in predicting how people with these characteristics would vote. Data from a recent poll show that 28 percent of Americans identify themselves as Republicans, 38 percent as Democrats, and 34 percent as independents.[15] We also know that many of these people who identify as Democrats have been voting for Republican presidential candidates in the last 52 years. Table 8.2 shows, for example, that, although union members are more likely to identify themselves as Democrats and to vote for Democratic candidates in general, in 8 of the last 14 presidential elections at least 40 percent of the union households voted for Republican presidential candidates. Therefore, while demographic data are useful in predicting voter behavior, they should not be taken to mean that all persons who carry a particular demographic will vote for the same candidates or, for that matter, will vote at all.

Sex

One possible explanation of why more women are found in the Democratic Party than in the Republican Party comes from the field of psychology. Women generally score higher on tests of compassion (sympathy, kindness, nurturing, caring about others, etc.) than do men. Since the Democratic Party currently is identified as the more liberal of the two parties, it is logical that, if nothing else interferes, more women would vote Democratic than Republican. In other words, in the last 60 years it is the Democratic Party that has championed the causes of the "underdog." Therefore, women, generally having a higher sensitivity to the "down-and-out," tend to vote for Democratic candidates. Feminists would tend to support the Democratic Party more often than the Republican because Democrats are more likely to give at least tacit support to feminist causes. (If you are a woman reading this and you generally vote Republican, don't feel bad. There are a number of factors involved in voting patterns other than a person's sex.) This tendency to support Democrats continued in the 2000 presidential election with women preferring Democrat Al Gore by a rather consistent margin of about 7 percent. Since women now constitute more than half the voters now, the party preferences of women take on added significance in any election.

Table 8.2   Union Households Voting for Republican Presidential Candidates

Year	Candidates*	Percentage
1952	Eisenhower/Stevenson	44%
1956	Eisenhower/Stevenson	57%
1960	Kennedy/Nixon	36%
1964	Johnson/Goldwater	17%
1968	Nixon/Humphrey	44%
1972	Nixon/McGovern	57%
1976	Carter/Ford	36%
1980	Reagan/Carter	45%
1984	Reagan/Mondale	43%
1988	Bush/Dukakis	41%
1992	Clinton/Bush	32%
1996	Clinton/Dole	30%
2000	Bush/Gore	34%
2004	Bush/Kerry	40%

*Winners are listed first

Source: *CQ Researcher*, (28 June 1996): 560; *New York Times*, 10 November 1996, 16. 2000 data excerpted from VNS Exit Polls posted on the MSNBC website, November 8, 2000. CNN.com Election 2004 exit poll results, November 3, 2004.

Race, Nationality, and Religion

Also falling into the ranks of Democratic voters are some racial, ethnic, and religious minorities. From the end of the Civil War (War Between the States) up to the Great Depression of the 1930s, African Americans were staunchly loyal to the Republican Party. It was, you will remember, the Republican Party under Lincoln that freed them from slavery. However, African Americans, like many others, began to switch their allegiance in the 1930s to the Democrats because the Republicans were identified with the poor economic conditions and the Democrat Franklin D. Roosevelt was credited with turning the economy around. (The perception of the Democratic Party as the "savior" of the poor, the unemployed, etc., has stuck.) African Americans were further persuaded to vote Democratic when that party championed the cause of civil rights against its own powerful Southern Democrat members. Today an overwhelming majority of the blacks who vote, (they do have low voter turnout) vote Democratic. For example, in the 2000 and 2004 presidential election, about 90 percent of African Americans who voted cast their ballots for the Democratic candidate.[16]

Similarly, ethnic minorities, such as Hispanics and those of Eastern European and Irish descent, most of whom were Catholics, did not feel welcomed in

FDR at the Grand Coulee Dam in Washington. October 2, 1937.
Poor Americans' admiration for FDR was something so powerful that it has survived for decades after his death. FDR, with his sense of stewardship and his personal experience with suffering, genuinely wanted to help the people. This most enigmatic of men became the most influential American political leader of the twentieth century. Although he did not achieve all his goals, his accomplishments are nevertheless impressive.
Photo credit: FDR Presidential Library

the Republican camp initially. When many of these people migrated from their homelands to the United States, there was a strong bias toward native-born Americans in the Republican Party. Consequently, the Republicans did not seek to recruit these people as Republican voters by offering them any programs that would be of particular benefit to them. In addition, these Catholic, Hispanic, and Eastern European immigrants usually settled in large cities such as New York, where the Democratic Party was highly organized at the time, often "boss" oriented. Hispanics of Cuban descent, however, tend to support Republicans more than Democrats because of the Cuban Americans' identification with the stronger anticommunist positions of the Republicans.

Social and Economic Class and Occupation

Closely related to minority-status voting patterns are those of social and economic class and occupation. In the ranks of the Democratic Party are found more lower-income people than are found in the Republican Party. These people do tend to vote Democratic as do blue-collar workers. However, as we move further away from the Great Depression, voting behavior based on social and economic class decreases. Still, the Republican Party still attracts the upper social and economic level of our society, such as physicians, lawyers, and upper-income business people, as well as the more highly educated (except perhaps college professors who tend to be more liberal and, therefore, are more frequently found in the Democratic Party). These alignments again probably have a great deal to do with perceptions of the two parties. The Republicans are seen as favoring "big" business and the "rich," while the Democrats are viewed as more interested in the "little" guy. Whether these beliefs are true or not really doesn't matter for our purposes here. What counts is that over the years various groups have thought they were true.

Age

As noted earlier, the younger the voter, the more likely he/she is not to vote. Still, the Democrats can claim slightly more younger people in their ranks than the Republicans. Yet, it is interesting that in the 1984 presidential election, Reagan (the Republican) got strongest support from young voters. Democratic Party identification appears to be strongest among those aged 50 and over. Again perceptions of the Democratic Party's willingness to support Social Security and Medicare programs may be a contributing factor here.

Place of Residence

Where a person lives also affects his/her voting behavior. People who live in big cities, such as New York, Chicago, Detroit, Atlanta, or Los Angeles, generally are placed in the Democratic camp. Urban dwellers tend to vote Democratic

partly because most minorities and blue-collar workers live in large urban areas also. On the other side of the coin, people who live in small cities or rural areas tend to vote Republican. These voters do not expect as much from government since they have had to depend more on their own resources for generations unlike those who live in big cities. In other words, "small-town-U.S.A" and rural America are populated by more independent folks than are found in the cities where various social services are more frequently offered. Consequently, those who do not live in big cities see no reason perhaps to vote for candidates who wish to produce more social service programs (usually for big-city dwellers, at least in the eyes of the rural voter). That means they don't vote for Democrats as often as they do for Republicans.

When regions of the country are considered, the Midwest boasts the highest percentage voters claiming to be independent. The West now has the distinction of having almost an even split among Republicans, Democrats, and independent-identified voters. The South, while still showing a tendency toward the Democratic Party overall, has been fairly consistent in its support for Republican presidential candidates since the 1960s, although it reverts to its Democratic roots for many other candidates. For example, in 2004, 58 percent of Southern voters voted for George W. Bush, the Republican, whereas 56 percent of Northeastern voters voted for John Kerry, the Democratic candidate.[17]

It should be noted, however, that this seeming inconsistency is not so strange when one considers that Southern Democratic candidates are usually more conservative than their counterparts in other areas of the country. Even in this region, however, independent-identified voters constitute the largest bloc of voters.

The percentage of voters who identify themselves as independents has risen somewhat over the years. While it is true that more people have indicated that they are independents, this most recent jump—a bit more than usual—is probably due to the candidacy of third-party/independent candidates like Ralph Nader in recent presidential elections. However, those who predict the demise of the Democrats and Republicans because of this so-called trend toward "independence" are engaging in flights of fancy for several reasons.

*Voters tend to show an interest in independent candidates early in the election year, but they almost always return to the two dominant parties by late fall.

*In the twentieth century, only thirteen states had voted for a third-party/independent candidate even once, and none has since 1968.

*Independent or third-party candidates suffer from a "can't win" image. Voters tell pollsters that they like these candidates but in the end decide not to vote for them because the voters think the candidates cannot win against the two major party candidates.

*Raising money and getting on the ballot in all fifty states poses a significant obstacle to third-party and independent candidates.

Unless some larger-than-life candidate, who has moderate views, and who can produce the funding necessary to mount a serious campaign comes along to deliver a death blow to one of the two dominant parties, it is likely that the Democrats and Republicans will continue along their merry way.

DOES YOUR VOTE REALLY MATTER?

Many times we hear people make excuses for not doing something they know they ought to have done—voting as well as other things. A candidate running for re-election for his seat on the Massachusetts Governor's Council continued to campaign till the last minute. When he arrived at his voting precinct, it was a few minutes after 8:00 p.m. The polls had closed, and he did not get to vote for himself. When the ballots were counted, he lost by one vote! On certain issues such as raising local or state taxes, those who are against such a move usually turn out in larger numbers than those who support it or are indifferent to it. Therefore, many times the true will of the people is thwarted merely because sufficient numbers of people who support something (or are against it) did not go to the polls. In effect, democracy in the United States certainly does not refer to majority rule! This country rarely has a majority of its eligible or even its registered voters going to the polls as we have seen. Those who point to the 2000 presidential election where it was often difficult to decide if the votes being counted were even valid cannot discount the importance of voting. Who knows what the outcome of that election would have been had the other 49 percent of eligible voters actually voted? The election may not have been close at all.

How important is your vote? This last little story is not about voting, but it does illustrate the point about getting involved in the political arena. Perhaps if the German people had paid more attention to their elections, the whole Nazi era might never have happened. A noted German Lutheran pastor, who lived in Germany during the Nazi regime, later made this statement about political involvement.

In Germany they came first for the communists, and I did not speak up because I wasn't a communist. Then they came for the Jews, and I did not speak up because I wasn't a Jew. Then they came for the trade unionists, and I did not speak up because I wasn't a trade unionist. Then they came for the Catholics, and I didn't speak because I was a Protestant. Then they came for me, and by that time no one was left to speak up.[18]

Think about it.

Chapter Eight Notes

[1]*Dunn v. Blumstein*, 405 U.S. 330.

[2]*New York Times*, 4 January 1984.

[3]Steven J. Rosenstone and Raymond E. Wolfinger, "The Effect of Registration Laws on Voter Turnout," in *Controversies in Voting Behavior,* 2d ed., eds. Richard G. Niemi and Herbert F. Weisberg (Washington, D.C.: CQ Press, 1984), 35.

[4]*The Book of States* (Lexington, Ky.: The Council of State Governments, 1992), 261.

[5]Bureau of the Census, *Statistical Abstract of the United States*, 116th ed. (Washington, D.C.: Government Printing Office, 1996), 285-287.

[6]Raymond Wolfinger and Stephen Rosenstone, *Who Votes?* (New Haven, Conn.: Yale University Press, 1980).

[7]Shawn W. Rosenberg with Patrick McCafferty, "Image and Voter Preference," *Public Opinion Quarterly* 51 (Spring 1987): 44.

[8]Arthur H. Miller, Martin P. Wattenberg, and Oksana Malunchuk, "Schematic Assessments of Presidential Candidates," *American Political Science Review* 80 (1986): 521-540.

[9]Arthur H. Miller and Martin P. Wattenberg, "Policy and Performance Voting in the 1980 Election." Paper presented at the 1981 Annual Meeting of the American Political Science Association, New York, New York.

[10]V. O. Key, Jr., and Milton C. Cummings, Jr., *The Responsible Electorate: Rationality in Presidential Voting 1936-1960* (Cambridge: Harvard University Press, 1966).

[11]Douglas A. Hibbs, Jr., and Heino Fassbender, eds. *Contemporary Political Economy* (Amsterdam: North Holland, 1981), 8.

[12]Edward G. Carmines and James A. Stimson, *American Political Science Review,* 74 (1980): 78-91.

[13]Carmines and Stimson, 78-91.

[14]Carmines and Stimson, 78-91.

[15]Data compiled from *American National Election Studies*, Center for Political Studies, The University of Michigan.

[16]Excerpted from VNS Exit Polls posted on the MSNBC website, November 8, 2000.

[17]CNN.com Election 2004 exit poll results, November 3, 2004.

[18]Statement attributed to Pastor Martin Niemoeller, 1892-1984.

Suggested Readings

Conway, M. Margaret. *Political Participation in the United States*, 2d ed. Washington, D.C.: CQ Press, 1990.

Key, V.O. Jr., and Milton C. Cummings. *The Responsible Electorate: Rationality in Presidential Voting 1936-1960*. Cambridge: Harvard University Press, 1966.

Patterson, Thomas and Robert McClure. *The Unseeing Eye: The Myth of Television Power in National Politics*. New York: G.P. Putnam's Sons, 1976.

Pivan, Francis, and Richard Cloward. *Why Americans Don't Vote*. New York: Pantheon, 1998.

Pivan, Francis, and Richard Cloward. *Why Americans Still Don't Vote: And Why Politicians Want It That Way*. Boston: Beacon Press, 2000.

Teixeira, Ruy. *The Disappearing American Voter. Washington*, D.C.: Brookings Institution, 1992.

Verba, Sidney, Kay Lehman Schlozman, and Henry Brady. *Voice and Equality: Voluntarism in American Politics*. Cambridge: Harvard University Press. 1995.

Chapter Nine

Campaigns and Elections:
Winning Ain't Everything But it Beats What's in Second Place

The mayor was making an important speech and he was becoming irritated by the unkempt man in the front row of the audience who would not stop heckling him. Finally, losing patience, the mayor turned to the man and said, "Will the gentleman who disagrees with me please tell the audience what he has ever done for the betterment of the city?" In a flash, the man replied, "Well, I voted against you."[1] The man may have been a bit rude, but his comment serves to remind us that campaigns and elections are a vital aspect of the democratic process. Here the politicians, who usually make the rules for everybody else, must (for once) submit to the judgement of the people they govern. Candidates for office use campaigns to promote themselves and attack their opponents, and on election day the people have the final say. In a healthy democracy, the public will be presented with a variety of real choices on the ballot, no person will be unfairly denied the right to vote, the votes will be counted honestly, and the side with the largest number of votes will win. Unfortunately, recent campaigns and elections in the United States have led some to doubt the health of our democracy—doubts which the 2004 presidential election did not entirely resolve.

The decade of the 1990s saw a drastic rise in campaign spending, as the political parties used legal loopholes to get around federal limits on contributions. Critics charged that public debate was increasingly becoming dominated by multi-millionaires and their friends. The U.S. electoral system was cast in a

183

very unflattering light when confusing ballots and faulty vote-counting procedures in Florida had kept the result of the 2000 presidential race in doubt for
over a month. Moreover, the ultimate winner—true to what is actually written
in the Constitution—became president even though he lost the nationwide
popular vote. Campaign spending set new records in the 2000 election, as
candidates and interest groups flooded the airwaves with attack ads. Influenced
by these events, and by fallout from the Enron financial scandal, Congress in
2002 passed laws to improve voting procedures and to limit campaign spending in the United States.

These well-meant efforts achieved—at best—mixed success in the 2004
election. The attempt to control expenditures failed completely. Spending on
the presidential race ballooned to two and one-half times the level of just four
years previously, as each of the two major presidential campaigns spent over one
billion (yes, billion) dollars on behalf of their candidate. Many states did up-
grade voting and vote-counting procedures, as a result of the federal Help America
Vote Act. Yet serious problems remain. There is no doubt that President George
W. Bush won re-election, defeating Senator John Kerry (D-MA) by a narrow
margin of 51 to 48 percent in the popular vote and by 286 to 252 in the electoral college. But charges that Bush's vote may have been electronically padded
in certain key states proved impossible to check or refute due to the lack of a
"paper trail" in electronic voting machines. Enough irregularities occurred in
various states to suggest that the United States still has a way to go before we
can have total confidence in our election process.

In this chapter we shall investigate how elections are conducted in the United
States, what governmental positions are elected, the methods of campaigning
for office, and the various current problems and efforts for reform that have
recently gained attention.

HOW ELECTIONS ARE CONDUCTED

You will recall that the United States operates under a federal system of government in which powers are divided between the national government in Washington D. C. and the state governments. Under this system the power to conduct elections—even presidential and congressional elections—is reserved to
the states. Most of the laws regulating aspects of the electoral process, such as
voter registration, polling places, ballot access, voting machines, petitions, and
so forth, are state laws, not national laws. The costs of elections are also borne
by the states. Procedures vary significantly from state to state. Some states are
more efficient than others; none are perfect. In addition, most states delegate
the job of actually running the elections to local officials, so the process can
vary from county to county within a state. This is not always a problem. Local
election officials often do an outstanding job under very trying circumstances.
However, local officials can also be corrupt or incompetent. The words of

former Soviet dictator Joseph Stalin can sometimes be true even in the United States: "The people who cast the votes decide nothing; the people who count the votes decide everything."[2]

How America Votes

Voting Technology. The United States uses five methods of voting. At the time of the 2000 election, punch cards were the most common method of voting in the United States. Unfortunately punch cards have a big disadvantage: the little cardboard squares, known as "chads," do not always drop off when they should. The may "hang," and if they do, the vote may not be counted. The ballot-counting difficulties in Florida in the 2000 presidential election stemmed partly from that state's use of punch-card voting. Democrats and Republicans engaged in prolonged squabbling over whether various chads were hanging or not. Other localities use optical scanning, where voters must fill in little ovals on the ballot. This technology also has problems. If a voter mistakenly marks an "X" or does not fill in the entire oval, the vote is not counted. Voting machines have been primarily used in East Coast states and Louisiana. These devices break down and can lend themselves to voter fraud. Votes might already be in the machine, for example, when the polls open. Paper ballots, an old-fashioned solution, are used by few Americans, mostly in rural areas. Paper ballots are very easy to deal with when there are few people in the voting precinct. However, to revert back to paper ballots in urban areas would be impractical today.[3]

In the aftermath of the 2000 presidential election, after considerable debate, Congress passed the Help America Vote Act (HAVA). The bill provided $3.5 billion over five years to the states to replace punch-card voting machines and for additional reforms in the voting process. Many states have switched to

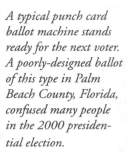

A typical punch card ballot machine stands ready for the next voter. A poorly-designed ballot of this type in Palm Beach County, Florida, confused many people in the 2000 presidential election.

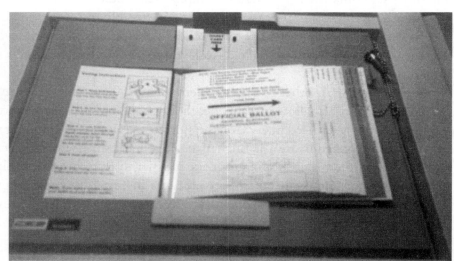

electronic "touch screen" voting systems that can eliminate the kinds of problems associated with mechanical devices or bits of cardboard. Indeed, electronic voting is probably the wave of the future, although it comes with a problem of its own—the possibility that a "hacker" might break into the system and cause it to report false vote totals. No electronic system is totally secure.

Unfortunately, experience with touch-screen voting in the 2004 election did little to relieve any concerns. Voters in several Florida counties reported that when they tried to select Democratic presidential candidate John Kerry, George W. Bush appeared on the screen, and voters in Youngstown, Ohio related similar happenings. An Associated Press story reported about a thousand such incidents around the country.[4] These could be chance occurrences, but electronic cheating is almost impossible to detect (or to disprove). A UC Berkeley study found that Florida counties using electronic machines awarded Bush between 130,000 and 260,000 "excessive" votes.[5] Other researchers have reached different conclusions—and Bush won Florida by 350,000 votes in any case—but enough doubts have lingered from the 2004 election to worry many people. Conspiracy theorists have observed that Diebold Inc., a company that makes many of the touch-screen systems used in the United States, is owned by one of President Bush's prominent supporters.[6] These suspicions may be unwarranted, but it is obviously not good to leave room for any kind of reasonable doubt about the fairness of our voting process.

These concerns have led to calls for all electronic voting machines to produce an actual paper record, verified by the voter, which can be kept by election officials and, if necessary, counted to confirm the electronic total. Bills to require such paper trails have been introduced into Congress—one co-sponsored by Senators John Kerry and Hillary Clinton (D-NY), two possible candidates for the presidency in 2008. Many state-level officials have made similar proposals in their respective states. Nevada used paper-verified voting in 2004, and other states may follow Nevada's example.[7] This could increase the public's confidence in our voting process, by making it possible to refute the kind of suspicions that arose after the last two presidential elections. Perhaps, eventually, the United States will have a high-tech voting procedure that actually satisfies everyone.

Ballot Design. Another Florida problem in the 2000 presidential race concerned the design of ballots in Palm Beach County—the so-called "butterfly ballot"—that may have led many Gore supporters to mistakenly cast their votes for Reform Party candidate Pat Buchanan. The local supervisor of elections had redesigned the ballot, hoping to make it easier to read, but the result was mass confusion. Although no sinister plot was involved, this incident does show how a "small" mistake by one official can have huge consequences. In 2004, a poorly designed electronic ballot in Burke County, North Carolina, may have caused over 10 percent of the voters in that county to cast no vote for president at all![8]   In fact, politicians have known for years that even the arrangement of names on the ballot can make a big difference in the outcome of the election.[9]

Many people reportedly were denied the right to vote in the 2000 election, due to inaccurate voter lists. The Help America Vote Act therefore required the states to allow the use of **provisional ballots** by voters. These are ballots cast by individuals who claim to be properly registered, but whose names do not appear on the official list at the polling place. Provisional ballots are sealed and kept separate and are only counted if the person in question indeed proves to be a legitimate voter. Each state was permitted to decide for itself the procedures used to handle provisional ballots, and some states imposed requirements that critics found excessive. This issue may well be a subject of contention in future elections.[10]

Types of Elections

Elections in the United States are either **primary elections** or **general elections**. Primary elections are those in which political party members choose their nominees for various offices. Any number of persons may wish to be a party's candidate for governor, state legislator, mayor, or some other position. The voters decide who these nominees will be by voting in that party's primary election, which is held several weeks or months before the general election. In the general election, voters decide who will actually hold the office from among those nominated by the parties. While a primary may feature a large number of candidates for each office, in the general election the field has usually been cut substantially since each party now has only one candidate per office. However, **independent candidates**, those not belonging to a political party, may also be on the ballot.

Types of Primaries. Types of party primaries vary from state to state In states that use **closed primaries** only registered party members can vote in a particular party's primary. Some of the most populous states have closed primaries, for example, New York, Florida, and Pennsylvania. A **semi-closed system**, in which registered independents may vote in any party's primary, is found in Oregon, New Jersey, California, and Massachusetts. The **open primary** is used in most southern states, as well as in Ohio, Wisconsin, Michigan, and other states in the upper Midwest. Here voters are not obligated to indicate their party preference. On primary-election day, voters have access to the ballots for all parties, and they decide at that time in the voting booth which party's primary they wish to participate in. In other words, the decision is made when people vote on election day and not when they register.

Louisiana uses a **blanket primary**.[11] In that state, voters can choose, for each elective office, any candidate from any political party in the primary election. If one candidate wins a majority of votes cast for a particular office, that candidate is declared the winner, and no run-off election is required. However, if no candidate wins a majority, the top two vote-getters, regardless of party affiliation, move on to the general election. (They could actually be from the same party.) In this blanket primary, voters can "mix and match," choosing to vote for candidates from more than one party. The only restriction is that they may not vote for candidates from more than one party for the same elective office. For example, voters who vote for a Democrat for U.S. senator may not also vote for a Republican for the same office.

With a choice of either open or closed primaries, most voters prefer the open primary since it gives them more choices on election day. Political parties, however, generally favor the closed primary because it prohibits **crossover voting or raiding.** This occurs when voters of one party vote in the primary of another party. Party leaders fear that such voters may purposely support a weak candidate of the other party to help their own side win the general election. It is rare, but it has happened.

There is one further type of primary that is often used in elections for local offices: the **nonpartisan primary.** In this case, political parties do not nominate candidates at all. All candidates for a given office run as individuals; they are listed together on the ballot with no mention of party affiliation. If a candidate receives a majority of the votes cast in the primary, he or she is elected with no need for a run-off. If no candidate receives a majority in the primary, the top two vote-getters, regardless of party affiliation, will compete in the general election that follows.

Initiatives, Referendums and Recalls. Voters use these to force the state or local governments to do something the voters want done or to punish politicians who have done something the voters do not like. Let's deal with them one at a time.

The **initiative** allows voters to sign a petition stating that they would like to have a certain legislative proposal put before the voters at the next election. For example, suppose a number of people in Michigan wanted to see the death penalty for murder included in that state's law. If these people could gather enough signatures of registered voters on their petition—the number required varies from state to state—then the state would be forced to put the question to the Michigan voters to see if they wanted such a law. If the majority of voters said "yes" to the proposal, then the death penalty would become law in Michigan. In other words, the initiative allows voters to make laws directly, thereby bypassing the state legislature that doesn't always see "eye to eye" with the voters. Although about half the states permit initiatives, this procedure is particularly popular in California, Oregon, Washington, North Dakota, Arizona, and Colorado. Some states require that the legislature approve a proposal before it is placed on the ballot.

Initiative proposals cover a wide variety of topics from taxation to environmental issues. In recent years, the voters of Missouri voted to legalize slot machines on river boats; Oregon approved a measure allowing doctor-assisted suicide, and a dozen states have voted to permit the use of marijuana for medical purposes. Voters in many states have used initiatives to impose term limits on their politicians—since, strangely enough, politicians are usually reluctant to impose term limits on themselves!

While the initiative allows voters to do things that politicians do not want to do, a **referendum** is an election that allows the voters to show their approval or disapproval of something their state or local politicians have already done or are about to do. In effect, the referendum is what we might call a "voters' veto." Just as the President of the United States can accept or reject bills passed by Congress, voters in a referendum can accept or reject measures taken by their state and local governments. The main difference between the initiative and the referendum is the source of each. The initiative comes from the voters, through a petition, to the voters on a ballot. The referendum, on the other hand, comes from a state or local legislative body to the voters in an election. As with the initiative, a referendum also requires a petition for a referendum to be held. Every year thousands of referendums are held on such matters as school bonds, taxes, the fluoridation of water, restrictions on nuclear power plant construction, and banning pornography. Most states require a referendum before an amendment is added to the state constitution, and Arizona, Colorado, Oklahoma, and Washington require a referendum before taxes can be raised.

Supporters of the initiative and the referendum call these procedures "direct democracy" and maintain that, "the more distant the legislators are from the people. . . the more likely there will be an environment in which initiatives are successful." Opponents observe, however, that wealthy special interest groups are best able to get items on the ballot and to fund a campaign to reach the public. In the 1998 election, supporters of Proposition 5, a California initiative legalizing casino-style gambling on Indian reservations, spent about $70 million to pass their measure. It won easily, since the opposition raised only $28 million.[12]

Unlike a regular election in which the voters decide whom to put in office, the **recall** allows them to throw someone out of office before his/her term has expired. As with the initiative and the referendum, recalls require that signatures of registered voters be gathered on a petition. If the required number of signatures is obtained, then the question is put to the voters whether to remove or retain the official. These recalls are usually begun when a significant number of voters are upset over public policy decisions made by the official in question. It is not required that the official do anything illegal—merely that a large enough number of voters do not *like* what he/she has done. A San Francisco politician was once recalled for attempting to ban call girls from that city's Barbary Coast district.[13]

Perhaps the most spectacular recall election in American history took place in California in 2003. Angered by a vehicle registration fee increase, and unhappy with "politics as usual" in their state government, the voters recalled unpopular Governor Gray Davis by a margin of 55 to 45 percent. Davis thus became only the second governor of any state to be recalled—the other case occurring in North Dakota in 1921. The race to succeed Davis became a Hollywood extravaganza when 135 candidates qualified for the ballot, including several actors of varying talents—one of whom, the "Terminator," Arnold Schwarzenegger, actually won the election. A political scientist has grumbled that the Davis recall was "like a zoo with the cages of the untrained animals pushed wide open"—a "manifestation of mob-ocracy."[14] Yet the fact is that more voters turned out for the special election to recall Davis than had turned out the previous year for the regular state election in which he was (temporarily) re-elected.

Types of Ballots

Whether you use voting machine, a computer punch card, or a paper ballot to cast your vote, all ballots have certain forms to follow.

There are two types of ballots used in general elections. **The Party-Column Ballot** (or Indiana Ballot), which encourages voting for candidates from one party, lists candidates in columns, with the party name and state party symbol at the top of the column. The list begins with the highest office at stake in the election and proceeds down to the lowest offices. Usually there is a place at the top of the column to make a mark or, on a voting machine, to pull one lever, and, in so doing, vote for all party candidates in that column. Voting for all the candidates of one party is called **straight-ticket voting.**

The office-group ballot (also called the Massachusetts Ballot) lists all the candidates under the major heading of the office they are seeking. In states using this ballot, voters who wish to vote a straight ticket must usually go through each office group to find their party's candidates. Office-group ballots were designed to encourage **split-ticket voting**—"mixing and matching" one's choices with some Democrats, some Republicans, and, if possible, an occasional independent, as well.

Federal law requires that ballots be printed in languages other than English if there is a significant language minority in the voting district. The most common language requiring such ballots is Spanish.

Arrangement of Names

There are generally two ways that states arrange names on the ballots: alphabetically or randomly. On the surface this alphabetical listing of candidates may seem unimportant. However, studies have shown that candidates whose names appear first on the ballot have about a 3 percent advantage over those whose names appear further down the ballot. Consequently, five states have adopted random listing of candidates' names on the ballots—the name that gets picked out of the hat first, so to speak, gets to be listed first. Officials sometimes even rotate candidates' names on the ballot from precinct to precinct or district to district, thereby equalizing the "first-name-on-the-ballot" advantage. In 2002, a judge reversed the result of the mayoral race in the city of Compton, California, because the city clerk neglected to randomize the candidates' names on the ballot as state law requires.[15]

Incumbent Advantage

The incumbent—the person who already holds the office—usually has a big advantage. According to Charles Madigan, reporter for the *Chicago Tribune*, "The only way a member of Congress leaves office is (a) on a stretcher, (b) in handcuffs, or (c) so embarrassed by a scandal that re-election chances evaporate."[16] In the 1994 election, many prominent Democratic legislators, including the Speaker of the House, were defeated—yet, even then, over 90 percent of the congressional incumbents seeking re-election found a way to win. There are several reasons for this high rate of success. First, incumbents are generally better known than their opponents just because they hold the office. Second, incumbents naturally receive more free publicity. If a prominent official wants attention, he or she simply calls a press conference, marches in a parade somewhere, or visits the zoo and comments on the cuteness of the baby pandas. Challengers must usually pay for their publicity. Third, incumbents frequently have had more campaign experience—they're street wise, so to speak. Fourth, they have a staff paid for by tax dollars to do all sorts of work for the voters. These constituent services (also known as casework) often translate into votes for "good old Senator Snark," who serves the public so faithfully. Fifth, incumbents can usually raise more campaign funds because many contributors believe the incumbents will win—a self-fulfilling prophecy. All of these factors make it very difficult for incumbents to be defeated.

WHO IS ELECTED?

There are half a million elected officials in the United States, but only 537 (besides the presidential electors) are elected to positions in the national government. The rest are state and local government positions. We certainly can not address them all in this textbook, but we will discuss the two groups of elected offices at the national level and give a general overview of those at the state level. Let's begin with the executive branch of the national government in which there are only two elected positions: president and vice president.

President and Vice President

The election for president and for vice president is the only at-large election in the United States. "At-large" means the voters in the entire United States are all allowed to vote for president and vice president. All other elected officials of the national government are chosen from states or from districts within the states. For example, Florida voters get to vote only for two U.S. Senators for Florida, not senators for all the other states also.

Nomination. We have already learned that political parties in the United States nominate candidates for political offices including the President and the Vice President of the United States. To be nominated for president by the Democratic or the Republican Party, a candidate must receive a majority of the delegate votes at the party's national convention. In the past, national conventions were very exciting events. Delegates were usually picked by party bosses and often went to the conventions **unpledged**, that is, uncommitted to any presidential candidate. Conventions might do surprising things, like nominate a **dark horse**, a candidate that no one had ever heard of before. Today, however, the conventions are very predictable (and rather boring). This change came about because, in recent years, most states required the parties to pick convention delegates in primary elections where the would-be-delegates generally run pledged to one of the presidential rivals. Thus, the presidential candidate who gets the most popular votes in the primaries will usually have a majority of the delegates sewed up ahead of time. So, the convention turns into a carefully scripted and dull coronation. This was certainly the case in 2004. President Bush had no opposition for the Republican nomination, and Senator Kerry had disposed of his Democratic rivals before the primary election season was half over. Nothing memorable happened at either party's convention that year.

New Hampshire was one of the first states to establish a presidential primary, and its primary comes very early in the fight for the nomination for each party. The candidates who win in New Hampshire often gain an important boost for their campaigns, although not always. United States Senator John McCain (R-AZ) won the New Hampshire Republican contest in 2000, but George W. Bush overtook him in the following primaries. Because of the large number of states that must be contested, the race for a presidential nomination often boils down to money, but that is true of most other political races too. "Money" in this context doesn't refer to corruption but to the cost of campaigning, particularly the price of television advertizing.

The national conventions meet to pick their nominees in the summer of every presidential-election year. The nomination for each party requires a simple majority of the delegate votes. In theory, it is the party's national convention that nominates whomever it wants for vice president. In truth, however, the presidential nominee almost always makes the selection and picks someone who seems likely to attract votes. For example, if the presidential nominee is a Protestant, then the vice presidential nominee might be selected because he or she is Catholic or Jewish, thus appealing to another segment of the voters. If the presidential nominee is from the West, then the vice-presidential running mate might be selected because he or she is from the East or the South. This kind of selection is called **balancing the ticket.** In 1984, Democratic presidential nominee Walter Mondale balanced the ticket in an historic way by choosing Geraldine Ferraro to be the first woman nominated for vice president by a major party. In 2000, Democratic presidential nominee Al Gore selected Connecticut Senator Joe Lieberman, who became the first Jewish person to run on a major party ticket. Senator Lieberman's reputation for honesty may have been the key factor in this instance because the scandals of the Clinton administration (some involving Mr. Gore himself) were in the news at the time. In 2004, Senator Kerry, who comes from Massachusetts, chose North Carolina Senator John Edwards as his vice presidential running mate, hoping to appeal to southern voters.

Balancing the ticket seems to have become less important in recent years. Bill Clinton and Al Gore, who were running mates in 1992 and 1996, are both male, white, Baptist Southerners and about the same age. When George W. Bush selected Dick Cheney to be his 2000 vice presidential candidate, both men were residents of the same state, Texas. In these cases, the personal "chemistry" between the individuals concerned outweighed any thoughts of political balance. It's actually not clear that the voters care much about where the vice presidential candidate comes from. The Kerry-Edwards ticket failed to carry a single southern state—not even Edwards' home state of North Carolina.

The Electoral College

To many people, the most surprising feature of the 2000 presidential contest was that the candidate with the most popular votes did not win. Republican George W. Bush finished a half million votes behind Democrat Al Gore in the nationwide count. Nevertheless, George W. Bush captured the White House. To understand how such a thing can occur, we must examine an institution called the electoral college. The Framers of the Constitution did not favor a direct popular vote for president and vice president. They feared that the common people (most of us) did not possess the wisdom and virtue necessary to make an informed choice, i.e., the correct choice in their view. Instead, the

Framers provided that the president would be selected by a special body of presidential electors, collectively known as the electoral college. The Framers hoped these electors would be smarter and better informed than the average person. So how does this body work? (As it happens, the electoral college is relatively complicated, so be sure you are not drifting off into "never-never land" at this point.)

• Each state is allotted the same number of electoral votes as it has representatives and senators in Congress. For example, Florida has 27 electoral votes, because Florida has 25 representatives and 2 senators. Since the number of representatives a state has is based on that state's population, we can see that the larger the state's population, the larger its electoral vote. The most populous state, California, has 55 electoral votes, while the least populous, Alaska, has only 3 votes. (See Chart 9.1) No state can have fewer than 3 electoral votes because all states must have at least 1 representative and 2 senators.

• Currently, the total number of electoral votes distributed among the states (and the District of Columbia) is 538. Congress has fixed the number of members for the House of Representatives at 435. Also, each of the fifty states is entitled to two United States Senators, making 100 in all. The three remaining electoral votes come from the District of Columbia. The Constitution, as it was originally written, did not provide for any electors for the District of Columbia, but the Twenty-third Amendment allowed the District of Columbia to have three electoral votes. Now we have accounted for all 538 votes: 435 based on the number of representatives in the House, 100 based on the number of senators, and 3 for the District of Columbia.

• Despite appearances, the people technically do not vote for president at all. It is true that the voters see on their ballots the names of the candidates for president and for vice president from each party along with any independent candidates. In reality, however, the people are voting not for president and vice president but for slates (lists) of presidential electors pledged to the candidate whose name appears on the ballot. Each candidate puts forward an electoral slate composed of faithful supporters, and the slate that wins the most popular votes in a state will cast that state's electoral votes.

• The electoral college system in the states, with two exceptions,[17] is based on a winner-take-all system. A candidate who receives just one popular vote more than any other candidate in a state will be given all that state's electoral votes. In 1992, Bill Clinton got 5.1 million popular votes in California, 46 percent of the total cast—the most of any candidate. He, therefore, won all of California's electoral votes, although Republican George Bush and independent candidate Ross Perot together got almost one million more popular votes than Clinton did in that state.

Chart 9.1: Allocation of Electoral Votes based on the 2000 Census

---

Total: 538;   Majority Needed to Elect: 270

ALABAMA - 9	MONTANA - 3
ALASKA - 3	NEBRASKA - 5
ARIZONA - 10	NEVADA - 5
ARKANSAS - 6	NEW HAMPSHIRE - 4
CALIFORNIA - 55	NEW JERSEY - 15
COLORADO - 9	NEW MEXICO - 5
CONNECTICUT - 7	NEW YORK - 34
DISTRICT OF COLUMBIA - 3	NORTH CAROLINA - 15
FLORIDA - 27	NORTH DAKOTA - 3
GEORGIA - 15	OHIO - 20
HAWAII - 4	OKLAHOMA - 7
IDAHO - 4	OREGON - 7
ILLINOIS - 21	PENNSYLVANIA - 21
INDIANA - 11	RHODE ISLAND - 4
IOWA - 7	SOUTH CAROLINA - 8
KANSAS - 6	SOUTH DAKOTA - 3
KENTUCKY - 8	TENNESSEE - 11
LOUISIANA - 9	TEXAS - 34
MAINE - 4	UTAH - 5
MARYLAND - 10	VERMONT - 3
MASSACHUSETTS - 12	VIRGINIA - 13
MICHIGAN - 17	WASHINGTON - 11
MINNESOTA - 10	WEST VIRGINIA - 5
MISSISSIPPI - 6	WISCONSIN - 10
MISSOURI - 11	WYOMING - 3

Source: National Archives and Records Administration home page
URL: http://www.nara.gov /fedreg/elctcoll/vote2004.html

•Candidates for president and vice president need a majority of the electoral vote to be elected; that is, they need at least 270 electoral votes—one more than half the total.   Presidential candidates campaign heavily in the biggest states. In fact, the eleven states with the largest electoral vote together total 274. A candidate winning the popular vote in these eleven states, even if by a small margin, would be a winner even if he/she lost every other vote in the country. Thus, a candidate can win the popular vote in the United States as a whole and still lose the election since the Constitution says that a majority of the electoral college vote is required, not the popular vote. In fact, this has happened three times now: in 1876, 1888, and 2000.[18] This is the biggest flaw in the electoral college system.

•Before the general election in November, each political party within the state and each independent presidential candidate's organization within the state selects a slate of electors. Being an elector is considered an honor, a way to reward people who have worked hard for the party or the independent candidate or have contributed financially in a significant way. Anyone may be chosen except people who already hold offices in the national government, such as senators. Once the winning slate of electors is chosen from each state in the general election in November, then the "real" election takes place. Early in December, the winning electors travel to their respective state capitals, where they cast their votes for president and for vice president. There should be no surprises at this point since the presidential electors are expected to be mere rubber stamps of the popular election in their state. The ballots are sealed and sent to the United States Congress, where in January they are officially read aloud and counted. By this time, of course, everyone usually knows the outcome, but in theory no one is elected until this count takes place in Washington, D.C.

We should note that, even though the presidential electors have pledged ahead of time to vote for a certain candidate, they do not actually have to do so in many states. The Framers of the Constitution wanted the electors, not the people, to pick the president. The Constitution, therefore, contains no legal requirement that the electors follow the popular will. Indeed, every now and then an elector does "bolt" his or her party and vote for some other candidate. This action has never changed the outcome of an election. However, to guard against the possibility, candidates try to choose only the most loyal of their followers to serve on their electoral slate. States can legislate that electors vote for the person they were pledged to; the latest to do so was Virginia in 2001.

•If no candidate receives a majority of the electoral vote, then the Constitution provides that the House of Representatives shall choose the president from the top three candidates. Each state would have only one vote, however, which means that Alaska's one House member would equal California's 55! This is a clumsy procedure that worked badly both times it was tried in 1800 and 1824.[19] The Constitution also provides that, if no vice-presidential candidate receives a majority, the Senate shall choose the vice president from between the two leading candidates. Each senator has one vote. It is most unlikely that the House and Senate will have to choose these officials as long as we have only two major parties. But when strong third party candidates come along—like George Wallace, who received 46 electoral votes in 1968, or Ross Perot, who pulled 19 percent of the popular vote in 1992—there is a real chance that no candidate will receive an electoral college majority.

A number of proposals have been made over the years to amend the Constitution's electoral college provisions. The most popular one among the voters is just to scrap the electoral college altogether and replace it with direct election by the people—whoever gets the most popular votes wins. Yet nothing has changed for several reasons. First, the electoral college is traditional in this country. It is very difficult to change something that has been going on for two hundred years. Second, the states with large populations may not really desire a change since they receive a great deal of attention from presidential candidates because of their significant electoral vote. (Remember the eleven largest states comprise a majority of the electoral college.) Third, the very smallest states probably would not desire a change either since they have slightly more electoral votes than their population strictly entitles them to. With all these forces in operation that tend to maintain things the way they are, it is highly unlikely that the method of electing the president and the vice president will change in the near future. Despite the heated debates about scrapping the electoral college shortly after the 2000 presidential election, the momentum to do so was gone within a few months.

Congress

Election to the United States Congress, whether as a member of the House of Representatives or of the Senate, is much simpler than election to the presidency or the vice presidency. Members of Congress are just directly elected by a popular vote. Whoever gets the most votes is the winner. In most states, all that is required is a **plurality**—the most votes of any candidate. In some states, however, a **majority**—over half the votes cast—is needed. For example, if, in the general election, the Democratic candidate gets 34 percent of the vote, the Republican candidate gets 33 percent, and an independent candidate gets 33 percent, then the winner in most states would be the Democrat because that candidate had more votes than any other candidate. However, in those states where a majority is required, there would be a run-off election between the top two finishers.

When Elections Are Held. Every two years in the even-numbered years there will be elections for the House of Representatives. Therefore, representatives[20] must stay in closer touch with their **constituents** (voters in their districts) because they must run for re-election more frequently. Senators have six-year terms, and their terms are staggered so that only one-third of the Senate seats come up for election at the same time that the entire House is up for election.

Geographic Regions. Voters elect senators from the entire state, while representatives are elected from districts within the state. You will recall that the 435 members of the House are distributed among the states according to their respective populations. This distribution occurs every ten years, immediately following the census. Every census always reveals that some states have gained population relative to other states and, therefore, deserve more representatives, while other states correspondingly must lose, while still others might remain the same. The need to redistribute the members of the House leads to one of the oldest problems of American politics: gerrymandering.

The redistribution of representatives is called **reapportionment**. The state legislature must divide the state into districts of roughly equal population—currently about 640,000. Reapportionment can create tremendous political upheaval within a state if the population of that state has changed. Some incumbents (current office holders) may face re-election against each other or may face re-election in newly drawn districts where they are not as well known. These things may occur because the state legislature must redraw district lines to meet the new number of representatives for the state. If the state legislature fails to redraw its district lines, when necessary, or draws them in a discriminatory way, then the federal courts may end up doing the job.

Creating discriminatory districts is called **gerrymandering**. The term got its name from Elbridge Gerry, a signer of the Articles of Confederation and delegate to the Philadelphia Convention, who also served a term as vice president. When the first district lines in Massachusetts were drawn on a state map, some people thought the result similar to the lizard-like animal called a salamander. Gerry was the leader of the majority political party in the state legislature, so his name was combined with salamander to produce the term *gerrymander*. The goal of a gerrymander is to cram as many of the other party's voters into as few districts as possible, while giving one's own party a majority in as many districts as can be managed.

Critics have long seen gerrymandering as a serious problem of American politics. Not only does it distort the public will, it tends to foster **one-party districts**—districts where one party has such a huge majority that the other party cannot possibly win. The elections in such districts tend to be boring and irrelevant. Political scientists generally agree that **swing districts**, where both parties have a chance, promote a more vigorous public debate. California's latest actor-turned-governor, Arnold Schwarzenegger, has proposed that the re-districting process in his state be taken away from the state legislature and given to a non-partisan panel of retired judges, who could be trusted to draw the lines fairly. The Democratic leadership in the state legislature, who created California's most recent gerrymander, have—somewhat surprisingly—shown a willingness to consider Schwarzenegger's plan. So it is possible that gerrymandering may soon be abolished in the nation's most populous state.[21]

The federal Voting Rights Act of 1982 required that district boundaries be drawn in such a way as to maximize the number of representatives from minority ethnic groups. Because of this requirement, the percentage of nonwhite members of Congress rose from about 8.5 percent to 13 percent in the 1992 election. The districts drawn for this purpose were just as odd-looking as Gerry's salamander. In 1996, the U.S. Supreme Court ruled that race-based reapportionment can be unconstitutional, and as a result, a number of "majority-minority" congressional districts had to be redrawn, mainly in Southern states.[22]

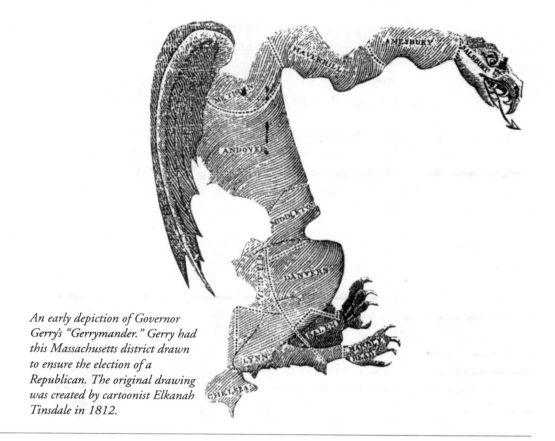

An early depiction of Governor Gerry's "Gerrymander." Gerry had this Massachusetts district drawn to ensure the election of a Republican. The original drawing was created by cartoonist Elkanah Tinsdale in 1812.

State and Local Offices

State governments, like the national government, have legislative, executive, and judicial branches. There are literally thousands of elected positions in the states. Governors and lieutenant governors are elected, as well as members of the state legislatures. Also, many executive and judicial offices that are appointive posts on the national level are elected in the states. Local offices—city councils, school boards, water districts, and so forth—are even more numerous. The 50 largest cities in the United States are governed by over 650 elective councils and boards. One out of every 500 Americans is an elected official of some sort. "Grass roots" politics is alive and well in this country. Indeed, voters can be overwhelmed by the number of decisions they must make on election day.

2. States can hold elections whenever they choose for state offices. Some hold their elections at the same time that the national elections are held while others prefer to hold them in the "**off years**" when no national elections are at stake or, at least, when there is no presidential election. States that choose these "off years" do so in hopes that the voters will focus on state and local issues. One drawback, however, is that voter turnout is generally lower than it is when

the election is held in conjunction with a national election. (You will recall that voter turnout is usually low in any election, state or national, in the United States.)

ELEMENTS OF A SUCCESSFUL CAMPAIGN

There is a very good reason why political campaigning has become a multibillion-dollar business in the United States today. As an astute politician once noted, "Winning isn't everything, but losing isn't anything."[23] There is no "silver medal" in politics. A well-run campaign can make the all-important difference between winning and losing.

The Candidate

The first ingredient of any successful campaign must be the candidate, and in today's political climate the most important characteristic a candidate can possess is the ability to raise money. This usually implies that the candidate will fall into one (or more) of three categories. The candidate will either (1) be extremely wealthy, so that he or she can finance the campaign personally, or (2) know lots of wealthy people, who can be called upon to contribute, or (3) be a veteran politician who has already developed a long list of faithful contributors. It is also helpful that the candidate have the right personality for raising cash—that he or she be willing to spend many long hours on the telephone asking both friends and total strangers to open their wallets and purses.

The candidate must be **marketable**. Marketable means "able to be sold"—sold to the public. The candidate must appear intelligent and highly qualified, while at the same time seeming to be "just one of the folks." This is not easy. Also, the candidate should have high marks in **name recognition**. In other words, when the candidate's name is mentioned, most people should already be familiar with it. Prominent business people, war heroes, movie stars, the sons and daughters of famous people, or people who have been elected to office before have a far better chance than people who are relatively unknown. It is also important to know the "right" people—those who have influence over others: business and labor leaders, ministers, people in civic and political organizations, and so forth. Generally speaking, successful candidates have been "joiners" for a long time and have lots of acquaintances.

Marketable candidates must enjoy all the handshaking, baby kissing, backslapping, talking, banquets, and speeches that go into making a campaign. Regardless of how busy candidates are, they must stop and listen to the "bag lady" on the street, as well as to the banker. Optimism is another good characteristic. Current research indicates that those who avoid unpleasant topics and speak about a bright future for the voters win more often than candidates who do otherwise.[24]

A marketable candidate must project the proper image. A candidate who dressed and acted like Ozzy Osbourne would undoubtedly not be elected to public office. In the past when fewer people actually got to see or hear candidates, especially for national offices such as president, the appearance or voice of the office-seeker may not have been as big a factor as it is today. But with the introduction of radio and television, millions of people get an opportunity to judge the candidates. A famous example can be found in the election debates between Senator Kennedy and Vice President Richard Nixon during the presidential election in 1960. Kennedy, a rather handsome man, wore make-up for his television appearances since the bright lights tend to make people on camera look like cadavers. Nixon, less eye-appealing to begin with, considered makeup effeminate and refused to wear it. Nixon began to realize his mistake when his mother called from California after the first debate to ask if he were "feeling all right."[25] Nixon narrowly lost that election, and most political analysts believe it was because of the image created in the televised debates.

In 2000, Democratic presidential candidate Al Gore's image brightened considerably after "the Kiss"—a long (televised) smooch with his wife, Tipper, during the Democratic National Convention. Polls showed that women were especially impressed. But Gore's image suffered later, during his first televised debate with George W. Bush, when he emitted loud sighs of disgust during his opponent's remarks.[26]

Spouses, like candidates, must project the right image. In the 1992 presidential campaign, and again in 1996, Hillary Clinton was almost as much a focus of attention as was the candidate, Bill Clinton, and her changes of hairdo were carefully noted by the media. The latter, of course, may say more about the stupidity of some of the media than it does about candidates' spouses. First Lady Laura Bush, a former teacher and librarian, is thought to be a major political asset to her husband—who once joked that he was living proof a "C" student could grow up to be president. On the other hand, Teresa Heinz Kerry probably did not help her husband's presidential prospects when she told a newspaper reporter to "shove it" during the 2004 campaign.

White males still seem to have an advantage running for office, but women have made inroads. There once was a time when female candidates were at a definite disadvantage. Today, however, females with well-financed campaigns are as likely to win elections as males. Five women were major party nominees for the U.S. Senate in 2000, and all of them won. The most prominent of these was former First Lady Hillary Rodham Clinton, elected for the state of New York. Results in more recent years have been mixed. Yet, overall, women have lost no ground. In the 2004 election, no fewer than ten women won major party U.S. Senate nominations. Five were incumbents, and all of them won, while the five non-incumbents all lost. Currently, fourteen women serve in the U.S. Senate and sixty-five serve in the House of Representatives. Eight women

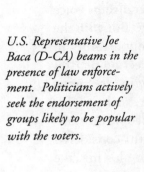

U.S. Representative Joe Baca (D-CA) beams in the presence of law enforcement. Politicians actively seek the endorsement of groups likely to be popular with the voters.

now serve as governors. No woman has been nominated by a major party for president, though Senator Hillary Clinton has been mentioned as a future possibility.

Non-white candidates are also winning elections in greater numbers than in the past. The 2004 election saw two Hispanics and an African American elected to the U.S. Senate. Two Asian-Americans were already serving in that body. Currently, forty African Americans, twenty-five Hispanics, five Asian-Americans, and one Native American serve in the House of Representatives.[27] These figures are much larger than a generation ago—yet we should remember that, even now, not one of these groups has congressional representation equal to its percentage of the population. White males are not as dominant as they once were, but they are still over-represented in political office.

Not long ago, any hint of homosexuality would have been fatal to a candidate's hopes, but the times are (slowly) changing. Currently, three members of the U.S. House of Representatives are openly gay or Lesbian.[28]

Today's marketable candidates may be increasingly diverse in some ways, but they are all alike in one respect: they must have a strong "killer instinct." That doesn't mean that they must have a "win-no-matter-what" attitude, but it does mean that they must have the determination to rise in the wee hours of the morning perhaps to speak at a Lion's Club breakfast meeting, speak at a college in mid-morning, continue on to a Chamber of Commerce luncheon for chicken and peas, eat kielbasa at a Polish festival in the afternoon, devour more chicken and peas at a fund-raising dinner at night, then meet with the campaign staff till well past midnight, and then be prepared to do it all over again the next day without having a stomach ache or looking as if they had been run over by a truck.

Good health is also necessary for a marketable candidate. This is not to say that people who are "physically challenged" by not being able to walk, for example, cannot get elected to office. However, persons who have a serious heart ailment or who have had numerous operations may find it quite difficult to convince voters that they have the stamina to hold office. If an operation should occur, the press will surely find a picture of whatever part of the candidate's body that was removed and put it on the nightly news. In recent years we have been treated to pictures from colon polyps to gall stones to hemorrhoids from various politicians.

Stamina and determination also apply to the spouse of the candidate, for he or she frequently campaigns with the candidate. Spouses, like candidates, must project the right image. In the 1992 presidential campaign and again in 1996, Hillary Clinton was almost as much a focus of media attention as was the candidate, Bill Clinton, and her changes of hairdo were carefully noted by the media. The latter probably says more about the stupidity of some of the media than it does about the candidates' spouses!

Campaign Organization

Besides a "marketable" candidate, a successful campaign must have effective organization. When important national or state offices are at stake, some of this need will be met by the national or state party committees. Despite this party involvement, however, campaigns today are usually **candidate centered, with the principal organizational focus being the candidate's personal operation, not the party's.**

Properly run campaigns, from presidential campaigns on down to campaigns for Commissioner of Drains, will be organized similarly. A candidate will form a **finance committee to raise money from large and small contributors, both individuals and from PACs.** Unfortunately, this is the single most important factor in any campaign. If enough cash is found, a candidate will hire a team of seasoned professional **campaign consultants. These are people who make their living by "marketing" politicians—that is, devising strategies to "sell" candidates to the voters.** They will decide what kinds of ads are used, what the candidate's hair style will be, and what, if anything, the candidate will say about the issues of the day. The candidate will also employ a professional **campaign manager and staff to coordinate the various day-to-day campaign activities.** Finally, there must be **volunteers to put up yard signs, pass out fliers door-to-door, make phone calls, stuff envelopes, help register supporters to vote, and get them to the polls on election day.** When major national or state offices are at stake, some of these activities may be handled by national or state party committees.

Money

A street-wise politician once observed, "Money is the mother's milk of politics,"[29] and never has that been more true in the United States than today. Campaign spending reached new heights in 2004. The presidential campaigns of George W. Bush and John Kerry spent about $1.1 billion apiece, while other presidential candidates spent almost $160 million among them, for a total of nearly $2.4 billion spent on this race alone.[30] That was (by far) the record for a presidential campaign. Just four years previously, the presidential campaigns all together had spent "only" one billion dollars. Campaigns for the U.S. House and Senate pushed total spending on races for national office in 2004 to about four billion dollars. The candidate with the biggest bankroll won 95 percent of all House races and 91 percent of all Senate races that year.[31] The record for total spending in a U.S. Senate election, incidentally, is held by the 2000 contest between Hillary Clinton and Representative Rick Lazio for the New York seat won by Clinton — $80 million.[32]

The big spenders are not only in national races. California Governor Gray Davis raised and spent $77.8 million to win re-election in 2002. His Republican opponent, Bill Simon, spent a mere $36.4 million—about $10 million of it his own money.[33] Local races can be expensive as well. The record for spending by a candidate for local office is held by Michael Bloomberg, victor in the 2001 New York City mayor's race, who spent $70 million, almost all of it from his own pocket.[34]

Unfortunately, campaign contributions may come with strings attached. Successful presidential candidates, for example, often reward large donors with political appointments, such as ambassadorships. After his 1972 election, Richard Nixon appointed 52 major Republican contributors to various federal positions. Upon being offered the ambassadorship to Costa Rica, one of these appointees complained: "Isn't $250,000 an awful lot of money for Costa Rica?"[35] She was then offered and she accepted the ambassadorship to Luxembourg. Former President George Bush's nominee as ambassador to Spain, a Florida real estate developer, spoke no Spanish but did contribute $126,000 to the Republican campaign. Former President Clinton's first choice for ambassador to France, the late society hostess Pamela Harriman, raised $12 million for the Democratic Party, including $3.2 million for Bill Clinton.[36] She did, at least, speak French!

Political fund-raising became an issue in the 1996 presidential race. About a month before the election, newspaper reports uncovered some $650,000 in illegal contributions to the Democratic Party — some of the money allegedly coming indirectly from the Chinese government![37] The fund-raising problems of the Clinton administration continued to unfold after the election. It was charged that government lists and facilities were used for political fund-raising purposes and that the historic Lincoln bedroom in the White House had, in effect, been "rented" to hundreds of rich Democratic Party contributors. Vice President Al Gore was accused of taking part in an illegal fund-raiser and of illegally making fund-raising calls on a government telephone. The scandals continued after Clinton left office, with serious questions concerning his pardon of the aptly-named fugitive financier, Marc Rich, wanted for tax evasion, price gouging, and trading with the enemy. Clinton's critics noted that Mr. Rich's former spouse was a heavy contributor to the Democratic Party.[38]

The Republicans had their share of problems, too. Bob Dole's chief fundraiser went to jail in the course of the 1996 campaign. In 1997, House Speaker Newt Gingrich was censured and fined $300,000 for untrue statements made to the House Ethics Committee about his fund-raising operations. George W. Bush raised eyebrows in 2000 when he refused public financing, which enabled him to avoid federal limits on his overall campaign spending. More recently, many Republican and some Democratic politicians have been embarrassed by revelations of past campaign contributions from Enron Corporation.

Where the Money Comes From

Individual contributions are the main source of campaign funds. Individuals often make contributions by purchasing tickets to fund-raising dinners, where they can rub elbows with the candidate and other notable people. It is common nowadays for these tickets to go for $1000 or more. For that kind of money, you might expect a little more than chicken and peas; however, the menu will probably be just that—chicken and peas. The purpose of the dinner is to raise money for TV commercials, not to produce gourmet food!

Funds are also solicited by mail. Potential donors receive a computer-generated letter that looks as if it were individually typed and addressed to them. It isn't. It is part of a mailing of perhaps hundreds of thousands of letters. The letters are frequently sent out by zip codes, focusing on areas where wealthier people or supporters of the candidate are likely to live. Professional fund-raising firms keep lists of persons who have contributed in the past and are, therefore, good bets to do so again.

Political Action Committees are another potent source of campaign funds although these donations have been much criticized. Critics observe that while individuals may be motivated by a sense of idealism or civic duty, most PACs exist to represent a special interest group. PACs appear to be mainly interested in supporting winning candidates: three-fourths of PAC money goes to incumbents seeking re-election.[39]

Political parties are, likewise, major contributors. In closely contested races Democratic and Republican Party candidates will get significant financial help from their party's national and state committees.

206   *Chapter Nine*

The **candidates' personal funds** can be of critical importance if the candidate is wealthy. The U.S. Supreme Court has ruled that contributions by candidates to their own campaigns cannot be limited unless the candidate receives public funding. Thus, Ross Perot ran for president as an independent in 1992, without accepting public funding, and spent $60 million of his own money in the process! In the words of Will Rogers, "politics has got so expensive that it takes lots of money even to get beat with." Jon Corzine set a record for candidate self-financing in 2000, when he parted with about $65 million of his personal funds to win a U.S. Senate seat from New Jersey with just 50.7 percent of the vote. That record was shattered just one year later by Michael Bloomberg's $70-million effort in New York City, hardly a dent in Bloomberg's $4.5 billion personal fortune.[40] The political parties are increasingly recruiting wealthy individuals to run for office to take advantage of their ability to fund their own campaigns.

Public financing is the only alternative to the use of private money in campaigns. The presidential contest is the only federal election funded in part by taxpayers. Candidates seeking the nomination for president can receive matching funds from the federal government if they meet certain requirements and agree to spending limits. If they do not accept any public funds, there are no limits on their expenditures. Once the presidential nomination fight is over, the successful major party nominees receive a large federal grant ($47 million in 2000). They are also forbidden to solicit or to spend private money in the general election, although the use of soft money and issue ads (discussed below) has rendered this restriction meaningless. Minor party presidential candidates can receive a subsidy if that party got over 5 percent of the nationwide popular vote in the previous election.

Public funding of the presidential election is dependent upon having enough tax money in the presidential campaign fund. In recent years, fewer and fewer people are using the checkoff box on their tax return to designate $3.00 of their taxes to this fund. In some cases people forget or they just don't understand what the box is for. However, some taxpayers just do not want their money being given to candidates they do not support.

Only a few state and local jurisdictions fund campaigns with tax dollars, but the practice seems to be slowly increasing. New York City used public financing for the first time in the 2001 mayor's race.

Federal Campaign Funding Rules (and Loopholes)

Until recently, the Federal Election Campaign Acts of 1971 and 1974 provided the legal framework for the funding of campaigns for president or for Congress. Under these laws, individuals have been limited to giving $1000 to a federal candidate in a given election and also limited in the total amount they could give to all candidates for national (federal) office. Limits on PACs were higher— $5000 per candidate per election. These laws also provided for public financing of presidential elections and for the **Federal Election Commission (FEC)** to enforce federal rules. Unfortunately, by the 1990s, these laws had become riddled with loopholes, several of which were of special concern to reformers.

The U.S. Supreme Court created one loophole— **candidate self-financing**— when it ruled in *Buckley v. Valeo* that candidates may use unlimited amounts of their own money for their own campaigns—if they do not accept any public funding. In addition, the Court ruled against any limit on spending for a candidate if the candidate has no voice in how the money is spent. Thus, if a PAC donates money to a candidate's official campaign, the limit if $5000. But, if the PAC spends money directly for advertising on behalf of the candidate, there is no limit—as long as the candidate has no say in what the PAC is doing. This kind of spending is called **independent expenditure**.

Another loophole, **soft money,** was created by the Federal Election Commission. The federal election laws allowed individuals to donate unlimited amounts to political parties but only so long as those funds were used for so-called "party building" activities, such as registering voters and taking them to the polls on election day. Soft money was never supposed to be used to advertise for candidates. However, beginning with the 1996 election, the political parties began doing exactly that. In that year, both the Democratic and the Republican Parties spent millions of dollars of "party-building" money on television commercials showcasing their presidential candidates. The FEC, made up of equal numbers of Democrats and Republicans, rejected the argument that these ads violated the rules. Instead, the FEC ruled that the commercials in question were only **issue ads**—efforts to inform voters on what the parties stand for—and that they just happened to feature the presidential candidates! Since the FEC permitted the practice, it continued to grow. In the 2000 presidential election, the two major parties together raised and spent well over $400 million in soft money contributions.[41]

The Triumph (?) of Reform

Serious efforts to reduce the impact of money on the electoral process began in 2000. That year, Senator John McCain (R-AZ) based his campaign for the Republican presidential nomination on a call for reform, and the following year introduced a reform bill into Congress. McCain's bill met fierce resistance from conservatives, until one more scandal tipped the balance in its favor. Following the collapse of Enron Corporation, a Texas-based energy company, it was revealed that Enron had been a generous political donor, having given $2.4 million to candidates in the 2000 election alone. Enron's contributions went to Republicans over Democrats by about a 3 to 1 margin and notably featured former Texas Governor George W. Bush. Bush administration officials pointed out, correctly, that they had pulled no strings to prevent Enron's collapse, but reformers observed that the failed company's misdeeds had long gone undetected because of toothless federal regulations sponsored by Enron's congressional allies.[42] Quite a few legislators suddenly decided they needed to look like crusaders against corruption, and a bill containing McCain's reform proposals — **Bipartisan Campaign Reform Act of 2002** — was passed by Congress and signed into law by President Bush. The measure was immediately challenged in the courts by conservatives, who claimed that it violated rights of free speech. But the major provisions of the new law were upheld, in late 2003, by a 5 to 4 ruling of the U.S. Supreme Court.[43]

The new reform law tightens existing federal regulations principally in two ways: (1) the bill bans the use of soft money by national political parties, while severely restricting its use by state parties, and (2) the bill forbids interest groups from running independently financed issue ads within 30 days of a primary or 60 days of a general election. To meet conservative objections that the limits established in 1974 have become too restrictive, the bill doubles (to $2,000) the amount that an individual may give to a candidate in an election. Finally, contribution limits were loosened even further in the case of federal candidates facing self-financed wealthy opponents. Reformers hoped that these provisions would eliminate some of the glaring abuses of the past.

The 2004 presidential election was in many ways a disappointment to reformers, but the news was not entirely bad. With soft money now forbidden to them, the Democratic and Republican Parties were forced to rely entirely on **hard money**—that is, contributions subject to the federal limits and therefore relatively small-scale. Yet aggressive marketing techniques and the use of the Internet enabled the parties to raise more than twice as much in donations as they had raised four years previously, when they could take soft money. Much of this came from PACs and persons with ties to interest groups. But much of it also came from ordinary citizens who simply felt moved to take part in the electoral process. The parties' ability to finance themselves with relatively small donations is a sign that there may be alternatives to big money dominance in American politics.

In other respects, the 2002 reform law may have done more harm than good. Soft money did not disappear in 2004, it was simply re-directed away from the parties to the so-called **527s**. These entities—named after the section of the IRS Code that applies to them—are formed to make independent expenditures on behalf of candidates running for office. As we know, if the candidate has no say in what the 527 does, it can take unlimited donations. Both presidential candidates benefited from spending by these 527s. The chief independent contributor on Senator Kerry's side was multi-billionaire businessman George Soros, who gave a total of $23.5 million to numerous anti-Bush 527 committees. The main independent contributor on President Bush's side was Houston developer Bob J. Perry who, among other ventures, gave $4.5 million to Swift Boat Veterans for Truth—a 527 committee that financed harsh commercials attacking Senator Kerry's record as a Vietnam War hero.[44]

The problem with 527 committees is that it is unlawful for them to communicate with the candidates they support. Candidates and committees cannot coordinate their efforts in any way. Consequently, candidates lose control over their own campaigns. Thus, Senator Snark may wish to emphasize foreign policy issues in his re-election effort, only to find that his wealthy supporters—who have agendas of their own—are spending money on TV ads praising his support for tax cuts for millionaires. On the other hand, candidates can escape responsibility for slanderous things said on their behalf. In 2004, President Bush could avoid any criticism based on the controversial Swift Boat Veterans ads, since they were financed by an independent expenditure. The advent of 527 committees seems likely to increase the amount of confusion and hypocrisy in American politics—and it is all due to the latest reform!

Where the Money Goes

All campaigns for national office will require professional management and expertise. The campaign consultants provide strategic planning and overall direction to the effort. Specialized firms handle polling, press relations, fundraising, media buys, computer services, television and radio production, mailing, and the rest. All this expert help costs money, but it is necessary. Candidates and their personal friends rarely have the knowledge or the temperament to manage a campaign.

Television and radio advertising is often the largest single item of expenditure in a campaign for a national or a statewide office. Television advertising is the surest way to reach virtually all of the voters with a brief, effective message. Television is by far the most expensive of the mass media. Thirty seconds of advertising on a highly-rated, prime-time program may cost $400,000 or more. The arrival of cable television has made this medium more affordable but that only means campaigns can buy more commercials. Since "you can't knock on everybody's door," a consultant noted, "the closer you can make your commercial to a personal visit from the candidate, the more. . . vital it is to the campaign." Unfortunately a 60-second commercial does not lend itself to an in-depth discussion of the issues. This observation led another consultant to note that you do have to be very conscious of the images because that's what it's all about.[45]

Another leading item of campaign expenditure is **direct mail**. The advantage of mail is that it can be **targeted, that is, designed to appeal to a particular segment of the population.** It is not uncommon for a candidate to send one mailer to Democrats, stressing compassion for the poor, and another mailer to

Republicans, stressing the need to kick deadbeats off welfare. Since mail can be directed specifically to those persons most likely to vote, it may be the most cost-effective way to campaign. Candidates also invest in billboards, signs, bumper stickers, buttons, potholders, and many other items. Some candidates even hire skywriters—airplanes that leave a message like "Vote for Honest John" written in the sky!

Internet advertising is another area that no candidate can afford to neglect. It is essential for a campaign to have a web site, where press releases, position papers, and other information (like how to contribute money) can be posted. There is no better way to find and communicate with like-minded voters.

One new campaigning method that has great promise involves the use of the Internet. Jesse "The Body" Ventura, former wrestler (yes, wrestler) and successful 1998 candidate for governor of Minnesota, pioneered the use of the Internet as an organizational tool. His committee raised $43,000 on the Internet, and a single e-mailed appeal generated 250 campaign volunteers. Senator McCain's 2000 presidential campaign, likewise, created a grassroots' operation with the assistance of the Internet. Within 48 hours of McCain's surprise victory in the New Hampshire primary, the fund-raising link to his Web site had collected $1 million. In California, over 300 candidates established campaign Web sites for the 2000 election while only two had done so just six years previously. If you are computer savvy, you may have a bright future in politics.[46]

Volunteers

Money is necessary to a successful campaign, but it is not always enough. Volunteers are also essential. While it is possible to hire a professional firm to, say, make telephone calls to voters, volunteers are much better for this purpose for two reasons. First, the money saved by using free, volunteer labor in place of paid workers can be shifted to other purposes such as television. Second, volunteers who are truly devoted to the candidate will be much more effective advocates than callers who are only doing it for the money. Volunteers who seem sincere can pick up votes that cannot be won in any other way and are worth their weight in gold to a candidate.

Individuals who wish to pursue a political career, or who simply wish to have clout in their communities, will make a point of volunteering to help candidates in their campaigns. Campaign volunteers are the sort of people who get hired for staff jobs or get picked to serve on local boards and commissions. You might keep this in mind if you are politically inclined—or just power hungry!

CONCLUSION

The United States is the world's leading democracy, but this country's system has also shown weaknesses in recent years. State and local governments conduct all elections, even those for national offices. In many respects, the ballot technology still needs improvement. Because of the electoral college, it is possible to have a president who cannot claim to speak for a majority of the voters. The high level of campaign spending and the open disregard for some of the campaign finance laws have given the impression of a political process that is not fully living up to democratic ideals. Reforms may eventually correct some of these problems, but some will probably persist for the foreseeable future.

Some critics long for a return to the "good old days" when candidates utilized less expensive and more personal methods of campaigning. However, television is not going to go away, and media campaigns require massive amounts of money. Fund-raising and professional management are essential to successful campaigns in today's world. Still, volunteers and the "personal touch" will always have a major role to play in the process. Maybe we should stress voter education so that the electorate will not be fooled by $1500 suits, perfectly capped teeth, hair styled by Sassoon, Hollywood makeup, and speeches loaded with meaningless slogans like "Who do you trust?" or "Don't stop thinking about tomorrow."

Chapter Nine Notes

[1]"Off the Record," *Campaigns and Elections: The Magazine for People in Politics,* February 2005, 54.

[2]"Off the Record," *Campaigns & Elections: The Magazine for People in Politics*, December/January 2001, 94.

[3]"A 'Modern' Democracy that Can't Count Votes," *Los Angeles Times*, December 11, 2000, A1-A17.

[4]"Touchscreen Voting Problems Reported," The Associated Press, November 5, 2004.

[5]Keith Olbermann, "All I know is what I don't read in the papers," countdown.msnbc.com posted November 19, 2004.

[6]"Who's Counting Our Votes?" *The Hightower Lowdown*, Oct. 2003, 5.

[7]Dan Seligson, "More Changes at the Polls?" Campaigns *and Elections*, February, 2005, 27. "Bills Would Alter Election Procedures," *Los Angeles Times*, February 18, 2005, A23.

[8]"Obscure Theory Fells a Mayor," Los Angeles Times, February 10, 2002, B1.

[9]"Florida: Controversy Centers on New Ballot," *Los Angeles Times*, November 9, 2000, B1-B7.

[10]Thomas Hargrove, "Election Study Finds Widespread Ballot-Counting Problems," newsobserver.com posted December 23, 2004.

[11]In the past, a number of states including Alaska, California, and Washington used a partisan blanket primary. These blanket primaries were declared unconstitutional by the Supreme Court in *California Democratic Party v. Jones*, (530 U.S. 567), 2000.

[12]"Citizen Initiatives," *Campaigns and Elections*, May 1994, 33-36. "A Gamble That Paid Off," *California Journal*, December 1998, 44-47.

[13]"The Politics of Recall," *California Journal*, July 1995, 17.

[14]Ron Faucheuz, "Inside Politics: the Follies," *Campaigns and Elections*, December 2004/January 2005, 13.

[15]"Obscure Theory Fells a Mayor," *Los Angeles Times*, 10 February 2002, B1. The judge ruled that the winning candidate, whose name was first on the ballot received 306 "extra" votes he might not have gotten, a figure which was more than his margin of victory.

[16]May, 21, 1989, sec. 4, 1

[17]Maine and Nebraska do not use the winner-take-all system for electoral vote.

[18]In 1876, Rutherford B. Hayes defeated the popular-vote winner Samuel J. Tilden in the electoral college. In 1888, Grover Cleveland won the popular vote but lost to Benjamin Harrison in the electoral college. In 2000, George W. Bush won the electoral vote but lost the popular vote to Al Gore by about 500,000 votes.

[19]In the election of 1800, Thomas Jefferson and Aaron Burr had an equal number of electoral votes. After 36 ballots, the House of Representatives chose Thomas Jefferson. Because of the way the Constitution was written before the 12th Amendment was passed, Burr automatically became vice president. Similarly, the House of Representatives on the first ballot elected John Quincy Adams president in 1824 even though Andrew Jackson, one of his opponents, had received more popular votes. The Senate has had to choose a vice president only once. The Senate selected Richard M. Johnson in 1837 after no one received a majority of the electoral vote in the 1836 election.

[20]Members of the House of Representatives are frequently referred to as "Congressmen." Although members of both the House and the Senate are technically members of Congress and, therefore, "Congressmen," the term is usually used to mean members of the House of Representatives.

[21]Nancy Vogel, "Foes Make Remap Offer to Gov." *Los Angeles Times,* March 1, 2005, Ba.

[22]"Shifting Racial Lines," *Newsweek*, 10 July 1995, 38-39.

[23]Quote attributed to Jess M. Unruh, former Speaker of the California State Assembly.

[24]*Saginaw News*, 12 May 1988, A14; article based on research by Martin Seligman and Harold Zullow of the University of Pennsylvania.

[25]Richard M. Nixon, *Six Crises* (New York: Doubleday & Co., 1962), 367.

[26]"The Follies," *Campaigns & Elections,* December/January 2001, 12.

[27]Mildred L. Amer, "Membership of the 109th Congress: A Profile," Congressional Research Service, The Library of Congress, Order Code RS22007, December/January 2001,12.

[28]"The Follies," op. cit., 18.

[29]Statement attributed to Jess M. Unruh.

[30]Thomas B. Edsall and James V. Grimaldi, "On Nov. 2, GOP Got More Bang for its Billion, Analysis Shows," *Washington Post*, December 30, 2004, A01.

[31]Micah L. Sifry, "Running Clean," TomPaine.com, posted December 6, 2004.

[32]"Cost of California Races Expected to Top $200 Million," *Los Angeles Times*, 6 November 2000, A3-A12.

[33]Margaret Taler, "Davis Raised Record Amount," *Sacramento Bee*, 1 February 2003, A-1.

[34]Jessica Kowal, "Bloomberg Spends Nearly $70M on Campaign," *Newsday*, 3 December 2001, Part 2/Features.

[35]Final report of the Senate Select Committee on Presidential Campaign Activities, 93rd Congress, 2nd sess. (Washington, D.C.: Government Printing Office, 1974), 904.

[36]Christopher Ogden, *Life of the Party* (New York: Warner Books, 1994), 484-498.

[37]"Campaign Money Spattering On," *The Economist*, 14 February 1998, 14.

[38]"L.A. Leaders' Support Cited in Decision to Free Vignali," *Los Angeles Times*, 19 February 2001, A1-A13.

[39]"PAC Poop Out," *Campaigns & Elections*, May 1995, 8-9.

[40]Kowal.

[41]"Spending: Records Fall as Campaigns Report Totals," *Los Angeles Times*, 8 December 2000, A44.

[42]Jonathan Chair, "Reform School: Enron and the Need for Campaign Finance Reform," *The New Republic*, 4 February 2002, 15-16.

[43]David G. Salvage, "High Court Upholds Most of Campaign Finance Law," *Los Angeles Times*, December 11, 2003, A1.

[44]"Top Individual Contributors to 527 Committees — 2004 Election Cycle," posted 01/15/2005 by Blurblogger, figures taken from IRS data.

[45]"Good Cinematography Brings Power to Political Ads," *Campaigns & Elections*, August 2000, 54-55.

[46]"Politicians Discover Wonders of the Web." *San Diego Union-Tribune*, 30 December 1998. "Clamoring for Cyberspace," *California Journal*, September 2000, 10-16.

Suggested Readings

Abramson, Paul R., John H. Aldrich, and David W. Rohde. *Change and Continuity in the 1992 Elections.* Washington, D.C.: CQ Press, 1995.

Ansolabehere, Stephenn and Shanto Iyengar. *Going Negative: How Attack Ads Shrink and Polarize the Electorate.* New York: Free Press, 1995.

Greive, R. R. *The Blood, Sweat, and Tears of Political Victory—and Defeat.* Lanham, Md.: University Press of America, 1996.

Kern, Montague. *30-Second Politics: Political Advertising in the Eighties.* New York: Praeger, 1989.

Nelson, Michael, ed. *The Elections of 1996.* Washington, D.C.: CQ Press, 1997.

Sabato, Larry J., ed. *Campaigns and Elections: A Reader in Modern American Politics.* Glenview, Ill.: Scott, Foresman, 1989.

Part Three
Representing the People

The Washington Monument

In the previous two sections we looked at how our government was put together, as well as how we, as citizens, elect public officials and influence their behavior. Now we turn our attention to the institutions of government, or the structure through which power is exercised.

In creating our government, the Framers thought it best to divide power among three separate branches: the legislative, the executive, and the judicial. This concept, separation of powers, was a unique and revolutionary idea in world government. The obvious intent in separating power was to safeguard against the potential of political abuse and, thus, guarantee the continuation of democracy within the nation. Not content, the Framers also chose to create a system of checks and balances among the three branches as a further safeguard. Each branch was allotted powers to check the powers of the other two branches. Although the Framers may or may not have been cognizant of it, two interesting by-products resulted from this move. First, it made cooperation among the branches an absolute necessity before governmental action could be taken. Second, it guaranteed that the personality of governmental leaders would greatly influence the balance of power from one branch to another.

With this in mind, we turn to the institutions of our government. We look briefly at some of the factors that influenced the structuring of each branch and the powers allotted to it. Likewise, we will examine the relationship between branches, as well as how personalities and changing times have influenced both their structure and political role. Also, we will examine some problems inherent within each branch and some suggestions for improvements. Finally, we conclude with a look at foreign policy in chapters thirteen and fourteen.

Chapter Ten

Congress:
The People's Branch

There is little doubt that the architects of the United States government had a grand vision for Congress. The Framers of the Constitution termed it the "people's branch," and they envisioned it as the first among equals in the three co-equal branches. It would make all laws, and both the executive and judicial branches, while not totally subordinate to it, would carry out its will. The Constitution charged the executive branch with enforcing the laws Congress made and charged the judicial branch with interpreting those laws. The expectation of the Framers that Congress would be the first among equals did not work out. While the power of Congress has fluctuated over the decades since this government first set up shop, there is little doubt that beginning with the 1930s and onward, it has steadily lost ground to the other two branches, particularly the presidency. Much of this can be attributed to a changing world that demands swift and decisive action; still, another part lies with the fragmentation of power and uncertainty of purpose that has frozen Congress in a seemingly permanent state of inertia. Nonetheless, the modern creature called the Congress is significantly different from the institution envisioned by the Framers.

With all branches of the government assembled in the House of Representatives, the president delivers his first "State of the Union" address.

THE INSTITUTIONAL CONTEXT OF THE CONGRESS

The institutions of governance, the Congress, the presidency, and the federal courts, are all political institutions, as well as functional institutions. That is, while the function of the Congress is to pass laws, that function is carried out by politicians. Politicians do things for political reasons; consequently, if one's perception of how Congress operates is based on the "how-a-bill-becomes-a-law" approach, one can be misled concerning the actual operating procedures of the Congress.

A "Congress" is considered to be one of the two-year election cycles of Representatives. It is divided into sessions that correspond with the calendar year. For example, the first session of the 109th Congress (the 109th Congress since 1789) began in January 2005.

Representation

A constituent is a person who lives in a representative's or a senator's electoral district. The electoral district is the whole state for a senator and a geographic part of a state for a representative. Members of Congress represent their constituents in a variety of ways.

Representing Individuals. Members of Congress represent their constituents as individuals primarily by means of casework. **Casework** occurs when a member of Congress intervenes with the bureaucracy on behalf of a constituent. The bureaucracy, for our purposes, can be understood as executive-branch employees. Bureaucrats typically have a range of discretion they can exercise without getting permission from their own superiors. In casework, the members essentially ~~ask bureaucrats to use their authority in a way that favors the constituent.~~ By analogy, if a police officer stops someone for speeding, that police officer can be considered a bureaucrat. (He or she is employed by the executive branch of the state or locality.) Police officers typically would have a range of discretion. They could give the person a warning, give him or her a ticket for speeding, or give the person multiple tickets: for speeding, broken tail lights, and other infractions. ~~In casework, constituents want someone to intervene so that they get a warning and not a fistful of tickets.~~ So why would the bureaucrats listen to members of Congress? They listen because Congress writes the budget used by the bureaucracy and writes the laws under which bureaucrats operate. ~~If the bureaucrats are not cooperative with members of Congress, the bureaucratic budgets can be cut or the laws which govern the bureaucracy can be rewritten.~~ The line that members of Congress cannot cross, however, is that they cannot ask the bureaucrat to do anything illegal or unethical.

Representing Interest Groups. Members also represent organized interests in their districts. These interest groups typically are not concerned with casework. Casework is aimed at solving people problems – lost social security checks and the like. Organized interests (e.g., the plumbers union or the National Wildlife Federation) are generally concerned with legislation that affects the group's agenda. Members then represent these interest groups by support or opposition to such legislation.

Representing the District or State. Members represent their districts or states by supporting or opposing all kinds of legislation. In representing their districts, members are primarily concerned with the impact of the legislation on their constituents in their respective districts. For example, in considering a trade agreement, most members would be primarily concerned with whether the trade pact would increase the number of jobs in their districts and less concerned with its impact on the country as a whole. If the member represents a coastal district that sees employment increase if international trade increases, the congressional member would probably support the trade pact even if it led to job losses, say, in North Dakota. The point of this scenario is that members generally consider the economic and political interests of their districts first and the rest of the country second. Representatives from California are expected to look after the interests of California first and be less concerned with how legislation affects Florida. In this sense, party is an almost irrelevant consideration. Whether the representatives from California are Republicans or Democrats, they will look after their districts first, irrespective of party label.

Members also represent their districts with **"pork barrel" legislation, also sometimes called "pork."** Definitions of pork vary. One representative's *pork* is another's *vital government program.* The concept behind pork is that ~~it is an economic benefit that is not economically justified.~~ For example, if a member had a small town in his or her district and that town had a post office, the member might try to get another post office for the town. The purpose of the second post office would not be to deliver the mail more effectively, since the first post office was doing a perfectly adequate job of that. On the contrary, the purpose of the second post office might be to provide additional jobs in a town that needs jobs. Citizens of the town, now grateful for the additional jobs, may be more inclined to vote for the member's re-election.

Voting on Legislation

There are a variety of ways by which members vote on legislation. Often when considering a given piece of legislation, however, many members have not actually read the proposed legislation from cover to cover, nor have they listened to the entire debate concerning that legislation. Yet, they often feel obliged to vote on this legislation. The result of this behavior is that many members vote based on factors other than having read or listened to debate on a given piece of legislation.

Personal Knowledge. One method whereby members vote is personal knowledge. It is expected that members of Congress develop expertise in several policy areas. If a member of Congress is voting on a piece of legislation concerning one of those policy areas, the member can vote based on his or her own expertise. Barack Obama, for example, a newly elected Democratic U.S. Senator from Illinois is well known for reaching across party lines to shape compromise. His knowledge of cross-party interaction could be very helpful in issues demanding such skills.

District Majority. Another voting modality is what can be called a district majority. If a member's office is getting stacks of traditional mail, faxes, phone calls, e-mails, etc., supporting a particular position on an issue, it is in the interest of the member to support that position. The letters and e-mails, of course, are not a scientific sampling of public opinion in the district. It is a self-selected sample. It may also be that the letters and e-mails are part of a "canned" campaign. Rush Limbaugh may get on the radio one afternoon, for example, and say that everyone should oppose House Resolution XYZ. Some portion of his listeners will, no doubt, call or write their member of Congress, reflecting Mr. Limbaugh's arguments. It does not matter that the persons making the phone calls and writing the letters may be completely uninformed about the issue. What matters is that they cared enough to write the letter or make the phone call. If they care enough to do those things, they are pretty well guaranteed to be voters, and members of Congress care a whole lot about voters! It is possible that other persons in the district feel differently about the issue, but the fact is that persons feeling differently did not care enough to communicate their position. The member, for his or her own electoral health, should pay attention to

Congressman Cliff Stearns takes time out from his busy schedule to speak to the press on issues of importance to his constituents. In the background are other members of Congress from the state of Florida. Not only is such work necessary to keep up with the issues at home, but it also pays big dividends at the ballot box.

the folks who are communicating with the office. Having said that, members cannot simply sit around waiting to see what their constituents say about an issue and make their voting decision based on constituents' views. Although members of Congress receive mountains of mail and "goboodles" of phone calls and e-mails about issues, these communications do not address every issue facing the Congress or even most issues. The largest number of messages typically involve what we sometimes refer to as "hot-button" issues, like abortion or gun control. Communications on more mundane issues, like a raise in pay for the military or insurance regulation, are negligible from individual constituents. What all this boils down to is this: If members of Congress are getting all those communications about an issue, they had better support that district majority. On most issues, however, they will not get an extraordinary amount of mail and phone calls.

Advice from Associates. Members also vote based on advice they receive from other trusted members. Generally this advice will come from someone from their own wing of their political party. A conservative Republican, for example, will get advice from some other conservative Republican. In addition, members of Congress employ a large number of people in their staff who are experts in particular areas of legislation. These staffers can wield tremendous influence over members of Congress who do not have that same expertise. Many times members of Congress can be seen walking to the floor of the House or Senate for a vote while being "briefed" by a staff member about how the member should vote.

Party Loyalty. Finally, members sometimes base their votes on loyalty to their own party. It is often the case that members don't really care if the bill passes or not, nor do their constituents particularly care. For instance, suppose the member is from Trenton, New Jersey, and the bill in question is an agricultural aid bill. As far as the people in much of New Jersey are concerned, the cows just walk into the supermarket and lay down. In that instance, the member from New Jersey might vote whatever position his or her party takes on the legislation. Similarly, when an urban aid bill comes up, a member from rural Texas probably won't care one way or the other, nor will his or her constituents. Therefore, the member will vote according to the position taken by his or her party.

Structure

The structure of Congress is **bicameral**, meaning it is a two-house legislative body. Representatives serve two-year terms and senators six-year, staggered terms. The entire House stands for re-election every two years, while only one-third of the Senate is up for election. Therefore, the Senate, barring some extraordinary circumstances, will always have experienced people in it.

Each state is allotted two senators, but membership in the House is based on the population of each state relative to the other states. In 1911, Congress voted to fix the size of the House of Representatives at 435. Every ten years after the census, these 435 seats are allocated to the states based on the latest census data.

Tenure of Office

It is generally taken for granted that members of Congress will seek re-election. Indeed, this has become the age of the career politician. This has not, however, always been true. In the early days Congress was a passing fancy for most members, with few running for re-election after having served one term. Long hours, poor pay, the difficulty of travel, and separation from family discouraged most members from seeking another term. Shortly after the Civil War the trend began to change. Members suddenly became interested in re-election, and the average length rose to two terms with many members serving more. This trend continued until today the average stay for a House member is five terms or ten years. Senators stay longer too. The vast majority serve two terms (twelve years) or more. However, it should be mentioned that the increased workload of Congress, as well as the expertise and specialization required of today's legislators, has greatly contributed to the emergence of the "professional politician."

FUNCTIONS AND RESPONSIBILITIES

Most people perceive the function of Congress as only that of enacting laws. While lawmaking is the primary function of Congress, it is not its only function. The duties and responsibilities of Congress are varied and complex.

Lawmaking

Although there is considerable variation in the structures of democratic governments throughout the world, the single, indispensable institution in each is that of the legislature. Regardless of what it is termed—Congress, Parliament, Knesset (Israel), etc.—there must exist a body within each democracy charged with making the laws. The Constitution provides Congress with additional powers through various amendments. If no presidential candidate receives a majority of the electoral vote, the Twelfth Amendment gives Congress the right to decide. This does not normally happen, but it almost occurred during the 2000 presidential contest. The Sixteenth Amendment provides Congress with the right to impose income taxes. And, under emergency conditions when both the president-elect and vice president-elect shall have died, resigned, or have been found not to qualify, the Twentieth Amendment designates that Congress will determine who will be the acting president.

Oversight

A common complaint voiced by most legislators is that they are so busy with current legislation that they do not have the time to review how legislation already passed is being implemented. Termed **oversight**, this function is crucial to maintaining a balance between Congress and the executive branch of government. The purpose of the oversight process is to allow Congress to determine that the laws are being implemented by the executive branch in the way that Congress intended. Although Congress has the power to enact laws, it must rely upon the executive branch to carry them out once passed. Often times, those in the position of implementing policy either do not understand the intentions of Congress or, perhaps, might disagree with the policy decision itself. These employees of the executive branch could either refuse to implement the policy by inaction (procrastination) or by interpreting the policy decision in a way that conforms to their own individual philosophy. If the executive agency is not enforcing the law the way that Congress intended, and if the executive agency is reluctant to change what it is doing, the Congress has some tools to get its attention. For instance, Congress can always rewrite the law or cut the agency's budget. If Congress is intent on having the executive branch enforce the law in a particular way, Congress can ultimately force the issue and, if push comes to shove, abolish the rebellious agency.

	Number in the House if it were representative of American society at large	Number in the 105th Congress	Number in the 106th Congress	Number in the 107th Congress	Number in the 108th Congress
Men	184	384	379	376	374
Women	226	46	56	59	61
Black	52	37	35	34	39
Hispanic	30	18	19	18	18
Poor	65	0	0	0	0
Lawyers	2	225	239	234	235
Under 45	300	124	136	140	141

Table 10.1

To What Extent Does the House Mirror Society?

Public Education

One often overlooked function of Congress is that of educating the public. Communication is a two-way street. Just as it is important for a member of Congress to listen to his/her constituency—to find out their problems, needs and opinions—it is also important to provide information that will help citizens understand the complexities of governmental action. Such understanding can lead to more responsible opinion formation, participation in local government affairs, and voting in elections. Members of Congress perform this function by speaking to local groups, writing articles in local papers, or communicating directly to constituents through the mail. The information revolution has also gone a long way in facilitating this public education function. Information on current activities in Congress and the times and subjects of congressional hearings are now readily available on the Internet.

Conflict Resolution

The United States is a pluralistic country. Abortion, school prayer, defense spending, commitment of resources to space exploration, welfare expenditures, and so forth are just a few areas in which Americans disagree. In many countries disagreement on any one of the above issues might erupt into violence with the street becoming the battleground for conflict resolution. In stable democratic governments, this is not the way in which conflict is handled. In our society, differences of view are resolved orderly and peacefully in Congress. Representatives of various views (lobbyists) meet and through persuasion convince the leaders of government that their position is correct. More often than not, neither side achieves total victory. ~~Both sides end up having an impact, and the difference between views are resolved through **compromise** with each side winning and losing as legislative leaders attempt to accommodate the interests of many different groups. Members of Congress refer to this process as *horse-trading*—"You give me this and I'll let you have that."~~ Some ~~political experts have criticized Congress as being too eager to compromise.~~ Thus, they insist, governmental ~~action is "watered down,"~~ and problems are not really resolved. Others, however, maintain that compromise in difficult situations where individuals hold strongly different beliefs is necessary. Not only does it legitimize governmental decision, it also prevents conflict from tearing the nation apart.

Constituent Service

As we saw earlier, ~~constituent service, also called casework,~~ regularly takes place, where legislators deal with various requests from the people back in their states and districts. The members of Congress also provide district or state-wide benefits. These services frequently are in the form of some economic gain to the district or state such as a defense contract for a major employer or repairs to highways and bridges. Securing these district and state-wide benefits for their constituents is a legitimate function for members of Congress to pursue.

POLITICAL ORGANIZATION OF THE CONGRESS

When we look at the political organization of Congress, we are looking at party organization in both the House of Representatives and the Senate. The important thing to remember is that ~~the majority party controls the operations of each chamber;~~ this means they control the agenda of the chamber, the administration of rules in the chamber, and the number of Democrats and Republicans on committees in the body (House or Senate). ~~The agenda, for our purposes, consists of the legislation that the Congress will debate and vote on,~~ and that agenda is set by the majority party. This is particularly important in the U.S. House of Representatives, where there is much less cooperation between Democrats and Republicans for reasons we will address a bit later.

This majority-party control has some real-world consequences. ~~In the last decade, Republicans have controlled the House, meaning that if you were a Democrat from Iowa, not only would legislation you proposed not be voted on, it probably would not even be debated.~~ Democrats, of course, also prevented Republican legislation from being debated or voted on in the House during the preceding four decades of Democratic control. Additionally, the ~~majority party controls the rules of the chamber~~ (under what circumstances to allow amendments to legislation, etc.). These rules will also be manipulated by the majority for their own political advantage. Unlike student government in high school, ~~in the U.S. Congress there is no attempt to be fair.~~ Members were not elected to be fair; they were elected, so many of them believe, to advance their particular political agenda.

Finally, the majority party controls the committees. In practice, control of the committees means that the majority party will see to it that every committee is stacked in that party's favor with important committees heavily stacked. For example, in the first session of the 109th Congress, there were 31 Republicans and 26 Democrats on the House Energy and Commerce Committee while the more important House Ways and Means Committee (the committee that proposes tax legislation to fund budgets) was stacked 24 Republicans to only 17 Democrats. This lopsided arrangement is done intentionally by the majority party to make sure it is not outvoted in committee. Both parties do this when they are in the majority, and it is used as a method of control by the majority.

It is worth noting that institutionally the House and Senate are very different creatures. In the House there is usually little cooperation between Democrats and Republicans because the majority party has the ability essentially to act while ignoring the minority party. By contrast, in the Senate there is genuine cooperation between Republicans and Democrats, irrespective of which party is in charge. Keep in mind, however, that no matter which party controls, there are times that some members will "bolt" their own party and vote with the opposition. This behavior demonstrates with clarity that representing the state, a district, or interest group supersedes party loyalty.

The political leadership in the House revolves around the position of **Speaker of the House.** The Speaker is the only constitutional officer in the House; that is, he or she is the only officer of the House required by the Constitution. The other officers, majority and minority leaders, the party whips, etc., were created in the nineteenth century and could be dispensed with any time the House membership would see fit. The Speaker cannot be dispensed with, and representatives elect a member to be Speaker every two years with each new Congress. One is elected Speaker in what amounts to a second election after the general election in November. Sometime in December or early January, the newly elected members of the House get together to begin this process. Conceptually all the Democratic members of the House are put in one room and all the Republican members of the House in another. The Democrats elect a Democratic candidate for Speaker and the Republicans elect a Republican candidate for Speaker. When it's time for the voting, there is a party-line (partisan) vote with all the Democrats voting for the Democratic candidate and all the Republicans voting for the Republican candidate. The party with the majority in the House wins this vote, and their candidate becomes Speaker. Voting for someone other than the candidate nominated by one's party is highly discouraged by means of punishment to rebellious party members. The political leadership of the respective party will remove the offenders from committee assignments that they wanted and, instead, will put them on committees that they did not want.

The Speaker is the most powerful position in the House in that he or she controls the chamber and plans the legislative agenda. Having said that, most modern Speakers content themselves to setting general legislative themes for the session, leaving the day-to-day operations of the House chamber under the control of the majority leader. The majority leader is also elected by his or her colleagues in the majority party. So, for example, with Republicans in control of the House, the Republican members elect one of their own to act as majority leader. If we think of the Speaker as being similar to the president of a bank, the majority leader would be analogous to the branch manager, making many of the day-to-day decisions about operations. The minority leader is elected by the members of the minority party and serves as their spokesperson. The minority leader is sometimes consulted by the political leadership of the majority party but is generally irrelevant to the legislative process. Without the votes to control anything in the chamber, the House minority leader is often left only to complain about events in the House on the Sunday morning talk shows.

In addition, both parties have whips, with some organizational differences between those from the Democratic Party and those from the Republican Party. The term "whip" derives from the nineteenth century "Whippers" who kept the dogs in line during English fox hunts. The whips and various assistant whips are all elected by their colleagues, with Democratic whips being elected by House Democrats and Republican whips elected by House Republicans. The whips serve as the "eyes and ears" of the political leadership in the ranks of the two parties. They count votes during debate and report their results to their respective political leadership. Legislative debate may span several calendar days and the number of Democrats and Republicans supporting a particular measure may change significantly as the debate progresses and amendments are added or removed from proposed legislation. The whips inform their respective political leadership as to where their members are in terms of supporting or opposing a bill at a given point in time. This information helps the political leadership of both parties to plan strategies to pass or derail the proposed legislation. The whips also serve the function of informing members what the party position is with respect to a given piece of legislation. With some legislation the party positions are obvious; if a piece of legislation deals with gun control or abortion, it does not take a rocket scientist to know how the parties will come down on it. However, most legislation is not so obvious as to indicate a party's position. For example, if a piece of legislation is proposed that would provide commercial assistance to merchants in Trinidad, the position that the Democratic and Republican Parties would take is not at all clear. At this juncture, the whips play a role in letting members know what the party position is on that piece of legislation. The Democratic and Republican Party caucuses will have talked about the legislation proposing assistance to the Trinidad merchants and arrived at a position on it. Members of the House that missed that caucus would then be informed by the whips as to what the party position is on the legislation. Whips also serve as "cattle drivers" to "round up" the party's members when a vote is about to take place and make sure that the members are present.

Political leadership in the Senate, as one might expect, is a bit different than in the House. Senate leadership is an example where the intent of the Framers went a bit astray. It was expected that the vice president would play a significant and substantive role as president of the Senate, but that's not how it worked out. The primary role of the vice president, beyond breaking tie votes in the Senate, has turned out to be attending the funerals of foreign leaders when the president is not interested in going. The role of the vice president has been changing somewhat during the last couple of decades of the twentieth century, and the importance of the vice president has been escalating. The vice president's role in the Senate, however, is still minimal and, with the exception of ceremonial events, the vice president generally will show up in the Senate only three or four times a year when a tie vote is anticipated. If there is a tie vote and the vice president is not in attendance, then the legislation would not pass. Since the vice president is rarely in attendance in the Senate, his or her place is taken by the president pro tempore (usually just referred to as president pro tem). By tradition, the president pro tem is the member of the majority party with the longest number of years of continuous service. This officer in theory presides over Senate floor debate. The president pro tem, however, usually delegates this task to other, more junior senators. The position is essentially one of a glorified clerk since the president pro tem acts on the advice of the Senate majority leader. The Senate majority leader is the "boss" of the Senate and, in that sense, is the equivalent of the Speaker of the House.

Table 10.2: Major Differences Between the House and Senate

Larger (435 members)	Smaller (100 members)
Shorter term of office (2 years)	Longer term of office (6 years)
Less flexible rules	More flexible rules
Narrower constituency	Broader, more varied, constituency
Policy specialists	Policy generalists
Power less evenly distributed	Power more evenly distributed
Less prestige	More prestige
More expeditious in floor debate	Less expeditious in floor debate
Less reliance on staff	More reliance on staff
Less press and media coverage, but floor proceedings televised	More press and media coverage

Source: Adapted from Walter J. Oleszek, *Congressional Procedures and the Policy Process*, 3rd. ed., (Washington, D.C.: Congressional Quarterly Press, 1989), p. 24.

While there are similarities, the Senate is quite unlike the House in that there is genuine cooperation between the majority and minority leaders. As in the House, the majority party elects the majority leader, and the minority party elects the minority leader. Unlike the House, however, legislative themes are set in consultation with the minority party. Likewise, there are whips in the Senate, but these positions are somewhat less relevant than they are in the House. Since the Senate is a much smaller body of 100 as compared to 435 in the House, it is relatively easier for the party leadership to keep track of the political intentions of their members.

The Congressional Committee System

Congress is organized along committee lines. Most legislative work in Congress takes place within the committee, not on the floor of the House or the Senate. The committee system is often referred to as Congress' *little legislatures*. The purpose of the committee is to study bills and make recommendations to the entire membership of their respective chambers. When the bill reaches the committee, it usually is referred to a subcommittee. Subcommittees are smaller

Table 10.3: PARTY LEADERS IN THE 108th CONGRESS, 2001-2003

Position	Incumbent	Party/State	Leader Since
House			
Speaker	J. Dennis Hastert	R., Ill	Jan. 1999
Majority leader	Tom DeLay	R., Tex.	Jan. 2003
Majority whip	Roy Blunt	R., Missouri	Jan. 2003
Chairperson of Republican Conference	Deborah Pryce	R., Ohio	Jan. 2003
Minority leader	Nancy Pelosi	D., Ca.	Jan. 2003
Minority whip	Steny Hoyer	D., Md.	Jan. 2003
Chairperson of the Democratic Caucus	Robert Menendez	D., NJ	Jan. 2003
Senate			
President *pro tempore*	Ted Stevens	R., Alaska	Jan. 2003
Majority floor leader	Bill Frist	R., Tenn.	Jan. 2003
Assistant majority leader	Mitch McConnell	R., Ky.	Jan. 2003
Secretary of the Republican Conference	Rick Santorum	R., Pa.	Jan. 2003
Minority floor leader	Tom Daschle	D., S.Dak.	June 2001
Assistant floor leader	Harry Reid	D., Nev.	Jan. 2003
Chairperson of the Democratic Caucus	Barbara Mikulski	D., Md.	Jan. 1995

units of the committee and are usually chaired by a ranking (senior) member of the majority party. In the House, subcommittees have become an important part of the legislative process, and their action on bills is usually considered critical to a bill's ultimate success. The Senate, on the other hand, has not made extensive use of the subcommittee system. This difference is probably a result of the Senate's smaller membership. In many cases subcommittees have become the burial ground for legislation deemed either inappropriate to the needs of the country or too controversial for consideration.

Institutionally the House and Senate have, at least, three layers of rules; there are the rules for the whole House or the whole Senate, the rules for a particular full committee of the House or Senate, and the rules for a particular subcommittee of the House or Senate. These rules accomplish a variety of things, one of which is to lay out the jurisdiction of the various committees and sub-committees. They define the scope of the committees' authority in considering legislation and determine the committees' powers and responsibilities.

The modern Congress has also established various types of committees, including standing, select, and joint committees. Standing committees are created at a particular point in time and last essentially forever, from Congress to Congress, and do not have to be re-created. The House Agriculture Committee, for example, was created by the House in 1820 with seven members and still exists today although with fifty-one members. Select committees are created by the House or the Senate but are generally expected to deal with problems that are limited in scope and in time. Select committees usually do not exist beyond two or three Congresses (four or six years). Joint committees are the only category of congressional committee where representatives and senators sit around the same table. The most common type of a joint committee is a conference committee that hammers out the differences between House and Senate versions of legislation. We will have much more to say about conference committees later in the chapter.

The Constitutional charge of the Congress is to legislate. Other functions are supposed to be related to that fundamental legislative charge. We sometimes hear of a congressional investigation into some public policy. While most congressional investigations have a political component (e.g., Democrats are trying to "get" Republicans, or Republicans are trying to "get" Democrats), in theory the purpose of the investigation is to determine whether congressional legislation is needed in the policy under investigation. If a congressional investigation uncovers evidence that the criminal statutes of the United States have been violated, the committee turns that evidence over to the U.S. Department of Justice, an executive agency. Since the executive branch does have the Constitutional charge of enforcing the law, the Department of Justice can have people prosecuted, and, if prosecuted successfully, put in jail. Congress, however, cannot jail anyone.

Table10.4: Standing Committees of the House and Senate

House	Senate
Agriculture	Agriculture, Nutrition and Forestry
Appropriations	Appropriations
Armed Services	Armed Services
Banking, Finance, and Urban Affairs	Banking, Finance, and Urban Affairs
Budget	Budget
District of Columbia	Commerce, Science and Transportation
Education	Energy and Natural Resources
Energy and Commerce	Environment and Publics Works
Foreign Affairs	Finance
Government Operations	Foreign Relations
House Administration	Governmental Affairs
Interior and Insular Affairs	Judiciary
Judiciary	Labor and Human Resources
Merchant Marines and Fisheries	Rules and Administration
Post Office and Civil Service	Small Business
Public Works and Transportation	Veterans' Affairs
Rules	
Science and Technology	
Small Business	
Standards of Official Conduct	
Veterans' Affairs	
Ways and Means	

[handwritten margin notes: "Spending" near Appropriations; "Agenda" near Rules; "Taxes" near Ways and Means; stars beside Appropriations, Budget, Government Operations, Rules, Ways and Means (House) and Appropriations, Budget, Rules and Administration (Senate)]

Now we come to an important component of the committee system, namely, the committee staff. **Committee staff are employees of Congress, not elected members of Congress, who work for a committee.** They are not to be confused with a member's personal or legislative staffs. These are different people altogether. While committee staffers are typically very bright, energetic, and talented persons, they are all **patronage** positions, appointments made to reward constituents for their support. The committee staff organizes and administers the hearings process and carries out much of the nuts and bolts work of the Congress. Members of Congress often do not read the entire text of every bill that comes before their respective bodies. Yet, someone has to read the bills, and frequently it is committee staffers who read every line of a piece of proposed legislation. This work allows the staff to write memos to committee members that may say that "line three of paragraph two on page ninety-eight appears to conflict with a Supreme Court decision in 1985." Then, the members can determine if a change is needed. Of course, it would be nice if every member read every piece of legislation in its entirety, but in the absence of that behavior, committee staffers help to fill the void. Committee staff also play a significant role in organizing and administering many congressional hearings. If a hearing involved the Al-Qaeda terrorist network responsible for the 9/11 attack against the United States, for example, committee members may not know the names of all of the relevant experts on Al-Qaeda. Committee staff, using academic and professional reference works, might then create a list of those experts along with contact information for them and present the list to the committee. Committee members may then choose some of their expert witnesses on Al-Qaeda from that list.

Congressional committees and subcommittees have a variety of options when considering legislation. They can report the legislation out favorably, unfavorably, or they can refuse to consider it. If legislation is reported out favorably it is usually with amendments (changes) to the original draft version of the legislation. That means the committee or subcommittee is saying to their colleagues that the bill is a good piece of legislation and they should vote in favor of it. If a committee or subcommittee reports a piece of legislation out unfavorably it, of course, means the contrary, that the legislation is flawed and does not deserve support from the rest of the Congress. The problem with reporting legislation out unfavorably, however, is that it makes the supporters of the legislation angry at the committee or subcommittee. For that reason, the preferred method to kill legislation is to refuse to consider it. That way it dies automatically at the end of the session, but no one has a political problem because no one has actually spoken against the legislation. It can even be reintroduced in the next session. Politically, this maneuver is quite relevant. About 10,000 bills are introduced every session that the sponsors (the members who introduce the legislation) know have no chance at all of passing the Congress. However, by introducing the legislation, the member can show a constituency group that they are "doing something" that furthers the constituency group's interest. This helps the member get political support from those constituents in the next election. For example, a member of the House from New York City might introduce legislation to ban the private possession of handguns in the United States. That member would know full well that such legislation would have no chance of passing the House, let alone the Senate, or of getting the signature of a president. The committee would just refuse to consider it. However, such a member could go back to gun-control groups in New York City and tell them that he or she was "doing something" about the availability of handguns. This might get the member the political support of the gun-control group in the next election.

Kay Bailey Hutchison (R-TX) became the first woman to represent her state in the U.S. Senate with her election in 1993. She was elected to a second full term in 2000 with the largest number of votes ever garnered in Texas, more than 4 million. With her election as Vice Chairman of the Senate Republican Conference, she became one of the top five leaders of Senate Republicans in the 107th Congress.

PASSING A LAW

Introducing a Bill

Bills for consideration by Congress can originate from a variety of sources: Congress, the executive branch, the bureaucracy, or special interest groups seeking legislation favorable to their memberships' well-being. Regardless of where the bill originates, it must be introduced (sponsored) by an elected member of Congress. Usually a bill will have a large number of sponsors. Not only does this practice provide a broader base of support for the bill, thus, enhancing its chances for passage, but also it allows members of Congress to claim credit for popular legislation without expending much time or effort. Usually, though, the first name on the bill is considered its major sponsor.

All bills must pass both chambers of Congress before becoming law. With the exception of appropriation bills and revenue bills, bills may be introduced in either chamber first or begin in both simultaneously. Appropriation bills (bills spending money) by custom originate in the House while the Constitution requires (in Article I Section XII) that bills raising revenues (tax bills) begin in the House.

In the House, the bill is placed in what is termed the *hopper*, a mahogany box near the Speaker's podium. Senators may introduce bills directly from the floor or hand them to the clerk for publication. The latter is preferable. After introduction, the respective clerk will assign a number to the bill and route it on to the government printing office for duplication and initial distribution to members of the relevant congressional committees. Along with numbers, bills are assigned prefixes to designate whether it is a House or Senate bill. An *HR* prefix would designate a House bill, whereas an *S* would be used for Senate bills.

Bills are classified as being one of three types: resolutions, private legislation, or public bills. They differ from each other in the following ways:

Resolutions: concern internal business of either chamber or, in some cases, reflect a sentiment of both the House and Senate on a particular matter.

Private Legislation: special acts that pertain only to the individuals for which the legislation was written. When Congress attempted to intervene in the Florida right-to-die case involving Terri Schiavo in the spring of 2005, it was in the form of a private bill. The bill requiring the federal courts to determine whether Ms. Schiavo's federal Constitutional rights were violated applied only to her and to no one else.

Public Bills: most numerous and undoubtedly the ones receiving the greatest attention, these bills concern issues that, generally speaking, affect everyone and the nation as a whole.

Once introduced and assigned a number, the bill is ready for its first reading. This simply means that it is assigned to a committee for study and action. In the House, the Speaker will make the assignment. In the Senate, it is the presiding officer. Usually, the subject matter of the legislation will determine to which committee it is assigned. However, in cases where there is overlapping jurisdiction, the wishes of its sponsor are usually honored. However, if the bill is extremely controversial, assignment can breakdown into a power play between competing interests. In some cases, a bill may be divided with parts referred to different committees. As one might imagine, a bill's assignment to the *right* committee, or a committee whose chairperson and membership are already favorably disposed toward it, greatly enhances its chances for success.

In Committee

If a subcommittee is serious about a bill, however, a full hearing will take place on its merits. The vast majority of hearings are open to the public although the hearings are sometimes in executive session, i.e., closed, if sensitive national security or law enforcement information is discussed.

Frequently experts or interested parties will be brought in to testify either in the bill's behalf or against it. Witnesses testifying at congressional hearings are testifying as to their opinion of the impact of the proposed legislation. Witnesses are normally invited to testify based on special knowledge (of the subject matter of the legislation) or special experience (relevant to the objectives of the proposed legislation). Afterwards, members submit amendments or offer different wording based, in theory, on testimony offered by the witnesses. Debate and compromise follows and, once finalized or "marked up," the bill, along with a comprehensive report explaining the revisions, is sent to the full committee.

Upon receiving the bill from its subcommittee, the full committee debates the bill. The full committee also will usually hold hearings and have a mark up session. Although this sounds redundant, the full committee is not actually duplicating the efforts of the subcommittee. The subcommittee's hearings and mark up session were focused on the policy area expertise of the subcommittee. The full committee's hearings and mark up session look at the subject matter of the legislation in terms of the wider policy area expertise of the full committee.

Three courses of action are possible. First, the full committee may accept the bill as reported to it by the subcommittee without revisions. This is uncommon. Second, the bill may be amended by the full committee, passed, and sent on for final action by the entire chamber. And third, it is possible that the full committee may reject the subcommittee's recommendation for passage and vote to kill the bill. It is possible, though it seldom happens, that the full committee will vote to report out a bill for consideration but attach to it an unfavorable recommendation. Nevertheless, when reporting a bill out, the committee must attach to it a comprehensive explanation of its handling and recommendations. Often members of the committee who disapprove of the majority view will attach their own reports urging the full chamber to overturn the committee's recommendation.

If a committee refuses to report out a bill that a majority of the chamber wants to consider, it is possible to pull the bill up after thirty days from the time the committee first received the bill. In the House, this action is achieved through a **discharge petition**, requiring the signatures of a majority (218) of the full House membership. The same action in the Senate is accomplished by enactment of a special resolution. Practically speaking though, formal methods are seldom successful. In a fifty-year period, 393 discharge petitions were circulated with 19 ending in successful results.[1] For the most part legislators are reluctant to sign such documents in fear that it might provoke affected committee members to seek revenge against them in the future. Up until now, the handling of a bill is fairly similar in both the House and Senate. After a bill clears the committee system, the procedure changes dramatically in the two chambers.

The Committee Chairperson

No discussion of leadership in Congress would be complete without a de account of the committee chairperson. As mentioned previously, the m of action in Congress takes place in the trenches—the committee system.

occurs within the trenches on a day-to-day basis is determined by the chairperson. This is true of both the House and Senate. Recent reforms have attempted to curb the power of chairpersons, but their influence still remains substantial. Currently chairpersons possess the power to call meetings, establish agendas, hire and fire committee staff, arrange hearings, designate conferees, act as floor managers, control committee funds and rooms, chair hearings and markups, and regulate the internal affairs and organization of the committee.

Each of these powers can be used in a variety of ways to influence legislation. Although not all chairpersons are this autocratic in the use of their power, each exerts considerable influence on the outcome of bills in the legislative process.

House Passage

A bill under consideration in the House is placed on a **calendar**. Five such calendars exist in the House with each designated for a particular type of legislation. Bills concerning the raising or spending of funds are placed on the so-called **Union Calendar**. The **House Calendar** contains all other major public measures. Bills that have to do with immigration requests, claims against the government, and other private matters are assigned to the **Private Calendar**. Noncontroversial bills are routed to the **Consent Calendar**. And lastly, all bills arriving by means of a discharge petition, and, as we have already seen, few of these exist, are placed on the **Discharge Calendar**.

With the exception of bills on the Private and Consent Calendars, all bills are routed through the **Rules Committee**, one of the most powerful committees in the House. The purpose of the Rules Committee is to act as a traffic cop to control the flow of bills to the House floor. It does this by scheduling bills for consideration in order of importance and organizing debate through the establishment of rules. In a body with 435 members it is easy to understand the importance of organization. The history of the Rules Committee is that its members use their power to create rules preventing legislation unfavorable to their constituents from either reaching the House floor or passing once there. As a result, the Rules Committee has been a political battleground with its members being among the most powerful members of Congress.

After clearing the Rules Committee, the next stop is the House floor where all 435 members will have the opportunity to voice their opinions in open debate. Usually debate is limited from four to eight hours with the time being divided equally between the two parties. Attendance at these sessions is sparse. The parliamentary device of the Committee of the Whole is used to allow debate in the House without an actual quorum. Normally, to do business, the House needs a minimum of 218 of the 435 members present. The Committee of the Whole allows debate to take place with as few as fifty-one members present. The limitation on the Committee of the Whole is that it can only use

Figure 10.5 HOW A BILL BECOMES A LAW

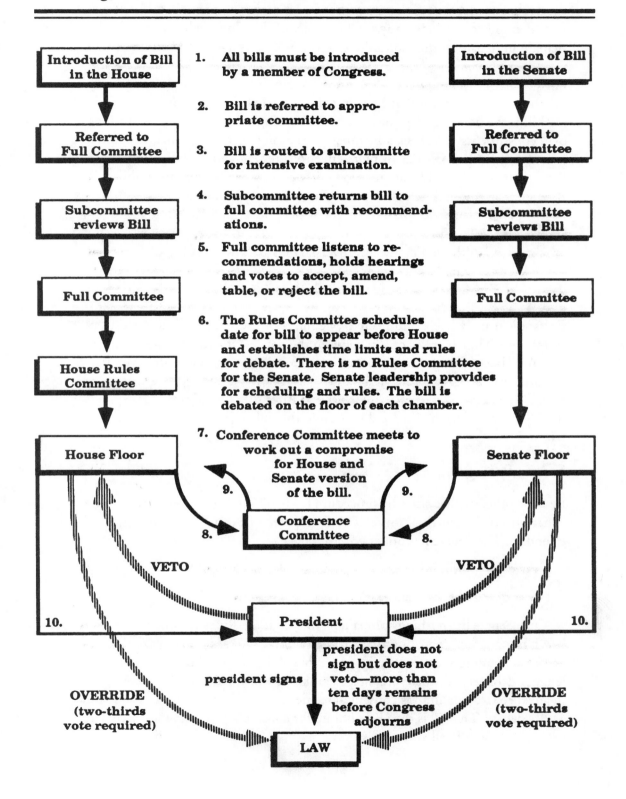

Introduction of Bill in the House

Referred to Full Committee

Subcommittee reviews Bill

Full Committee

House Rules Committee

House Floor

1. All bills must be introduced by a member of Congress.

2. Bill is referred to appropriate committee.

3. Bill is routed to subcommitte for intensive examination.

4. Subcommittee returns bill to full committee with recommendations.

5. Full committee listens to recommendations, holds hearings and votes to accept, amend, table, or reject the bill.

6. The Rules Committee schedules date for bill to appear before House and establishes time limits and rules for debate. There is no Rules Committee for the Senate. Senate leadership provides for scheduling and rules. The bill is debated on the floor of each chamber.

7. Conference Committee meets to work out a compromise for House and Senate version of the bill.

8.

9.

Introduction of Bill in the Senate

Referred to Full Committee

Subcommittee reviews Bill

Full Committee

Senate Floor

Conference Committee

VETO

VETO

President

10.

10.

OVERRIDE (two-thirds vote required)

OVERRIDE (two-thirds vote required)

president signs

president does not sign but does not veto—more than ten days remains before Congress adjourns

LAW

up debate hours and cannot actually pass anything. This device is used to allow the House to debate legislation without 218 members present, but it is not intended to keep anyone away. Any member of the House who wishes to participate in debate in the Committee of the Whole is able to. The reason that attendance is sparse at these debates is that for a given member debating a given bill may not be the best use of their time. For example, a member from a heavily urban area may not feel that listening and participating in debate over a farm aid bill is the best use of his or her time. They might better spend it with their own constituents. Likewise, a member from a rural area might spend time at a farm event in their district in preference to listening and participating in the debate on an urban aid bill. Congress has also allowed members to hand in their speeches without actually making them. Instead, they are merely recorded in the *Congressional Record.* Once debate concludes, the amendment process begins if the bill came up under what is called an **open rule,** which allows for amendments. Although many controversial bills are brought up under a **closed rule** where no amendments are allowed, an open rule brings the legislative process alive. The **five-minute rule** is invoked giving each member exactly five minutes to speak either in favor of or against amendments that modify the bill. Debate is usually lively and heated. Members of the House wishing to speak simply rise. Time is split equally between the parties. If two or more members rise, members of the committee that considered the legislation are given first opportunity. In all other cases the rights of seniority usually prevail. Amendments are accepted by simple majority vote. After the allotted time has expired, the House votes on the finalized version of the bill, and it is either accepted or rejected.

Senate Passage

Because of its smaller size, the procedure for handling legislation differs in the Senate from that in the House. The first difference can be seen in terms of calendars. The Senate has only two:

Calendar of General Orders—all public and private bills

Executive Calendar—all treaties and nominations

The Senate has nothing comparable to the House Rules Committee. Legislation reaches the Senate floor in typically two ways: by *unanimous consent* or by *motion.* Unanimous consent is the preferable of the two methods since it avoids lengthy debates and, therefore, helps crank out work. Here, both parties agree in advance to a unanimous consent agreement outlining the rules and time for a bill's debate. The bill is then brought up for consideration and either accepted or rejected by roll-call vote.

In the absence of unanimous consent, bills are brought to the Senate floor by motion. Usually controversial, bills brought by motion are subject to the hazard of the **filibuster**, a long-standing tradition of unlimited debate allowed only in the Senate. Here, a senator or group of senators strongly opposed to a particular bill, ultimately destined to pass, can block passage or force compromise on the majority by continuous debate. A filibuster begins when one senator who is opposed to the bill is recognized by the presiding officer to speak. Once recognized, the senator begins to speak (what is said has little consequence) and refuses to yield the floor. Occasionally, a round-robin effect occurs with the senator who initiates the filibuster yielding the floor to other senators participating in the filibuster. Consequently, the floor remains in the hands of those opposed to the legislation, and a long and effective filibuster is thus guaranteed.

Only one legislative method exists to end a filibuster. Termed **cloture**, the procedure begins with a petition requiring sixteen signatures. If obtained, debate halts and a vote is taken on the cloture motion. Sixty votes are needed (a three-fifths vote) to invoke cloture, and, if gained, a thirty-hour cap is set for debate on the bill on a first-come, first-serve basis. Once this time expires, the bill is voted on and either accepted or rejected. Filibusters and delay tactics are now used across party and ideological lines. Recently we have seen filibusters used primarily against judicial nominees with whom the persons conducting the filibuster have ideological differences. This is a novel use of the filibuster, which historically was used in legislative disputes rather than presidential nominations.

Conference Committee

Although bills may start out with identical language in both the House and Senate, they generally wind up very different once clearing the respective chamber's floor. Since only one bill can be sent to the president, representatives of the two chambers must meet and iron out differences. This is done in **conference committee**. A room in the Capitol building, somewhere halfway between the two chambers, is selected and work begins. In conference committee each chamber has one vote with the vote being cast by majority agreement. Membership is not limited but usually ranges from three to seven members from each chamber. The Speaker appoints members to conference committee within the House. In the Senate the selection is made by the presiding officer. However, it is usually the bill's chairperson in agreement with the committee's ranking minority member that informally makes the selection, with members from the bill's committee being given first choice based upon seniority. Seats on a conference committee are distributed according to party dominance in each chamber. Members of the Conference Committee (often called "conferees") are generally from the full committee (the full House committee and the full Senate committee, the House and Senate Agriculture Committees, for example) where the legislation originated. Once an agreement is reached, the bill is returned to both chambers for approval by the entire membership. Usually, such approval is readily forthcoming since the compromises made on a particular bill have already been run through the leadership of both chambers by conferees. Likewise, most legislators instinctively understand that haggling and bickering over each conference committee's report would bring the legislative process to a screeching halt.

Executive Consideration

Next, a bill must be sent to the president for consideration. The president has four options to exercise within a ten-working-day period of time (holidays and weekends are excluded). **First**, the president could sign the bill in which case it would become law. **Second**, the president could opt not to sign the bill, but not veto it either. Here, after ten days, the bill would become law. If less than ten working days remain before adjournment of Congress, the president could exercise a **pocket veto**. The Constitution gives the president ten days to decide on a bill. Should Congress adjourn before the ten-day period ends and the president does not sign the legislation, it dies automatically. Finally, the president can veto the bill.

Congress sometimes makes use of a device termed the **rider amendment**, usually just called a **rider**. This allows Congress to slip legislation by the president that he might ordinarily veto. A bill of extreme importance to the president would be found and to it would be attached an piece of legislation in the form of an amendment that the president disliked. When the president received the bill, he would then be faced with a dilemma. To secure the desired legislation, he would be forced to accept the rider. Conversely, to reject the rider, he would lose that portion of the legislation he wanted. Unlike governors in over three-fourths of the states, the president does not have the power of **item veto.** These governors can veto a portion of a bill while accepting the rest. The vetoed portion would then be returned to the state legislature for a possible override. The item veto would obviously limit Congress in its use of riders. The Constitution, however, grants the president only the authority to veto a bill completely, not just parts of it.

It should be noted that Congress and the president are cautious in their use of riders and vetoes. An overuse of either would be taken by the other side as an abuse of power, necessitating retaliatory action. Thus, in the long run the effectiveness of the method would be lost.

The Override

If the president vetos the bill, all is not lost as far as the Congress is concerned. The bill returns to both houses of Congress, where the members might try to override it. A two-thirds vote in both chambers is needed to override the veto and enact the bill into law. Historically only 1 in 25 vetoes are overridden. This tendency has proven remarkably consistent even when public support for a president is low.

CONCLUSION

Although Congress is primarily a law-creating institution, the persons creating those laws are politicians. Those politicians are motivated by politics—the process of who gets what, when, and how[2]—and are not merely following the technical process of passing laws. They use the technical process to achieve political ends, that is, to redistribute wealth, prestige, and security.[3] While the uninformed usually conclude that Congress enacts laws directed at the betterment or protection of the United States as a whole, the reality is that members put together coalitions of votes for enacting laws that reflect usually the particular interests of a state, a district within a state, or interest groups Although critics contend that this characteristic is a serious flaw in congressional representation, they seem to forget that the United States is organized into states, districts within states, and, yes, even interest groups to which most of us are members at some time or other.

Chapter Ten Notes

[1]Nadine Cohodas, "Discharge Petition Derailed?" *Congressional Quarterly Weekly Report*, 12 July 1980.

[2]Harold Lasswell, *Politics: Who Gets What, When and How*. (New York: McGraw-Hill, 1936).

[3]Lasswell.

Suggested Readings

Davidson, Roger H., and Walter J. Oleszek. *Congress and Its Members*, 5th ed. Washington, D.C.: CQ Press, 1996.

Deering, Christopher J., and Steven S. Smith. *Committees in Congress*. 3d ed. Washington, D.C.: CQ Press, 1997.

Fox, Harrison W., and Susan Webb Hammond. *Congressional Staffs: The Invisible Force in American Lawmaking*. New York: Free Press, 1977.

Kaptur, Marcy. *Women of Congress*. Washington, D.C.: CQ Press, 1996.

Sinclair, Barbara. *Legislators, Leaders and Lawmaking: The U.S. House of Representatives in the Postreform Era*. Baltimore, Md.: Johns Hopkins University Press, 1995.

Sneier, Edward V., and Bertram Gross. *Congress Today*. New York: St. Martin's Press, 1993.

Chapter Eleven

The American Presidency:
Uneasy Lies the Head that Wears the Crown

When the delegates who gathered in Philadelphia began to draft a new Constitution for the United States, it appeared, from what they wrote, that they considered the most important branch of the government to be the legislative branch, i.e., Congress. The largest portion of the Constitution is devoted to the powers of that branch. Article II, which deals with the executive branch, seems to be describing an administrator—an executor—of the programs Congress decides to have implemented rather than the powerful leader that the president has become. It would not be too bold to say that today's president actually has power over the existence or nonexistence of the entire planet in that presumably he or she could, with a single phone call, destroy by means of nuclear weapons all that exists. In this chapter we shall address what the Constitution says about the executive branch, what it has come to be today, and most importantly—why.

However, before we launch into what the Constitution says, we should acknowledge the tremendous influence former presidents have had on the presidency even to this day. One particular president deserves special recognition, namely George Washington. When Washington became president, there was little or no guidance about what he should be doing as chief executive of the

United States. The Constitution was of little help. George Washington is said to have "invented the presidency." Since Washington was the first president, much of what he did became traditions that presidents today still feel obligated to comply with. A good example of one of these is the Cabinet. This body of advisors to the president is nowhere mentioned in the Constitution. It is an idea the first president borrowed from the English parliamentary system; however, the Cabinet in the United States does not function the same as it does in the United Kingdom. Washington may have borrowed the concept of a Cabinet, but he then structured it to his needs. Every president since Washington has had a Cabinet although some presidents have made more use of it than others. Much of what President George W. Bush does today is not so much because of the dictates of the Constitution as it is because of what the first president did more than 200 years ago.

Washington was also the first president to use **co-optation**, whereby he tamed two potentially dangerous enemies to his administration by bringing them into his Cabinet. Bringing Alexander Hamilton, founder of America's first political party (the Federalists), and Thomas Jefferson, founder of America's second political party (the Democrats), into the Cabinet was even more of a political coup because the two men were also political enemies. Washington, in addition, to everything else, was a very good politician in the best sense of that word. He effectively controlled his opposition while simultaneously bringing two of this country's brightest, most ambitious men to the service of building the United States into a strong country at a time when it needed such men the most. Thus, subsequent presidents of the United States owe a tremendous debt to the man who first held the office.

QUALIFICATIONS FOR THE OFFICE OF PRESIDENT

Formal Qualifications

Article II of the United States Constitution sets forth only three requirements for the office of president: (1) age: 35, which in 1787, when the Constitution was written, was considered at least middle aged if not older; (2) native-born citizen, which means that the person must be a United States citizen at birth either by being born on American soil or by being born to American-citizen parents; (3) a resident of the United States for at least fourteen years. This last requirement was intended to insure that individuals who were not living in the United States, although native-born citizens of this country, were familiar enough with the customs, traditions, and thinking of Americans. It can be readily seen that these three requirements would prohibit very few individuals from seeking the office of president. Most of those who would not be eligible would be persons who had not yet attained the age of 35 and a few—relatively speaking—who were not native-born citizens. However, over the years certain informal qualifications have developed, although not stated in the Constitution, which would limit severely the number of people who would be eligible for the office.

Informal Qualifications

The first of these informal requirements and one that should be obvious to any elementary student who has ever had to memorize the names of all the presidents of the United States is that a president must be a **male**. The United States has had only forty-three presidents, and all of them have been males. The phenomenon of male leadership in the position of head of state is not found throughout the world. In recent history, illustrations can be found of a number of countries being led by women; for example, Golda Meier in Israel, Indira Gandhi in India, Margaret Thatcher in Great Britain, Corizon Aquino in the Philippines, or Benizir Butto in Pakistan. Of course, if we go further back in history, we find significant numbers of women in leadership positions in powerful countries, for instance, Queen Elizabeth I of England. However, in the United States if we base the informal qualifications for the presidency on past experience, we must conclude that presidents are males. This requirement may find some exceptions in the not-too-distant future since the first female was nominated by a major party for the vice presidency in 1984.[1] Still, even if a female receives a major-party nomination, it is doubtful that she will win against a male opponent, and, if she does win, it is doubtful that this win will create a real trend. The bottom line is that most Americans, rightly or wrongly, perceive this position to be a male province.

The second informal qualification should also be quite obvious to those who have managed to live long enough to have seen a number of presidents: a president must be a **Caucasian (white)**. Again there is no constitutional restriction on other races seeking the office; however, no nonwhite person has ever received the nomination from a major party.[2] This restriction may also be eroding somewhat; like the nomination of a female, the nomination of a minority person has yet to come to pass.

A third informal requirement can be found in the ethnic descent of the individual. Perhaps it is natural that presidents are selected from the majority ethnic groups in this country, i.e., **Northern Europeans**. A reading of the list of former heads of state reveals names like Pierce, Johnson, Wilson, Adams—descendants of the English or Scots. We find no Kowalskis, Difattas, Mendozas, or Korsakoffs. Although these names, at least on the surface, indicate persons of the Caucasian persuasion, so to speak, they are Polish, Italian, Hispanic, and Russian, respectively, and no one of these ethnic descents has ever been elected president. Therefore, we must also conclude that besides being a white male, a person must also be of Northern European descent to be elected president.

Age can also be considered a fourth informal qualification. Most presidents, when elected, have been in their **fifties**, although with the election of Ronald Reagan at age 68 this age bracket may be changing. To a person in his/ her teens or early twenties, age 56, for example, may seem quite old. Yet in reality, being in one's fifties today is considered by many to be middle aged since Americans are living longer now than they did previously. (The average life span for Americans today is about 75.) Therefore, age 55 or 56 is relatively young, and many countries do not even consider a person fit to rule until he/ she has reached the seventies. Individuals in this last age group are considered by the people of countries such as China to be wise enough to rule others. (Please note, however, that China does not elect its rulers as the United States does.) Be that as it may, Americans tend not to support the candidacy of persons who are "too old." In fact, even though he won, many questions concerning his age were raised during the campaign and the presidency of Ronald Reagan. Age was also an issue when Republican Robert Dole sought the presidency in 1996. Most political scientists assert that the United States has seen the last of the World War II-era presidential candidates.

Age discrimination, like racial and ethnic discrimination, may be a factor in the selection of "qualified" candidates for the presidency. While we tend to think of age discrimination in terms of older age groups, it also comes into play with younger people. In other words, it is highly unlikely that a 35-year-old person would be nominated for president, much less get elected. That person would be perceived as *too young*, even though he or she met the constitutional age requirement.

Fifth, we should consider **religion** as an informal requirement for the presidency. The Constitution does not require any religious test for political office. In fact, the Constitution expressly prohibits such a test: "...no religious Test shall ever be required as a Qualification to any Office or public Trust under the United States." (Article VI) However, all chief executives of the United States, with three exceptions, have at least been professed Christians—meaning that they *said* they were this or that religion whether they actually practiced that religion or not. Ten of the thirty-eight who declared a religious preference have been Episcopalian with the next most numerous group being six Presbyterians. The remainder are spread out among Unitarians (4), Methodists (4), Reformed Dutch (2), Roman Catholics (1), Disciples of Christ (3), Baptists (4), Quakers (1), and Congregationalists (1). Thomas Jefferson considered himself a deist, one who believes in a Creator but does not believe this Creator interferes at all in the operations of that which He created. The Creator is revealed through nature and reason and not through organized religion; hence, Jefferson was not a member of any church and was often accused of being an atheist. Like Jefferson, Andrew Johnson and Abraham Lincoln professed no church membership either. In regard to Lincoln, one scholar writes:

One of the many ironies of American history is the fact that a man who had so little truck with [use for] organized religion should have been bracketed with Christ as the central figure in the American passion play. The cultists have not failed to point out that Jesus, born in a manger, died on a cross on Good Friday, and that Lincoln, born in a log cabin, died under an assassin's bullet on Good Friday. Both were redeemers (of those in bondage), saviours (the one of sinners, the other of the Union), and martyrs (to their objectives).[3]

No person of Jewish faith has ever been nominated for president, and only two Roman Catholics have been nominated with one being elected. The election of 2000 made history when, for the first time, a major political party, the Democrats, nominated someone of the Jewish faith for the vice presidency of the United States, Senator Joseph Lieberman of Connecticut. Many observers believe that, since the election of John Kennedy, religion is not as much of a factor as it used to be. However, it should be noted that, although he won, Kennedy's popular-vote margin of victory was only about 100,000 votes. In addition, Jimmy Carter found his "born-again" Christian status was very much a factor in the 1976 presidential election. Likewise, Pat Robertson of "The 700 Club" fame found himself defending his "born-again," television-evangelist background in the 1988 campaign.

Sixth, more presidents are drawn from the ranks of **lawyers with previous political experience as governors or senators**. Unlike many countries of the world very few of United States presidents have come to the office as a result of military fame. Nonetheless, the presidents who did come to office due, at least partially, to military fame are notable; among them are George Washington, Andrew Jackson, Theodore Roosevelt, and Dwight Eisenhower. One president, before he became a professional politician, was actually a men's clothing salesman (Harry Truman) and another an actor (Ronald Reagan). Only one president with a doctorate degree, Woodrow Wilson, who had a political science Ph.D., was ever elected to this office. Perhaps there is some justification for Americans having a preference for persons with previous political experience in that the most successful presidents (those who accomplished a great deal of what they set out to do) have had prior political experience. Yet, in every election campaign, particularly for lesser offices, we hear candidates state that, if elected, they will "run the government like a business." Those who have tried have not usually been successful. Running the government is not like running a business where the bottom line presumably is making a profit.

The marital status of a presidential office seeker is the seventh informal qualification. Almost all presidents have been **married** men, although some have been widowers at the time of election. James Buchanan was elected as a bachelor and remained unmarried throughout his term of office. Grover Cleveland was elected as a bachelor but got married while occupying the White House

Few presidents could get elected without the support of their wife and family. Here, George W. Bush proudly stands with his wife, Laura, and Bill Clinton proudly stands with his wife, Hillary Rodham Clinton, who is now a Senator from New York. Many political observers believe that Bill Clinton could not have survived without the support of his wife during his impeachment trial.

during his first term. Woodrow Wilson's first wife died during his time as president but he remarried while occupying the White House. Additionally, only one president (Ronald Reagan) has been divorced, but he had been married to his second wife for over twenty years before he was elected president. It would seem that, since divorce is so prevalent in American society today, voters might no longer consider a divorced person an unsuitable candidate for the country's highest office. There are perhaps some grounds for seeking a person who is married for the office of president: married men live longer than single men—assuming that the voters want the president to finish his term of office before leaving them permanently! We could certainly wonder, however, with the recent revelations of marital infidelity by President Clinton, both in and out of office, whether a divorced or single president might not be preferable to one who has a "wandering eye!"

Eighth, despite the old adage that any boy can grow up to be president, only a select few have. At least in recent times, many of these select few have started their campaigns with the advantage of being relatively wealthy men and, therefore, knew other wealthy individuals or potential support groups who could help them raise the millions of dollars needed to finance a successful campaign. Americans like to think that people of humble origins like Abraham Lincoln are the "typical" president. In reality they are not. Very few were born in log cabins, so to speak. While substantial wealth is not necessarily required, poor people do not seek, nor would they be elected to, the presidency.

Finally, to be elected president a person must usually be **ideologically moderate**. You will recall in the discussion of political parties that because of the nature of these parties and the presidential type of government that the United States has, a candidate for office cannot afford to be too far to the left or to the right ideologically. Too many potential voters would be "turned off" because the American voter is also ideologically moderate. Both major political parties are centrist parties, meaning they are ideologically moderate. Candidates who have been perceived by the voters as being too conservative or too liberal have gone down in flames at the polls on election day. The name of the game for a presidential candidate is moderation—"I believe in motherhood and apple pie but not too much of either!"

The classic example of a presidential candidate being perceived as too far *right* was the election of 1964 when Barry Goldwater ran for president as a Republican. His Democratic opponent, Lyndon Johnson, won overwhelmingly partially due to his portrayal of Goldwater as an extremist on the right who would get rid of social security and who was too eager to use nuclear weapons even at the risk of starting a nuclear war. Likewise, the classic example of a presidential candidate being perceived as too far *left* was the election of 1972 when George McGovern ran for president as a Democrat. His Republican opponent, Richard Nixon, won overwhelmingly in part because of his portrayal of McGovern as an extremist on the left who was a socialist at best, a communist at worst, or at the very least a left-wing lunatic.

Interestingly, the United States has also had two father-son combinations elected to the presidency. The first was John Adams and John Quincy Adams. The second, of course, was George Bush and George W. Bush. Both John Adams and George Bush served only one term as president, and both became president after first serving as vice president. Often, as history shows us, the office of vice president is not the best stepping stone to the presidency unless the vice president assumes office upon the death of the president. Another similarity between these father-son combinations is that John Quincy Adams, like George W. Bush, was elected president even though he lost the popular vote. Adams's election went to the House of Representatives when the electoral college failed to choose a winner by majority vote.

ELECTION OF THE PRESIDENT AND LENGTH OF TERM

Election

The president and the vice president of the United States are elected by the electoral college. (See Chapter 9) The origins of the electoral college as a means of selecting the president are open to scholarly dispute. Since the Founding Fathers were, for the most part, products of a classical education, they were very familiar with the works of Plato and his notion of the philosopher king, whereby the leader chosen was among the "best of the best." Since Plato was not a democrat and did not trust the masses, this explanation would seem to be plausible. Another theory asserts that the electoral college was borrowed from the Iroquois confederacy that peacefully ruled what became New York State for over 500 years. Benjamin Franklin had much contact with these Indians. Franklin supposedly borrowed the Iroquois method of selecting a chief by the council. The major difference was that the Iroquois council was made up entirely of women who picked a male as chief! Obviously our electoral college was, at least, originally designed to be exclusively comprised of males who, in turn, selected a male to be president.

This system of indirect election was chosen by the writers of the Constitution to insure the electoral independence of the presidency from any existing governmental institution and presumably to keep the office free from too much influence from the voters. Election by the electoral college requires a majority vote (currently standing at 270 out of a total of 538 electoral votes). Such an election procedure has not produced the independence that the Founding Fathers seemed to have wanted. However, for better or worse, that is the system under which the presidency operates today and under which it will continue to operate unless changed by constitutional amendment—a prospect that is not very likely in the near future.

Term of Office

The Constitution sets the term of office of the president and the vice president at four years. Originally presidents could serve as many terms as they could get themselves elected to. Twenty-one of them only served one term. Yet, no president attempted election for more than two terms, following a tradition established by George Washington. However, when Franklin Roosevelt was elected to four consecutive terms, fear of a chief executive becoming too powerful produced the Twenty-second Amendment, which now prohibits a person from serving more than two terms (either consecutively or nonconsecutively) or ten years as president. The ten-year stipulation was a result of circumstances under which a vice president might become president upon the death, resignation, or removal of a president. If this situation occurs, he may serve the remainder of the former president's term and then be elected for a four-year term of his own. At this point, if the total number of years (to the day) is no more than six years, he may seek re-election for another four-year term because the total number of years he would possibly be in office would not equal more than ten years.

Even when the Constitutional Convention was considering the length of a president's term, there was considerable debate about what it should be. Suggestions ranged from a two-year term like members of the House of Representatives to a life term like a king. The four-year term seems to have been settled upon more because it was between the two-year term of the House and the six-year term of the Senate than anything else. Today there are those who advocate lengthening a president's term of office to six years with possible re-election for one more term and others who suggest that it be changed to one, ten-year term. Supporters of these changes argue that the complexity of the presidency and of the United States government in general requires a longer time in office to accomplish what the president sets out to do. Considering that the entire governmental budget under George Washington amounted to about $100,000 while today's budget is about $1.7 trillion, perhaps these recommendations have merit.

Sometimes people wonder how a president supports himself once he has retired from the presidency. Have no fear! While recent presidents drew salaries of $200,000,[4] plus other funds that were used to operate the White House, to travel on government business, etc., recently retired presidents have done well. Former President Bush receives a presidential pension of $143,800 annually, plus a $44,000 annual pension as a former member of Congress. In addition, he got $1.5 million to spend in his "transition" from president to private citizen. Thereafter, he, like other former presidents, received a mere $150,000 for his office and staff requirements for two and a half years and then $96,000 a year after that until he dies.[5] As of 2001, there are four other living, former presidents of the United States drawing similar benefits. It's pretty easy to sit back and say these guys are and continue to be overpaid. However, when compared to the salary George Washington got, today's presidents are grossly underpaid. Washington's annual salary of $25,000 is equivalent to about $600,000 per year in current dollars!

Table 11.1: Twelve Best Presidents

Rank/President	Height	Personality Type	Assassination/Attempts
1. Abraham Lincoln	6'4"	Positive	Yes
2. George Washington	6'2"	Positive	No
3. Franklin Roosevelt	6'2"	Positive	Yes
4. Woodrow Wilson	5'11"	Negative	No
5. Thomas Jefferson	6'2.5"	Positive	No
6. Andrew Jackson	6'1"	Positive	Yes
7. Theodore Roosevelt	5'10"	Positive	Yes
8. Harry Truman	5'9"	Positive	Yes
9. Lyndon Johnson	6'3"	Negative	No
10. John Adams	5'7"	Negative	No
11. James Polk	5'8"	Positive	No
12. John Kennedy	6'0"	Positive	Yes

Table 11.2: Twelve Worst Presidents

Rank/President	Height	Personality Type	Assassination/Attempts
1. Jimmy Carter	5'9.5"	Negative	No
2. Benjamin Harrison	5'6"	Negative	No
3. Andrew Johnson	5'10"	Negative	No
4. John Tyler	6'0"	Negative	No
5. Zachary Taylor	5'8"	Negative	No
6. Millard Fillmore	5'9"	Positive	No
7. Calvin Coolidge	5'10"	Negative	No
8. Franklin Pierce	5'10"	Positive	No
9. James Buchanan	6'0"	Negative	No
10. Richard Nixon	5'11.5"	Negative	No
11. Ulysses Grant	5'8.5"	Negative	No
12. Warren G. Harding	6'0"	Positive	No

Source: Jack Holmes and Robert Elder, Jr., "Our Best and Worst Presidents: Some Possible Reasons for Perceived Performance," *Presidential Studies Quarterly*, XIX (Summer, 1989), 534 and 541.

WHAT MAKES A "GOOD" PRESIDENT

What is the mark of a good president? Asking the experts has become the accepted way of judging presidential performance. The presidential greatness game began in the late forties, when Arthur Schlesinger asked fifty-five prominent historians to grade past presidents. A grade of "A" meant that president was considered *great*; "B," *near great*; "C," *average*; "D," *below average*; and "E," *failure*.[6] Interesting as the survey was, it completely side-stepped the issue of how to measure the performance of a president in office. That particular issue was addressed when Thomas Bailey identified forty-three criteria for measuring presidential greatness or lack of it. They included such items as achievement, administrative capacity, quality of appointees, blunders, industriousness, and scandals.[7] If the Schlesinger survey suffered from lack of guidelines, the Bailey study included everything and excluded nothing. The reader was left with a broader view of the many facets of the presidency but still unable to evaluate presidential performance in a meaningful way.

A study by Jack Holmes and Robert Elder, Jr., indicates that a number of factors may be influential in making a "good" president, i.e., one who is perceived to be successful in office.[8] The study ranked presidents from "best" to "worst" and analyzed characteristics of each. Interestingly, Holmes and Elder found that the twelve "best" presidents were two inches taller on the average than the twelve "worst" presidents. Four presidents have been left-handed. (Left-handed people make up about 10 percent of the U.S. population.) However, only one of them is considered a successful president by Holmes and Elder (Harry Truman), and he was short. In addition, the "best" category had positive attitudes toward their jobs and toward people in general, while the "worst" category had negative orientations. It was also noted that the "best" presidents were more likely to be assassinated or to have attempts made on their lives while in office and were more likely to go to war than their "worst" counterparts. The

Table 11.3: Barber's Presidential Personalities

	Active	Passive
Positive	Franklin Roosevelt Harry Truman John Kennedy Gerald Ford Jimmy Carter George Bush	William Howard Taft Warren G. Harding Ronald Reagan
Negative	Woodrow Wilson Herbert Hoover Lyndon Johnson Richard Nixon	Calvin Coolidge Dwight Eisenhower

Source: James D. Barber, *The Presidential Character: Predicting Performance in the White House*, 3d ed. (Englewood Cliffs, N.J.: Prentice Hall, 1985).

factors isolated in the study are not the only characteristics that make a president successful, but they are intriguing to consider. Table 11.1 indicates some of the findings of Holmes and Elder.

Part of the work of Holmes and Elder was based upon previous studies done by James D. Barber who holds that presidents, like others, exhibit behavior patterns that can be used to predict presidential success or failure. Barber asserts that presidential character is either active or passive in activity level and positive or negative in outlook. According to this analysis, active/positive presidents are more successful than passive/negative ones. Active/positive presidents come to the presidency with enthusiasm and a drive to lead and succeed. They are always ready to grab the brass ring. In contrast, passive/negative presidents are reactive by nature; they wait for something to happen and then react to it instead of causing things to happen. They are likely to take direction from others, look upon the job of president as a chore, a duty, and fail to use the enormous resources at their disposal. Table 11.2 illustrates Barber's classifications of presidents from Taft through Bush.

At least one former presidential candidate believes that highly successful presidents must also possess a healthy sense of humor about themselves and their jobs. In his book *Great Political Wit*, former Senator and presidential candidate Bob Dole quotes a number of presidents and presidential candidates including America's heaviest president. President William Howard Taft, who tipped the scales at a generous 350 pounds, was offered a *chair in law* (teaching position) at his alma mater Yale University after he left office. Taft replied that a *sofa of law* would be more appropriate![9]

PRESIDENTIAL SUCCESSION

Constitutional scholars have debated whether the Constitution actually meant the vice president to become president upon the death, resignation, or removal of the president. The debate arose because the document only stated that the vice president would assume the duties of the president should any of these events occur or should the president become unable to perform his duties. Nevertheless, traditionally the vice president became president, beginning with John Tyler, who became president in 1841 when William Henry Harrison died shortly after he was inaugurated. Article II, Section I, Clause 6 also provided that Congress would be able to pass a law stating the order of presidential succession after the vice president. Currently this law, adopted by Congress (1947), places the Speaker of the House of Representatives next in line for the presidency after the vice president, then the president pro tempore of the Senate, then the secretary of state, followed by the other Cabinet members in the order in which their posts were created.

Although an order of presidential succession had been created, there was a strong feeling that the Constitution should be amended so that a vice president

Secret service agents subdue John Hinkley after he had shot President Reagan. Press Secretary James Brady and patrolman Thomas Delahanty lie on the ground after being hit by the gunfire. In all, Hinkley fired six shots before being subdued.

could be appointed by the president with the approval of the Congress in cases where the vice-presidential office was vacant. Many times during American history that office has been vacant, but no president died while that vacancy existed. The suggestion to appoint a vice president became the Twenty-fifth Amendment. In addition to providing for the appointment of a vice president, the amendment also settled the dispute whether the vice president actually becomes president upon the death, resignation, or removal of a president. The amendment states directly that he does.

The Twenty-fifth Amendment was ratified in 1967 and was used for the first time in 1973 when Vice President Spiro Agnew resigned and Representative Gerald Ford was appointed to serve out his term. The irony here was that Ford himself succeeded to the presidency when President Richard Nixon resigned. Ford then appointed former New York Governor Nelson Rockefeller to serve as vice president. (Keep in mind that these appointments must be confirmed by a majority vote of both houses of Congress.) This event was the first time in the history of the United States that neither the president nor the vice president was elected.

PRESIDENTIAL DISABILITY

The Twenty-fifth Amendment also supposedly took care of another thorny problem—namely presidential disability. Because the Constitution was not especially specific about what constituted a president's inability to perform his duties or who was to decide if he was unable to perform them, this amendment makes the case fairly clear. First, the president can inform the Speaker of the House and the president pro tempore of the Senate that he is incapacitated and that the vice president should assume the president's duties. When his incapacity no longer exists, he informs the Congress and resumes his duties as president. However, suppose a president is so incapacitated that he cannot inform Congress, e.g., unconscious, or, wild as it may seem, suppose he goes "whacko" and streaks around the White House lawn in his "birthday suit"? The amendment also takes care of these events in that it provides that the vice president and a majority of the Cabinet can inform Congress that the president is unable to perform his duties. The vice president then will become acting president until the president is back to "normal." However, human nature being what it sometimes is, it is conceivable that the vice president, in cahoots with the Cabinet, could declare the president disabled in order to "take over." The amendment provides that, if there is a dispute between the president and the vice president and the Cabinet concerning this matter, then a two-thirds vote of both houses of Congress will settle the issue. So far, presidential disabilities have been handled with apparent smoothness. If there was any argument about the matter, it was never brought to the attention of Congress or the public. There have been occasional hints that presidents have been reluctant to surrender their powers to the vice president, perhaps even when they should, and that vice presidents, often having political ambitions of their own, are reluctant to press the matter for fear of alienating the president and party leaders, whose support they may need for their own bids for the highest office at a later date. *The Los Angeles Times* and *The Associated Press* reported that President Reagan, while "ill or under sedation," may have approved a shipment of arms "to Iran by Israel, which would have been [prohibited by law] without congressional approval."[10]

We might legitimately wonder why all this worry about who becomes president if the president dies or is disabled or about who becomes vice president. Perhaps we will find the answer by looking at what normally happens in dictatorships when the leader dies—power struggles. There are usually several people waiting in the wings, so to speak, in dictatorships. Frequently no single one of them has enough control of the military or of the important positions in the government just to take over immediately, so they begin to fight. In the end, one person manages to kill off the others or drive them out of the country, so that he eventually becomes the leader. Sometimes these "fights" turn into all out revolutions that last for years. In other words, when there is no written rule that everyone abides by concerning succession to leadership, governments become unstable and frequently unable to function, occasionally for long periods of time. Consequently, having a written rule tends to reduce the anxiety produced by the death, resignation, or removal of a president.

THE VICE PRESIDENT

Qualifications and Nomination Process

The Constitution sets the same requirements for the office of vice president as it does for that of president: (1) at least 35 years old, (2) a native-born citizen, and (3) a resident of the United States for at least fourteen years. That the qualifications for this office are the same as for the higher office is logical since it was intended that the vice president, at the least, would assume the duties of the president should the latter die, resign, be removed, or become disabled.

For years the nomination of a person for vice president by the political parties did not assume much importance and still doesn't attract as much attention as that of president. However, in recent times the person nominated for the lower office has managed to gain more notice than previously. Still, vice-presidential candidates are usually selected more on their abilities to "balance the ticket" than on their abilities to lead the country should the need arise. In practical terms, balancing the ticket means that, if the presidential nominee comes from the West, as Ronald Reagan did, then the vice-presidential nominee should come from another part of the country, as George Bush did (Texas). When Walter Mondale from Minnesota was nominated in 1984 by the Democratic Party, he selected Geraldine Ferraro of New York, who was not only from a different state but also a woman and a Roman Catholic. It is even preferable that the vice-presidential nominee come from a state with a large electoral vote, such as Ferraro of New York or John Kennedy's running mate in 1960, Lyndon Johnson of Texas. Many times the vice-presidential candidate had sought his party's nomination for president and only accepted the nomination for the lesser office when he could not reach his original goal. We should keep in mind that, although the party convention officially nominates the vice-presidential candidate, the nominee almost always is the person whom the presidential nominee has indicated he wants for his running mate. Frequently, the presidential and vice-presidential nominees for each party have very little in common because of this balancing-of-the-ticket phenomenon. We should also remember that balancing the ticket makes sense only in the context of the American political party system that requires that the parties appeal to as large a number of voters as possible to win the election. Therefore, balancing the ticket should be seen as an attempt to draw as many voters of different backgrounds as possible to the party ticket.

There are exceptions to this balancing the ticket business, however. President Bill Clinton, a relatively young, white, male, Southern Baptist, from the South, chose as his running mate Al Gore, who was also a relatively young, white, male, Southern Baptist, from the South.

Duties of the Vice President

Vice-presidential duties can be divided into two categories: (1) **official duties** required by the Constitution and by congressional acts and (2) **unofficial duties** that have been given to vice presidents by some presidents.

The Constitution merely states that the vice president should do three things: (1) preside as president of the Senate (presiding officer of the Senate), (2) vote in the Senate only in case of a tie, and (3) wait for the president to die, resign, be removed, or become incapacitated. Now the Constitution does not state item #3 in those exact words, but that is the essence of what it means. At times it must be uncomfortable for a president to know that the person following him around, so to speak, is just waiting for him to "kick the bucket!" By law today the vice president has also been made a member of the president's Cabinet and a member of the National Security Council.

Over the years many vice presidents have complained that being vice president is the most boring job because there really is very little to do officially. John Nance Garner, one of Franklin Roosevelt's vice presidents, said that the office "wasn't worth a bucket of spit." They have also expressed the idea that they are often kept in the dark about what the president is doing; therefore, if they had to assume the presidency, they would be at a disadvantage because of this lack of knowledge. Harry Truman, who became president when Franklin Roosevelt died, had no idea that the United States had developed an atomic bomb. He was told when he assumed the chief executive's position.

Some recent presidents have alleviated some of the boredom and perhaps some of the ignorance of the vice presidents by giving them a number of "unofficial" duties. As was the case with Lyndon Johnson, the vice president has been used as a substitute for the president on ceremonial occasions such as greeting lesser heads of state who come to the United States or for saying "good-bye" at their funerals!

Along these same lines, vice presidents have been used to carry official messages from the president to other governments and to make fact-finding trips or goodwill trips to other countries. These kinds of trips provide a vice president with very little freedom to be "his own man." An aide to Vice President Hubert Humphrey, who served under President Lyndon Johnson, noted:

> We did a lot of traveling for the president, but were never allowed to negotiate anything. . . .When we went to Vietnam, we were Johnson's eyes and ears, without any kind of authority. When we talked, we talked for Lyndon Johnson, not Hubert Humphrey, and had to get every syllable cleared with the White House."[11]

Some presidents have used their vice presidents as spokespersons and campaigners for the administration. Particularly adept at this practice was President Nixon, who used Vice President Agnew in this capacity to launch verbal attacks on those who disagreed with the president's policies. By using Agnew instead of doing it himself, Nixon could always seem above all the turmoil and name-calling.

Depending on the vice president's background and qualifications, some presidents have used them as ombudsmen, a person to hear complaints, gather support, and smooth out any problems with such people as governors, mayors, pressure group leaders, and the like. This function takes a great deal of time and carries with it no authority to solve any of the complaints that may be presented. As one Agnew aide noted: "Every time a governor would come to town, we would have to schedule a meeting, show him around the grounds, listen for an hour to all the problems of his state, and give him a vice-presidential pen."[12]

Because of his official function as presiding officer of the Senate, the vice president, it would seem, should have some lobbying activity. On occasion presidents have used them in this capacity but only sparingly. The major reason is that most vice presidents have perceived their roles as presiding officer of the Senate as one of impartiality. However, although one rarely occurs, the vice president does get to vote in the Senate in case of a tie. Needless to say, he votes the way the president wants him to vote, or he would never be seen in the Senate again! As president of the Senate, probably the most important activity a vice president carries out for a president is to give the chief executive a sense of how the Senate feels about his policies in general, as well as particular policies as they come before that body. The truth of the matter is that the vice president spends very little time presiding over the Senate.

Some historians argue that countries with large standing armies and, therefore, many generals need to involve themselves in wars about every twenty-five years to give the generals something to do. Otherwise, they might be plotting to overthrow the government at home. A similar situation can be found with the vice president's "unofficial" function as a member of various task forces, councils, and forums. The idea is that, if the vice president is given "busy work," he will be less likely to be a problem to the president. Although the committees have high-sounding titles, they rarely have any real policy impact. This function is time consuming but goes nowhere.

As can be seen from the preceding descriptions of "unofficial" vice-presidential functions, there has been no mention of a role for the vice president as an advisor to the president. The vice president has such a role, but it is usually quite small and can be easily cut off by the president. The major advisory function of the vice president occurs in his role as a member of the Cabinet and of the National Security Council (NSC), an advisory body made up of the heads of the branches of the military and the secretaries of state and defense among others.[13] Lyndon Johnson became so angry at Hubert Humphrey's opposition to the president's decision to bomb North Vietnam that Johnson refused to call an NSC meeting for some time to isolate Humphrey from his advisory function. Strange as it may seem, a vice president has very little access to the ear of the president—especially if the president doesn't want to hear what he has to say. It seems that high government officials, as well as others, to be sure, suffer from tremendous ego problems at times.

Even when these unofficial duties are added to his constitutional duties, the vice president still appears to be a relatively bored person. The public frequently forgets who the vice president is. However, circumstances can immediately catapult him into the very powerful position of president with the wink of an eye. In the past forty years Harry Truman, Lyndon Johnson, and Gerald Ford could attest to that fact. All were vice presidents who became president upon the death or resignation of a president.

DUTIES OF THE PRESIDENT

The Constitution outlines a number of things that the president either *can* or *must* do. From the time that George Washington served as president to the present day, many of these duties have taken on a different flavor than they previously had. In other words, various presidents have interpreted their powers differently than perhaps others did or even differently from what was seemingly intended in the Constitution. In addition, some of the duties of the president have been expanded or even lessened by Congress, as well as by the Supreme Court of the United States at times.

Foreign Affairs Powers

The term *foreign affairs* is not in the United States Constitution. Nor does the document make absolutely clear who has authority to "conduct foreign relations" or to "make foreign policy." After 200 years, however, the president has dominated American foreign affairs far beyond what the Constitution expresses or implies and far beyond what the writers of the Constitution contemplated or might have foreseen. Two hundred years of history have given the presidency a virtually exclusive role in the conduct of foreign relations and a paramount role in the making of foreign policy. International law requires that there be one person who can speak on behalf of a sovereign state, and the president fulfills that role for the United States. Congress, as well as the courts, recognizes the president's superior position in this area. But the president's part can be understood only in relation to that of Congress, which retains "the power of the purse." In other words, the president's ability to conduct some foreign affairs may be limited by Congress' unwillingness to fund the activity the president wishes to pursue.

Table 11.4: United States Military Involvement without Declarations of War from 1950 - 2002

Country	Year(s)	Country	Year(s)
Korea	1950-1953	Libya	1986
Lebanon	1957	Panama	1989
Cuba	1962	Kuwait	1991
Vietnam	1964	Somalia	1993
Dominican Republic	1965	Iraq	1993
Laos	1970	Haiti	1994
Cambodia	1970	Bosnia	1995
Cambodia	1975	Zaire	1997
Iran	1980	Yugoslavia	1999
Grenada	1983	Afghanistan	2002
Mediterranean Sea	1985	Iraq	2003

Source: Data from the *Congressional Record*.

Commander-in-Chief. As commander-in-chief of the armed forces, the president has the power to blow us all away with one simple command. This is not to say that he has that intention; rather, the statement is intended to stress that the superpower status of the United States and its destructive capabilities, both offensive and defensive, make the president's control of the military of paramount importance. However, there is a continuing debate concerning the actions of presidents in this capacity. Learning lessons from the American Revolution, the Framers sought to create a single command and to ensure civilian control of the military; they did not consider the office of commander-in-chief to have any independent political authority. What they intended was that, if Congress maintained an army and navy, the president would be their commander; if Congress declared war or if the United States were attacked, the president would command the armed forces. On the face of the Constitution, that is the sum of presidential power as commander-in-chief. Some scholars, as well as a number of members of Congress throughout the years, have contended that the president's power as commander-in-chief does not include engaging in war without a declaration of war from Congress except in emergencies. Despite their arguments, presidents have engaged United States battle forces over 130 times without declarations of war from Congress. Table 11.4 shows the countries to which the United States sent troops just since the end of World War II.

President Harry Truman committed American fighting forces to South Korea in 1950, an action that involved this country in a prolonged and costly war, and Presidents Eisenhower, Kennedy, Johnson, and Nixon initiated and executed a chain of events that created massive American involvement in Southeast Asia during the 1950s, 1960s, and 1970s, the effects of which can still be felt.

U.S. Marines move down a street in Panama in search of troops loyal to General Manuel Noreiga. President Bush ordered the invasion to protect American lives in the country after an American serviceman was shot. Noreiga eventually surrendered and was brought to the United States for trial.

With the rise of congressional activism in the 1970s, presidents no longer thought it necessary to argue that they had the implied powers they had been exercising. Instead, they insisted that such powers were exclusive and that Congress did not have the power to monitor or to regulate presidential activity as commander-in-chief.[14]

Congress, perhaps feeling more overwhelmed by the presidency than believing such presidential actions were unwise, responded to these events in 1973 with the passage of the **War Powers Resolution**. This act seemingly provided some curbs on the president's ability to make war, although certain provisions of the act are constitutionally questionable: (1) the president can commit troops only after a declaration of war by Congress or by specific authorization by law or in a national emergency created by an attack on the United States or its armed forces; (2) if there is a national emergency, the president must report to Congress within forty-eight hours; (3) he must remove troops within sixty days unless Congress authorizes them to stay; and (4) he must consult Congress "in every possible instance" before committing troops to battle.

As stringent as the law sounds, it has not yet curbed the presidential appetite for "playing soldier." President Gerald Ford complied with the forty-eight-hour report provision after authorizing a rescue attempt for a captured American merchant vessel in Southeast Asia; President Jimmy Carter did the same after approving the rescue attempt of Americans held hostage in Iran; and President Ronald Reagan submitted his reports when he committed American marines to Lebanon, when he ordered the invasion of the Caribbean island of Grenada, and when he ordered the bombing of Libya. Congress has never refused to allow troops to remain when committed by a president since the act was passed. It is likely that this situation will continue because sentiment is quite divided even among the American population whether these actions are correct foreign policy or not. Table 11.4 shows United States military involvement around the world without declarations of war in the second half of the twentieth century. It illustrates the point made above that presidents commit the military pretty much as they please even after the War Powers Resolution was passed.

Not only does the president have the power to command the troops in foreign affairs, but he also has the authority to use them domestically. An example of a president exercising this authority occurred when President George Bush sent troops to Los Angeles in 1992 to curb riots in that city. The use of the armed forces or federal marshals in this manner falls under the president's authority and obligation to enforce the laws of the United States, which will be discussed later on. The use of troops domestically has always created a great deal of controversy since the troops are employed against the people of the United States. Therefore, presidents have rarely used their authority in the domestic arena.

Treaty-Making Power. The president is granted the authority to negotiate treaties with foreign governments. However, because of the system of checks built into the Constitution, these treaties must have the approval of two-thirds of the Senate. Although there have been sixteen treaties rejected by the Senate, whatever the president wants in the way of treaties he usually gets. Notable exceptions were the Treaty of Versailles, which was the official end of World War I, and the second Strategic Arms Limitation Treaty (SALT II), which was intended to limit certain weapons for the United States and the former Soviet Union. These treaties were never officially approved by the Senate.

The Senate also may insist upon numerous amendments to a treaty before it agrees to ratify. When President Carter, for instance, put forth the controversial Panama Canal Treaties in 1977, the Senate demanded that a number of things be changed before it would give its approval.

Executive Agreements. When a president believes that the Senate may balk at a particular treaty arrangement or if he feels that an agreement needs to be made hurriedly or secretly, he can exercise his authority to make executive agreements. An **executive agreement** is an agreement between the president of the United States and the head of some other country. It has the force of a treaty but does not require Senate approval. However, an executive agreement, unlike a treaty, is not binding on future presidents. The authority to make such agreements is not found explicitly in the Constitution; rather, it is done under the president's general authority in foreign affairs and by congressional authorization. Customarily, presidents use executive agreements for routine business matters, such as acquiring and maintaining embassies, and most involve trade matters, some of them quite controversial. For example, one president used an executive agreement to sell huge quantities of wheat to the then Soviet Union, thus, driving up the price of wheat here at home. Still, there have been significant and far-reaching executive agreements made by presidents that did not concern trade. Many of President Johnson's commitments to South Vietnam in the early 1960s were made through executive agreements, and the end of our involvement in the war in that country was also concluded by executive agreement. One of the secret provisions of the latter agreement was that the United States would help finance the rebuilding of North Vietnam. When that part of the agreement became known, the public was so outraged that it was never implemented. (There are those who contend that there was never any intention of implementing it.) In response to a number of unpopular executive agreements, in 1972 Congress passed the Case Act, which requires that they be reported to that body within sixty days. This requirement in no way limits the president's ability to make them. Furthermore, the law allows the president to report an agreement to the Senate Foreign Relations and the House International Relations Committees in secret if he believes that disclosure of the agreement would threaten national security. Since World War II, executive agreements have accounted for about 95 percent of all agreements made between the United States and other countries.

Extend Diplomatic Recognition. The Constitution gives the president the authority to send and receive ambassadors. By receiving a country's ambassador, the president is stating that the United States recognizes the government of that country as legitimate; i.e., he extends diplomatic recognition. It is difficult for countries to function without the diplomatic recognition of at least the United States or countries of Western Europe. Very little, if any, trade or travel goes on between the United States and countries with whom there is no diplomatic recognition. On the flip side, countries that receive diplomatic recognition from the major economic/military powers have significant advantages. The state of Israel was granted quick recognition by President Harry Truman in 1948, an act that essentially told the world that the United States would support the newly formed state's right to exist. Diplomatic recognition was extended to mainland (Communist) China by President Carter, which opened the way for trade and friendlier relations between China and the United States. China is one of the United States' major trading partners today. However, the U.S. runs its second largest trade deficit with China, the first being with Japan.

In the past withdrawal of diplomatic recognition (returning ambassadors to their home states) was a prelude to declarations of war between countries. Now since countries are reluctant to declare war on each other because of the possible use of nuclear weapons, it merely means that relations are strained: one is "mad" at the other and wishes to express this displeasure short of all out war. The United States withdrew its diplomatic recognition from Cuba, for example, in the 1960s and from Iran in the 1970s. Both of these countries have been relatively isolated from the rest of the world since then, especially in terms of trade.

The Growth of Presidential Power in Foreign Affairs. From the beginning the nature of the presidential office and the character of foreign relations and of diplomacy contributed to the increase of presidential power in the area of foreign affairs. Unlike Congress, the president is always in session. Unlike Congress, he can act informally, quickly, and secretly.

Presidential authority in foreign affairs has grown in proportion to the growth and power of the United States. Early in the nineteenth century the international relations of the United States were modest, and presidents were still cautious politically, as well as constitutionally. Opportunities for asserting extraordinary presidential authority became more frequent later in the nineteenth century and early in the twentieth. President Theodore Roosevelt claimed the power to do whatever was not expressly forbidden to him by the Constitution or by the law, so he dispatched troops, annexed territory, and made international agreements on his own authority. President Bush invaded Panama and claimed powers to pursue the Gulf War against Iraq, and President Clinton sent American troops into Somalia and Bosnia as part of a United Nations operational agreements on his own authority.

More recently, the events of 9/11 and the "war" on terrorism have also provided yet another opportunity to increase the power and prestige of the president. In the immediate wake of the crisis, President Bush's popularity ratings went sky high in response to the public's perceived need to turn to one person in times of crisis. The numbers continue to remain high despite some criticism of the way in which he handled the pre- and post- 9/11 situation. Much of the criticism could be political posturing for the coming elections in November 2002. The long-term effects of this crisis on the presidency, as well as President Bush's reaction to it, remains to be seen.

In terms of the structure of the executive office of the presidency (See Chapter 12), there are already some changes. We now have a Department of Homeland Security. In addition, both the president and Congress appear to be ready to restructure the Immigration and Naturalization Service. This restructuring results from problems with issuing visas to persons who want to enter and remain in the United States for a specified period of time, as well as problems with keeping track of those who are in the United States on visas to make sure they leave when they are supposed to leave.

The Legislative Powers of the President

Near the top of any presidential job description would be "leading Congress." Since the American system of separation of powers is actually one of shared power, presidents can rarely operate independently of Congress. If they are to

George W. Bush chats with Cliff Stearns (R-FL) and colleagues aboard Air Force One. Today, the president constantly travels throughout the United States and all over the world.

succeed in leaving their stamp on public policy, much of their time in office will be devoted to trying to persuade the legislative branch to support their proposals.

Chief Legislator. Nowhere does the Constitution use the term "chief legislator"; it is strictly a phrase invented by textbook writers to emphasize the chief executive's importance in the legislative process. The Constitution, however, directs that the president "give to the Congress Information of the State of the Union and recommend to their Consideration such Measures as he shall judge necessary and expedient." Congress added to this function a great deal of authority so that today presidents make annual presentations to Congress called the State of the Union Message, the Economic Message, and the Budget Message. The **State of the Union Message** is an address to Congress, as well as to the people, in which the president conveys his ideas about what the problems of the country are and what laws can presumably solve them. According to the Constitution, the State of the Union Address could be a written document delivered to the Congress. Over time, however, presidents have decided to give their State of the Union Address to a joint meeting of Congress, the Supreme Court, and the Cabinet, since all the major television and cable networks give live coverage to the speech. To a certain extent the State of the Union Address has become more of a public relations campaign aimed at the American people as much as, or more than, a communication to the Congress on the State of the Union.

The **Economic** and **Budget Messages** deal with narrower topics such as unemployment and the president's budget proposals. After these addresses are delivered, Congress receives actual legislative proposals formulated in the executive branch and introduced in Congress usually by members of the president's party.

Since the **Budget and Accounting Act of 1921** was passed, which gave the president control over the presentation to Congress of the entire national budget, the president's role in the legislative process has increased so much that today about 80 percent of all legislation passed by Congress is begun in the executive branch. The Budget and Accounting Act brought about the executive budget process first experimented with by the government of the State of New York. Under the executive budget process the "president proposes, while the Congress disposes." This executive budget process became part of the way the U.S. government does business when the budget grew to such a size that one person making the budget made more sense than 535 members of Congress. The president's **Office of Management and Budget (OMB)** has primary responsibility for making the budget. Congress now acts as a watchdog, reviewing and amending the president's proposals rather than formulating very many of them itself. The president's legislative role has become a major means of judging how effective he is in office by measuring his success in persuading Congress to act on his proposals.

The Constitution also grants the legislative function of the veto to the president as part of its system of checks. Usually for a bill to become a law, the president's signature is required. However, he may have objections to the bill, which he expresses when he refuses to sign the bill. He itemizes his objections and sends the bill back to the Congress. This action is called a **regular veto** or just a veto. Congress at this point has the option of agreeing with his objections and changing the bill or of overriding his veto by a two-thirds vote of both houses. Overriding a veto is not the easiest thing to do. To date only about 4 percent have been overridden.[15]

Many recent presidents have argued for legislation, if not a constitutional amendment, to grant them a power that some state governors have, namely, the **line-item veto**. This allows the president to veto certain items of a budget bill while leaving others intact. It would be particularly useful to presidents in cutting spending on relatively unnecessary items that benefit a particular state. Congress passed a bill in 1996 that gave the president the power of line-item veto; however, the law was quickly challenged. The law was declared unconstitutional since it altered what was in the Constitution. If Congress seriously wants the president to have this power, then they must submit a constitutional amendment to the states. Thus far, none is forthcoming.

There is also another type of veto called a **pocket veto**. With this procedure, when the president receives a bill within ten days or less (Sundays excluded) of Congress' going out of session, (final adjournment, not holiday recesses) he can just refuse to sign it—stuff it in his pocket, so to speak. When
Congress goes out of session, the bill just dies without his signature. If the
lawmakers wish to have the bill, they must begin the process of introducing it,
etc., all over again. Hence, the pocket veto is said to be the only veto that
Congress cannot override.

Another of the president's legislative powers is the power to issue executive
orders. **Executive orders** are issued by the president and have the same force as
if they were laws passed by Congress. They involve filling in details of congressional acts, carrying out treaties, or creating or changing practices of executive
agencies. Although there is no specific grant of this authority in the Constitution, presidents have issued such orders over the years, and the practice has
become customary as well as more frequent. President Truman used an executive order to ban racial discrimination in the armed forces, and President Reagan
employed this device to decontrol the price of crude oil, gasoline, and propane
in 1981.

Besides executive orders, the president also has some legislative power actually delegated to him by the Congress. For example, the legislative branch has
authorized the chief executive to award federal contracts and to select the sites
of government installations. Awarding these contracts and selecting these sites
are called **preferment**, and with it the president has a very powerful tool with
which to manipulate members of Congress, as well as the economy. Since these
sites and contracts provide powerful boosts to local economies, members of the
House and the Senate are particularly interested in seeing that their states get at
least their "fair" share. Thus, the president can bargain for votes in Congress
with his power of preferment and has done so particularly with the congressional committees dealing with defense, whose members frequently receive
military installations in their states and districts. It should not go unnoticed
that the national government is this country's largest single buyer of goods and
services, purchasing around $600-billion worth annually.[16] That much buying
power produces a great deal of leverage for the president and the executive
branch in general.

Party Leader. No matter what other resources presidents may have at their
disposal, they remain highly dependent upon their party to move their legislative programs. Representatives and senators of the president's party frequently
form the nucleus of coalitions supporting presidential proposals and provide
considerably more support than do members of the opposition party. Thus,
party leadership in Congress is every president's principal task when seeking to
counter the natural tendencies toward conflict between the executive and legislative branches inherent in the American government's checks. However, de-

spite the pull of party ties, all presidents experience substantial slippage in the support of their party in Congress and can count on their own party members for support no more than roughly two-thirds of the time. Therefore, presidents are forced to take an active role in party matters and to persuade and to mobilize members of their own party, as well as members of the opposition.

The President's Legislative Skills. The president's legislative skills come in a variety of forms. Of these, bargaining receives perhaps the most attention from media commentators on the presidency. There is no question that many deals are struck. Some of these "deals" might be characterized as **legislative log rolling**—"You scratch my back and I'll scratch yours." Others might more appropriately be called **pork barrel legislation**—legislation designed to bring construction dollars to a particular district for such things as river and harbor projects, highway construction, new post offices, etc. Frequently the projects are not really needed. In either case the president trades his support for legislation that some members of Congress want in return for their support on legislation the president wants. Obviously the president needs to bargain only if he does not have enough votes for passage of his programs.

Presidents may improve their chances of success in Congress by making certain strategic moves. It is wise, for example, for a new president to be ready to send legislation to the Hill (Congress) early in his first year in office to exploit the favorable atmosphere that typically characterizes this "**honeymoon**" period. Obviously this is a one-shot opportunity.

Another important aspect of presidential legislative strategy is establishing priorities among legislative proposals. The goal here is to set Congress's agenda. If presidents are unable to focus attention on their priority programs, these programs may become lost in the maze of the legislative process.[17]

The Executive Powers

One of the most important roles of the president is that of chief executive. In that role, presidents have substantial powers granted by the Constitution, delegated by Congress, and derived from the nature of their office. The most important are the appointment and removal powers, the power to issue executive orders, and the power to prepare the annual budget and to regulate expenditures.

The Appointment and Removal Power. Like the treaty-making power, the president's appointment power is subject to the approval of two-thirds of the Senate and in one instance the approval of two-thirds of the House and the Senate (required for the appointment of a vice president). The Constitution and various congressional acts grant the chief executive the authority to appoint all federal judges, diplomats, other government officials such as the Cabinet members, and even a vice president should a vacancy occur in that office. Today with the growth of the federal government, the president can appoint about

2000 people to his administration, and, if military officers are included, that figure becomes approximately 100,000. That gives the president a great deal of **patronage** to dispense—appointing people to government offices to pay off political debts. Although only about half of these nonmilitary appointments fall into policy-making positions, the appointment power of the president gives him a significant impact on policy making. His ability to appoint persons to the federal courts even gives the chief executive policy-making influence long after his term of office has ended since federal judges are appointed for what amounts to life terms. Rarely does the Senate refuse to approve the person the president has selected. When a nominee appears to be "in trouble," presidents often withdraw the nomination or hint that it would be a good move for the nominee to do so. Occasionally the Senate has withheld its approval as was the case with two of President Bush's nominees to the Supreme Court in 1989. Likewise, President Clinton's nomination of Lani Guinier to head the Civil Rights Division of the Justice Department produced such an outpouring of disapproval by the Senate that she withdrew her name from consideration. In 1991, President Bush's nominee to the Supreme Court, Clarence Thomas, was confirmed for appointment by a vote of fifty-two to forty-eight. Despite charges that Thomas had sexually harassed a former employee—charges that produced a media "feeding frenzy"— he became the second black Supreme Court justice.

While the president can send any name to the Senate that he desires, the practice of **senatorial courtesy** often grants senators of the president's party a virtual veto over appointments to jobs in their states, especially U.S. District Court judges. Senatorial courtesy, although merely a tradition, demands that other senators accept or reject presidential appointments based on the judgment of the senators from the state wherein the appointment is to be made— assuming these senators are from the president's party. In other words, the president is not going to submit a name to the Senate without first getting the "okay" from the home state's senators—again assuming they are from the president's party.

The removal power is the logical complement of the appointment power. The ability to remove subordinates is fundamental to presidential control of the executive branch. Without the removal power, the president could not be held fully responsible for the actions of those under him or for the failure of departments and agencies to achieve his objectives. While the president can remove many officials he appoints whenever and for whatever reason he wants, others may require removal for "cause" specified in the law. Still, the president may exert informal pressure on some officials to resign. For example, he may call publicly for someone's resignation, or he may revoke authority he has delegated to an official as a means of indicating displeasure and lack of confidence. However, presidents do not like to do this since it makes their administration appear weak if there is a great deal of turnover.

Financial Power. Presidents have substantial financial powers delegated by Congress that they use in their efforts to control the executive branch. The most important of these is the power to create the budget, which is an annual plan for spending by the national government. Among other things, the budget establishes the president's spending priorities. By trying to control how much money is spent, the chief executive hopes to influence the performance of the economy—a task that is not always very easy to do in the manner the president intends.

Besides budgeting, presidents have certain discretionary spending powers that increase their leverage over the bureaucracy. Presidents have substantial nonstatutory authority (not given by laws, i.e., informal), based on "understandings" with congressional committees, to shift funds within a program, as well as from one program to another.

Enforce Laws of the United States

When the president is inaugurated, he promises to "faithfully execute the laws of the United States." He performs this task with the help of a huge bureaucracy consisting of about two million people. We will discuss this bureaucracy later, but for the moment let's give an example or two of how a president enforces a law Congress has made.

Congress has authorized the national government to collect income taxes. It created an agency in the executive branch called the Internal Revenue Service (sometimes jokingly referred to by taxpayers as the "Infernal" Revenue Service). This agency issues rules and regulations concerning the payment of these income taxes and is ultimately responsible to the president for the performance of this function. Silly as this sounds, the 1989 *Internal Revenue Service Manual* contained guidelines for the collection of income taxes after a nuclear attack!

Another example comes not from the enforcement of a congressional act but, rather, from the enforcement of a Supreme Court order. As already mentioned, the Supreme Court ordered the desegregation of public schools in the 1954 case *Brown v. Board of Education of Topeka, Kansas*. When schools in Little Rock, Arkansas, refused to desegregate, President Eisenhower ordered army troops into the city to enforce the court order. This kind of enforcement is not the norm in the United States; on the contrary, most of the president's enforcement power is employed in an administrative capacity as described previously with the Internal Revenue Service example.

Judicial Functions

The Constitution authorizes the president to grant **executive clemency** (pardons), **amnesty** (group pardons), **reprieves** (delays in the execution of a sentence), and **commutations** (lessening of sentences). These "judicial" functions can be exercised only on behalf of persons who may be or who are involved in federal crimes, not state crimes. Therefore, the president cannot commute a death sentence to life in prison for a person convicted of murder in Florida. The Constitution further limits the president's pardoning power in that he cannot grant someone a pardon who was impeached.[18]

In recent years these presidential powers have been the topic of much public debate. A cry of "foul" was heard when President Nixon pardoned Jimmy Hoffa, former president of the powerful Teamsters Union, shortly before the union endorsed Nixon for president. Many also felt that President Ford's pardoning of former President Nixon in regard to the Watergate scandal before Nixon was even charged with a crime was inappropriate. Defenders of President Ford countered that the country had been bogged down in "Watergate" for too long and that to continue in this mire by possibly trying a former president in court was not worth the effort since Nixon had been punished sufficiently by being forced out of office.

President Carter did not escape criticism in 1977 either when he granted amnesty to all Vietnam War draft evaders (but not to deserters). Strangely enough, this type of amnesty had been granted after every war the United States has ever fought but not so soon after the war had ended as in the case of Vietnam. Carter came under fire again when he commuted the sentence of Patricia Hearst, who had been convicted of armed robbery, among other things. Many believed the commutation was a result of Hearst's being the daughter of millionaire, newspaper magnate, William Randolph Hearst. However, Carter defended his action on humanitarian grounds saying that Hearst had originally been an unwilling participant and had subsequently been rehabilitated. Regardless of why presidents exercise their "judicial" functions, the courts have upheld their constitutional right to do so.[19]

CONCLUSION

The Office of the President of the United States has changed dramatically over the past two hundred years since its beginnings with George Washington. Customs begun by various presidents years ago, together with authority given to the chief executive by Congress, have expanded the presidency to such an extent that many people long to return to the simplicity of its earlier years. Such a reversal, however, is not likely to be forthcoming as long as the United States continues to be the powerful and complex country that it is with its huge bureaucracy. Some presidents have come to the office with the idea that the government could be run like an army or perhaps like a business. Those who adopted these approaches usually have not been considered too successful. The primary reason, it seems, for their lack of success has been a failure to understand that the office of the presidency is like no other. Many have tried to understand it, analyze it, explain it, but no one yet has seemed to be its master.

Those presidents who have been deemed successful have apparently been men of intelligence, great political savvy, and integrity; have surrounded themselves with advisors and administrators with the same qualities; and perhaps have had a large dose of luck to boot.

Chapter Eleven Notes

[1]Geraldine Ferraro was nominated by the Democratic Party for the office of vice president in 1984. She and her presidential running mate, Walter Mondale, were defeated by the Republican ticket of Ronald Reagan and George Bush.

[2]The Communist Party of the United States and one other minor party once nominated a black female for president. Needless to say, they did not win the election.

[3]Thomas Bailey, *Presidential Greatness: the Image of the Man from George Washington to the Present* (New York: Appleton-Century-Crofts, 1966), 68.

[4]At this writing, Congress is discussing whether to raise the president's salary to $400,000 annually.

[5]*The Saginaw News,* 27 December 1992, 7(A).

[6]Arthur M. Schlesinger, *Paths to the Present* (New York: Macmillan Co., 1964).

[7]Bailey, *Presidential Greatness.*

[8]Jack Holmes and Robert Elder, Jr., "Our Best and Worst Presidents: Some Possible Reasons for Perceived Performance," *Presidential Studies Quarterly*, XIX (Summer 1989): 529-557.

[9]Robert Dole, *Great Political Wit* (New York: Doubleday & Co., 1998).

[10]20 December 1986.

[11]Paul C. Light, *Vice-Presidential Power: Advice and Influence in the White House* (Baltimore: The Johns Hopkins University Press, 1984), 28.

[12]Light, 34.

[13]There is some debate concerning the function of the National Security Council. Facts surrounding the sale of arms to Iran beginning in July of 1985 and continuing into late 1986 indicate that at least some members of the NSC were acting on their own and making policy and strategic decisions sometimes without the consent of the president.

[14]Louis Fisher, *Constitutional Conflicts between Congress and the President* (Englewood Cliffs, N.J.: Princeton University Press, 1991.)

[15]Lyn Ragsdale, ed. *Vital Statistics on the Presidency: Washington to Clinton* (Washington, D.C.: Congressional Quarterly Press, 396.

[16]See the most recent *Statistical Abstract of the United States* for the exact figure.

[17]Jon R. Bond and Richard Fleisher, *The President in the Legislative Arena* (Chicago: University of Chicago Press, 1990).

[18]Some confusion may result with this last statement regarding President Ford's pardoning of former President Nixon. Nixon resigned before the vote on his impeachment. Therefore, Ford was within his rights to pardon the former president for crimes he may have committed connected with the Watergate scandal. Otherwise, Nixon may have been subjected to criminal prosecution by the United States government.

[19]See *Ex parte Grossman*, 267 U.S. 87 (1925).

Suggested Readings

Campbell, Colin, S.J., and Bert Rockman, eds. *The Clinton Presidency: First Appraisals*. Chatham, N.J.: Chatham House, 1995.

Corwin, Edwin S. *The Presidential Office and Powers*, 4th ed. New York: New York University Press, 1957.

Drew, Elizabeth. *On the Edge: The Clinton Presidency*. New York: Simon and Schuster, 1994.

Edwards, George C., III, and Stephen J. Wayne. *Presidential Leadership: Politics and Policy Making*. New York: St. Martin's Press, 1997.

Kernell, Samuel. *Going Public: New Strategies for Presidential Leadership*, 3d ed. Washington, D.C.: CQ Press, 1997.

McDonald, Forrest. *The American Presidency: An Intellectual History*. Lawrence, Kans.: University of Kansas Press, 1994.

Neustadt, Richard E. *Presidential Power and the Modern Presidents: The Politics of Leadership from Roosevelt to Reagan*. New York: Macmillan Co., 1990.

Thomas, Norman, and Joseph A. Pika. *The Politics of the Presidency*, 4th ed. Washington, D.C.: CQ Press, 1996.

Watson, Richard A. *Presidential Vetoes and Public Policy*. Lawrence, Kans.: University of Kansas Press, 1995.

Chapter Twelve

The Executive Bureaucracy:
Making Government Work

It does not require much thought to conclude that no one person today could conceivably carry out all the duties of the president without a great deal of help, and some suggest that even with help the president is not capable of controlling all that goes on. However, when things go well, the chief executive gets all the credit; on the other hand, when things go wrong, he gets all the blame. As President Truman said in referring to the office of president: "The buck stops here."

Nonetheless, the assistance that the chief executive does get comes from what is called the executive bureaucracy—administrative units that carry out the day-to-day activities of the executive branch of government. These administrative units are divided into four large groupings: The Executive Office of the President, the Cabinet, independent agencies and regulatory commissions, and government corporations.

The sheer size of the executive bureaucracy is staggering. Including both civilian and military personnel, which number almost 3 million civilians and over 1 million military, the federal government bureaucracy employs about 5 percent of the work force in the United States. The number of people it employs in its computer work force is larger than the population of the city of St. Petersburg, Florida.[1] In addition, the executive bureaucracy of the national government has budgets amounting to around $2 trillion annually. This figure

275

may have more meaning when put this way: The federal bureaucracy spends more than $2 million per minute! With a civilian payroll of about $100 billion annually, the national government is the fifth largest "industry" in the United States.[2] To house this huge work force and to carry out its functions, the federal government owns about one-third of all the land in the United States, about 437,000 nonmilitary vehicles, as well as 400,000 buildings, which contain 2.6 billion square feet of office space.[3]

Approximately 18 percent of all public (government) workers are employed by the national government, and of these nearly 98 percent work for the executive branch. The Defense Department and the Postal Service account for more than half of all civilian employees.[4]

Despite popular misconceptions, the federal civilian work force is distributed throughout the country, as well as abroad. Nearly 88 percent of federal employees work outside the Washington, D.C., metropolitan area, with California actually having more than the District of Columbia itself. About 4 percent work outside the United States.[5]

While most Americans believe the national government's bureaucracy is too large, the actual size of the U.S. government is proportionally smaller than most large industrialized countries. In addition, when compared to state-government bureaucracies, which employ almost 20 million workers, the federal bureaucracy looks puny.

The reasons for the expansion of all bureaucracies include:

• An increasing population, coupled with the growing complexity of society. For example, before there were rockets, there was no need for the National Aeronautics and Space Administration. Likewise, before 9/11 there was no Department of Homeland Security.

• A greater public acceptance of business regulations such as product safety rules, drug standards, and environmental policies.

• A general public acceptance of social welfare programs such as Social Security and Medicare.

• The bureaucracy's own necessity to increase its services.

The executive bureaucracy is a major source of information and power for the president, but its clumsy structure requires control and may often work against the job in itself. Members of the bureaucracy may work to protect their own interests or their departments when threatened by budget cuts. They may ignore the president's demands and delay or sabotage his agenda. To gain the support of this huge bureaucracy, presidents must bargain and persuade, much more often than they can order and demand. Let us proceed now to look at the executive bureaucracy to try to make some sense out of this huge "machinery" of government. Then we'll see how one goes about becoming a part of the federal bureaucracy since it is such a significant employer and contributes substantially to the economy of the United States every year.

Table 12.1: THE EXECUTIVE OFFICE OF THE PRESIDENT

White House Office	Office of Management and Budget
The Cabinet	Office of Global Communications
Office of Administration	National Security Council
Council on Environmental Quality	Council of Economic Advisors
Office of Science and Technology Policy	Office of the U.S. Trade Representative
Domestic Policy Council	Office of National Drug Control Policy
National Economic Council	Military Office
Office of Faith-Based and Community Initiatives	Office of National Aids Policy
USA Freedom Corps Volunteer Network	President's Foreign Intelligence Advisory Board

HOW THE FEDERAL EXECUTIVE BUREAUCRACY IS ORGANIZED

As with any large organization, the federal bureaucracy covers a lot of ground, so to speak. If we brought in a chart of the hierarchy of the federal executive bureaucracy, we could spend days just following the lines of authority—who reports to whom, etc. However, we can make a bit more sense out of the maze merely by focusing on the major components: the Executive Office of the President, the White House Office, the Cabinet, the independent agencies, the independent regulatory commissions, and government corporations.

The Executive Office of the President

This administrative unit contains offices or councils with an estimated budget of over $387 million in 2003.[6] The persons who work here are the president's closest advisors—some closer than others—and they are appointed by the president with the consent of the Senate and serve at "the pleasure of the president." This phrase means that he can fire them whenever he pleases. Presidents do not usually fire members of the Executive Office unless there is some crisis that brings such action about. For example, President Reagan fired (or caused to resign) Lt. Col. Oliver North and Adm. John Poindexter in December of 1986 when it was learned that these two members of the National Security Council had been involved in a possibly illegal transfer of government funds. Thus, a president is free to "dispose" of members of the Executive Office at will.

The make-up of the EOP varies from president to president, depending on what seems to be getting attention and on the preferences of the chief executive. Table 12.1 lists a recent configuration of the EOP. Some of the offices and councils contained in the EOP are discussed below.

The **White House Office** consists of the president's closest advisors. Their offices are usually located in the West Wing of the White House. It is here that we find, among others, the White House Chief of Staff; an economic advisor; a national security advisor; speech writers; a press secretary; an appointment secretary; and a number of persons who convey the president's views to members of Congress, to other governmental agencies, the media, and the public in general.

To assume that the White House Office is a small group of assistants for the president would not be correct. In fact, the office today has over four hundred people in it. Because of this large number of people, the charge is often leveled that the president is too insulated from the Cabinet and other members of the government. White House staffers insist that they do not make policy decisions and never inject themselves between the president and members of the Cabinet, etc. Yet it appears that this bureaucratic layer, which does seem to buffer the chief executive from whatever is outside the inner circle, has caused many a president in recent times much grief.

Created in 1970 to replace the Bureau of the Budget, the **Office of Management and Budget (OMB)** has two primary tasks: (1) to assist the president in the preparation of the budget and (2) to help get that budget enacted into law. The OMB also keeps the president informed about the performance of the various agencies in the executive branch. The director of this office is in one of the most powerful positions in the executive branch since he/she usually has great influence over budget decisions and, therefore, great influence over who gets what, when, and how.

The OMB would have to deal with any budget cuts that the president might want to make in his proposals to Congress. Recently the interest group Citizens Against Government Waste,[7] a nonprofit "watchdog" group, proposed a list of budget cuts. These recommendations included:

Reducing the number of political appointees: About 2700 patronage jobs are awarded annually in Washington. Reducing that number to 2000 could save over $300 million over five years.

Privatizing military commissaries: Now most military posts are near civilian stores. While privatization would save the taxpayers about $4 billion over five years, the costs to commissary users would rise.

Imposing a moratorium on federal land purchases: The national government now owns about one-third of all the land in the United States. Yet, it spends about $300 million annually to acquire more. Not buying any more land would save that $300 million annually.

Eliminate the Export Enhancement Program: U.S. companies that export agricultural products are paid a bonus by the government to do so. This

Col. Oliver North is sworn in at the "Iran-Contra" trial.

subsidy puts more money in the coffers of big agribusinesses with little or no impact on increasing those exports. Ending this practice would save about $2 billion over five years.[8]

In previous years the same group has recommended the elimination of unproductive programs starting with the Department of Commerce! (Can you imagine how Commerce Department employees greeted that suggestion?)

Closely tied to the OMB by subject matter is the **Council of Economic Advisors**, which is responsible for advising the president concerning economic matters by analyzing and assessing the economic health (or lack of it) of the United States. The council also prepares economic reports for the president that present and analyze data and forecast coming growth, decline, or stability in the economy. These tasks were formerly a bit easier perhaps in some ways than they are today since it is extremely difficult to predict economic activity accurately over an extended period (perhaps a year) and since this economy is so intimately intertwined with those of other countries from which we buy or sell goods. To be sure, there are today very sophisticated methods of gathering and analyzing data, but economists, like political scientists, differ about whose analysis is correct.

We also find in the Executive Office of the President an agency created in 1947, namely the **National Security Council (NSC)**. Although some presidents have included others on the NSC, it usually consists of the president, the vice president, the secretary of state, the secretary of defense, the director of the Central Intelligence Agency, and the chairman of the Joint Chiefs of Staff (heads of the various branches of the military). The NSC is charged with advising the president on matters of national security, both domestic and international. Beginning in December 1986, the council came under fire because of its role in the "Iran-Contra" affair, which involved the possibly illegal sale of weapons to Iran and the illegal transfer of profits from that sale to the Contras in Nicaragua. The NSC was criticized, particularly by members of Congress, because it appeared to be formulating and executing policies of its own rather than merely advising the president. Still, with a staff of about two hundred, the NSC is perhaps the most powerful agency in the area of national security. How well it functions is a question for debate. Detractors would claim that it makes far too many mistakes, while supporters state that it must be doing something right since the United States is still a free country. Both of these views appear a bit too simplistic since the NSC, like any other government agency, is a political institution that must juggle many interests at the same time. What may be an efficient national security policy may not be acceptable politically to the many interests within the country. For example, few would argue that United States domestic security could be enhanced considerably by sealing its borders with barbed wire, machine guns, and military patrols. But we can imagine the "weeping and gnashing of teeth" that would be heard if such actions were taken. This is not to say that the NSC, or any other governmental agency for that matter, should be above criticism but merely to point out that the area in which it has responsibility is highly complex.

The **Office of the United States Trade Representative** is responsible for developing and carrying out the foreign trade policies of the United States. With more and more imports coming into the country that threaten domestic industries, this office has attempted, sometimes successfully, to negotiate voluntary quotas from such countries as Japan. Congress, however, does not seem too pleased with the way trade policy has been developed of late and has imposed or threatened to impose strict import quotas or higher tariffs (import taxes) if a more balanced trade between the United States and other countries, particularly Japan, is not forthcoming. The head of this office is the United States Trade Representative, who holds the rank of ambassador. He or she is responsible for any negotiations or meetings dealing with foreign trade.

The year 1988 brought the **Office of National Drug Control Policy (ONDCP)** to the Executive Office of the President. Headed by a director who is commonly referred to as the "drug czar," this office is responsible for preparing and maintaining a national strategy for the control of illegal drugs. Additionally, it makes recommendations to the president regarding the organization, administration, and budgets of all federal departments and agencies engaged in enforcing the drug laws. Critics contend that, while its role sounds impressive, the office has no real control over what it is supposed to be doing. For example, it cannot require other drug enforcement agencies to follow the national strategy or to use their budgets in ways that the ONDCP wants.

President George W. Bush was the driving force behind the creation of the **Office of Faith-Based and Community Initiatives.** This office focuses its efforts on only six areas: the homeless, prisoners, at-risk youth, addicts, senior citizens in need, and families moving from welfare to work. That being the case, there are Centers for Faith-Based and Community Initiatives in the U.S. Departments of Justice, Labor, Health and Human Services, Housing and Urban Development, Education, and Agriculture.

For example, the Juvenile Mentoring Program of the Department of Justice, known as JUMP, supports one-to-one mentoring projects for youth at risk of failing in school, dropping out of school, or becoming involved in delinquent behavior, including gang activity and substance abuse. In 2002, the program made $12 million available to nonprofit organizations, including religious organizations to carry out juvenile mentoring programs at the local level.

Another office created during the administration of George W. Bush is the **Office of National AIDS Policy.** It focuses on coordinating continuing domestic efforts to reduce the number of new infections of the virus in the United States, particularly in segments of the population that are experiencing increases in the rate of infection. In addition, this office coordinates an increasingly integrated approach to the prevention, care, and treatment of HIV/AIDS. With the United States just recently approving huge amounts of money to fight AIDS in Africa, the office will also emphasize the integration of domestic and international efforts to combat this disease.

The Cabinet

The presidential Cabinet is composed of the secretaries of the various departments. The Constitution does not provide for the Cabinet specifically; rather, it was a practice begun by George Washington that has continued on a larger scale to the present day. Most members of the Cabinet are appointed by the president with the consent of the Senate, but they may be removed by the president whenever he no longer desires their services. As in the White House Office, shake-ups in the Cabinet do not occur too frequently unless there is some crisis to bring them about. The offices included in the Cabinet can vary from president to president; however, the secretaries of the various departments are always included. Since it is not possible for purposes of this book to go over in detail what each Cabinet position does, Table 12.2 indicates the primary functions of the fourteen departments included in the Cabinet.

Table 12.2   THE CABINET

Name	Function
Department of State	Makes and executes foreign policy; negotiates treaties and agreements with foreign governments; carries out day-to-day activities with foreign countries; issues passports and visas; provides information and propaganda programs in foreign countries; plans and executes foreign aid programs.
Department of Defense	Formulates military policies and maintains the armed forces; plans and executes civil defense programs.
Department of the Treasury	Formulates and executes polices for fiscal management; collects and disperses tax revenues; administers laws on firearms, counterfeiting, narcotics, alcohol, imports, tobacco; licenses ships; protects the president and his family through the Secret Service.
Department of the Interior	Responsible for development of territories of Guam, Samoa, Virgin Islands, and Pacific Trust Territories; administers conservation and outdoor recreation programs; administers national parks and Indian reservations; conducts research on surface and sub-surface mining; inspects mines; conducts geologic research; constructs and operates public facilities for generating electric power, provides irrigation and flood control programs.
Department of Agriculture	Provides soil and forestry conservation programs; insures farmers against damage to or loss of crops; does research on the production and marketing of crops and livestock; provides low interest loans to farmers; regulates trading on commodity exchanges where farm products are bought and sold; makes loans for electric power and phone service to rural areas; administers farm subsidy programs.
Department of Commerce	Conducts a census every ten years; forecasts the weather and other environmental phenomena; promotes trade; provides economic analyses; regulates and maintains the basic units of measurement; promotes minority business enterprises; grants patents, copyrights, and trademarks; gives assistance to areas with substantial, long-term unemployment.
Department of Labor	Administers unemployment compensation; studies national labor requirements and the impact of technology on employment; administers laws relating to welfare and pension plans and those relating to labor union operations; administers industrial health and safety laws and wage and hour laws; administers programs for training and employing of veterans.

Department of Health and Human Services	Administers Social Security and welfare programs; conducts research and other programs on health, hospital care, and disease; administers Medicare and Medicaid programs.
Department of Housing and Urban Development	Administers programs for the development and financing of public and private housing, urban renewal, community planning; administers laws pertaining to civil rights in housing.
Department of Transportation	Administers programs dealing with aviation, highway construction and safety, railroads, mass transit, waterways, and the Coast Guard.
Department of Energy	Conducts programs and research to find new energy sources and to promote energy conservation; administers nuclear weapons programs and major electric power generation programs.
Department of Education	Administers vocational programs, special education programs, bilingual programs, and adult education and rehabilitation programs; oversees educational programs through local elementary, secondary, and post-secondary schools.
Department of Justice	Provides attorneys for the national government; interprets federal law for other governmental agencies; prosecutes violators of national law; administers immigration law, federal prisons, and parolees from federal prisons; investigates possible federal crimes through the Federal Bureau of Investigation (FBI).
Department of Veterans Affairs	Newest cabinet post (1989); administers all federal programs for veterans and their families; e.g., monetary benefits for disabilities or death of veterans, life insurance, education hospitalization, home loans, and burial.
Department of Homeland Security	Combines 22 formerly disparate agencies, including the FBI and the Coast Guard, with the express purpose of defending the nation's homeland.

Despite the appearance of being a major advisory body for the chief executive, the Cabinet has rarely been used for that purpose. Individual Cabinet members actually have more influence with the president and discuss more substantive issues with him than does the Cabinet as a whole. The agenda of Cabinet meetings is usually a general discussion rather than meetings to set any type of overall policy. Policy decisions are normally made in conferences between the president and two or three Cabinet members, rather than with the Cabinet as a whole.

Since it has garnered a large share of media attention, let's take a moment to look at the newly created **Department of Homeland Security.** Obviously it grew out of the horrendous events of 9/11. Created in June 2002, and headed by the Assistant to the President for Homeland Security, its mission is to create and coordinate the execution of a broad national strategy to secure the United States from terrorist threats or attacks. The department is responsible for coordinating the executive branch's efforts to identify, prepare for, stop, guard against, respond to, and recover from terrorist events within the United States.

While the mission of the Department of Homeland Security is indeed a noble one, it is also political and overwhelming. Understandably Americans and others were shocked by the horror of 9/11 and wanted, and still want, some "guarantees" that everything will be done to prevent such events in the future. Part of the response from the government to address this demand is the Department of Homeland Security. It is a step in the right direction, according to most authorities, since coordination of many government programs is frequently lacking. For example, sharing of information among police and intelligence agencies was and, in many respects, still is lacking. However, the creation of the

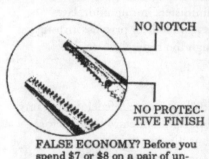

NO NOTCH

NO PROTEC-TIVE FINISH

FALSE ECONOMY? Before you spend $7 or $8 on a pair of unmodified duckbill pliers, consider this quotation from an Air Force memo to Senator Charles Grassley, who had asked if notched pliers were really worth $740 more than unnotched ones. "Anyone who has tried to perform minor maintenance on their car or kitchen," said the unsigned memo, "knows that the lack of the proper tool can make a simple task almost impossible."

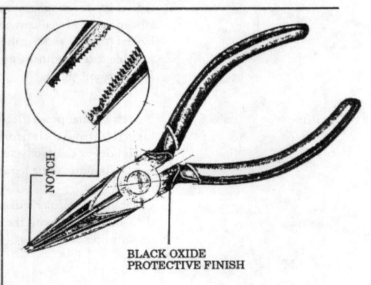

NOTCH

BLACK OXIDE PROTECTIVE FINISH

Department of Homeland Security was also political pabulum to calm the public. Politicians must, at least, *appear* to be doing something about domestic terrorism even though the United States borders are like a sieve, full of little holes through which both the "good guys" and the "bad guys" can pass frequently undetected.

With all the media attention focused on terrorism, we must remember that domestic terrorism could also come from our own homegrown variety of terrorist. Timothy McVeigh, who was executed for the destruction of the Federal Building in Oklahoma City, was a native-born, American citizen, whose ancestors were probably Scots!

Presidents over the years have utilized the Cabinet more of less, depending on the administrative style of particular presidents. One Cabinet member admitted that he was so bored during Cabinet meetings that he used to read news magazines "carefully hidden on [his] knees below the edge of the Cabinet table."[9] Although individually they are often employed as advisers to the president, Cabinet members are frequently closer to their executive departments as administrators than they are to the president.

While the Cabinet always consists of the heads of the Cabinet departments, the president may invite anyone else he chooses to sit in on the meetings. In the last quarter of this century, presidents have included the vice president in the Cabinet and frequently the Director of the Central Intelligence Agency, the Budget Director, and the United Nations Ambassador.

Independent Agencies

There are a number of agencies in the executive branch that are not under the jurisdiction of any department in the Cabinet. They have independent status because they either don't fit into any one department, because they perform a service for many or all departments, or because Congress wanted a particular function to be separated from others. The president appoints the heads of these agencies with the consent of the Senate, usually for specific terms, which may not necessarily coincide with his term of office. His power to remove these officials is usually severely restricted. Examples of independent agencies that perform services include the Office of Personnel Management and the General Services Administration (GSA), a "watchdog" agency that oversees spending by other government agencies. Although the GSA did not catch this particular goof, the picture on the opposite page shows a $748.00 pair of pliers purchased by the Air Force. Such purchases might come under the scrutiny of the GSA.

Probably the most powerful and most well-known independent agency is the Environmental Protection Agency (EPA). It is charged with carrying out national laws dealing with clean air, safe drinking water, solid waste disposal, radiation, pesticides, and other toxic substances. While the agency is not universally liked, it does have the support of some powerful interest groups such as

Table 12.3: Major Independent Regulatory Commissions

Commission	Date Established	Functions
Federal Reserve Board	1913	Regulates money supply and banking industry
Federal Trade Commission	1914	Administers antitrust laws and laws forbidding false advertising
Food and Drug Administration	1930	Issues regulations regarding foods, drugs, and medical equipment, e.g., pacemakers
Federal Communications Commission	1934	Regulates radio, television, telephone, and telegraph industries
Securities and Exchange Commission	1934	Regulates buying and selling of stocks and bonds
National Labor Relations Board	1935	Enforces fair labor practices laws
Occupational Safety and Health Administration	1970	Issues workplace rules; investigates penalizes violations
Consumer Product Safety Commission	1972	Issues standards for product safety and prohibits unsafe
Nuclear Regulatory Commission	1974	Regulates nuclear power industry
U.S. International Trade Commission	1974	Investigates unfair trade practices by foreign companies and can penalize offenders
Federal Energy Regulatory Commission	1977	Regulates production and transportation of electricity and transportation and sale of natural gas

the National Resources Defense Council, the Sierra Club, the Wilderness Society, Friends of the Earth, the National Audubon Society, and the Environmental Defense Fund.

A new independent agency was created on December 17, 2004, when President George W. Bush signed the Intelligence Reform and Counterterrorism Act of 2004. This law, resulting from the intelligence inadequacies of 9/11, created the National Intelligence Office with a director reporting directly to the president. The Director of National Intelligence (DNI) is particularly responsible for insuring that intelligence gathered by more than a dozen intelligence-gathering agencies is shared with *all* intelligence agencies and other relevant government agencies and departments.

Accordingly, the Office of Counterterrorism was created to "serve as the primary organization in the United States government for analyzing and integrating all intelligence . . . pertaining to terrorism and counterterrorism." It does not have direct responsibility for domestic terrorism. The Center's director serves as the principal advisor to the Director of National Intelligence. Additionally, the Center serves as the "central and shared knowledge bank on known and suspected terrorists and international terror groups, as well as their goals, strategies, capabilities, and networks of contact and support." In other words, all intelligence gathered by the United States is stored and to some degree analyzed by the Center for Counterterrorism so that those seeking intelligence are not required to look for it from one end of the government to another in hopes that maybe some agency will want to share that intelligence.

Independent Regulatory Commissions

Instead of performing service functions as most agencies do, the independent regulatory commissions and boards perform regulatory functions. They regulate important areas of economic activity in the United States such as communications and the stock market, by making rules regarding activity in these areas and then adjudicating these rules. Political scientists characterize these agencies as **quasi-legislative** and **quasi-judicial**, that is, they make the rules (as a legislative body would do) and punish those who violate the rules (as a court would do). As in the service agencies, the heads of these commissions and their members are appointed by the president with the consent of the Senate, usually for fixed terms. The president's removal power here is also quite limited.

Although most independent regulatory commissions are not part of any Cabinet department, a few very powerful ones are located within the Cabinet structure. Probably the ones most recognized by the general public are such agencies as the Internal Revenue Service (Treasury Department), the Occupational Health and Safety Administration (Department of Labor), and the Food and Drug Administration (Department of Health and Human Services), Table 12.3 lists some of these commissions and their general functions.

Government Corporations

Government corporations are agencies of the government that operate businesses to provide a service to consumers either free or at a reduced cost. The first of these corporations was established during the Great Depression of the 1930s. Primary examples include the Tennessee Valley Authority (TVA), which was created to provide inexpensive electric power to parts of the rural South; the Federal Deposit Insurance Corporation (FDIC), which insures member banks' deposits up to $100,000 per account; Amtrak, which operates passenger railroad service for the United States, and the United States Postal Service, which, we all know, delivers the mail. These corporations have been given considerable management flexibility, but they are still subject to government control. And, contrary to popular belief, they do attempt to make a profit. As a matter of fact, the Postal Service made more than $1 billion annually in profits in recent years, and yet the price of a first-class stamp increased in 1999 and again in 2001. Ah . . . the power of bureaucracies! The last increase resulted from the decrease in mail volume going through the U.S. Post Office. E-mail has begun to take its toll on the postal system.

THE CIVIL SERVICE SYSTEM

Until the 1880s government employees were hired mainly on the basis of their support for the person who won the presidential election, rather than on their ability to do a particular job. This system of rewarding supporters with government jobs was called **patronage** or the **spoils system** and was especially associated with President Andrew Jackson, who was the first president to use it openly and extensively. Every time a new president was elected, many who did not support him in the election were fired and replaced by those who did. The spoils system was not a very efficient way to run the government since many unqualified persons were employed, while others who could perform the job better were left out because they did not support the "correct" candidate.

Finally, in 1883 Congress passed the Pendleton Act, which created the Civil Service Commission—now called the **Office of Personnel Management (OPM)**—to oversee the hiring of government employees. The system has been refined to the point that today about 90 percent of all government positions are covered under the "**merit system**." Hiring is now based on "merit"—competitive examinations, education, and work experience, rather than on the person's political positions. There are also provisions in the civil service, as in the private work force, for preferential hiring of veterans, women, the physically challenged, and racial and ethnic minorities. Although most federal government employees are now covered under the merit system, it should be noted that the president still can hire and fire at will a significant number of people in the bureaucracy. Presidents can appoint over 2000 people to various offices in the bureau-

A disappointed office seeker assassinated President Garfield. Civil service positions began to replace the "spoils system."

cracy. For example, when President Clinton came into office, he fired all the attorneys in the Justice Department and replaced them with "his" people—meaning he rewarded a number of supporters and their friends with patronage jobs.

While the merit system's intent was to remove the hiring and firing of government employees from the political arena, an unwanted side effect has been mediocrity. Civil service employees cannot be removed from office except for "gross negligence," and even with gross negligence many are not fired. A postal worker who dumped his mail every day in a garbage bin was merely fined but not fired. In the view of historian Daniel J. Boorstin, the bureaucracy is characterized by ". . . caution, concern for regularity of procedures, avoidance of the need for decision."[10] If you have ever tried to figure out your own income taxes or probably any other form from the government, you know what Boorstin means. In this famous example of bureaucratic ineptitude, the government issued a 700-page description of something it wanted to buy called "rodent elimination devices."—translation: mouse traps!

Besides often cumbersome procedures that sometimes contribute to bureaucratic inefficiency, in a normal year, only about 200 people will be fired for incompetence and another 2000 for misconduct, out of the nearly two million civil service employees with the federal government. Director of the Office of Personnel Management James King asserts that "only someone who aggressively seeks to be terminated" is likely to be discharged. As you can see in Table 12.4, the process of firing a civil servant seems to be designed to make it easier to "promote" the problem employee to some area where he or she will do less damage than it is to just get rid of the person!

Table 12.4: Rules for Firing a Bureaucrat

• Written notice at least thirty days before a hearing to determine incompetence or misconduct.

• Statement of cause, noting specific dates, places, and actions cited as incompetent or improper.

• Right to a hearing and decision by an impartial official, with the burden of proof falling on the agency that wishes to fire the employee.

• Right to have a lawyer present and to provide witnesses favorable to the employee at the hearing.

• Right to appeal any unfavorable action to the Merit Systems Protection Board.

• Right to appeal any unfavorable action by the board to the U.S. Court of Appeals.

• Right to stay on the job and be compensated until all appeals are exhausted.

Reforms

Some reforms have been attempted in the realm of merit pay increases for civil service employees, but so far there has been little effect on the efficiency level of the bureaucracy. However, in defense of the bureaucracy, many people enter government service in the hope of performing a service for the country and its people. Yet, the mere size of the government today, along with the political pressures that are always exerted on administrators in the bureaucracy, often makes government service in any capacity a thankless and frustrating position to hold. For instance, the EPA has attempted over the past decade to do something about a highly polluted river that flows from Mexico into California. This river is so full of toxic material that animals that drink from it are often found dead shortly after quenching their thirst. Presidents from Carter to Reagan have made agreements with the Mexican government to clean up the river, but political maneuverings have thus far prevented the EPA from being able to perform its functions. Lest we cast the blame solely on the Mexican government's shoulders, we should be aware that the largest polluters of the river are United States companies operating in Mexico.[11]

With a view to making the bureaucracy more open and responsive to the needs of the citizens, in 1976, Congress passed the **Government in the Sunshine Act** (silly as that sounds). This law requires that about 50 federal agencies hold their meetings in public. The only exceptions concern discussions of court proceedings and personnel problems.

Sunset laws, another attempt at reform, place federal programs on a definite schedule for congressional oversight. Unless Congress specifically reauthorized a particular program at the end of the designated period, it would be ended automatically; that, its sun would set. Very few "suns have set," thus far. For example, the federal Helium Program was started in 1925 to keep our blimps afloat. The U.S. does not use helium-powered blimps any more, but 32 billion cubic feet of helium are still stored today in Amarillo, Texas.

The eight years of the Clinton administration (1993-2001) saw a reduction in the overall number of bureaucrats by about 11 percent. However, of the 250,000 jobs cut during those years 212,000 came from the Defense Department and from the end of the process of bailing out some of the nation's savings and loan associations. The most ironic figure of all is that many who were "downsized" were later rehired as private consultants. Thus, they did not qualify as government employees.[12]

In another move to improve the civil service, Congress passed the Civil Service Reform Act in 1978, which prohibits reprisals against whistleblowers by their superiors. The law also set up the Merit Systems Protection Board as part of this protection. *Whistleblowers* in this context refer to bureaucrats who report serious governmental inefficiency or illegal action. They can be low-level clerks, managers, or even highly specialized employees, such as scientists. Many federal agencies also have toll-free numbers that employees can use anonymously to report bureaucratic waste and inappropriate behavior. About a third of all calls result in agency action or follow-up.

While it certainly is easy to point the finger at the bureaucrats and say they are inefficient and wasteful. This is especially true when we discover that 80,000 buttons bearing the message "For Kids' Sake, Think Toy Safety," designed and distributed by the Consumer Product Safety Commission, had to be recalled because they could be accidentally swallowed, the pinpoint was too sharp, and paint was toxic! However, we must remember that many times their partners in crime, so to speak, are members of Congress who appropriate money for what most citizens would view as frivolous things. For example, no civil service reform yet envisioned would prevent Congress from appropriating $5 million to build a new military golf course at Andrews Air Force Base, when there were already nineteen military golf courses around Washington, D.C. Similarly, new reforms would not have prevented Congress from appropriating $330,000 to build a deluxe, earthquake-proof, outdoor "john" for hikers in a remote recreation area in Pennsylvania. Finger pointing goes both ways.

Employment with the Federal Government

The Office of Personnel Management (OPM) is frequently thought of as a central hiring agency for the federal government, but it is not. In general, the role of the OPM is one of helping individual government agencies, offices, bureaus, etc., to meet their personnel requirements; originating and enforcing government personnel rules; supervising some application, testing, and screening procedures; ranking some, but not all, applicants for particular positions; maintaining some registers; organizing and distributing job vacancy information; offering limited training services; certifying and auditing personnel records; and providing benefits to employees and retired government employees. Since the mid-1980s, hiring authority has been delegated mainly to the individual agencies.

The federal government does not have a single "personnel office" as a private company might have. Instead, federal employees are classified into competitive and exempted services and positions, the majority of which are competitive, i.e., merit-system positions. Those government agencies that fall outside the jurisdiction of the OPM—**exempted services**—include congressional and judicial bureaucratic positions, as well as some executive agencies, for example, the CIA, U.S. Postal Service, the FBI, the federal courts, and the General Accounting Office. Persons who want to be employed in one of these exempted positions must apply directly to the agencies themselves since they have their own personnel procedures.

Besides the exempted services, the federal government also has **exempted positions**, which include, among others, teachers in overseas schools for dependents of persons in the Department of Defense; medical personnel in the Department of Veterans Affairs, National Science Foundation scientists and engineers, and drug enforcement agents.

Classifications and Compensation

The federal work force is divided fairly evenly into "blue-collar" and "white-collar" positions. Most white-collar (administrative, scientific, clerical, and technical employees) are paid according to the **General Schedule (GS)**, which has a salary range from about $16,016 (GS-1, entry level) all the way up to about $116,517 (GS-15, highest level).[13] Some blue-collar workers are paid according to the **Federal Wage System (WG)**. The WG wages vary depending on the geographic location of the employee. Senior management positions within the bureaucracy are paid according to a different schedule called the **Executive Schedule (EX)** with salaries ranging from EX-1 at the top of $180,100 annually to EX-5 at the low end, earning approximately $131,400.[14]

Despite the fact that salaries lag behind the private sector, most federal workers are generally satisfied with their jobs. In a recent survey done by the Office of Personnel Management, just over 40 percent of respondents said they *would* recommend their organization as a good place to work. The remaining 60 percent was divided among those who disagreed, strongly disagreed, or who were neutral about the idea. In fact the respondents' biggest gripe, so to speak, concerned recognition and rewards, as well as the failure of managers to deal with poor performing or nonperforming employees. Yet, when asked if they were considering leaving their current jobs, 64 percent answered "no."

Examinations

Not every position with the federal government requires a test. In fact, most do not. All the applicant is required to do is submit a resume. However, some jobs, e.g., typist and many jobs in the Postal Service, may require a skills test. State Department positions as Foreign Service Officer specify both the written and oral Foreign Service Examinations, which are given annually. Each vacancy announcement will indicate whether a test is required.

THE ~~ROLE~~ *Problems* OF THE BUREAUCRACY

Bureaucracies serve as both implementors of policy and as regulators of some of the private sector. In short, they govern. How well they do their jobs is highly dependent on the quality of personnel, the motivation of personnel, the willingness of the public to be "governed," as well as the wisdom and political savvy of the high-level policy makers, such as the president. In all of these areas the federal bureaucracy, as well as other government bureaucracies, both domestic and foreign, has had its problems. Recruiting highly qualified persons to positions in the bureaucracy is time consuming and frustrating, both for the hiring agency and for the applicant. In addition, salaries for bureaucratic positions are not always competitive with those of the private sector. The sheer size of the bureaucracy and the monumental tasks demanded to govern a country the size of the United States creates its own set of logistical problems, not to mention that the public often views the word "bureaucrat" as a "dirty word." If an Internal Revenue Service agent is at a social gathering and lets it be known what his or her occupation is, people literally flee as if the agent were infected with bubonic plague! Let us not forget that people don't always want to be governed or, at least, don't want to be governed in the fashion that the government, through its bureaucracy, wants to govern.

The Implementation Function

When Congress, the president, the courts, or some regulatory agency passes legislation, or issues an executive order, judicial decision, or regulation, it is the bureaucracy that carries out these policy decisions. In other words, once someone decides that the country should do something, the bureaucracy is supposed to "implement" that decision—see that whatever was decided is actually done.

On the surface the role of the bureaucracy as implementors sounds simple enough. However, any number of things can go wrong in trying to execute policy. "Murphy's Law" seems to apply: whatever can go wrong will go wrong.

Faulty Program Design. One of the things that can go awry results from faulty program design. Suppose Congress decided that the federal government should eliminate poverty in the United States. To do so, an agency would be created; it would hire consultants to define the term poverty and to determine the causes of poverty. Then it would design programs to eliminate the causes. *Voila!* No more poverty. The problem is, however, that poverty is a relative term. To be poor always is seen in relation to something else. As long as people have differing incomes and expenses—even different tastes—someone will always be deemed poor. Even if the plan merely intended to give "poor" people extra money, that money would have to be obtained from taxation, which would take away income from people not deemed to be poor, thus, making them "poor" also!

Lack of Clear Directions. Besides faulty design, sometimes Congress does not want to deal directly with certain "hot potatoes." So it passes a law so vague that the bureaucrats responsible for implementing the congressional policies must try to figure out for themselves what Congress meant by certain words in the law. For example, in 1972, Congress passed a law that seemed to be saying that colleges and universities that receive any federal funding (most of them do) could not discriminate against women in the field of athletic competition. The Department of Health, Education, and Welfare (now the Department of Education) issued a 30-page report interpreting what it thought the act required. Naturally there was substantial disagreement, and dozens of lawsuits were filed in which the courts had to decide whether Title IX of the Education Amendments of 1972 required that equal amounts of money be spent on women's and men's athletics programs. There still is no clear-cut decision.

Inadequate Resources. While conventional wisdom always says that bureaucracies are loaded with money that they proceed to waste, the real issue is does the bureaucracy in question have adequate funding to do the task required. Sometimes the answer is a resounding "no". Complaints abound, for example, about "near misses" at airports because of overwork or understaffing in air traffic controllers. It takes forever and a day for a new drug to be tested and cleared for marketing in the United States, in part, because of underfunding in the Food and Drug Administration. The number of ships, planes, and personnel used to stop drug trafficking into the United States is grossly inadequate. The list could go on for pages. The bureaucracy is expected to perform when it has not often been given the necessary resources to do the job mandated.

To say the bureaucrats do not always have adequate resources to fulfill their role does not mean that bureaucrats do not waste money. Indeed, agencies whose job it is to audit the spending of other agencies issue report after report indicating that they do. One recent report indicated that the federal government has 26 programs that are labeled as "wasteful." Ten of those twenty-six programs had been on the list for a decade.[15] In addition, a report issued from the Health and Human Services Department indicated that improper Medicare payments amounted to $12.6 billion.

Other examples seem equally as outrageous. The CIA and the Pentagon paid over $11 million to psychics to find out if those psychics would offer insights about foreign threats to the United States. If that one did not cause your heart to fail, this one might. The Social Security Administration made payments of over $20 million a year to thousands of prisoners through the Supplemental Income Program. Your author's favorite, however, is this one. The Department of Energy paid out $10 million a year to its employees to encourage them to lose weight!

Bureaucratic Red Tape. To function with relative efficiency, bureaucrats must follow certain routines. Otherwise, they would constantly be reinventing the wheel every day when they reported for work. These routines, however, can become obstacles to implementing policies and programs and very frustrating to those on the receiving end of the "red tape." In other words, sometimes bureaucracies do things in a certain way because they have always done them that way, regardless of whether the procedure retains any merit in solving a particular problem.

Bureaucrats Who Have Minds of Their Own. Most people would agree that some discretion—the ability to make decisions on one's own authority—is good. However, it can produce some problems also, especially regarding uniformity of treatment of each person. The IRS serves as an excellent example. No amount of written rules could possibly cover every deduction that a taxpayer might want to include on his/her tax return. The agents who deal with the public every day, as well as the agents' supervisors, exercise some discretion about whether something is deductible or not, given no written rule. For example, if a man teaches at a college that requires him to wear a sport coat and tie to work, do these clothes constitute a uniform and are their costs deductible? Airline flight attendants can deduct their uniforms. Could this teacher? Expenses connected with investments are deductible according to the written rules of the IRS. But is the cost of a taxi ride to visit a stockbroker deductible? In other words, is that ride an investment expense?

Sometimes bureaucrats themselves do not maintain a neutral stand toward certain policies. Where there is discretion, i.e., where the policy is not perfectly clear with all the i's dotted and the t's crossed, there will be some bureaucrats who will use their discretion to undermine the policy or program if they don't like it. For instance, we often think that whatever the president orders will be immediately carried out, but this is not always the case when the person responsible for executing the order does not like it. President Nixon once ordered his secretary of state to bomb a terrorist camp. The secretary disagreed with the idea and just said that bad weather prevented him from doing so.[16]

Decentralization. Instead of being under the control of one agency, responsibility for implementing government policies and programs is sometimes scattered among several agencies. For example, over one hundred human service programs are dispersed among ten different agencies and departments, including the Department of Health and Human Services, the Department of Agriculture, the Department of Housing and Urban Development, and the Department of Labor. Lack of central responsibility for programs makes coordination difficult and time consuming, and many times "turf wars" result as with drug enforcement policy. The agencies and departments involved—the Drug Enforcement Agency, the Customs Service, the State Department, and the Federal Bureau of Investigation, among others—are notorious for not cooperating with one another.

Capture. Another characteristic that causes problems for the bureaucracy is called capture. The term refers to the tendency of an agency to develop a very close relationship with the special interests it oversees and, thus, to protect rather than regulate those interests. Capture is especially problematic for regulatory commissions. At various times in its history, for example, the Federal Communications Commission was made-up of commissioners who were very supportive of the industries they regulated. Many of the commissioners, in fact, were former employees of the regulated industries. Interest groups put continuing pressure on presidents and on senators to staff the bureaucracy with personnel who are sympathetic to the industries they will be regulating.[17]

The Regulatory Function

Bureaucracies also function as regulators of some segments of the society. While Americans like to think of themselves as leading unregulated lives—free spirits—the fact is almost everything is regulated from birth to death and almost everything in between! In a report the Office of Management and the Budget estimated that federal regulations cost consumers around $200 billion annually, while providing anywhere from $32 billion to $1.621 trillion in benefits. The latter figures seem a bit self-serving since the range of benefits seems to be too wide to be credible. The Rochester Institute of Technology estimates that the cost is much higher than the OMB's estimate. The Institute claims that government regulation has an annual consumer price tag of about $700 billion!

The OMB also estimated that Americans spend 7.3 billion hours on regulatory paperwork. At a cost of $26.50 an hour, that's more than $190 billion.

Over 80 percent of this total is for compliance with tax laws and internal Revenue Service regulations. Astounding as it may seem, the federal bureaucracy instituted almost 5000 rules annually in recent years! The various agencies that do this "regulating" were discussed previously in this chapter, but perhaps it might be useful to see just how we come in contact with these regulations every day.

Let's assume that Minerva Maven gets up this morning and prepares to go to work. She goes into the kitchen to make coffee with an electric coffee maker. The coffee maker was manufactured under product safety standards issued by the Consumer Product Safety Commission. In fact the coffee itself meets the Department of Agriculture and the Food and Drug Administration specifications regarding the use of chemicals and cleanliness when it was grown and also during its processing by the marketer. The kitchen Minerva is standing in, when constructed, had to meet certain building specifications (local usually, although some are national). Martha's little girl, Mavis Maven, comes into the kitchen, probably wearing a robe and pajamas that are flame retardant because of government regulation. In addition, most of the food, appliances, and other materials and utensils in the kitchen were shipped in trucks or on railroads, both of which are heavily regulated by the federal government.

After getting herself and the rest of the family ready—Minerva is not yet "liberated"—she drops off Mavis at a day-care center that is probably regulated by the state and drives a car that has to meet so many government standards that it is a wonder that cars are manufactured at all!

Arriving at work, Minerva enters a building that not only meets the building codes but also has to deal with the EPA and the Occupational Safety and Health Administration (OSHA) to protect worker health and safety. The company she works for must file papers with various government agencies and possibly submit to inspections by some. It must demonstrate annually to the federal government that it does not give any benefits to one group of employees that it does not give to another and may have to prove that it does not discriminate on the basis of sex, physical handicap, race, religion, etc., in its hiring and promotion practices and that it has a written and enforced policy against sexual harassment.

That night after she and Melvin Maven, her husband, have prepared supper (Melvin was feeling guilty about Minerva's doing all the housework.) in the well-regulated kitchen with well-regulated food, they watch TV that is regulated to the hilt even though the government would deny that it has any direct regulatory function in this area. Later they prepare for bed and set their alarm clock, whose time is regulated by the federal government. In other words, it is 7:00 a.m. EST because the government says it is!

This scenario could go on forever, but the point is that we take for granted all these regulations without much thought about the people, i.e., the bureaucrats, who provide them and implement them every day. Their jobs are often unglamorous. While we may not agree with every rule and regulation implemented by the bureaucracy, few of us would want to trust our fellow man or woman completely, knowing that there were no regulations at all regarding their behavior. For instance, how many of us would invest in the stock market if we knew there was no Securities and Exchange Commission looking over the stockbroker's shoulder?

CONCLUSIONS

Government—the legal apparatus that makes, enforces, and interprets laws—cannot be understood merely in the context of the authority granted by the Constitution to the president, the Congress, and the courts to do something. There must be something or someone to see to it that the policies and programs of the government are carried out. That something or someone is the bureaucracy. Organized in hierarchical fashion into departments, bureaus, agencies, commissions, and offices, the executive bureaucracy has personnel numbering in the millions, some of whom are political appointees—patronage—and others who must qualify for the positions under the civil service merit system. Whatever else can be said of the bureaucracy, without it life in a modern society could not function as smoothly as it does, despite appearances to the contrary. However, it must also be noted that, although recent presidents have tried to decrease the number of regulations and the Congress has enacted some legislation to take away much of the regulatory authority, these agencies and commissions still are major players in governing our behavior. They exercise legislative authority when they make policies (rules); they perform a judicial function when they hear complaints as a court would about the rules they make; they also exercise executive authority because they enforce their rules and decisions. Therefore, the three functions of any government—to legislate, to adjudicate, and to administer laws—are performed by some regulatory agencies over which elected officials, such as the president, have only minimal control.

Chapter Twelve Notes

[1]*U.S. News & World Report*, 30 December 1985/6 January 1986, 25.

[2]*U.S. News*, 28 January, 1985, 52.

[3]*U.S. News*, 30 December 1985/6 January 1986, 25.

[4]Ronald L. Krannich and Caryl Rae Krannich, *Find a Federal Job Fast!* 2d ed. (Woodbridge, Va: Impact Publications, 1992), 55.

[5]Krannich and Krannich, 55.

[6]*Budget of the United States Government, Fiscal Year 2003* (Government Printing Office, 2004).

[7]Citizens Against Government Waste publishes its annual report entitled *Prime Cuts Summary*. One can secure a copy by writing the group at CAGW, P.O. Box 98222, Washington, D.C. 20090-8222. There is a small fee per copy of about $5.00.

[8]"More Prime Cuts From Federal Pork," *Parade Magazine*, 16 February 1997, 23.

[9]Zbigniew Brzezinski, *Power and Principle: Memoirs of the National Security Adviser, 1977-1981* (New York: Farrar, Straus & Giroux, 1983), 67.

[10]*U.S. News*, 30 December 1985/66 January 1986, 25.

[11]Paul C. Light, *The True Size of Government* (Washington, D.C.: Brookings Institution Press, 1999).

[12]This story was reported on "Sixty Minutes," CBS Television Network, December 28, 1986.

[13]Source: U.S. Office of Personnel Management, Washington, D.C.

[14]Source: U.S. Office of Personnel Management.

[15]Karen Gullo, "Wasteful Government Spending Eyed," Associated Press, February 10, 1999.

[16]Seymour Hersh, *The Price of Power: Kissinger in the Nixon White House* (New York: Summit, 1983), 235-236.

[17]See Arthur Belonzi, *The Weary Watchdogs: Governmental Regulators in the Political Process* (Wayne, N.J.: Avery, 1977).

Suggested Readings

Bennett, Linda M. and Stephen E. Bennett. *Living with Leviathan.* Lawrence, Kan.: University of Kansas Press, 1990.

Bernstein, Marver. *Regulating Business by Independent Commission.* Princeton, N.J.: Princeton University Press, 1955.

Derthick, Martha. *Agency Under Stress.* Washington, D.C.: Brookings Institution, 1990.

Edwards, George C., III. *Implementing Public Policy.* Washington, D.C.: Congressional Quarterly Press, 1980.

Goodsell, Charles T. *The Case for Bureaucracy*, 3d. ed. Chatham, N.J.: Chatham House, 1993.

Kerwin, Cornelius. *Rulemaking: How Government Agencies Write Law and Make Policy.* Washington, D.C.: CQ Press, 1994.

Chapter Thirteen

The Relations of Nations:
The Shrinking Globe

Governments, you will recall, regardless of whether they are democratic or non-democratic, perform three functions. They make laws, they enforce laws, and they resolve disputes. When governments perform these functions, they issue policies that fall into two categories: domestic policy or foreign policy.

A country's **domestic policy** consists of the objectives the government hopes to carry out within country's own borders, as well as the means of achieving those objectives. For example, providing every qualified student with the means to go to college would be considered a domestic policy as would building an interstate highway. The means to achieve these things, also domestic policy, would probably involve passing a tax for this purpose or earmarking money from an existing tax for these purposes.

Foreign Policy

In this chapter we shall consider the other side of the governmental policy coin, namely, foreign policy. **Foreign policy** is defined as a country's national interest pursued abroad. To be more specific, it is a set of objectives that the country has outside its borders. These objectives and the tools to achieve them are designed to maintain the country's survival and its expectations of quality of life. Sometimes the distinction between foreign policy and domestic policy becomes blurred since internal policies may directly affect external policies and vice versa. Therefore, there is often no clear line to separate where one begins and the other ends.

For example, in April 1996, the U.S. Congress voted to eliminate most farm subsidies to American farmers within seven years. Farm subsidies in the **European Union**, a trading bloc consisting of 25 countries, often reach 35 percent. And the Japanese government protects its rice farmers with severe import restrictions, a foreign policy known as **protectionism**. As a result, the Japanese and European consumers pay much higher prices for food than an American consumer. Are these examples of domestic policy? Yes. But, they relate to foreign policy as well. Today, domestic markets are increasingly subject to **global competition**. The subsidizing of industries cannot survive the comparative advantage of efficient production. Today countries that formerly restricted trade are now embracing capitalism without borders. In *The Wealth of Nations*, an eighteenth-century, free-trade advocate, Adam Smith, championed low tariffs as a way to economic prosperity for the largest numbers. There seems to be no turning back from greater integration of global trade. **Interdependency** best describes the world of the twenty-first century.

OBJECTIVES OF FOREIGN POLICY

The foremost objective of foreign policy is national self-preservation, which consists of five elements.

Preserving the Country's Sovereignty. **Sovereignty** means that no authority is legally above the authority of the state. Keep in mind here that the term *state* is used to denote a country (geographic area) with sovereignty. It does not refer to what in the United States is called a *state*. Those geographic areas such as Michigan, Florida, or California are not *sovereign*. On many issues they must answer to a higher authority other than their own, namely the United States government. The United States, Russia, Mexico, Honduras, and Canada are examples of what we mean by *states* because these countries possess *sovereignty*, i.e., they answer to no higher authority other than their own laws and treaties that they agreed to.

The foreign policy of a country is designed to allow that country to continue to exist and not to be swallowed up by other countries. Poland is a good example of a country whose foreign policy has not met that major objective during much of its history. Poland has been run over, divided, incorporated, or erased many times since it first appeared on the map of Europe in the eleventh century. In the case of the United States, continuation as a legal entity has been successful primarily because of the two oceans that separate it from Europe and Asia and because of a powerful military in the twentieth and twenty-first centuries.

A state's continued existence results sometimes from a strong military, but also from long-standing observance of **international law**, the compilation of treaties, conventions, and covenants signed by states over the centuries. **Hugo Grotius**, writing in the 1600s in Holland, is considered the father of international law. He pointed out the right of states to exist, given an identifiable people, government, and territory. Thus, a country's sovereignty, or independence from other countries, is a cornerstone of international law today.

Sovereignty, of course, isn't absolute. After the Persian Gulf War the United Nations passed Security Council Resolution 688 (April 5, 1991) requiring Iraq to relinquish its sovereignty to permit international humanitarian aid to minority Kurds and religious dissidents within Iraq. By strict international legal standards, Iraqi sovereignty has been violated by the sanctions imposed by the United Nations.[1] Likewise, Afghanistan's and Iraq's sovereignty was violated when American troops and others invaded the country and toppled the government of the Taliban in Afghanistan and Saddam Hussein in Iraq. Wars are always an example of violation of sovereignty. Some, as in these instances, are considered by some to be justified.

Preserving the System of Government. A country may remain legally intact but be forced to change its system of government. Imperial Japan is a good example. Prior to the end of World War II, Japan was governed—at least on paper—by an emperor. In reality that country was ruled by a very powerful military not subject to civilian control. When Japan's dreams of controlling Asia came to an end in 1945, the United States forced the Japanese to accept a republican form of government with a constitution similar to that of the United States. Japan's failed foreign policy contributed to the collapse of its traditional system of government. Changing the governmental structure does not necessarily mean a radical change in a people's culture and socioeconomic activities. American economist Francis Fukuyama maintains that trust among Japanese is the most distinguishing feature of that society. This trait helps explain Japan's political stability and that country's transformation to an economic giant.[2]

Preserving the Ideology. You will remember the term **ideology** refers to our way of organizing and interpreting the world around us. Capitalism, communism, socialism, Christianity, Islam, Zionism, and Nazism are all examples of ideologies. Part of national self-preservation involves the country's deciding what the world is like as well as deciding what it thinks the world *should* be like. In other words, is the world full of hostile countries (Snarling Pit Bull dogs), or is it populated with friendly folks (happy Cavalier King Charles Spaniels)? The country's foreign policy is designed to present this ideology to others in a positive light and to persuade others that this ideology is superior to other ideologies. A country's existence is perceived to be threatened when faced with ideologies hostile to its own. Thus, the United States and the former Soviet Union for about four decades spent vast amounts of time, energy, and money on their

A group of citizens protest United States's policy in the Middle East. Such protest, they hope, will influence the leaders of this country to force the Israelis to resolve their differences with the Palestinians and, thus, bring peace to that region of the world. In light of recent events in the area, peace is still very far away.

respective foreign policies because each perceived the other as threatening its ideology, among other things.

Maintaining Physical Security. Foreign policy is designed to maintain a country's physical security. This is accomplished by a strong army, intimidating weapons systems, alliances with other countries, and by acquiring other territory to make the country more defensible. Israel is a prominent illustration of a country whose foreign policy has been driven by a powerful need for physical security since it came into existence in 1948. Israel was dependent on western democracies to defend it in the Persian Gulf War and still debates the advisability of returning the strategic Golan Heights captured from Syria in 1967. On the other hand, there are countries that attempt to achieve physical security by not having armies or security treaties. Switzerland has managed to survive intact through two world wars without a significant military presence. Costa Rica, in Central America, maintains its physical security without an army. Whichever method is chosen, maintaining physical security allows the country, its system of government, and its ideology to continue.

To this end, states in the post-World War II era entered into many **bilateral treaties,** such as the Strategic Arms Reduction Treaties (START I and II). Under START, both Russia and the U.S. agreed to reduce their nuclear arsenals by at least one-half. In such **multilateral treaties** as the Nuclear Non-Proliferation Treaty of 1968, the U.S. and others agreed to contain the spread of nuclear weapons.[3] Unfortunately such arrangements do not always achieve their goals completely since many countries besides the United States and Russia now have nuclear weapons. India, for example, a country that does not have enough food for its one billion people, has "tested" a number of nuclear weapons, presumably in an attempt to intimidate its neighbor, Pakistan. Pakistan is presumed also to have nuclear weapons. In addition, the communist regime in North Korea has continued to develop its nuclear capability despite international pressure to do otherwise. And now Iran has presumably gotten into the nuclear mix having the capability to make nuclear weapons from the nuclear waste of nuclear power plants supplied by Russia. And the beat goes on. . . .

In 2001, President George W. Bush announced that the United States would not continue to be a part of the Anti-Ballistic Missile Treaty, which had been in effect with Russia (and the former Soviet Union) since 1972. In a speech on May 2, 2001, Bush stated: "We need new concepts of deterrence that rely on both offensive and defensive forces." Apparently Bush maintains that U.S. security can best be achieved with more sophisticated missile technology, among other things. Bush also openly subscribes to "preemptive strikes." This concept is a change from long-standing policy of not attacking until someone attacks the United States. Now, the United States reserves the right, so to speak, to "pounce" on some country before it "pounces" on the United States.

Maintaining Economic Security. A country's existence can be threatened in an economic sense. Foreign policies are aimed at securing the economic well-being of a country through such means as **embargoes** (refusal to buy or sell to another country), **tariffs** (taxes on imported goods), **quotas** (restricting the quantity of an imported product), or by advocating **free trade** (no restrictions). Economic security as a goal of foreign policy also includes the economic security of a country's trading partners through such things as **most favored nation** (MFN) trade status, loans, or grants. The formation of what is now called the **European Union** in 1958 is an example of an attempt to maintain economic security in Western Europe. The United States, feeling threatened by this economic alliance, established its own **North American Free Trade Agreement** (NAFTA) with Canada and Mexico in 1993, which may soon include other countries in the Western Hemisphere, most notably Chile.

As a result of global interdependence, maintaining economic security today has less to do with benefiting at the expense of others (called a **zero-sum game**) as it has with cooperating so all can benefit. Every state wishes to partake of the bounty of trade. Former Clinton Secretary of Labor Robert Reich points out that companies that operated in only one country are succumbing to webs of interaction between companies worldwide. This event, in turn, has contributed to the decline of government-directed industrial policy, which is very difficult to carry out when multinational corporations are the major economic players. In fact, governments in the future may play an increasingly limited role in determining their economic security.[4] Reich and others stress the need for a population with value-added skills as a way to render a workforce more competitive. As the industrial age has moved steadily into the information age, learning styles and technological advances have a great say in determining which states provide the most agreeable climate for economic security.[5]

THE "TOOLS" OF FOREIGN POLICY

Just as a carpenter needs tools to build a house, so governments need "tools" to make foreign policy and to carry it out. These "tools" fall into five categories.

Diplomacy as a Tool of Foreign Policy. Diplomacy involves communication between governments. Through diplomacy governments negotiate, threaten, propagandize, confuse, or embarrass other governments. Diplomacy is used to collect intelligence and to negotiate agreements. The purpose of diplomacy is to gain something that governments want without war; to gain something before a war begins; to gain time so that the country can prepare for war; to salvage as much as possible of the country's power or territory if the country has already lost the war; to divide the "spoils" of war; and to secure truces during a war. Diplomacy may also be used simply to gain the other side's point of view.

Economics as a Tool of Foreign Policy. As a tool of foreign policy, economics involves putting tariffs on foreign goods to protect domestic industries and workers from competition; developing new industries (e.g., computer manufacturing), new products, and technologies (e.g., super-conducting materials, lasers, and cell phones); and securing raw materials vital to economic survival (e.g., oil). This tool of foreign policy might also involve expanding a country's exports by developing new markets so that others become dependent, or it might mean an attempt to damage or destroy a rival economically (e.g., the Arab oil embargo against the West in 1973 or the Japanese "dumping" microchips on the U.S. market below cost in 1987, or the UN embargo on trade with Iraq and Libya during the late twentieth century and early twenty-first century). Sometimes this economic tool takes the form of economic alliances in which a group of countries come together to trade with one another under a most-favored-nation agreement while excluding others from their "club" (e.g., the European Union or NAFTA).[6]

This exclusiveness may also be imposed. The former Soviet Union required countries in its economic alliance, Comecon, to purchase products from the U.S.S.R. sometimes at higher prices than the products could be purchased elsewhere. The economic tool of foreign policy is also in use when the United States or other countries provide **foreign aid** to others in the form of grants, loans, or free goods such as food or medicine. Although on the surface the motive for this kind of aid may seem charitable, the underlying, and perhaps more realistic, purpose is to "buy" friendship.

Propaganda as a Tool of Foreign Policy. The use of words, pictures, and actions to promote a foreign policy is called **propaganda**.[7] For example, the United States broadcasts radio programs to Cuba in which the listeners are told about life in noncommunist countries. While the negative aspects of these "western" countries may be discussed, emphasis is more likely to be placed on the positive side, such as the higher standard of living in the United States or

France or Germany. Propaganda designed to weaken an "enemy" by publicizing its actions in a negative light is called **subversion**. For example, in the United Nations, the United States has brought evidence about China's mistreatment of its own citizenry.

The Military as a Tool of Foreign Policy. The military as a tool of foreign policy is probably the most widely recognized because it has such devastating effects. Sometimes the military option is used in an all-out war, e.g., World War II. The purpose of war is to end a real or potential danger or to expand the territory of a country to obtain more room, more goods, or more resources. War, however, is expensive and is not without risks. Someone loses, and today, because of the nuclear potential, the planet itself could be exterminated.[8]

Since World War II, the more likely scenario has been either **targeted warfare** where the struggle is confined to a specific geographic area such as the Middle East or Kosovo, or surrogate warfare. **Surrogate warfare** involves the use of someone else's army or the use of rebels (guerrillas, freedom fighters, etc.). Rather than get involved themselves directly with their own military, the United States and the former Soviet Union chose to utilize a surrogate—a substitute. Cuba played this role quite well for the U.S.S.R. by sending its army to Angola in Africa when the Soviet Union wanted to ensure the survival of a Marxist government in that country. Since Cuba was so closely tied to the U.S.S.R. economically and militarily and had no one to turn to, Cuba did what the Soviets wanted.

Likewise, rather than send its own troops to Nicaragua to overthrow the Marxist regime there, the United States supplied and trained the Contras (anti-communist Nicaraguan rebels) to do the job throughout the 1980s. Both the United States and the former Soviet Union experienced defeat in recent history when they tried to use their own armies to enforce a particular foreign policy: the United States in Vietnam and the Soviet Union in Afghanistan. It is much safer and much cheaper to use a surrogate. And, if per chance the surrogate loses, the country using the surrogate does not have to bear as much loss of face itself.

The military option can also be used as a deterrent to the foreign policy of the opposing side. The prevailing notion among the more powerful countries in the twentieth century had been that each side should arm itself to the teeth so that the other side would not dare attack. This idea is usually referred to as **balance of power,** but some have called it *balance of terror* because of the potential for planet-wide destruction as a result of nuclear war. Some suggest, however, that it is this very threat of world annihilation that has actually prevented another world war.

Considering the collapse of communism and the expense of continued maintenance and expansion of the military sector, military budgets in most advanced countries have fallen dramatically. Reduction of military expenditures, the so-called **peace dividend**, was supposed to provide more human services and to bolster the consumer sector of the world's economies. In recent years the U.S. budget for the military, which included atomic energy defense activities and defense-related matters, accounted for less than 20 percent of the total U.S. government budget.   Human resource spending, which includes education, training, unemployment compensation, health care, income security, Social Security, veterans benefits, pensions and other entitlements, is estimated to be 75 percent of the budget.[9] While these figures represent huge amounts of money, they do correct a misrepresentation frequently touted by opponents of military spending. The United States budget is not primarily spent on the military. In addition, now that the Soviet Union is merely a paragraph in a world history book, ongoing negotiations between Russia and the United States have produced significant cuts in recent years in weapons and weapons systems in these two countries. Yet, military spending increases when the United States becomes involved in such military operations as the invasion of Afghanistan and Iraq. Being a "super power" is expensive. Now the United States is involved in what is said to be a long-term war with terrorists and the countries that support them. We have already seen a large increase in proposed military spending. However, that noted, the military budget still does not approach that of other government sector expenditures, as stated above.

The arms race continues in less developed countries, ready markets for countries wanting to sell weapons. The continuing economic crisis in Russia creates a danger that Russia may decide to sell even some of its nuclear technology to sustain itself. Because of that likelihood, the United States has been buying missiles from the Russians to keep them out of the hands of other countries and possibly terrorists. For the moment at least, the flood of nonnuclear arms to shore up dictatorships has the potential to destabilize large areas of Africa and the Middle East.[10] It may surprise some to learn that the U.S. is the largest merchant of arms to the world.

International Terrorism as a Tool of Foreign Policy. The Office for Combating Terrorism, a part of the Department of State, in its publications defines terrorism as ". . . premeditated, politically motivated violence perpetrated against noncombatant targets by subnational groups or clandestine state agents. International terrorism is terrorism involving citizens or territory of more than one country." Put another way, terrorism is the ability of a person or a group of people to extract compliance from another person or group through the use of force or the threat of it illegally[11] or without regard for human rights. Terrorism aims to extract this compliance through massive intimidation to bring about specific changes in the behavior, thought processes, and emotions of the masses. These desired changes include pity, sympathy, indignation, and hatred, depending upon who the terrorist targets are. Such a definition is much more neutral in that it can be applied to any form of terrorism, whether from a relatively small, unorganized group, an individual, or from the power of the state itself.

Terrorism, or power, is arbitrary. There are few, if any, rules for its employment. As such, the victims of terrorism do now know when to expect it, where to expect it, how to expect it, or even if to expect it. Hence, the very uncertainty and arbitrary nature of terrorism adds to its potency as a weapon to achieve either long- or short-range goals.

Terrorism can be divided into two broad categories: terrorism from above and terrorism from below.[12] Terrorism from above is state terrorism, in other words, the ability of the government to extract compliance from the masses with force or the threat of it. Dictatorships usually qualify as governments that use terrorism from above, e.g., Nazi Germany and the Taliban government in Afghanistan.

By contrast, terrorism from below is the use or threat of force by those who are not in control of the machinery of government, i.e., private citizens. It is this kind of terrorism that makes most of the headlines in the news media today, although terrorism from above (governmental terrorism) goes on daily and probably has greater historical longevity. Groups such as Hamas, the Irish Republican Army, the Red Army, the Islamic Jihad, the Symbionese Liberation Army, Al-Qaeda, Shining Path, and numerous others exemplify terrorism from below.

In states that practice terrorism from above, there is usually some sort of "secret police" organization that is used as the official, yet unofficial, executors of power. In Nazi Germany, there was the Gestapo; in early Soviet Russia, there was the Cheka. These organizations are frequently populated by two types of people: those who believe the end (usually the survival of the state in its present form) justifies the means and those who merely enjoy inflicting pain on other people, i.e., sadists. Regardless of which type of individual one is unfortunate enough to encounter, the result is the same; however, the sadistic type frequently likes to prolong the agony.

Like terrorism, the terrorists themselves come in different "flavors": criminals, insane persons, and persons with a "cause."[13] Probably the easiest to understand are criminal terrorists. According to the rules of law and "civilized" behavior, all terrorists, by definition, are criminals. However, it is useful to distinguish terrorists who are motivated by individual greed from those who are motivated by some particular "cause" and from those who have essentially lost touch with reality. Whether practicing terrorism from above or below, criminal terrorists have a material motive, usually power and money. They are selfish and professional, i.e., business-like. ("Do Not take this personally, but I am *gonna* kill you because it is my job.") Criminals are realistic and concrete rather than abstract in their motivations. These people are predictable in their behavior and usually quite determined and ruthless. They are not the kind of individuals who can sustain long-term goals; hence, they are interested in concrete, immediate success, not success of a cause twenty, fifty, or a hundred years down the road. The common thug, the mugger, the bank robber, the "hit man," or the Mafia members fit well into the category of criminal terrorists from below; while dictators such as Samosa of Nicaragua, Marcos of the Philippines, or Peron of Argentina were typical of criminal terrorists from below. (Many criminal terrorists from above would use some propaganda ploy to try to cover up their real interests. For example, Peron was the champion of the working class—"The Working Man's Friend"—while he lined his pockets.) These people do not like to take risks. The criminal terrorist from below, for example, does not like the spotlight on himself and, consequently, usually keeps a low profile. While the state terrorist is frequently well known, he, like his counterpart from below, is usually surrounded by loyal, well-paid, highly-trusted bodyguards to insure that no one practices terrorism on him. However, this preventive measure does not always ensure safety as evidenced by the number of assassinations of both types of criminal terrorists. One further feature of criminal terrorists runs as a common thread throughout all of them: they are definitely homicidal. Although there is probably no way to measure with any accuracy the number of people murdered throughout history by criminal terrorists from above or below, the number must run into the millions.

Unlike the criminal terrorists, insane terrorists are not rational. They are self-centered and willing to sacrifice themselves to achieve their abstract, irrational goals such as ridding the world of sin, obtaining salvation for themselves by making amends for their own perceived guilt or the guilt of someone close to them. In other words, their actions are motivated by highly personal reasons usually known only to them and most of the time do not make sense to anyone other than themselves. Consequently, their behavior is very unpredictable. Since the aggression that they direct at the outside world is frequently a substitute for inwardly directed aggression, these people may not only be homicidal but also suicidal. And, unlike the criminal terrorist, the "crazy" terrorist will take enormous risks, often times with the subconscious intent of being caught. "Son of Sam," the "Boston Strangler, " California's "Hill-Side Strangler," and Jeffrey Dahmer serve as excellent examples of insane terrorists.

While "crazy" terrorists like Jeffrey Dahmer and criminal terrorists like Al Capone can garner a good share of media attention, the "crusading" terrorist, i.e., terrorists with a cause, can capture the lion's share of any nightly news broadcast. Crusading terrorists thrive on publicity. The more dramatic and showy the terrorist event, the better they like it. This type of terrorist has both concrete and abstract goals, e.g., a homeland for the Palestinians (concrete) and justice or the will of Allah (abstract). Therefore, their motivations can be material, like the criminal terrorist, or symbolic, like the insane terrorist. Since they are willing to kill and be killed in the service of the "cause," they can definitely be characterized as homicidal, as well as suicidal, just like the "crazy" terrorists. However, crusading terrorists are not usually insane in the normal sense of the word. They are, to use Karl Mannheim's terminology, functionally rational, meaning the tactics they employ have a rational, although conventionally immoral, relationship to the desired goal. However, the goal itself may not be rational. Like "crazy" terrorists, the crusaders are also unpredictable. One might even say that crusaders are predictable in their unpredictability. They are concerned with both immediate and long-range success and are very creative in their quest for publicity. Horrible as it was, crashing jet liners into the World Trade Center was definitely creative.

The type of terrorism that one usually focuses attention on in the present day is terrorism perpetrated by "crusaders." Individuals, it appears, have become accustomed to the "crazies" and the "crooks" running around killing people. Indeed, television and motion pictures have perhaps played a major role in most people's rather casual attitude toward kidnappings and murders committed by the insane and the criminals. Everyone has seen these events portrayed on the "tube" or the "big screen" scores of times. (For the uninitiated, see "Death Wish, Parts I, II, III"; "The Texas Chain Saw Murders"; or "Halloween, Parts I, II, III—adnauseum.") However, the masses have not yet been saturated with crusading terrorists and their activities, although the prospects are good that they will be since the depiction of violence is a money-making proposition.

If today a terrorist means a crusading terrorist, i.e., a terrorist with a cause, then precisely what is (are) the cause(s)? If one could arrange to have representatives from each of the terrorist organizations to state their "causes," one would certainly hear a vast array of "causes." However, if the superficial is disregarded, a number of commonalties can be discerned.

First, it must be clearly understood that some crusading terrorists are actually criminal terrorists in disguise as previously mentioned. No terrorist who desires mass support will announce that he/she just wants to become a dictator. The inner circle of cohorts may be well aware that assumption of governmental power through terrorism is the actual goal, but the "troops" in the field or the "fellow-travelers" are rarely aware that this is the case until the goal has been reached, e.g., the defection of "Commandante Zero" from the ranks of the Sandinistas in Nicaragua once they had assumed power.

If some terrorists, perhaps even most terrorists, are really motivated by the desire for dictatorial power at the state level, and if, as is assumed here, they are fairly intelligent souls who are not willing to reveal that motivation, then they must come up with some other justification for their activities. These justifications usually fall into one or more of the following categories and can be used by "closet" criminal terrorists as well as by true crusading terrorists: (1) lack of democratic structures with which to initiate change, (2) unequal distribution and consumption of resources/anti-modernism, and (3) nationalism.

Many terrorists will argue quite convincingly and most hypocritically that the reason they are terrorists is that they had no other choice. In fact, they have done their homework in "Propaganda 101" so well that one can hear even non-

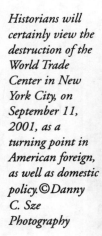

Historians will certainly view the destruction of the World Trade Center in New York City, on September 11, 2001, as a turning point in American foreign, as well as domestic policy.©Danny C. Sze Photography

terrorists agreeing with them! For example, a few weeks after the attack on the World Trade Center on September 11, 2001, there were some Americans who were saying that the United States deserved this action as punishment for certain perceived evils like abortion. While the argument may seem compelling, one must not lose sight of the fact that only by means of unlimited and constant justification can terrorism become a real threat to the status quo. "...Terrorism flourish(es) whenever the critical intellect is ready to abdicate in favor of an oceanic sense of belonging. The frustration of felt impotence seeks escape in fantasies of unlimited omnipotence that lead to immoral acts performed in good conscience and with impunity under the cover of sanctimonious justification."[14] The United States possesses some of the most democratic institutions for change that have ever been conceived and implemented, and yet acts of terrorism have been carried out in that country in the form of kidnappings, murders, maimings, and bombings by such groups as the Symbionese Liberation Army, Puerto Rican terrorist groups, anti-abortionists, and the Weather Underground, and individuals such as Timothy McVeigh, of Oklahoma City bombing fame, to name a few. To assert that any country is governed by a majority of its people all the time is an absurd proposition. At best, it is governed by a plurality of its people (a group larger than any other group but not necessarily a majority). That plurality will shift its membership depending upon the issue addressed. Change does not have to be brought about by terrorism;

however, people who choose this method are not willing to wait the length of time that the use of non-violent means admittedly often takes. In addition, the controlling plurality at any given point in time may not desire the change that some individual or group wants. For example, public opinion polls reveal that a major change in the status of the availability of abortion during the first twelve weeks of pregnancy is not desired by the American public. A major change in abortion laws may never be desired by a sufficient number of Americans; therefore, the practice of bombing abortion clinics in true terrorist fashion is the chosen response of some who advocate such a change. Thus, the claim of some anti-abortionists that the government won't listen, in reality is that the government responded to what appears to be the current majority or plurality of United States public opinion on the subject. In other words, the child-like mentality of the terrorist has demanded that, if he cannot get what he wants legitimately, he will get it illegitimately.

Nevertheless, lack of democratic institutions and its para-state structure of terrorism from above in a number of countries are contributing factors to terrorist activity. Certainly if governments would rid themselves of their terrorism from above, there would be one less "justification" for terrorists from below to use.

Although the problem of unequal distribution and consumption of the world's resources has been around perhaps from the beginning of time, this inequality still stands as a justification for terrorist activity. The word justification is significant to the understanding of terrorism, for without constant justification for their actions terrorists would soon be out of business. Although the United States, for example, has about one-sixth of the world's population, it consumes approximately one-third of the world's natural resources. Terrorists can cite this statistic as an example of the "righteousness" of their actions. Why should one-sixth of world's population have one-third of the resources? Indeed, there is inequity here, but the point is not that the inequity exists but rather how it is used. To terrorists the "cause" is the driving motivation; belonging to the "group"; experiencing danger and the feeling of omnipotence are their driving force or life's blood.

Much of the wealth accumulated by the United States and other highly developed countries is the result of their embracing of capitalist economies centuries ago. Other countries did not go through this change from their traditional societies to more modern ones. Hence, unequal distribution of wealth as an "excuse" for terrorism is really a cover for an ideology of anti-modernism. As the influences of democratic capitalism, with its emphasis on individual rights and ambitions, spread around the world, they pose uncomfortable challenges to established cultures and political regimes. In so far as one becomes "modern," one may lose one's traditional ideological or religious identity. Asian societies, such as Japan and Singapore, seem to have made this transition more successfully than more traditional societies in Africa and the Middle East. In these societies, people who find it most difficult to cope with modern changes may strike out, hence, the rise in political terrorism by religious fundamentalists around the world. As global capitalism continues to develop, this conflict between "new" and "old" ways of organizing societies will continue to grow. Much the same thing occurred in Western Europe when the medieval period gave way to the Renaissance and the beginnings of modern capitalism.

Nationalism also serves as another excellent justification for terrorist acts. The Middle East is replete with examples from almost all quarters with the use of nationalism as an excuse for committing all sorts of atrocities. Palestinians want a country to call their own. So do the Israelis. Unfortunately they both want to occupy the same ground. Nationalism is frequently expressed in terms of "us" against "them." In this regard, many acts of terrorism perpetrated by Middle Eastern terrorist groups against the United States, both at home and abroad, were justified by these groups because of nationalism. They view United States support for the existence of the state of Israel as an attempt at genocide against Palestinians. It is not the purpose here to argue who is right and who is wrong. Rather, the intention is to explain that terrorism needs justification to survive.

Finally, the availability of suppliers of weapons, training, strategy, and sanctuary lend their support to the on-going slaughter. Supplying weapons is a profitable business. The United States is the world's largest exporter of weapons. Unfortunately sometimes these weapons are used by governments to terrorize their own people, and sometimes even against the United States itself. While the elimination of weapons would indeed eliminate most terrorism, it would probably take a large dose of state terrorism on the masses to accomplish this goal. So we are presented with another situation of "the end justifies the means," the motto of all terrorists.

Although every country openly is against terrorism and views such action as abhorrent, there are still governments that "fudge" a bit when the violent group happens to be friendly toward the governments in question. Hence, the old cliché, "One man's terrorist is another man's freedom fighter."

What makes international terrorism an intriguing tool of foreign policy is that it is very difficult to combat since it is frequently carried out by persons who are not working for governments. If the "terrorist" is working for a government, that government will most likely refuse to acknowledge any connection with him/her and usually has gone to great lengths to make it difficult, if not impossible, to trace the terrorist to that government.

Modern-day international terrorism does not pose a threat of overthrow of any government or the collapse of any institutions, such as capitalism, which are the normal targets of terrorism. The most frequent result of terrorist acts is that they are major annoyances that require governments to expend much money

Reactionary Muslim terrorists of the Al Qaida organization, led by Osama bin Laden, crashed an American Airlines flight into the Pentagon with the resulting destruction seen here.

and manpower to prevent. Although the acts on 9/11 were certainly more than an annoyance, most terrorist acts are not of such magnitude. The events of 9/11 are good examples of how terrorism can also result in embarrassment for the governments involved particularly if they are considered "major" powers in the world and are not able to defend themselves or their citizens against attack by small groups of people. Governments such as Libya, Syria, Cuba, Iran, Iraq, and North Korea have from time to time been named as sponsors of international terrorism. If the accusation is true, and there is substantial evidence to indicate that it is true, then the use of terrorism to execute some foreign policy goals still seems to be a safer tool to use by these countries than is direct, warlike confrontation with such countries as the United States, Great Britain, France, Israel, or Germany. To engage directly the military forces of these states would, to say the least, be dangerous. On the other hand, to "attack" them through terrorism is safer since the "sponsoring" state can always deny any connection with terrorist groups. Keep in mind, these people do not wear military uniforms designating for whom they work. It is also true, however, that, although terrorist actions may benefit the foreign policy goals of a particular country, that country may not actually be a controlling factor in the terrorist group. Therefore, it is wrong to assume that if the "sponsoring" state could be eliminated, terrorism would stop. From the perspective of a country's foreign policy, terrorism can be looked upon as a type of surrogate warfare, but remember that terrorist groups often have their own agenda that may or may not coincide with any particular state's foreign policy goals.[15]

PATTERNS OF FOREIGN POLICY

A state's foreign policy displays observable patterns. These patterns can be seen in a country's relations with its allies, its neighbors, and its enemies. These patterns are isolationism; neutrality; diplomatic and judicial accommodation; social, economic and cultural cooperation; balance of power; collective security; and conflict.

Isolationism

Isolationism as a pattern of foreign policy refers to a country's refusal, as much as possible, to become involved with the rest of the world or with the region in which it is located. To say the least, this foreign policy pattern was easier to accomplish in years past than it is today for a number of reasons. **First**, until recently many areas of the world were securely separated from one another by vast distances or even large bodies of water, making it difficult to become involved with others even if the country wanted to. The United States at one time exhibited a pattern of isolationism. George Washington in his farewell address upon leaving office in 1798 warned of getting involved in "foreign entanglements." Later on in the years following World War I (1919-1939), the United States, tired of war and fearing that its peace could only be ensured through isolating itself from the rest of the world, refused to join the **League of Nations** and the **World Court**. The U.S. discouraged international trade by imposing tariffs on foreign goods, adopted legislation prohibiting the sale of weapons to warring countries, banned loans to those countries, prohibited Americans from sailing on ships of warring countries, and forbade American merchant ships to enter war zones. Japan and China also practiced isolationism rather readily at times in their long histories because they were literally isolated by vast distances from what was happening in Europe.

Second, isolationism is difficult to achieve today because of substantial international interdependency on trade and because the vast distances and huge oceans that used to separate one country from another now can be bridged in a matter of minutes or hours. Technology has made isolationism almost impossible.

Neutrality

This term expresses a desire for noninvolvement with the rest of the region or world in time of conflict; it exhibits a moral condemnation of conflicts; it expresses a fear of involvement; and it anticipates avoiding destruction in case of war or profiting from foreign aid from one or all belligerents. Switzerland is probably the best-known example of a modern, neutral state and has certainly profited from that status in that Switzerland serves as the banker for the rest of the world, regardless of ideology.

Neutrality is the act of nonbelligerency, a formal policy of taking no sides in a specific conflict. Argentina during World War II fit this category. During that war ships and sailors from belligerent countries such as the United States and Germany entered Argentine ports and took R & R (Rest and Recreation) all in the same place, only to resume hostilities once out to sea again.

Neutrality may be imposed on some area by others. After World War II, Austria, like Germany, had been divided into four zones, each governed by one of the victorious "allies": the Soviet Union, Great Britain, the United States, and France. The Soviet Union refused to allow Austria to reunify and govern itself until 1955 when the U.S.S.R. finally agreed to full independence. Austria, however, according to the treaty, had to pledge that it would not take sides with either the United States or the Soviet Union. Today Austria is a full member of the European Union, an option the former Soviet Union once denied her.

Diplomatic and Judicial Accommodation

Still another pattern of foreign policy is diplomatic and judicial accommodation. This is a foreign policy aimed at solving problems by direct diplomacy or seeking diplomatic arbitration from another country or group. Sometimes less powerful countries exhibit this foreign policy pattern by seeking to negotiate directly with a more powerful country with which it has a dispute or by getting some other country to act as an intermediary. Countries also utilize international bodies such as the **World Court** in The Hague to resolve their disputes just as an individual might go to court to solve a problem with his/her neighbor.

For this kind of policy to work, of course, all sides must agree to the mediation and to abide by the decision of the mediator or court. That doesn't always happen. When Nicaragua took its dispute with the United States about the latter's mining of Managua's harbor (Managua is Nicaragua's capital.) to the World Court in The Hague (in Holland) in the late 1980s, the United States refused to accept the Court's judgment. Mediation seems to work better between equals rather than between a powerful country and a weak country.

Social, Economic, and Cultural Cooperation

This pattern of foreign policy involves the pursuance of common goals by two or more countries. Such cooperation can be accomplished through international organizations such as the United Nations, the International Postal Union, or the World Health Organization—all of which involve a great deal of international cooperation among most of the countries of the world. It can also be accomplished bilaterally, for example, the **most favored nation** trading status granted to China by President Clinton in 1995 to the present, or multilaterally (among three or more countries), for example, the European Union. Social, economic, and cultural cooperation can also be accomplished through private **nongovernmental organizations (NGOs)** such as the International Chambers of Commerce or the International Red Cross.[16]

Balance of Power

This particular pattern of foreign policy is born out of a real fear of war. A country that utilizes it shifts its allegiance from side to side in hopes of creating an equilibrium—one side equal to the other in power. We associate **Balance of Power** with early Greek city-states and with the nineteenth-century alliances that produced World War I. A variation of this policy is referred to as **appeasement**—giving the "enemy" some of what it wants in hopes that war will be averted. Britain practiced this policy until Germany's invasion of Poland in 1939. It stems from a desire for the country's own security, an attitude of "peace at all costs," or an attempt to avoid war until the country is prepared for it.

Collective Security

A foreign policy whereby countries join together and pool their resources to increase their individual strengths is referred to as **collective security**. The idea here is to hinder a potential aggressor collectively—to present a united, powerful front—because each individual state is not powerful enough to do so alone. Of course, it also rests on the assumption that the "enemy" is stronger than any individual state. Here we come back to the balance of power concept where each side—in this case the United States and its allies within the **North Atlantic Treaty Organization (NATO)** and the former Soviet Union and its allies (**Warsaw Pact**)—armed itself with exotic weapons, as well as massive conventional forces, so that neither side would feel comfortable about the outcome of a war. Collective security is not a twentieth-century phenomenon although we sometimes tend to think so. Actually it is quite an ancient tactic. In 490 BCE, the Persian King Darius invaded Greece but was defeated by Athenian armies. Later, led by Themistocles, Athens prepared to repel further Persian attacks by building up its military and by organizing most of the Greek city-states, including Sparta, into a defensive alliance. Although initially defeated, eventually the Greek alliance was victorious. In modern times, this pattern of foreign policy is exemplified by NATO and the United Nations.

Conflict

The final pattern of foreign policy is **conflict**. Conflict does not mean a failure of foreign policy as some would suggest; rather, it is itself a foreign policy. If a country feels threatened or feels it can defeat the enemy and still survive, conflict is the foreign policy choice. However, conflict does not always mean all-out warfare. Instead, it ranges from such things as mob violence (e.g., ongoing Palestinian *Intifada* [uprising] in the occupied territories), **guerrilla warfare** (e.g., Afghanistan in 1979), **targeted warfare** (e.g., the Persian Gulf War in 1991 or Kosovo in 1999 or the wars in Afghanistan and Iraq in the early twenty-first century), **conventional war** (e.g., World War II, the Korean War, the Vietnam War), and **nuclear war** (e.g., the 1945 bombing of Japan).

So why fight wars? There are at least seven reasons why countries employ conflict as a foreign policy. **First**, it usually produces fast results. With some notable exceptions like the Hundred Years' War (1337-1453), most wars are over in a reasonable amount of time. **Second**, wars tend to produce "permanent" results. **Third**, wars enhance the prestige of the winner. **Fourth**, wars bring to an end an uneconomical, undeclared, "cold" war. Two or more countries can be belligerent toward each other for years and years with one never really getting the upper hand over the other. Although a war is costly, "cold" wars that drag on and on can also be very draining of national wealth. **Fifth**, wars strengthen the social "glue" that holds a country together. Things can appear rotten at home with almost everyone dissatisfied, but as soon as a war comes along, all the domestic problems are forgotten. **Sixth**, wars strengthen the position of the rulers (the elite) and improve their chances of survival, especially if they are victorious! **Seventh**, wars provide an excuse for eliminating anyone within the country who wishes to overthrow the government. With all these reasons to go to war, we must remember that war is always a risky business because if you lose, things are not so rosy. And today, since so many countries, even small ones, have weapons of mass destruction, the risk is even greater.[17]

THE FUTURE

The world's peoples welcomed the new millennium with much fanfare and anticipation. We live in exciting times, where technology presents us with interesting, exciting, and sometimes dangerous opportunities. The recent past took us through two world wars, then through a forty-five year cold war. In the 1990s, the collapse of most communist systems around the world, signaled by the demise of the U.S.S.R., ushered in an era of what some call a **new world order**. The new world order is touted as one of peace and cooperation among all the countries of the world. (Cooperation may be what is hoped for, but your author does not see much of it currently.) Others view this phenomenon with fear—primarily fear of a loss of national identity. For example, if the UN were to become the world's government, individual state sovereignty would cease to exist. While the world seems to be less threatened by nuclear war since the collapse of the Soviet Union, there remain significant dangers stemming from smaller, "rogue" states and terrorists, who may have nuclear capability themselves.

Implicit in the concept of this new order are confederations like the United Nations and NATO, which are capable of imposing order whenever disputes arise. In the years following its creation in 1945 with a membership of just forty-four countries, the UN never was able to surmount the divisions posed by the cold war. Now in the seemingly less hostile climate, the UN and NATO have a real opportunity to make collective security a reality. Thus, NATO forces moved into Bosnia-Herzegovina in 1996 in an attempt to restore order between ethnic factions and bombed Yugoslavia in an attempt to stop that country's genocide (ethnic cleansing) of ethnic Albanians. Elsewhere, NATO moved to expand it membership eastward to include the former communist satellites, Poland, the Czech Republic, and Hungary. These moves are not without their detractors. Russia feels threatened by NATO, especially if surrounded by NATO member countries. The UN, offered an opportunity to remove a brutal dictator in Iraq who was threatening the world with his support for terrorism, allowed national jealousies to thwart attempts by some countries, e.g., the U.S., to make his removal a global affair. The UN stands today as a much weaker organization than it was prior to the Iraq War.

In addition, the world still faces an uneven distribution of resources. The former communist countries, attempting to change from their centrally planned economy to a free market economy, continue to experience severe economic hardship. Furthermore, famines are commonplace in poor countries, ravaged by climatic change and intertribal strife. Many of these countries, in attempting to generate income, are contributing to the demise of both animal and plant species, as well as the overall quality of the world's environment. At the 1992 United Nations Conference on Environment and Development, states addressed worldwide concerns over the environment. Environmental concerns come not only from activities in the Third World but also from highly sophisticated societies such as Japan and the United States, where pollution of the air and water continues, although much progress has been made in the last three decades. Keep in mind that the more advanced countries do a great deal more to prevent and clean up pollution than the rest of the world does.

As it stands now, the United States is the driving force, both economically and militarily, behind the UN and NATO. The United States currently has the world's strongest economy, and when it sneezes, the world catches a cold. How long will this country be willing or able to continue in this role? How does the United States apply the principles and tools of foreign policy to achieve its primary objective of self-preservation? That, dear readers, is the subject of the next chapter, *Foreign Policy American Style*.

Chapter Thirteen Notes

[1] Jarat Chapra and Thomas G. Weiss, "Sovereignty Is No Longer Sacrosanct: Codifying Humanitarian Intervention," in Steven L. Speigel and David J. Pervin, *At Issue: Politics in the World Arena.* 7th ed. (New York: St. Martin's Press, 1994), 46.

[2] Francis Fukuyama, *Trust: The Social Virtues and the Creation of Prosperity* (New York: The Free Press, 1995), 185-193.

[3] Abdul Aziz Said, Charles O. Lerche, Jr., and Charles O. Lerche III, *Concepts of International Politics in Global Perspective*, 4th ed. (Englewood Cliffs, N.J.: Prentice Hall, 1995), 180-184.

[4] Robert B. Reich, *The Work of Nations* (New York: Vintage Books, 1992), 228-281.

[5] Lewis J. Perelman, *School's Out: A Radical New Formula for the Revitalization of America's Educational System* (New York: Avon Books, 1992), 66-70.

[6] Joshua S. Goldstein, *International Relations*, 2d ed. (New York: HarperCollins, 1996), 18-20.

[7] John T. Rourke and Mark A. Boyer, *International Politics on the World Stage*, Brief Edition (Madison, Wis.: Brown & Benchmark, 1996), 12-13.

[8] James Lee Ray, *Global Politics*, 7th ed. (Boston: Houghton Mifflin Co., 1995), 230-240.

[9] *Budget of the U.S. Government, Fiscal Year 1997* (Washington, D.C.: U.S. Government Printing Office, 1997), 60-66.

[10] Bruce Russett and Harvey Starr, *World Politics: the Menu for Choice*, 5th ed. (New York: W.H. Freeman, 1996), 12-14.

[11] This definition suits terrorism although it was used to define the term power in Harold Lasswell's political analysis. See, Harold Lasswell, Politics: Who Gets What, When and How. New York: McGraw-Hill, 1936.

[12] Frederick J. Hacker, M.D., Crusaders, Criminals, Crazies: Terror and Terrorism in our Time. New York: W.W. Norton & Company, Inc., 1976.)

[13] Hacker.

[14]Hacker, 8.

[15]Michael G. Roskin and Nicholas O. Berry, *IR: The New World of International Relations,* 2d ed. (Englewood Cliffs, N.J.: Prentice Hall, 1993), 18-24.

[16]Robert O. Keohane, "Hegemony in the World Political Economy," in Robert C. Art and Robert Jervis, eds. *International Relations: Enduring Concepts and Contemporary Issues,* 4th ed. (New York: HarperCollins, 1996), 88-92.7

[17]Donald M. Snow and Eugene Brown, *The Contours of Power: An Introduction to Contemporary International Relations.* (New York: St. Martin's Press, 1996), 119-120.

Suggested Readings

Ambrose, Stephen E. *Rise to Globalism: American Foreign Policy since 1938.* 7th ed. New York: Penguin Books, 1993.

Diehl, Paul F. *International Peacekeeping.* Baltimore: Johns Hopkins University Press, 1996.

Gottlieb, Gideon. *Nation Against State: A New Approach to Ethnic Conflicts and the Decline of Sovereignty.* New York: Council on Foreign Relations, 1993.

Greenfield, Liah. *Nationalism: Five Roads to Modernity.* Cambridge: Harvard University Press, 1992.

Grosscup, Beau. *The New Politics of Terrorism.* Far Hills, N.J.: New Horizons Press, 1991.

Kennedy, Paul. *The Rise and Fall of the Great Powers: Economic Change and Military Conflict from 1500 to 2000.* New York: Random House, 1987.

Kissinger, Henry. *Diplomacy.* New York: Simon and Schuster, 1994.

McCormick, J. M. *American Foreign Policy and Process.* 2d ed. Itasca, Ill.: F.W. Peacock, 1992.

Rourke, John T. *International Politics on the World Stage.* 5th ed. Guilford, Conn.: Brown & Benchmark, 1996.

Weiner, Myron. *The Global Migration Crisis: Challenge to States and to Human Rights.* New York: HarperCollins, 1994.

Chapter Fourteen

Foreign Policy:
American Style

Thus far, we have talked about foreign policy without trying to put a particularly "American" slant on it. Now, however, we shall take a look at the content, the process, the "machinery," and the people involved in formulating and executing foreign policy in the United States. Keep in mind that what is described here fits within the overall framework of foreign policy that the previous chapter has outlined for you.

THE CONSTITUTIONAL GRANTS OF POWER

The Constitution divides the authority in the foreign policy arena between the executive branch and the legislative branch. While on the surface it may appear that the two branches of government have almost equal authority over foreign policy matters, presidents and their staffs have come to exercise more day-to-day, practical control in this area than the Congress. As we have already seen in the chapter on the executive branch, the president can make an executive agreement (an agreement between the president and the head of another country) rather than negotiating a treaty. By using the executive agreement instead of a treaty, the president avoids having to get the consent of the Senate to carry out

Chart 14.1: Constitutional Allocation of Authority in Foreign Policy Making

Legislative Authority	Executive Authority
Make laws	Command armed forces
Declare war	Negotiate treaties
Appropriate money	Appoint diplomats and
Call out the militia	cabinet members
Raise and maintain armed forces	Recognize other governments

the agreement. (Remember treaties must be approved by the Senate, but executive agreements can be made without anyone's permission.)

Congress has also given away some of its own control to the president. For instance, Congress passed laws allowing the chief executive to spend what are called "**discretionary funds**." This money is appropriated by Congress for the president to spend for unforeseen needs in the national interest. It was with these funds that President Kennedy began the Peace Corps. President Lyndon Johnson also used more than $1 billion in discretionary funds in 1965-1966 in Vietnam.[1] In addition to the use of discretionary funds, Congress has given the president the authority to transfer money that was appropriated for one program to some other program. The chief executive can also appoint certain foreign policy assistants without the consent of the Senate.

Even though Congress must appropriate money for programs connected with the foreign policy of the United States, such as the Defense Department budget, the scales tip in favor of executive control rather than congressional. Part of the defense budget has come to be called the "**black budget**" because what the money is spent on is ultra secret with only a few congressional leaders having any notion at all about its content.[2] When reading the budget requests for various Defense Department agencies and services, the black budget requests appear as a multi-billion-dollar request for projects with code names like *Classic Wizard*, with vague descriptions such as "selected activities" or "special programs." These black budget accounts are not audited in the same fashion as other government spending because "few federal investigators have the security clearances necessary to audit black programs, which usually are classified as 'sensitive compartmented information,' a classification above top secret."[3] Intelligence agencies such as the Central Intelligence Agency (CIA), the National Security Agency (NSA), the National Reconnaissance Office (NRO), and the various intelligence services of the military get 75 percent of their funds through the black budget, none of which ever appears in a public document.[4] According to the U.S. Center for Strategic and Budgetary Assessments, classified or

ace Corps member Philip
sniewski is a volunteer
orking in rural
velopment and secondary
ojects including forestry.
oking at water pulled
m a shallow well outside
is child's house, Lesniewski
gins to deal with the
oblem of contaminated
ter.

"black" programs account for more than $23 billion (about 17 percent) of recent budget requests for the Defense Department.[5] While the United States has the largest black budget, other countries, especially Britain and France, have black budget projects also.

Just like the space programs of NASA, black-budget spending does have some positive side-effects for the commercial market. Many of its technological developments ultimately make it to consumers in such products as phased-array antennae that allow a driver to park a car in tight spaces, for example, with a voice guiding the driver.

It is also true that despite the War Powers Resolution, which attempted to limit the president's ability to wage war without congressional consent, presidents still sidestep Congress on this issue. Since the resolution was passed in 1973, presidents have committed troops to battle or potential battle many times, most recently in such countries as Iraq, Afghanistan, Yugoslavia, Kuwait, Somalia, Haiti, Bosnia, and Zaire.

With these ways of "getting around" Congress, we can probably safely conclude that, despite appearances, the executive branch of government has the upper hand in matters of foreign policy today.

THE INPUTS

Keep in mind that in foreign policy matters the president usually has the last word, but he does receive information, pressure, and advice from various sources. To make it easier to understand, let us imagine that we have a computer (the president). Like all computers, thus far, someone has to put information into the computer so that it can produce output. We will call the output *foreign policy*. What we are interested in here is who "inputs" data into the computer and what kinds of "viruses" might enter the system to make it malfunction.

The State Department

This executive department can and frequently does have major input into foreign policy matters. It is not only supposed to help formulate American foreign policy, but it is also supposed to assist in the execution of that policy. The department is headed by a secretary of state. Despite its important role, the Department of State has fewer personnel than any other executive department. It is this department that actually connects on a daily basis with the governments of almost 200 countries around the world through the United States ambassadors, consuls, and other career diplomats. It is also responsible for administering United States foreign, economic aid programs, which used to be considerably larger than the military aid programs. However, this is not the case any more.

Once the State Department and particularly the secretary of state consistently dominated the "input" into American foreign policy. However, in the twentieth century various presidents tended to weaken the role of the State Department by appointing weak persons to the office of secretary of state, by essentially ignoring the advice given to them by the secretary of state, or by appointing and then openly accepting the advice of a national security advisor instead of the secretary of state. In addition, the State Department's position is almost constantly being challenged now by the Defense Department, the Central Intelligence Agency (CIA), and the National Security Council (NSC). The former often sees aid in the humanitarian sense while the others are more inclined to see aid as a protection against threats to the United States. In 2004, the United States spent $19.6 billion in both economic and security assistance around the globe.[6]

There are always complaints from various interest groups and individuals in the public that the government spends too much money on what is generically called *foreign aid* (economic and security aid). While it is true that this expenditure could be used domestically, it is not a huge chunk of the total budget of the United States. In fiscal year 2004, this kind of spending amounted to less than 1 percent of the total budgetary expenditures.

Foreign policy can have an impact on domestic affairs as well. Contrary to popular opinion, foreign aid has a positive impact on the domestic economy. When the United States grants credit to foreign governments to purchase military equipment, almost all such purchases must be made in the United States. When the United States grants economic aid through international development organizations, it frequently purchases American goods for projects in foreign countries. Both types of aid have a positive effect on the U.S. economy by generating a larger gross domestic product, more jobs, and more tax revenues.

Defense Department (DOD)

Like the State Department, the Defense Department has responsibilities in the area of foreign policy, particularly in the area of military aid and the use of military force. Sometimes the two departments come into direct conflict with each other because their inputs don't "jive" with each other. What may be "good" military policy may not be viewed by the State Department as "good" diplomatic policy. Although the secretary of defense is always a civilian (non-military), the secretary's sympathies usually lie with the military. It would be illogical to assume that a president would appoint a person as secretary of defense who was not in tune with military problems and solutions. Hence, the Departments of State and Defense are sometimes at odds with each other over which policies are the best to pursue. Like the secretary of state, the secretary of defense can be strong or weak and will perform his/her role accordingly.

Besides the difficulty presented when the two departments don't see eye to eye, policy inputs from the DOD are often very expensive and difficult to monitor as we have already seen in the black budget references. For example, an Air Force missile called the AIM120A Advanced Medium Range Air-to-Air Missile (AMRAAM) was supposed to cost a mere $68,800 when Congress agreed to purchase the weapon in 1981. Now, however, each missile will average $461,000. Since 17,127 of AMRAAMs were scheduled to be purchased, the total bill would be around $7,895,547,000—no small change.[7] It should be obvious that the defense contractor who proposed to manufacture and sell this missile to the government has a vested interest in it other than national security, as do the people who work for this defense contractor and the members of Congress who come from the state where this defense contractor operates.

Foreign policy inputs from the Defense Department can also be expensive because apparently the military has not yet developed or refuses to implement a better program for testing proposed, new weapons before multimillion-dollar investments of tax money are made. A report issued by the General Accounting Office (Congress' "watchdog on waste") states: "the Pentagon's weapons testing program still cannot adequately assess whether weapons would work in combat . . . ."[8] Furthermore, the Pentagon[9] has been known to pay outlandish prices for items that could be bought in a hardware store for practically nothing. For example, the Air Force purchased from Lockheed, a prominent defense contractor, toilet pots for its C-5A transport planes, which were described as resembling a common roasting pan. The price paid for each was $317.79. To make matters worse, the Air Force purchased sixty-seven of these $317.79 toilet pots

American women saw combat in the Gulf War. Here a female MP stands guard at a critical post with members of the UN forces.

after the plane's toilet system was redesigned to eliminate the need for them![10] Similarly, a report released in May 1997 stated that the DOD "has made hundreds of millions of dollars in overpayments to contractors because of . . . computers that can't talk to one another and the use of over 100 different accounting systems."[11]

Foreign policy difficulties can result even within a given context. Leaving aside the question of whether the United States *should* provide foreign aid, something the American public generally disapproves of, given that Congress does provide this aid, who gets it becomes a volatile, political question. Currently Israel receives the lion's share of all security assistance.

The military services themselves have a huge stake in foreign policy. They must convince the public, as well as other members of the government, these defense forces, together with all of their weapons, are needed. Former Defense Secretary William Cohen stated: "We need forces that are agile, flexible and responsive in a dynamic and uncertain world, forces that can quickly descend on and dominate any situation, and forces that can halt and defeat military aggression by major regional powers, even in two places across the globe.[12] Convincing Congress and the American public to maintain this kind of military force was difficult in the post-cold-war era because of the demand for a "peace dividend." Consequently, the defense budget was reduced from 24 percent of the total budget in 1990 to less than 15 percent in 1996.[13] Now, with terrorism and other threats around the globe to deal with, the defense budget in 2004 stood at 18 percent of the total budget. Consider the following: 67 percent of the national government's total budget is considered mandatory spending. Only

33 percent is discretionary spending. In other words, the U.S. government gets to spend only 1/3 of its annual budget on almost anything it wants. In fiscal year 2004, that would have amounted to about $873 billion out of a budget of about $2.5 trillion. Of that $873 billion, about $400 billion was devoted to defense spending. The overwhelming amount of all U.S. government funding goes to items such a Medicare, Medicaid, education, the criminal justice system, salaries of government employees, upkeep of government buildings, maintaining highways, managing air traffic, regulating the safety of food and drugs, etc.

While we tend to think of defense spending as "foreign" policy, be aware that the money spent does impact the domestic economy. Somebody has to build the airplanes, ships, guns, and missiles. Somebody has to make the uniforms, feed the troops, make the computers, cell phones, satellites, boots, and tanks. These "somebodies" are almost always U.S. companies, located in U.S. states, like Georgia, Massachusetts, Texas, and California.

The Socioeconomic Elite

The term **socioeconomic elite** refers to the upper class. They have "position" and money in the society. Like other groups in society, they have an influence on foreign policy. Some of these socioeconomic elites, although not all, who make their money in defense-related industries, fear any major shifts in foreign policy because they do not know what those shifts may produce for increasing or decreasing their wealth and status. Therefore, these socioeconomic elites influence foreign policy in a conservative direction.

As it stands now, the United States and the countries of the former Soviet Union (primarily Russia) run neck and neck with one another as the world's largest producers/exporters of weapons. These weapons are manufactured in the United States by such companies as General Electric, Boeing, General Dynamics, Lockheed Martin, Westinghouse— just to name a few. Since 1990, the United States has exported around a quarter billion dollars worth of weapons to seventy countries. In the mid-1990s when the U.S. was cutting back on big-ticket weapons and weapons systems, many of these companies laid off employees and closed plants. These companies that manufacture weapons lost billions of dollars. The stockholders lost massive amounts of money also. Some of these stockholders are part of the socioeconomic elite we've been talking about. Would they really welcome such a change in United States foreign policy? Undoubtedly it would be an extremely rare occasion that one of these people would admit that world peace wasn't really on his/her agenda, but given the choice of world peace *without* money or the continuation of things as they are *with* money, we could assume that some of these folks would choose the latter. While the U.S. and Russia may continue their friendlier posture toward each other, as long as the Defense Department asserts the need for a military capable of fighting and winning two major, regional wars, it is doubtful that defense contractors will go out of business.

Now there would be circumstances when these conservative socioeconomic elites might wish to see a change in foreign policy. Let's look at United States policy toward Israel and the Arab countries. Because the Arabs control substantial amounts of oil and can affect the price of it as evidenced by the embargo of the early 1970s and gasoline price fluctuations, some of the American elite would like to see the United States develop a more favorable policy toward the Arabs and a less favorable one toward Israel. After all, the United States does need oil to continue in the manner it is accustomed to, they might argue. Therefore, it would not always be accurate to say these conservative socioeconomic elites support status-quo foreign policy. Elite groups do not always have a unified position; they, too, have differences of opinion or conflicts of interest just as everyone else does.

The Intelligence Community

Throughout history, certain events have caused the world to change so much that these events take on special importance. One such event was the destruction of the World Trade Center and the damaging of the Pentagon by terrorists on September 11, 2001. At that time there were over a dozen American intelligence agencies operating more or less independently. Having very few people to report to, other than the agencies' own directors, these "spy" organizations did not do much communicating with one another either.

As a result of the rather severe wake-up call the United States received with "9/11," the U.S. intelligence community was reorganized with the passage of the **Intelligence Reform and Terrorism Prevention Act of 2004**. The law is designed to impose a measure of central authority over the fifteen agencies charged with gathering and processing intelligence in the U.S. Among its provisions are the following:

- Creates a new position, Director of National Intelligence, who will be the principal adviser to the president. This position oversees all other intelligence agencies, oversees the billions of funds set aside for intelligence agencies, and reports directly to the president.

- Establishes a National Counterterrorism Center for planning intelligence missions and coordinating information on terror threats and responses.

- Creates a Privacy and Civil Liberties Board of private citizens to oversee privacy protections.

- Makes information-sharing mandatory among government agencies.

- Establishes minimum standards for birth certificates and driver's licenses and improves security of Social Security cards.

- Calls for more airline-passenger prescreening.

- Increases border patrols.

- Tightens visa requirements for visitors to enter the country.

- Strengthens government's ability to investigate terrorist suspects.

The **Intelligence Community**, or the **IC**, as it is called in "bureaucratic-speak," is a federation of executive branch organizations that pursue intelligence activities necessary for the conduct of foreign relations and for ensuring the national security of the United States. IC members collaborate together both to meet their own missions and to satisfy overall IC objectives. Each agency has its own area of expertise and responsibility, but all report to the Director of National Intelligence. Chart 14.2 lists and gives a brief description of the agencies now included in the IC.

Central Intelligence Agency. While all of these intelligence entities are important and interesting in their own right, some of them deserve an extra look. Probably the most well-known American intelligence agency is the **Central Intelligence Agency**, more commonly called the **CIA**. Created in 1947, the CIA is charged with the coordination of intelligence gathering from all sources. It is also supposed to collect and analyze national security data on its own. Thus, on the one hand, the CIA is a coordinating agency for all intelligence gathering and analyzing for the United States, and, on the other, it is itself an intelligence gatherer and analyzer with agents of its own. Despite popular belief, most of the information the CIA gathers is obtained from public sources such as newspapers and books. Although the best known, it still has the smallest budget of the three major intelligence agencies. Nevertheless, the information presented by the CIA often has a major impact on the direction of U.S. foreign policy. During the cold war era, the CIA consistently overestimated the military capacity of the former Soviet Union, and, consequently, played a significant role in persuading presidents and Congress to take a confrontational approach toward that country.

The law establishing the CIA also calls for the agency "to perform such other functions and duties related to intelligence affecting the national security." It is these "other functions" that have led to some interesting, if not altogether pleasant, footnotes in American foreign policy history. For example, the CIA plotted and assisted in the overthrow of the government of Iran in

Chart 14.2: The American Intelligence Community

Central Intelligence Agency (CIA)
Central clearing house for all intelligence; obtains intelligence, and conducts other covert operations related to national security.

National Security Agency (NSA)
Conducts worldwide intelligence operations; conducts electronic surveillance within the United States; codes and decodes information.

National Reconnaissance Office (NRO)
Operates system of spy satellites that, among other things, supply photographic data to the rest of the intelligence community.

Army Intelligence (G2)
Primarily obtains information on ground forces and new weapons of other countries.

Air Force Intelligence (A2)
Primarily obtains data on aircraft and space technology/weapons of other countries.

Office of Naval Intelligence (ONI)
Primarily collects information on foreign naval capacity and operations.

Bureau of Intelligence and Research (I & R)
Part of the State Department; collects data of an economic, scientific, sociological, and political nature in order to forecast trends.

Defense Intelligence Agency (DIA)
Part of the Department of Defense; analyzes the capabilities of both allies and enemies of the United States.

Department of Energy
Obtains and analyzes information about foreign energy supplies, production, intentions, and policies.

Federal Bureau of Investigation (FBI)
Secures information about security threats within the United States.

Department of the Treasury
Collects information on foreign investment, as well as on foreign monetary and economic policy and status.

Drug Enforcement Administration (DEA)
Secures data on both foreign and domestic drug production and distribution.

1953 and installed Shah Rezza Pahlavi as the head of the new government. The
Shah remained a faithful ally of the United States till his government was over-
thrown in 1979. Iranian resentment of United States interference in their affairs ultimately culminated in the Iran hostage crisis during the Carter administration. The CIA has also been implicated in plots to assassinate or the actual
assassinations of such people as Fidel Castro of Cuba, Salvador Allende of Chile,

Ngo Dinh Diem of South Vietnam, and Muammar Qaddafi of Libya. The agency was also found to have spied on American citizens in the United States, although it is specifically forbidden to do so by law.

As long as the CIA and other similar agencies engage strictly in intelligence-gathering operations, there is usually very little criticism of their activities. It is in the area of covert (undercover) operations that may, as noted above, involve assassinations, revolutions, or illegal transfer of funds that Congress begins to get a bit testy about their activities. When these things are discovered, Congress usually attempts to "fix" the problem by making some type of institutional change within the offending organization. In 1981 Congress passed the **Intelligence Authorization Act** that requires intelligence agencies to report to two congressional committees about their current covert activities, as well as their "significant anticipated operations." The problem remains, however, not with who reports what to whom but, rather, with the type of people who authorize and carry out these operations. If they themselves are unethical (i.e., believe they can make their own rules, that the end justifies the means, etc.), then no law regarding the reporting of covert activities will change their behavior. In fact, they will sometimes attempt to find other avenues for their activities to get around the law as happened in the Iran-Contra affair. The **National Security Council (NSC)** was used as a vehicle to carry out a covert operation involving the possibly illegal sale of weapons to Iran and to give the profits to the Nicaraguan Contras. (Rebels fighting against the communist government of Nicaragua.) Giving the money to the Contras was forbidden by law, but the NSC apparently decided on its own to do it anyway. The NSC was accused of running a "phantom government" by the *Miami Herald* newspaper, which asserted that Lt. Col. Oliver North (an aide to the NSC) was so powerful that he could order the orbits of surveillance satellites changed to follow Soviet ships and ordered secret missions over Cuba and Nicaragua with high-altitude, spy aircraft. If that wasn't disturbing enough, the *Herald* also reported that North drafted a secret plan for suspending the Constitution and turning over the government to the Federal Emergency Management Agency, essentially declaring martial law throughout the country. The point is that sometimes foreign policy input from the CIA and other intelligence agencies becomes more than mere input. It becomes output—the foreign policy itself—and that's not the way the game is supposed to be played.

One of the unfortunate side effects of Congress' discovering CIA misconduct is that, in trying to "fix" the problem, the legislative branch frequently forces the retirement, firing, or demotion of high-level CIA personnel. As a result, the agency is left with inexperienced leadership for years to come.

National Security Agency. Referred to as a "global vacuum cleaner of intelligence," the **National Security Agency (NSA)** gathers information around the world, as well as within the United States, not only from ground stations but also from KH11 spy satellites. Its internal surveillance operations are approved by a panel of eleven (**Foreign Intelligence Surveillance Court**), who meet twice a month essentially to grant search warrants. These search warrants allow the NSA to conduct legal, electronic surveillance of suspected foreign agents (some of whom are United States citizens). President Reagan also gave the NSA permission to use "the computer systems of the Internal Revenue Service, the Social Security Administration, and every other civilian government agency."[14] Interestingly enough, there is no congressional act creating the NSA because it was established by executive order in 1952, and perhaps of more importance there is no law limiting its powers!

National Reconnaissance Office. The **National Reconnaissance Office** (**NRO**) was such a secret organization that the letterhead used on its stationery was classified material! In fact, the United States government did not officially acknowledge the existence of the NRO until 1992. The NRO operates satellite reconnaissance systems and provides photographic evidence to other intelligence agencies from its space platforms that are disguised as weather and research satellites. Its budget is about $5 billion annually.[15] Secretive as the organization is, tourists who visit the NASA space flight launch center near Titusville, Florida, are likely to see on a sign posted regarding NASA's upcoming flight schedule that reads "NRO project."

Department of Homeland Security. Created in the aftermath of the disastrous events of "9/11," the **Department of Homeland Security** brought together 22 agencies and 180,000 employees, unifying once-fragmented national-government functions in a single agency dedicated to protecting America and Americans from terrorism. The broad range of responsibilities includes prevention and deterrence of terrorist incidents against the United States and its citizens, as well as response to any incidences that may indeed occur. It is the Department of Homeland Security that issues the color-coded terror alert warnings. Since these warnings came into the existence, they have almost always been "elevated," orange. Sadly, most people do not pay much attention to these alerts any more. Therefore, the department may have to find another, less *routine* way of sounding alarm.

The National Security Council

Another input into American foreign policy decisions is the **National Security Council** (**NSC**). It was established in 1947 to analyze the security situation of the United States and to advise the president of that assessment. Usually composed of the vice president, the secretaries of state and defense, the CIA director, the Chairman of the Joint Chiefs of Staff, the Assistant for National Security Affairs, and a number of support people, the NSC is supposed to be a policy advisor to the president, not a policy executor. The staff members meet in the White House Situation Room, which is a security area in the basement of the west wing of the White House. Here they put together a daily report of intelligence from around the world gathered from various sources. While its influence varies from president to president, the NSC, as indicated above, received a great deal of attention during the latter part of the Reagan administration because of its involvement in the Iran-Contra affair when it became an executor of policy rather than an advisor.

The **Assistant for National Security Affairs**, usually just called the **national security advisor**, is the title of the person who heads the NSC staff. This person can be extremely influential in foreign policy matters, again depending on how the president feels about that person and that position. President Nixon, for example, relied quite heavily on the NSC and Henry Kissinger when Kissinger was national security advisor. Kissinger was extremely skillful at undercutting the influence of then Secretary of State William Rogers. It has been said that United States foreign policy during the Nixon years was Kissinger's, not Nixon's, so strong was the former's influence. On the other hand, Presidents Truman and Kennedy hardly ever met with the NSC.

Public Opinion. While public opinion has some influence on the formulation of American foreign policy, its effects are usually on the short-term rather than long-term policies. Characteristically only about 15 percent of the public actually keeps up with foreign affairs, and also characteristically opinion is highly unstable, depending on how successful the public tends to view the effects of the policy decision in the short run. Americans tend to "rally around the flag" when they feel their interests threatened but easily become discouraged when pleasant solutions do not come about in a relatively short period of time. For example, when the hostages were first taken by Shiite extremists with the blessing of the Iranian government, Americans rallied behind the president. "How dare the Iranians do such a thing?" However, when the affair dragged on and on, support for the president's foreign-policy decision (essentially to do nothing but wait) waned and actually turned to almost complete lack of support. Americans typically favor nonmilitary solutions to international problems and are not willing to support foreign policies that require long-term solutions and/or hardships unless they are absolutely forced to do so, for example, by being attacked by the Japanese at Pearl Harbor. Also characteristically Americans are much more inclined to express opinions about what *not* to do rather than what *to* do or how to do it. A public opinion poll conducted in March of 1969 revealed that 52 percent of the respondents thought that American involvement in Vietnam was wrong. But when asked what the government should do about this "wrong policy," 32 percent thought the war should be escalated, 26 percent wanted all Americans out of Vietnam, 19 percent advised an end to the war as soon as possible, 19 percent supported the current way of fighting the war, and 4 percent offered other ideas.[16]

Part of the reason for our ignorance of what's "out there" results from our isolation from most of the world during much of our history. It has just been in recent times that air travel has made it relatively easy to go to other countries. Perhaps because of this isolation many Americans also developed a provincial and ethnocentric attitude. That's a fancy way of saying some of us—maybe a lot of us—think that "our" way is the best way, "our" stuff is better than "their" stuff, "our" people are better than "their" people, and "our" country is better than "their" country. With that kind of attitude why bother to find out about anyone else? Americans still do not travel abroad very much as evidenced by the fact that only about 11 percent of Americans have passports.

The American news media cannot escape some of the credit for American global ignorance. The media pay very little attention to global news unless it directly affects the average American. When British news reporting, for example, is compared to American news reporting, the difference is striking. There seems also to be much less of a tendency to sensationalize the news among British reporters than there is among American reporters. Unless one reads such newspapers as the *Christian Science Monitor*, subscribes to foreign newspapers, travels abroad frequently, or listens to the British Broadcasting Company reports that some public radio stations subscribe to, he/she is left with a very slanted view—an American news media view—of what the world is all about.

Foreign policy is also a rather complex subject. It requires a level of sophistication and education that most Americans do not have and apparently do not want to acquire. There is a move in the educational system toward what is termed *global education* or *global awareness*. The intent of this curriculum is to make Americans more aware of the rest of the world, to rid them of their provincialism and ethnocentrism. If the attempt is successful, in the long run perhaps individual American citizens will have more of an impact on foreign policy than they do now. At this time, most Americans who express an interest in foreign policy are manipulated by the current administration, pressure groups or socioeconomic elites because many Americans do not really know enough to make a truly informed judgment. Rather, they "mouth" whatever the current *line* might be. People are *told*, for example: "We are trustworthy, but the Chinese are not." People *believe*: "We are trustworthy, but the Chinese are not." Therefore, foreign policy is to remain as it is. There is no point in exploring any alternatives because "they are not to be trusted." The point is this: it may well be that Americans are trustworthy and the Chinese are not. However, without even elementary knowledge about China and what is going on around the world, how can a person make such a judgment?

The result of the individual's lack of interest in foreign affairs is what is termed the **"professionalization" of foreign policy**. This term means that foreign policy is made by "experts" who are typically appointed civilians and military personnel. It is true that the President of the United States may have the last say so in many areas of foreign policy, but he/she does not make these decisions in a vacuum. Instead the president depends on the advice given by such people as the secretary of state, the secretary of defense and the National Security Advisor—all of whom are civilian appointees—as well as such military types as the Chiefs of Staff of all four branches of the military—who were not elected to those positions either.

There is a tendency among the uninformed American public to regard foreign policy as the domain of these "professionals," these "experts," or to regard foreign policy as such a dangerous, uncertain game that the United States should just stay out of it completely—isolate itself from the rest of the world. This policy of isolation—at least from those outside its own hemisphere—was one that the United States had followed for a good deal of its short history. There are also those who think all foreign policy is best carried out by using the military. The point is that Americans do not pay enough attention to what is going on elsewhere and do not have even elementary knowledge of most parts of the world and their history to make a reasoned judgment.

Interest Groups. As with domestic issues, foreign policy issues get considerable attention from interest groups. Therefore, another source of input into the making of foreign policy is such groups as the American Legion, the Arms Control Association, the AFL-CIO, or the American Israel Public Affairs Committee. Generally, the effect of interest-group input varies from issue to issue, but it seems to have greater impact when the lobbying effort is done out of public view and when the issue is not considered a crisis issue.

The influence of interest groups on foreign policy, as with domestic policy, frequently produces a maintenance of the status quo—things as they are—because various groups tend to counterbalance one another. In other words, interest-group support, like socioeconomic elite support, is usually conservative. Labor unions, like defense contractors, might have a vested interest in maintaining the "war machine." How many thousands of people, many of whom are union members, would be unemployed if the world became terribly peaceful all of a sudden? Not only would there be economic hardship on those who would lose jobs, but the union itself would lose power. As a result of this conservative tendency, foreign-policy making has been described as "a taffy-pull: every group attempts to pull policy in its own direction while resisting the pulls of others with the result that policy fails to move in any discernible direction. The process encourages solutions tending toward the middle of the road . . . ."[17]

Some interest groups, however, are highly successful in their lobbying efforts. The **American Israel Public Affairs Committee (AIPAC)**, for example, boasts a membership of 35,000, wealthy constituents across the United States, many of whom have personal relationships with members of Congress. In other words, the group can call upon these people to put forth the AIPAC position to members of Congress personally—friend to friend. "Its ability . . . in Congress to block or water down a weapons sale to any Arab nation . . . has been firmly established."[18] Israel is the number one recipient of United States foreign aid, which amounts to approximately 30 percent of the annual foreign aid budget. The point here is not to dicker about whether such aid should be given. Rather, it is merely to point out that organizations such as AIPAC can have an influence on Congress and the White House on American foreign policy.

The Mass Media. As with domestic issues, the mass media's role involves agenda setting rather than actual shaping of public opinion. You will recall from the chapter on public opinion that the media usually manage to tell us what to think *about* rather than *what* to think. In foreign policy matters, since most Americans are ignorant and apathetic about them, the media perhaps have even less effect, except on that 15 percent who actually pay attention to global affairs, as well as on the foreign policy makers themselves. The media's effect on the other 85 percent, according to one scholar, is indirect, occurring when someone might come into contact with a member of the "attentive public"—those 15 percent who pay attention to global happenings.[19]

Still, if interest groups who try to influence foreign policy are most successful "behind the scenes" on matters that have not captured public attention, then media exposure of these matters may have a negative impact on the interest group's ability to have its way. On the other hand, if no interest group has taken up the cause of a particular policy issue, media attention to that issue increases the likelihood that some interest group will direct its attention to it.[20]

Multinational Corporations and Banks. A **multinational corporation** is one that operates in more than one country. The largest American-based, multinational corporations, International Business Machines (IBM), Mobil, Standard Oil of California, General Electric, International Telephone and Telegraph (ITT), Exxon, Union Carbide and Ford, have assets greater than most countries of the world. Because they operate in more than one country, their interests and policies may at times collide with those of the United States government. For example, when King Faisal of Saudi Arabia announced his country's oil embargo on the United States in 1973, Frank Jungers, chairman of the board and chief executive officer of ARAMCO (Arab/American Oil Company), ordered oil production cut further than the King had ordered. Jungers justified his decision by saying, "The important thing was to give the immediate image of being with the government, not trying to fight it."[21]

Yet multinational corporations are in many ways like other important political/economic inputs in current world politics. "They possess interests and a . . . capacity to act in pursuit of those interests, but . . . their corporate officers and administrators remain overwhelmingly American and reflect prevailing American attitudes toward international relations."[22]

United States banks also have input into foreign-policy making. These banks have made over a quarter trillion dollars worth of loans to foreign countries and business enterprises. A good chunk of these loans was made to Mexico. When oil and gas prices decline and negative economic events occur, many of these governments have not always been able or have not been willing to make their loan payments. On the one hand, loans to developing countries may lend support to American foreign policy in these countries, but, if the country defaults on the loan, the American economy suffers and possibly even the tax payer. If banks fail, the United States government is obligated through the FDIC (Federal Deposit Insurance Corporation) to make good on each deposit in a failed bank up to $100,000 per account (assuming the bank had FDIC insurance). If there isn't enough money in the FDIC to cover such losses, then tax money will be used.

The banking community in 1981 apparently was more concerned about being able to collect on loans it had made to the government of Poland than it was about seeing the Solidarity trade union movement succeed in that country. With Solidarity disrupting the Polish economy, the government's ability to repay those loans was threatened; therefore, big banks, like the Chemical Bank of New York with outstanding loans to Poland, were at odds with United States policy and were not supportive of Solidarity. While it may appear that at times the multinational corporations and the big international banks do not have the national interest at heart, keep in mind that good economic policy may not always be good political policy, whether domestic or foreign.

Congress. We have already seen in the beginning of this chapter that the Constitution grants Congress considerable power in the area of foreign policy. But we have also noted that Congress has given away some of its power in the foreign policy area either directly or indirectly to the executive branch. Yet Congress does have input into the foreign policy process when it wishes to assert itself. Laws were passed that require that the president seek congressional approval of all arms sales of more than $25 million (**Foreign Assistance Act of 1974**) and any transfers of major military equipment of more than $7 million (**Arms Export Control Act of 1976**). The president is now also required to submit a quarterly report to Congress on any anticipated arms sales or transfers.

In addition, Congress controls the "purse strings" and can, if it so desires, refuse to appropriate money for various defense and/or foreign policy initiatives. For example, in 1985 Congress refused to continue to fund military aid for the Contras despite the president's plea for the continuation of such assistance. However, most of the time the executive branch gets what it wants from a more than agreeable Congress. Remember, it is Congress that authorizes such covert spending of tax dollars as the black budget.

Individual members of Congress and certain committees have more input than the Congress as a whole. The House **Armed Services Committee** and

Senate **Foreign Relations Committee** with their respective chairpersons some-times have been known to put a stop to something the White House wanted to do.

Other Countries. The foreign policies of other countries have an impact on the foreign policy (and even the domestic policy) of the United States. To most governments, the world is divided into "us" (the "good guys") and "them" (the "bad guys"). Then the effect on foreign policy comes from two sources, namely, friends and enemies.

With friends, i.e., allies, country "A" may be put into the position of having to support something an ally (country "B") has done even though country "A" would not have done the act itself. For example, the Americans are, more or less, forced to support, or at least not openly oppose, the actions of the British in Northern Ireland because Britain is an American ally. Similarly, the British supported American actions regarding Libya. Such support is not always forth-coming. However, when allies do not support each other, there is always a price to pay in terms of perceived weakness of the alliance, anger on the part of the country that expected the support, or perhaps even "revenge" from the ally who did not get supported. For example, in 1954, when the French, an ally of the United States, asked for American support in its war in what was then French Indo-China (now Vietnam, Cambodia, and Laos), the Americans denied that assistance. When the Americans were caught in a similar situation in South Vietnam about twenty years later, the French sat by and watched the American defeat. More recently with the Iraqi war, Germany, France, and Canada—all considered U.S. allies—withheld their support and even openly opposed the invasion of Iraq to remove Saddam Hussein by the American-led coalition of countries.

It may be true also that relatively powerless countries can also be very de-pendent on a very powerful country with which they are friends. Honduras serves as an illustration of this concept. Honduras, considered an ally of the United States, is not in a position to balk at much of anything the United States wants to do in Honduras. Honduras is extremely dependent on the United States at present for its economic survival. When the United States said: "Let the Nicaraguan Contras use Honduras as a base of operations against the Nica-raguan government," what was little Honduras supposed to say—"No?" Of course not. Complain as the government of Honduras did, the Contras still used Honduras because that's what the United States wanted.

A country's foreign policy is also obviously affected by its enemies. Power-ful countries play games of who can build the biggest, most destructive nuclear arsenal, together with the shiniest conventional weapons, and the heftiest armies. They also build alliances with other countries to make themselves even more powerful, while trying to maneuver themselves into potent economic positions so that goods can be used as leverage, e.g., oil, food, gold, diamonds, etc. Countries that lack power are usually forced to agree with one or the other "side" to survive. Which side they go with often depends on where the country is located in relation to the powerful countries or which country gets there first with the most "aid." (Sometimes "aid" comes with "advisors," who are often soldiers in civilian clothes.)

Sometimes the powerful countries get a little tired of playing the game and retreat into isolationism or at least try to do that. Today such a policy is more difficult to achieve since countries are more dependent on one another probably than they ever have been before. If, for example, the United States wished to isolate itself, where would it get most of the oil it uses? The U.S. does not have that much oil left on its own soil.

AN OVERVIEW OF AMERICAN FOREIGN POLICY SINCE 1789

Isolationism

After the battle for independence was won, the United States began to chart a course for itself in the field of foreign policy. Since the country was new to independence and particularly weak, it chose, at least in some respects, a policy of isolationism. Despite this country's stated policy of not becoming involved in the affairs of others, the United States carried on a lively trade with anyone who wanted to trade. Soon it actually began to envision that the Western Hemisphere was its own little private domain and that European countries should keep their hands off. This "hands off" attitude was announced officially in 1823 in what has become known as the **Monroe Doctrine**. The Monroe Doctrine proclaimed the United States as a "protector" of the Western Hemisphere, although most Latin American countries, once they had gained independence, usually viewed this role as one of interference in their affairs. In its desire to stretch from "sea to shining sea," this country acquired territory previously belonging to Mexico, France, Spain, and Russia either by war or by purchase.

Neutrality

Despite its avowed policy of isolation, the United States never really has isolated itself. The more accurate description of American foreign policy throughout most of its history, at least regarding countries outside the Western Hemisphere, has been one of attempted neutrality while protecting American interests. It is worth mentioning that American leaders seem always to have had a greater tendency to wrap their foreign policy in morality more so than the leaders of other countries.[23] These moral overtones reflect "a tendency to treat

American soldiers inspect a Vietnam village for Viet Cong fighters.

international relations as a morality play—a struggle of the good against the bad. While idealistic tendencies can be refreshing, they can also lead to policy confusion and charges of hypocrisy when morality loses out, as it so often does, to concrete interests."[24] For example, the proclaimed reason for American involvement in South Vietnam was to "save" the country and presumably all of Southeast Asia from communism—for most Americans a noble purpose. However, when push came to shove, the United States abandoned South Vietnam to the communists rather than continue in that lengthy, costly war. Likewise, the Clinton administration's stated purpose of intervening in Somalia was to secure transportation routes so that food could be distributed to starving Somalians caught in the fighting between warring factions. Again a noble purpose. However, when American soldiers were killed, the president withdrew his forces, and presumably the Somalians went back to starvation. In other words, the concrete interests of the United States overrode any moral interests it may have had in either South Vietnam or Somalia.

Before World War I, the United States proclaimed a policy of neutrality toward what appeared to be worsening unrest in Europe. Yet, despite its best intentions, it was drawn into the war or got into the war, depending on how one interprets the situation. Rather than just saying that the United States believed its involvement on the side of the Allied Powers was in its own best interests, President Wilson declared the country's involvement as a war "to end all wars" and to "make the world safe for democracy." A new morality play had begun. After the war Americans wanted no part of the League of Nations supported by Wilson and returned to their neutral stance while advocating free trade, leaving the Europeans to find their own way of maintaining peace. However, when the Great Depression struck, self-interest got in the way of the morality play once more, and successive American presidents erected trade barriers to protect domestic industries. "With the world's greatest trading nation withdrawing, total world trade dried up and unemployment spread, contributing to the rise of fascism and militarism in Europe and Japan."[25]

Interventionism and Collective Security

When World War II did break out in Europe and in Asia, President Roosevelt adopted, with congressional backing, a policy of massive aid to the British and the Soviet Union—certainly not a neutral position. Although public opinion was against American involvement, ultimately the United States entered the war after the attack on Pearl Harbor by the Japanese.

After World War II, the United States never again postured itself in neutrality or isolationism. It assumed a role of "world policeman"—keeper of the peace, so to speak. It adopted a policy of **interventionism**[26]—involving itself from one end of the globe to another. Its major enemy since the end of the war was, until the early 1990s, the Soviet Union. Relations with that country had gone from so-so, to bad, to worse, and back again over the years. To protect itself and others from the perceived Soviet/communist threat, the United States executed a number of foreign policy initiatives such as the **Truman Doctrine**, which offered military aid to those fighting communist takeovers from outside their own countries. Another such initiative, the **Marshall Plan**, provided massive economic aid to war-torn Europe in the hope that a return to economic prosperity would allow the "free" European countries to remain free of communism. Expanding on previous foreign policy, the **Nixon Doctrine** proclaimed that the United States would provide weapons and training for "Third World" countries fighting "communist" takeovers from within. One of these beneficiaries of the Nixon Doctrine was Iran. Ultimately, as we know, it was not communists who took over Iran but fundamentalist, Shiite Moslems led by the Ayatollah Khomeini. In the 1980s, the **Reagan Doctrine** continued the policy of American support for Third World countries that were fending off communist revolutions. The policy also included active support with weapons and training of noncommunist, pro-American rebels in countries where weak, leftist governments existed such as Nicaragua.

After World War II, the United States for the first time in its history tied itself to a string of worldwide alliances during peacetime, the most noteworthy of which was NATO. In doing so, it also stationed troops on foreign soil for the first time except during war. In addition, the Americans became founding members of the United Nations. (Remember that just 25 years previously they had refused to join a similar organization, the League of Nations.) It did not take long for such "entanglements," as George Washington referred to them, to produce United States involvement in Korea under the sponsorship of the United Nations that the U.S. had helped to create.

Today there is a growing public, as well as some official, sentiment for the United States to remove itself from the United Nations. Opponents to the UN cite the cost of membership (the U.S. pays 22 percent of the U.N. budget), the alleged anti-American attitudes expressed by members of the institution, and the failure of the UN to act effectively in averting conflict and tragedy, as in the case of Rwanda in 1994. Recently, a U.S. ambassador to the United Nations, John Danforth, left his post after only five months in the job. His reason was that he saw the futility of trying to persuade the UN members to intervene in Sudan to stop the genocide that has been going on in that country for years. Proponents of continued U.S. participation in the body argue that the UN continues to represent the best opportunity for dialogue between nations and that its ability to act more effectively as peacekeepers in over a dozen nations underscores the utility of the organization. Despite this growing debate, no administration, either Republican or Democrat, has actively sought to limit or end U.S. involvement at the UN over the past sixty years.

Still considering itself as the only thing preventing communism from taking over the world, the United States embarked on its longest war (ten years) in Southeast Asia. The defeat (or at the very least, the tactical withdrawal) of the United States from Southeast Asia in 1974 produced the realization that the United States could not continue to play the role of "world policeman" alone. It had actively pursued a reduction of tensions with its major rival in Moscow. Despite the Reagan years, where there were an American military buildup, a great deal of "sword rattling," and sometimes out and out confrontation—but wisely never with anyone who could really do the Americans any damage—the 1990s ushered in a seemingly new era of cooperation among former enemies. Now that the Soviet Union is "out" and Russia is "in," current American policy, tempered by economic constraints, seems to be a friendly, but cautious, attitude toward all the changes in the world, except where American interests seem to be directly and severely threatened, e.g., Kuwait, or where an American president feels constrained for domestic, political reasons to intervene, e.g., Haiti.

Summary of Some Major American Foreign Policy Directions Today

Present-day American foreign policy still mixes morality with self-interest—with self-interest usually winning out, although it may not always seem that way. Current United States foreign policy directions include these significant areas.

First, the prevailing climate between Russia and the United States is toward more cooperation and continued reduction of conventional, as well as nuclear, weapons. However, please note that both sides still maintain awesome military capability, and each country's interests do not always coincide with each other.

Second, the United States continues to rely on collective security through its major alliance NATO and any other alliances (coalitions) the U.S. may enter into for specific shorter-term goals, the preemptive strike against Iraq. While the United States is still a member of the United Nations, it seems that current policy will include that body in a much more limited way than in the past since the Americans have demonstrated a willingness to "go it alone" when necessary. An example of this continued, if sometimes ambivalent, American recognition of the relevance of the United Nations may be found in the 2003 invasion by a coalition of nations led by the United States and Great Britain. In the runup to the war, the United States actively sought to secure a resolution of support for the war from the UN Security Council. When the Security Council failed to provide this resolution, the US still went to war against Iraq, but did so citing earlier UN Security Council resolutions which the American and British Governments claimed already sanctioned an invasion of Iraq due to the continued violation of UN resolutions by Saddam Hussein. Thus the Bush administration, even as it pursued its own objectives in Iraq, tried to provide at least some justification for its actions under UN resolutions.

Third, in the area of trade, American foreign policy supports free trade officially, while unofficially it bows to domestic pressure and has significant numbers of price supports, tariffs, and quotas. In response to the European Union, the United States, Canada, and Mexico have entered into a free trade agreement of their own, and similar arrangements with the rest of the Western Hemisphere are likely to occur. While some domestic industries are not happy with this support of free trade, the makers of foreign policy have thus far been unmoved. However, the United States self-interest dictates that it does not eliminate its trade barriers without its trading partners doing likewise, unless there is some compelling external reason to do so.

Fourth, after the terrorist attack on September 11, 2001, terrorism is now a top foreign policy concern. President Bush has formulated a new security policy for the United States, based on two principles. The first is unilateralism, taking independent action without seeking prior consent from other world powers or international organizations like the United Nations. The second principle is the preemptive strike, which means attacking enemies first before they can attack you. Some people have already referred to this foreign policy as the "**Bush Doctrine**." However, international cooperation was actively sought in the global fight against terrorists. The U.S. is pushing ahead with very tough actions, such as the invasion of Iraq, which ended with the collapse of Saddam Hussein's government. Hussein was known to have helped terrorists and was in the process of making weapons of mass destruction.

This last item—cooperation—includes efforts to reduce the threat of nuclear terrorism. Since the collapse of the Soviet Union, crime and corruption in the former Soviet republics, even among high-ranking officers in the military, have increased. Nuclear weapons and uranium for making bombs are not as well guarded as they were during the cold war. Over one hundred attempts at nuclear smuggling have been detected, including one by an impoverished electrical engineer who initially kept radioactive cesium hidden in his vegetable garden! There is continuing concern that the promise of large sums of money will result in the transfer of nuclear material, technology, and scientists to terrorists or to countries eager to build nuclear weapons, such as Iraq, Libya, or North Korea.

Fifth, the United States will support recent efforts by former communist countries to democratize their governments by granting loans and preferential trade status within the budget constraints imposed by budget deficits, a continuously rising national debt, and a domestic public opinion negative to foreign aid.

Finally, there is the China issue. Although the U. S. has established permanent, normal, trade relations with China, tensions continue to exist between the two countries. Part of this tension stems from U. S. support of Taiwan, an island off the coast of mainland China and once a part of China. At the end of World War II, the Chinese civil war between the communist forces of Mao Tsetung and the noncommunist (nationalist) forces of Chiang Kai-shek continued. In 1949, the defeated nationalist government fled to Taiwan. The U.S. helped save the regime and consequently prevented the communists from taking over Taiwan. The Chinese government still considers Taiwan a part of China while Taiwan considers itself the legitimate government of all of China. In recent years, the Taiwanese and their government officials have become increasingly in favor of establishing complete independence. The U.S. will face a tough policy choice ahead should Taiwan declare independence, an action that clearly might provoke a war with China. China is a nuclear power, a permanent member of the Security Council of the United Nations, and an emerging economic power. The bottom line is China could be a formidable enemy, more so than it was in the Korean War in the early 1950s. The one bright spot here is that China is one of the United States' largest trading partners. Americans buy more Chinese goods than the Chinese buy American goods—a trade imbalance. China is less likely to jeopardize such a profitable relationship.

CONCLUSION

After reading this chapter, you should now have a "feel" for how very complex making and carrying out foreign policy is. There are so many variables to be considered, and some situations require instantaneous responses. The United States, like every other country in the world, must make foreign policy choices on a daily basis, and like other countries, it does not always choose wisely. Although some might argue that a country should forget "morality" and always act in what it believes to be its best interests, it isn't all that easy to see what those "best interests" are sometimes. As the poet Robert Burns said: "The best laid plans of mice and men often go awry."[27]

Chapter Fourteen Notes

[1]James A. Nathan and James K. Oliver, *Foreign Policy Making and the American Political System,* 2d ed. (Boston: Little Brown & Co., 1987), 125.

[2]*Detroit Free Press*, 8 February 1987, 6 (A).

[3]*Detroit Free Press*.

[4]*Detroit Free Press*.

[5]Cited in Nick Easton, "New Technology from "Black World, CNN.com, 8 September, 2003.

[6]Source: Appendix E: Economic and Security Assistance, *Country Reports on Human Rights Practices, 2004*. U.S. Department of State, Bureau of Democracy, Human Rights, and Labor, February 28, 2005.

[7]*Detroit Free Press*, 3 August 1986, 6 (B).

[8]*Saginaw News*, 27 July 1988, 3 (A).

[9]The Pentagon is the building in which the Defense Department is housed, but the word can be used, as it is here, to mean the Defense Department.

[10]*Saginaw News*, 19 January 1986, 7 (G).

[11]Reuter News Service, "GAO Says Pentagon Made Millions in Overpayments," *Mercury Mail*, 12 May 1997.

[12]Reuter News Service, "U.S. Military Must Keep Two-War Force," *Mercury Mail*, 12 May 1997.

[13]Harold W. Stanley and Richard G. Niemi, *Vital Statistics on American Politics*, 1997-1998 (Washington, D.C.: Congressional Quarterly, Inc., 1998), 339.

[14]*Detroit Free Press*, 8 February 1987.

[15]*New York Times*, 16 November 1992, 16 (A).

[16]Kenneth Janda, Jeffrey M. Berry, and Jerry Goldman, *The Challenge of Democracy: Government in America,* 2d ed. (Boston: Houghton Mifflin Co., 1989), 718.

[17]Charles W. Kegley and Eugene Wittkopf, *American Foreign Policy: Pattern and Process,* 2d ed. (New York: St. Martin's Press, 1982), 287.

[18]*Saginaw News,* 16 October 1988, 1 (D).

[19]Elihu Katz, "The Two-Step Flow of Communications," *Public Opinion Quarterly* (Spring 1957): 61-78.

[20]Bernard C. Cohen, "The Influence of Special Interest Groups and Mass Media on Security Policy in the United States," in *Perspectives on American Foreign Policy,* ed. Charles W. Kegley and Eugene Wittkopf (New York: St. Martin's Press, 1983), 222-241.

[21]Nathan and Oliver, 288.

[22]Nathan and Oliver, 283.

[23]George F. Kennan, *American Diplomacy 1900-1950* (Chicago: University of Chicago Press, 1951); see also Stanley Hoffmann, *Gulliver's Troubles: The Setting of American Foreign Policy* (New York: McGraw-Hill Book Co., 1969), chap. 5.

[24]Frederic S. Pearson and J. Martin Rochester, *International Relations: the Global Condition in the Late Twentieth Century,* 2d ed.; (New York: Random House, 1988), 113.

[25]Pearson and Rochester, 114.

[26]As a pattern of foreign policy, interventionism is conflict, one of the seven patterns of foreign policy discussed earlier in Chapter 13.

[27]Robert Burns, "To a Mouse," 1785.

Suggested Readings

Barnet, Richard J., and John Caranagh. *Global Dreams: Imperial Corporations and New World Order*. New York: Simon & Schuster, 1994.

Cumings, Bruce. *The Origins of the Korean War*. Princeton: Princeton University Press, 1990.

Freedman, Lawrence, and Efraim Karsh. *The Gulf Conflict 1990-1991: Diplomacy and War in the New World Order*. Princeton: Princeton University Press, 1993.

Gordon, Michael R., and General Bernard E. Trainor. *The Generals' War: The Inside Story of the Conflict in the Gulf*. New York: Little, Brown & Co., 1995.

LaFeber, Walter. *America, Russia, and the Cold War, 1945-1990*. New York: McGraw-Hill Book Co., 1991.

Litwak, Robert S. *Détente and the Nixon Doctrine: American Foreign Policy and the Pursuit of Stability, 1969-1976*. New York: Cambridge University Press, 1984.

Markusen, Ann, and Joel Yudken. *Dismantling the Cold War Economy*. New York: HarperCollins, 1992.

Nathan, James, ed. *The Cuban Missile Crisis Revisited*. New York: St. Martin's Press, 1992.

Smoke, Richard. *National Security and the Nuclear Dilemma: An Introduction to the American Experience in the Cold War*. New York: McGraw-Hill Book Co., 1993.

Snow, Donald M. and Eugene Brown. *Puzzle Palaces and Foggy Bottom: U.S. Foreign and Defense Policy-Making in the 1990s*. New York: St. Martin's Press, 1994.

Chapter Fifteen

The Judicial Branch:
The Grand Ole Umpire

Although most Americans believe they understand their judicial system, three general misconceptions persist. The first is that the law is fixed and unchanging; what was law yesterday is law today. And, furthermore, in matters of law things are either right or wrong—in every instance and in every court of law. Nothing could be further from reality. American law is fluid, constantly changing, and often applied differently in seemingly identical cases. As former Justice Oliver Wendell Holmes once remarked, "A word is not a crystal, transparent, unchanging. It may vary greatly in content according to the circumstance, the time in which it is used."

The second misconception has to do with the ability of the courts to take action. Americans are an assertive people. When problems exist, they expect action. This same standard is applied to our judicial system, and citizens are frustrated when the courts fail to respond. The truth, however, is that the American system of justice is *passive*, meaning that before any action can be taken on a legal matter, the issue must be *brought* to a court. The courts cannot and do not go out looking for issues to resolve. In the words of Justice Robert H. Jackson, "Courts have no self-starter." When Congress enacts a law, it is not first reviewed by a court to see if it conforms to the Constitution before enforcement. Enforcement begins and continues until such time that a citizen brings the law before a court and demands a review to determine its constitutionality. In short, laws are assumed to be constitutional unless or until they are brought through the long appellate process and ruled unconstitutional.

Finally, most Americans see the judicial system strictly as an institution that enforces or oversees policy. This is not true either. Courts are more than mere dispensers of justice. By the way that they interpret the Constitution or laws written by the legislature, courts create policy. To appreciate this point, one only has to consider the controversy surrounding the Supreme Court's decisions on abortion, integration, affirmative action, school prayer, euthanasia, and a host of other issues that impact on the lives of American citizens.

In this chapter we will undertake a study of American judicial system. We will come to understand its power, its structure, the way it conducts its business, and the controversy surrounding its decisions. Finally, we will conclude with thoughts on its future direction.

Understanding Law

Law is a set of rules or regulations enacted by public officials and enforced by the courts (or other legally appointed bodies) to govern the conduct of citizens. In the United States two broad categories of law exist: criminal and civil.

Civil law attempts to govern relationships between people or settle disputes when people feel that they have been either injured or treated unfairly by others. For example, let us say that your neighbor decides to burn leaves one fall day and, due to carelessness, burns your house down to the foundation. Understandably you are upset and sue in an attempt to recover your losses. In such a case you will become the **plaintiff** and your neighbor would be the **defendant**. The trial would take place in a civil court and be presided over by a civil-court judge. A jury may or may not be present depending upon the wishes of the defendant. What would be absent would be a public prosecuting official since the state has no vested interest in the outcome. The outcome of civil cases is measured in dollars. If the plaintiff wins, the jury (if used) or the court (judge) will determine the extent of injury and award a settlement. Civil suits are not always just between individuals. It is possible for a person to sue the government or the government to sue an individual. Here a public official would act on behalf of the government, i.e., the government would have an "attorney" representing it.

Criminal law deals with wrongs committed against the general public. Local, state, and the national governments establish laws that regulate behavior for the purpose of creating a just and orderly society. Should an individual break a criminal law, the government will prosecute the offender because it has a vested interest in enforcing the laws of the society so that the society continues to function. Unlike a civil case, a public official representing the interest of the public as a whole will prosecute the case.

Under criminal law, crimes are classified by their seriousness. **Felonies** are serious offenses punishable by death (**capital punishment**) or imprisonment for more than a year depending upon the offense. **Misdemeanors** are less serious and usually punishable by a fine or imprisonment up to a year.

The Origins of American Law

American law has its roots in the English system of **common law**. Often referred to as "judge-made" or "bench-made" law, this type of law evolved during the medieval period in England to establish some uniformity in the way in which disputes were settled throughout the land. Prior to this attempt, conflicts were resolved according to local custom that varied considerably from one place to another. In the year 1066, the King's Court was created, and judges, acting under its authority, began traveling around the country hearing cases and rendering decisions. Cases were decided on the basis of custom and common sense as they applied to the facts. In time as the number of cases grew, the most important ones were gathered together and placed into annual yearbooks. Judges would then refer to these cases for guidance in resolving disputes currently before them. If no similar case could be found, a new decision would be made, and it would become a precedent for all future cases like it. **Precedent** refers to a court decision in an earlier case with facts and legal issues similar to those in a case currently before a court. Precedents are extremely important in the American judicial system since it creates stability and continuity in the law.

Other Sources of American Law

Important as it is in our legal system, common law does have its limitations. As a result, other sources of law have come into play.

One weakness in common law is its inability to prevent something from happening in advance. Suppose Elmer Schmaltz and his neighbor Beulah Bolt share a property line, and in the middle stands a magnificent oak tree. Elmer develops a sudden interest in growing vegetables, and the only place he has to put his garden is by the oak tree. Now we all know that a lot of sunshine is required for a good garden. Since the oak tree blocks out the sun, Elmer informs Beulah that he plans to chop it down over the weekend. Beulah protests, but he refuses to listen to reason. Under common law, Beulah would have to wait until the tree were cut down before taking action, but by then the damage would already have been done. To avoid this problem, a type of law termed **equity** was created. In this example, Beulah could just trot herself up to the court and get, if the court agreed with her position, an **injunction** prohibiting Elmer from cutting the tree down. A violation of the injunction would place him in **contempt of court** for which he could be heavily fined or, in some cases, jailed.

Modern society has moved more and more away from common law in favor of **statutory law**. Originating from legislatures or other legally empowered governmental bodies, this law, specifically detailed in the form of statutes, has replaced most areas previously governed solely by common law. In laymen's terms, statutory law just means laws that are actually written down by some legislative body, e.g., state legislature, Congress, city council, etc. The major role of the courts here is to determine what the elected officials intended when enacting the law and then applying that intention (meaning) to the facts in individual cases. In modern societies most law is statutory.

With the expansion of the federal government came a growth of bureaucratic agencies designed to regulate various activities in the marketplace or society. The Food and Drug Administration, Federal Communications Commission, and the Environmental Protection Agency are just a few examples. Such agencies function in a quasi-legal/judicial capacity; they establish rules and regulations (based upon statutory law), oversee compliance, and, in cases of violations, hear cases and assess penalties. These rules and regulations constitute a separate body of law called **administrative law**.

Constitutional law is the last and perhaps most important branch of law in our society. As we have discussed previously, our society is founded upon constitutional government. That means the supreme law of the land is the Constitution, which is superior to all the other types of law. For example, suppose Congress makes a law establishing a state religion. While not requiring people to belong to this state religion, everyone would be taxed to support it. Such a

An early drawing of an English judge scanning one of the annual yearbooks in hopes of finding some guidance for a case before him. The American system of law is rooted in the English system of "common law."

law would be an example of statutory law. However, this law would be in direct conflict with the First Amendment of the Constitution that expressly forbids the establishment of a state religion. Using its power of **judicial review**, a concept discussed later, the law would be declared "null and void" (unconstitutional). That court decision would be an example of constitutional law.

AMERICAN COURTS

Laws have little meaning or impact until applied. The purpose of a court of law is to function as a meeting area for the application of law. Due to our unique governmental structure, the American court system is quite different from those of other countries of the world.

An Adversary System

Courts in America function on an **adversary system**. What this means is that when a case comes before the court, the parties—plaintiff and defendant or, in the case of criminal law, state and defendant—function in the role of adversaries or, in other words, they compete against each other for a favorable ruling. For its part the court maintains a position of neutrality. It listens to both sides and then, based upon the facts of the case as they apply to the law, makes a ruling. One side will win; the other side will lose.

This adversary system is prescribed by Article III of the Constitution, which limits courts to hearing only "cases" and "controversies." Legally, this means that courts, as stated previously, must wait for cases to come to them. It is not within their realm to seek out cases for trial. Likewise, courts are not permitted to offer opinions before matters are brought before them. Consequently, the president, or anyone else for that matter, could not seek advice from a court in advance of any action he/she might want to take.

Jurisdiction and Standing

Your first task in taking a case before a court would be to determine **jurisdiction**. Jurisdiction is the power of a court to hear and decide a particular case. Three basic types of jurisdiction exist: subject matter, geographic, and hierarchical.

Subject matter refers to the nature of the subject brought before a court. Subject matter is divided into two broad classifications: **general jurisdiction** and **special jurisdiction** (sometimes termed "limited jurisdiction"). The majority of courts, both at the federal level and state level, possess general jurisdiction. These courts that have general jurisdiction are not limited (for the most part) in the types of cases they can hear. On the other hand, special jurisdiction is more focused on a special area. At the state level special jurisdiction courts would likely be those handling cases in highly technical areas such as probates and wills, divorce, child custody, juvenile matters, etc. Special jurisdiction courts at the federal level are those in the areas of taxation, customs, patents, and claims. State courts further divide subject matter into criminal and civil matters. Thus, some courts would hear only civil cases, and other courts would hear only criminal matters. This is not true of federal courts.

Geographical jurisdiction deals with the location of the court where the case is heard. The United States is divided into districts and regions with each court having jurisdiction over cases within its boundaries. It would not be possible for a defendant or the state to shop around for a court of its liking to try a case. Sometimes courts will surrender their jurisdiction in favor of another when a specific need arises. An example would be in a criminal case when it would be impossible, because of the publicity a particular case might have generated, to find an impartial jury. The case would then be moved to a different location to ensure that the constitutional rights of the defendant were observed. This change of location for the trial is called a change of venue.

Hierarchical jurisdiction is used to determine the level at which a case is brought to trial. On a hierarchical level, courts have either original or appellate jurisdiction. Original jurisdiction applies to courts in which cases are first heard. Once a trial is over, if any question concerning its outcome remains, as applied to rights or facts, it may be appealed to a higher court with appellate jurisdiction, meaning a court with the power to review decisions of lower courts. Upon review, the court would either *affirm* (let stand) or *reverse* (overturn) the original decision. Under certain circumstances, it is possible that the appellate court may order that the case be reheard in the lower courts. With the exception of the Supreme Court of the United States and state supreme courts, all other courts are limited to either original or appellate jurisdiction.

Standing is yet another important ingredient in our court system. By standing we mean that an individual must have a substantive interest in the outcome of a case before he/she can bring it to trial. In other words, individuals must be affected by the resolution of the conflict in some important way to affect their well being. Let's say that an airplane crashes in my community, and a number of passengers are killed. In a class-action lawsuit, the victims' relatives sue the airline responsible for negligence. Because the accident has so frightened me that I am no longer able to fly, I also feel injured and, thus, attempt to join the class-action suit of the others seeking a share of the settlement. The court would have to determine if my position merited standing. If so, I would be allowed to join the suit; if not, I would not be permitted to do so. Before standing is granted, a definable *legal* injury must occur. With regard to standing, injuries are classified as either public or private. A public injury would, of course, be a crime. A private injury is termed a tort. (Remember this is a *tort*, not a *torte*. The latter is wonderful layer cake with various kinds of tasty "goo" between the layers. It tastes much better than a tort.)

Duality of American Courts

Back to the concept of federalism. As we already understand, this means that we have a dual system of government in our country: we have state governments, and we have a national government. This same pattern of duality is reflected in the court system. With two separate governments enacting law, we require two separate court systems—state and national (federal).

Whereas the jurisdiction of state courts is somewhat open-ended, that of the federal courts is limited. The Constitution, in Article III, Section 2, states that the federal courts' jurisdiction is based upon **subject matter** (what the case is about) and, or, the **nature of the parties** (who the people are) in the case. In terms of subject matter, federal courts are limited to the following:

1. cases involving a constitutional issue,

2. violations of federal law,

3. questions concerning treaties,

4. matters involving admiralty and maritime law.

In regard to the nature of the parties, federal court jurisdiction is limited to the following:

1. any cases affecting ambassadors, or public ministers, and consuls of other countries

2. any case in which the United State government is a party,

3. any case in which citizens of different states would be a party,

4. any case between citizens of the same state claiming lands under grants from different states (relevant to the 18th and early 19th centuries, more than today),

5. any case between a state and a citizen of another state.

This distinction between federal and state jurisdiction is not as clear as represented by the above description. Sometimes, matters heard in state courts eventually are considered in federal courts. This is true where constitutional issues are present. For example, if a suspect is prosecuted and convicted of a robbery in a state court, it is possible for the case to end up in the Supreme Court of the United States. However, the case would center not on the defendant's guilt or innocence, but on whether the rights of the accused had been violated. Likewise, in some instances where the federal courts have jurisdiction, a case will first be sent down to the states for resolution. One such example would be cases involving a lawsuit between citizens of different states where the amount of damages sought is more than $50,000. Though clearly within federal district court's jurisdiction, the court generally requires that the individuals first seek a remedy at the state level.

STATE JUDICIAL SYSTEMS

Don't need to know all the way to 363.

Wide variation exists in both the structure and operation of state courts. Nevertheless, a general pattern is apparent. Most state court systems consist of four basic components: trial courts, special jurisdiction courts, intermediate appellate courts, and, at the very top, a state supreme court.

Trial Courts

Trial courts are those in which defendants face an accuser, testimony is given, and a decision is rendered. Three levels of trial courts are discernible in most state systems. The first is the **magistrate court**. Magistrates, or justices of the peace as they are more commonly titled, are either appointed or elected to serve the judicial needs of a smaller community. Ironically, though they have little formal legal training, they are the legal profession's "jack-of-all-trades," handling everything from disturbing the peace to performing marriages and everything of a minor civil or criminal nature in between. What legal training these individuals lacked, they made up for in judicial zeal, having a conviction rate exceeding 80 percent.[1] Soon the justice of the peace will only be a legend as most states are currently in the process of phasing out the magistrate court.

The second layer of trial courts is the one most familiar to Americans. Included here are traffic courts, police courts, small claims courts, night courts,

A local courthouse built at the turn of the century in the process of repair. Courthouses like this remind us of the duality of our judicial system.

and municipal courts. Though called by different names, their function is the same— to provide quick and inexpensive justice. Generally speaking, most trials at this level are bench trials. However, if a sentence of jail is possible, the defendant has the right to request a jury trial.

Circuit courts, the third level, are the real workhorses of the state trial system and the place where serious criminal and civil disputes are handled. This is also the first level that makes use of a **trial jury** (more formally termed a **petit jury**) to render a verdict in a case. Whether a jury is used is dependent upon the wishes of the defendant. If a jury is not used, the presiding judge would determine guilt or innocence.

The number of jurors used in a trial varies depending upon the requirements of the state and the charge against the defendant. Criminal juries normally have twelve jurors but can have as few as six. The Supreme Court has set six as the absolute minimum. The process of jury selection begins when potential jury members are seated in the jury box and questioned by attorneys from the opposing sides. Each side is permitted a specified number of **peremptory challenges**. Peremptory challenges are a limited number of challenges each side in a trial can use to eliminate potential jurors without stating a reason. However, they may not be used to keep members of a particular race or sex off the jury. Once the challenges are used up, the attorneys must appeal to the presiding judge stating grounds why an individual should not serve. These kinds of appeals to the judge are referred to as **challenges for cause**. Jury selection has become a science in itself with psychologists devoting their entire careers to it. Often the outcome of a trial hinges on jury selection.

Once a case has gone to a jury in a criminal trial and an acquittal verdict is returned, the judge must honor it and release the defendant. This is not true in civil cases. If a jury returns with a verdict that, in the opinion of the judge, is inconsistent with the evidence, he/she may throw it out and declare a mistrial. The case would then have to be retried.

Special Jurisdiction Courts

Special jurisdiction courts are characterized by their limited jurisdiction. Each court in the system oversees a particular area such as probates of wills and estates, divorces, juvenile, etc. Two basic purposes underlie the creation of these courts. The first is to take some of the pressure off the circuit courts so that they can concentrate on more serious matters. Second, the business of these courts is so specialized that a high level of expertise is needed. Focusing on a single area allows judges to develop this expertise and, thus, provides some measure of consistency in rulings.

One court with special jurisdiction that has attracted a great deal of attention lately is the small claims court. Few Americans have not heard about or seen "The People's Court." Although a television show, "The People's Court" is based on the real **small claims court** that provides an invaluable service. Before its creation many citizens were victimized by a legal system too expensive in which to seek a just remedy to their grievances. For example, let us say that one day your neighbor backs out of his driveway and destroys your mailbox. He promises to completely cover the expense of replacing it, so you hire a local handyperson to come dig out the old post that is set in concrete and replace it and the mailbox. You submit the bill to your neighbor, and he refuses to pay for it. Before the creation of the small claims court, you would have been helpless. The cost of hiring an attorney would not justify the cost of seeking a legal solution to the problem. Now with small claims court, you may bring your neighbor to court without having to hire an attorney. The process begins when the plaintiff (that's you) files a complaint with the court and pays a small filing fee.

Once filed, a court date is set, and a **summons** (a court order telling your neighbor to appear in court) is issued. Both plaintiff and defendant, without the aid of lawyers, present their case. Evidence is submitted, and the judge renders a binding verdict. In seeking a remedy in small claims court, the plaintiff is limited by two conditions. First, the claim cannot exceed a fixed dollar amount (usually $2,500). Second, the claim must be for actual loses. In other words, you cannot seek money for pain and suffering. One note of caution is in order. Your claim must be reasonable. Should you sue your neighbor and lose, he might well turn around and counter-sue to compensate for lost time. The burden would then fall upon you to prove that your case was not frivolous. This, of course, applies to all suits and is designed to protect against unreasonable harassment and frivolous litigation.

Intermediate Appellate Courts

Intermediate appellate courts have appellate jurisdiction only. They do not hear testimony or take evidence. Rather, they review transcripts and, on the basis of evidence presented during the original trial, make a decision either to sustain (let the original verdict stand), overturn the verdict, or order that a new trial be held.

State Supreme Court

Each state has one court that is the final court of appeals, usually referred to as the state supreme court. This court possesses both original and appellate jurisdiction. However, most of its cases arrive by means of appeal. Once it has ruled on an issue, all other state courts must fall into line and comply with its decision. Having lost in this court, a defendant's only other alternative would be to appeal to the Supreme Court of the United States. However, to do so, the defendant must prove that a substantial federal question is involved.

Arbitration: An Alternative to the Courts

Nearly every state now recognizes and provides for binding arbitration to settle legal problems. Like small claims courts, arbitration provides an alternative to lengthy and costly court proceedings. Here is how the process works. Let's assume that you and a neighbor decide to go into business together, making and selling greeting cards. Because you are better off financially, you agree to purchase all the necessary equipment, and your neighbor promises to reimburse you from his/her share of the profits. Unfortunately the business fails, and, realizing that there is no potential for future profits, you and your neighbor decide to close shop for good. You request payment for half of the company's losses that total $10,000. Your neighbor refuses, citing the original agreement whereby he/she would repay with profits from the sale of greeting cards. But, since you closed the company, there will never be any profits. You threaten a suit, but neither you or your neighbor wants to be subjected to the costs and publicity of a civil suit. Your alternative would be to select an outside arbitrator to hear and settle the case.

You and your neighbor would obtain a list of arbitrators licensed to hear your type of case from either the state or the American Arbitrators Association. Once you have agreed upon an arbitrator, he/she would set a mutually agreeable time to hear the dispute. Each of you would agree in writing to abide by the decision of the arbitrator. If you and your neighbor cannot agree upon an arbitrator, the following procedure is used. Each of you selects an arbitrator who, in turn, selects a third. All three arbitrators would then hear the case. However, your costs have now tripled since it is the contesting parties who must compensate the arbitrator(s). The arbitrator would hear the case and make a decision. If you disagree with the arbitrator's decision, your only recourse would be to appeal. But as is true of all appeals, you must have grounds to appeal (your neighbor lied, the arbitrator was biased, etc.), and it is up to the court to decide whether to grant your appeal.

Selection of State Judges

A high degree of variation also exists in how state judges are selected. In some states judges are elected directly by voters in popular elections. Here, when a judgeship becomes available, each party will select a candidate in accordance with state law and party rules. These candidates will then face one another, along with independents (if state law permits), in the general election. After the election the winning candidate will, at least theoretically, cut party ties and serve in a nonpartisan capacity for an initial term. Once this term has expired, the judge will, in most systems, face the voters again. However, in this election, the incumbent judge does not face a challenger but, rather, runs on his/her record and voters cast ballots either to retain or not to retain. A vote of 60 percent is usually required for the incumbent to gain another term. In some states judges are appointed either by the governor or by a special commission established to review candidates and make selections to the bench. Continued service is then conditional, based upon "good behavior." It is generally true that most state systems have both elected and appointed positions, depending upon the court. Also, should a vacancy suddenly appear in an elected position, most states allow for an appointment until an election can be held.

Both of the above systems have weaknesses. In an elected system, the rule of thumb is that to be a judge one must "play ball" with the dominant political organization in the district. If not, it is difficult to secure the party's endorsement for a spot on the ticket. Judgeships in these systems are often used as political "plums" to reward good party members, and unfortunately the best candidate is not always endorsed. The end result is a system where "it is the politicians who select the judges. The voters only ratify their choices."[2] Systems in which judges are appointed also have disadvantages. Voters are denied direct input into the selection and retention of their judges. If a judge does perform poorly or perhaps is found to be unethical, the voters have no recourse except to rely upon the wisdom and integrity of review boards who themselves are appointed. Furthermore, the membership of such boards represents political compromises between parties and, thus, is either slow or incapable of taking action when needed.

To overcome these disadvantages, many states have moved to a system that has been termed the **Missouri Plan**. Adopted in Missouri in 1940, this system attempts to combine elements of both election and appointment. When a seat on the bench becomes vacant, a nonpartisan commission, consisting of lawyers, a judge, and citizens, reviews applicants and selects three worthy candidates. This list is then sent to the governor who will make the final selection from the three names. The winning candidate serves an initial term and then, on the merit of his/her record, must face the voters directly to gain additional terms. Seventeen states employ some version of the Missouri Plan.[3] Citizens from states using this method have expressed overwhelming satisfaction with the plan, replacing only thirty-three judges of the more than 14,000 seeking re-election.[4] The average citizen, however, feels strongly that judges should be elected.

Tenure of State Judges

In elected systems judges serve anywhere between four and ten years. In Maryland the term is fifteen years. Judges in appointive systems generally serve longer with some being appointed for life (Rhode Island and Massachusetts). Judges in New Jersey are appointed by the governor for a term of seven years and then, if reappointed, serve for life as long as they perform properly.

Until recently, the only way to remove an unfit or unethical judge was through election or impeachment and conviction. However, as statistics would demonstrate, few judges ever are not re-elected or impeached even though many are deserving. Now, in most states judges can be removed by judicial conduct committees or special courts for a variety of reasons relating to unfitness.

THE FEDERAL JUDICIAL STRUCTURE

Compared to that of the state's, the federal judiciary is relatively simple. At its core are the U.S. District Court, U.S. Court of Appeals, and the U.S. Supreme Court. While there exist other courts both in and out of the judicial system, these three courts define the federal judicial structure.

U.S. District Courts

The U.S. District Courts (not to be confused with state district courts) carry the load in the federal judiciary, handling over 300,000 criminal, civil, and bankruptcy cases annually. Less than 20 percent of these cases is criminal. Currently there are ninety-four of these courts spread across the United States and its territories. Each state has its own U.S. District Court, and boundary lines never cross state lines. Some districts cover just part of a state, like the Northern District of California. The number of judges serving each district court varies, depending upon the amount of population and litigation (lawsuits) in the area. Currently there are about 662 serving the U.S. District courts. Also, within each district is a **U.S. Bankruptcy Court**, a part of the District Court that administers the bankruptcy laws.

All federal cases, both criminal and civil, begin in the district court. Having only original jurisdiction, these courts are the trial courts for the federal judiciary. As such, they are the courts where federal juries are formed, testimony is given, evidence is weighed, and verdicts are rendered based upon federal law and the facts in the cases. Federal juries must have twelve members, and all decisions must be unanimous. **Bench trials** (trials without juries where the judge makes the final determination) are permissible if so desired by the defendant and agreed upon by the presiding judge. Federal civil cases also have juries if the amount in question is greater than $20 (set by the Constitution and never amended). However, federal civil juries are smaller, sometimes consisting of as few as six members, and their decisions need not be unanimous.

U.S. Courts of Appeals

Congress placed each of the ninety-four districts in one of twelve regions, or circuits, as they are frequently called. Each circuit has a court of appeals. If you lose a case in a district court, you can ask the court of appeals to review the case to see if the district judge applied the law correctly. While there are twelve circuits, there are actually thirteen separate courts of appeals. The Twelfth Court of Appeals is for the District of Columbia. The thirteenth, which has nation-wide jurisdiction, was added in 1982 and hears appeals from certain courts and agencies, such as the U.S. Court of International Trade, the U.S. Court of Federal Claims, the U.S. Patent and Trademark Office, and certain types of cases from the district courts (mainly lawsuits by people claiming their patents have been infringed). There are about 180 judges serving in the U.S. Court of Appeals.

Federal appeals court judges must hear the case of any party who has lost a case in the lower court, including regulatory agencies. When reviewing cases, judges sit in panels ranging from 3 to 15 members. Each side presents its argument in what is termed a **brief**. Usually briefs are presented in written form, and the court simply reviews the evidence presented in the original trial. However, in cases judged by the court to be of extreme interest, oral arguments are permitted with each side being allotted a specified period of time in which to present its views. In either case, no new evidence is allowed. After hearing oral arguments or reviewing briefs separately, the judges meet privately to discuss their views and vote. The decision is then announced publicly.

The U.S. Supreme Court

There is only one Supreme Court of the United States, and it dominates the judicial system. Once the Court, as it is usually referred to, decides an issue, all other courts, both federal and state, must "fall into line." Although the number of judges sitting on the Court has varied over time, being as low as five (1789) at one time and as many as ten at another (1863), it has not changed since 1869 when Congress fixed the number at nine. The Supreme Court possesses both original and appellate jurisdiction. Its original jurisdiction is limited to four types of cases:

1. a case involving the United States government and a state,

2. a case between two states,

3. a case involving a foreign ambassador,

4. a case in which a state brings suit against a citizen of another state, alien, or a foreign country.

The Supreme Court sits atop the federal judiciary and is the final arbitrator of all disputes on matters concerning the Constitution, federal laws, and treaties. Furthermore, once the Court has spoken, its decision is final. There is no higher authority in our country to which to appeal, however, an amendment may be added to the Constitution to negate the Court's decision, but this action is rare.

The Court's Work Schedule

The work of the Supreme Court begins on the first Monday in October and normally ends sometime around the latter part of June or early July. The Court may extend its session on an emergency basis as it did in 1974 to resolve the conflict between President Nixon and Congress over the "Watergate tapes," but this is rarely done. Most cases of interest or those needing attention are simply placed on next year's calendar. When in session, the Court hears oral arguments from 10:00 in the morning to noon and 1:00 to 3:00 in the afternoon on Mondays, Tuesdays, Wednesdays, and Thursdays, if needed. Fridays are reserved for conferences in which the judges meet to discuss and vote on cases. The Court organizes the presentations of oral arguments into seven, two-week segments scattered throughout its session with the recesses between being used for research and opinion writing. Contrary to popular opinion, the workload of a justice is substantial and demanding. It has been estimated that the justices read an average of twenty-five pounds of briefs each week the Court is in session.

Cases: Making it to the Supreme Court

Relatively speaking, the Supreme Court hears very few cases. Of the 10 million or so cases heard in all courts in the United States each year, about 7,000 will eventually end up on the Supreme Court's docket. Of these, the Court will usually schedule fewer than 200 for oral arguments with the rest being affirmed, dismissed, or reversed through a **memorandum of decision,** or **memorandum opinion**. This is a brief statement by a judge announcing his/her ruling without detail or without giving extensive reasons. Such memoranda (plural) are issued by appeals courts in language such as: "The petition of appellant is denied for the reasons stated in *Albini v. Younger,*" or "The decision below is affirmed."[5]

There are three ways to appeal a case to the Supreme Court. The first, and least successful method, is by **certification**. Here a lower court would request technical instructions from the Supreme Court. The second method of appeal is by a **writ of appeal** in which the appeal is based upon a "theoretical right" to have the case reviewed by the Supreme Court. This method is used when a question arises whether a state law or provision of the state's constitution conflicts with a federal law, treaty, or the national Constitution. However, simply raising the issue is no guarantee that the appeal will be granted. The Court must determine first that a "substantial" constitutional question exists, and in the vast majority of cases the Court refuses to grant the appeal.

The most successful method of having a case brought before the Court is through a **writ of certiorari**, a Latin phrase meaning "made more certain." The process is initiated by the petitioner (losing party) from either a lower federal court or the court of last resort in a state (usually the state supreme court). In determining which cases to review, the Court uses the "rule of four." If four justices agree that "there are special and important reasons" for reviewing a case, and so vote, a writ of *certiorari* is issued directing the lower court to send the records of the case to the Supreme Court for review.

Appealing a case to the Supreme Court can be an extremely expensive affair, costing up to over $100,000. Likewise, the rules for filing an appeal are very complicated, requiring a great amount of technical skill. Realizing the potential this procedure has for injustice, namely, that unless one has a great deal of money, it is impossible to appeal, the Court has allowed a more relaxed standard for petitions filed **in forma pauperis**, or petitions filed "in the manner of a pauper." Though crudely prepared by "jailhouse lawyers" and often handwritten on a single sheet of paper, such appeals have contributed much to our understanding of justice and the Bill of Rights. In the event that the petitioner cannot afford the filing fee, this fee will be waived.

Oral Arguments

To be selected to argue a case before the Supreme Court is considered the highest honor of the legal profession. In cases involving the United States, the solicitor general of the Justice Department is the government's lawyer. Litigants (the plaintiff and the defendant) are expected to furnish their own attorneys, if able. If a defendant is too poor to hire an attorney, the Court will appoint one without fee. Once notice has been served that oral arguments will be taken, both sides must submit lengthy briefs citing both law and precedent favoring their positions. The contending party (the one wishing to overturn the original verdict) is given forty-five days thereafter in which to submit a brief. Once filed, the answering party (the one wishing to have the original verdict sustained) has thirty days in which to submit a brief. Upon occasion the Court will request that an interested third party participate by submitting **amicus curiae**, or "friend of the court" briefs.

The rules for presenting oral arguments are rigid and strictly adhered to. Each side is allotted a half-hour, sometimes an hour if the case is complicated, in which to present its brief. The reading of briefs is highly discouraged. Attorneys must present their case in a lively and forceful manner if they expect to win. During the presentation itself, judges are allowed to, and often do, interrupt to ask questions. Many times the questions are so pointed that lawyers have complained that the judges are actually baiting them. Even if interrupted, the lawyer is still expected to finish on time. The lectern from which the presenter speaks contains two lights—one white, the other red—that inform the lawyer of the time. When the white is lit, five minutes remain; when the red light flashes, time has expired, and the presenter must quit immediately even if in the middle of a sentence.

Conference Friday

Each Friday the justices file into the oak-paneled conference chamber to review cases. Here again formality dominates. Upon entering, each justice shakes the hand of all others present, just as they do before entering upon the bench to hear arguments, and then takes his/her place around a rectangular table. Conferences are strictly private with only the justices in attendance. Once the justices enter, the doors are locked, and no record of any conversation is kept. After each justice has spoken and the case has been thoroughly reviewed, the Justices vote. A simple majority of those voting decides the issue. In some cases, because of a potential conflict of interest, a justice will not vote on a case. For example, most Supreme Court Justices served as judges in lower federal courts. If one of the justices had rendered a decision in a case in a lower court, the Justice merely excuses himself/herself from the case before the Supreme Court.

Opinion Writing

Once a decision is reached, the Court usually puts it in writing. The chief justice, if voting with the majority, will decide who shall write the opinion. If the chief justice does not vote with the majority, the next most senior member will decide who will write the opinion. Opinions are extremely important because the wording will set the precedent for all other courts in the land to follow. Preparing an opinion is a satisfying but demanding task. Even though a majority of the Court agreed with the decision, more often than not, they agreed for different reasons. The opinion's author must take this into consideration and find a compromise that will appease all members voting with the majority. Once completed, this becomes the **majority opinion** and for practical purposes the new law.

If a justice who has voted with the majority does not believe that the Court's opinion reflects an understanding of his/her views, a **concurring opinion** may be written. Such opinions generally are an elaboration of the views of a single justice. **Dissenting opinions** are also permitted. Here, a justice having strong views on the case, but having voted with the minority, will offer a personal opinion in opposition to the majority opinion. Though it will have no current value, it can set the stage for a future attempt to reverse the Court's view.

The decision is presented to the public, in open session, in summary form. The author of the majority opinion will speak for the Court. Justices who have written concurring and dissenting opinions are also permitted to summarize their views. After the necessary editing, the Court logs its opinions in the *United States Reports,* a journal available in most college and public libraries.

Entry way to the Supreme Court of the United States.

Special Courts

There are other courts in the federal system. Two of them are part of the Judicial Branch, but the remainder are not. They were created by Congress at various times to serve in a very limited jurisdiction. Besides the courts listed below, some United States territories (Guam, the U.S. Virgin Islands, and the Northern Mariana Islands) also have district courts that function as both federal and "state" courts.

The **Court of Appeals for the Armed Forces** was designed to insure a military judicial system that balanced the need to maintain discipline in the armed forces with the desire to give military personnel rights paralleling as nearly as possible the rights enjoyed by accused persons in the civilian community.

The **Court of Appeals for Veterans Claims**, was created in 1988. This federal court is not part of the Department of Veterans Affairs (VA), and it is not connected to the Board of Veterans' Appeals (BVA), which is an administrative body within VA. Cases come to this court from the BVA, and most cases deal with disability or survivor benefits, but a few deal with education benefits, life insurance, home loan foreclosure, or waiver of indebtedness.

Established in 1982, the **United States Court of Federal Claims** is a part of the Judicial Branch and is authorized to hear primarily money claims founded upon the Constitution, federal statutes, executive regulations, or contracts, express or implied-in-fact, with the United States. This court has been given new jurisdiction in the area of bid protests, as well as jurisdiction in vaccine compensation, civil liberties, product liability, oil spills, and various other areas of the law over the last two decades.

The **United States Tax Court**, established by Congress in 1924, decides controversies between taxpayers and the Internal Revenue Service involving underpayment of federal income, gift, and estate taxes. Its decisions may be appealed to the federal courts of appeals and are subject to the review of the U.S. Supreme Court on *writs of certiorari*. The Tax Court hears cases in approximately 80 cities, and its offices are located in Washington, D.C.

Congress established the **Foreign Intelligence Surveillance Court in 1978.** The Court was created for the purpose of passing on requests for surveillance and physical searches that are aimed at foreign powers and their agents, and ensuring that the rights of "United States persons" are protected in the process. No finding of probable cause that a crime has been committed is required, as is required for search warrants issued by federal and state courts. This court's ability to grant such warrants was expanded by the passage of the Patriot Act, which was aimed at preventing future terrorist acts. There has been an increase in requests for warrants since the antiterrorism law was enacted.

The existence of the court in question is no secret. It consists of eleven U. S. District judges appointed by the Chief Justice of the United States. Appeals from this court are heard by a court of review, consisting of three district court judges, also appointed by the Chief Justice. Of course, as with any application for a search or surveillance, the target of the request is not given notice or an opportunity to respond, for obvious reasons. Therefore, there is no procedure to take an appeal from an order *granting* a request. Supposedly, this court has granted between 7500 and 10,000 warrants for surveillance of some kind since its inception and has denied the government's request rarely.

Finally, there is the **United States Court of International Trade, which,** like the Court of Federal Claims, is part of the Judicial Branch. In the Customs Court Act of 1980, Congress created the U.S. Court of International Trade to deal with cases involving international trade and customs duties. Most of its cases concern the classification and valuation of imported merchandise, customs duties, and unfair import practices by trading partners.

SELECTION OF FEDERAL JUDGES

The Constitution of the United States clearly sets forth the procedure for the selection of Supreme Court judges. Article II, Section 2, dictates that the president shall nominate people to the Supreme Court with the advice and consent of the Senate. The method of selection for other federal judges was left for Congress to determine. To avoid confusion, Congress elected to follow the same procedure—presidential nominations followed by senatorial confirmation. Although the procedure seems straightforward, the fact that the president and the Senate are jointly responsible for filling the federal judiciary ensures each appointment, regardless of the level, will contain a heavy dose of politics.

Nomination of Federal Judges

Interestingly, the Constitution establishes no requirements to qualify as a candidate to the federal judiciary. Likewise, there are no congressional laws on the subject. Does that mean that any one of us could become a federal judge tomorrow? Theoretically yes; practically no. Custom and politics dictate that all nominees must have a law degree and some prior judicial experience; otherwise, they would be rejected as unworthy. Although the first qualification, that of a law degree, is taken as a must, the second, prior experience, has been a debatable item. More specifically, debate has raged over what constitutes prior experience and how much is necessary to qualify an individual to such a high position. President Reagan's appointment of Daniel Manion, a small-town Indiana lawyer, to the U.S. Court of Appeals is a case in point. With no experience on the bench (state or national), Manion's main qualification seemed to be his conservative philosophy. Although many senators complained bitterly and attempted to block the confirmation, others pointed out that if experience were an absolute prerequisite, some of the great justices in our country's history (Chief Justices Taney, Fuller, and Warren and Associate Justices Story, Brandeis, Sutherland, and Frankfurter) would never have served. In the end Manion was confirmed.

Although the politics of nomination change, the nomination procedure remains the same. When a federal judicial seat needs to be filled, the president selects the individual and forwards the name to the Senate. The Senate Judiciary Committee will open hearings on the nomination. Testimony is offered by individuals familiar with the nominee, background checks are reviewed, and finally the individual is questioned personally by committee members in open hearings. In the meantime, as mandated by custom, a blue slip is sent to the senators from the state where the judge will serve. This practice, termed senatorial courtesy, provides senators a nonverbal way to pass judgment on the nominee. Not returning the blue slip would constitute disapproval.

Although the process is the same for all federal judges, the politics differs considerably, depending upon the level of the court for which the appointment is made. The difference, of course, is reflects the importance both the Senate and the president attach to each of the three basic courts in our judiciary. In the case of district court judges, senatorial courtesy is the rule. Here the president will contact the senator or senators of the state in which the seat is available and request a nomination. If neither senator is from the president's party, then an independent panel is formed to search for an appropriate candidate. It is well understood by all, even independent panels, that the candidate should be a member of the president's party. In the case of appeals court judges, senatorial courtesy is not an important factor because judges here serve more than one state. Also, since cases at the appeals level are more important, the president will take a greater interest. Selections to the Supreme Court are considered the strict domain of the president. An appointment to the Supreme Court can, in some respects, be viewed as the most important decision the president has to make. Members of the Supreme Court will serve for life unless removed from the bench through impeachment and conviction, something that has never happened in our history. Only one Supreme Court justice has been impeached (Samuel Chase in 1805), and in that case the Senate failed to vote for conviction. Thus, a president who is careful in his selection has the opportunity to influence future policy decisions long after leaving office.

The Supreme Court: The Nomination Process

Politics and Selection. The single most important factor in the selection of a Supreme Court nominee is political philosophy. The president will attempt to select a candidate whose political view comes closest to matching his own. This usually means that a president will select an individual from the ranks of his own political party. Of course, this is no guarantee that the candidate's views will not change once on the bench. In fact, history has demonstrated that many presidents have been sorely disappointed by individuals they have elevated to the Supreme Court. President Eisenhower's appointment of Earl Warren for chief justice illustrates this point. With Earl Warren at the helm, the Court was launched into a "liberal revolution" emphasizing human rights over property rights and national standards over state standards in Bill of Rights' issues. Eisenhower was later to have remarked, "It was the biggest damn-fool mistake I ever made."[6] Many legal experts consider Earl Warren's leadership to have been the most important to the Court since that of our nation's first Chief Justice John Marshall.

Background Factors. Age, race, sex, religion, and area of residence are also important factors taken into consideration by a president when making selections to the Court. President Reagan's appointment of Sandra Day O'Connor to the Supreme Court is one such example. Never before had a woman served on the Court. In the 1960s, various women's rights groups began to exert electoral pressure on presidential candidates to nominate a woman. These efforts finally produced results when Ronald Reagan promised, if elected, to nominate the first woman. Though seen as a campaign ploy to counter growing criticism of his insensitivity toward the women's rights issue, President Reagan made good on his pledge with the retirement of Potter Stewart. Generally known for her conservative views, Sandra Day O'Connor believes the Court should limit its role in the policy-making area of our government.

In terms of other background factors, the Court has been overwhelmingly white. Only two African Americans, Thurgood Marshall and Clarence Thomas, have ever served on the Court. From a religious standpoint, Protestants have dominated with the majority coming from the higher-status denominations of Episcopalians, Presbyterians, and Methodists. Catholics, Lutherans,

Table 15.1

The Supreme Court, 2005

Name	Birth Year	Appointment Year	Political Party	Law School	Appointment President	Religion
William H. Rehnquist	1924	1971/1986*	R	Stanford	Nixon	Lutheran
John Paul Stevens	1920	1975	R	Chicago	Ford	Nondenominational Protestant
Sandra D. O'Connor	1930	1981	R	Stanford	Reagan	Episcopalian
Antonin Scalia	1936	1986	R	Harvard	Reagan	Catholic
Anthony Kennedy	1936	1988	R	Harvard	Reagan	Catholic
David Souter	1939	1990	R	Harvard	Bush	Episcopalian
Clarence Thomas	1948	1991	R	Yale	Bush	Catholic
Ruth Bader Ginsburg	1933	1993	D	Columbia	Clinton	Jewish
Stephen Breyer	1938	1994	D	Harvard	Clinton	Jewish

*Chief Justice

and Baptists have traditionally been underrepresented while Unitarians (a liberal denomination that stresses individual choice and an acceptance of all beliefs) have been overrepresented in terms of their numbers. Presidents have attempted to maintain a Catholic and a Jewish seat on the bench although interruptions have occurred. This has been done to balance the Court as well as to gain the favor of these two, large voting blocks.

The vast majority of justices have graduated from college. Those who didn't were generally appointed in the nineteenth century when a college education was not as commonplace. Perhaps our most famous justice, John Marshall (1801–1835), had only six weeks of legal training. Today, all justices have advanced degrees beyond the baccalaureate, a fact reflected by their occupational backgrounds, the most common of which is either a private law practice or state or federal judgeships. A substantial number of our justices has come from the ranks of executive federal posts such as secretary of state, secretary of the navy, etc. Seven U.S. Attorney Generals, as well as two of their deputies, have found their way to the Court. Other appointments can be seen in Table 15.2.

Confirmation. As we know, presidents appoint Supreme Court justices, but the Senate has a check on this power through its own power of confirmation. A simple majority is needed to win approval. Rarely does the Senate not approve the president's choice. Generally speaking, the selection of Supreme

Court justices is viewed almost as an inherent right of the president, a way of carrying out the mandate upon which he was elected. In the entire history of our country, the Senate has failed to confirm less than 30 nominations to the Supreme Court with most occurring in the nineteenth century. Most recently failure to confirm nominees has revolved around the issue of ideology. Many liberal members of the Senate are threatening to filibuster the nomination of conservative Supreme Court nominees. Republicans, who currently control the majority in the Senate (2005), have countered with proposals to eliminate filibusters from the judicial nominating process. Some scholars assert that the Senate's confirmation power of "advise and consent" should be limited only to ensuring the nominees are legally qualified, not whether they espouse the correct political ideology. Others have noted that, since the justices have a lifetime appointment and the power, in effect, to say what the law is, a thorough examination of their philosophy is not only appropriate but necessary. The conflict remains unresolved, and future nominations are sure to rekindle the controversy.

THE POWER OF THE COURT

The United States Supreme Court is "distinctly American in concept and function," as Chief Justice Charles Evans Hughes (1930-1941) observed. Few other courts in the world have the same authority of constitutional interpretation and none have exercised it for as long or with as much influence. Alexis de Tocqueville, the same French political commentator who essentially described the United States as a nation of joiners in reference to pressure groups, also noted more than 150 years ago that "A more imposing judicial power was never constituted by any people." Once the Court has spoken, neither the president, Congress, or the states can overrule it, except by constitutional amendment or another Supreme Court decision.

Judicial Review

We are a constitutional government. All laws and actions of public officials must be in harmony with the Constitution. If not, they are subject to being declared "null and void" by the Court. The Court's right to invalidate acts that are in conflict with the Constitution is referred to as **judicial review.**

Curiously, judicial review is not mentioned anywhere in the Constitution. Rather, the Court has conferred upon itself this power through its own interpretation of constitutional language. In terms of state laws and state court decisions, the Supreme Court points to Article VI of the Constitution, which declares that all federal statutes and treaties "shall be the supreme Law of the Land." Likewise, the Constitution further states that "judges in every state shall be bound thereby, anything in the Constitution or laws of any State to the

Table 15.2: Background of Supreme Court Justices

Occupational Position before Appointment

Private legal practice	25
State judgeship	21
Federal judgeship	28
U.S. Attorney General	7
Deputy or Assistant U.S. Attorney General	2
U.S. Solicitor General	2
U.S. Senator	6
U.S. Representative	2
State Governor	3
Federal executive posts	9
Other	3

Religious background

Protestant	83
Roman Catholic	11
Jewish	6
Unitarian	7
No religious affiliation	1

Age on Appointment

Under 40	5
41-50	31
51-60	58
61-70	14

Political Party Affiliation

Federalist (to 1835)	13
Democrat-Republican (to 1828)	7
Whig (to 1861)	1
Democrat	44
Republican	42
Independent	1

Educational Background

College graduate	92
Not a college graduate	16

Sex

Male	106
Female	2

Race

Caucasian	106
Other	2

Source: Congressional Quarterly, *Congressional Quarterly's Guide to the U.S. Supreme Court*, (Washington, D.C.: Congressional Quarterly Press, 1996) and author's update.

contrary notwithstanding." Few legal scholars would take exception to the Court's interpretation on this point. However, in regard to acts of the national legislature or the president, the Constitution is less clear. Nevertheless, early in our nation's history, Chief Justice John Marshall, in the famous case of *Marbury v. Madison*, stated:

> *It is emphatically the province and duty of the judicial department to say what the law is. Those who apply a rule to particular cases, must of necessity expound and interpret that rule... A law repugnant to the Constitution is void; ...courts, as well as other departments, are bound by that instrument.*[7]

What Marshall attempted to point out here was that, if we were to remain a constitutional government, the national government, as well as the states, would have to be bound by the Constitution. Furthermore, according to his logic, the judiciary, basically because it is in the position of applying law to individual cases, should be the institution in charge of safeguarding the Constitution.

Although no Supreme Court in the history of the United States has reversed Marshall's position, it has not always been, nor is it today, totally accepted. Many critics maintain that the Court should not have the power of judicial review. They base their argument on the following propositions.

1. The Constitution does not expressly delegate this power to the courts.

2. Abuses or errors of the other two branches, the legislative and the executive, are best corrected either by themselves or by each other through constitutional checks and balances built into our government. If not, the people are capable of correcting the problem themselves through the electoral process.

3. And finally, judicial review violates the principle of majority rule by putting supreme power in the hands of nonelected officials who serve for life terms.

On the other hand, those who accept the concept of judicial review argue that without it the judicial branch would have no way to check the other two branches, and, thus, it would not be an equal partner in our government as originally intended by the writers of the Constitution.

Also, advocates of judicial review point out that the Court, though possessing this power, has rarely used it to nullify acts of Congress. Since the origins of judicial review (1803), the Court has declared fewer than 125 congressional laws unconstitutional. If anything, the Court has used its power of judicial review to affirm the vast majority of legislative acts that have been challenged, a point often overlooked by those who oppose the concept. For the most part, the Court has exercised its power of judicial review as a means to strike down acts of state legislatures that conflict with the national Constitution. Thus, judicial review has been far more important in controlling states than it has been in controlling the president or Congress.

Activism versus Self-Restraint

Despite all the debate, judicial review is accepted by most legal scholars as a legitimate and defensible constitutional position. More often than not, the debate regarding judicial review now centers on the *extent* and *purpose* the Court should use its power. Two basic positions prevail. The first is **judicial activism**, which advocates a strong and forceful judiciary very much involved in the policy-making arena. This attitude dominated the thinking of the Supreme Court during the Warren years (1953 to 1969). Led by Chief Justice Warren, the decisions of the Court went far beyond simply applying the Constitution to cases before it. Instead, it began to use its power either to create or alter policies enacted by the Congress or by the states. In 1954, the Court began its trek toward activism with the case of *Brown v. Board of Education,*[8] in which it officially outlawed segregation of public schools. A series of rulings followed, directing schools to desegregate even if it meant busing children from one district to another. Likewise, in the area of criminal rights, the Court pushed the meaning of individual rights in criminal matters far beyond that which the national and state legislatures were willing to afford suspects. Miranda, Gideon, and Escobedo became household names as the courts freed hundreds of suspects denied basic rights by law enforcement officials. Schools and local communities were instructed by the Court to cease activities such as school prayer, Christmas plays with religious overtones, or the expenditure of public funds to purchase items that might violate the principle separation of church and state as prohibited in the First Amendment.

For its part the Warren Court defended its activism on four basic points:

1. Many groups in our society do not receive adequate representation in our government—minorities, women, the handicapped, the poor, etc. This is not the way democracy should ideally work, but it is reality in a popularly elected government in which public officials are easily swayed by powerful and highly organized interest groups. All too often, the Court is the last hope for many of our citizens.

2. The Court also has an obligation to protect citizens from their own inattentiveness. It is a complicated and busy world. Too often we, as citizens, are unaware, unprepared, or too preoccupied with the immediate day-to-day problems in our own lives to worry about rights. This does not mean that we do not want our political and civil liberties protected. Activists argue that the creators of our government intended the Court to function in this role by acting as an "intermediate body" between the government and the people.[9]

3. Judicial activism is necessary to an ever-changing society relying upon a Constitution written over two hundred years ago. If the Court did not continually reinterpret the Constitution based upon the changing values of each new generation, the Constitution would rapidly outlive its usefulness. The only alternative to judicial activism would be to update the Constitution through the amendment process. But this would have required literally hundreds of amendments that, in the end, would produce a legal nightmare for both the courts and the citizens.

4. And finally, the Court has a solemn obligation to uphold the Constitution even if no constituency exists or even if the view might be contrary to the wishes of the public. Such cases, because of their potential unpopularity, are going to be avoided by the other two branches. As one political observer noted, "Few American politicians even today would care to run on a platform of desegregation, pornography, abortion, and the 'coddling' of criminals."[10] Likewise, maintain advocates, if the Court's views are so repugnant to the public as to be intolerable, constitutional amendments can be added to correct the situation.

While accepting the practice of judicial review, many, including some justices, believe the Court has gone too far in its use. Associate Justice Felix Frankfurter urged the Court to accept the doctrine of judicial restraint in matters of law. This doctrine holds that judges should decide a case on its own merit according to legally established precedent and refrain from interjecting their own values and policy preferences. Judicial restraint also advocates a literal reading of the Constitution when called upon to decide the constitutionality of laws or acts of public officials. The arguments most commonly mentioned in support of this position are as follows.

1. Judicial activism encourages the development of big government at the expense of the states and the individual. Big government ultimately leads to the centralization of decision making in the hands of the few and, thus, constitutes the single, greatest threat to democracy.

2. Judicial activism encourages people to be lazy and inattentive to government because they believe that the Court will protect their political and civil rights. This undermines that spirit that is most needed in democratic government—citizen participation.

3. Federal judges are not elected and serve a life term. Thus, they are not accountable to the voters. Policy making, according to the constitutional framework of this nation and in line with the intentions of the framers, was placed in the hands of the legislature. If a legislative act clearly contradicts a provision of the Constitution, it should be declared "null and void." If not, then the Court should allow the legislative branch

and the people to work their will rather than trying to interpret the Constitution to include the justices' personal values.

4. The Constitution will not become outdated as suggested by those advocating "judicial activism." The task of keeping up will merely pass to the national and state legislatures as well as other public officials elected to serve the people. After all, contend supporters of judicial restraint, such officials are better equipped to determine the "public will" because of their direct election and accountability to the people.

Regardless of one's views associated with the debate over activism versus self-restraint, the history of the Court demonstrates a consistent pattern of adherence to the following rules of self-restraint:

1. The Court will not pass upon the constitutionality of legislation in a non adversary proceeding but only in an actual case. The court will thus not act in an advisory capacity to either the executive or legislative branch of government.

2. The Court will not decide hypothetical cases; it is not an anticipatory institution.

3. The Court will not pass upon a constitutional question if some other ground exist upon which it may dispose of the case.

4. The Court will not formulate a rule of law broader than required by the precise facts to which it must be applied.

5. The Court will not pass upon the validity of a law if the complainant fails to show that he or she has been injured by the law or if the complainant has availed himself or herself of the benefits of the law.

6. The Court will make every effort to hold a law constitutional. This is a clear example of the Court honoring the principle of separation of powers.

7. A litigant must have exhausted all remedies available in lower federal or state courts before the Supreme Court will accept the case for review.

8. The constitutional issue must be both crucial to the case and substantial rather than trivial before the Court will invalidate a law.

9. The Court has usually (but not always) stayed out of foreign affairs and military policy areas.

10. If the Court rules a law unconstitutional, it will limit its decision to the section of the law in question leaving the rest of the law intact.

It is easy to see that ideology plays a prominent role when discussing any aspect of the judicial branch of the United States. The liberal position, of course, support judicial activism, and the conservative position supports judicial restraint.

LIMITATIONS ON THE COURT

The Court is limited in its use of power in several important ways. The most obvious limitation to the Court's power is that which speaks to compliance. Once the Court has taken a stand on an issue, it must rely upon other institutions of the government, usually the executive branch, to guarantee compliance. But what if the other institutions of the government are in disagreement? One of the most celebrated examples of this occurred during the presidency of Thomas Jefferson. Displeased with a ruling by the Court, Jefferson stated, "Marshall has made his decision; now let him enforce it." Nor are recent examples hard to find. In 1954, the Court in the *Brown v. Board of Education* case ruled that segregation of schools was "inherently unconstitutional" and ordered that racial integration proceed "with all deliberate speed." Nearly a decade passed before Congress finally decided to assist the Court in its ruling by passing legislation authorizing federal enforcement of local desegregation. A more recent example can be seen with President Reagan, who strongly criticized the Court's action in civil rights matters and forced busing to obtain school integration. Statistics reveal that the criticism was not mere campaign rhetoric. In the first year of his administration the Justice Department issued less than half the citations to schools for violation of civil rights than it did during the last year of the Carter administration. The same pattern can be observed in the job market in regard to affirmative action ordered by the Court in favor of racial minorities and women. Although numerous examples could be offered, the point is clear—the Court is capable of making policy, but it is powerless to carry it out.

In addition to his power to control the Justice Department, the president also limits the power of the Court through appointments. A Court that is too liberal runs the risk of incurring the wrath of the public. This could eventually, as it did with the Warren Court, produce an electoral backlash that aided the candidacy of a conservative presidential candidate, Ronald Reagan, who, once elected, began to appoint more conservative judges to the federal judiciary.

Congress is also a factor limiting the Court. Should Congress disagree with a particular interpretation the Court has given to a law, it can always rewrite or modify it to clarify its original intentions. However, this is true only if a constitutional question is not present. If it is, Congress' only remaining alternative would be to amend the Constitution. In 1970, for example, the Court ruled that Congress did not have the power to give 18-year-olds the right to vote in state and local elections. The Twenty-sixth Amendment was proposed and enacted to get around this ruling. Congress also has the ability to change the size of the judiciary. In 1863, Congress increased the number of Supreme Court judges to ten so that a more militant unionist majority could be obtained. A few years later, it lowered the number to seven to deny President Andrew Johnson the opportunity of making any appointments. When President Johnson's term expired, the number was again raised to nine. Congress can also, through its confirmation power, influence the character of the judiciary. Presidents usually confer with legislative leaders to see if a particular appointment might run into problems. If so, a president might decide to compromise and offer another name to avoid a lengthy and potentially embarrassing floor fight with the Senate. Congress also controls the size of the Court's personnel and the Court's budget. Cuts in these areas could seriously affect the Court's ability to function effectively. And finally, if all else fails, Congress has the constitutional right to alter or deny jurisdiction in certain matters. The use of this tactic has been suggested by groups opposed to the Court's rulings on abortion and school prayer.

In the final analysis, if the rulings of the Court are too offensive, they can be ignored. Again Alexis de Tocqueville understood this better than anyone else. Commenting on the power of the Court, he stated:

> Their power is enormous but it is clothed in the authority of public opinion. They are the all-powerful guardians of a people which respects law; but they would be impotent against public neglect or popular contempt.[11]

An example of this can be seen with school prayer. Although the Court has consistently ruled against prayer in public school, many school districts, particularly those in rural areas, still continue the practice. Local leaders are well aware of the Court's ruling but simply choose to look the other way. Frequently, if a local community's values and customs are in one direction and the rule of law is in another direction, the community's values prevail unless a legal issue is made of the conflict. The practice of ignoring the Court's decisions is not confined only to local communities. President Nixon informed the Court that, unless its ruling were "definitive" in regard to handing over the White House tapes in the Watergate investigation, he would ignore it. However, the Court's vote was unanimous, and President Nixon eventually complied.

THE COURT: AN ASSESSMENT

In the *Federalist Papers*, Alexander Hamilton remarked that "the judiciary is beyond comparison the weakest of the three departments of power . . . capable of doing the least harm to the public."[12] Certainly history has not proved this to be the case. With its power of judicial review, a concept even Hamilton supported, the Court has been catapulted into the center of a raging storm of ethical and political conflicts. Besieged by contesting opponents, the Court is pressed upon to decide issues that impact hard on our everyday lives: abortion, equal rights, integration, surrogate mothering, euthanasia, incarceration, execution, etc. Likewise, in the political area, the Court literally has the opportunity to reshape government by its rulings on reapportionment, states rights, integration, governmental regulation, tax laws, presidential and congressional power, etc. In fact, if Hamilton were alive today to witness the controversy surrounding the Court, he would probably be more inclined to agree with the assessment of Robert Dahl, a noted political scientist, who commented, "To consider the Supreme Court of the United States strictly as a legal institution is to underestimate its significance in the American political system."[13]

All of this leads us to an interesting observation. With all this power one might easily conclude that the Court is in a most enviable position. However, the exercise of this power has brought the Court few friends. In fact, seemingly no one is totally happy with its actions. Conservatives complain that the Court has gone too far in undermining state's rights as well as usurping the power of popularly elected institutions—Congress and the president. Racial minorities accuse the Court of institutionalizing racism through its rulings that appear to benefit white, corporate America. Many whites could not disagree more. Pointing to affirmative action, desegregation rulings, and other actions taken on behalf of minorities, many whites insist that the Court has gone too far and now is guilty of reverse discrimination. In criminal matters, police and other law enforcement officials complain bitterly at being handcuffed by the Court in dealing with offenders. The accused, particularly the poor offenders, insist the opposite is true and point to the preferential treatment given to "white-collar" criminals in comparison to poor "street criminals." Feminists denounce the judicial system as being male dominated and sexist in its treatment of women. Newly formed, male rights organizations have leveled counter charges at the Court in matters of divorce, child custody, and alimony payments. Business and industry are not without their criticisms of the Court, charging that rulings in the areas of monopolies, trusts, unions, and consumer protection have destroyed individual initiative and our country's ability to compete in the world market. For their part, the poor attack the Court as the lackey of the rich and powerful, protecting property rights and upholding laws designed to keep the rich, rich and the poor, poor.

Why has the Court been surrounded by such controversy? First, the questions in need of the Court's attention are not easy ones; otherwise, they would have been resolved long before reaching its doorstep. Also, the very nature of our adversary system that dictates a win-or-lose situation adds to the controversy. Nevertheless, at some point in time in a nation of conflicting values and competing interests, there must be a final arbitrator, and it is the Court that has assumed this responsibility for our society. As former Chief Justice Earl Warren stated, "The Court sits to decide cases, not to avoid decision. . . . When cases come to us, we should not sweep them under the rug, only to leave them for future generations."[14] Viewed in this context, it is easy to understand why some decisions of the Court have been and, undoubtedly, will continue to remain controversial.

Chapter Fifteen Notes

[1]Henry J. Abraham, *The Judicial Process*, 4th ed. (Oxford University Press, 1980), 148.

[2]Glen R. Winters and Robert E. Allard, "Judicial Selection and Tenure in the United States," in *The Courts, the Public, and the Law Explosion*, ed. Harry W. Jones (Englewood Cliffs, N.J.: Prentice-Hall, 1965), 157.

[3]*The Book of States*, 1992-93 edition, (Lexington, Ky.: The Council of State Governments, 1993), 233-34.

[4]William Jenkins, Jr., "Retention Elections: Who Wins When No One Loses?" *Judicature* 61 (1977): 79-86.

[5]http://dictionary.law.com/

[6]Joseph W. Bishop, Jr., "The Warren Court is not likely to be Overruled," *New York Times Magazine*, 7 September 1969, 31.

[7]*Marbury* v. *Madison*, Cranch 137 (1803).

[8]*Brown* v. *Board of Education, Topeka, Kansas*, 347 U.S. 483 (1954).

[9]"Judicial Authority Moves Growing Issues," *Lincoln Journal*, 24 April 1977.

[10]Martin Shapiro, "The Supreme Court: From Warren to Burger," in *The New American Political System*, ed. Anthony King (Washington, D.C.: American Enterprise Institute, 1978), 180-81.

[11]Alexis De Tocqueville, *Democracy in America*, vol. I (New York: Schocken, 1961), 166.

[12]See "The Federalist, No. 78," in Alexander Hamilton, James Madison, John Jay, *The Federalist Papers*, ed. Clinton Rossiter (New York: The New American Library, 1961).

[13]Robert Dahl, "Decision-Making in a Democracy: The Role of the Supreme Court as a National Policy-Maker," in *Readings in American Political Behavior*, ed. Raymond E. Wolfinger (Englewood Cliffs, N.J.: Prentice-Hall, 1966), 166.

[14]Earl Warren, *The Memoirs of Earl Warren* (Garden City, N.Y.: Doubleday & Co., 1977), 523.

Suggested Readings

Abraham, Henry. *The Judicial Process.* 6th ed. New York: Oxford University Press, 1993.

Baum, Lawrence. *American Courts: Process and Policy*, 3d ed. Boston: Houghton Mifflin, 1994.

Craig, Barbara, and David M. O'Brien. *Abortion and American Politics.* Chatham, N.J.: Chatham House, 1993.

Cannon, Mark, and David M. O'Brien, ed. *View from the Bench: The Judiciary and Constitutional Politics.* Chatham, N.J.: Chatham House, 1985.

Hall, Kermitt L., ed. *The Oxford Companion to the Supreme Court of the United States.* New York: Oxford University Press, 1992.

O'Brien, David, *Storm Center: The Supreme Court in American Politics.* 4th ed. New York: W.W. Norton and Company, 1996.

Rosenberg, Gerald. *The Hollow Hope: Can Courts Bring About Social Change?* Chicago: University of Chicago Press, 1991.

Woodward Bob, and Scott Armstrong. *The Brethren: Inside the Supreme Court.* New York: Simon and Schuster, 1979.

Part Four
Living Up to the Dream

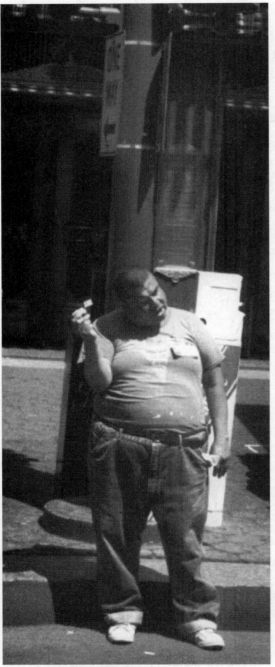

Selling the flag for pennies.

Justice is a dominant and reoccurring theme in the American system of government. Americans cherish it, political philosophers write about it, and, naturally, politicians talk about it. But, what is the meaning of "justice"? Interestingly enough, the answer to this question in America depends on the context in which it is used. To some, particularly lawyers and legal scholars, justice is a concept that determines how we, as citizens, are treated individually and collectively by the laws of our society. A just society is one that treats all its citizens equally. Consequently, in a court of law, it matters not whether one is rich or poor, black or white, Christian or Jew, etc. In other words, in America "justice is blind." As small children, we all learned this lesson when discussing why it was that the statue of the lady holding the scales of justice was blindfolded. In a different context, justice can also be used as a measure of opportunity. Here a just society provides equal access to the riches of our nation. This does not mean that everyone's slice of the pie is going to be the same size, but it does mean that each of us will be afforded the same opportunity to compete fairly. Again, we learn this early in life when our teachers proudly announce to us that America is the "land of opportunity."

In this section we consider these two separate meanings of justice. Justice as a matter of rights, both civil and criminal, are discussed in chapters sixteen and seventeen. In the concluding chapter, we consider how just our society is and what needs to be done to narrow the gap between the ideal of equal opportunity and its practice.

Chapter Sixteen

Citizens and the Law:
The Rights of the Accused

The Incident

It is late at night—midnight. You're alone and traveling one of the city's main streets on your way home after having attended a party for a friend who is being transferred to another city. The streets are unusually dark as the sky is covered by a thick and ominous layer of clouds. Heavy rains are forecast, but they have not yet begun to fall. While listening to the radio, your mind wanders casually back to the party. It was nice, relaxing, filled with gaiety and laughter. And though it is true that you consumed several drinks while there, it was over a three-hour period and in no way do you feel that your driving is impaired.

Looking down, you check your speed to find that you are well within the legal limit. Everything seems perfect. The warm summer air, laced ever so lightly with the promising scent of a summer rain, rushes in through open windows to swirl haphazardly about the car's interior. On the radio is one of your favorite songs. You gently sip the soft drink in the paper cup you brought with you from the party. Then, as you approach an intersection, it happens. A large weather-beaten dog suddenly darts into the street. Blinded, the animal freezes helplessly in the path of your car, its eyes locked on the onrushing headlights. You pump the horn in an attempt to break the dog's trance. The effort is futile, and at the last moment, just before impact, you pull the wheel sharply to the right to avoid collision. Instantly the tail end of the car veers wildly to the left. The cup of soft drink tumbles from your hand, spilling its contents over the seat and floorboard as you enter a sideward skid. Your first impulse is to hit the brake, but you resist. Releasing the wheel, you let the force of the road realign the car's momentum. The wheel reverses spin thus averting a roll, and after a few quick swerves, you regain control.

Inside your chest you can feel your heart pounding furiously like a mad drummer, but you take solace in the fact that the dog's life is saved and the incident is over—at least that is what you think before seeing the red lights flashing behind you. You panic, though there is no reason to do so. Your mind races. Now you think about the drinks you had at the party. Will the officer think you are drunk? Pulling over to the side of the road, you reach down to retrieve your paper cup and set it in the car caddie. Quickly, you open the glove compartment, grab a piece of gum, flick the compartment door closed, and stick the gum in your mouth to mask any lingering trace of alcohol. With the squad car parked directly behind, you wait nervously.

For most Americans this is the way their first encounter with the police begins—a simple traffic violation. And, though usually it is nothing too serious, most of us who have experienced it would admit to a slight moment of panic as we sit watching the officer slowly approach our car through the rear view mirror. Do we have anything to worry about? Probably not, but there is always that slight chance things could go awry, and, if so, it is then that first thought of civil rights pops quickly into our minds. We think to ourselves— exactly what rights do I have? What type of questions will be asked? Do I have to answer? Will my car be searched? Will I be searched? Do I have any privacy rights when being searched? "Drats," you mutter to yourself admonishingly, "if only I had paid more attention to that unit on civil rights during my government class!"

In this first chapter on civil liberties, we take up the topic of the rights of the accused in criminal proceedings. Most of the Bill of Rights—the first ten amendments to the Constitution—deal with the rights of persons accused of a crime. These include all of the Fourth Amendment, most of the Fifth Amendment, all of the Sixth Amendment, and all of the Eighth. Since these rights comprise the major portion of the Bill of Rights, it is clear that the Founding Fathers appreciated the importance of providing constitutional protections to individuals facing possible deprivation of their life or liberty. In addition to these constitutional provisions, there are two other important rights in the Fourteenth Amendment (which is addressed to the states): the right to due process of law and the right to the equal protection of the laws. We will also be discussing other basic rights accorded to everyone but not found in the U.S. Constitution. These include rights such as presumption of innocence, right to a jury of your peers, proof (of guilt) beyond a reasonable doubt, and the right of appeal.

We started this chapter with a traffic-stop scenario we feel everyone could relate to in terms of its believability. We use this incident and its aftermath as a backdrop for describing the criminal justice system and the rights of those who undergo prosecution. You will be in the shoes of an individual who goes through the system, from arrest to trial, through the post-conviction appellate process. The above incident is used as a starting point because of its familiarity. And, while it is true that what has happened or is about to happen in our scenario would probably not occur in most similar situations, it is perfectly reasonable to assume that it could. So, let us follow this drama then, as it unfolds and, in the process, gain an understanding of the rights of persons accused of a crime.

Before proceeding, it should be noted that as originally interpreted by the United States Supreme Court, the Bill of Rights did not protect against *state* action, only federal. Speaking for a unanimous Supreme Court, Chief Justice John Marshall said: "The Constitution was ordained and established by the people of the United States for themselves, for their own government, and not for the government of the individual states. . . ."[1] However, over the years the Court has extended most of the protections of the Bill of Rights to citizens in matters of state criminal proceedings. (The typical defendant in this country is charged with a violation of a *state* criminal law). This was done through the Court's interpretation of the due process of law clause of the Fourteenth Amendment.[2] Now, let us return to our incident.

The Stop

When you see the flashing lights, you pull your car off the road onto the shoulder, making sure that you are in no danger from oncoming traffic. Should you

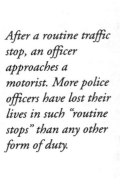

After a routine traffic stop, an officer approaches a motorist. More police officers have lost their lives in such "routine stops" than any other form of duty.

step out of your car or remain seated inside? Generally, it is preferable for you to remain inside. In all situations, even traffic violations, well-trained police officers will assume they are at risk. Before approaching you, the officers will make a few initial checks by radio to see if the car is reported stolen, who it belongs to, and if the owner has any outstanding warrants. Too, before leaving their squad car, they will report on their location and activities. This is standard operating procedure.

Having completed the above checks and finding everything in order, it is now time for you and the officers (there are two of them) to get acquainted. You wait nervously watching through the rear view mirror as they slowly approach on opposite sides of your car. Though holstered, each has a hand resting upon his or her revolver. You wonder if the gum has done its job. You chew faster and swallow hard—so hard that the gum accidentally slips to the back of your throat choking you. Pounding on your chest, you cough violently trying to force it up and forward but no amount of effort works. The gum slips even farther back and realizing you have no choice, you swallow. Looking up through red, teary eyes, you see one of the officers standing by your window. Rolling down the window, you point quickly to your throat and choke out an explanation, "Gum."

The officer asks you for your driver's license, registration certificate, and proof of insurance and informs you as to why you were stopped. You are not surprised to hear that the issue is your driving skills. Both officers—the one talking to you and the other one—now standing on the opposite side of your car—will visually scan the interior of your car, looking for any weapons or contraband that might be *in plain view*.[3] The Supreme Court has ruled that such a "search" is reasonable because the courts accord a lesser protection of privacy to persons in vehicles as compared to when they are in their homes. Also the police have the right to protect themselves and the public. How much further can the officers proceed in their search? Can you be searched? Can the police do a thorough search of your car? Within the scope of a routine traffic citation stop, the visual scanning is as far as the officers have a right to intrude into your privacy. If nothing out of the ordinary is observed, the search ends. Your Fourth Amendment rights protect you against *unreasonable searches and seizures*. Under normal conditions the police must first arrest you before conducting a search of your person. If any illegal substance or material is then found, it becomes admissible in a court against you. However, before you can be arrested, the police must have **probable cause**[4] to believe that you are somehow involved in a criminal act. If there is no *probable cause* then the search is unconstitutional and, under the **exclusionary rule**,[5] any substance or material seized will not be admissible in court. (A corollary to the *exclusionary rule* is the **fruit-of-the-poisonous-tree rule**, which states that evidence traceable to an illegal search, seizure, arrest, or interrogation is inadmissible, as "fruit of the poisonous tree—the illegal police or governmental activity.) Thus, if key evidence is declared inadmissible because it was the result of an illegal search or seizure the charges, in all probability, will be dismissed.

The above procedure of *arrest, search, and seizure,* as has been stated, applies to normal situations, where the chief criterion is the presence or absence of probable cause. Under certain circumstances, however, the Court has granted police officers the right to stop and temporarily detain individuals and to subject them to a limited search and brief questioning. These are "stop and frisk" scenarios based on **reasonable suspicion,** a lesser standard than probable cause.[6] If the police reasonably believe that you are behaving suspiciously, they can stop you and question you. For their protection, they will "pat down" the outer garments of your clothing. If, while you're being "frisked," they find an illegal weapon or contraband of some sort, you will be arrested, and the evidence would be admissible in court. If the search is challenged and a court rules there was no reasonable suspicion to justify the "stop and frisk," the evidence obtained would be declared inadmissible, as mentioned before. The *exclusionary rule* would apply and, in all likelihood, the charges would be dismissed.

Let us analyze the incident we have described up to this point, in terms of whether the circumstances meet the criteria of *reasonable suspicion.* Unfortunately for you, it certainly appears the criteria are easily met, on three counts:

1. Your car was careening recklessly about the street. A reasonable possibility exists that you could be under the influence of alcohol or drugs.

2. You were observed by the officers reaching (or grabbing) beneath the seat. You might be concealing a weapon or hiding contraband.

3. Additionally, the officers noticed that you reached into the glove compartment and placed something in your mouth. It is reasonable to assume that you might be attempting to hide or destroy evidence of a crime.

From your standpoint such assumptions are ludicrous. After all, you are a pillar of your community. But, from the vantage point of the officers, who neither know you or your lifestyle, your actions are well within the bounds of what the Court has ruled as *suspicious behavior.* At the very least, you were not in proper control of your vehicle. Thus, from the officers' perspective, there are reasonable grounds for stopping you, briefly questioning you, and conducting a more extensive search of your person and your vehicle.

The Initial Search

Normally, after asking for your driver's license and other documents, the officers would run your name through their car computer to see if you have any outstanding arrest warrants. (This procedure is known as a "lien check.") But,

A suspect is cuffed before being transported to the police station. Standard police procedure requires such action to guarantee both the safety of the officer and suspect.

because of your suspicious behavior, you are asked to step out of the car immediately.

Upon exiting the car, you are instructed to, as they say on television, "assume the position!" This means that while facing the car at a distance of approximately three feet, you are required to lean well forward, place your hands on the hood, and spread your feet apart. At this point one of the officer will "pat-you-down" to ensure that you do not have a concealed weapon on your person. The officer will also be looking for other types of contraband since, given your behavior, it is reasonable for the officer to assume that you might be in possession of illegal drugs. While one officer is searching your person, the other proceeds to search the interior of your car. You can't quite see exactly what the officer searching your car is doing, as you are struggling to keep your balance in the awkward position you were asked to assume.

The Supreme Court has ruled that an officer's right to search in these circumstances is limited to an area within the suspect's immediate control.[7] The glove compartment, trunk, closed purse, suitcase, or any other area where there is an "expectation of privacy," whether locked or not, is off-limits to the officer.[8] However, if the officers ask for your permission to do a more thorough search of the interior of your car as well as your trunk, and you oblige, then they are free to do so and seize any evidence subject to seizure. If you refuse to give consent they are not free to search such areas without a warrant. Is it possible for the officers to obtain a warrant if you refuse? After all, if you are reluctant to agree to a wider search of your vehicle, might there be reason to suspect you are hiding something? Quite naturally, the answer would be no, and no magistrate would issue a warrant to the police simply because you refused to give the hoped-for consent. Simply exercising your constitutional rights against "unreasonable searches and seizures" does not constitute grounds for the issuance of a warrant! Otherwise, carried to its extreme, this type of logic would make a mockery of the Fourth Amendment.

It should be noted that there are numerous situations—involving emergency circumstances—where a warrant may not be required to conduct a search. (The Supreme Court refers to these emergency circumstances as **exigent circumstances**). There are the typical "stop and frisk" situations, where no vehicles are involved, just individuals behaving suspiciously. There is the plain-view doctrine already referred to. There are other *vehicle exceptions* to the requirement of a warrant. For example, a motor vehicle that the police have good reason to suspect is transporting drugs or contraband could be searched on the grounds that it would be gone (along with the evidence) before a warrant could be obtained. The "exigent circumstance" here is the ready *mobility* of the vehicle.[9] The Court has also ruled that customs and border police have the right—without a warrant—to search persons and things coming into the country to enforce customs and immigration laws. To protect citizens against hijackings, airport guards have the right to search passengers and luggage—without a warrant.[10] Public school students are subject to search by teachers and administrators—without a warrant.[11] And, the Court has ruled that the police can search open fields for marijuana despite "No Trespassing" signs without a warrant.[12]

The Arrest

Again, back to our incident scenario. With your hands still on the hood, you wait anxiously while your car is being searched. Nothing has been found on your person, and the police have chosen not to exercise their right to administer a sobriety test. Then, an unexpected twist develops. Emerging from your car, the police officer who approached your car from the passenger side holds a small revolver in his hand. A flood of adrenaline suddenly surges through your body as you recall having put it in the glove compartment after target practice at a pistol range in a neighboring community. It's your hobby. Of course, you knew you were supposed to carry it in the trunk as instructed by the teacher of your original firearms safety class. But, it was raining when you finished your target practice session. And what difference does it really make anyway, you thought. The law was written for criminals—dangerous types—not for good citizens like you, right? Wrong! The officer approaches and asks if you have a permit to carry the gun in your car. Your answer is no. Is the gun registered, he inquires. Again the answer is no. You quickly explain the gun was given to you by your father who lives in a state that doesn't require registration. The officer informs you that you are under arrest for the illegal possession and transportation of a firearm.

Reading Your Rights

Unceremoniously, one of the officers handcuffs your arms behind your back while the other begins to read you your **Miranda rights**:

1. "You have the right to remain silent."

2. "Anything you say can and will be used against you in a court of law."

3. "You have the right to be represented by an attorney."

4. "If you cannot afford an attorney, one will be appointed for you by the court to represent you free of charge."

5. "Do you understand your rights?"

You do know about *Miranda* and you tell the officer, "Yes, I know my rights and I don't want to waive them." The truth is you are in shock and too scared to think straight. So you decide you should just keep quiet, at least for a while until you figure out what is going to happen to you. It is standard practice for the police to read a suspect his/her rights upon being arrested. You are now in *custody* and about to be subjected to *interrogation*. At this point you must be informed of your right not to answer any questions, as well as other rights. These so-called "*Miranda* rights" (or "*Miranda* warnings") were established in 1966, in the case of *Miranda v. Arizona*.[13] The Court ruled that any person about to be subjected to **custodial interrogation** must be provided certain "procedural safeguards." The Court defined *custodial interrogation* as "questioning initiated by law enforcement officers after a person has been taken into custody or otherwise deprived of his freedom in any significant way." The "procedural safeguards" are the warnings that came to be known as the *Miranda* rights. Once you have been properly "Mirandized," if you wish to talk, you are free to do so, but you can stop at any point. Always keep in mind, however, that any information you provide will come back to haunt you in court!

How important is it that you be read your rights prior to interrogation? Very important. The *Miranda* warnings are designed to protect your Fifth Amendment right not to incriminate yourself—your right to remain silent. Further, the Supreme Court has ruled that defendants who are unaware of their rights essentially possess no rights. Consequently, the burden falls upon the state, principally through its law enforcement agents, to make suspects aware of their rights at the time of their arrest. And, it must be clear to anyone who is being Mirandized that he/she understands the rights being read. A suspect who does not speak English must be Mirandized in the suspect's native tongue. The Court requires that if suspects choose to answer questions posed to them by the police, it must be clear that they are doing so knowingly, intelligently, and voluntarily.

At the police station the suspect is questioned before being formally charged.

The issue of reading the Miranda rights in the suspect's native language has come under fire by critics of the *Miranda* ruling. However, one must keep in mind that not all persons in the United States, whether visiting this country or working here on a temporary basis, speak English. Not to advise such persons of their rights in their native tongue would deprive them of the same constitutional rights enjoyed by the rest of us.

Additionally, while the Court has consistently upheld Miranda, it has allowed several exceptions. First, the Court will allow statements obtained in violation of Miranda to be used to *impeach* the testimony of the defendant who takes the stand at trial.[14] This means that prior inconsistent or contradictory statements made by the defendant may be used to challenge the defendant's credibility at trial should the defendant choose to testify. Second, the Court will allow the use of statements obtained from a suspect who had not been Mirandized prior to questioning if an immediate threat to public safety prevented the police from giving the warnings.[15] Finally, the Rehnquist Court has held that in some situations what appears to be a violation of *Miranda* could be a simple matter of a "harmless error" and not impermissible self-incrimination.[16]

Impoundment

After you are placed under arrest, handcuffed, and Mirandized, you will be placed in the back seat of the squad car and transported to the police station for booking and processing. As for your car, the officers will make a decision whether to impound it or lock it up and leave it on the side of the road for you to reclaim after making bail. The decision generally depends upon the seriousness of the charge against you (misdemeanor or felony) and the circumstances of your arrest. For example, in this case the officers have reasonable suspicion to believe that you might be harboring contraband. (Remember the gum you placed in your mouth after being stopped—and your coughing/choking?). With these suspicions, and the finding of the gun, it is likely that a closer look at your car might be desired. This is accomplished through impoundment and inventory. So, your car will be towed away to the police impoundment yard or garage. Once your vehicle is in their possession, the police will inventory the car. What this means is that a very thorough search of the car will be conducted—the interior, the glove compartment, the trunk; all boxes or containers found will be opened. An inventory list will be made of all items found. The Court has ruled that any contraband (things illegal to possess) found in the process of inventorying is admissible in court as evidence against you. The police do not have a right to strip the car down—tear out the seats, remove the tires, pull out the dash, etc. This would require a warrant, and it is highly unlikely that one would be issued since there is no reason to assume that you are a major drug or arms dealer. However, it should be noted that the invention of micro-cameras, such as those used in surgery, now make it possible for the police to look into many areas of the car that before were hidden from view. Likewise, if there was strong suspicion that you were trafficking in drugs, a specially trained dog could be brought in to "sniff out" the car. If the results were positive, then probable cause to obtain a warrant would exist for a more extensive search of your car. Also, be aware, that new "zero tolerance" drug laws provide for the forfeiture of property used in the commission of crimes involving controlled substances. Let's say you have just purchased a new $35,000 automobile and, while driving it around, are stopped and caught with a substantial amount of drugs in your possession. Under the provisions of these laws you have now forfeited title to your car to the state. Your vehicle now belongs to the state and can be auctioned away to obtain money to fight the war on drugs. These laws apply to homes, cars, boats, planes, etc.

Booking

The procedure used by police during this stage varies according to the size of and the resources available to the department. In smaller departments, the arresting police officer generally handles most matters. In larger departments, where specialization is the rule, you will probably be turned over to another officer for booking.

The first stage of booking is information-gathering. The officer will obtain your name, place of residence, age, sex, race, etc. The arresting officer will fill out a report detailing the events surrounding your arrest. The officer will inquire as to why you were in the vicinity at the time you were stopped, what you were doing with the gun, your past police record, and similar information. This stage is critical to the disposition of your case because it provides information upon which the officer will make a final judgment as to the charge against you.

It is, of course, your right to refuse to answer any questions. You also have the right to make a phone call after arriving at the station. However, you must verbally request to do so.

You decide to cooperate and provide all the information asked of you. After all, in your heart and soul you are no criminal. Upon completion of the initial questioning, you will be fingerprinted and photographed, front and both sides. Afterwards, you will be taken to a holding cell. Belts, shoestrings, ribbons, and anything else that you might use to inflict harm on yourself are removed. All personal effects are inventoried and placed in an envelope. An itemized list of your possessions is presented to you to inspect. After you sign the itemized list, it is placed inside, and the envelope is sealed.

While you're striking up new friendships with your cell mates, the officer will process your papers and run a check on your prints with the FBI. Once this information has been gathered and reviewed, the officer will usually call a state's attorney to discuss your case and decide which charges will be brought against you in court. Again, in most states, the possession of a weapon can either be a serious misdemeanor or felony. How the charge will go will depend a lot upon how the officer views the case.

Interrogation

All things being normal, meaning that your background and story check out, you will probably be charged with a *Class Four* misdemeanor, a charge that in most states could result in incarceration for up to one-year and/or a fine up to $1000. Although serious, it is certainly less so than the sentence for the felony charge. You are hoping for a misdemeanor charge. If so, you will be able to post bail immediately as soon as it is set by the court. Upon posting bail, your possessions (everything except contraband) would be returned, and you would be assigned a date to appear in court. Since the charge against you (*Class Four* misdemeanor) could result in a jail sentence, you would be entitled to a court-appointed lawyer to represent you, if you could not retain private counsel.[17]

Your hopes for a quick resolution of the problem disappear when two new officers appear and escort you back to the interview room for more questioning. You sit anxiously at the desk while one reviews the file. The other leans casually against the door. "Is there a problem?" you ask. There is no reply. Finally you are asked to recount your story. Again, you go through it in excruciating detail. It's now 2:30 in the morning, and fatigue is setting in. You become irritable, which, of course, does not help your case. The officers respond with shortness and irritability of their own. The problem then surfaces. The officer seated in front of you reveals that while checking your background, it was discovered that you were once charged with possessing an illegal narcotic—cocaine. In effect, you have a police record, an interesting fact, they point out that you failed to mention when questioned earlier.

You're stunned. You were only sixteen at the time, having troubles at home and had fallen into bad company. It happens to many teenagers. Besides, the charges were dropped, and you haven't touched the stuff since. You had no idea that records were still kept on the incident. You attempt to communicate all this, very excitedly, to the officers, but they appear unimpressed. They ask about the arresting officer's report of your putting something into your mouth.

"Gum," you yell. "It was gum! I told them so!"

They nod, but the expressions on their faces tell you they're not buying your story. The officer by the door speaks up and remarks, casually, that they have *a way* to find out what's in your stomach.

What? You wonder. Can they pump your stomach? X-ray your body? Take a blood test? Make you take a lie detector test? The answers are no, yes, yes, and no. The Court has ruled that pumping a stomach is a violation of your rights against unreasonable searches.[18] Conversely, though, the Court has ruled that x-rays and blood tests are permissible under certain conditions.[19] And lastly, you cannot be forced to take a lie detector test because it violates your Fifth Amendment rights not to be compelled to be a witness against yourself. It should be noted that even if you agree to voluntarily take a lie detector test and the results prove unfavorable, the findings cannot be used in court as evidence against you.

While you're thinking over your options, if any, and what procedure you may be subjected to, one of the officers begins to talk about a series of armed robberies in the neighborhood where you were stopped. Descriptions given by several eyewitnesses seem to fit you. Also, a gun similar to yours was used! Matters appear to be going from bad to worse, and you decide that discussing the matter further is not in your best interest. Can you refuse to continue the interrogation even though you had decided to cooperate and answer all police questions? The answer is yes. At this point you have the right to demand legal counsel, retained or appointed. You inform the new officers that you want to call your attorney. The officers cease questioning instantly, as required by *Miranda*. After you call your lawyer, you are taken back to your cell where you wait anxiously for him to arrive.[20]

The Lineup

Daylight is approaching as you are led back to your cell. A few hours later you make a call to a friend and instruct him to find you a lawyer. At 10:00 a.m., you are taken from your cell and escorted back to the interrogation room where you meet with your attorney. He discusses the case and the suspicions of the police with you. He also informs you that you are going to be placed in a line-up. Must you submit to a line-up? The answer is yes. However, before doing so, the state must inform you of the following:

1. Although you do not have a right to refuse to appear in a lineup, you do have a right to have a lawyer present when witnesses to the crime view the line-up.

2. If you are unable to pay for a lawyer (not an issue as you have a lawyer), a lawyer will be appointed to represent you during the line-up free of any cost to you.[21]

3. You and the other participants in the line-up will be asked to repeat certain words, phrases or sentences spoken by the person who committed the crime. You have no right to refuse. (A lineup can also be a photo lineup, where the witness is shown a number of photos, including one of the suspect. In addition, police sometimes use what is termed a *showup*, where the witness is merely asked if the suspect in custody is the perpetrator of the crime.)

The results of the line-up prove inconclusive. Apparently, there *is* a strong resemblance between you and the robber, but the witnesses are unable to make a positive identification. Your attorney informs you that although the police are unable to charge you with the robbery, they remain suspicious. However, regarding the illegal possession of a firearm, the prosecutor has decided to file *felony* charges (which carry imprisonment of a year or more) against you, and you are due to appear in court within the hour. Hastily, you consult with your attorney regarding strategy. Should you wish, it is at this point that you will attempt, based on advice of counsel, to **plea bargain**. What this means, your attorney explains, is that he/she will contact the prosecutor's office and offer to plead you guilty if the charge is reduced to a misdemeanor and the state recommends probation rather than the maximum one-year prison term. At the very least the attorney will try to negotiate the best plea bargain possible. You agree with your attorney's proposal (after all, jail is no fun-place) and instruct him/her to proceed with "the deal." But, your attorney quickly finds out that the District Attorney is currently under tremendous public pressure to "put hand-gun offenders away" and has decided that nailing your hide to the courthouse door might be good politics! There's no choice now, explains your attorney. You've got to go the distance; you have to go to trial.

Bond Hearing

The next step in the process is the bond hearing. This must occur within twenty-four hours of your arrest. The purpose of the bond hearing is twofold:

1. To inform the individual of the charges against him/her;

2. To set bail.

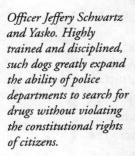

Officer Jeffery Schwartz and Yasko. Highly trained and disciplined, such dogs greatly expand the ability of police departments to search for drugs without violating the constitutional rights of citizens.

Concerning the first point, the most important, if this first court appearance was not to occur, you have a constitutional right to file a writ of *habeas corpus*,[22] which directs the state to bring you before a court for a review of the legality of your detention. When you are brought before a judge, you are formally informed of the exact charges filed against you. In your case, you are officially informed you are facing the felony charge you at first thought you probably needn't worry about.

Your attorney will request that **bail** be set in your case. In its simplest explanation, bail is a sum of money you pay to secure your release from jail until such time that your case comes to court. The necessity of bail results from our unique system of justice in which a defendant is presumed innocent until proven guilty by the state. Because of this basic presumption, it then follows that defendants should maintain their right to liberty while awaiting trial. However, this poses a problem for the court. If set free, how can the court guarantee that the defendant will bother to appear for trial? Bail solves this thorny issue. The court usually attempts to set bail at an amount that is large enough to guarantee that the defendant will attend all required court proceedings but reasonable enough so that the defendant can raise the sum and remain free until trial.

Although you do not have a constitutional right to bail, the Eighth Amendment prohibits the state from setting "excessive bail" in cases where it is granted. In other words, the sum set by the court must be reasonable and in line with the charge against the defendant. In setting the sum, the court will also take into account your personal background, previous arrest record, and ability to pay. In certain cases bail can be denied to individuals charged with capital offenses

(offenses that carry the death penalty) or who have, by past actions, demonstrated that they cannot be trusted to reappear in court. Likewise, individuals who pose a serious threat to others in society can be denied bail.

It has been common practice for defendants unable to raise the entire bail amount to have to rely on the services of a bail bondsman. Bail bondsmen post the bail for you and will usually charge between 5 to 15 percent of the set amount for their services. (They may also require you to put up property as collateral.) This fee is nonrefundable. If you "jump bail," the bail may be forfeited; you will become liable for the entire amount, and the property you put up as collateral can be confiscated by the bail bondsman. Abuses of this system, as well as the accusation that the system favors the rich, have led states to establish court-administered bail systems. For example, many states have bail systems that include some or all of the following features:

1. I-Bond—(Individual Recognizance Bond) the defendant is released on his/her own recognizance. A predetermined amount of money is set so that if the defendant fails to appear in court he/she will forfeit the money when apprehended.

2. D-Bond—(Deposit Bond) bail is established, and the defendant must put up 10 percent of its value. When the defendant appears in court, 90 percent of it is returned with the remaining (10 percent) retained by the court to cover processing costs.

3. Cash Bond—the defendant is required to cover the full amount. Most states allow defendants to pledge property of equal value instead of cash.

The type of bond a judge will use depends upon the seriousness of the crime and the background of the defendant. *Cash bonds* are generally used in serious cases in which the defendant is recognized as a threat to society. Let's say that in our case the judge decides upon a *Deposit Bond* of $15,000, a reasonable sum considering the charge against you. You post $1500 with the Circuit Clerk, and you are "free on bail." You are released from custody pending further court proceedings as the prosecution of your case goes forward.

What would happen if you could not come up with the $1500? You would be returned to jail to await trial and pre-trial proceedings. Again, critics remind us that bail (where money has to be deposited or property pledged) is an institutionalized privilege of those with financial means. People who are unable to post bail and have no property to pledge— primarily the poor—return to jail to await further court proceedings, including going to trial. This puts them at a disadvantage in two ways. First, they lose their rights to liberty and are forced to suffer the humiliation of incarceration, even though they may ultimately be found not guilty. And second, since they are confined, they are not able to participate actively with their attorney in planning their defense.

Search and Seizure: Special Rules

Having obtained your freedom, your immediate concern is your security and privacy. Will the police attempt to search your house to obtain additional evidence to use against you in court? After all, from their standpoint, you are a prime suspect in some very serious crimes. Your attorney advises you that there are strict rules regarding when the police could enter your house without a warrant. For example:

1. If you or, in your absence, someone who lives with you voluntarily grants permission for the police to enter and conduct a search of the common areas of the house, such as the living room or kitchen. No one but you can give permission to search your own private areas of the residence, e.g., your bedroom, your bathroom, your closet.

2. If, after witnessing a crime, they are in "hot pursuit" of a suspect (whether it is you or someone else) who enters your house.

3. If, through an open window or door, they see a crime being committed within.

4. If they have reason to believe that someone's life is in danger.

If the circumstances do not justify waiving the procuring of a warrant, then the police must obtain a warrant to execute a search of your house. Warrants are obtained through the courts, but before the issuance of a warrant, a magistrate requires that the police establish *probable cause.* Two points are worth mentioning here. First, suspicion alone does not constitute grounds for establishing *probable cause.* Second, the mere possession of a warrant does not permit the police to enter your house on a "fishing expedition."[23] In other words, they could not tear out walls or rip up floor boards just to see if they could find evidence subject to seizure. Warrants contain limits in that they must describe the "place to be searched and the persons or things to be seized." However, your lawyer points out two very important facts. First, the Court has allowed police wide latitude with respect to searches of houses and buildings. For example, if in the process of searching a house for drugs, the police discover a printing press and counterfeit money, the owner would be subject to arrest and the evidence seized would be admissible in court. The key point here is that the press and counterfeit money were in a place the police would normally be expected to search for drugs.[24] Second, decisions by the Burger and Rehnquist Courts have expanded the powers of police in searches based on the doctrines of "good faith," "inevitable discovery," and "retroactive probable cause." The **good faith rule** allows the use of evidence obtained under a warrant police believed to be legal but later proved invalid.[25] The **inevitable discovery rule** applies if police obtained evidence illegally but can prove that it would have been discovered eventually.[26] Finally, the "retroactive probable cause" rule (the **independent source doctrine**) allows prosecutors to use evidence traceable to illegal police or governmental activity if the evidence has a lawful independent source.[27]

Your final question to your lawyer concerns your phone. Can the police put a "tap" on it without a warrant? The answer is no. A warrant would be required, and, to obtain a wiretap warrant, the police must have probable cause with respect to anticipated criminal activity conversations.[28]

Arraignment

Your attorney informs you that your case has been scheduled for *arraignment*. You must appear in court, where you will be informed of the charges filed against you, and you will be asked to enter a plea. If you plead "guilty" your case will be set for sentencing. If you plead "not guilty" your case will be set for trial. Constitutionally, you have the right to a trial *before an impartial jury* (under the Sixth Amendment). At the federal level, juries must be composed of twelve individuals. States, on the other hand, are constitutionally required to have a minimum of *six*. Likewise, the number of votes needed for conviction is higher at the federal level (unanimous) than at the state level (where less than a unanimous verdict may be allowed; though most states follow the federal standard). Additionally, the Constitution requires that the trial be held in the state and in the community in which the crime was allegedly committed (Article III, Section 2 of the Constitution and the Sixth Amendment). In some cases this may pose a problem. If the accused is extremely disliked in the community or if the crime has received an inordinate amount of local pretrial publicity, then it may be difficult to find impartial jurors. In such a case, a **change of venue** would be in order. The defense could file a motion to change the trial site to a different locale within the state to ensure due process of law for the defendant.

A defendant may choose to waive the constitutional guarantee of the right to trial *by jury* and, instead, ask to be tried by a judge, known as a **bench trial**. In a *bench trial* the judge hears the case, weighs the evidence, and determines guilt or innocence. There is no doubt that you were transporting a weapon illegally. The entirety of your defense rests upon the evidence (the gun) being declared inadmissible under the *exclusionary rule*. And since only the judge can rule on this point of law, a trial *by jury* would be pointless. Therefore, your attorney decides on trial by judge.

Preliminary Hearing

The Fifth Amendment of the Constitution provides that a defendant cannot be brought to trial on felony charges unless a *grand* jury issues an *indictment*. The **indictment** serves as the formal charging instrument, signifying a determina-

The Constitution guarantees the right to a "speedy trial." However, many times individuals charged with crimes spend months in jail before trial due to the backlog of cases in the courts.

tion on the part of the grand jury that probable cause exists to bring the defendant to trial. The Supreme Court has ruled that the Fifth Amendment's requirement of indictment by a grand jury applies only to *federal* crimes.

Composed usually of sixteen to twenty-three citizens, the grand jury is convened to hear evidence presented by the prosecutor and to determine if they should issue a **true bill** of indictment. Issuance of a *true bill* means that the accused must stand trial. If the grand jury fails to find sufficient evidence to indict, a *no bill* is issued, and your troubles are over.

In state criminal proceedings many states do not use grand juries. Many of them use the *information* as the basis for bringing a defendant to trial. The information serves as the indictment. The majority of the states require a *preliminary hearing* prior to formal charging in felony cases.

A **preliminary hearing** is a preliminary examination of the state's evidence in felony cases. The defendant is brought before a judge to determine if there is *probable cause* to believe a crime was committed by the defendant and whether the evidence justifies *binding* him/her over for trial. The state is obligated to present sufficient evidence to convince the judge that the case should proceed to trial (be *bound over*). During your preliminary hearing, your attorney, in a *Motion to Suppress* evidence, attempts vigorously to prevent the state from introducing the gun as evidence against you at trial. He/she argues that it was discovered in your glove box, an area that the police had no right to search, and, therefore, any evidence found in the glove box is inadmissible under the *Exclusionary Rule*. Had the judge agreed with your attorney, the state's case would have collapsed, and the charges against you would have been dismissed before coming to trial. In practice, the state usually has little difficulty meeting its burden of proof at the preliminary hearing and convincing the judge that the prosecution should go forward. And, unfortunately, such is the case here. The judge denies your attorney's motion, rules in favor of the prosecution, and binds you over for trial.

Speedy Trial

The Sixth Amendment guarantees you the right to a speedy trial. However, the Court has refused to set a time limit in defining what *speedy* means. Concern with the seriousness of court delays led to the passage of the **Speedy Trial Act** by Congress in 1974. Applying only to federal courts, the act demands that a defendant be brought to trial within sixty days of arrest. If not, the charge against the defendant must be dropped.

State courts are not bound by the above act. State courts have attempted to stay within a time span of 120 to 180 days, depending on whether the defendant is in jail or free on bail. For those out on bail, the court normally schedules cases 180 days from the date of arrest; whereas, for those in jail and waiting, the court will reduce the time to 120 days.

Trial Rights and Procedures

Presumption of Innocence

As a defendant in our judicial system, you have a number of very important trial rights, all of which will be explained by your attorney prior to the commencement of your trial. The most fundamental right of a person accused of crime is the *presumption of innocence*. The state must prove your guilt; they have the burden of proof. And the standard of proof is *proof beyond a reasonable doubt*. You need not prove your innocence. You need not call any witnesses. You need not present any evidence. You need not put on a defense. And, if the state fails to meet its burden, you will be acquitted. You will be found **Not Guilty**.

Right to Counsel

You have the right to be represented by an attorney at your trial. You will be provided with a court-appointed attorney if you cannot afford to retain one. This basic right is guaranteed by the Sixth Amendment. Originally applied only to federal courts, the Court has expanded the right to counsel to state criminal cases in which the defendant is at risk of incarceration.[29]

Right Not to Testify

If you will recall, you were informed of your right to remain silent when your Miranda Rights were read to you at the time of your arrest. The Fifth Amendment protects you against self-incrimination. Specifically, you have the right not to take the stand at trial; you have the right not to be compelled to testify. However, should you choose to testify in your own behalf, you will be answering questions advanced by your own attorney (**direct examination**); but then you must also submit to questions from the prosecution (**cross examination**).

Right of Confrontation

Related to the above is the right (Sixth Amendment) of a defendant to confront witnesses testifying against him/her. What this means is that although you are not required to take the stand, those accusing you must. As each witness for the prosecution takes the stand, under oath, to testify against you (*direct examination*), you have the right (through your attorney) to question (*cross examine)* each. This basic right has created considerable controversy in rape cases in which the victim (usually a woman) is forced to undergo humiliating cross-examination while the defendant (normally a man) sits idly by, comfortably shielded from such grueling questioning by the Fifth Amendment. Likewise, in such cases it is permissible (within justifiable range) for the defense to probe into and make known the victim's past sexual history while the prosecutor is generally forbidden to bring up the defendant's past criminal record. If such information about the defendant's past be revealed, the judge would, in all likelihood, be forced to declare a *mistrial,* and the state would have to initiate a whole new trial against the defendant. Except for very specific limited purposes at trial, the only point in the criminal process where the defendant's past criminal record can be brought to light is at the time of sentencing. Although this whole business might seem unfair in some cases, as in those involving rape victims, think of what life in America would be like if you could be accused of a crime, brought to trial, convicted, and sent to prison without ever knowing who accused you or without you having the right to dispute their accusations.

Right to Subpoena Witnesses

A defendant has the right to **subpoena** witnesses to testify in his/her behalf. What this entails is the court issuing an order compelling an individual to testify at trial. This Sixth Amendment right is fundamental to our concept of fair trials because it provides the means by which defendants can prove their innocence. Returning to a key issue in your case, the question as to why you were carrying a gun on the day of your arrest, is of great relevance. You wish to prove that your possession of the gun was related to your marksmanship hobby and you were not carrying an illegal concealed weapon for a criminal purpose.

In preparation for trial you have already discussed with your attorney—in minute detail—all the circumstances preceding your arrest. You informed your attorney that on the day of your arrest a young friend, by the name of Jerry, had accompanied you to the pistol range for target practice. His testimony would certainly be helpful in establishing your original intention with respect to carrying the gun. Unfortunately, when you contacted Jerry, you found that he was reluctant to become involved. It turns out that Jerry is younger than he had always led you to believe. (He is 20.) Under federal law he is not legally eligible to purchase handgun ammunition, but he had done so on several occasions. He did it by using false identification and is afraid that if he testifies this might come out at the trial. Is this the end of it? Of course not! You can exercise your right to subpoena Jerry. He would be legally obligated to come to court and testify. He could lie, deny knowing you or anything about the pistol club, but to do so would subject him to the penalty of perjury, which could ultimately land him in jail. A much better strategy would be to tell the truth, and on any related question about his purchase of handgun ammunition, "plead the Fifth," meaning to not answer any questions pertaining to the ammunition.

The Trial

The moment of truth has arrived—your day in court! Being an adversarial system, the American criminal justice system is relatively straightforward—the state against you. Court proceedings begin with the reading of the formal charge against you. Then both sides will offer an opening statement (opening arguments) outlining their view of the case. The defense may choose not to make an opening statement at this point. Next, the prosecution will presents its case. As has already been pointed out, the state has the burden of proof and must go first. You are the beneficiary of the "presumption of innocence" and have no obligation to present a case or defense in your behalf. Each witness is sworn in before giving his/her testimony. Undoubtedly, both your attorney and the prosecution will object to certain questions posed by each other to the witnesses, and it will be the responsibility of the judge either to overrule the objection (allowing the question) or to sustain it (not allowing the question). Both sides can also raise objection to witness responses, trial procedures, and to the admissibility of evidence.

Your attorney has made it clear that the entirety of the state's case against you rests upon the testimony of the arresting officers and the legality of the search that uncovered the handgun. (The issue of the legality of the search and seizure was first raised at the Preliminary Hearing). The prosecution calls as the first witness one of the two officers who stopped you—the officer who did the search leading to the discovery of the gun in the glove compartment. Skillfully, the prosecutor leads the officer through his testimony, recounting every detail of the evening of your arrest, including your every movement and activity. Obviously, the state is attempting to lay the groundwork for the *reasonable suspicion,* which, in the state's opinion, justified the officers stopping you, and then they could explain the justification for the search and arrest that followed.

On cross examination, your attorney asks the officer, "So, you and your partner were of the opinion that because you saw my client swerving his car that he might be driving under the influence of drugs or alcohol."

"Yes."

"But, he told you he swerved to avoid hitting a dog, correct?"

"Yes."

"He told you also he was gagging on some gum, correct?"

"Yes."

"Officer, is it unusual for someone who has consumed liquor to have a soft drink and pop some gum when they get behind the wheel and start driving again?"

"No."

"And, you did notice, did you not, the spilled soft drink on the floorboard near the driver's seat?"

"Yes."

"And, did you search the person of the defendant?"

"Yes," answers the officer.

"And why was such a search deemed necessary?"

"For safety purposes," answers the officer. "The defendant was behaving suspiciously; he appeared to be reaching underneath his seat, and he also grabbed something from the glove compartment and put it in his mouth.

"Did you find anything when you did the pat-down search of my client?"

"No."

"Did he appear to be intoxicated or under the influence of drugs?"

"No."

The prosecutor asks, "Did you search the car?"

"Yes."

"For what purpose, exactly."

"For safety purposes."

"Is that all?"

"No," he continues. "We suspected that there might be a weapon in the defendant's car and perhaps contraband or evidence of a crime as well. His behavior led us to believe that he may have been trying to conceal or destroy evidence. We concluded, therefore, that there was justification to support a non-warrant search of the defendant's vehicle, based upon 'exigent circumstances.'"

"Could you be a bit more specific regarding what you mean by 'exigent circumstances'?"

"Well, if we were correct as to what might have been in the car, if the defendant had been released, without the vehicle being searched, all that would have been lost."

"How extensive was your search of the defendant's car?"

At this point the officer begins to describe his search of the interior of your car. Leaning over, you try to whisper something to your attorney, but he raises his hand, silencing you. Obviously, this testimony is critical to your case, and he wants to hear it all.

The officer continues his testimony up to the discovery of the gun. When he finishes, the prosecutor turns and walks quickly back to the table. Picking up your gun, he returns to the witness stand and hands it to the officer. "Is this the gun you found in the defendant's vehicle?"

"Yes," he replies, after a brief inspection. "It has my mark and my initials."

Taking the gun from the officer, the prosecutor approaches the bench and hands it to the judge. "Your Honor, at this point the state wishes to enter this gun, marked 'state exhibit A,' into evidence."

"Objection," shouts your attorney, springing from his chair. "Defense requests that State Exhibit 'A' be suppressed on the basis that it is the product of an illegal search." Immediately, the prosecutor counters the objection from your attorney, and a brief and heated exchange occurs between the two before the judge raps his gavel and instructs both to approach the bench.

"Counselor," he addresses your attorney, "is this not essentially the same motion you made at the preliminary hearing?"

"Yes, your Honor," he readily admits, "but as we all know, in practice, many judges are reluctant to suppress evidence prior to trial, especially in cases like the present one. Also, as the court is no doubt aware, there is a difference of opinion among judges on this point. Some feel that rulings on admissibility are best handled at trial, not pretrial. The fact that our motion was denied at pretrial does not deprive us of the right to challenge the admissibility of the same evidence at trial. Further, the pre-trial ruling should in no way prejudice our present objection."

The judge nods in agreement before signaling your attorney to elaborate on his objection.

"Our objection is founded upon three points, your Honor. First, the search of my client's car was conducted prior to arrest. The Supreme Court gives the police broader search power if the warrantless search follows (is 'incident to') a lawful arrest. Second, it was a non-consent search. And third, the search that produced the gun was of areas expressly forbidden by the Supreme Court to police without a warrant. These include the areas under the front seat, the trunk, and the glove compartment."

"And the state's position," questions the judge, turning to the prosecutor.

"The Court has ruled that law enforcement officers do not need a warrant in *exigent circumstances*, and certainly no warrant is required to conduct 'plain-view' searches," notes the prosecution. "And the evidence in question was found during a lawful plain-view search."

"Your honor," admits your attorney, "it is true that police officers do have the right to conduct plain-view searches, but the officer clearly went outside the bounds of the plain-view doctrine when he searched the glove compartment."

"The glove compartment was not locked," the prosecutor quickly states.

"It was not locked, but it was **closed**," responds the defense. "The contents of the glove compartment were not in plain view! Further, according to Supreme Court rulings, the glove box cannot be searched in a case like this because it is protected by the principle of *expectation of privacy*.

Turning to the judge, the prosecutor remarks, "The court should consider the officer's testimony as to why they wanted to do a more thorough search of the defendant's car. The Supreme Court has granted police officers the right to conduct non-warrant searches of vehicles based upon their *'mobility.'*"

"Your honor," responds your attorney, "we do not dispute there was "reasonable suspicion" to justify the initial stop of my client. We do not challenge the "pat-down" search immediately following. But there was no reasonable basis for the belief that there was a weapon inside the car. There was no reasonable basis for a belief that there was contraband or evidence of a crime in the car or that my client was trying to hide or destroy evidence. What the officers observed did not qualify as 'exigent circumstances' to justify the extended search of the vehicle. Be that as it may, your Honor, you just heard the state's argument that the chief justification for the search of the glove compartment was that it was not locked, and that that fact made it subject to a 'plain view' search and legitimized the seizure of the gun."

"Your Honor," protests the prosecutor, "we maintain that . . . ."

"Thank you both," interrupts the judge. "I believe I have an understanding of both positions. Please step away from the bench."

Both attorneys return to their tables, sit in their chairs, and wait for the ruling. The judge sifts through his papers, stopping occasionally to briefly study his notes on the officers' testimony. You sit nervously on the edge of your own chair. Beads of perspiration dot your forehead and inside your stomach churns. Finally, after a few moments of contemplation, the judge looks up, signifying that he is ready to rule. "There is little doubt that the defendant was unlawfully transporting a weapon. With respect to issues of search and seizure, it is clear that the Supreme Court is in a process of transition, redefining Fourth Amendment rights and granting law enforcement authorities greater latitude in apprehending felons. Quite naturally, this impacts the applicability of the Exclusionary Rule."

Suddenly you feel sick to your stomach. You waver faintly on the edge of your chair as images of prison life flood your mind. Your attorney places a comforting hand on your arm as if to steady you. And then the judge's decision. . . .

"However," continues the judge, "based upon current Supreme Court rulings, I am compelled to agree with the defense that the arresting officers exceeded their authority under the Constitution. As the state is well aware, the determinative factor in deciding whether a search and/or seizure violates the Fourth Amendment is the element of *reasonableness*. This is especially true with respect to non-warrant searches. There is no quarrel with the circumstances that prompted the stop of the defendant by the officers, nor the 'pat-down' search immediately following. There is no quarrel with the initial 'plain view' search—glancing into the interior of the car upon the defendant being pulled over. The defense did not object to any of these points."

"The defense objects to the conclusion on the part of the officers that 'exigent circumstances' existed and to the expanded search that followed, which led to the discovery of the gun. The defense vehemently objects to the search of the glove compartment under the auspices of the 'plain-view' doctrine. I find the initial stop was lawful; the initial search of the defendant was supported by *reasonable suspicion*. However, I find no 'exigent circumstances,' nor reasonable suspicion, nor *probable cause* to support the expanded search of the defendant's vehicle. And, I find that the search of the glove compartment represented an unreasonable search and seizure, and the state's interpretation of the 'plain-view' doctrine is **plainly wrong**! Accordingly, defense's objection as to the admissibility of the gun is sustained." Addressing both the defense and prosecution, the judge explains that since the state's case was built solely upon the seized weapon, the court will dismiss the charges against the defendant. It is over—you are free!

Post-Trial Counsel

Before leaving the courthouse, you confer with your attorney for the last time. You ask if you can ever be tried for this offense again. Your attorney explains that the Fifth Amendment of the Constitution protects citizens against **double jeopardy**. In other words, you are forever immune from prosecution by the state for this incident. However, if you had violated federal law as well as state law in transporting the weapon, it would be possible for the federal government to arrest you and prosecute you in a federal court. Such an event would be unlikely, however, since the gun taken from you was ruled inadmissible as evidence based upon a constitutional guarantee against unlawful search and seizure.

What about the money you lost in attorney fees and time away from work? Can you sue the government for compensation? The answer is generally no. To sue, you would have to prove that the government had knowingly and with malicious intent sought to harm you by false arrest.

Final Thoughts

Though thankful at having secured your freedom, a nagging question lingers in the back of your mind as you walk slowly the length of the courthouse steps. There is no doubt that you were in fact guilty of transporting a gun illegally. But, you were saved from prison by what many refer to as a constitutional technicality. Your attorney explained it all to you—your civil rights and the importance the Court attaches to these rights. Without such safeguards, believe some legal experts, the United States could become a "police state." That's why the Exclusionary Rule was instituted—to force law enforcement authorities to respect your rights. But then there are other legal experts who have argued, in an equally persuasive voice, that the Exclusionary Rule has freed murderers, rapists, drug dealers, and other felons to walk the streets and prey upon even more law-abiding citizens. They argue that it is possible to discipline police without throwing out the evidence. In the past you have tended to side with the critics of the Exclusionary Rule and have been outraged when you heard that in many cases the rule results in the release of dangerous felons. But now, having faced the state and the threat of prison, all because of an illegal search, you are left with doubts. Which side is right? You wonder. . . .

A Postscript

The trial court judge was quite correct in his comment that the U.S. Supreme Court has been granting law enforcement authorities greater latitude in apprehending criminals and that this naturally impacts the Exclusionary Rule. Numerous Court doctrines have made evidence heretofore deemed inadmissible, because the evidence was obtained as a result of an illegal search, seizure, arrest or interrogation, no longer automatically so. Most of these doctrines are discussed in this chapter; such as "exigent circumstances," "good faith," "independent source," "inevitable discovery." Others, still, includes the "harmless error" doctrine, the "attenuation" doctrine, and the popular "totality of the circumstances" doctrine.

All these doctrines speak to the Supreme Court more and more upholding police practices against constitutional challenges. The Court has given the police the power to search a passenger's belongings if they found evidence of drug use by the driver. The Court upheld the right of police to stop and frisk a fleeing suspect.

Recently, the high Court did some things that curtailed the power of the government in criminal matters. However, the overall trend of the Court's last five years reflects increasing conservatism in the field of criminal procedure.

(Notwithstanding this observation, the Supreme Court this year, 2005, declared the death penalty for juveniles unconstitutionally cruel and unusual.) The Court's rulings have been tilted toward conservatism:

- Reaffirmed the *Miranda* Rule;[30]
- Ruled that police may not use thermal-image sensing devices to find evidence of criminal activity unless they obtain a warrant;[31]
- Held that drugs found in an automobile search were admissible even though the police officers may have stopped the defendant for a routine traffic offense as a pretext to search for drugs;[32]
- Ruled that police officers can detain a suspect outside his or her house while they obtain a warrant to search for drugs in the home;[33]
- Agreed that life sentences for habitual criminals did not routinely violate the Eighth Amendment's ban on cruel and unusual punishment;[34]
- Held that police, in routine drug and weapons interdiction effort, were not required to inform passengers on a bus that they did not have to cooperate and could leave the bus.[35]
- Ruled that the police can demand an individual stopped on the basis of *reasonable suspicion* to identify him/herself.[36]

In the area of automobile searches the Supreme Court continues to give law enforcement officers greater and greater leeway based on the trilogy of *inherent mobility-minimal expectation of privacy-exigent circumstances*. Further, the great expansion in the powers given to the government after 9/11, in the name of national security, especially the federal government, is still being felt. Strong efforts must be made to defend and strengthen individual liberties and individual rights, including rights of persons accused of a crime. As this goes to press, two or more justices on the Supreme Court are on the verge of retiring, including Chief Justice Rehnquist. Their replacements will no doubt be conservative, as the president who is likely to appoint them, George W. Bush.

Chapter Sixteen Notes

[1]*Barron v Baltimore*, Pet. 243, (1883)

[2]In a series of cases, beginning in the 1930s and accelerating in the 1960s, the Supreme Court has applied most of the rights in the Bill of Rights to the states (all rights except those in the Second, Third, Seventh and Tenth Amendments, and the Grand Jury requirements in the Fifth Amendment. This was done through what came to be known as the Incorporation Doctrine, which involves interpreting the word, *"liberty,"* in the due process of law clause in the Fourteenth Amendment to include certain rights in the Bill of Rights. By doing this, the rights in question become applicable to the states because the Fourteenth Amendment is addressed to the states.

[3]The Supreme Court has ruled that criminal evidence in "plain view" of an officer may be seized, without a warrant. *Coolidge v. New Hampshire*, 403 U.S. 443 (1971); *Horton v. California*, 496 U.S. 128 (1990).

[4]*Probable cause* is a reasonable belief by a police officer that there is justification to conduct an arrest or a search. *Illinois v. Gates*, 462 U.S. 213 ((1983).

[5]The Exclusionary Rule, propounded by the Supreme Court, states that illegally seized evidence is inadmissible in court. The illegal police activity may be a violation of the Fourth Amendment (illegal search, seizure, or arrest); Fifth Amendment (illegally obtained statements or confession); or the Sixth Amendment (denial of right to counsel). The Fourth Amendment's exclusionary rule was made applicable to the states in *Mapp v. Ohio*, 367 U.S. 98 (1977).

[6]*Terry v. Ohio*, 393 U.S. 1 (1968).

[7]The power of the police to search the area within the suspect's immediate control comes under a "search incident to arrest." *Chimel v. California*, 395 U.S. 752 (1969). And if the suspect is driving a vehicle when placed under arrest, the police can search the entire passenger compartment of the vehicle (including the console, glove compartment, and all containers. *New York v. Belton*, 453 U.S. 454 (1981). The challenged search in our Incident occurred *before* the arrest.

[8]The search power of the police at this point in our Incident is grounded in *reasonable suspicion* and, according to the Supreme Court, is more limited than if you are under custodial arrest. The police may conduct a limited search for weapons of the passenger compartment if there is reasonable suspicion that an occupant in the vehicle is dangerous and may gain immediate access to a weapon in the car. *Michigan v Long*, 463 U.S. 1032. (1983). The doctrine of *reasonable expectation of privacy* was enunciated in *Katz v. United States*, 389 U.S. 347 (1967).

[9] *Carroll v. United States*, 267 U.S. 132 (1925).

[10] *United States v. Ramsey*, 431 U.S. 606 ((1977).

[11] *New Jersey v. T.L.O.*, 469 U.S. 325 (1985).

[12] *Oliver v. United States*, 466 U.S. 170 (1984).

[13] *Miranda v. Arizona*, 384 U.S. 436 (1966).

[14] *Harris v. New York*, 401 U.S. 222 (1971).

[15] *New York v. Quarles*, 467 U.S. 649 (1984).

[16] *Arizona v. Fulminante*, 499 U.S. 279 (1991).

[17] *Gideon v. Wainwright*, 372 U.S. 335 (1963).

[18] *Rochin v. California*, 342 U

[19] *Schmerber v. California*, 384 U.S. 757 (1966).

[20] *Miranda v. Arizona.*

[21] *United States v. Wade*, 388 U.S. 218 (1967) and *Gilbert v. California*, 388 U.S. 263 (1967).

[22] *Habeas Corpus*, Latin for "you have the body," is court order directing that a person in custody be brought before a court or judge to challenge the lawfulness of his/her detention. This personal liberty right was protected under British common law and is preserved in the U.S. Constitution, in Article I, Section. 9.

[23] *Dunaway v. New York*, 442 U.S. 200 (1979).

[24] *Harris v. United States*, 390 U.S. 234 (1968).

[25] *United States v. Leon*, 468 U.S. 897 (1984).

[26] *Nix v. Williams*, 467 U.S. 431 (1984).

[27] *Murray v. United States*, 487 U.S. 533 (1986).

[28] *Katz v. United States.*

[29] *Gideon v. Wainwright*, 1963.

[30] *Dickerson v. United States*, 530 U.S. 428 (2000).

[31] *Kyllo v. United States*, No. 99-8508 (2001).

[32] *Arkansas v. Sullivan*, 532 U.S. 769 (2001).

[33] *Illinois v. McArthur*, 531 U.S. 326 (2001).

[34] *Ewing v. California*, No. 01-6978 (2003).

[35] *United States v. Drayton*, No.10-631 (2002).

Suggested Readings

Abraham, H.J. *Freedom and the Court.* 4th ed. New York: Oxford University Press, 1982.

Acker, James R., and David C. Brody. *Criminal Procedure: A Contemporary Perspective.* Boston: Jones and Bartlett Publishers, 2004.

Baker, Liva. *Miranda: Crime, Law and Politics.* New York: Atheneum, 1983.

Berns, Walter. *The Death Penalty: Cruel and Unusual Punishment,* New York: Basic Books, 1979.

Black, Charles L., Jr., Rev., ed. *Capital Punishment: The Inevitability of Caprice and Mistake.* New York: W.W. Norton and Company, 1982.

Bondeson, Ulla V. *Alternatives to Imprisonment: Intentions and Reality.* Somerset, N.J.: Transaction Publishers, 2002.

Cushman, Robert. *Cases in Civil Liberties.* 6th ed. Englewood Cliffs, N.J.: Prentice Hall, 1994.

Dershowitz, A.M. *The Best Defense.* New York: Random House, 1982.

Drips, Donald A. *About Guilt and Innocence: The Origins, Development, and Future of Constitutional Procedure.* Westport, Conn.: Praeger Publishers, 2002.

Fleming, Macklin. *The Price of Perfect Justice.* Basic Books, 1974.

Graham, Fred. *The Self-Inflicted Wound.* New York: The Macmillan Co., 1970.

Kalven, Harry, Jr., and Hans Zeisel. *The American Jury.* Chicago: University of Chicago Press, 1986.

Levy, L.W. *Against the Law: The Nixon Court and Criminal Justice.* New York: Harper & Row, 1974.

Lewis, Anthony. *Gideon's Trumpet.* New York: Vintage, 1964.

Walker, Samuel. *In Defense of American Liberties—A History of the ACLU.* New York: Oxford University Press, 1990.

Wall, David and Richard Young, eds. *Access to Criminal Justice: legal Aid, Lawyers, and the Defence of Liberty.* Holmes Beach, FL: Wm. Gaunt & Sons, Inc., 1996.

Chapter Seventeen

Civil Liberties:
Freedom in America

In the previous chapter we looked at the rights of the accused. These rights, based upon the Bill of Rights, assure that our freedom is guaranteed against arbitrary and capricious action by law enforcement officials who act on behalf of the government. The Bill of Rights also guarantees other rights considered "fundamental" to a free society. These include freedom of religion, speech, the press, the right to acquire and possess property, and others too numerous to mention here. In this chapter we embark upon an examination of some of these rights.

The Bill of Rights were proposed by Congress in 1789 and ratified by the states in 1791. Ten of the twelve proposed amendments were thus added to the Constitution. Civil liberties can be defined as Constitutional and legal protections against government interference in one's life. The Bill of Rights were designed to provide Americans with basic and fundamental rights that the government could not take away. The Founding Fathers feared that government, particularly like the one they had suffered under British rule, would enslave a free people unless it were restrained from doing so.

The First Amendment contains what some call the four basic freedoms: religion, speech, press and assembly. The remaining Bill of Rights deal with other basic rights such as quartering of troops, the right to bear arms and rights of the accused (from the preceding chapter). It is important to realize that even these fundamental rights are not absolute. Although Americans may indeed enjoy more freedom than any other people on earth, there are some limitations on how much liberty we can exercise. The government (known as the state) can deprive us of liberty in some cases. Usually, if the state can prove a "compelling" interest or an individual's freedom to exercise his rights may harm others, then it can limit rights. It may be helpful to picture an imaginary boundary that separates the individual from the arbitrary powers of the state. The state can penetrate that boundary only if it can prove that compelling interest. When the individual and the state are in dispute over such freedoms, the Supreme Court is the final arbiter. The Court must interpret the Constitution and decide what these rights actually mean and when and if they can be limited.

When the Bill of Rights were added to the Constitution, they had a major flaw. They start out by saying "Congress shall make no law," meaning that the national government could not take away our basic rights. However, it failed to mention that the states were also prohibited from taking away individual freedoms. States were free to deprive people of basic rights. In 1833, the Court said "these amendments contain no expression indicating an intention to apply them to the State governments."[1] In other words, the Bill of Rights applied only to the national government. To close this loophole, the Fourteenth Amendment was passed (but not until 1868!) to make sure the states were prevented from making laws that would violate fundamental freedoms. The Fourteenth Amendment stated that "No state shall make or enforce any law which shall deprive a person of life, liberty or property without due process." However, the Fourteenth Amendment was not enforced for many years. In 1925, the Supreme Court ruled in *Gitlow v. New York* that the Bill of Rights also applied to the states. The Fourteenth Amendment thus incorporated or took over the Bill of Rights and prevented the states from taking away basic rights. Think of the Bill of Rights as a shield that stood between the national government and the individual. The Fourteenth Amendment took that shield and placed it between the state and the individual. Since the *Gitlow* decision, the Supreme Court has had to expand that shield by applying most of the Bill of Rights to the states. We will look at how the Supreme Court had either allowed that shield to protect the individual or the state to cross that boundary and interfere with those rights. We will start with the First Amendment freedoms.

FREEDOM OF RELIGION

It may be no accident that the Founding Fathers deliberately chose religion as the first freedom in the First Amendment. To many Americans, this is the most sacred freedom we enjoy. This nation was founded on the notion of freedom of religion as evidenced by the Pilgrims and Puritans who settled here in the early seventeenth century. (Ironically, some of the first colonists did not believe in freedom of religion for those who disagreed with them!) The first two parts of the First Amendment are known as the Establishment Clause and the Free Exercise Clause. They need to be examined separately although they both deal with religion.

The **Establishment clause** means different things to different people. However, the Supreme Court offered this interpretation:

> *Neither a state nor the federal government can set up a church. Neither can pass laws which aid one religion, aid all religions, or prefer one religion over another. Neither can force or influence a person to go to or to remain away from church against his will or force him to profess a belief or disbelief in any religion. No person can be punished for entertaining or professing religious beliefs or disbeliefs, for church attendance or nonattendance. No tax in any amount, large or small, can be levied to support any religious activities or instructions, whatever they may be called, or whatever form they may adopt to teach or practice religion. Neither a state or the federal government can, openly or secretly, participate in the affairs of any religious organizations or groups or vice versa.[2]*

It is clear from this ruling that there is a so called "wall" between the government and religion. It is commonly referred to as the doctrine of "separation of church and state." Why is this concept so critical to Americans? Remember that under British rule, there was an official church headed by the monarch. This is still the case today as the Church of England is headed by Queen Elizabeth II. However, this wall may be a little ambiguous in some cases. For example, printed on all our money is the motto "In God we Trust." Children still recite the Pledge of Allegiance, which proclaims "One nation, under God." Both Houses of Congress start their day with a prayer. When taking the oath of office, the president swears to defend and protect the Constitution "so help me God." What the Founding Fathers may have meant is that there should be tolerance for all religious beliefs. People have a right to believe whatever they wish or nothing at all! Basically, they may have concluded government and religion should have nothing to do with each other and have no relationship whatsoever.

The Establishment Clause touches on issues such as aid to public schools, prayer in schools, and the recitation of the Pledge of Allegiance. The Supreme Court must decided if under what conditions, if any, the wall between church and state should be breached. In addition, the Court must arbitrate if it thinks the government and religion have become entangled and involved in each other's affairs. One of the most controversial church-state issues is prayer in school.

Why won't the Court let children pray in school? After all, don't the United States Congress and state legislatures open their sessions with prayer? In ad-

dressing this question, two important distinctions need to be made. The first is that the Court's ruling applies only to public schools, those supported through the expenditure of tax dollars. Children who attend private or **parochial** (church-affiliated) schools have and will always be allowed to exercise their right to organized prayer.

The second distinction is that the Court is not opposed to prayer in school. Students in public schools have always prayed, especially around test times or before they ate cafeteria food! What the Court has objected to is sponsorship or encouragement of prayer by public-school authorities. Such activity violates what is commonly referred to as the **establishment clause** of the First Amendment that states that "Congress shall make no law respecting an establishment of religion." The Court's position was clearly laid forth in the 1962 case of *Engel v. Vitale*.[3] Here the New York State Board of Regents approved the daily recital in their public schools of a short, nondenominational prayer that read as follows:

> *Almighty God, we acknowledge our dependence upon Thee, and we beg Thy blessings upon us, our parents, our teachers, and our country.*

In a 6-1 decision, the Court ruled that the prayer was an attempt on the part of the government to establish a religion. One year later, the Court followed up its ruling by declaring a Pennsylvania state law that required daily recitation of the Lord's Prayer and Bible readings unconstitutional.[4] The Court has also ruled against the posting of religious materials, for example, the Ten Commandments, on school walls.[5] In 2003, the Chief Justice of the Alabama Supreme Court was removed because he refused to remove a Ten Commandments monument from the courthouse.

As might be expected, these decisions generated a storm of controversy that, to date, continues to rage. Since the terrorist attacks of 9/11, supporters of school prayer have asked the Court and school officials to reconsider the ban on organized prayer. Recently, advocates have attempted to include school prayer in the classroom through a period of silent meditation, like an Alabama law that allowed teachers to include within the curriculum a one-minute period for "meditation or voluntary prayer." The Court struck this act down since it was clearly established by the state legislature as an attempt to bring back school prayer.[6] However, some experts suggest that the Court may yet allow silent meditation if properly handled by state legislatures and done without pre-established religious intentions. An example of this was a Virginia law that required a moment of silent reflection at the beginning of the school day. A federal court ruled this was not a violation of the Establishment Clause because it did not mandate prayer. The moment of silence does not even mention prayer. Students could pray, be silent, or just close their eyes! Unlike in the *Engel* case, a teacher or other school official was not forcing students to pray in an organized manner. The Supreme Court refused to hear an appeal and let the lower court decision stand.

In 1992, the Supreme Court struck down the use of clergy, selected by school officials, to lead prayers at public school graduation ceremonies. In a 6-3 vote in 2000, the Court also barred school officials from letting students lead stadium crowds in prayer before a football game.[7] This decision reversed what it had said about student-led prayer at sporting events less than a decade earlier.

Despite these previous defeats, supporters of religion in public schools continue to do what the courts say they cannot do. On February 8, 2002, a federal judge ordered Reah County (Dayton, Tennessee) to stop Bible study classes in the public schools when parents of two school children anonymously challenged the program in a lawsuit. Ironically this is the same county that is remembered as the site of the famous Scopes Monkey trial in 1925, which challenged the teaching of evolution instead of creationism in the public classrooms.

It should be noted that the Court permits the study of the Bible or religion in public schools, but only as part of the regular secular curriculum, like a course on comparative religion or the Bible as literature. Conversely, the state could not prevent the study of a particular subject, such as evolution, just because a certain religion objects to its implications.[8] And, in 1987 the Court struck down a Louisiana law that required "creationism" (the Bible's version of how the world was created) to be taught along side of evolution. Here the Court ruled that creationism was not a scientific, but, rather, a religious doctrine.

In another 1993 case, the Supreme Court confronted the issue of when religious groups faced having their right to free speech violated simply because they were religious groups. Voting 9-0, the Court struck down a New York state school district's policy forbidding the use of school facilities after hours by religious groups while allowing other community groups access. The Court proclaimed that this practice violated the First Amendment free speech guarantees by discriminating against religious organizations.[9] In June of 1995, the Court ruled in a 5-4 decision that the University of Virginia's refusal to fund the printing of a student, religious newspaper was unconstitutional.[10]

Regarding the final part of our question, how is it that the national Congress and state legislatures can get away with opening prayers? Are they not subject to the same rules as children in public schools? Interestingly enough, the Court has considered this question and ruled that it is, indeed, legal for legislators, both national and state, to open their sessions with a public, nondenominational prayer. The Court ruled that the critical difference here was that, as adults, the legislators were not "susceptible to religious indoctrination or peer pressure."[11]

Recently, one of the most controversial issues regarding religion in schools has been the Pledge of Allegiance. In 2002, the Ninth Circuit Court of Appeals struck down the words "under God" because it violated the Establishment Clause.

A great furor in much of the nation ensued, and the case was appealed to the Supreme Court. There was a great deal of anticipation by the advocates of the pledge (including the Bush administration which supports the words "under God") who were hoping the Court would clearly say the entire pledge was not a violation of the Establishment Clause. However, they could only claim a hallow victory after the ruling. The Court dismissed the case without reaching any decision because the father, who had sued on behalf of his daughter because she had to recite the pledge, did not have full custody. Therefore, the father had no standing to sue. Yet, Justice Sandra Day O'Connor said in a separate opinion "the Pledge has become, alongside the singing of the Star-Spangled Banner, our most routine ceremonial act of patriotism"[12] The words "under God" can be said once again, but this issue will surely be headed back to the Supreme Court again.

Not all subjects taught in parochial schools are religious in nature, so why can't the government provide some money to help support the secular (non-religious) curriculum? Contrary to what many may think, some tax money finds its way to parochial and private schools. The crucial difference, however, at least from the standpoint of the Court, is the *purpose* for which the money is to be used. For example, the Court has allowed states to give money for transporting students to and from private and parochial schools, for the purchasing of secular textbooks, and providing lunch programs. Likewise, parochial and private schools have benefited from assistance in diagnostic services for speech and hearing problems, for certain types of remedial help, and reimbursement for the cost of scoring state-required standardized tests. The Court has justified the continuation of these expenditures on the basis of its **child benefit theory**, which held that providing such assistance benefits the child rather than the school or religious institution.[13] Similarly the Court ruled that parents could deduct a large portion of what they paid for tuition, books, and transportation for their children from their state income taxes if the state law permitted such deductions.[14] Similar tax deductions have not yet been granted for federal income taxes.

What the Court has taken exception to is any activity that could be construed as "sponsorship, financial support, and active involvement of the sovereign [government] in religious activity."[15] As such, the Court has ruled against the following types of state support to parochial elementary and secondary schools:

1. salaries of teachers other than for remedial work,

2. reimbursement for equipment,

3. purchases or loans of maps and other instructional materials,

4. counseling for students,

5. preparation of teachers' tests,

6. repair of school facilities,

7. transportation of students to and from field trips.

The Court has also ruled that religious instructors are not permitted to enter public schools on school days to provide religious training on a voluntary basis. However, the Court recently voted 5 to 4 to allow public school teachers to conduct remedial classes at parochial schools.[16] Likewise, the Supreme Court upheld the **Equal Access Act** that prohibits high schools receiving federal funds from discriminating against certain groups because of their religious, political, or philosophical beliefs. Schools that allow some community groups to hold meetings on school property must now provide meeting space for after-school activities for all groups. Although the suit was brought on behalf of *Bible* clubs, the Court ruled that all clubs, including devil worshipers and the Ku Klux Klan, are entitled to meeting space in public high schools.[17] In other words, if the school allows one group to hold meetings in its buildings, then it must admit any group, regardless of its ideology.

The Court's rulings regarding public aid for colleges and universities are considerably more relaxed. The state is allowed to provide funds for the construction of buildings and operation of educational programs so long as they are not used as worship centers or to teach classes specifically designed for religious training.[18] The Court's rationale here is basically the same as it was with Congress; that is, college students are older and less susceptible to indoctrination. A variation of this issue was discussed by the Court in a recent decision. The state of Washington sponsored a scholarship program for students but recipients could not use the money to pursue a devotional theology degree. The Court upheld the state's policy and said it did not violate the rights of students who wanted to obtain such a degree.[19]

Is the display of religious artifacts on public property, such as a nativity scene, legal? The answer to this question is, yes—at least in some cases. In a 5-4 decision, the Court ruled that Pawtucket, Rhode Island, was within its legal rights to purchase and display a nativity scene in the center of its shopping district. The Court's rationale was based upon three points. **First,** the purchase and display of the nativity scene were motivated from the celebration of a national holiday. **Second,** since the nativity scene was displayed alongside a "Santa's house" and other holiday symbols, it was reasonable to assume that its display had a commercial intention. And **finally,** no excessive entanglement could be established between the government and a special religious group. If any benefit did occur, it was in the words of the Court, "indirect, remote and incidental."[20] In a recent ruling, *Capital Square v. Pinette and Knights of the Ku Klux Klan*, the Court has expanded the use of public property for religious artifact use. In 1995, the Court ruled that the Ku Klux Klan could erect a cross on state property used for public purposes. The Court reasoned that (1) the property was a genuinely public forum, (2) the state could not discriminate against religious speech alone, and (3) religious expression could not violate the establishment cause where the expression was purely private and occurred in a traditional public forum.[21] However, to muddy the waters a bit further, the 7th U.S. Circuit Court of Appeals ruled in a Wisconsin case in February 2000, that a statue of Jesus Christ that stands on privately owned land within a city park violates the law because people could assume the city government endorses a religion. Just a month earlier, the U.S. Supreme Court let stand a Maryland law that required the annual closing of all public schools on Good Friday.

What should a person understand from all these rulings? If nothing else, it should be clear that, on matters of church and state, there is no agreement about the meaning of "establishment of religion."

Does the Constitution protect all religious practices? Even though the Constitution seems rather clear on this point—"Congress shall make no law . . . prohibiting the free exercise [of religion]"—the Court has never taken the position that all religious practices are legal. Rather, what it has attempted to do is to distinguish religious beliefs from behavior or actions based on such beliefs. In plain language, while the government recognizes your right to believe in anything you want, it will not necessarily permit you to act out those beliefs if they are deemed antisocial or harmful to the society. If your religion believes in sacrificing young virgins to the gods, then this is clearly not protected under the Free Exercise Clause! The Court has ruled that the handling of poisonous snakes or the use of mind-altering drugs such as peyote (used in the religious ceremonies of some native Americans) is illegal. The Court reaffirmed this decision by striking down the Religious Freedom Restoration Act enacted by Congress to protect religion from government interference.[22] Likewise, the Court continues to rule against the practice of polygamy, even though some recent reactionary religious groups profess it as part of their religious beliefs.[23] And, too, while the Court has recognized that adults may refuse medical treatment for themselves, they could not prevent medical authorities from intervening with blood transfusions and other measures to save the lives of their children.[24] A Pennsylvania couple whose son nearly died of cancer because they chose to treat his condition with faith healing instead of medicine were sentenced to 14 months' probation and lost custody of their son. Similarly, others have been convicted of manslaughter when their child died of complications from diabetes after the parents refused to allow treatment. Moreover, the state may require vaccinations for school children whose parents are opposed to such measures to protect

The price of a free society! The Court has ruled that the constitutional right to free speech and assembly apply to all citizens regardless of how offensive their beliefs might be to the majority.

the community from disease.[25] In the words of the U.S. Supreme Court in 1944, "Parents may be free to become martyrs themselves. But it does not follow that . . . they are free to make martyrs of their children . . . before they have reached the age . . . where they can make the decision for themselves."[26]

On the other hand, the Court has declared some controversial religious practices valid. Jehovah's Witnesses are not required to salute the American flag because doing so conflicts with their belief of worshiping graven images.[27] Amish parents, whose beliefs run counter to "worldly values," are not required, as are people of other faiths, to educate their children beyond the eighth grade. In the suit against them, the Court ruled that the state had failed to prove that the lack of a secondary education impaired such children from becoming productive and healthy adults later in life. The Court was careful to point out that the decision applied only to the Amish and not to "faddish new sects and communes."[28] The Court has also decided that employees cannot be fired from their jobs for refusing to work on Saturday or Sunday because of religious convictions.[29] And finally, the Court has ruled that conscientious objectors cannot be drafted into the military. Furthermore, the Court has ruled that one need not be a member of a particular religious group to claim such status. Even atheists can be exempt if their "consciences, spurred by deeply held moral, ethical, or religious beliefs, would give them no rest or peace if they allowed themselves to become part of an instrument of war."[30] In these instances and others similar to them, the Court has attempted to walk a fine line in cases involving religious practices. Again, the key question from the Court's standpoint, is the practice "antisocial" or "harmful."

While these cases serve as examples of the constitutional protection of religious practices *Oregon Department of Human Services v. Smith,* a 1992 case, can be viewed as the potential reversal of this era of protection. Until the Oregon case, the state was required to show a compelling state interest to overcome a religious group's objections to comply with recognized standards. Since this Oregon case, the government can order religious groups to comply as long as the law is content neutral, that is, the law is not aimed only at religious groups. Rather, its application is intended for everyone.[31] For example, in south Florida, there are a number of people of Caribbean descent who practice a native Caribbean religion called Santeria. Among their religious practices is the "sacrifice" of chickens and goats. The city of Hialeah enacted an ordinance forbidding such practices. However, the Supreme Court struck down the ordinance because the law did not make the killing of chickens and goats outside of religious practices illegal. In other words, the Santerias *would* have been compelled to comply *if* the law had applied to all and not just to them.[32]

Needless to say, this shift in protection has religious groups upset and working hard to restore what they feel to be religious freedom. Groups that were previously exempt from all sorts of laws, such as the Amish being allowed to keep their children out of school after the eighth grade, can no longer be as sure that they will be exempt from certain types of legal compliance. As time passes, these issues that were seemingly resolved may be revisited by courts in light of these more recent rulings.

FREEDOM OF SPEECH AND THE PRESS

Along with religion, freedom of speech and the press has generated equal amounts of controversy within our society. Although the Constitution seems relatively straightforward in stating that "Congress shall make no law . . . abridging the freedom of speech, or of the press," the Court has never granted people an absolute right to say anything they wish, either verbally or in writing. Keep in mind that no right is absolute. The Supreme Court is very protective of most basic rights, but there is a limit to how far a person can exercise his or her rights. A good example is freedom of speech. It is perhaps better to give a better definition of what we mean by speech. When we think of speech, we think of verbal speech. However, there are so many ways to express yourself without ever opening your mouth! The term expression is probably a much better and accurate word than speech. The Court has been particularly sensitive to cases dealing with expression and have generally sided with the rights of the individual. However, not all forms of expression enjoy a great deal of protection.

Types of expression could be: (1) Verbal speech, (2) Political speech, (3) Symbolic speech, (4) Commercial speech, (5) Slander, (6) Libel, (7) Art, (8) Pornography, and (9) Obscenity. We will discuss some of these in greater detail to examine how much freedom each is accorded.

Most reasonable individuals have little difficulty grasping this point in light of an understanding that some forms of speech may violate the rights of others or hold potential harm for the society. The trick, however, is to determine what speech violates others' rights or has legitimate potential for societal harm. Your freedom of expression ends when it infringes on the rights of others or causes harm to the public. You do not have the right to blast your stereo at 3 a.m. in the morning or stand up in front of an audience and tell lies about someone! Although the interpretation of the First Amendment regarding freedom of speech and the press has undergone changes over time, in this chapter we will take a look at only those interpretations currently used.

The Preferred Position Doctrine

Sometimes referred to as the "absolutist position," this doctrine comes closest to declaring all forms of censorship unconstitutional. Justices Hugo Black and William O. Douglas, who both served the Court until the early to mid-1970s, were avid supporters of this doctrine. In the issue of the Pentagon Papers, perhaps the most celebrated case settled by this doctrine, Justice Black wrote, "Both

Dr. Daniel Ellsberg, antiwar activist who was arrested for releasing the secret "Pentagon Papers," holds an impromptu news conference outside a federal building in Boston while his wife, Patricia, waits behind him after he was released on bond. The Court later reversed Ellsberg's conviction when it was demonstrated that the government used illegal means to obtain evidence against him.

the history and language of the First Amendment support the view that the press must be left free to publish views, whatever the source, without censorship, injunctions, or prior restraints" *(New York Times Co. v. United States)*.[33] In summary then, this position maintains that speech and press are essential to the continuation of democracy in America and are of the "highest priority." Judges, therefore, should be especially vigilant when encountering laws restricting speech and the press. The preferred position doctrine is still viewed by the Court as relevant in cases with political overtones.

Direct Incitement Test

As noted earlier, your freedom of expression can be limited. When can and should the government stop one's freedom of speech? A landmark case in 1919 addressed the issue. The Court ruled "Whether the words used are used in such circumstances and are of such nature as to create a clear and present danger that they will bring about the substantive evils that Congress has the right to prevent"[34] The Court stated here that speech can be limited if it threatens public safety, and, thus, we have the establishment of the Clear and Present Danger Doctrine. Later in the *Gitlow* decision (yes, we talked about this case before earlier in the chapter) the Court established the "bad tendency rule," which stated that speech could be limited if it leads to some sort of evil. For example, someone can be stopped from screaming "FIRE" in a crowded movie theater. That action will obviously result in injuries. The issue with this is knowing what someone will say. Unless you are a psychic, how do you know that someone will say something evil that will lead to harm? It is not possible to follow people around and tackle and gag them in the event they MAY say something evil!

During the half century following the issuance of the clear and present danger rule, the Supreme Court struggled with the meaning of the word "danger." Exactly what constituted a "danger"? Finally in 1969, the Court created a new test to determine if certain kinds of speech could be regulated by the government, namely the **direct incitement test.** Under this test, the government could punish people who advocate illegal action only if "such advocacy is directed to inciting or producing imminent lawless action and is likely to incite or produce such action."[35] Requiring that the "harm" be "imminent" (near at hand) made it more difficult for the government to punish speech and is consistent with the principle that speech plays a very special role in a democratic society. For example, if a member of some militia group openly advocated the eventual overthrow of the United States government by force, he could not be prosecuted for this speech. Unless the militiaman starts handing out the guns to his supporters, he is still within the protections of the First Amendment. The courts interpret the First Amendment to mean that there is a distinction between advocating something illegal and actually doing it or conspiring to do it.

Prior Restraint

Prior restraint is the action of government to prevent the publication of materials or the utterance of speech that it views harmful. The Court regards this form of censorship as potentially the most dangerous threat to the functioning of a free society. Although the Court has permitted the government some areas in which to exercise "prior restraint," its use comes with what the Court in one ruling stated as "heavy presumption against its constitutionality."[36] The government has been most successful in obtaining prior restraint in military and security matters.

Least Drastic Means

Having determined that a particular law restricting freedom of speech or the press is a legitimate end, the Court will next attempt to ascertain if the method used is the **least drastic means**. If another method, less restrictive on speech or the press, could accomplish the same purpose, then the law would be declared unconstitutional. For example, if there was a fly in your house, you could certainly kill it by blowing up the house with dynamite! Or, you could just use a fly swatter. The fly swatter would be the least drastic means of achieving the goal.

Content Neutral

In rulings on laws restricting speech and the press, the Court has tended to be more favorable to those that are **content neutral**. Such laws generally concentrate on regulating the process as opposed to ideas. For example, a law prohibiting the distribution of handbills at a traffic intersection during rush-hour traffic would, in all likelihood, be declared constitutional. However, including within the same law a phrase restricting only political handbills would result in an unconstitutional ruling. The difference is that one law restricts all handbills and, thus, is content neutral. The second bill, however, attempts to regulate a specific form of free speech and, as such, is not content neutral.

Centrality of Political Speech

The right to criticize the government is essential to maintaining a free society. It is not only the right of citizens to openly question their government, but it is also their duty as Americans to do so! America was a nation founded on protest. The American colonists were extremely harsh and critical toward King George III and Parliament, and the Founding Fathers were aware that any government must tolerate and allow political dissent. Americans are given a great deal of latitude when criticizing public officials. Short of threatening his life, one is allowed to say almost anything he or she wants about President Bush. (Just look at the extremely harsh criticism he received in the bitter election of 2004!) All of our public officials may be criticized by the public, and they are free to criticize their colleagues. It is obvious how negative and nasty political campaigns have become by their brutal tone. Consequently, the Court has always granted greater latitude on matters of public policy. In defending its favorable treatment, the Court declared that "Not all speech is of equal First Amendment importance. It is speech on matters of public concern that is at the heart of the First Amendment protection."[37]

Admittedly, our previous review of historical and current doctrines is rather lengthy. However, it does provide us with the necessary information to understand the complexities of the issues before the Court, as well as the rationale it uses to justify its decisions. With this in mind, let's turn to some questions commonly asked by students when discussing this topic.

Can I be sued for spreading a false rumor about my neighbor, even though I believed it to be true? You bet! Your freedom of speech does not give you the right to harm others. The Court has consistently upheld the illegality of **slander** (oral defamation) and **libel** (written defamation). The fact that you believed the rumor to be true at the time you spread it makes no difference whatsoever. However, for your wrongdoing to become **actionable**, the plaintiff would have to furnish proof that the statement was observed by a third party. For example, suppose you walk up to a fellow-employee and privately accuse him of having an affair with the boss. You could not be held accountable for slander. The same would be true if you wrote your accusation in a private letter. Your action would not be libelous. However, suppose, unknown to you, the intercom system was on broadcast, and the remark was heard by other employees throughout the store. Now we're talking *big bucks*! Also, in regard to our other example, if your secretary types the letter of accusation, then you could be sued for libel. (You really don't want to do these things, so just keep your mouth shut!)

Interestingly enough, the same protections against slander and libel do not extend to public officials and public figures (for example, movie and television personalities). The Court has ruled that before such individuals can sue, they must prove that the statements made against them were false and made with *actual malice*, that is, intention to harm (*New York Times v. Sullivan*).[38] Why make it so difficult for public officials and public figures? Basically, to ensure that "unfettered discussion" of public issues is not discouraged. If we are to remain free, then it is necessary for citizens to feel secure in criticizing public figures without fear of retaliation.

Can I be prosecuted for swearing in public? Yes and no, depending upon the circumstances. Generally, the act of swearing in public is not illegal. As one justice commented, "one man's vulgarity is another's lyric." But this is not an absolute. The Court has ruled that certain words and abusive forms of speech can be banned if they, by their utterance, tend to incite violence from the person or group to whom the remarks are directed.[39] Under this ruling, racial and ethnic slurs could be banned. Likewise, while the utterance of some four-letter words would not be punishable under most circumstances, if directed at a person in such a way that could provoke violence, it could be punishable. However, it is important to note that the Court applies rather strict standards on the side of free speech. For example, in one case, when a teenager burned a cross on the front lawn of a black neighbor, the police charged the youth with a bias-motivated crime of race, color, creed, religion, or gender. Upon challenge, the city defended its action maintaining the crime provoked alarm and anger, which could incite violence. The Court ruled against the city, stating that the law was too broad. The city could well have arrested and prosecuted the youth for trespassing and destruction of property. The same rule applies to signs and words worn on clothing. It should be mentioned that some communities have circumvented this free speech issue with laws dealing with disturbing the peace (yelling, shouting, screaming, etc.). It would be wise, however, again to keep your mouth shut when you think about swearing in public. Not all state laws regarding this issue have been brought before the courts on appeal. For example, in Michigan, it is against the law to make such utterances in the presence of children, and the state has successfully prosecuted people for doing so.

Does the above rule apply to symbolic speech? For example, what if I give someone "the finger"? The Court has held that speech may be symbolic. Consequently, some acts, gestures, or symbols can convey a message or political viewpoint. Not that any of us would make this gesture, but giving someone "the finger," therefore, is speech and could be declared unlawful because of its tendency to incite violence. It is on this basis that some city governments have attempted to ban the display or the wearing of certain gang symbols. The issue of symbolic speech becomes considerably more complicated when done to express a political belief. In a recent controversial ruling, the Court struck down a congressional act making it illegal to desecrate the American flag. Hence, even burning the flag is currently a legitimate political expression.[40] The Court has also ruled that, while schools could enforce reasonable dress codes, they could not prohibit students from wearing armbands to protest governmental action unless the schools could first prove that the action would incite violence.[41] However, not all politically symbolic speech is legal. In the late 1960s, the Court refused to approve draft-card burning by Vietnam-War protesters.[42] The Court's reasoning was that the act itself (destroying draft cards) was illegal under the Selective Service Act.

Another issue dealing with symbolic speech is cross burning. Many states and local governments passed hate crimes legislation in the past 15 years that

Not all areas of free speech are protected. The Court has ruled that some practices are clearly illegal. Here, Goddard C. Graves, 22, burns his Selective Service classification card in front of a local draft board office. Although this gesture of symbolic speech is prohibited, a recent ruling by the Court gave such protection to burning the American flag.

would ban activities such as cross burning. It is commonly known that the KKK has burned crosses in the past as a symbol of their hatred for such groups as African Americans and Catholics and to declare their opposition to Civil Rights legislation. However, since a burning cross is silent, the intent is not always clear, and it doesn't necessarily constitute a clear and present danger to public safety, the Supreme Court has granted some amount of protection to it. In fact, in a 2004 decision, the Court struck down a state law that banned cross burning. The Court said that burning a cross with the "intent to intimidate" can be outlawed. However, it also argued "It may be true that a cross burning, even at a political rally, arouses a sense of anger or hatred among the vast majority of citizens who see a burning cross. But this sense of anger or hatred is not sufficient to ban all cross burnings."[43]

While we are on the subject of the KKK, the Court has again extended the protection of freedom of speech to them in a recent case. As many civic groups do, the Klan wanted to adopt a stretch of highway in Missouri to pick up litter and trash. Missouri thought it would be inappropriate to allow a hate group to participate in the Adopt a Highway program. The state feared that it would encourage people, who have contempt and loathing for the Klan, to deliberately throw trash on the highway! The Court ruled that barring the Klan from volunteering to pick up trash was a violation of their freedom of speech.[44]

Do students in public schools have the same rights as adults in the public? In attempting to decide between the greater issue of order and Fourth Amendment privacy rights of students, the Court has consistently ruled in favor of order. In a 1985 case, the Supreme Court gave school officials the right to search students without a warrant or "probable cause" if they believed a crime had taken place. In this case a fourteen-year-old girl was detained by school officials who believed she was in possession of drugs. In searching the girl's purse, they found marijuana, a pipe, and letters indicating she was selling the drug to other students. Attorneys for the student maintained that the search was illegal and, as such, the evidence seized was inadmissible. In a 6-3 decision the Court upheld the conviction stating that the officials needed only knowledge of drug activity in the school.[45]

In 1995, the Court extended the rights of school officials by allowing mandatory drug tests of athletes and, in 2002, extended this ruling further by allowing random drug testing of any student participating in extracurricular activities, which included, not only sports, but also choir, student clubs, and cheerleading squads, among others.[46]

Although not necessarily related to drugs, one federal court has also ruled that teenagers do not have the right to wander the streets late at night. In upholding a Washington, D.C., curfew law for children younger than 17, the court stated that the law does not violate children's rights or interfere with the rights of parents to bring up their children as they see fit. Therefore, in answering the original question about minors and adults having the same rights, the answer is it depends, but the courts tend to lean toward society's safety and order rather than toward consideration of a minor's freedom.

Can I be arrested for something that I might say in cyberspace? The Founding Fathers could have never foreseen the use of the Internet as a tool of expression. Certainly this will be an area of great change. At this point in time it appears that the Court is squarely on the side of free speech. No where is this more clearly seen than with the area of obscene materials. In 1996, Congress passed the Communications Decency Act. The act made it illegal to transmit "indecent" and "patently offensively" materials over the Internet, which would be available to minors. One year later, the Court struck down the act citing that it was too broad since it suppressed a large amount of constitutionally protected speech to adults.[47] The Court sent mixed signals (as it sometimes does) with two other cases dealing with the Internet and free speech. In 2003, the Court upheld a portion of the 1998 Child Internet Protection Act (CIPA) when it said that Congress could deny funds to libraries that did not use filtering blocking software to prevent patrons from accessing pornographic websites. This act would also authorize a fine of up to $50,000 for placing material on the Internet that would be harmful to minors if seen by children online.[48] However, the Court struck down the entire CIPA in 2004!

In another case, a man named James Baker was arrested for transmitting e-mail messages to a college woman in which he threatened to kidnap and assault her. The case was short-lived as the indictment was thrown out before it reached trial. In doing so, the judiciary came down on the side of free speech by ruling that Baker's messages failed to meet the "true threat" standard. Controversial as it was, the ruling stated that "Discussion of desires, alone, is not tantamount to threatening to act on those desires."[49] Needless to say, many people vehemently disagreed with the Court's ruling in this case.

In still another case, a lower federal court, restricted a company's ability to flood the Internet with junk mail. When America On-line (AOL), the largest on-line service provider, attempted to stop Cyber Promotions from sending commercial advertisements to its customers, the company sued. Cyber Promotions maintained that their advertisements were protected by First Amendment rights of free speech. The Court disagreed maintaining that AOL had the right to block such transmissions to its subscribers.[50] This decision was reaffirmed when Cyber Promotions brought suit against CompuServe.[51]

In 1998, a U.S. District Court also decided in favor of a high-school student who had established a personal home page on the Internet, using his parents' home computer for the project. Spiced with occasionally vulgar language, the home page criticized the school's official Web site. The school had suspended him for posting the page critical of the school.

The Internet will undoubtedly continue to be fertile ground for conflict as those concerned about the potential harm of unfettered access and transmission of all materials square off against those who fear that any infringement will lead to an erosion of free speech. The frustration of the judiciary in this arena is clearly echoed in the words of Supreme Court Justice Souter, "I have to accept the real possibility that if we had to decide today. . . just what the First Amendment should mean in cyberspace, . . . we would get it fundamentally wrong."[52]

When running for office, do I have the right to post my campaign literature where I want? Sorry. Again the answer is no. The right of citizens to distribute handbills, leaflets, and pamphlets in support of religious and political ideas or candidacy has long been upheld by the Court. However, communities can regulate how they may be distributed as long as such ordinances are content neutral. Sound trucks, ruled the Court, may be regulated in the same manner. For example, a law that prohibited all sound trucks from operating in residential areas between midnight and 7:00 a.m. would be considered "content neutral" and allowable. A law that forbade only religious sound trucks from operating in the same time period would not.

One of the most difficult and controversial expression issues deals with the issues of pornography and obscenity. In 1964, United States Supreme Court Justice Potter Stewart said, "I can't define pornography, but I know it when I see it." Although the Court has ruled that pornography and obscenity are not protected speech, it is often difficult to ban them because it is not easy to define

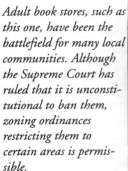

Adult book stores, such as this one, have been the battlefield for many local communities. Although the Supreme Court has ruled that it is unconstitutional to ban them, zoning ordinances restricting them to certain areas is permissible.

what they are! Obviously, there is near unanimous agreement that child pornography should always be forbidden. However, one could make the argument that we have seen an explosion in questionable material in almost every segment of society. With the universal use of the Internet, it is now possible to view some of the most graphic and shocking material imaginable. Just check your spam mail and you will discover we are bombarded with pornography and obscenity on a daily basis! As previously mentioned, the Court has been very protective of the Internet. Until recently, local authorities were responsible for establishing the laws which govern pornography and obscenity, but now citizens can bypass these regulations by using the Internet to view whatever they choose or have this material delivered to the comfort and privacy of their homes! Nonetheless, the Court has the power and responsibility to make rulings dealing with these thorny issues.

Can local communities prohibit stores from selling magazines such as "Playboy" and "Penthouse"? Again we enter into a mine field. In no area has the Court had more trouble providing a definitive ruling than in the area of obscenity. The Court has consistently held that "obscenity" is not protected by the freedoms of speech and the press (*Roth v. United States*).[53] Although a majority of the Court agreed with this position, its attempt to establish guidelines about what constituted obscenity ran into trouble. In the *Roth* case, the Court defined obscenity as that material "which deals with sex in a manner appealing to the prurient interest." Furthermore, its test revolved around the question of whether the average person, applying "contemporary community standards," would be offended by the material. However, the Court stated that "the portrayal of sex .

. . in art, literature, and scientific materials" enjoyed First Amendment protection. Obviously, considerable confusion resulted in applying the test—even by members of the Court. In 1973 in the case *Miller v. California*,[54] the Court attempted to clear up the confusion. Here it outlined three major guidelines for local officials: (1) would "the average person, applying 'contemporary community standards' find that the material, taken as a whole, appeals to the prurient interest...; (2) whether the work depicts or describes, in a patently offensive way, sexual conduct specifically defined by the applicable state law; and (3) whether the work, taken as a whole, lacks serious literary, artistic, political, or scientific value." In essence, the Court threw the issue back to local governments with an admonition that it would no longer review their decisions on a case by case basis. However, a year later in the case *Jenkins v. Georgia*[55] the Court warned that local juries did not have "unbridled discretion in determining what is patently offensive."

In *United States v. X-Citement Video, Inc.*, the Court upheld a ban on interstate transportation of child pornography.[56] However, in late 1999, the 9th U.S. Circuit Court of Appeals ruled that the federal Child Pornography Prevention Act went too far when it outlawed, not only sexual images of actual children, but also images that only appeared to be minors. That Court ruled that child pornography was clearly unconstitutional, but outlawing images that did not involve the use of real children violated the First Amendment rights of people in the adult entertainment industry.

As already noted, in 1996, Congress enacted the Communications Decency Act. The intent of the law was to protect children from pornography through the Internet. One year later, the Court declared the law unconstitutional. Justice John Paul Stevens speaking for a unanimous Court stated:

> It is true that we have repeatedly recognized the governmental interest in protecting children from harmful materials. But that interest does not justify an unnecessarily broad suppression of speech addressed to adults. The government may not reduce the adult population. . . to . . . only what is fit for children.[57]

So where does that leave us? Currently the Court's position is best represented by the following two statements:

1. Obscenity is not entitled to constitutional protection.

2. In proceeding against obscenity, local governments must do so under specifically defined laws detailing what sexual conduct is prohibited in words or pictures.

Local officials have found that enacting such laws is no easy task. At present, here are some of the finer applications of obscenity laws:

1. Sexually explicit materials about minors ("kiddie porn") or aimed at them are not protected by the First Amendment. In a 1990 case, the Court upheld a strict Ohio law making it illegal to possess and view such material even in the privacy of one's own home.[58]

2. Local communities can ban the sale of what is commonly described as "girlie" magazines to minors.

3. The location of "X-rated" movie theaters, as well as adult bookstores, can be regulated by special zoning laws.

4. Zoning bans on live entertainment to prohibit nude dancing in adult bookstores are illegal if they specifically single out such places.

5. Antipornography ordinances banning the sale of magazines such as "Playboy," "Penthouse," and others are unconstitutional.

As a result of these Court rulings, recent efforts by local communities have been more directed at restricting locations where sexually explicit materials can be viewed and who can view them, rather than at banning them.

What does the public think about freedom of speech? Results of a poll conducted in 1997 by Market Shares Corporation for the *Chicago Tribune* newspaper revealed that 27 percent of those polled believed that the First Amendment went too far in the rights it guarantees, 55 percent said the guarantees were about right, eight percent said the amendment did not go far enough, and 11 percent said they did not have an opinion.

When specifically asked about speech on the Internet, 50 percent said the government should restrict what goes on the Internet, 31 percent disagreed with that idea, eight percent did not have an opinion, and 12 percent were not familiar with the Internet. In addition, regarding the use of sexual expressions by radio personalities on the air (Howard Stearns and others, for example), the survey resulted in 58 percent thinking they should not be permitted to do so, 35 percent asserting they should, and seven percent who had no opinion. The bottom line here is that free speech or not so free speech is still generating a great deal of controversy.

Let's say that my boss is involved in fraudulent business activities, and I reveal the information to a reporter who later prints a story about it in the newspaper. Can the reporter legally refuse to reveal me as his/her source on the grounds of confidentiality? Much to the dismay of reporters, the answer is a definite no. The Court's position on this matter is best illustrated by the now famous case of *New York Times' Co. v. Jascalevich*.[59] A *New York Times* reporter, Myron Farber, refused to turn over his notes, as ordered by the presiding judge in a murder case. Farber claimed a reporter's notes and records were protected by a *shield of* *confidentiality*. The judge disagreed and jailed Farber for an indefinite period. The matter was appealed before the New Jersey Supreme Court, and Farber lost. The state court based its decision on the 1972 Supreme Court case of *Branzburg v. Hayes*,[60] in which the Court concluded that "the public has a right to every man's evidence, except for those persons protected by a constitutional, common law, or statutory privilege." What this means is that Congress could, if it so desired, protect reporters by enacting a **shield law**. Naturally reporters have argued in favor of shield laws stating that without this type of protection valuable information will not be published, and the public will suffer. Apparently Congress has not been persuaded since no such laws have been passed.

The press have also claimed to be exempt from surprise warrant searches of their files and working papers. They maintained that material could only be viewed through a subpoena issued by a judge after a hearing. In the case *Zurcher v. Stanford Daily*,[61] the Court disagreed. In this case police officers of Santa Clara, California, obtained a warrant to search the files of the *Stanford Daily* to obtain pictures of a student takeover of the university hospital. The paper objected citing confidentiality but again lost for essentially the same reasons as above. However, in this case Congress did choose to write a law prohibiting the issuance of warrants to police for searches of "work products" of the press unless the persons involved are suspected of a crime or the material to be seized could prevent death or bodily harm to others.

If I am being tried for a crime, can I exclude the press to protect my reputation? The Court has ruled that the press has a right to attend public trials. This right is based upon the decision that trials are public forums, and the public has a right to know.[62] Former Chief Justice Burger went so far as to state that the press may be granted priority entrance to trials and provided special seating. The only instance in which the defendant might have a right to exclude the press is if it could be shown that media coverage would interfere with his/her constitutional rights to a fair trial. However, in such instances judges have generally ruled in favor of the press.

Although the press has a right to attend trials, they have no right to photograph or televise a trial's proceedings. Some states permit these activities; others do not.

ADDITIONAL RIGHTS

Can the government compel citizens to submit to drug testing? With the widespread use of drugs in our society, it became an increasing concern that many people in extremely sensitive areas of employment might well be putting the country as a whole or individuals at risk. In 1986, President Reagan signed the first executive order mandating drug testing for a wide range of governmental employees. However, in the same year, a lower federal court ruled that a "mass roundup urinalysis" violated the constitutional protections of individuals against unreasonable searches. The Court ruled that the fear of drug abuse was not a reason for trampling on "fundamental principles and protections."[63] However, the courts have not ruled out mandatory testing altogether. It has been allowed in cases of public employees in which there is a compelling national interest (Defense Department employees) or in which the public safety is at stake (e.g., customs inspectors, prison guards, train engineers, etc.). In 1997, Congress passed a law authorizing random drug searches of all congressional employees. (Note: The members of Congress did not include themselves in this law.)

Private employers and professional sports organizations have required pre-employment drug screening for some time. The Court has upheld these actions. In 1989, the Court went further in ruling that mandatory drug and alcohol testing of employees involved in accidents was constitutional.[64] However, in 1997, the Court ruled unconstitutional a Georgia law that required all candidates for state offices to pass a drug test 30 days before qualifying for nomination or election.[65] As in other areas of search and seizure (See Chapter 16), the Court makes a distinction between searches conducted by government and those conducted by nongovernmental agencies. Those conducted by government are much more restricted.

Didn't the Court once declare the death penalty "cruel and unusual punishment"? If so, why are some inmates still being executed? The Court has never taken the position that the death penalty was "cruel and unusual punishment." It has, however, questioned the manner in which it is applied. For example, a study of those executed in America between 1930 and 1965 revealed that nearly all were male and that over half were black. Few women and disproportionately few white males convicted of capital crimes were put to death.[66] On the basis of this evidence, the Court in 1972 declared the death penalty illegal until such

The gas chamber at San Quentin Prison was hermetically sealed by twisting the wheel affixed to the iron door. The executioner stood by the lever at the upper right, looking into the gas chamber through blinds slanted so that he could see the victim, but the victim could not see him.

time that states eliminated the arbitrary way in which the death penalty was applied.[67] In 1986, the Court further refined its view when it required that before the death penalty could be imposed, the state must prove that the defendant "had actually killed, attempted to kill, or intended that lethal force be used."[68] In addition, the Court has ruled that a state may not automatically impose the death penalty for capital offenses. Each case must be handled individually with the circumstances of the crime and the character of the guilty party taken into account.[69] At present, a majority of states (39) have revised their laws to comply with the Court's guidelines and are currently executing death-row inmates. In two separate decisions in 1989, the Court decreed that both juvenile offenders and the mentally retarded may be executed.[70] However, about half the states that have death penalty laws do not execute retarded persons, and more than half do not execute persons under the age of 18.

In June 2002, the Supreme Court dealt another blow to the death penalty in an Arizona case that affected about eight hundred people scheduled for execution in the United States. The Court ruled in *Ring v. Arizona* (122 S.CT. 2428) that trial judges by themselves could not impose the sentence of death on defendants convicted of possible capital offenses (death penalty sentences). That determination must be made by a jury in a separate hearing. Since Arizona and a number of other states had allowed the trial judges to impose the death sentence, all those inmates awaiting execution who had sentencing decided solely by the judge at their trials were granted stays of execution while the entire mess was sorted out.

How can the government prohibit citizens from owning and carrying guns when the Second Amendment clearly states that "the right of the people to keep and bear Arms, shall not be infringed"? This is, perhaps, the most misinterpreted amendment in the Bill of Rights. Historically, the Court has never interpreted the Second Amendment to mean that individual citizens have a right to arm themselves. Rather, the Court has interpreted this amendment as a right of states to create an armed militia. Thus, we have the national guard. Indeed, we are fortunate that the Court has chosen to view the Second Amendment from this perspective. Otherwise, it would be possible for your neighbor, with whom you might be quarreling, to purchase a cannon and place it in his front yard with the barrel pointing toward your house!

Every state has laws restricting the use of guns, some more restrictive than others, to be sure. There are also federal laws that prohibit certain people from legally purchasing guns. They include people convicted of or under indictment for felony charges, fugitives, the mentally ill, those with dishonorable military discharges, those who have renounced U.S. citizenship, illegal aliens, illegal drug users and those convicted of domestic violence misdemeanors or under domes-

Senator Dick Durbin (D-IL) talks at the podium on the issue of handgun control. In the wheelchair to his left is Jim Brady, who was hit by gunfire when John Hinkley shot at President Reagan. The Brady Act is a congressional law mandating that state law enforcement agencies conduct criminal background checks prior to allowing an individual to purchase a handgun.

tic violence restraining orders. State laws add other categories. On November 30, 1999, the computerized, instant check system established by the Brady Act began operation. It is designed to prevent gun sales to criminals, drug users, and others barred from buying handguns, rifles, or shotguns. In the first 41 days of the system's operation, the FBI blocked almost 12,000 guns sales and took steps to catch over 1500 would-be gun buyers who were wanted for criminal offenses. Strangely enough, the heaviest gun-buying period in the United States is the Christmas season.[71]

State laws usually set up rules regarding how and under what circumstances a person may "carry" weapons. The meaning of the word *carry* was recently expanded by the Supreme Court in a 5-4 decision. According to this ruling, a person is considered to be carrying a weapon even if the weapon is locked in the glove compartment or the trunk of a car.[72]

If the state plans to build a new highway through the living room of my house, which has been in my family for three generations, do I have to sell or can I refuse? <u>The answer is you must sell</u>. Should the state decide that it wants your property for some purpose it deems necessary for the public interest, it can claim your property. This principle is referred to as **eminent domain** and is a right the national government also possesses. Many students find it appalling that the government can seize private property. But consider how difficult it would be to build highways, schools and hospitals, establish communication networks, lay power lines, etc., without a procedure to acquire property. This is why every government has historically laid claim to the principle that the <u>public good overrides private property rights</u>.

It is interesting to note that before the Fourteenth Amendment was put in place, the Supreme Court ruled that states could seize property without paying for it. Just compensation applied only to the national government. However, the Court now, under due process rights of the <u>Fourteenth Amendment, requires states to compensate people for their loss</u>.

What if the Ku Klux Klan wanted to march through an all black neighborhood or a Neo-Nazi group wanted to goose step through an area where many are Jewish and survived the Holocaust of World War II? One would think this could definitely be a clear and present danger to public safety. Surprisingly, the Court has been very supportive of controversial groups and their right to speech (as show in the previous example of the *Capital Square v. Pinette* decision). In other words, even Nazis or Klan members have the right to express their views publicly so long as they do it in a peaceful manner. As for potential violence, the Court has mandated local officials to protect peaceful demonstrators who themselves may be targeted for violence.

Local governments do have some rights in these matters. The Court has ruled that certain time, place, and manner restrictions can be placed upon demonstrators as long as such restrictions are **content neutral**. For example, the courts have ruled that groups have a right to public places—streets, sidewalks, parks—for marches and demonstrations, but no group has the right to trespass on private property. Hence, a corporate office would be off limits to demonstrators. Likewise, groups have the right to peaceful assembly, but demonstrators who shout offensive slogans that could produce a riot or block traffic would be subject to arrest. And too, it is well within the right of local officials to prohibit marches through quiet residential areas at 4:00 in the morning. Although these are only a few of the many examples that could be offered, they serve to illustrate that when it comes to assembly, it's a two-way street between the rights of demonstrators and those of local government.

There is an on-going argument between those who support a loose interpretation of freedom of assembly and those who support a more restrictive view. According to the former, the measure of a just society is its willingness to protect the rights of unpopular groups. In doing so, we protect our own rights. Those who disagree contend that the world has experienced too many horrors such as the Nazi holocaust and other "ethnic cleansing" as in the former Yugoslav republics, racially motivated violence, violence against women, etc. Because of these horrors, societies should not grant forums to those who wish to argue for the continuation of such deeds. Very few societies interpret freedom of speech, press, religion, and assembly as liberally as the United States judicial system.

Is it constitutional for a state to outlaw certain sexual practices among consenting adults? Historically, laws have often been written restricting certain sexual practices deemed inappropriate by the majority. In recent years, with the evolution of "gay power," homosexuals have organized against such legislation contending that they, most often, are the targeted victims of so-called "sex laws." In 1986, the Court agreed to hear the case of Michael Hardwick, a homosexual who had been arrested by police in an Atlanta motel room when discovered having sex with another man. In this particular case, the police went to the motel room to arrest Hardwick for failing to pay a fine for drinking in public. When they arrived, they found Hardwick engaged in a homosexual act outlawed by Georgia law. Hardwick was arrested, tried, and convicted. He then appealed, contending that sexual acts between consenting adults, performed in the privacy of one's home, were beyond the reach of the government. Hardwick's

Gay rights groups march in protest over rulings by the Supreme Court that upheld the constitutionality of laws banning certain types of sexual practices. The intent of this march was to persuade Congress to act in their behalf.

attorney argued that sexual preferences, as well as acts, differed little from other privacy rights granted by the Court in matters of contraception and abortion. In a 5-4 decision, the Court disagreed maintaining that only heterosexual choices, such as whom to marry, whether to conceive a baby, or whether to abort, fell into the "*zone of privacy*."[73] However, the Court reversed the *Hardwick* decision in 2003. The case stems from a 1998 incident in which Houston police were responding to a weapons disturbance. Upon entering the home, they found two gay men engaging in consensual sex. The two men were arrested, convicted, and fined for violating the Texas sodomy law. They appealed the conviction, and the Supreme Court ruled that all state sodomy laws were unconstitutional since "it is within the liberties of people to choose without being prosecuted as criminals."[74]

Consequently, in answer to the question, it *is* constitutional for the government to restrict certain sexual practices of both homosexuals and heterosexuals, but individual states have chosen not to continue to do so for some actions. Currently, thirty-five states have either rescinded laws restricting sodomy between consenting adults or had these laws declared unconstitutional by courts. However, there are some really strange laws regarding sexual behavior still on the books in some local communities. For example, a town in Wyoming bans couples from having sex while standing inside a store's walk-in freezer. Not to be outdone by Wyoming, a town in Utah prohibits couples from having sex while riding in an ambulance![75]

Do terminally ill patients have a right to end their lives? Historically, the Court has taken a dim view of suicide. How we see ourselves and how we value life are essential ingredients to the stability of our society. But what about cases where humans are trapped in hopeless situations and must endure endless pain? Should they be made to suffer despite the inevitability of death? Or, should they be granted the right to end their own lives? Many see this issue as one of privacy, an individual decision to be made by rational, thinking human beings acting in their own best interest. Others see it as a threat to the values that sustain a well-ordered society.

In a very early case (1976), the state Supreme Court of New Jersey allowed the parents of a comatose young woman to remove her feeding tube.[76] However, in 1990 and again in 1997, the U.S. Supreme Court held that individuals, even mentally competent people, do not have the *right* to terminate their lives with or without assistance from a physician.[77] In other words, the Court was saying that the state could enact laws to permit or *not* permit suicide or assisted suicide. These issues were not about individual rights, according the Court's interpretation, but about the state's right to govern certain individual behavior. All states have laws against suicide, and almost all states ban assisted suicide either by law or by court interpretations of state laws and constitutions. Only the state of Oregon allows physician-assisted suicide on a limited basis. Despite all the laws and judicial decisions, 61 percent of the public, according to one poll, believes that physicians should be allowed to assist terminally ill patients who are in pain to die.[78] This attitude may explain why it took the State of Michigan five tries (on five different charges) to convict Dr. Jack Kevorkian of second-degree murder. On that fifth charge, Dr. Kevorkian defended himself—usually a very foolish thing to do!

LIMITATIONS ON RIGHTS

By no means were those who wrote the Bill of Rights (basically the Anti-Federalists) of limited intellectual ability or foresight. Again, the Bill of Rights grew out of a compromise between the Federalists and the Anti-Federalists. To secure ratification of the new constitution, the Federalists sought to appease the Anti-Federalists by promising to incorporate a bill of rights into the document once it was approved. As we have already seen, the Anti-Federalists were very suspicious of a strong central government. Hence, the purpose of the Bill of Rights was to ensure that the government was kept in check. Work on the Bill of Rights had not progressed too far when its authors suddenly became aware that they were wielding the proverbial "double-edged sword." For, although they had a wonderful opportunity to secure some very basic rights, they realized that it would not be humanly possible to write down, or even think of, all rights possessed by people. Could it later be interpreted that those rights written into the Constitution were the only rights people had? Certainly not. How was the dilemma to be resolved? Having completed their basic work, the Anti-Federalists added the Ninth Amendment. It reads as follows:

> *The enumeration in the Constitution, of certain rights, shall not be construed to deny or disparage others retained by the people.*

Simply stated, this means that just because some rights are listed in the Constitution does not mean that these are the only rights people possess. Considering the complexity of current society and the tremendous changes the United States has undergone in a little more than 200 years of independence, authors of the Bill of Rights showed exceptional foresight by including the Ninth Amendment.

CONCLUSION

One of the distinguishing features of governments and societies that endure is their recognition of human freedom. While no government or society is perfect, it is the striving for perfection that most impresses those who live where freedoms are ignored. Debate about the meaning and extent of various liberties enjoyed by those who live in the United States will certainly continue. In the meantime, Americans would be wise to reflect from time to time on how we exercise these liberties and, probably more importantly, how we allow others to do the same. One of the most daunting tasks of the government in the post 9/11 era is to balance the rights of the individual and the need to provide safety. The Patriot Act of 2002 was passed in the wake of the 9/11 attacks and has sparked a tremendous debate in America. While some say the Patriot Act is a necessary evil to prevent additional terrorist attacks, others claim it has had a chilling effect on individual freedom in the U.S. Although the Patriot Act should be debated, (and everyone should know what it contains. There is simply not enough space in this chapter to provide a detailed analysis!) the large issue here is how can we live up to the American ideals of providing all citizens with these precious rights yet prevent another tragedy like 9/11. Finding this delicate balance will no doubt be one of the biggest challenges to America for many years.

Chapter Seventeen Notes

[1]Barron v. Baltimore, 32 U. S. 243 (1833).

[2]Everson v. Bd. of Education,m 330 U. S. 1 (1947).

[3]*Engel v. Vitale*, 370 U.S. 421 (1962).

[4]*Abington School District v. Schempp*, 374 U.S. 203 (1963).

[5]370 U.S. 421 (1962).

[6]*Wallace v. Jaffree*, 86 L Ed 2d 29 (1985).

[7]*Sante Fe Independent School District* v. *Doe,* (2000) No. 99-62.

[8]*Larkin v. Grendel's Den*, 459 U.S. 116 (1982).

[9]*Chicago Tribune*, 8 June 1993, 1 and 13.

[10]*Rosenberger v. University of Virginia*, 132 L.Ed. 1995.

[11]*Marsh v. Chambers*, 463 U.S. 783 (1983).

[12]Elk Grove School District v. Newdow 02-1624 (2004).

[13]330 U.S. 1 (1947).

[14]463 U.S. 783 (1983).

[15]*Lemon v. Kurtzman*, 403 U.S. 602 (1971).

[13]*Agostini v. Felton*, 1997.

[17]*Chicago Tribune*, 5 June 1990, 1 and 12.

[18]*Tilton v. Richardson*, 403 U.S. 672 (1971).

[19]Locke v. Davey 02-1315 (2004).

[20]*Lynch v. Donnelly*, 465 U.S. 668 (1984).

[21]*Capital Square Review v. Pinette and Knights of the Ku Klux Klan*, 132, L.Ed. 1995.

[22]*Reno, Attorney General of the U. S. v. American Civil Liberties Union*, 117 S.Ct. 2329 1997.

[23]*Reynolds v. United States*, 98 U.S. 145 (1879).

[24]*Jacobson v. Massachusetts*, 197 U.S. 11 (1905).

[25]*Jacobson v. Massachusetts.*

[26]*Prince v. Massachusetts,* 321 U.S.1958 (1944).

[27]*West Virginia State Board of Education v. Barnette*, 319 U.S. 624 (1943).

[28]*Wisconsin v. Yoder*, 406 U.S. 205 (1972).

[29]*Sherbert v. Verner*, 374 U.S. 398 (1963).

[30]*Welsh v. United States*, 398 U.S. 333 (1979).

[31]*Chicago Tribune*, 7 January 1990, 1 and 6.

[32]*Church of the Lukumi Babalu Aye, Inc. v. City of Hialeah*, 508 U.S. 520 (1993).

[33]403 U.S. 713 (1971).

[34]*Schenck v. U. S.*, 249 U. S. 47 (1919).

[35]*Brandenburg v. Ohio*, 395 U.S. 444 (1969).

[36]*Nebraska Press Assn. v. Stuart*, 427 U.S. 539 (1976).

[37]*Dunn & Bradstreet v. Greenmoss Building*, 86 L Ed 2d 593 (1985).

[38]*Chaplinsky v. New Hampshire*, 315 U.S. 568 (1942) and *NAACP v. Claiborne Hardware Co.*, 458 U.S. 886 (1982).

[39]*McIntyre v. Ohio Election Commission*, 131 L.Ed. 1995.

[40]A ruling reported by the Court in the first two weeks of June, 1990.

[41]*Tinker v. Des Moines School District*, 393 U.S. 503 (1969).

[42]*United States v. O'Brien*, 391 U.S. 367 (1968) and *Brown v. Glines*, 444 U.S. 348 (1980).

[43]Virginia v. Black 01-1107 U. S. (2003).

[44]Rahn v. Robb, 04-629 (2005).

[45]*New Jersey v. T.L.O.*, 469 U.S. S. 325 (1985).

[46]*Board of Education v. Earls*, 122 S.Ct. 2559 (2002)

[47]*Reno v. Americans Civil Liberties Union.*

[48]*ACLU v. Ashcroft* 03-0218 (2004).

[49]*United States v. Gonda*, 890 FSupp. 1375 (1995)

[50]*Cyber Promotions, Inc. v. America Online, Inc.*, 948 F.Supp. 436 (E.D.Pa. 1996).

[51]*CompuServe, Inc. v. Cyber Promitons, Inc.*, 962 F.Supp 1015 (S.D. Ohio 1997)

[52]*Denver Area Educational Telecommunications consortium, Inc. v. Federal Communications Commission*, 116 S.Ct. 2374 (1996).

[53]354 U.S. 476 (1957).

[54]413 U.S. 15 (1973).

[55]418 U.S. 153 (1974).

[56]*Time*, 30 April 1990, 85.

[57]*Reno, Attorney General of the United States v. American Civil Liberties Union.*

[58]99 S.Ct. 6 (1978).

[59]439 U.S. 1301 (1978).

[60]408 U.S. 665 (1972).

[61]436 U.S. 547 (1978).

[62]*Richmond Newspaper, Inc. v. Virginia*, 448 U.S. 555 (1980).

[63]*Anderson v. Creigton*, 483 U.S. 635 (1987).

[64]*Skinner v. Railway Labor Executives' Association*, 489 U.S. 602 (1989).

[65]*Chandler v. Miller*, 520 U.S. 305 (1997).

[66]Steffen W. Schmidt and others, *American Government and Politics Today* (St. Paul, Minn.: West Publishing Company, 1985), 117.

[67]*Furman v. Georgia*, 408 U.S. 238 (1972).

[68]*Cabana v. Bullock*, 88 L Ed 2Ed 2d 704 (1986).

[69]*Roberts v. Louisiana*, 431 U.S. 633 (1977).

[70]*Chicago Tribune*, 27 June 1989, 1 and 12.

[71]Michael J. Sniffen, "FBI Blocks 11,584 Guns Sales" (Associated Press: Washington, D.C., January 11, 1999).

[72]James Vicini, "Gun 'carried,' even locked in car--top U.S. court" (Reuters: Washington, D.C., June 8, 1998).

[73]*Bowers v. Hardwick*, 478 U.S. 186 (1986).

[74]Lawrence v. Texas 02-102 (2003).

[75]Robert Wayne Pelton, *Loony Sex Laws That You Never Knew You Were Breaking* (Walker and Company, 1992).

[76]*n re Quinlan*, 70 N.J. 10 (1976).

[77]*Cruzan by Cruzan v. Director, Missouri Department of Mental Health*, 497 U.S. 261 (1990); *Vacco, Attorney General of New York, et al. v Quill, et al.,* 117 S.Ct. 2293, 138 L.Ed.2d 834 (1997).

[78]*USA Today*/CNN Poll (Novermber 22, 1999): 21A.

Suggested Readings

Brigham, John. *Civil Liberties and American Democracy*. Washington, D.C.: Congressional Quarterly Press, 1984.

Friendly, Fred W. *Minnesota Rag: The Dramatic Story of the Landmark Case That Gave New Meaning to Freedom of the Press*. New York: Random House, 1981.

Gates, Henry Louis, Jr., ed. *Speaking of Race, Speaking of Sex: Hate Speech, Civil Rights, and Civil Liberties*. New York: New York University Press, 1995.

Hentoff, Nat. *The First Freedom: The Tumultuous History of Free Speech in America*. New York: Delacorte, 1980.

Levy, Leonard W. *Emergence of a Free Press*. New York: Oxford University Press, 1985.

Lewis, Anthony. *Make No Law: The Sullivan Case and the First Amendment*. New York: Random House, 1992.

Miller, W.L. *The First Liberty: Religion and the American Republic*. New York: Knopf, 1968.

O'Brien, David M. *Constitutional Law and Politics: Civil Rights and Civil Liberties*. 3d ed. New York: W.W. Norton and Company, 1997.

Chapter Eighteen

Equality:
Promises and Realities

Perhaps no issue has proved more troublesome to Americans than equality. For over two hundred years the people of the United States have agonized over it, debated it, attempted to legislate both its meaning and existence, and warred over it from the battlefields of the War Between the States, fought over it in the streets of nearly every urban community, and, more recently, agonized over it in attempting to prevent another terrorist attack. And still the conflict continues to produce strong, divisive reactions. Public opinion polls have asked Americans about the issue of equality for several decades. Some of the questions asked and statements that seek responses are:

1. If your party nominated an African American for president, would you vote for him if he were qualified for the job?

2. If African Americans came to live next door, would you move?

3. Do you approve or disapprove of marriage between whites and non-whites?

4. Do you think white students and African-American students should go to the same schools or to separate schools?

5. In general, do you favor or oppose the busing of African-American school children and white school children from one district to another?

6. White people have a right to keep African Americans out of their neighborhoods if they want to, and African Americans should respect that right.

7. Homeowners should be able to decide for themselves to whom to sell their house, even if they prefer not to sell to African Americans.

8. Once affirmative action programs for women and minorities are started, the result is bound to be reverse discrimination against white men.[1]

How would you have responded? Do you think members of your family and friends would feel the same? Why?

For those who did respond, the results revealed a surprising pattern of inconsistency between values and actions. On the one hand, most Americans seem to be aware of the discriminatory barriers faced by minorities and, largely, disapprove of these obstacles. This disapproval was demonstrated by the overwhelmingly receptive response to the first four questions that measured the respondent's *values*. However, in a sharp contrast, an intolerant pattern was found on the remaining four statements concerning actions. These results suggest that, while possessing liberal values about the rights of women and minorities, few Americans support *governmental* efforts to resolve the problems of discrimination. Speculation about why this conflict between values and actions exists has led to much debate among scholars. One analysis suggests that Americans generally are committed to expanding the opportunities for victims of discrimination; however, governmental efforts to accomplish these goals collide with another equally cherished ideal within the culture: liberty (See Chapter One). The resulting clash between these two values has left programs, values, and commitments to equality in a state of confusion.

This chapter will explore the issue of equality. It will reveal that, while the United States has made good on its promise to some in our society, there still remains a substantial segment of its population for whom equality and opportunity remain difficult to achieve. The remainder of the chapter will examine what is being done to extend the equality of opportunity to these citizens.

THE STRUGGLE FOR POLITICAL EQUALITY

The present barrier faced by minorities and women to social mobility has its roots embedded deep within history. The experience of women, in general, and racial minorities, in particular, is illustrative of this point.

The Experience

Only an irrational few would assert that the experience of the African-American minority in the United States has been one of fairness and equality. No

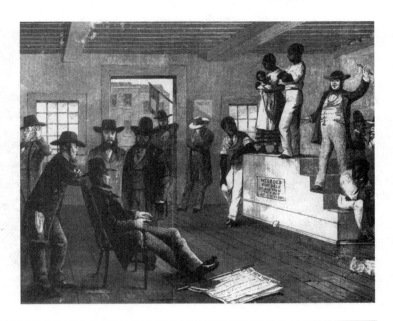

A slave auction at Richmond, Virginia, in 1856.

group could endure a long history of slavery and the social and political disruption that slavery entails without sustaining a severe collective and individual trauma. Slavery, coupled with the discrimination and intimidation that resulted after slavery was abolished, has left the black American psyche deeply wounded. It has been only in recent decades that efforts began to reverse these undemocratic patterns of behavior and to attempt to heal the wounds this history has produced.

The Freedom Amendments. Immediately following the close of the War Between the States, Congress proposed the Thirteenth Amendment, which officially ended slavery in the United States. On its heels came the Fourteenth Amendment, which bestowed citizenship upon all persons born or naturalized in the United States. In addition, state governments were forbidden to take any action that would interfere with the rights of citizenship.

One problem still remained. Since the responsibility of conducting elections was wholly within the constitutional jurisdiction of the states, many Americans feared that some states might deny African Americans the privilege of voting. To alleviate that fear, the **Fifteenth Amendment** prohibited any attempt to limit the privilege of citizens to vote on the basis of "race, color or previous conditions of servitude."

Besides two constitutional amendments, Congress passed a number of civil rights laws. The most important was the *Civil Rights Act of 1875*, which, among other things, prohibited racial discrimination in public accommodations such as hotels, hospitals, parks, etc. This law responded to the southern states' ever-increasing legislation designed to limit the civil rights of black Americans through segregation.

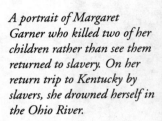

A portrait of Margaret Garner who killed two of her children rather than see them returned to slavery. On her return trip to Kentucky by slavers, she drowned herself in the Ohio River.

The Rise of "Jim Crow"

The African-American hope for equality faded quickly with the end of Reconstruction. With the departure of federal troops came the rise of **Jim Crow laws**. The aim of such laws was twofold: **first**, to deny the political rights of African Americans to vote and, **second**, to segregate African Americans, as well as other racial minorities, from the white population. The attempt of African Americans to undo these injustices through civil suits proved futile. In fact, the Court ultimately sided with the segregationists. Perhaps the two most damaging cases to be decided were *United States v. Resse* (1876) and *Plessy v. Ferguson* (1896).

In *United States v. Resse,*[2] the Court declared that the Fifteenth Amendment did not guarantee an absolute right to vote but only the right of an individual not to be discriminated against in voting because of race, color, or previous condition of servitude. Quickly southern states enacted a number of devices designed to disenfranchise African-American voters. Chief among these were:

1. **Literacy tests:** a device whereby voters would be required to pass a test to prove literacy prior to voting;

2. **Grandfather clauses:** exempted all people and their descendants who had voted before 1867 from taking the literacy test;

3. **Poll tax:** required voters to pay a fee to vote;

4. **White Primary:** a device that denied African Americans the right to vote in primary elections on the basis that political parties were private organizations and beyond the reach of the Fifteenth Amendment.

In the case of *Plessy v. Ferguson,*[3] African Americans tested segregation in public accommodations. On June 7, 1890, an African-American man, Homer Adolph Plessy, bought a ticket and boarded a train in New Orleans bound for

Covington, Louisiana. Taking a seat in a coach section reserved for whites, Plessy refused to move to a "Jim Crow" car when requested. He was arrested, and the incident set the stage for one of the great civil rights cases of the century—*Plessy v. Ferguson* (1896). Anchoring their case on both the Thirteenth and Fourteenth Amendments, attorneys for Plessy argued that segregation differed little from slavery in that it perpetuated a "servile character" and, likewise, denied African Americans "equal protection under the law." Unmoved by the arguments, the Court ruled against Plessy. Writing for the majority, Justice Henry Billings Brown laid forth the "separate-but-equal" doctrine, maintaining that as long as equal accommodations for whites and African Americans were provided, no constitutional issues were in question. The effect of the *Plessy* case was devastating to African Americans. Almost overnight, America was transformed into a dual society—one for whites and one for "coloreds."

An African-American Child Awakens America

Although it was the Supreme Court that had legally bound them to segregation, black leaders continued to use the courts to push their claims for equality. In part this decision can be attributed to congressional and presidential apathy toward resolving racial inequalities, a condition that was rooted in the lack of African-American suffrage (right to vote). After much deliberation and search for the perfect test case, African-American leaders anchored their hopes for a better society on the case of a black child by the name of Linda Carol Brown, a resident of Topeka, Kansas.

According to the law, Linda Brown attended an all-black elementary school nearly two miles from her home. To arrive on time, Linda was required to catch a bus at 7:40 a.m., with a drop-off time thirty minutes prior to the opening of the school's doors. In harsh, cold weather students huddled against the outside walls of the building waiting for the 9:00 a.m. bell. Angered by the insensitivity of the arrangement, Linda's father attempted to enroll his child in the all-white school only seven blocks from his home, an easy distance for his daughter to walk. When his request was turned down, Oliver Brown sued.

Brown v. Board of Education (1954)[4] differed from previous civil rights cases. Rather than claiming equal facilities were not being provided, it instead argued the question of whether a country founded on the proposition that "all men are created equal" could remain true to this commitment while permitting segregation to exist. Ruling for a unanimous Court, Chief Justice Earl Warren delivered the historic decision:

> We conclude that in the field of education. . . . Separate educational facilities are inherently unequal.

The Court's decision in the *Brown* case proved important not only in the field of education but in all sectors of our society. Less than one week after the

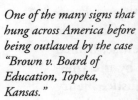

One of the many signs that hung across America before being outlawed by the case "Brown v. Board of Education, Topeka, Kansas."

historic ruling, *Brown* was being applied to cases involving public beaches, golf courses, buses, dining counters, etc. As jubilant black Americans celebrated the death of "Jim Crow," the courts, under the ever-vigilant and persistent efforts of civil rights leaders, began the slow and difficult task of dismantling all segregation laws.

THE QUEST FOR COMPLIANCE

Simply mandating an end to segregation did not provide equal opportunity to minorities in our society. The decision of the Court in the *Brown* case was largely ignored. Compliance came only through rigorous and assertive action by Congress and the president.

Education

On the basis of its decision in the *Brown* case, the Court had ordered school districts to desegregate with "all deliberate speed." The southern states' interpretation of "deliberate speed" varied considerably from the Court's. When it became obvious that their intent was not to comply with desegregation, many lawsuits were initiated. In the late 1950s and early 1960s, barriers to education began to fall in the public schools, both lower grades and colleges, but not without violence.

Eventually, as the pressure over desegregation reached a boiling point between civil rights activists and local school officials, Congress intervened with the passage of the *Civil Rights Act of 1964*. The importance of this measure is that it attacked school segregation on an economic level by denying federal educational funds to school districts that refused to comply with the law. Since

southern communities relied heavily on the infusion of federal money to operate their schools, the measure proved most effective. In 1963, one year prior to
the passage of the act, only 2 percent of all southern blacks attended an integrated school. By 1972 the figure rose to a startling 91 percent.

Comparatively speaking, the integration of southern schools proved to be a
"cakewalk" compared to the problems faced by civil rights leaders in the urban
North. Southern communities, because of their smaller size, relied upon **de jure**
segregation, which means segregation by law. The North, on the other hand,
practiced **de facto** segregation. This form of segregation is rooted in residential
patterns. Larger communities are broken into neighborhood school districts,
and children are assigned to specific schools depending upon the location of
their home. Since discrimination also occurs within housing, it is possible to
draw district boundaries to create a segregated school system. In 1973, the courts
began grappling with the problem of de facto segregation. School districts in
cities such as Chicago, Denver, Detroit, and Boston were ordered to submit
desegregation plans. In many cases, when it was determined that the city had
not acted in good faith or that more conventional methods of achieving integration would not work, the courts ordered **busing**. However, critics charge
that busing has aggravated the problem by producing **white flight** (people moving
from the cities to the suburbs to avoid integrated schools). Politically, most
politicians find it expedient to oppose busing as a means to achieve integration.
In spite of political problems with busing, a more important question has arisen.
In many of the large cities, the proportion of minority students has increased to
an extent where they vastly outnumber white students. Under such conditions,
the question arises "integrate with whom?"

Friend or foe? To a large extent it depends upon how it's being used. When transporting kids to and from neighborhood schools, it receives an overwhelming round of applause. However, when used for integration purposes, it has become a symbol of bitter racial strife.

Graduation rates provide yet another dimension of the problem. Current statistics available indicate that approximately 85.1 percent of whites have completed a high school education in comparison to 80 percent of the black population. For college graduation, approximately 27.6 percent of whites have completed four or more years of college while for blacks the percentage is only 17.3. Such data suggest a wide disparity still exists in educational opportunities between blacks and whites.[5]

The Ballot

Following the enactment of the Fifteenth Amendment, black males were eligible to vote, however the responsibility of running elections and determining qualifications for voting is within the constitutional jurisdiction of the states. Unfortunately after Reconstruction ended in the South, a number of states moved to disenfranchise its potential African-American voters. The effect of this was devastating, for without suffrage African Americans were bound to their heritage of servitude almost as effectively as they had been under the institutions of slavery. African-American leaders complained bitterly, but, for the most part, these complaints were ignored by an apathetic Congress and president. The first hope appeared in 1915, and again it would be the courts that would take the first action. In that year, the Supreme Court struck down Oklahoma's grandfather clause.[6] A number of years later, in 1944, the white primary was declared an illegal discriminative device in the important case of *Smith v. Allwright.*[7]

As the barriers preventing minorities from voting started to fall, increased numbers of African Americans began to register. Suddenly the black American vote became important, not only to state and local officials but also to national candidates. By 1966 poll taxes had been eliminated by means of court decisions as well as by the Twenty-fourth Amendment. Additionally, the Civil Rights Act of 1964 limited the use of literacy tests by exempting any voter with a sixth-grade education.

In response to further pressure by African-American leaders, Congress enacted the *Voting Rights Act of 1965.* Earmarking areas in which less than 50 percent of the eligible, voting-age population had registered to vote prior to November 1, 1964, the act forbade literacy tests altogether. In addition, a **preclearance test** was established for these areas that required that any change in election procedures be approved by the Justice Department prior to its implementation. By 1975, states were required to provide bilingual ballots for "language minorities" where they exceeded 10 percent of the population. States began redrawing districts taking race into account according to the 1982 Voting Rights Act. As a result of these efforts, the past two decades have seen a dramatic increase in the number of minorities registering to vote and those being elected to national, state, and local office. In 1993, white voters challenged a district drawn in North Carolina on the grounds of racial gerrymandering, drawing a district for racial advantage in violation of the "equal protection clause." Appellants argued that segregating voters on the basis of race is unconstitutional. The Supreme Court agreed. In 1996, the Court affirmed its opposition to race-based districting by declaring that three Texas districts and one in North Carolina were unconstitutionally drawn because boundary lines were drawn solely to increase the number of minorities.[8] And, in 1997, a federal court upheld the Court's position by overturning the boundary lines of a district in the state of New York, which used ethnicity and race as dominant factors.[9]

Public Accommodations and Facilities

Along with the struggle to desegregate the schools, civil rights leaders waged a simultaneous battle to open up public accommodations and facilities to African Americans. Again, the bulk of the battle occurred within the South. The first shot was fired in 1955 when an African-American woman named Rosa Parks refused to surrender her seat to a white man on a crowded public bus. This action was a violation of law in Montgomery, Alabama, and she was promptly arrested. Dr. Martin Luther King, Jr., a young Baptist minister, joined the battle and, together with Rosa Parks and other civil rights leaders, initiated a boycott against the bus company. The action precipitated the arrest of King and much violence against the city's African-American citizens, but the boycott continued. Finally, after being faced with massive layoffs and rising fares, the bus company capitulated to the demands of the boycotters to desegregate.

For his part, King, along with his nonviolent protest methods, sparked the imagination of the country. Suddenly African Americans were caught up in a new wave of hope. Breaking with the NAACP (National Association for the Advancement of Colored People), which stressed legal action, King, in 1957, formed the Southern Christian Leadership Conference (SCLC), which emphasized nonviolent protest as a vehicle for change. Actions against two other southern cities followed the formation of the SCLC: Birmingham and Selma, Alabama. In both cases King's nonviolent marches touched off violent responses by racially bigoted whites. The brutality with which the peaceful protesters were treated, especially by Birmingham police, caught the attention of the national media, and across the country millions of Americans watched as African Americans struggled for their rights in the streets of southern cities. As the violence continued, thousands of whites joined King's cause. Together with African Americans they became known as **Freedom Riders**, so called because of their travels throughout the South to desegregate public facilities and accommodations. In general, these efforts were successful.

These efforts culminated on August 23, 1963, when, under the combined leadership of King (SCLC), Roy Wilkins (NAACP), Whitney M. Young (National Urban League) and James Farmer (Congress of Racial Equality), nearly a quarter of a million people from all races participated in a "March on Washington." Speaking in his trademark style, King delivered perhaps one of the most passionate and memorable speeches ever written on behalf of racial equality.

Although the Civil Rights Act of 1964 has been very effective in controlling overt incidences of discrimination, de facto segregation remains a reality of minority existence.

Housing

Perhaps no right is more fundamental to the concept of human equality than housing. Similarly, no denial more clearly constitutes the basis of inequality than segregated housing, for it serves as a springboard to discrimination in all other aspects of life: jobs, education, health care, etc. A number of devices, now illegal, had prevented minorities from living in racially integrated neighborhoods. However, although now illegal, some people still break the law!

The **restrictive covenant**, used extensively before being declared illegal by the Court in 1948, entailed the signing of legal agreements that prohibited homeowners from selling their property to African Americans and other minorities.[10] This device effectively kept neighborhoods segregated.

Blockbusting represented (and still does to some) a very real fear to many white communities. In an attempt to maximize profits by playing on fear, unscrupulous realtors tried to persuade whites through rumors to sell their property and move before the neighborhood turned all black. In a spree of panic selling, the realtor bought homes at rock-bottom prices and then sold them to blacks desiring to move into an integrated neighborhood. Similarly, realtors

The mule-drawn wagon bearing the body of Dr. Martin Luther King, Jr., moves up Auburn Avenue toward downtown Atlanta after funeral services for the slain civil rights leader. Winner of the Nobel Peace Prize and a staunch supporter of nonviolence, Dr. King was assassinated in Memphis, Tennessee, on April 4, 1968.

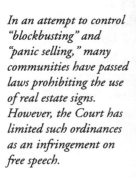

In an attempt to control "blockbusting" and "panic selling," many communities have passed laws prohibiting the use of real estate signs. However, the Court has limited such ordinances as an infringement on free speech.

have been known to steer minorities away from predominately white neighborhoods and into segregated areas of the community. Lending institutions and insurance companies had discouraged integration with **redlining**, a practice that denied mortgage money and insurance to certain portions of the city considered to be high risk because of their racial composition.

In 1968, the Court moved against discrimination in housing in the case of *Jones v. Mayer*[11] when it affirmed the rights of all Americans in buying or renting property. In essence it declared that property owners could not refuse to sell or rent property on the basis of race. Likewise, the Court ruled that minorities could sue if denied this basic right.[12] Congress, in its attempt to curb abuses, passed the *Open Housing Act of 1968*. This measure outlawed blockbusting and redlining, as well as the practice of steering minorities away from predominately white neighborhoods.

Within the last two decades a few communities have experimented with a plan termed **integration maintenance**. The focus of this plan is to stem white-flight in an integrated community perceived as being in danger of becoming resegregated. To avoid "panic selling," quotas are set for each block of the neighborhood. This quota is generally set at 30 percent and referred to as the **tipping point** (point at which white flight will begin if exceeded). Once the quota is reached, a strong effort is made to discourage African Americans from buying property on a particular block. Instead, they are steered to other areas within the community that have not yet attained the pre-established quota. In some cases, especially apartment complexes, quotas are rigorously maintained without exception. The plan has received mixed reviews from both white and African-American community leaders. Advocates of integration maintenance insist that it is the only sensible way to integrate and preserve the stability of the community, which, they maintain, is in the interest of both African-American and white residents. Critics chastise the plan as demeaning to the dignity of African Americans and represents just another way for whites to regulate the freedom of African Americans. Furthermore, they insist that the plan violates the language of the Civil Rights Act of 1968. The judicial system, however, maintains that integration maintenance is legally just, and the plan has been upheld at the state level in the past.[13] When that case was brought before the federal Supreme Court it upheld the ruling of the lower state court by refusing to review the case and thereby upholding the constitutionality of integration maintenance.[14] What do you think about integrated maintenance?

Job Discrimination

The fact that minorities face discrimination in employment is not a new discovery. When the Civil Rights Act of 1965 was passed, African-American family income was 55 percent of white family income.[15] In 2002, the median income in constant dollars for blacks was $29,026 compared to $45,086.[16] An even more alarming picture is revealed. In 2002, 7.8 percent of whites lived 125 percent below poverty level while 21.5 percent of blacks did.[17]

Much of this income difference is traced to discrimination within the job market, which also in part results from lack of education, skills, and experience. In other words, for many blacks the picture is still bleak. Although unemployment rates vary with the economy, unemployment for blacks is always higher than for whites. In one typical year (2003) white unemployment was 4.3 percent. For the same year, black unemployment was 8.3 percent. This trend held true even for blacks with college degrees—4.5 percent for blacks and 2.8 percent for whites. And, as one might suspect, the unemployment rate for minority young people was even greater. The percentage of white teens unemployed was 15.2 percent compared to 33 percent for black teens. For those 20 to 24 years old the unemployment rate for blacks more than doubled that of whites (8.4 percent for whites and 19.8 percent for blacks).[18]

Racial discrimination, the lack of educational opportunities, and institutional barriers such as "last hired, first fired" policies are leading contributors to wage disparities.[19] Even when employed, African Americans face enormous barriers to equal wages. On average, the median income for African Americans is 36 percent less than for whites.[20]

Early in the 1960s, Congress took definitive steps to reduce job discrimination. The **Equal Employment Opportunity Commission** (EEOC) was created with the passage of the Civil Rights Act of 1964. The EEOC investigates complaints of job discrimination and, when found, attempts to resolve the situation through voluntary means. If not successful, it reports the matter to the Justice Department. Should a company be found guilty of job discrimination, it would be subject to loss of future governmental contracts. Under both the 1866 and the 1964 Civil Rights Acts, individuals were able to bring suit against a business for discrimination in the workplace. However, in a recent decision in *Wards Cove Packing Co. v Antonio*, the Supreme Court greatly restricted this right by shifting the burden of proof to the employee to demonstrate why a particular practice was discriminatory. Previously, it was the employer who had to justify any practice that limited the opportunities of minorities or women. Likewise, the Court ruled that employees, in attempting to prove their case, could not base their discrimination suit solely on statistics showing racial imbalances.[21] In the many court cases that followed this ruling, the decision to shift the burden of proof to the employee has been upheld. Critics charge that the ruling "has the practical effect of denying to those who suffer the emotional pain and indignity of on-the-job racial harassment any effective remedy." Supporters, on the other hand, praised the ruling as freeing business from the unwarranted and costly potential of "being dragged into court every time there was a racial or gender imbalance between one segment of their work force and another."[22]

COMPLIANCE FADES—THE EMERGING OF AN INCREASING ELITIST CLASS

The 1980s and 1990s economic restructuring and the increasing global competition placed crippling ceilings on wages and benefits, often times greatly reducing them. Most Americans felt the impact; but those without college degrees have been most severely challenged in trying to make the paychecks cover the cost of living or in obtaining employment. The poor become poorer; the middle class becomes less affluent as their assets dwindle; while the rich become even richer from returns on their investments and substantial net worth. Opportunities for the poor and middle class to acquire asset-producing resources have been virtually eliminated by the new economic restructuring policies. The struggle to pay household bills and high interest credit cards pushes the middle class and the poor into precarious economic positions and reduce what few assets they owned.

By the turn of the century, the US had become "the most unequal society of advanced democratic nations. The top 20 percent of the households earned 50 percent of the nation's income and commanded an astonishing 83 percent of the nation's wealth. Even more striking, the top 1 percent earned about 17 percent of national income and owned 38 percent of the national wealth. In nearly two decades the number of 'deca-millionaires'—those worth at least $10 million—had more than tripled, from 66,500 to 239,400."

"In contrast, the bottom 40 percent of Americans earned just 10 percent of the nation's income and owned less than 1 percent of the nation's wealth. The bottom 60 percent did only marginally better, accounting for about 23 percent of income and less than five percent of wealth. The racial gaps are even more disheartening. The typical African-American household had fifty-four cents of income and twelve cents of wealth for every corresponding dollar in the typical white American household. Hispanics had sixty-two cents of income and four cents of wealth."[23]

The acquisition of assets—land, home, a business, savings, investments- are essential in planning for future generations. It transfers to succeeding generations while earned income stops when the job ends, meaning little in transferable wealth.

Political influence is obtained through wealth. For example, many members of congress spend more time courting wealthy constituents outside their districts (seeking contributions) than they spend with the residential constituents who vote them into office. Consequently, most policies that are directed toward providing tax breaks pave the way for the rich to increase their assets, yet are of little benefit for the middle class and the poor. These regressive policies benefit the wealthiest 55 percent of the taxpayers. The poorest citizens are locked out because their earnings are too low and income-supported assistance limits earnings as an eligibility factor.

OTHER MINORITIES IN AMERICA

We have looked closely at the situation of African Americans, but other minority groups should be considered as well. Blacks are not the only minority group in the United States to receive less than equitable treatment. In fact, although we will not deal with it here, white, ethnic minorities have experienced discrimination at the hands of other whites, as well as other minorities. Discrimination is not just practiced by one particular group.

Native Americans

Perhaps the most overlooked minority in our society are Native Americans. According to 2003 statistics, if one includes Alaskan natives, Eskimos and Aleuts, the population of Native Americans totals just over 4.1 million.[24] Most reside on reservations or in rural communities out of sight from most other Americans. Also, since the oil embargo of 1973 and the subsequent energy crisis that brought some tribes large sums of money, many Americans have developed a stereotype of affluent reservation life with wealth-laden Native Americans driving Cadillacs. Such a stereotype is far from reality for the majority of Native Americans. Only half of all Indians live on the 267 federal reservations (excluding Alaska), and for those who do, only a few tribes have benefited from mineral wealth.[25] For most Native Americans, life remains a precarious, daily struggle for existence. Life on many reservations is sub-standard. Poverty is rampant.

A 1910 boarding school in Geno, Nebraska, established under the "General Allotment Act." The sole purpose of the school was to transform Native Americans to "white ways."

Addiction to alcohol and tobacco is common. The quality of water is often inferior. Housing, health care, and education are poor. Many die early.

It is not that past experience has had a tremendous effect on present circumstances. Native Americans were exploited from the "get go," so to speak. With the arrival of the first Europeans, Indians were unable to resist encroachment upon their land. Organized into scattered bands, lacking a common language, and divided by cultural differences, Native Americans were not able to pool their resources or mobilize their power to resist the highly centralized, political military might of the Europeans. At best their attempts to protect their land amounted to little more than sporadic retaliation. In the end their story would be one of complete and total victimization. With the conclusion of the Indian Wars in 1880, the fate of Native Americans would be exclusively in the hands of the federal government. Under federal control they have been lied to, cheated, robbed, and herded like cattle onto barren reservations far from their homelands. Even then, defeated and humiliated, their subjugation would not be finished. In 1887 Congress, in an attempt to destroy Indian culture, passed the **General Allotment Act**. Later to be termed *indigenismo*, its singular goal was total assimilation of Native Americans into white culture. Under this policy, Indian children were forcibly removed from their homes and taken to government boarding houses where they were educated and socialized to fit better into the white man's industrial society. Perceived correctly as cultural genocide (elimination of a way of life), Native Americans bitterly resisted the program, and finally it was abandoned in 1934 by the **Indian Reorganization Act**. However, the enactment and implementation of the General Allotment Act remain a bitter memory.

In the wake of the civil rights movement, Native Americans joined other minorities in expressing their frustration over the procrastination of the federal government in addressing their grievances. One of the most dramatic incidents occurred when, late in February 1973, a small band of militant Oglala Sioux led by the A.I.M. (American Indian Movement) occupied the hamlet at Wounded Knee, South Dakota. Historically significant, Wounded Knee was the site of the infamous and senseless slaughter of more than three hundred Sioux, mostly women and children, and marked the end of Indian resistance to white supremacy in 1890. With the national press looking on, the small band of Indians held authorities at bay for seventy days. Two people were killed and several injured before the occupation ended. Although all those participating were indicted, few were convicted due to legal irregularities in their prosecution.

More recently, Native Americans have achieved some measure of success in the courts. At present, over $1.4 billion has been awarded to Native Americans in 284 suits. In one of the largest settlements, Alaskan natives received 40 million acres of land and nearly $1 billion in 1971.[26] And in the second largest settlement, the Puyallup tribe signed away its claim to much of its traditional land in return for $162 million.[27] Unfortunately, although the money and land have provided a measure of relief and much of it has been placed in holding corporations to ensure that future generations of Native Americans will benefit, the settlements are small in comparison to both the numbers of Native Americans involved and their problems. Recent budget cuts, as well as the Bush and Reagan administration's belief in encouraging Native Americans toward a goal of independence, have seriously cut into aid provided to federal reservations. In commenting on the cuts, Dan Bomberry, director of the privately funded Tribal Sovereignty Program, states, "We are seeing people in desperation going after oddball forms of economic activity. There has been a big push on bingo; the Mowapa Paiutes outside Las Vegas wanted to put a whorehouse on the reservation; and the Fort Mojaves even considered having a hazardous waste dump on the reservation."[28] Recently, internal disagreement within the Indian movement over leadership has led to splits in the organization that, in turn, have severely hindered their ability to achieve gains through political action.

Asian Americans

The Chinese and the Japanese share a legacy not uncommon to that of African Americans. All arrived in this country as immigrants and, as racial minorities, have been victimized by prejudice and discrimination. A large percentage of Asian Americans arrived in the country between 1848, the beginning of the California Gold Rush, and the completion of the Transcontinental Railroad in 1869. With the completion of both, work became scarce, and conflict between white workers and Asian Americans intensified due to fears by the former that a cheap labor supply would ultimately undercut both working conditions and wages of white ethnic groups. As a result of this fear, the first *Chinese Exclusion*

Act was passed in 1882 with the purpose of halting the immigration of all Chinese into the United States for a period of ten years. However, it was eventually made permanent. Not until recent changes in immigration laws did the doors of America again open to the Chinese. As a result, Chinese immigration jumped from a low of 105 per year[29] to 65,000 in 1993 alone.[30] The number of Asian Americans in the United States doubled between 1980 and 1994.[31] Since 9/11 immigration has dropped 9.4 percent to 61,282 with the tightening of immigration laws.

The plight of Japanese Americans was only slightly better. Japan, a world power, was in a better position than China to protect its immigrants from outright discrimination and exploitation. However, during sporadic outbreaks of "yellow phobia," Japanese immigrants suffered greatly. Perhaps the most tragic incident of "yellow phobia" occurred on February 19, 1942, during World War II when President Franklin D. Roosevelt signed Executive Order 9066 that stipulated that virtually all Japanese Americans were stripped of citizenship rights and interned in relocation camps. Not only degrading and humiliating, the incident resulted in substantial loss of property. Although the United States was also at war with both Germany and Italy, Americans of neither heritage suffered a similar fate. The Supreme Court, on December 18, 1944, ruled that such activity was illegal and abolished the camps.[32] It wasn't however, until 1988, that Congress provided compensation in the amount of $1.2 billion for the 65,000 survivors of the relocation camps.

Despite the many obstacles to success, Asian Americans have, on the whole, fared better than other racial minorities. In fact, their median family income of $52,626 per year is higher than whites at $45,086.[33] Likewise, in terms of education, they again appear to achieve a disproportionately larger number of ad-

A Japanese child, tagged and packed, awaits shipment to a concentration like camp for the duration of World War II. Executive Order 9066, signed by President Roosevelt, affected all Japanese-Americans, regardless of how long they had resided in America.

vanced educational degrees with 49.8 percent having achieved four or more years of college.[34] These statistics have provided ammunition to some researchers and politicians who argue against providing special consideration or preferential treatment for racial minorities in general.

Arab/Muslim Americans

Since the terrorist attacks of September 11, 2001, the United States has been struggling to define what constitutes adequate security without sacrificing fundamental liberties. It seeks the balance between security and liberty. The United States is a country full of targets. It has a very mobile population, moving around every day in millions of cars, trucks, trains, and planes. In addition, U.S. ports receive about 59,000 cargo shipments on any given day. How can all this be made secure in a free society? Is ideal homeland security really compatible with the American culture that embraces personal freedom, thrives upon freewheeling commerce, and an open society? These are the very foundations of this country that made it a world leader. These basic creeds are exactly what make the United States vulnerable. *The New York Times* put it rather succinctly by saying "This . . . nation must weigh carefully the tradeoffs it wants to make between vigilance and its ideals."[35]

The events of September 11, 2001, have caused some ordinary citizens, as well as some policing agents, to treat Arab/Muslim Americans with disdain, even with violent physical and verbal attacks attacks and lengthy incarcerations without filing charges. By November 2001 the federal authorities stopped issuing information regarding the number of Muslim men being held as suspected terrorists. According to the tally, kept by the Amnesty International U.S.A., the total held at that time was 1,147. Of those, 3 were indicted on terrorists related charges, and 400 were deported. Hady Hassan Omar was held in solitary confinement for 73 days without being charged. He has filed a lawsuit in the Western District of Louisiana, claiming his days of captivity rose "to the level of torture." The Amnesty International U.S.A. claims to have many documented records describing U.S. authorities' cruel and degrading treatment of immigrants from Middle East and South Asian countries.[36]

Even individual citizens, who prior to 9/11 peacefully waited their turn in neighborhood establishments, were literally trying to kill one another. Local police forces became very aggressive in detaining, arresting, and searching Arab/Muslim Americans and their properties, again, often in the absence of the application of the due process standard. These actions stemmed from fear, anger, a sense of horror, and an overwhelming feeling of helplessness.

President Bush has frequently cautioned the country that the struggle to secure the homeland is tenuous because some of the same forces that executed the attacks of September 11 are among us and perhaps are waiting and preparing to strike again. The United States cannot become too relaxed or too rigid and still maintain the quality of life that it is famous for. It must balance securing the homeland with assuring equality for all citizens and seek world peace all at the same time. Accomplishing these tasks may be impossible; however, not trying to accomplish them would be a cardinal error.

Puerto Ricans

Puerto Rico is a territory of the United States, and its people are American citizens. Therefore, they face no barrier to immigration. The first great wave of Puerto Ricans migrating to the mainland, termed *La Migracion*, occurred following World War II. Most possessed little education, were unskilled agricultural workers, and settled in New York City and a handful of other northern industrial cities. Facing language and cultural barriers, as well as ethnic prejudice, most have not fared well on the mainland. Yet each year approximately 30,000 more islanders choose to leave Puerto Rico and come to cities like New York.[37] In fact, by 1983, nearly one-third of the entire population of Puerto Rico had migrated to the mainland.[38] Between 1980 and 1990, the number of Puerto Ricans on the mainland had increased by over 35 percent.[39] Why? They migrate mainly for economic reasons. Typically, with unemployment running at over 15 percent, and median income at under $6,000 per year, Puerto Rico holds little promise for those seeking a better life.[40]

Like other minority groups, Puerto Ricans are becoming increasingly more active in the political process. Although, as a territory, Puerto Ricans have a nonvoting representative in the United States House of Representatives, most political gains have come from local efforts in cities where large voting blocs of Puerto Ricans reside. Few candidates in such cities can afford to ignore their demands for better jobs, education, and health care. Within the last two and a half decades the society has also had to contend with the F.L.A.N. (Fuerzas Armadas de Liberacion Nacional), a terrorist organization whose goal is Puerto Rican independence from the United States by violent means, if necessary. Since the early 1960s, the F.L.A.N. has claimed responsibility for over one hundred bombings.[41] The question of Puerto Rico, as well as the status of its people, remains a dilemma.

Mexican Americans

The disenfranchisement of Mexican Americans closely resembles that of Native Americans. In the early period, most Mexicans were incorporated into American society by expansionistic military conquest. This period of military conquest is normally recognized as beginning in 1819 when Mexico granted permission to Anglo immigrants, mostly Southerners, to settle in its northern region, now Texas. Only two conditions were required: a pledge of allegiance to

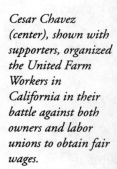

Cesar Chavez (center), shown with supporters, organized the United Farm Workers in California in their battle against both owners and labor unions to obtain fair wages.

the Mexican government and a conversion to Catholicism. Both were initially accepted and then, after settlement, rejected. These and other conflicts soon turned into hostilities, and eventually, as a result of the **Texas Revolt** of 1835-1836, the territory broke away from Mexico. In 1845, the United States, believing Mexico to be weak and racially/ethnically inferior, granted statehood to Texas and, thus, touched off war between the two countries. By the time the war ended, Mexico was forced to concede over half of its country to the United States in the **Treaty of Guadalupe Hidalgo**, signed February 2, 1884. Thus, in a stroke of the pen, the United States acquired what is now Arizona, California, Colorado, New Mexico, Texas, Nevada, and Utah, in addition to portions of Kansas, Oklahoma, and Wyoming. In 1853 one more strip of territory was added by the **Gadsden Purchase**. Originally purchased for a railway through New Mexico and Arizona, the territory later proved to be exceedingly rich in copper. As for the Mexican citizens living within the territories, they were given one year in which to decide whether to relocate south of the new border or become U.S. citizens. Those who elected to stay, however, were guaranteed full citizenship rights, including the protection of their property and religious rights.

In spite of treaties and guarantees by the federal government, Mexicans who chose to remain soon found themselves the victims of violence, tax schemes, and border disputes. It is generally estimated that four-fifths of Mexican landholdings were transferred into the hands of Anglos.[42] By the end of the century, dispossessed of their land and victimized by prejudice and discrimination, most Mexican Americans would become a poverty-stricken, mobile, labor force serving the interests of their Anglo conquerors.

In the decades to follow, Mexicans would cross the border in record numbers. For the most part their presence was a matter of active recruitment by agricultural and mining interests who organized "barrio programs" that assisted in their migration. Mexicans represented a cheap and exploitable source of labor and possessed a willingness to perform demeaning and dangerous work refused by other ethnic groups.

To date, the conditions of Mexican Americans are unavoidably tied to their past. Overrepresented in agriculture, they constitute the lowest-paid minority within the country. Likewise, they lag behind all other Americans in health, education, employment, and occupational status. Prior to World War II, most Mexican Americans resided in the Southwest, but within the last two decade this pattern has changed with more migrating to urban centers across the country, particularly those states within the Midwest. Mexican Americans have now become the largest minority group in the United States, constituting about 12 percent of the population, according to the 2000 census.

Like other minority groups, Mexican Americans have become increasingly active politically. Spearheading what was to become collectively known as the *Chicano movement*, Cesar Chavez organized California grape pickers into the **United Farm Workers Organizing Committee**. A follower of the nonviolent methods of Gandhi, he was successful in obtaining recognition for some of the most oppressed migrant workers in the country through fasts, strikes, and a national campaign to boycott grapes. Other Chicano organizations would follow in an attempt not only to improve social and economic conditions of Mexican Americans but to elect political officials.

Emerging Disadvantaged Groups

The success of racial minorities in politicizing their demands for equal opportunity has not escaped the attention of other groups in the society who, likewise, perceive themselves as victims of discrimination. As such, across America there has been an increase of groups, each seeking support from the government in addressing their special grievances. The elderly, gays, and the physically handicapped represent just a few examples of the most successful emerging groups within society. Each has caught the attention of politicians, and each has been relatively successful in obtaining special consideration in employment, housing, and access to public facilities and services, as well as to grants of federal dollars to help resolve their problems. Although these groups have been useful in pointing to the inequalities of the society in areas other than race or gender, they have posed new problems for politicians. The success of each group further encourages the formation of additional groups that, in turn, places new and mounting demands on elected officials. Faced with limited funds and a growing national debt, politicians are frequently placed in the potentially dangerous position of slighting one group for another and, thus, paying the price at the ballot box in the next election. Also, minority and disadvantaged groups currently face a situation very much different from that of the free-spending days of the 1960s. As always, whether the groups represent minorities or the disadvantaged in general or any other segment of American society, the nature of the governmental system requires that all groups compete for the limited resources available from the taxpayers. While few would argue that there are enough resources to eliminate poverty, the reality of the U.S. situation is that the national government itself spends a substantial amount of money on what are termed in the budget *Human Resources*. This budgetary category includes such line items as funding for education, training, employment, social services, health, medicare, social security disability benefits (SSD), social security income benefits (SSI), and veterans benefits and services. (Please note the Human Resources budget does not include traditional social security retirement benefits, which amount to another enormous sum of money.) In 2002, the United States government spent $1.3 trillion ($1,300,000,000,000) on human resource items.[43] In addition, in 2002, the national government spent $18.2 billion ($18,200,000,000) on food stamps. That figure is up from $14.9 billion in 2000 and up again from $15.5 billion in 2001.[44] The reality of federal spending today has created a situation in which each group cannot hope to achieve its demands fully. With the rising federal deficit, groups will have to compete for a smaller and smaller piece of a shrinking federal social budget. This will probably reflect a shift in budgeting ideology from funding federal programs that focus on eradicating poverty to funding federal programs that remove or reduce entitlements. One such example of inadequate federal funding is health care. According to the Journal of American Medical Association: Annuals of Emerging Medicine, some 60 percent of Latinos and over 40 percent of African Americans nationwide had no health care insurance in 2002 and 2003. There is no doubt that their number will continue to increase especially in high unemployment areas. Lack of or inadequate health care is a serious problem in the U.S. today.

WOMEN

Emerging Feminism

Like racial minorities, women have suffered a similar denial of equal opportunity. The only difference between the two groups is the pattern in which the denial has been exercised. For racial minorities, white supremacy has been the cause; for women, it has been male supremacy. Supreme Court Justice Brennan summarized the problem in the following fashion:

> Throughout much of the nineteenth century the position of women in our society was, in many respects, comparable to that of blacks under the pre-Civil War slave codes. Neither slaves nor women could hold

A rare photograph of the early leaders of women's rights. Susan B. Anthony is seated in the front row, second from the left, and Elizabeth Cady Stanton, third from the right. Matilda Joslyn Gage, second from right, front row, joined with Stanton and Anthony to edit the "History of Woman Suffrage."

office, serve on juries, or bring suit in their own names, and married women traditionally were denied the legal capacity to hold or convey property or to serve as legal guardians of their own children.[45]

In a case before the Supreme Court in 1873, a member of the Court proclaimed:

> Man is, or should be, woman's protector and defender. The natural and proper timidity and delicacy that belongs to the female sex evidently unfits it for many of the occupations of civil life.[46]

Not all women concurred with this opinion. In July of 1848, over one hundred women convened the **Seneca Falls Convention**, where a *Declaration of Sentiments* was drafted calling for equality for women. Principally at issue was the right of women to vote and to participate in political affairs. Early leaders of the women's rights movement included Lucretia Mott, Elizabeth Cady Stanton, and Susan B. Anthony. Although many men at the time supported the notion of equality for women, others did not. A great majority of newspaper editors termed the movement "the shrieking sisterhood" and labeled their leaders as unfeminine, slandering them even to the point of accusing them of immorality and drunkenness. With the conclusion of the Civil War, abolitionists, from which the women's rights movement was born, pressed for the adoption of the Fifteenth Amendment guaranteeing the right to vote regardless of race, creed, or color. Women complained bitterly since no provision was made to include gender within the language of the amendment. For their part, male abolitionists were steadfast in their refusal to include gender for fear it would jeopardize the passage of the amendment. This conflict ultimately led to a split between women suffragists and abolitionists. In 1869 the National Woman's Suffrage Association was created with its main goal being the achievement of women's suffrage (right to vote). After fifty years of struggle, this fundamental right would be achieved with the ratification of the Nineteenth Amendment in 1920.

Protectionism and the Courts

With their right to vote firmly secured by constitutional guarantee, women launched an all-out attack on other discriminative processes that disenfranchised them because of their sex. Some of the items principally targeted included discrimination in employment, inheritance, property ownership, and the inability in many states to serve on juries. But, like the right to vote, the road to equality in these other areas would require years of struggle. Under the prevailing norms of the society, a **protective policy environment** had been established to protect women from exploitation both at home and in the labor market. For example, men who abandoned families were compelled to pay alimony and child support. Likewise, legally binding statues were enacted limiting the rights of employers regarding female workers. Not only were these laws deemed necessary to protect women from backbreaking labor but also to shield them from sexual harassment. In general such laws enjoyed overwhelming support by society—men and women alike. But as women's rights groups were quick to point out, while protecting some women, such policies increasingly served to further disenfranchise women as a group as more and more women entered the labor market.

The first subtle shift away from protectionism came in 1971 in *Reed v. Reed*.[47] Here the Court struck down a state law that gave mandatory preference to males in the selection of estate administrators. Since then the Court has struck down numerous other laws that discriminated on the basis of sex. Unlike race, however, the Court has ruled that under certain circumstances, sex discrimination may well be appropriate. In one of the most recent and far-reaching decisions, a federal appeals court let stand a company policy denying women the opportunity to work in situations that might be hazardous (chemical or otherwise) to their unborn babies. Termed **"fetal protection policies,"** the ruling encompasses all women of potential childbearing age even if they have finished raising their families or have no intentions of having children.[48] Similarly, the Court has ruled that sex discrimination could be used in matters of military service. (The Court has ruled that it is not discriminatory to draft men but not women.)

In 1973 the Court in the precedent-setting case of *Roe v. Wade*[49] established the constitutional right of women to **abortion-on-demand** during the first trimester of their pregnancy. In subsequent decisions the Court would rule that

Although no woman has been elected president, many have influenced the policy decisions of their husbands who occupied the Oval Office. After being First Lady, Hillary Rodham Clinton was elected to the U.S. Senate from the state of New York. She waits to speak from the United States Senate podium beside Senator Dick Durbin. (D-IL)

neither the state nor a husband could interfere with this right. As the number of abortions increased (over 1.5 million abortions were performed per year from 1973 through 1980,[50] so did the pressure by anti-choice groups to reverse abortion rights. With the lone exception of the **Hyde Amendment**, which prohibits the use of federal welfare money to pay for abortions except in life-threatening situations, rape, or incest, these attempts failed. However, pro-lifers were able to score a majority victory with the 1989 Missouri case of *Webster v. Reproductive Health Services*.[51] In this landmark decision the Court allowed two restrictions on abortion. First, it permitted states to bar public employees from assisting in abortions and to prohibit abortions from being performed in state hospitals or public facilities. Second, it allowed states to require doctors to perform viability tests on women twenty weeks into their pregnancy to see if the fetus could survive outside the womb. *Planned Parenthood v. Casey* allowed that once the fetus is viable a state may "regulate, and even proscribe, abortion except where it is necessary" as long as the restrictions do not place an "undue burden" on the mother's rights.[52] By1996, abortions had decreased slightly to 1.3 million per year.[53]

With the Court appointments of Presidents Ronald Reagan and George H. Bush, the Court has allowed the states increasing latitude in restricting abortions. By 1997, 31 states had enacted 44 separate measures limiting abortions in one way or another. The lone surprise to pro-life advocates in this period was the decision by the Court granting abortion clinics the right to sue pro-life groups for damages under the federal racketeering law. President Clinton reversed the onslaught on abortion rights with the appointments of two liberals—Ruth Bader Ginsburg and Stephen G. Breyer in 1993 and 1994.[54] However, on January 21, 2001, President George W. Bush, on his first full day in the Oval Office, reinstated (by executive order) the Reagan/Bush (G.H.W.) abortion restrictions on aid given to international family planning groups that support abortions.[55] President George W. Bush and Vice President Dick Cheney are strong supporters of the pro-life position. Now in his second term, the president continues his adamant support of the Republican Party platform by advocating an absolute ban on abortion.

During the Clinton administration, abortion issues rested in the state legislatures rather than the federal courts. This may change during the administration of President George W. Bush. During his term in office, the president will undoubtedly have an opportunity to appoint several Supreme Court justices who share his pro-life views. Such appointments could place the abortion battleground back in the federal arena. For now, women still have the right to abortions in some facilities but not necessarily state-operated ones. It appears that the battle over this highly volatile issue of abortion will not end any time soon.

Equal Rights Amendment

The issue of protectionism played a major role in the defeat of the Equal Rights Amendment (ERA). Proposed by Congress in 1972, the amendment simply read as follows: "Equality of rights under the law shall not be denied or abridged by the United States or by any state on account of sex." Ironically, the amendment split women basically into two groups. For those who opposed ERA (principally an organization known as STOP ERA), the issue was one of protectionism. If ratified, they maintained women would lose their special position within the legal system. As such, they would be subject to the draft, loss of child support, and alimony. Additionally, property and pension rights that they shared with their husbands would be in jeopardy, as well as maternity leaves and benefits. Some ERA opponents even went so far as to claim that the passage of the amendment would mean the Court would require unisex bath and locker rooms! However, no constitutional expert took such claims seriously. On the other side, proponents of ERA, notably the National Organization for Women (NOW), argued that, if passed, sex discrimination would legally disappear, and all women would benefit as a result. However, such a claim, like many of those advanced by ERA opponents, must be viewed cautiously since it would be the responsibility of the Court to interpret the meaning of the amendment. On June 30, 1982, the Equal Rights Amendment died—three states short of the required number needed for passage.

Present Discrimination

Is an equal rights amendment really needed by women? Yes, maintain feminists, and to support their claim, they point to current economic data that show women as a group suffering enormous barriers to income and occupational equality. Recent studies of income differences between the sexes show that white, male, high-school graduates earned a median annual income of $30,414, while, their female counterparts earned $18,092. Similarly, males with at least a bachelor's degree earned $66,810 annually while females with the same degree earned $36,755.[56] Even after accounting for differences in education, the gap remains. Other factors such as work continuity and training level fail to account for all of the difference. After a review of numerous national studies taking such variables into account, the National Research Council concluded that one-half to three-fourths of the income difference between male and female workers could be attributed to discrimination.[57] The basis of this discrimination lies in traditional, sex-role expectations, coupled with poor, inadequate, child-care facilities. As a result, women as a group are relegated to lower-status/lower-income occupations. It is for this reason that women's rights groups advocate a concept termed **comparable pay**. Under this plan employers would be required to pay men and women with similar skill levels equal income even though they occupied different jobs within the company, for example, secretaries and loading dock workers. The obvious intent is to overcome discrimination between male-dominated and female-dominated occupations. At least one state, Washington, has already implemented a comparable pay plan for state employees. However, recent attempts to force other states to adopt similar plans through federal court action have failed.[58] In 2000 the U.S. Court of Appeals for the 6th Circuit upheld the right of employees to discuss pay levels. It ruled that to prohibit such discussion violated the National Labor Relations Act (NLRA) and interfered with an employee's right to engage in protected concerted activity.[59] Employees should be able to share wage level information without fear of job loss retaliation. Also, high on the priority list of women's rights groups is better child-care facilities with extended hours of service, improvement in maternity benefits, shared and flextime jobs, and professional-level, part-time work. Some employers have initiated paternity leave programs and have been instrumental in locating child-care facilities on or near the work sites. Such measures could drastically improve the opportunities for women in America.

While the business community has made a number of accommodations for working parents, they raise the issue of the cost of doing these things. When someone goes on maternity or paternity leave, the business must often hire someone to replace that person on a temporary basis. The jobs that these temporaries are taking are not always the routine types of jobs that someone could easily and quickly learn. Hence, many times, not only is there the cost of replacing the employee on leave, but also the cost of training the temporary, who will lose the position when the regular employee returns. In addition, most government employers and many business employers continue the salary of the employee on leave for a specified period of time. The issue is not as "clean" as it seems at first glance.

Politics and Contemporary Women

The turbulent and often dramatic events of the 1960s radically transformed women's groups within the country. Older groups like the United Methodist Women, Women's Christian Temperance Union, and the League of Women Voters concentrated on traditional values and concerns of women. These groups have now been joined by new ones such as the National Organization for Women, Women's Equity Action League, and the National Women's Political Caucus, seeking to radically alter the social, political, and economic conditions of women. Although smaller in membership than their older counterparts, they were far more vocal and better organized to politicize their demands through the national media. While these groups had early success in uniting women on mainline issues like equal pay, extended social security benefits for wives and widows, sexual crimes, pornography, etc., they splintered when adopting aggressive stands on the more recent controversial issues of abortion and homosexual rights. As such, membership declined and, what is more important, new more conservative, better funded women's groups emerged to challenge their leadership position. This division, as was the case with minority groups, has tended to dilute their political strength. Still, even though divided, politicians are well aware of the potential voting power of women. Today, women, though still seriously underrepresented, occupy elected positions at all levels of the political stratum. Women have obtained only moderate increases in their total numbers in Congress in recent years—7 percent from the 105th to the 109th Congress.

Women in Congress[60]

Congress	Total	Percent
105th	44	8.2
106th	54	10.1
107th	74	13.8
108th	76	14.2
109th	82	15.3

Women have yet to make a significant impact upon laws for and about women. One example is the insurance coverage for such drugs as Viagra, Levitra, and Cialis that alleviate male dysfunction. Most insurance companies covered these drugs as they entered the market. On the other hand birth control drugs for women were not covered until recently, due to concentrated efforts and bitter protests launched by women's advocacy groups. Also, helpful drugs for women are not readily forthcoming. Now, seven years after Viagra received the Food and Drugs Administration's approval, with many warnings and cautions, there is nothing for women, even though more problems are reported. Recently, Intrinsa, a testosterone patch, which female research studies reported to be very successful, was rejected. FDA stated that years' more research is necessary. Yet, some doctors are quietly prescribing the hormone to some women. Drug relief for male issues seems practically instantaneous while female issues are repeatedly delayed or placed on the back burner. All the cautions are in the literature for men but for women, most often, it is not enough. As a result, women do not get the opportunity to evaluate and decide with their medical practitioners as their male counterparts do.[61]

Pay rates continue to be one of women's biggest political concerns while the number of women in the work force continues to grow. Currently women make up nearly half of the work force.[62] The Michigan Women's Foundation reported in their Fall 2002/Winter 2003 newsletter, Trillium, "the wage gap between men and women has closed at a rate of less than one penny per year since 1963, when the Equity Pay Act was signed.[63] Progress is being made at a snail's pace. Yet as women become more prominent in the workforce and enter nontraditional occupations there is a thread of optimism that opportunities for women in America will improve in the future.

SEXUAL PREFERENCE

Sexual preference issues have increased over the past several years as homosexuals become more aggressive in demanding equal treatment. Although it ignited heavy debate in Congress, in 1993 President Clinton ended the ban on homosexuals in the military. Inquiries into a service member's sexual orientation were prohibited. Over protests of violating the First Amendment, freedom of speech, the Supreme Court left the military's policy of "don't ask, don't tell" intact. This 1999 decision was the fifth time that the Court refused to invalidate the military's policy.[64] The following year in another case the Court left room for one to interpret that the Boy Scouts of America could bar homosexual boys from membership when it ruled that First Amendment rights would be violated if the Scouts were forced to accept gay troop leaders. The Court said forcing acceptance violated the Scout's right to "expressive association" and infringed upon the group's right to advocate its viewpoint.[65]

In a 6-3 ruling, the Court delivered on June 26, 2003, the most significant civil rights decision for gays and lesbians. The opinion rejected a Texas sodomy law (*Lawrence, et. al. v. Texas*) and emphasized that gays and lesbians are "entitled to respect for their private lives." The Court struck down state laws that make consensual homosexual sex a crime and opened the door to other laws that discriminate against gays and lesbians. This ruling over-ruled the 1986 decision, *Bowers vs. Hardwick*, that upheld a Georgia law similar to the Texas statute. This ruling invalidates laws in 13 states, four of which had prohibited only homosexual activity. All states outlawed sodomy as recently as the 1960s. Illinois was the first to repeal its law in 1961.

One of President George W. Bush's campaign issues was the sanctity of marriage being between a man and a woman. He has vowed to seek a constitutional amendment. There seems to be growing support through various religious groups. Gays and lesbians are fighting back. Here is an issue that will be debated back and forth for some time to come.

AFFIRMATIVE ACTION: A Mandate For Change

By 1960 it had become evident to many that governmental insistence on "color blindness" and "gender neutrality" was simply not enough to dismantle the discriminatory barriers faced by minorities and women. Also, the debate on civil rights had suddenly shifted by this time. The demands for equal opportunity, as well as for political equality, became increasingly more vocal and, in many cases as witnessed by urban riots, more violent. To restore order to American society and to fulfill the promise of equality would require direct and positive intervention by the government. Such intervention would appear in the form of **affirmative action**.

Justification and Use of Affirmative Action

The justification for affirmative action rests on the premise that discrimination against minorities and women in our society has become self-sustaining. By self-sustaining we mean prejudices interact with attitudes that, in turn, give birth to discriminatory actions. These actions tend to confer advantages upon some, mainly white males, and disadvantages on others, principally minorities and women. Once established, these attitudes are continuously recycled, thus, perpetuating the discriminatory process in future generations. In other words, discrimination is a vicious and never-ending circle of intolerance. Nothing short of direct governmental intervention, insist advocates of affirmative action, will remedy the situation. The primary purpose is very simple but difficult to attain—a workforce that mirrors the community in which it serves.

The Plan

An affirmative action plan consists of goals, measures, and a timetable. *Goals* represent an ideal ratio between minority group members and white males that should be achieved if an organization selected among qualified applicants in the absence of discrimination. In determining the ratio, the courts and enforcement agencies rely heavily upon the percentage of minority group members living within the community. *Measures* are the means by which the goals are achieved. Some of the more common measures include the following:

1. deliberate and extensive recruiting among qualified applicants,

2. revising selection procedures so as not to exclude qualified minorities,

3. using race, sex, and national origin as positive factors in the selection process (preferential treatment),

4. mandating that a specified number of minorities will be selected from a pool of qualified applicants (quotas). In each instance, qualified applicants are sought.

The last element of an affirmative action plan is the *timetable*. Since it is impossible to remedy problems overnight, the government establishes a timetable in which the goals of the plan can be achieved.

Criticisms and Defense of Affirmative Action

Although an overwhelming majority of Americans desire an end to discrimination, disagreement occurs on the means to achieve this common objective. One criticism has always been that affirmative action rests on the assumption that lack of diversity in the workforce stems from discrimination. This assumption has not always proven true. However, the bulk of criticism revolves around two measures (preferential treatment and quotas) and focuses on three basic concerns.

First, critics charge that the use of these two methods substitutes numerical equality for the traditional standard of merit without regard to effects on the economy. Supporters of affirmative action indicate that this is not true. Contrary to popular notions, they say, affirmative action does not require the selection of minority candidates or women if they are not qualified. The Court, on the basis of the **Griggs Principle**,[66] simply states that the standards used to judge applicants must relate to job performance. For example, the use of a written test to demonstrate mathematical skills could not be used to select applicants for custodial work. On the other hand, such a test could be used in the selection of candidates for an architectural position.

Second, affirmative action programs have been roundly condemned as constituting **reverse discrimination**. Although advocates admit that incidences have occurred in which white males were deprived of their rights by faulty administration or interpretation of civil rights laws, the courts have consistently ruled that affirmative action plans must not *unnecessarily trammel* (restrict) the inter-

On the tenth anniversary of the Court's historical decision in the case "The Regents of the University of California v. Bakke," protesters gather in front of the Supreme Court to urge the justices to overturn its orignial decision.

est of white males. The Court has established three criteria to judge affirmative action plans in this regard:

1. the plan must not require that white workers be discharged and replaced with minorities;

2. the plan must not constitute an absolute bar to white workers;

3. and the plan must be a temporary measure.[67]

Affirmative action has also been criticized as perpetuating existing beliefs in the inferiority of minorities and women. Measures that use race and sex, maintain critics, reinforce a prevailing attitude by many in our society that minorities or women are incapable of achievement through merit but, rather, must rely upon government assistance. Again advocates disagree. Stereotypes, they insist, are not the result of affirmative action but, rather, predate it. In many cases minorities and women have been the unwitting victims of **tokenism**. (Hiring minorities and women because the employer had to.) Placed in hostile situations just to fill an employer's quota, they lacked the necessary help and cooperation to succeed. Therefore, they failed. Their failure then became the employer's rationale for not hiring more minorities and women. Affirmative action, they insist, has proven to be an effective method of placing qualified minorities and women in those competitive processes previously denied to them, and their eventual success will prove the only effective method of altering present negative stereotypes.

Challenges to Affirmative Action

The implementation of affirmative action plans has not gone without challenge in our society. Within the last two decades numerous suits have been filed by white males who perceive themselves as victims of reverse discrimination.

The first major challenge to affirmative action occurred in 1978, with the case of *Regents of the University of California v. Bakke*.[68] Here, Allen Bakke, a white male, was unsuccessful in obtaining admission to Davis Medical School at the University of California even though his scores were better than those of some minority students who were admitted. At issue was a quota system instituted by the school in which 16 of 100 seats were reserved for qualified minority students. Charging reverse discrimination, Bakke sued. In a 5-4 decision, the Court ruled for Bakke stating that the use of quotas in this case did, in fact, constitute reverse discrimination since white applicants were denied an opportunity to compete for *all* seats in the medical school. In a second 5-4 decision within the *Bakke* case, the Court did allow for preferential treatment if treated as a positive factor in the selection process much like the ten bonus points awarded to veterans on civil service examinations.

Although the use of quotas suffered a severe blow in the *Bakke* case, the issue was far from over. One year later in the case of *Steelworkers v. Weber*,[69] the Court seemingly reversed itself. Fearing multimillion-dollar suits by minorities and women, Kaiser Aluminum & Chemical Corporation negotiated an affirmative action plan that would increase African-American participation in skilled jobs. To accomplish this goal, 50 percent of the openings for training and promotion in such jobs were set aside for African-American employees. This action resulted in white employees with more seniority than African Americans being passed over for promotion. A rejected applicant, Brian Weber, sued. In a 5-2 decision, the Court upheld the plan. The difference between the two cases centered on the issue of how the Court chose to read civil rights legislation. In *Bakke*, the Court chose a literal interpretation and, thus, quotas were viewed as discriminatory to white males. Conversely, in *Weber* the Court concentrated on the intent of civil rights legislation, which was to eliminate discrimination against minority groups. Quotas accomplished this goal and, therefore, were ruled constitutional. Likewise, in 1980 the Court upheld the constitutionality of a congressional program requiring that 10 percent of certain federal construction grants be awarded to minority contractors.[70]

With the election of Ronald Reagan in 1980 and the mood of the nation turning more conservative, the battle over affirmative action took a swing to the right. Instrumental in this shift was Ronald Reagan's three appointments to the Court: Sandra Day O'Connor, Antonin Scalia, and Anthony Kennedy. The first attack on affirmative action came with a 1984 case in which the Court declared unconstitutional a Memphis, Tennessee, plan in which white firefighters with more seniority were laid off first to protect the jobs of newly hired minorities.[71] Advocates of the plan defended the plan as necessary to avert the discriminatory practice of "last hired-first fired" among minorities. The Court disagreed and reaffirmed its opposition to the practice in the 1986 case of *Wygant v. Jackson Board of Education*[72] in which white teachers with more seniority were laid off to preserve the jobs of minority teachers. Within these two cases the Court was able to make clear its position for lower courts to follow in evaluating proposals that would strip employees of their jobs to open positions to minorities, but it was unable to agree on a set of guidelines for hiring new employees. This would occur three years later in the case of *Wards Cove Packing Co. v. Antonio*.[73] Here the Court declared that simply having a disproportionate number of white men in upper management or any other job was not sufficient proof of discrimination. Rather, evidence would have to be presented that qualified minorities were passed over because of racial reasons rather than factors relating to job performance. And, furthermore, the burden of presenting this evidence rested not with the employer but with the employee. Likewise, in the case of *Richmond v. J. A. Croson Co.*,[74] the Court overturned a "job set aside" program adopted by the city council of Richmond, Virginia, in which 30 percent of all contracts were to be awarded to minorities. In rejecting the plan, the Court said it failed to specify any Richmond contractors who had been discriminated against, so that the quota could not be tied to the injury of anyone.

This trend has been followed in the lower courts also. In a case decided in 1997, *Hopwood* v. *State of Texas,*[75] two white students seeking entry to the law school at the University of Texas at Austin sued when their applications were denied because the university's affirmative action program took race into account in selecting applicants. This, they maintained, violated the students' Fourteenth Amendment rights. A federal appellate court agreed. When asked to consider the case on appeal, the Supreme Court declined, thus, letting the decision of the lower court stand.

Many educators believe that diversity in the classroom provides exposure to various interracial and cultural backgrounds that directly impact upon how students interact with people different from themselves. The Supreme Court put a chilling effect upon some ways of attaining classroom diversity when it allowed a lower Maryland court decision to stand. It denied school administrators leeway to stop a white boy from transferring from a minority-dominated neighborhood school to a primarily white magnet school.[76]

In contrast, a lower federal court in Michigan upheld the University of Michigan's undergraduate admission procedures, which includes race as one of several factors considered. The Center for Individual Rights (C.I.R.), a Washington, D.C. law firm, that conducts nationwide campaigns to dismantle affirmative action provides the funds for the plaintiffs in the two University of Michigan cases. Jennifer Gratz was an unsuccessful applicant for admission to the University's largest undergraduate college—the College of Literature, Science & Arts—for the 1995 fall term. More than 360 higher educational institutions and 21 international corporations filed amicus curiae briefs in support of U. of M in the *Gratz v. Bolinger* case. In his decision, Judge Patrick Duggan wrote, "university defendants have presented this court with solid evidence regarding the educational benefits that flow from a racially and ethnically diverse student body."[77] Later, he added that affirmative action could not be justified in attempting to remedy past and present inequalities. In the same federal district court, Judge Bernard Friedman ruled the University of Michigan's law school admissions policies unconstitutional in *Gutter v. Bolinger*. Here again, the challenge focuses on the race factor. However, this time the complaint referenced the *Bakke* case. The university defended its position by contending that it is in full compliance with *Bakke* as it allowed race to be a consideration but outlawed quotas. Both cases were appealed to the Six Circuit Court of Appeals. The court supported the university's position in *Gutter v. Bollinger*; thus overturning the district court decision. It said that the law school's use of race and ethnicity is "narrowly tailored" to achieve a diverse student body and the benefits of diversity are compelling. The decision referenced Harvard University's admission policies—cited by the U.S. Supreme Court's decision in the *Bakke* Case.

On August 9, 2002, the law school plaintiffs filed a petition for *certiorari* to the U.S. Supreme Court. On October 1, 2002, the undergraduate plaintiffs also filed a *certiorari* petition to the U.S. Supreme Court although the Court of Appeals had not rendered a decision. The Supreme Court agreed to hear both cases as a class action and scheduled oral arguments for April 1, 2003. Here again, over 300 *amici* briefs have been filed in support of the university. Among those filing briefs against the university was President George W. Bush. His brief states that the admission program is unconstitutional because it violates Fourteenth Amendment rights.

The university claims the admission program complies with the *Bakke* case and does not set quotas. Each applicant is reviewed individually. Consideration is given to the whole person. Academic strength, personal achievement, life experiences are among the factors considered. Academic qualifications, i.e. grades, test scores, strength of curriculum, are the overwhelming criteria examined in making admission decisions. There are no set-asides, or separate tracks, no targets, and no quotas. Each applicant competes with the applicant pool. Race is one of many factors considered. It accounts for 20 points of a 150-point Selection Index. Admissions counselors, to assure consistent assessment of a large pool of applicants each year, use the index. Academic factors account for 110 of the 150 points. The same 20 points used for race can be earned for those who are socioeconomically disadvantaged or who came from predominately minority populated high schools regardless of race. The 20 points can only be awarded once. Geographic diversity is considered as well. Students from the predominately white communities in Michigan's Upper Peninsula earn 16 points. Special consideration is given to men entering nursing and women entering engineering. Every year there are some white students admitted with lower test scores and lower grade point averages than some rejected minority students. The university receives 25,000 undergraduate applications each year for 5,000 spaces in the freshman class and 5,000 applications for 350 spaces in the law school.

Further, the number of underrepresented minority students varies from year to year based solely upon the characteristics of the applicant pool. There is no predetermined goal or quota. For example, over the years, the percent of minority law school students ranges from 12.5 to 20. The base line for admission is accepting only those students who are academically qualified.[78]

The Supreme Court, ruling 5-4, rendered its decision on June 23, 2003 in *Gutter v. Bollinger*. In the most significant and wide-ranging affirmative action ruling and decision on race in a generation, the Court ruled that colleges and universities can consider an applicant's race as a factor in attracting a diverse student body but reiterated that *quotas* violate the Constitution. The Court stated that colleges and universities have compelling educational reasons for seeking a diverse student body. It marked the first time a majority of the Court endorsed this view. The ruling involved affirmative action in admissions to the University of Michigan's undergraduate school, as well as to its law school. While striking down the formula-method in Michigan's undergraduate school, it upheld the admissions policy at the University of Michigan Law School, where officials consider race along with other factors when making admission decisions. The majority decision was written by Justice Sandra Day O'Connor. In an interview the day after announcing the decision, Justice O'Connor said, "if America provided adequate educational opportunities for young people, it could someday achieve the goal of ending affirmative action in college admissions." Looking toward the future she also stated, "I hope it looks as though we don't need artificial help to fill our classrooms with highly qualified students at the graduate level. And, if we do our job on educating young people, we can reach that goal."

Although hailed by affirmative action supporters as a huge victory, the case still is a "mixed bag of tricks." The Court's decision was vague in its language when it supported the "narrow" use of race as an admission factor. How is "narrow" to be defined? How is a school's particular use of affirmative action, *narrowly employed*, acceptable but another school's *narrow* use of affirmative action not acceptable? These are questions that will continue to plague the judiciary for years to come.

The University of Michigan discovered that the number of black freshman fell 15 percent after the Supreme Court decision. This has prompted the University to develop the M-PACT Program that will provide educational grants to assist lower-income undergraduate students to meet the costs to attend. This effort demonstrates the university's commitment to maintaining diversity.[79]

Until recently colleges and school districts were subject to losing their federal funding if they were found to be negligent in taking appropriate action in sexual harassment allegations. Title XI of the Education Amendments of 1972 prohibits discrimination based upon a person's sex. It applies to schools and colleges receiving federal funds. Victims of sexual harassment or other forms of sex discrimination in schools may sue for monetary damages. It does not matter who the victim is or who is doing the harassing. It could be an allegation of one student harassing another. The school district or college should take timely action in thoroughly investigating and penalizing when appropriate. There could be multimillion-dollar verdicts against colleges and school districts where it is determined that action was inadequate. Presumably, these potential penalties will force educational institutions to review current policies and not only adopt but enforce firm policies prohibiting sexual harassment and take preventative measures.[80]

The battles over diversity do not end with education or jobs; rather, it extends to language. English is the dominant language in the United States; yet, in government offices, hospitals, schools, and many other public facilities other languages are spoken and written. In 1998, Arizona passed a constitutional amendment that declared English the state's official language and required its use in most government transactions. The amendment actually prohibited the *use* of other languages in all government matters. However, the Arizona Supreme Court concurred with a lower court, which found the amendment a violation of free speech and equal protection guaranteed under the United States Constitution. Further, the Court said it created, "a linguistic barrier between persons and the government they have a right to petition.[81] The debate over language, like so many other issues connected with the Bill of Rights, continues with some advocating making English the *official* language of the United States.

Through the years, the impaired have made us more aware of equal access and discrimination issues. Recognizing that unequal treatment existed, in 1990, Congress passed the Americans with Disabilities Act to enforce constitutional guarantees of equal protection. The scope of this law was challenged in a recent case in which the Court ruled that the intent of the law did not extend to disabilities that could be corrected with medication or with certain devices such as glasses.[82]

In addition to challenges in the courts, affirmative action is being attacked in state legislatures. In 1996, "Proposition 209" was proposed to the citizens of California as an initiative to amend their state constitution. The main clause of the initiative read as follows:

The state shall not discriminate against, or grant preferential treatment to any individual or group on the basis of race, sex, color, ethnicity, or national origin in the operation of public employment, public education, or public contracting.

Nine million voters cast a ballot on the initiative. Over 54 percent agreed with it. The ballots had barely been counted when opponents filed suit seeking an injunction against enforcing Proposition 209. Initially, a federal judge granted the injunction. However, on appeal, an appellate court reversed the decision of the lower court. Again, the Supreme Court was asked to review the case. And, once again, the Court declined.[83] Thus, the initiative stood. Today, more than a dozen states have passed or are about to consider similar initiatives and measures.

Where Are We Now?

Understandably, decisions by the Court have brought an outpouring of both criticism and praise. Nowhere is this division of opinion more evident than on the Court itself. Justice Harry Blackmun wrote, "One wonders whether the majority still believes that race discrimination—against nonwhites—is a problem in our society, or even remembers that it ever was."[84] On the other hand, Justice Sandra Day O'Connor stated, "Classifications based on race carry a danger of astigmatic harm. Unless they are strictly reserved for remedial settings, they may in fact promote notions of racial inferiority and lead to a politics of racial hostility."[85]

The issue of equality in this country is one of turmoil and change. As the United States moves further into the new millennium, affirmative action and all other related topics will undoubtedly continue to be hotly contested. The Supreme Court decision in the University of Michigan cases may well define the structure of future policies related to education and employment that will affect everyone in the United States.

CONCLUSION

Ideals are of paramount importance to the survival of a country. In essence, they provide the social glue necessary to bind citizens together into a stable and orderly society. If a country is successful in the implementation of its ideals, peace and harmony will prevail—if not, conflict and disunity are destined to follow. Against this rule, how then are we to judge the United States?

As we have seen, the American thinkers staked their hope for their new society on the twin ideals of liberty and equality. In the wake of September 11 many Americans have been far more willing to trade some liberty and equality for more security. Are our fears causing the delicate balance of liberty and equality to teeter as on a seesaw? Similarly, as we have also seen in Chapter One, for a substantial number of citizens, white males, the implementation of these two ideals was achieved successfully. In fact, few countries in the world can compare favorably with the American record of social and economic mobility. For the most part, the success of the United States in the implementation of its ideals is the reason why the government has enjoyed a relatively stable political climate over its existence. The acceptance of the ideals and the belief in their practice lends a sense of legitimacy that, in turn, equates to stability. But is this true for all citizens? Unfortunately, as we have seen in this chapter, the answer is no. For minorities and women, equality has been an ongoing struggle spanning the length of the nation's history and to this day is yet to be achieved completely. In addition, the world is such a very different place than it was in the late eighteenth century. Today's threat of terrorism challenges the very fabric of equality as the United States searches for ways to balance security with freedom.

Chapter Eighteen Notes

[1]Scholarly Resources, *The Gallup Poll 1983* (Wilmington, Del.: Scholarly Resources, 1984), 144.

[2]92 U.S. 214 (1876).

[3]163 U.S. 537 (1896).

[4]347 U.S. 483 (1954).

[5]*Statistical Abstracts on the United States*, 2004-2005, The National Data Book. 124th edition.

[6]*Guinn and Beal v. United States*, 238 U.S. 347 (1915).

[7]321 U.S. 649 (1944).

[8]*Shaw v. Reno*; 509 U.S. - 125L.Ed. 2d. 511. *Bush v. Vera*, 116 S.Ct. 1996.

[9]Clifford Levy, "New York's 12th District is Ruled Invalid," *New York Times*, February 27, 1997, p. A12.

[10]*Shelley v. Kraemer*, 334 U.S. 1 (1948).

[11]392 U.S. 409 (1968).

[12]*Jones v. Alfred H. Mayer*.

[13]*The South Suburban Housing Center v. Greater South Suburban Board of Realtors*, 89-2115 (7th Cir. 1988).

[14]Federal Supreme Court dockett # 91925, September 27, 1992.

[15]Oliver, Melvin L., and Thomas M. Shapiro. *Black Wealth/White Wealth*. New York: Routledge, 1995.

[16]Statistical Abstract 2004-2005, Table 665.

[17]Statistical Abstract 2004-2005, Table 689.

[18]*Statistical Abstract*, 2003-2004, Tables 603 and 608.

[19]Richard B. Freeman, *The Declining Value of Higher Education and the American Social System* (New York: Aspin Institute for Humanistic Studies, 1976), 68.

[20]*Statistical Abstract*, 2004-2005, Table 665.

[21]*Wards Cove Packing Co. v. Antonio*, 490 U.S. 642 (1989).

[22]*Chicago Tribune*, 6 June 1989.

[23]Ray Boshara, "The $6000 Solution-Wealth Inequality," *Atlantic Monthly*, January/February 2003.

[24]*Statistical Abstract*, 2004-2005, Table 35.

[25]Steve Huntley, "America's Indians: Beggars in Our Own Land," *U.S. News & World Report*, 23 May 1983, 70.

[26]Nicholas von Hoffman, "Righting Old Wrongs," *New Republic*, 30 August 1980: 14-17.

[27]*Wichita Eagle*, 25 March 1990, 5A.

[28]Art Winslow, "Speaking With Forked Tongue," *Nation*, 12 February 1983, 178.

[29]Joseph Hraba, *American Ethnicity* (Itasca, Ill.: F.E. Peacock Publishers, Inc., 1979), 298.

[30]*Statistical Abstract*, 2003-2004, Table 10.

[31]*Statistical Abstract*, 1999, Table 18 and Statistical Abstract 2003-2004, Table 8

[32]Dylan S. Meyer, *Uprooted American: The Japanese-American and the War Relocation Authority During World War II* (Tucson, Ariz.: University of Arizona Press, 1971).

[33]*Statistical Abstract, 2001*, Table 668. It should be noted that the gap has significantly decreased in the past four years according to the data presented in 121st Edition of the Statistical Abstract. Whites have increased their median income by nearly $12,000. It is not the object here to determine what brought about this rapid change. Nonetheless, the "culprit" could very well be that the methods used to compile the data have changed.

[34]*Statistical Abstract,* 2003-2004, Table 212 and 665.

[35]*New York Times*, 20 January 2001, 5wk.

[36]H. Bray, "The New Wave of Puerto Rican Immigrants," *N.Y. Times Magazine*, 3 July 1983.

[37]New York Times Magazine, 27 October 2002

[38]Bray.

[39]Bray.

[40]*Statistical Abstract, 1992,* Table 17.

[41]*Statistical Abstract 1992,* Table 1344.

[42]L.F. Estrada and others, "Chicanos in the United States: A History of Exploitation and Resistance," *Daedalus*, 110 (Spring 1981): 107.

[43]United States Office of Management and the Budget, *Budget of the United States Government*, Historical Tables, annual.

[44]U.S. Department of Agriculture, Food and Nutrition Service. http://www.fns.usda.gov/pd.

[45]*Frontiero v. Richardson*, 411 U.S. 677 (1973).

[46]*Bradwell v. State*, 83 U.S. (16 Wall) 130, 141 (1873).

[47]404 U.S. 71 (1971).

[48]*Chicago Tribune*, 2 October 1989, 1A.

[49]401 U.S. 113 (1973).

[50]*Statistical Abstract,* 2001, Table 93.

[51]109 S. Ct. 3040 (1989).

[52]*Planned Parenthood v. Casey* 112 S. Ct. 29 (1992).

[53]*Statistical Abstract,* 2001, Table 93.

[54]*National Organization for Women v. Scheidler*, 114 S.Ct. 798 (1994).

[55]*New York Times*, 23 January 2001, 1A.

[56]*Statistical Abstract, ,* 2001, Table 676.

[57]David Shapiro and Timothy J. Carr, "Work Attachment: Investments in Human Capital and the Earnings of Young Women," in Women, *Work, and Family*, ed. Frank L. Mott (Lexington, Mass.: Lexington Books, 1978), 28.

[58]Reported in the *Chicago Tribune*, 5 October 1989. Note: a 1985 ruling by the 9th U.S. Court of Appeals said states can rely on market rates in setting salaries even if they knowingly pay less to women.

[59]*NLRB v. Main Street Terrace Care Center,* 2000 FED App. 021P (6th Cir.)

[60]www.House.gov and www.Senate.gov

[61]Ager, Susan, "Where's the Viagra for Women?," *Detroit Free Press*, February 6, 2005, p,H-1.

[62]*"Working Women Count! A Report to the Nation, Executive Summary," Women's Bureau, U.S. Department of Labor, 31 August 2000.*

[63]*Holmes v. California Army National Guard,* 98-500.

[64]Boy Scouts of America v. Dale, 99-699.

[65]Deb Price, "Gay Conservatives Open New Options," *Detroit News, 29 January 2001, 7A.*

[66]*Griggs v. Duke Power Co.,* 401 U.S. 424 (1971).

[67]"Affirmative Action in the 1980's: Dismantling the Process of Discrimination. A Statement of the United States Commission on Civil Rights," *Clearing House Publication* 70, November, 1981.

[68]438 U.S. 265, 364, (1978).

[69]443 U.S. 193 (1978).

[70]*Fullilove v. Klutznick*, 448 U.S. 448 (1980).

[71]1984—Memphis firefighters' case in which the Court said that whites with more seniority cannot be laid off to protect the jobs of minorities with less seniority.

[72]476 U.S. 267 (1986).

[73]490 U.S. 642 (1989)

[74]*City of Richmond v. J.A. Croson Co.,* 488 U.S. 469 (1989).

[75]*Hopwood v. The State of Texas*, 78 F.3d 932 (5th Cir.), 1997.

[76]Eisenburg v. Montgomery County Public Schools, No. 98-2503 (CA-98-2797-AW), 4th Circuit Court.

[77]Gratz v. Bollinger, 122 F. Supp.2d 811 (E.D. Mich. Dec. 13, 2000).

[78]http://www.umich.edu

[79]Schultz, Marisa, "U-M Seeks Diversity With More Tuition Aid," *Detroit News*, February 28, 2005, p.1.

[80]*Franklin v Gwinnett County Public Schools*, 2000.

[81]*Arizonans for Official English v. Arizona*

[82]*Board of Trustees of University of Alabama v. Garrett,* No. 99—1240, 2001.

[83]*Coalition for Economic Equity v. Wilson*, 110 F.3d 1431 (9th Cir.), 1997.

[84]109 S.Ct/ 706 (1989)

[85]*City of Richmond v. J.A. Croson Co.*, 488 U.S. 469 (1989).

Suggested Readings

Bowen, William G., *The Shape of the River: Long-Term Consequences of Considering Race in College and University Admissions.* Princeton, N.J.: Princeton University Press, 1998.

Brown, Dee. *Bury My Heart at Wounded Knee.* New York: Holt, Rinehart & Winston, 1971.

Browne Miller, Angela. *Shameful Admissions: The Losing Battle to Serve Everyone in Our Universities.* San Francisco: Jossey-Bass Publishers, 1996.

Chomsky, Noam, Mitchell, Peter and Schoeffel, John, *Understanding Power,* The New Press, 2002.

Curry, George E. and Trevor W. Coleman, "Hijacking Justice," *Emerge,* October, 1999, pp. 42-49.

Freeman, Jo. *The Politics of Women's Liberation.* New York: David McKay, 1975.

Kozol, Jonathan, *Savage Inequalities*, Crown, 1991.

Kaplan, Robert D., "Was Democracy Just a Moment," *Atlantic Monthly,* December, 1997.

Mansbridge, Jane J. *Why We Lost the ERA*. Chicago: University of Chicago Press, 1986.

McGlen Nancy E. and Karen O'Connor. *Women, Politics and American Society*. Englewood Cliffs, N.J.: Prentice Hall, 1995.

Steele, Shelby, *A Dream Deferred*, Harper Collins, 1998.

Unger, Roberto Mangabeira and West, Cornel. *The Future of American Progressivism*, Beacon Press, 1998.

Washburn, Wilcomb. *The Indian in America*, New York: Harper and Row, 1975.

Williams, Juan. *Eyes on the Prize: America's Civil Rights Years, 1954-1965*. New York: Penguin Books, 1987.

Declaration of Independence

Congress, July 4, 1776

When, in the course of human events, it becomes necessary for one people to dissolve the political bonds which have connected them with another, and to assume, among the powers of the earth, the separate and equal station to which the laws of nature and of nature's God entitle them, a decent respect to the opinions of mankind requires that they should declare the causes which impel them to the separation.

We hold these truths to be self-evident: That all men are created equal; that they are endowed by their Creator with certain unalienable rights; that among these are life, liberty and the pursuit of happiness; that, to secure these rights, governments are instituted among men, deriving their just powers from the consent of the governed; that whenever any form of government becomes destructive of these ends, it is the right of the people to alter or to abolish it, and to institute new government, laying its foundation on such principles, and organizing its powers in such form, as to them shall seem most likely to effect their safety and happiness. Prudence, indeed, will dictate that governments long established should not be changed for light and transient causes; and accordingly all experience hath shown that mankind are more disposed to suffer, while evils are sufferable, than to right themselves by abolishing the forms to which they are accustomed. But when a long train of abuses and usurpations, pursuing invariably the same object, evinces a design to reduce them under absolute despotism, it is their right, it is their duty, to throw off such government, and to provide new guards for their future security. Such has been the patient sufferance of these colonies; and such is now the necessity which constrains them to alter their former systems of government. The history of the present King of Great Britain is a history of repeated injuries and usurpations, all having in direct object the establishment of an absolute tyranny over these states. To prove this, let facts be submitted to a candid world.

He has refused his assent to laws, the most wholesome and necessary for the public good.

He has forbidden his governors to pass laws of immediate and pressing importance, unless suspended in their operation till his assent should be obtained; and, when so suspended, he has utterly neglected to attend to them.

He has refused to pass other laws for the accommodation of large districts of people, unless those people would relinquish the right of representation in the legislature, a right inestimable to them, and formidable to tyrants only.

He has called together legislative bodies at places unusual, uncomfortable, and distant from the depository of their public records, for the sole purpose of fatiguing them into compliance with his measures.

He has dissolved representative houses repeatedly, for opposing, with many firmness, his invasions on the rights of the people.

He has refused for a long time, after such dissolutions, to cause others to be elected; whereby the legislative powers, incapable of annihilation, have returned to the people at large for their exercise; the state remaining, in the mean time, exposed to all the dangers of invasions from without and convulsions within.

He has endeavored to prevent the population of these states; for that purpose obstructing the laws for naturalization of foreigners; refusing to pass others to encourage their migrations hither, and raising the conditions of new appropriations of lands.

He has obstructed the administration of justice, by refusing his assent to laws establishing judiciary powers.

He has made judges dependent on his will alone, for the tenure of their offices, and the amount and payment of their salaries.

He has erected a multitude of new offices, and sent hither swarms of officers to harass our people and eat out their substance.

He has kept among us, in times of peace, standing armies, without the consent of our legislatures.

He has affected to render the military independent of, and superior to, the civil power.

He has combined with others to subject us to jurisdiction foreign to our constitution, and unacknowledged by our laws, giving his assent to their acts of pretended legislation:

For quartering large bodies of armed troops among us;

For protecting them, by a mock trial, from punishment for any murder which they should commit on the inhabitants of these states;

For cutting off our trade with all parts of the world;

For imposing taxes on us without our consent;

For depriving us, in many cases, of the benefits of trial by jury;

For transporting us beyond seas, to be tried for pretended offenses;

For abolishing the free system of English laws in a neighboring province, establishing therein an arbitrary government, and enlarging its boundaries, so as to render it at once an example and fit instrument for introducing the same absolute rule into these colonies;

For taking away our charters, abolishing our most valuable laws, and altering fundamentally the forms of our governments;

For suspending our own legislatures, and declaring themselves invested with power to legislate for us in all cases whatsoever.

He has abdicated government here, by declaring us out of his protection and waging war against us.

He has plundered our seas, ravaged our coasts, burned our towns, and destroyed the lives of our people.

He is at this time transporting large armies of foreign mercenaries to complete the works of death, desolation and tyranny already begun with circumstances of cruelty and perfidy scarcely paralleled in the most barbarous ages, and totally unworthy the head of a civilized nation.

He has constrained our fellow-citizens, taken captive on the high seas, to bear arms against their country, to become the executioners of their friends and brethren, or to fall themselves by their hands.

He has excited domestic insurrections among us, and has endeavored to bring on the inhabitants of our frontiers the merciless Indian savages, whose known rule of warfare is an undistinguished destruction of all ages, sexes, and conditions.

In every stage of these oppressions we have petitioned for redress in the most humble terms; our repeated petitions have been answered only by repeated injury. A prince, whose character is thus marked by every act which may define a tyrant, is unfit to be the ruler of a free people.

Nor have we been wanting in our attentions to our British brethren. We have warned them, from time to time, of attempts by their legislature to extend an unwarrantable jurisdiction over us. We have reminded them of the circumstances of our emigration and settlement here. We have appealed to their native justice and magnanimity, and we have conjured them, by the ties of our common kindred, to disavow these usurpations, which would inevitably interrupt our connections and correspondence. They, too, have been deaf to the voice of justice and of consanguinity. We must, therefore, acquiesce in the necessity which denounces our separation, and hold them, as we hold the rest of mankind, enemies in war, in peace friends.

We, therefore, the representatives of the United States of America, in General Congress assembled, appealing to the Supreme Judge of the world for the rectitude of our intentions, do, in the name and by authority of the good people of these colonies, solemnly publish and declare, that these United Colonies are, and of right ought to be, FREE AND INDEPENDENT STATES; that they are absolved from all allegiance to the British crown, and that all political connection between them and the state of Great Britain is, and ought to be, totally dissolved; and that, as free and independent states, they have full power to levy war, conclude peace, contract alliances, establish commerce, and do all other acts and things which independent states may of right do. And for the support of this declaration, with a firm reliance on the protection of Divine Providence, we mutually pledge to each other our lives, our fortunes, and our sacred honor.

JOHN HANCOCK

BUTTON GWINNETT
LYMAN HALL
GEO. WALTON
WM. HOOPER
JOSEPH HEWES
JOHN PENN
EDWARD RUTLEDGE
THOS. HEYWARD, JUNR.
THOMAS LYNCH, JUNR.
ARTHUR MIDDLETON
SAMUEL CHASE
WM. PACA
THOS. STONE
CHARLES CARROLL OF
    CARROLLTON
GEORGE WYTHE
RICHARD HENRY LEE
TH. JEFFERSON
BENJ. HARRISON

THOS. NELSON, JR.
FRANCIS LIGHTFOOT LEE
CARTER BRAXTON
ROBT. MORRIS
BENJAMIN RUSH
BENJA. FRANKLIN
JOHN MORTON
GEO. CLYMER
JAS. SMITH
GEO. TAYLOR
JAMES WILSON
GEO. ROSS
CAESAR RODNEY
GEO READ
THO. M'KEAN
WM. FLOYD
PHIL. LIVINGSTON
FRANS. LEWIS
LEWIS MORRIS

RICHD. STOCKTON
JNO. WITHERSPOON
FRAS. HOPKINSON
JOHN HART
ABRA. CLARK
JOSIAH BARTLETT
WM. WHIPPLE
SAML. ADAMS
JOHN ADAMS
ROBT. TREAT PAINE
ELBRIDGE GERRY
STEP. HOPKINS
WILLIAM ELLERY
ROGER SHERMAN
SAM'EL HUNTINGTON
WM. WILLIAMS
OLIVER WOLCOTT
MATTHEW THORNTON

The Constitution of the United States of America

PREAMBLE

We the people of the United States, in order to form a more perfect union, establish justice, insure domestic tranquility, provide for the common defense, promote the general welfare, and secure the blessings of liberty to ourselves and our posterity, do ordain and establish this Constitution for the United States of America.

Passages no longer in effect are printed in italic type.

ARTICLE I.—THE LEGISLATIVE ARTICLE

Section 1. All legislative powers herein granted shall be vested in a Congress of the United States, which shall consist of a Senate and a House of Representatives.

House of Representatives: Composition, Qualification, Apportionment, Impeachment Power

Section 2. The House of Representatives shall be composed of members chosen every second year by the people of the several States, and the electors in each State shall have the qualifications requisite for electors of the most numerous branch of the State Legislature.

No person shall be a Representative who shall not have attained to the age of twenty-five years, and been seven years a citizen of the United States, and who shall not, when elected, be an inhabitant of that State in which he shall be chosen.

Representatives and direct taxes shall be apportioned among the several States which may be included within this Union, according to their respective numbers, *which shall be determined by adding to the whole number of free persons, including those bound to service for a term of years and excluding Indians not taxed, three-fifths of all other persons.* The actual enumeration shall be made within three years after the first meeting of the Congress of the United States, and within every subsequent term of ten years, in such manner as they shall by law direct. The number of Representatives shall not exceed one for every thirty thousand, but each State shall have at least one Representative; *and until each enumeration shall be made, the State of New Hampshire shall be entitled to choose three, Massachusetts eight, Rhode Island and Providence Plantations one, Connecticut five, New York six, New Jersey four, Pennsylvania eight, Delaware one, Maryland six, Virginia ten, North Carolina five, South Carolina five, and Georgia three.*

When vacancies happen in the representation from any State, the Executive authority thereof shall issue writs of election to fill such vacancies.

The House of Representatives shall choose their Speaker and other officers; and shall have the sole power of impeachment.

Senate Composition: Qualifications, Impeachment Trials

Section 3. The Senate of the United States shall be composed of two Senators from each State, *chosen by the legislature thereof,* for six years; and each Senator shall have one vote.

Immediately after they shall be assembled in consequence of the first election, they shall be divided as equally as may be into three classes. The seats of the

Senators of the first class shall be vacated at the expiration of the second year, of the second class at the expiration of the fourth year, and of the third class at the expiration of the sixth year, so that one-third may be chosen every second year; and if vacancies happen by resignation or otherwise, during the recess of the legislature of any State, the Executive thereof may make temporary appointments until the next meeting of the legislature, which shall then fill such vacancies.

No person shall be a Senator who shall not have attained to the age of thirty years, and been nine years a citizen of the United States, and who shall not, when elected, be an inhabitant of that State for which he shall be chosen.

The Vice President of the United States shall be President of the Senate, but shall have no vote, unless they be equally divided.

The Senate shall choose their other officers, and also a President *pro tempore*, in the absence of the Vice President, or when he shall exercise the office of President of the United States.

The Senate shall have the sole power to try all impeachments. When sitting for that purpose, they shall be on oath or affirmation. When the President of the United States is tried, the Chief Justice shall preside: and no person shall be convicted without the concurrence of two-thirds of the members present.

Judgment in cases of impeachment shall not extend further than to removal from the office, and disqualification to hold and enjoy any office of honor, trust or profit under the United States; but the party convicted shall nevertheless be liable and subject to indictment, trial, judgment and punishment, according to law.

Congressional Elections: Time, Place, Manner

Section 4. The times, places and manner of holding elections for Senators and Representatives shall be prescribed in each State by the legislature thereof; but the Congress may at any time by law make or alter such regulations, except as to the places of choosing Senators.

The Congress shall assemble at least once in every year, and such meeting *shall be on the first Monday in December, unless they shall by law appoint a different day.*

Powers and Duties of the Houses

Section 5. Each house shall be the judge of the elections, returns and qualifications of its own members, and a majority of each shall constitute a quorum to do business; but a smaller number may adjourn from day to day, and may be authorized to compel the attendance of absent members, in such manner, and under such penalties, as each house may provide.

Each house may determine the rules of its proceedings, punish its members for disorderly behavior, and with the concurrence of two-thirds, expel a member.

Each house shall keep a journal of its proceedings, and from time to time publish the same, excepting such parts as may in their judgment require secrecy; and the yeas and nays of the members of either house on any question shall, at the desire of one-fifth of those present, be entered on the journal.

Neither house, during the session of Congress, shall, without the consent of the other, adjourn for more than three days, nor to any other place than that in which the two houses shall be sitting.

Rights of Members

Section 6. The Senators and Representatives shall receive a compensation for their services, to be ascertained by law and paid out of the treasury of the United States. They shall in all cases except treason, felony and breach of the peace, be privileged from arrest during their attendance at the session of their respective houses, and in going to and returning from the same; and for any speech or debate in either house, they shall not be questioned in any other place.

No Senator or Representative shall, during the time for which he was elected, be appointed to any civil office under the authority of the United States, which shall have been created, or the emoluments whereof shall have been increased, during such time; and no person holding any office under the United States shall be a member of either house during his continuance in office.

Legislative Powers: Bills and Resolutions

Section 7. All bills for raising revenue shall originate in the House of Representatives; but the Senate may propose or concur with amendments as on other bills.

Every bill which shall have passed the House of Representatives and the Senate, shall, before it become a law, be presented to the President of the United States; if he approve he shall sign it, but if not he shall return it with objections to that house in which it originated, who shall enter the objections at large on their journal, and proceed to reconsider it. If after such reconsideration two-thirds of that house shall agree to pass the bill, it shall be sent, together with the objections, to the other house, by which it shall likewise be reconsidered, and if approved by two-thirds of that house, it shall become a law. But in all such cases the votes of both houses shall be determined by yeas and nays, and the names of the persons voting for and against the bill shall be entered on the journal of each house respectively. If any bill shall not be returned by the President within ten days (Sundays excepted) after it shall have been presented to him, the same shall be a law, in like manner as if he had signed it, unless the Congress by their adjournment prevent its return, in which case it shall not be a law.

Every order, resolution, or vote to which the concurrence of the Senate and House of Representatives may be necessary (except on a question of adjournment) shall be presented to the President of the United States; and before the same shall take effect, shall be approved by him, or being disapproved by him, shall be repassed by two-thirds of the Senate and House of Representatives, according to the rules and limitations prescribed in the case of a bill.

Powers of Congress

Section 8. The Congress shall have power

To lay and collect taxes, duties, imposts and excises, to pay the debts and provide for the common defense and general welfare of the United States; but all duties, imposts and excises shall be uniform throughout the United States;

To borrow money on the credit of the United States;

To regulate commerce with foreign nations, and among the several States, and with the Indian tribes;

To establish an uniform rule of naturalization, and uniform laws on the subject of bankruptcies throughout the United States;

To coin money, regulate the value thereof, and of foreign coin, and fix the standard of weights and measures;

To provide for the punishment of counterfeiting the securities and current coin of the United States;

To establish post offices and post roads;

To promote the progress of science and useful arts by securing for limited times to authors and inventors the exclusive right to their respective writings and discoveries;

To constitute tribunals inferior to the Supreme Court;

To define and punish piracies and felonies committed on the high seas and offenses against the law of nations;

To declare war, grant letters of marque and reprisal, and make rules concerning captures on land and water;

To raise and support armies, but no appropriation of money to that use shall be for a longer term than two years;

To provide and maintain a navy;

To make rules for the government and regulation of the land and naval forces;

To provide for calling forth the militia to execute the laws of the Union, suppress insurrections, and repel invasions;

To provide for organizing, arming, and disciplining the militia, and for governing such part of them as may be employed in the service of the United States, reserving to the States respectively the appointment of the officers, and the authority of training the militia according to the discipline prescribed by Congress;

To exercise exclusive legislation in all cases whatsoever, over such district (not exceeding ten miles square) as may, by cession of particular States, and the acceptance of Congress, become the seat of the government of the United States, and to exercise like authority over all places purchased by the consent of the legislature of the State, in which the same shall be, for erection of forts, magazines, arsenals, dock-yards, and other needful buildings;—and

To make all laws which shall be necessary and proper for carrying into execution the foregoing powers, and all other powers vested by this Constitution in the government of the United States, or in any department or officer thereof.

Powers Denied to Congress

Section 9. *The migration or importation of such persons as any of the States now existing shall think proper to admit shall not be prohibited by the Congress prior to the year 1808; but a tax or duty may be imposed on such importation, not exceeding $10 for each person.*

The privilege of the writ of habeas corpus shall not be suspended, unless when in cases of rebellion or invasion the public safety may require it.

No bill of attainder or ex post facto law shall be passed.

No capitation, or other direct, tax shall be laid, unless in proportion to the census or enumeration herein before directed to be taken.

No tax or duty shall be laid on articles exported from any State.

No preference shall be given by any regulation of commerce or revenue to the ports of one State over those of another; nor shall vessels bound to, or from, one State, be obliged to enter, clear, or pay duties in another.

No money shall be drawn from the treasury, but in consequence of appropriations made by law; and a regular statement and account of the receipts and expenditures of all public money shall be published from time to time.

No title of nobility shall be granted by the United States; and no person holding any office of profit or trust under them, shall, without the consent of the Congress, accept of any present, emolument, office, or title, of any kind whatever, from any king, prince, or foreign state.

Powers Denied to the States

Section 10. No State shall enter into any treaty, alliance, or confederation; grant letters of marque and reprisal; coin money; emit bills of credit; make anything but gold and silver coin a tender in payment of debts; pass any bill of attainder, ex post facto law, or law impairing the obligation of contracts, or grant any title of nobility.

No State shall, without the consent of the Congress, lay any imposts or duties on imports or exports, except what may be absolutely necessary for executing its inspection laws: and the net produce of all duties and imposts, laid by any State on imports or exports, shall be for the use of the treasury of the United States; and all such laws shall be subject to the revision and control of the Congress.

No State shall, without the consent of Congress, lay any duty of tonnage, keep troops or ships of war in time of peace, enter into any agreement or compact with another State, or with a foreign power, or engage in war, unless actually invaded, or in such imminent danger as will not admit of delay.

ARTICLE II.—THE EXECUTIVE ARTICLE

Nature and Scope of Presidential Power

Section 1. The executive power shall be vested in a President of the United States of America. He shall hold his office during the term of four years, and, together with the Vice President, chosen for the same term, be elected, as follows:

Each State shall appoint, in such manner as the legislature thereof may direct, a number of electors, equal to the whole number of Senators and Representatives to which the State may be entitled in the Congress; but no Senator or Representative, or person holding an office of trust or profit under the United States, shall be appointed an elector.

The electors shall meet in their respective States, and vote by ballot for two persons, of whom one at least shall not be an inhabitant of the same State with themselves. And they shall make a list of all the persons voted for, and of the number of votes for each; which list they shall sign and certify, and transmit sealed to the seat of government of the United States, directed to the President of the Senate. The President of the Senate shall, in the presence of the Senate and House of Representatives, open all the certificates, and the votes shall then be counted. The person having the greatest number of votes shall be the President, if such number be a majority of the whole number of electors appointed; and if there be more than one who have such majority, and have an equal number of votes, then the House of

---

Representatives shall immediately choose by ballot one of them for President; and if no person have a majority, then from the five highest on the list said house shall in like manner choose the President. But in choosing the President the votes shall be taken by States, the representation from each State having one vote; a quorum for this purpose shall consist of a member or members from two-thirds of the States, and a majority of all the States shall be necessary to a choice. In every case, after the choice of the President, the person having the greatest number of votes of the electors shall be the Vice President. But if there should remain two or more who have equal votes, the Senate shall choose from them by ballot the Vice President.

The Congress may determine the time of choosing the electors, and the day on which they shall give their votes; which day shall be the same throughout the United States.

No person except a natural-born citizen, *or a citizen of the United States at the time of the adoption of this Constitution*, shall be eligible to the office of President; neither shall any person be eligible to that office who shall not have attained to the age of thirty-five years, and been fourteen years a resident within the United States.

In case of the removal of the President from office or of his death, resignation, or inability to discharge the powers and duties of the said office, the same shall devolve on the Vice President, and the Congress may by law provide for the case of removal, death, resignation, or inability, both of the President and Vice President, declaring what officer shall then act as President, and such officer shall act accordingly, until the disability be removed, or a President shall be elected.

The President shall, at stated times, receive for his services a compensation, which shall neither be increased nor diminished during the period for which he shall have been elected, and he shall not receive within that period any other emolument from the United States, or any of them.

Before he enter on the execution of his office, he shall take the following oath or affirmation: —"I do solemnly swear (or affirm) that I will faithfully execute the office of President of the United States, and will to the best of my ability preserve, protect, and defend the Constitution of the United States."

Powers and Duties of the President

Section 2. The President shall be the commander in chief of the army and navy of the United States, and of the militia of the several States, when called into the actual service of the United States; he may require the opinion, in writing, of the principal officer in each of the executive departments, upon any subject relating to the duties of their respective offices, and he shall have power to grant reprieves and pardons for offenses against the United States, except in cases of impeachment.

He shall have power, by and with the advice and consent of the Senate, to make treaties, provided two-thirds of the Senators present concur; and he shall nominate, and by and with the advice and consent of the Senate, shall appoint ambassadors, other public ministers and consuls, judges of the Supreme Court, and all other officers of the United States, whose appointments are not herein otherwise provided for, and which shall be established by law: but the Congress may by law vest the appointment of such inferior officers, as they think proper, in the President alone, in the courts of law, or in the heads of departments.

The President shall have power to fill up all vacancies that may happen during the recess of the Senate, by granting commissions which shall expire at the end of their next session.

Section 3.   He shall from time to time give to the Congress information of the state of the Union, and recommend to their consideration such measures as he shall judge necessary and expedient; he may, on extraordinary occasions, convene both houses, or either of them, and in case of disagreement between them, with respect to the time of adjournment, he may adjourn them to such time as he shall think proper; he shall receive ambassadors and other public ministers; he shall take care that the laws be faithfully executed, and shall commission all the officers of the United States.

Section 4.   The President, Vice President and all civil officers of the United States shall be removed from office on impeachment for, and on conviction of, treason, bribery, or other high crimes and misdemeanor.

ARTICLE III.—THE JUDICIAL ARTICLE

Section 1.   The judicial power of the United States shall be vested in one Supreme Court, and in such inferior courts as the Congress may from time to time ordain and establish. The judges, both of the Supreme and inferior courts, shall hold their offices during good behavior, and shall, at stated times, receive for their services a compensation which shall not be diminished during their continuance in office.

Jurisdiction

Section 2.   The judicial power shall extend to all cases, in law and equity, arising under this Constitution, the laws of the United States, and treaties made, or which shall be made, under their authority;—to all cases affecting ambassadors, other public ministers and consuls;—to all cases of admiralty and maritime jurisdiction;—to controversies to which the United States shall be a party;—

to controversies between two or more States;—*between a state and citizens of another state*;—between citizens of different States;—between citizens of the same State claiming lands under grants of different States, and between a State, or the citizens thereof, and foreign states, citizens or subjects.

In all cases affecting ambassadors, other public ministers and consuls, and those in which a State shall be party, the Supreme Court shall have original jurisdiction. In all the other cases before mentioned, the Supreme Court shall have appellate jurisdiction, both as to law and fact, with such exceptions, and under such regulations, as the Congress shall make.

The trial of all crimes, except in cases of impeachment, shall be by jury; and such trial shall be held in the State where said crimes shall have been committed; but when not committed within any State, the trial shall be at such place or places as the Congress may by law have directed.

Treason

Section 3. Treason against the United States shall consist only in levying war against them, or in adhering to their enemies, giving them aid and comfort. No person shall be convicted of treason unless on the testimony of two witnesses to the same overt act, or on confession in open court.

The Congress shall have power to declare the punishment of treason, but no attainder of treason shall work corruption of blood, or forfeiture except during the life of the person attained.

ARTICLE IV.—INTERSTATE RELATIONS

Full Faith and Credit Clause

Section 1. Full Faith and credit shall be given in each State to the public acts, records, and judicial proceedings of every other State. And the Congress may by general laws prescribe the manner in which such acts, records and proceedings shall be proved, and the effect thereof.

Privileges and Immunities; Interstate Extradition

Section 2. The citizens of each State shall be entitled to all privileges and immunities of citizens in the several States.

A person charged in any State with treason, felony or other crime, who shall flee from justice, and be found in another State, shall on demand of the executive authority of the State from which he fled, be delivered up, to be removed to the State having jurisdiction of the crime.

No person held to service or labor in one State, under the laws thereof, escaping into another, shall, in consequence of any law or regulation therein, be discharged from such service or labor, but shall be delivered up on claim of the party to whom such service or labor may be due.

Admission of States

Section 3. New States may be admitted by the Congress into this Union; but no new State shall be formed or erected within the jurisdiction of any other State; nor any State be formed by the junc-
tion of two or more States, or parts of States, without the consent of the legislatures of the States concerned as well as of the Congress.

The Congress shall have power to dispose of and make all needful rules and regulations respecting the territory or other property belonging to the United States; and nothing in this Constitution shall be so construed as to prejudice any claims of the United States, or of any particular State.

Republican Form of Government

Section 4. The United States shall guarantee to every State in this Union a republican form of government, and shall protect each of them against invasion; and on application of the legislature, or of the executive (when the legislature cannot be convened) against domestic violence.

ARTICLE V.—THE AMENDING POWER

The Congress, whenever two-thirds of both houses shall deem it necessary, shall propose amendments to this Constitution, or, on the application of the legislatures of two-thirds of the several States, shall call a convention for proposing amendments, which, in either case, shall be valid to all intents and purposes, as part of this Constitution, when ratified by the legislatures of three-fourths of the several States, or by conventions in three-fourths thereof, as the one or the other mode of ratification may be proposed by the Congress; *provided that no amendment which may be made prior to the year one thousand eight hundred and eight shall in any manner affect the first and fourth clauses in the ninth section of the first article*; and that no State, without its consent, shall be deprived of its equal suffrage in the Senate.

ARTICLE VI.—THE SUPREMACY ACT

All debts contracted and engagements entered into, before the adoption of this Constitution, shall be as valid against the United States under this Constitution, as under the Confederation.

This Constitution, and the laws of the United States which shall be made in pursuance thereof; and all treaties made, or which shall be made, under the authority of the United States, shall be the supreme law of the land; and the judges in every State shall be bound thereby, anything in the Constitution or laws of any State to the contrary notwithstanding.

Supremacy Clause

The Senators and Representatives before mentioned, and the members of the several State legislatures, and all executive and judicial officers, both of the United States and of the several States, shall be bound by oath or affirmation to support this Constitution; but no religious test shall ever be required as a qualification to any office or public trust under the United States.

ARTICLE VII.—RATIFICATION

The ratification of the conventions of nine States shall be sufficient for the establishment of this Constitution between States so ratifying the same.

Done in Convention by the unanimous consent of the States present, the seventeenth day of September in the year of our Lord one thousand seven hundred and eighty-seven and of the Independence of the United States of America the twelfth. In witness whereof we have hereunto subscribed our names.

GEORGE WASHINGTON
President and Deputy from Virginia

New Hampshire
JOHN LANGDON
NICHOLAS GILMAN

Massachusetts
NATHANIEL GORHAM
RUFUS KING

Connecticut
WILLIAM S. JOHNSON
ROGER SHERMAN

Virginia
JOHN BLAIR
JAMES MADISON, JR

South Carolina
J. RUTLEDGE
CHARLES G. PINCKNEY
PIERCE BUTLER

New York
ALEXANDER HAMILTON

New Jersey
WILLIAM LIVINGSTON
DAVID BREARLEY
WILLIAM PATERSON
JONATHAN DAYTON

Pennsylvania
BENJAMIN FRANKLIN
THOMAS MIFFLIN
ROBERT MORRIS
GEORGE CLYMER
THOMAS FITZSIMONS
JARED INGERSOLL
JAMES WILSON
GOUVERNEUR MORRIS

Delaware
GEORGE READ
GUNNING BEDFORD, JR.
JOHN DICKINSON
RICHARD BASSETT
JACOB BROOM

Maryland
JAMES MCHENRY
DANIEL OF ST. THOMAS JENIFER
DANIEL CARROLL

North Carolina
WILLIAM BLOUNT
RICHARD DOBBS SPRAIGHT
HU WILLIAMSON

Georgia
WILLIAM FEW
ABRAHAM BALDWIN

THE BILL OF RIGHTS

The first ten Amendments (the Bill of Rights) were adopted in 1791.

AMENDMENT I.—RELIGION, SPEECH ASSEMBLY, AND PETITION

Congress shall make no law respecting an establishment of religion, or prohibiting the free exercise thereof; or abridging the freedom of speech, or of the press; or the right of the people peaceably to assemble, and to petition the government for a redress of grievances.

AMENDMENT II.—MILITIA AND THE RIGHT TO BEAR ARMS

A well-regulated militia being necessary to the security of a free State, the right of the people to keep and bear arms shall not be infringed.

AMENDMENT III.—QUARTERING OF SOLDIERS

No soldier shall, in time of peace, be quartered in any house without the consent of the owner, nor in time of war, but in a manner to be prescribed by law.

AMENDMENT IV.—SEARCHES AND SEIZURES

The right of the people to be secure in their persons, houses, papers, and effects, against unreasonable searches and seizures, shall not be violated, and no warrants shall issue but upon probable cause, supported by oath or affirmation, and particularly describing the place to be searched, and the persons or things to be seized.

AMENDMENT V.—GRAND JURIES, SELF-INCRIMINATION, DOUBLE JEOPARDY, DUE PROCESS, AND EMINENT DOMAIN

No person shall be held to answer for a capital, or otherwise infamous crime, unless on a presentment or indictment of a grand jury, except in cases arising in the land or naval forces, or in the militia, when in actual service in time of war or public danger; nor shall any person be subject for the same offense to be twice put in jeopardy of life or limb; nor shall be compelled in any criminal case to be a witness against himself, nor be deprived of life, liberty, or property, without due process of law; nor shall private property be taken for public use without just compensation.

AMENDMENT VI.—CRIMINAL COURT PROCEDURES

In all criminal prosecutions, the accused shall enjoy the right to a speedy and public trial, by an impartial jury of the State and district wherein the crime shall have been committed, which district shall have been previously ascertained by law, and to be informed of the nature and cause of the accusation; to be confronted with the witnesses against him; to have compulsory process for obtaining witnesses in his favor, and to have the assistance of counsel for his defense.

AMENDMENT VII.—TRIAL BY JURY IN COMMON LAW CASES

In suits at common law, where the value in controversy shall exceed twenty dollars, the right of trial by jury shall be preserved, and no fact tried by a jury shall be otherwise reexamined in any court of the United States, than according to the rules of the common law.

AMENDMENT VIII.—BAIL, CRUEL AND UNUSUAL PUNISHMENT

Excessive bail shall not be required, nor excessive fines imposed, nor cruel and unusual punishments inflicted.

AMENDMENT IX.—RIGHTS RETAINED BY THE PEOPLE

The enumeration in the Constitution, of certain rights, shall not be construed to deny or disparage others retained by the people.

AMENDMENT X.—RESERVED POWERS OF THE STATES

The powers not delegated to the United States by the Constitution, nor prohibited by it to the States, are reserved to the States respectively, or to the people.

PRE-CIVIL WAR AMENDMENTS

AMENDMENT XI.—SUITS AGAINST THE STATES [Adopted 1798]

The judicial power of the United States shall not be construed to extend to any suit in law or equity, commenced or prosecuted against one of the United States by citizens of another State, or by citizens or subjects of any foreign state.

AMENDMENT XII.—ELECTION OF THE PRESIDENT [Adopted 1804]

The electors shall meet in their respective *States*, and vote by ballot for President and Vice President, one of whom, at least, shall not be an inhabitant of the same State with themselves; they shall name in their ballots the person voted for as President, and in distinct ballots the person voted for as Vice President, and they shall make distinct lists of all persons voted for as President, and of all persons voted for as Vice President, and of the number of votes for each, which lists they shall sign and certify, and transmit sealed to the seat of the government of the United States, directed to the President of the Senate;—the President of the Senate shall, in the presence of the Senate and House of Representatives, open all the certificates and the votes shall then be counted;—the person having the greatest number of votes for President shall be the President, if such number be a majority of the whole number of electors appointed; and if no person have such majority, then from the persons having the highest numbers not exceeding three on the list of those voted for as President, the House of Representatives shall choose immediately, by ballot, the President. But in choosing the President, the votes shall be taken by States, the representation from each State having one vote; a quorum for this purpose shall consist of a member or members from two-thirds of the States, and a majority of all the States shall be necessary to a choice. And if the House of Representatives shall not choose a President whenever the right of choice shall devolve upon them, before *the fourth day of March* next following, then the Vice President shall act as President, as in the case of the death or other constitutional disability of the President.

The person having the greatest number of votes as Vice President shall be the Vice President, if such a number be a majority of the whole number of electors appointed; and if no person have a majority, then from the two highest numbers on the list the Senate shall choose the Vice President; a quorum for the purpose shall consist of two-thirds of the whole number of Senators, and a majority of the whole number shall be necessary to a choice. But no person constitutionally ineligible to the office of President shall be eligible to that of Vice President of the United States.

CIVIL WAR AMENDMENTS

AMENDMENT XIII.—PROHIBITION OF SLAVERY [Adopted 1865]

Section 1. Neither slavery nor involuntary servitude, except as a punishment for crime whereof the party shall have been duly convicted, shall exist within the United States, or any place subject to their jurisdiction.

Section 2. Congress shall have power to enforce this article by appropriate legislation.

AMENDMENT XIV.—CITIZENSHIP, DUE PROCESS, AND EQUAL PROTECTION OF THE LAWS [Adopted 1868]

Section 1. All persons born or naturalized in the United States, and subject to the jurisdiction thereof, are citizens of the United States and of the State wherein they reside. No State shall make or enforce any law which shall abridge **the privileges or immunities** of citizens of the United States; nor shall any State deprive any person of life, liberty, or property, without **due process of law**; nor deny to any person within its jurisdiction the **equal protection of the laws**.

Section 2. Representatives shall be apportioned among the several States according to their respective numbers, counting the whole number of persons in each State, excluding Indians not taxed. But when the right to vote at any election for the choice of Electors for President and Vice President of the United States, Representatives in Congress, the executive and judicial officers of a State, or the members of the legislature thereof, is denied to any of the male inhabitants of such State, being twenty-one years of age and citizens of the United States, or in any way abridged, except for participation in rebellion, or other crime, the basis of representation therein shall be reduced in the proportion which the number of such male citizens shall bear to the whole number of male citizens twenty-one years of age in such State.

Section 3. No person shall be a Senator or Representative in Congress, or Elector of President and Vice President, or hold any office, civil or military, under the United States, or under any State, who, having previously taken an oath, as a member of Congress, or as an officer of the United States, or as a member of any State legislature, or as an executive or judicial officer of any State, to support the Constitution of the United States, shall have engaged in insurrection or rebellion against the same, or given aid or comfort to the enemies thereof. Congress may, by a vote of two-thirds of each house, remove such disability.

Section 4. The validity of the public debt of the United States, authorized by law, including debts incurred for payment of pensions and bounties for services in suppressing insurrection or rebellion, shall not be questioned. But neither the United States nor any State shall assume or pay any debt or obligation incurred in aid of insurrection or rebellion against the United States, or any claim for the loss or emancipation of any slave; but all such debts, obligations and claims shall be held illegal and void.

Section 5. The Congress shall have power to enforce, by appropriate legislation, the provisions of this article.

AMENDMENT XV.—THE RIGHT TO VOTE   [Adopted 1870]

Section 1. The right of citizens of the United State to vote shall not be denied or abridged by the United States or by any State on account of race, color, or previous condition of servitude.

Section 2. The Congress shall have power to enforce this article by appropriate legislation.

AMENDMENT XVI.—INCOME TAXES [Adopted 1913]

The Congress shall have power to lay and collect taxes on incomes, from whatever source derived, without apportionment among the several States, and without regard to any census or enumeration.

AMENDMENT XVII.—DIRECT ELECTION OF SENATORS [Adopted 1913]

Section 1. The Senate of the United States shall be composed of two Senators from each State, elected by the people thereof, for six years; and each Senator shall have one vote. The electors in each State shall have the qualifications requisite for electors of (voters for) the most numerous branch of the State legislatures.

Section 2. When vacancies happen in the representation of any State in the Senate, the executive authority of such State shall issue writs of election to fill such vacancies: Provided, that the Legislature of any State may empower the executive thereof to make temporary appointments until the people fill the vacancies by election as the Legislature may direct.

Section 3. This amendment shall not be so construed as to affect the election or term of any Senator chosen before it becomes valid as part of the Constitution.

AMENDMENT XVIII.—PROHIBITION [Adopted 1919; Repealed 1933]

Section 1. *After one year from the ratification of this article the manufacture, sale, or transportation of intoxicating liquors within, the importation thereof into, or the exportation thereof from the United State and all territory subject to the jurisdiction thereof, for beverage purposes, is hereby prohibited.*

Section 2. *The Congress and the several States shall have concurrent power to enforce this article by appropriate legislation.*

Section 3. *This article shall be inoperative unless it shall have been ratified as an amendment to the Constitution by the legislatures of the several States, as provided by the Constitution, within seven years from the date of the submission thereof to the States by the Congress.*

AMENDMENT XIX.—FOR WOMEN'S SUFFRAGE [Adopted 1920]

Section 1. The right of citizens of the United States to vote shall not be denied or abridged by the United States or by any State on account of sex.

Section 2. The Congress shall have power to enforce this article by appropriate legislation.

AMENDMENT XX.—THE LAME DUCK AMENDMENT [Adopted 1933]

Section 1. The terms of the President and Vice President shall end at noon on the 20th day of January, and the terms of the Senators and Representatives at noon on the 3rd day of January, of the years in which such terms would have ended if this article had not been ratified; and the terms of their successors shall then begin.

Section 2. The Congress shall assemble at least once in every year, and such meeting shall begin at noon on the 3rd day of January, unless they shall by law appoint a different day.

Section 3. If, at the time fixed for the beginning of the term of the President, the President-elect shall have died, the Vice President-elect shall become President. If a President shall not have been chosen before the time fixed for the beginning of his term, or if the President-elect shall have failed to qualify, then the Vice President-elect shall act as President until a President shall have qualified; and the Congress may by law provide for the case wherein neither a President-elect nor a Vice President-elect shall have qualified, declaring who shall then act as President, or the manner in which one who is to act shall be selected, and such persons shall act accordingly until a President or Vice President shall have qualified.

Section 4. The Congress may by law provide for the case of the death of any of the persons from whom the House of Representatives may choose a President whenever the right of choice shall have devolved upon them, and for the case of the death of any of the persons from whom the Senate may choose a Vice President whenever the right of choice shall have devolved upon them.

Section 5. Section 1 and 2 shall take effect on the 15th day of October following the ratification of this article.

Section 6. This article shall be inoperative unless it shall have been ratified as an amendment to the Constitution by the Legislatures of three-fourths of the several States within seven years from the date of its submission.

AMENDMENT XXI.—REPEAL OF PROHIBITION   [Adopted 1933]

Section 1. The eighteenth article of amendment to the Constitution of the United States is hereby repealed.

Section 2. The transportation or importation into any State, Territory, or Possession of the United States for delivery of use therein of intoxicating liquors, in violation of the laws thereof, is hereby prohibited.

Section 3. This article shall be inoperative unless it shall have been ratified as an amendment to the Constitution by conventions in the several States, as provided in the Constitution, within seven years from the date of submission thereof to the States by the Congress.

AMENDMENT XXII.—NUMBER OF PRESIDENTIAL TERMS [Adopted 1951]

Section 1. No person shall be elected to the office of President more than twice, and no person who has held the office of President, or acted as President, for more than two years of a term to which some other person was elected President shall be elected to the office of President more than once. But this article shall not apply to any person holding the office of President when this article was proposed by the Congress, and shall not prevent any person who may be holding the office of President, or acting as President, during the term within which this article becomes operative from holding the office of President or acting as President during the remainder of such term.

Section 2. This article shall be inoperative unless it shall have been ratified as an amendment to the Constitution by the legislatures of three-fourths of the several States within seven years from the date of its submission to the States by the Congress.

AMENDMENT XXIII.—PRESIDENTIAL ELECTORS FOR THE DISTRICT OF COLUMBIA [Adopted 1961]

Section 1. The District constituting the seat of Government of the United States shall appoint in such manner as the Congress may direct:

A number of electors of President and Vice President equal to the whole number of Senators and Representatives in Congress to which the District would be entitled if it were a State, but in no event more than the least populous State; they shall be in addition to those appointed by the States, but they shall be considered for the purposes of the election of President and Vice President, to be electors appointed by a State; and they shall meet in the District and perform such duties as provided by the twelfth article of amendment.

Section 2.   The Congress shall have power to enforce this article by appropriate legislation.

AMENDMENT XXIV.—THE ANTI-POLL TAX AMENDMENT [Adopted 1964]

Section 1.   The right of citizens of the United States to vote in any primary or other election for President or Vice President, for electors for President or Vice President, or for Senator or Representative in Congress, shall not be denied or abridged by the United States or any State by reason of failure to pay any poll tax or other tax.

Section 2.   The Congress shall have power to enforce this article by appropriate legislation.

AMENDMENT XXV.—PRESIDENTIAL DISABILITY, VICE-PRESIDENTIAL VACANCIES   [Adopted 1967]

Section 1.   In case of the removal of the President from office or his death or resignation, the Vice President shall become President.

Section 2.   Whenever there is a vacancy in the office of the Vice President, the President shall nominate a Vice President who shall take office upon confirmation by a majority vote of both Houses of Congress.

Section 3.   Whenever the President transmits to the President pro tempore of the Senate and the Speaker of the House of Representatives his written declaration that he is unable to discharge the powers and duties of his office, and until he transmits to them a written declaration to the contrary, such powers and duties shall be discharged by the Vice President as Acting President.

Section 4.   Whenever the Vice President and a majority of either the principal officers of the executive departments or of such other body as Congress may by law provide, transmit to the President pro tempore of the Senate and the Speaker of the House of Representatives their written declaration that the President is unable to discharge the powers and duties of his office, the Vice President shall immediately assume the powers and duties of the office as Acting President.

Thereafter, when the President transmits to the President pro tempore of the Senate and the Speaker of the House of Representatives his written declaration that no inability exists, he shall resume the powers and duties of his office unless the Vice

514 / Constitution of the United States

President and a majority of either the principal officers of the executive department{s} or of such other body as Congress may by law provide, transmit within four days to the President pro tempore of the Senate and the Speaker of the House of Representatives their written declaration that the President is unable to discharge the powers and duties of his office.   Thereupon Congress shall decide the issue, assembling within forty-eight hours for that purpose if not in session.   If the Congress, within twenty-one days after receipt of the latter written declaration, or, if Congress is not in session, within twenty-one days after Congress is required to assemble, determines by two-thirds vote of both Houses that the President is unable to discharge the powers and duties of his office, the Vice President shall continue to discharge the same as Acting President; otherwise, the President shall resume the powers and duties of his office.

AMENDMENT XXVI.—EIGHTEEN-YEAR-OLD VOTE   [Adopted 1971]

Section 1. The right of citizens of the United States, who are eighteen years of age or older, to vote shall not be denied or abridged by the United States or by any State on account of age.

Section 2.   The Congress shall have power to enforce this article by appropriate legislation.

AMENDMENT XXVII.—VARYING CONGRESSIONAL COMPENSATION   [Adopted 1992]

No law varying the compensation for the service of the Senators and Representatives shall take effect until an election of Representatives shall have intervened.

Glossary

Administrative law Rules, regulations, and laws relating to the authority and procedures of administrative agencies.

Amendment The addition to or the deletion of a clause to a constitution or law.

Amicus curiae brief also called a friend of the court brief An action filed with the permission of the court which provides additional arguments to those presented by parties immediately involved with the case.

Annapolis convention A convention called in August 1786 which delegates from five states attended to originally consider trade and navigational problems. It was at this convention that the call was made to Congress and the states for what became the Constitutional Convention.

Anti-Federalists Persons opposed to the 1787 Philadelphia Constitution and to a more nationally centralized government.

Appellate jurisdiction Authority to review lower court decisions and administrative tribunals.

Articles of Confederation Drafted in 1777, ratified in 1781, this was the first constitution of the newly independent United States. It was replaced in 1789 with the present Constitution.

Autocracy Government in which all power is held by one person.

Bad tendency doctrine Interpretation of the First amendment that allows legislatures to make laws banning speeches that may have a tendency to cause people to engage in illegal activities.

Bicameralism Government use of a two-house legislature.

Bicameral legislature Format used by the U.S.Congress and forty-nine of the states that employs a two-house legislative system.

Bill of Attainer Legislation used to punish named individuals or easily identifiable groups.

Binding Arbitration When the law dictates that the stalemated dispute between management and labor be resolved by an impartial third-party whose decision must be accepted as compulsory by all parties.

Bipartisanship Policy that makes it appear that there is cooperation and unison between the major political parties.

Block Grant Funds granted by one level of government to another for broad programs such as health care or law enforcement.

Bureaucrat Government official; usually appointed rather than elected.

Categorical formula grant Funds granted by one level of government to another for specific programs, under specific circumstances.

Caucus Meeting of party members to choose party officials and candidates for public office and to decide policy questions.

Checks and balances In order for the government to run effectively, all three branches must work together and share equally in the power so that no one branch dominates the others and the business of government in efficiently run.

Civil law   The legal code that regulates the conduct between private individuals. Under this system, the government acts as negotiator of disputes among individuals and businesses.

Class action suit   Lawsuits brought by a person or a group of people on their own behalf as well as on the behalf of all persons in a similar situation. Class action suits are often brought against the auto industry and their outcome often mandate the replacement, at no cost, of car parts found to be defective or unsafe to all cars of the same make and model.

Clear and present danger doctrine   This interpretation of the First amendment does not allow laws that directly or indirectly restrict freedom of speech to be utilized unless the particular speech or writing presents a clear and present danger that it's presentation will lead to acts that the government defines as illegal.

Cloture   Method used to end filibusters in particular and debates in general in the U.S. Senate.

Coattail effect   The electoral success or failure that one candidate has impacts the success or failure of other candidates in the same party.

Commerce clause   The Constitutional clause giving Congress the power to regulate business activities that involve more than one state. This clause also prohibits states from disrupting the business activities of other states or nations.

Comparable worth   Notion advocated by those who believe that jobs traditionally held by women-nursing, childcare, secretarial, teaching-have been systematically held down in wage. These jobs are traditionally held by women because of pervasive stereotyping and discrimination while the higher paying jobs, such as plumbers and janitors are held by men. The idea that jobs should be paid at the same rate if they require comparable skills and contributions made to society.

Concurrent powers   Powers given to both the states and the national government by the Constitution.

Concurring opinion   An opinion offered by a Supreme Court justice which agrees with the decision of the majority but for different reasons than those of the majority.

Confederation   Government created when nation-states agreed to create a new government and allowed it certain powers. The power to regulate the conduct of individuals is not allowed in this form of government.

Conference committee   Committee appointed by each the House and the Senate to adjust differences on bills. Once out of committee, the bill must be accepted or rejected as it stands and may not be amended.

Connecticut Compromise   The original delegates of the Constitutional Convention agreed to give each state two senators regardless of population to compromise for the House of Representative's method of picking numbers of representatives according to population density. The compromise was made at the demand of the less populous states for agreeing to the new Constitution.

Conservatism   Political belief that favors state and local government over the Federal government involvement in private lives and businesses.

Conspiracy   Collaboration between two or more people to engage in illegal activity or in an activity that is lawful by itself but not when orchestrated by a particular group, under particular circumstances.

Constitution Rules and procedures of those who govern as outlined by agreement to allow for effective government.

Constitutional convention The Philadelphia convention of 1857 that determined the Constitution of the United States which was ratified by nine states and adopted in 1788.

Constitutional government Governments that follow a code of ethics that apply to those who govern and enforce that code when need be.

Constitutional law The Supreme Court interprets the meanings of the Constitution of the United States through its opinions. Laws are focused around these interpretations and people and government behave according to these laws.

Containment The foreign policy strategy employed by the Truman Administration and to some extent by all of the presidential administrations after World War II which was aimed at preventing the emerging powers of Europe and the Middle East from falling under Soviet control.

Curtiss-Wright case The 1936 Supreme Court case which upheld the sovereignty of the National Government in foreign affairs and declared the President to be its prime agent.

De facto segregation racial segregation that results from sources other than government practices.

Defendant In any court action, the individual or group defending itself against charges brought either by another person or by the legal authorities.

De jure segregation see Jim Crow laws   Racial segregation that results from government policies and practices.

Delegate Legislators, as the delegates of the people whom they represent, representing the views of their constituents rather than views that they hold personally.

Demagogue Charismatic leaders who appeal to the prejudices and emotions of the masses to retain their power.

Democracy Direct or indirect government by the people where there are frequent free elections.

Deregulation Hands-off approach that calls for less interference via rules and regulations by government.

Detente Policy aimed at reducing the tension between nations.

Deterrence U.S. defense policy to prevent nuclear attack by being able to survive a first attack by an adversary and respond with a massive counter attack that would inflict costly damage. The idea is that an initial attack would not be forthcoming because of fear of retaliation. Thus, an ever increasing arsenal of weapons on all sides.

Direct primary Election in which voters who are members of the party choose who will be nominated for the party's nominees in the general election.

Discharge petition Petition signed by a majority of the members of the House of Representatives which forces a bill from Committee onto the House floor for consideration.

Domino Theory Theory that assumes that if some key nations fall under Communist control, other nations will subsequently fall.

Double jeopardy Practice forbidden by the Constitution in which a person is tried for the same trial by the same government.

Dual Federalism   Idea that state and national governments, each granted certain rights and powers by the Constitution, are equal partners with the Supreme Court arbitrating conflicts between the two.

Due process clauses   Clauses in the fifth and fourteenth amendments that guarantee individuals that neither the state or national governments can deprive individuals of life, liberty or property without due process of law.

Electoral College   This formality gathers the states electors together and counts their votes as cast to formally represent their parties choice for president and vice president.

Eminent domain   The Constitution makes allowances for the government to take private property for public use, but just compensation must be made to the individual citizen.

Equal protection clause   A constitutional restraint imposed by the fifth and fourteenth amendments on the power of government to discriminate on the grounds of race, national origin or sex.

Equal Rights Amendment (ERA)   Proposed Constitutional amendment by the Congress of 1972 designed to give women equal protection under the law. Ratified by only thirty-five states, just three short of the number needed, time ran out and the amendment failed in June, 1982.

Equal-time requirement   Requirement by Congress and the Federal Communications Commission that requires television and radio licensees to give opposing candidates for public office equal amounts of free air time.

Equity   Remedy used by the courts when suits for money do not provide justice.

Establishment clause   First and fourteenth amendment clauses that forbids the government to make laws about any established religion. The Supreme Court further interpreted this clause to forbid government to support any or all religions.

Ethnocentrism   The belief held by most people in most societies that their own group is superior to others.

Excise tax   Tax imposed on the consumer of particular items such as cigarettes, liquor and gasoline.

Executive agreement   An international agreement that carries the weight of a treaty made by the president that does not need the approval of Congress.

Executive office of the President   The Reorganization act of 1939 established a group of offices to help the president carry out his tasks. These staff agencies change as the needs of government change.

Executive privilege   Claim made by presidents that justify the witholding of certain information from the public, the courts and even Congress in the interest of national security. Questioned by the *United States* v. *Nixon* case, the Supreme Court ruled that while presidents do have this privilege, its extent is subject to judicial review.

Ex post facto law   "After-the-fact" law not allowed by the Constitution that would punish criminals for an act not illegal at the time of its commission.

Extradition   Legal process whereby a criminal caught in one state is surrendered to another state.

Fairness Doctrine Doctrine that imposes on television and radio licensees the opportunity for differing viewpoints to be presented.

Federal Reserve System Created by Congress in 1913 to ensure regulated currency and amount of credit available and to establish banking practices.

Federalism Governmental arrangement that allows for two levels of government, one at a central level and the other at each of the state levels both of which have jurisdiction over individuals.

Federalist, The Written by Hamilton, Jay and Madison during the debate over ratification of the Constitution, this series of essays favored its adoption.

Filibuster A lengthy speech given by a member of the US Senate that impedes the introduction of a controversial matter by stalling until time runs out.

Full faith and credit clause Clause in the Constitution that requires that each state recognizes civil judgments made in other states.

Gerrymandering The practice of drawing or redrawing the boundaries of a voting district in such a way as to prevent the opposition from establishing a majority of votes.

Grand jury Twelve to twenty-three people who sit in private at a hearing where the government presents evidence. The grand jury then decides whether the evidence warrants an individual to stand trial.

Gross national product (GNP) The total monetary value of all goods and services given in any one year in the nation.

Habeas corpus Court orders that require jailers to show just cause for holding an individual.

Hatch Act Federal statute that disallows federal employees from certain political actions and protects them from being fired on partisan grounds.

Ideology A set of political attitudes and beliefs about the role of government, power and the role of the individual in society.

Ideologue Person with a stable and fixed ideology.

Immunity Exemption from prosecution given to a witness as a result of testimony given in return.

Implied Powers Constitutional powers given to Congress to do whatever is necessary to carry out expressed powers.

Impoundment Presidential act refusing to allow an agency to spend funds authorized by Congress.

Inflation Rise in the cost of goods purchased. Same as the decline of monetary value.

Inherent powers Powers attributed to the national government that deal with foreign relations. Supreme Court ruled that these powers do not need to be granted by the Constitution, rather they naturally grow out of the nature of governments and their relationship with other governments.

Initiative petition Petition by a group of voters to create a new law. May be submitted either directly to the people or to the legislature first, and if refused, to the voters.

Interest groups Collection of people sharing a common interest or concern willing to interact with other groups to meet their demands.

Interstate compacts Agreements among states usually approved by Congress.

Isolationism 1930's attitude that the US should stay out of everyone's business, especially militarily, and look after its own self-interest.

Item veto Power granted to state executives that allows them to veto part of a bill without having to veto it all. Presidents do not have this power.

Jim Crow laws Laws requiring that public facilities and accommodations, public and private, be segregated by race.

Joint committee Intended to speed up legislative processes, these committees are formed by members consisting of both the House and the Senate.

Judicial activism As opposed to judicial restraint which asks for a conservative interpretation of the Constitution, judicial activism asks that judges interpret the Constitution to reflect current trends and the desires and values of current people.

Judicial restraint The Constitution should be interpreted in the context of wording and intent meant by the authors of the document and changes should be made via the formal amending process.

Judicial review Supreme Court case *Marbury* v. *Madison* defines the authority of judges to decide on the validity of actions taken by executive officials according to the judges interpretation of the Constitution.

Ku-Klux-Klan Organization of white supremists characterized by white flowing robes and hoods espousing inferiority and hatred of blacks, ethnic groups and various religious factions.

Lame duck Elected official serving out a term of office after being defeated for reelection before the inauguration of the successor.

Legislative veto Declared unconstitutional in 1983, provisional law that allowed Congress or a committee of Congress to reject by majority vote an act or regulation of an agency of the national government.

Libel Written defamation of another person.

Liberalism Philosophical approach that favors governmental action to achieve equal opportunity and equality for all.

Libertarianism Philosophical approach that favors a free-market economic policy and non-interventional foreign policy along with a general limited role approach to government in general.

Lobby Seen as part of a citizens right to petition the government, lobbying involves activities aimed at influencing government officials to enact desired policies.

Lobbyist Person who acts for an organized group aimed at influencing decision making of public officials.

Maintaining election An election that runs in a similar pattern as the last election maintaining partisan support.

Majority floor leader The majority floor leader helps frame party policy and keeps the membership in line, determines the agenda and has strong influence in committee selection. This legislative position is held by an important party member selected in caucus or conference.

Massachusetts ballot Method of voting in which all candidates are listed under the office for which they are running. Also called office group ballot or office block ballot.

McCulloch v. *Maryland* Celebrated 1819 Supreme Court decision that established the doctrine of National supremacy and established the principal that the implied powers of the national government be generously interpreted.

Medicaid A state and national government project that pays as much as 80% of medical costs for those who do not qualify for the national medicare program. This financial assistance ensures that impoverished individuals whose medical expenses exceed social security and pension benefits have medical assistance available to them.

Military-industrial complex Alliance between top industry and top military personnel who protect their common interests in arms production and use.

Minority floor leader Elected spokesperson for the minority party who acts as party leader in the House and the Senate.

Misdemeanor Criminal offense punishable by fine and/or imprisonment of usually less than one year.

Missouri Plan System of selecting judges whereby the governor makes an appointment and then after one year the electorate votes whether to retain or reject. After the initial term, the judge comes up for reelection if she wishes to serve again.

National Security Council Planning committee including the president, vice president, secretary of defense, secretary of state and the chair of the joint chiefs of staff which confers on matters of national security.

National supremacy Constitutional doctrine that advocates that when a conflict between national, federal and local governments occur, the national government actions take priority.

Necessary and proper clause The clause in the Constitution that sets forth the implied powers of Congress. This clause grants Congress not only the enumerated powers, but also grant Congress the authority to make any new and additional laws needed in order to carry out those enumerated powers.

New Jersey Plan Presented by Paterson of New Jersey, this plan advocated modification of the Articles of Confederation and provided for strong states rights rather than a new Constitution and strong national government.

Nixon Doctrine 1970's policy suggested by President Nixon that would have the United States come to the defense of allies and friendly nations only if they would do most of the main fighting themselves.

Nonproliferation Treaty An international agreement that pledges that nations possessing nuclear devices not distribute that technology to those nations that do not posses nuclear devices.

Obscenity Defined by legislation or judicial interpretation as material presented in a patently offensive way that appeals to prurient interest in sex lacking serious literary, artistic, scientific or political interest.

Office group ballot Also called Massachusetts ballot or office-block ballot, this is a method of voting in which all candidates are listed under the office for which they are running.

Office of Management and Budget (OMB)   Agency that serves as clearinghouse for budgeting requests and management improvements.

Oligarchy   Form of government where control lies within a small group of people based on wealth or power.

Oligopoly   Occurs when a small group of business dominate an industry.

Ombudsman   Governmental official or office that handles complaints made against the government or its officials.

Override   An action of Congress attempting to override a presidential veto of congressional legislation. Veto overrides are rare, succeeding only 3% of the time, as a two thirds vote in both the Senate and the House are required.

Oversight   Process of monitoring and evaluating how a program has been carried out.

Party column ballot   Also called the Indiana ballot, this method of voting lists all candidates under their party designations allowing for easy casting of votes for only one party.

Party convention   Held on county, state and national levels, these conventions decide on policy matters and sometimes select party candidates for public office.

Party primary   Election open only to members of the party where nominees for office are presented and the candidate to run for the party for a particular office is chosen.

Party realignment   Seeking to maintain its competitiveness, a party sometimes makes fundamental changes in economic, social and other electoral foundations.

Patronage   Procedure whereby government jobs are given to supporters of the winning party.

Petit jury   Ordinary jury convened in criminal or civil trials. Not the grand jury.

Plaintiff   Party initiating court action seeking legal remedies for injuries received.

Plea bargaining   Negotiations between the prosecutor and the defense attorney whereby the defendant will plead guilty to a lesser crime.

Pocket veto   After the legislative body adjourns, if the president or governor does not sign a bill, rather "puts the bill in his/her pocket", the bill dies and does not become law.

Political Action Committee (PAC)   Major agencies through which congressional campaigns are financed, these groups are the political arm of well organized special interest groups.

Political machine   Political "boss" along with supporting ward and precinct workers who provide various services to constituents between elections and then call in these favors when it is time to reelect their candidate.

Political socialization   Process whereby we develop our political attitudes, values and behaviors usually started before we go to school and continuing throughout our lifetime.

Poll tax   Payment required to vote. Some states formerly required a poll tax, but it is now outlawed.

Populists   Political party of the 1880's and 1890's based in the rural South, Southwest and Midwest that waged reformist actions against banks, railroads and other establishments. Populist issues influenced the Democratic party and the progressive movements after 1892.

Preferred position doctrine Interpretation of the first amendment that disallows any law to be made that limits expression unless the government can convince the courts that the law is necessary to prevent serious injury to the public welfare.

Presidential primary Statewide primary in which members of a party choose delegates to go the national party convention and the nominee who will be the party's candidate running for president.

President pro tempore In the absence of the vice president, this official serves as the president of the Senate. Chosen from the members of the U.S. Senate, he is usually the senior member of the majority party.

Prior restraint Order made prior to the delivery of a speech, publishing of a book or newspaper or the release of a motion picture until certain conditions have been met.

Progressive tax Tax that imposes higher tax payments on those who are more wealthy.

Project grant Government funds earmarked for specific purposes based on merits.

Public defender Officer of the court whose job it is to provide free legal services to those who are accused of crimes and are unable to afford an attorney.

Public opinion Views and attitudes held by people on significant issues.

Public policy Intentions and actions practiced by the government on all issues.

Quasilegislative and quasijudicial Words coined by the Supreme Court to permit noncourt and nonlegislative bodies to decide disputes and make rules. Decisions are subject to court review and rules must be within general guidelines established by the legislature.

Random sampling A representative selection picked at random to sample public opinion.

Realigning election Election in which existing party loyalties change.

Reapportionment Redrawing the legislative district lines to acknowledge the existing population distributions.

Recall After a certain number of voters petition to have an elected official removed from office, this election is held where all voters have their say in the matter.

Referendum Submission for approval to the general voters of measures passed by the legislature.

Regressive tax Taxes imposed most heavily on those least able to afford them.

Representative democracy Also called a Republic The form of government where power is derived directly or indirectly from the people. Those elected to govern are responsible for their actions to the people who have given them their power. In this form of government, people elect representatives who make the rules as opposed to making rules themselves as occurs in a direct democracy.

Revenue sharing Program that allows for federal funds to be used by state and local governments to be spent at the discretion of the receiving governments.

Runoff election Election held when neither candidate receives a required number of votes.

Sales tax Tax charged on sales transactions.

Salience Significance of an issue or an event.

SALT Strategic Arms Limitations Treaty Agreement made between the US and the Soviets limiting both offensive and defensive weapons.

Sampling error The degree to which a sample is distorted and does not perfectly represent the entire population.

Sedition Attempt to overthrow the government by force or violence.

Seditious Descriptive word for a speech made to advocate forcefully overthrowing the government. The Supreme Court has ruled that Congress can outlaw seditious speech but that proof of specific urgings to commit violence were advocated by the speech giver.

Senate majority leader Elected leader of the majority party in the U.S. Senate. This is the most influential person, the chief power broker and the setter of the agenda.

Senatorial courtesy U.S. Senate custom of referring the names of prospective appointees to senators from the states where these appointees reside and withdrawing the names of any prospective appointees that these senators deem objectionable.

Separation of powers Constitutional division of power between the judicial, legislative and executive branches. The judicial branch interprets laws, the legislative branch makes laws and the executive branch applies the laws.

Shays's Rebellion Led by Daniel Shays in 1786-87 this rebellion in rural Massachusetts protested the foreclosing of mortgages. It resulted in support for a stronger national government.

Shield law Law establishing the right under certain circumstances of reporters and other media people to refuse to reveal sources of information.

Socialism Philosophical approach to government that allows for public ownership of businesses.

Speaker Selected by the majority party, elected by the entire House, this is the presiding officer of the House of Representatives.

Stare decisis The rule of precedence commonly held as binding; when a judge must decide on a case where the same question is presented as had been previously decided.

Statutory law Law enacted by legislature.

Subpoena A court order that demands the presence of an individual or certain materials before a judicial agency.

Suburbs Residential communities that surround an existing city.

Sunset process Legislative review of programs after a set number of years to determine whether the program is still viable or has outlived its usefulness.

Sunshine law Law requiring public agencies to operate in public except under certain circumstances.

Tariff Taxes levied on imports to help protect a nations own industries from international competition or simply to raise revenues by taxing products from abroad rather than raising taxes internally.

Third world Those nations that are rather poor and non-industrialized but are seeking to modernize and compete in the world market.

Three-Fifths Compromise An agreement between the north and the south at the Constitutional Convention in 1787 to count only three-fifths of the slave population in determining the number of representatives sent to the House of representatives.

Ticket splitting Practice of some voters who vote for the candidate rather than the party that the candidate represents. This means that a particular voter might vote for a candidate in a one office who is a democrat while at the same time voting for another candidate in a different office that is a republican.

Treason No person can be convicted of this crime unless he confesses in an open courtroom to the crime or two witness testify that they personally witnessed actions specified as treasonous. Only levying war against the U.S., adjuring to its enemies, or giving aid and comfort to its enemies constitute crimes of treason.

Truman Doctrine 1947 doctrine sponsored by Harry Truman aimed at halting the spread of communism in southeastern Europe. This plan called for the financial support of all free people in the world who wanted to resist outside forces of repression.

Trustee This view of a legislator holds that when elected, an officer of the people represents independent views for the general welfare of the people and that the legislator need not vote as their constituents demand, rather as general welfare dictates.

Unicameral legislature One house legislature. The state of Nebraska and almost all cities use this system.

Unitary system Form of government where power is concentrated in the form a national government.

Virginia Plan Plan presented at the Constitution Convention which favored the larger states proposing that the number of representatives in each of the houses be determined by the population density in each state.

Watergate 1972 incidents involving various misdeeds by the Nixon administration among which was the break-in that occurred in the Watergate Office Building in Washington, D.C. when the National Democratic Committee headquarters was raided. Among the other incidents were misuse of the CIA, FBI and IRS and the break-in of a psychiatrists office along with "dirty tricks" being played on Nixon's opponents during his election in 1972. Nixon eventually was forced out of the presidency and others in his administration were tried and spent time in prison.

Whip Party leader in the legislature who is the liaison between the rank and file and the leaders.

White Primary Declared unconstitutional in 1944 (*Smith* v. *Allwright*), this type of Democratic party primary held in the South allowed only white persons to participate. Because during this time period the democratic party candidates were the only one that had a chance to win in the elections held after the primaries, this effectively eliminated all of the black vote.

Writ of certiorari The formal device used to regularly bring lower court decisions before the Supreme Court.

Writ of habeas corpus Court order demanding jailers to explain to a judge why a person is being held in custody.

Writ of mandamus Court order demanding that a person perform a nondiscretionary act as required by law.

Index

534   *Index*